PROCEEDINGS OF THE IMF

GLOBAL MODERNIZATION REVIEW II

Modernity and Diversity in New Era

Editors-in-chief
Alberto Martinelli   Chuanqi He

Science Press
Beijing

Global Modernization Review (II):
Modernity and Diversity in New Era

Copyright © 2018 by Science Press

Editors-in-Chief
Alberto Martinelli   Chuanqi He

Responsible Editors
Yan Fu   Wenyan Cui   Li Song   Hua Shao

Published by Science Press
16 Donghuangchenggen North Street
Beijing 100717. P. R. China
Printed in Beijing

www.sciencepress.com

ISBN 978-7-03-058626-1 (Science Press, Beijing)

All rights reserved. No part of this publication may be reproduced, stored in a retrieval system, or transmitted in any form or by any means, electronic, mechanical, photocopying, recording or otherwise, without the prior written permission of the copyright owner.

Printed in China

Alberto Martinelli

Professor Emeritus, Political Science and Sociology, University of Milan
President, International Social Science Council, ISSC
Co-chairman, Scientific Advisory Committee of the International Modernization Forum

Chuanqi He

Professor and director, China Center for Modernization Research, Chinese Academy of Sciences
Academician, International Eurasian Academy of Sciences
Co-chairman, Scientific Advisory Committee of the International Modernization Forum
Chairman, Organization Committee of the International Modernization Forum

Scientific Advisory Committee of the International Modernization Forum and the Editorial Committee of the Proceedings of the IMF 2016

Editors-in-Chief

Prof. Alberto Martinelli, Political Science and Sociology, University of Milan, Italy

Prof. Chuanqi He, China Center for Modernization Research, Chinese Academy of Sciences, China

Members of Editorial Committee

Prof. Liping Bu, Alma College, USA

Prof. Zhengping Chen, Tsinghua University, China

Prof. Maurie J. Cohen, New Jersey Institute of Technology, USA

Prof. Diego Coletto, University degli Studi di Milano-Bicocca, Italy

Prof. Zhenghua Dong, Peking University, China

Prof. Zhulan Fang, Renmin University of China, China

Prof. Quanan Ha, Nankai University, China

Prof. Chuanqi He, China Center for Modernization Research, Chinese Academy of Sciences, China

Prof. Geoff Hodgson, University of Hertfordshire, UK

Prof. Eliseeva Irina, Institute of Sociology, RAS, Russia

Prof. Martin Janicke, Free University Berlin, Germany

Prof. Yihua Jiang, Fudan University, China

Prof. Müller Karel, University of Karlovy, Czech Republic

Dr. Juha Kotilainen, University of Eastern Finland, Finland

Prof. Edwin Pak-wah Leung, Seton Hall University, USA

Prof. Wen Li, Institute of Asia-Pacific Studies, Chinese Academy of Social Sciences, China

Prof. Jie-Hyun Lim, Hanyang University, Public of Korea

Prof. Alberto Martinelli, University of Milan, Italy

Prof. Arthur P. J. Mol, Wageningen University, Netherlands

Prof. Munir Morad, Anglia Ruskin University-Chelmsford, UK

Prof. Jose Antonio Ocampo, Columbia University, USA

Prof. Chengdan Qian, Peking University, China

Prof. Gert Spaargaren, Wageningen University, Netherlands

Prof. Piotr Sztompka, Jagiellonian University at Krakow, Poland

Prof. Edward Tiryakian, Duke University, USA

Prof. Catalin Turliuc, Romanian Academy, Romania

Prof. Fedotova Valentina, Institute of Philosophy, RAS, Russia

Prof. Hellmut Wollmann, Humboldt University Berlin, Germany

Prof. Zhengzhong Xu, Chinese Academy of Governance, China

Prof. Yiyong Yang, Academy of Macroeconomic Research, China

Prof. Xian Zhou, Nanjing University, China

Prof. Lixing Zou, China Development Bank, China

Foreword

Modernization has been a worldwide phenomenon since about the 18th century. It changed not only people's lives in all aspects including political, economic, social and cultural life, but also the human development, ecological and world system, etc. Modernization movement is just like an international marathon game of national development, in which the countries running ahead become developed countries while the rest become developing ones, and cultural diversity exists across time and space.

Today, almost all countries in the world are undergoing some kind of modernization consciously or unconsciously, and the modernization drive can also be set as a national goal directly or indirectly. The need has arisen to promote people's understanding of modernization process through the international comparative and interdisciplinary study.

The Second International Modernization Forum: Modernization and Diversity (IMF 2016) was held at China Hall of Science & Technology in Beijing on May 20-22, 2016. The China Center for Modernization Research of Chinese Academy of Sciences, International Social Science Council of UNESCO, Law & Development Academy of Peking University, and the *Theory and Modernization* magazine were the co-sponsors of the IMF 2016. The forum had received more than 60 papers and 90 scholars had attended the meeting. The Association for Modernization Studies (AMS) of China Society for Futures Studies (CSFS) was founded and Prof. Chuanqi He became the president of AMS of CSFS.

The Global Modernization Review (II): Modernity and Diversity in New Era presents the proceedings of the IMF 2016. It includes modernization and diversity in the new era, multiple modernities and cultural diversity, dynamics and paths of modernization, ecological modernization and green development, social modernization and human development, regional modernization and reduction of poverty and inequalities, and finally the appendix with world modernization indexes 2012.

The international modernization forum is an international arena for modernization study and its result is an important contribution to our collective understanding of modernization phenomenon. It provides valuable guidance for the further study, and opens the way to significant international and interdisciplinary cooperation for modernization researches.

Alberto Martinelli, Chuanqi He
Editors-in-Chief of the proceedings of the IMF 2016 and the Global Modernization Review (II),
co-chairmen of the Scientific Advisory Committee of the International Modernization Forum

Acknowledgments

This book was the selections of the main outputs of the Second International Modernization Forum held in Beijing in 2016 (IMF 2016). The China Center for Modernization Research (CCMR) of Chinese Academy of Sciences (CAS) is the host of the conference. The organization committee of the IMF 2016 includes the honorary chairman Academician Guangzhao Zhou — former president of the CAS, the chairman Prof. Chuanqi He — director of CCMR, the members including Prof. Zhenghua Dong, Prof. Xiwen Liu, Prof. Zhulan Fang, Mr. Xifang Tang, and Prof. Lixing Zou, and the secretaries including Dr. Qing Ye, Dr. Jing Jin, Dr. Lei Liu and Dr. Wenyu Zhu.

Each section of the IMF 2016 has been chaired separately by the leading scientists Prof. Alberto Martinelli, Prof. Boying Zhang, Prof. Edward Tiryakian, Prof. Chuanqi He, Prof. Eliseeva Irina, Prof. Lixing Zou, Prof. Jinyuan Liu, and Prof. Atle Midttun, Prof. Catalin Turliuc, Prof. Zhulan Fang, Prof. Jin Feng, Dr. Juha Kotilainen, Prof. Zhigang Wang. Prof. Chuanqi He, Prof. Alberto Martinelli and Prof. Boying Zhang presented the opening speech, welcome speech and closing speech respectively. Prof. Alberto Martinelli, Prof. Piotr Sztompka, Prof. Edward Tiryakian and Prof. Chuanqi He presented the keynote speeches.

The participants and contributions of the IMF 2016 came from 14 countries including: Czech Republic, Finland, Germany, Italy, Republic of Korea, the Netherlands, China, Poland, Romania, Russia, the United Kingdom, the United States, Norway and India.

This item was edited by the editorial committee of the proceedings of the IMF 2016. Prof. Alberto Martinelli and Prof. Chuanqi He are the editors-in-chief of the editorial committee and co-chairmen of the Scientific Advisory Committee of the IMF 2016. Members of the editorial committee and the Scientific Advisory Committee are the same.

The staffs of the CCMR of CAS have contributed to the IMF 2016. They are Dr. Jing Jin, Dr. Qing Ye, Dr. Wenyu Zhu, Dr. Xijun Zhao, Dr. Yang Li, Dr. Lei Liu and Dr. Li Li. Dr. Wenyu Zhu is also the secretary of the editorial committee.

The Bureau of International Cooperation of CAS and Bureau of Development and Planning of CAS have provided the financial support to the IMF 2016 and its publications.

Contents

Foreword

Acknowledgments

Part One　Modernization and Diversity in the New Era ·································· 1

    Modernization and the Sustainable Development Goals: The Case of the

        European Union ·· 3

    Moral Capital: An Important Prerequisite for Social Change and

        Successful Modernization ·· 26

    Global Challenges of Modernization ·· 33

    Three Paths Towards National Modernization ·· 46

    What's Modernization in the 21st Century: A Chinese Version ·························· 62

Part Two　Multiple Modernities and Cultural Diversity ······································ 71

    Harmonious Coexistence of Tradition and Modernity — Inspirations from

        the Lasting Survival of the Amish Community in Modern American Society ········ 73

    Cultural Diversity and Social Contradictions of the Modernization ···················· 77

    Culture Trend of Modernization as Reflected in Office Space Design ··················· 80

    Consolidation, Integration, Modernization: From the Shaping of the

        Framework "Mitteleuropa" to the European Union ·· 85

    Global Modernization Trend in the Perspective of Human History ····················· 90

    Urban Diversification and Social Diversity ·· 108

    Attitudes Toward Modernization and Rural-Urban Relationship:

        A Comparison Between Modern China and Japan ·· 115

Three Trends of Chinese Learning and Construction of Multi-modernity
 in China ··· 123

The Contours of Russian Modernization ·· 134

Part Three   Dynamics and Paths of Modernization ·················· 141

Modernization of Russia: Contemporary Trends ·· 143

How Did Romania Become Modern? A Southeastern European Experience
 During the 20th Century ··· 150

Specifics and Differentiation of the Balance of Modernization Processes
 in Russian Regions ·· 161

Progressive Reform: Path of Political Modernization in Britain and
 Its Inspirations ·· 170

The Guarantee of Progress and Harmony: Modernization and
 Livelihood Improvement in Modern America ··· 177

International Inequality and the Global Crisis: Managing Markets for
 Sustainable Growth ·· 184

A New Institutional Economy Growth Theory from the Angle of the
 Economic Rights ·· 201

A Historical Review of World Industrial Modernization ······························· 208

Challenges and Policy Suggestions on China's Agricultural Modernization ········ 220

Analysis on Diversity and Imbalance of Service Modernization:
 A View Based on the Second Modernization Evaluation ······························ 228

Part Four   Ecological Modernization and Green Development ················ 239

Staging Pathways Towards Ecomodernity ··· 241

Ecological Modernization and Resilience of Resource Communities ··············· 260

Ecological Civilization Construction Demonstration Areas
 in China from a Three-dimensional Theoretical Perspective ·························· 269

After Paris: Global Trend of Green Development and China's Ecological
    Modernization Strategy ············ 284
Establishment of Low-carbon City Construction Policy Toolkit and
    Analysis of the Policy Tools' Effectiveness ············ 295
Rural Ecological Modernization: Evaluation Indicators and Case Study ············ 302
Time to Reinstate Poise of Nature ············ 310
On Promoting the Construction of Ecological Civilization from
    the Perspective of Ecological Modernization Theory: A Case Study
    of the Wuhan International Garden Expo ············ 312

Part Five   Social Modernization and Human Development ············ 319

Social Modernization and Quality of Life Measurement in Russia ············ 321
A Study on China's Structural Reform in Social Fields ············ 326
Historical Experience of Modernization in Russia ············ 335
The Deepening of the Division of Labor, Social Structure and the Modernization of
    National Governance ············ 343
The Youth Entrepreneurship as a Factor of Social Modernization of Society ············ 351
To Explore a Chinese Discourse of Modernity Research Paradigms ············ 358

Part Six   Regional Modernization & Reduction of Poverty
and Inequalities ············ 365

Socio-economic Development of Region in the Context of Modernization
    Processes: A Case Study of St. Petersburg ············ 367
Regional Modernization and Sustainable Development in a Mining
    Region from the Habsburg Monarchy (Transylvania) in 1750-1914 ············ 376
Evaluation of Regional Modernization of China's 52 Regions ············ 388
Interactive Mechanism Between Regional Economic Integration and
    Regional Modernization ············ 400

Appendix ············ 410

Part One

Modernization and Diversity in the New Era

Modernization and the Sustainable Development Goals: The Case of the European Union

Alberto Martinelli

Professor Emeritus, Political Science and Sociology, University of Milan

The Sustainable Development Goals (SDGs), which were approved in September 2015 at the UN General Assembly in New York, provide the basic framework for successful, equitable and inclusive modernization, with each country deciding which path to follow toward and through modernity. There can be a positive relation between modernization and SDGs: On the one hand, the attainment of many goals — such as ending poverty, eradicating hunger, ensuring healthy lives, inclusive and equitable education, full employment, affordable modern energy, sustainable production and consumption patterns — depends on successful modernization strategies, based on the shared premise that there is more than one way to build a full-fledged modern society; on the other hand, the various paths toward and through modernity require that SDGs are taken seriously by every country and are considered common goals by all. The approach of multiple modernities — or varieties of modernity — provides a better framework for the attainment of SDGs than a unique model of modernization, since it allows to take into consideration the specificities of any given country and the various impacts of the historical time in which the various phases of the process take place. The core values and institutions of a society, as well as its position in the world economy and geopolitics, influence development outcomes and SDGs attainment. The positive relation between modernization and SDGs cannot, however, be taken for granted, because different types of modernity and different development models are unevenly committed to the various SDGs on the basis of different priorities and are unevenly fit to attain them. The strategies for achieving many SDGs, such as fostering gender equality and women empowerment, reducing inequalities within and among countries, achieving inclusive and sustainable industrialization, developing inclusive, safe and resilient cities, and taking urgent action to combat climate change, do conflict with the economic interests and political strategies of powerful actors, both at the national and global level.

In order to discuss the relationship between modernization and sustainable development goals, I will start with a brief summary of my own approach which is a critical reappraisal of the multiple modernities approach, and I will then examine the major strengths and weaknesses of the SDGs. In the following sections, I will discuss whether and to what extent the European variety of modernity as it is embodied by the European Union (EU) is fit to pursue and attain the various SDGs. To answer this question I will review the EU core values and distinctive institutions, and then instead of assessing the performance of the EU on each single goal and target, I will analyse the key questions the EU is facing nowadays which influence its ability to pursue SDGs, i.e. first, the exit strategy from the global financial-economic crisis and the consequences for Europe of the wars in the Middle East (massive flow of asylum-seekers, terrorism, etc. states); and second, the EU internal cleavages and the unaccomplished process of political integration. I will conclude by arguing that the solution to these conflated crises cannot be provided by nationalist closures and the re-nationalization of policies, but on the contrary by the construction of an even greater union.

1. My Conception of Modernization and Modernity

I have developed my conception of modernization and modernity in several writings, among which the book *Global Modernization: Rethinking the Project of Modernity* (2005) and the essay *Global Modernization and Multiple Modernities* (2015) both are available in Chinese. My conception shares some key ideas of the "Multiple modernities" approach (which is the most innovative approach in contemporary studies of modernization, and which has its best known and most articulated proponent); but I criticize, qualify and correct this approach on the basis of some insights of classical modernization theory — too hastily forgotten in the contemporary debate — and of the findings of empirical research. My aim is to contribute to develop the comparative analysis of the cultural and institutional patterns of modern Western societies with those of emerging economies and modernizing countries.

To briefly summarize my view, I argue, first, that modernity has become a common global condition, which in spreading to the whole world takes different forms and distinct patterns. I agree with Wittrock (2000: 56) that "the existence of a common global condition does not mean that members of any singular cultural community are about to relinquish their ontological and cosmological assumptions, much less than their traditional institutions; it means however that the continuous interpretation, reinterpretation and transformation of those commitments and institutional structures cannot but take account of the commonality of the global condition of modernity". Modern societies are not converging toward a single model, as both the classical sociology of Marx, Durkheim and to a large extent Weber (although they greatly differ in their analyses and predictions) and the 1950s and the 1960s theorists of convergence of industrial societies thought; but they are not diverging either, to the extent that Eisenstadt (2000) and multiple modernities scholars' pretend. What is happening in today's world is rather a complex dialectics of convergence and divergence.

Second, I maintain that modernization cannot be simply identified with Westernization. The civilization of modernity first arose in Western Europe and then spread to the rest of Europe, America and throughout the world; the original Western project constituted the crucial (and usually ambivalent) reference point for non-Western countries (to the extent that even movements with strong anti-Western and anti-modern themes were distinctively modern). But non-Western societies were capable of adapting, reinterpreting, reinventing institutional and cultural patterns, and providing different responses to the challenges and possibilities inherent in the core characteristics of the distinct civilizational premises of modernity. These outcomes of the modernization process were, in their turn, influenced by deep-seated cultural and cosmological differences among, say, Western Europe, China and Japan. A basic difference exists here among those scholars who think that in their core identities, these societies remain characterized by the form they acquired during much earlier periods of cultural crystallization and are bound to conflict with each other (as in Huntington, 1996) and those who stress change and transformation of commitments, values and institutional structures which cannot neglect the commonality of the global condition of modernity. I stand with the latter scholars and I think this commonality of global modernity is good for the commitment to pursue SDGs.

Third, different from the proponents of the multiple modernities approach, I argue that in defining modernity structural processes and institutions matter (Acemoglu and Robinson, 2012), modernization is not "first and foremost a cultural program" (Eisenstadt, 2000), and it is more than just a set of promissory notes, i.e. a set of hopes and expectations that entail some minimal conditions of adequacy which may be demanded of macro-sociological institutions no matter how much these institutions may differ in other respects"(Wittrock, 2000). The development of processes of structural differentiation across a wide range of institutions is a key and distinctive feature of all modernizing societies, although these societies produce quite different and specific forms of family, firm, government and welfare, since they are influenced by endogenous cultural traditions and historical experiences and by the specific epochs in which the different phases of the journey toward and through modernity take place.

I reiterate that there is not a unique successful model of modern society, a single legitimate way being modern (as in Fukuyama's post-cold war book *The End of History and the Last Man*, 1993), but several multiple modernities and varieties within them do exist. At the same time, I affirm once again that recognizing multiplicity and diversity does not imply denying the existence of common distinctive features in any process of modernization; if the concepts of modernity and modernization have a meaning at all, they must be defined in terms of few distinctive features, structural as well as cultural. The facts that the path toward and through modernity has been characterized from the start by internal antinomies and contradictions, social conflicts and political protest, and that these contradictions have fostered growing differences in the modernizing countries of the different regions of the world, do not imply that we cannot identify a core of key common features in all processes of modernization, as well as a set of similar problems that receive both similar and different, both common and specific, solutions.

2. The Sustainable Development Goals

The SDGs were solemnly approved and launched at the UN General Assembly in September 25-27, 2015 in New York. In July 2014, the UN General Assembly's Open Working Group (OWG) on SDGs forwarded a proposal for the SDGs to the UN General Assembly. The proposal contained 17 goals with 169 targets covering a broad range of sustainable development issues. In December 2014, the UN General Assembly accepted the Secretary-General's Synthesis Report which stated that the agenda for the post-2015 SDGs process would be based on the OWG proposals. Following the intergovernmental negotiations on the Post-2015 Development Agenda beginning in January 2015 and ending in August 2015, the final document transforming our world—The 2030 Agenda for Sustainable Development was adopted at the UN Sustainable Development Summit in September 2015.

The decision to move from the Millennium Development Goals (MDGs) to the SDGs was caused by the recognition that the MDGs had been only partially met and that much had still to be done. A few examples are drawn from the OWG proposal of July 2014: The goal to reduce by half the number of people living with less than 1.25 dollars a day by 2015 had been achieved, but one billion and two hundred million people still lived in conditions of extreme poverty; the percentage of children who did not attend primary school had been halved and gender equality had been achieved, but in developing countries 10% of children still did not receive any kind of education; the number of deaths below five years of age had been reduced to half, but there were still more than six million who did not reach that age in life; the global maternal mortality ratio had dropped by 46%, but the probability of maternal mortality was still fourteen times higher in developing countries compared with the developed ones. But the most discouraging data are those on environmental degradation due to climate change: compared to 1990 carbon emissions into the atmosphere had increased by 50%.

The agreement on SDGs resolutions of the September 2015 as well as that on climate change in the Paris COP 21 Conference in the following December had been reached adopting a smart device: all underwriting parties, first of all sovereign nation states, agreed on the goals, but kept their decision-making freedom as far as means are concerned, with the further qualification that they accepted to be monitored and evaluated for their performances. This device is a smart compromise between national sovereignty and global governance. In the contemporary globalizing world we live in a basic contradiction between growing economic, technological interdependence and social interconnectedness on the one hand, and persistent political fragmentation and cultural diversity on the other (Martinelli, 2003). As human beings, we face the same challenges — wars, climate change, inequality, but as citizens of sovereign countries we tend to recognize legitimate decision-making power only to our national governments. Sovereign governments are compelled by the gravity and urgency of the problems of the global agenda to cooperate and coordinate their actions, but they do not accept targets which are imposed from the outside.

The United Nations is not a world government but an international organization of sovereign states; it can draw attention to problems, recommend appropriate strategies, discourage dangerous courses of action, but can very seldom impose its will on the member states. Global governance can only be of multiple actors, multi-lateral and multi-level, but sovereign states continue to be the key players; international organizations, market actors and the various components of civil society — like NGOs and epistemic communities — also exert their influence in different ways and to different degrees on the various issues, but political power continues to stay mostly at the nation-state level (Martinelli, 2015). In world politics the best option to mobilize the international community to act in the pursuit of common global goals and targets is, therefore, an agreement among all the actors involved to implement their own autonomous strategies and policies. And to accept that, their performance is periodically assessed on the basis of agreed indicators and assessment procedures. The method agreed upon in the SDGs and COP 21 conferences is not easy to implement, as it is shown by the practice of the EU, which has first experimented it under the name of Open Method of Coordination (OMC). This method requires a set of conditions to work successfully: a clear definition of targets, guidelines and deadlines, constant monitoring and periodical assessment of performances by independent evaluators, the involvement of main stakeholders, and mutual learning of best practices. Wherever powerful interests prevent these requirements to be met, the OMC risks to become an exercise in symbolic politics in which national governments revise existing policies in order to prove their acceptance of the shared goals. Applying this method to the attainment of the SDGs will be even more difficult, because interests' conflicts and ideological divergences are more pronounced in the world at large than in the EU. Major obstacles are on its way both at the global level (economic and social inequalities, asymmetries of power, and conflicting Weltanschauungen) and at the country level (vested interests, power encroachments, corruption, and illegal activities).

In spite of these difficulties, the UN's post-2015 sustainable development agenda is a significant example of international cooperation and deserves the effort of all good willing partners, first of all of scientific communities all over the world. Global solidarity is still insufficient but is growing, and it is encouraging that, alongside international organizations, national, regional and city governments, many non-governmental organizations, collective movements, socially responsible corporations, labour unions, professional associations, religious institutions, universities and research centers have contributed to defining the goals and targets, and more importantly, are cooperating to achieve them. The two most important international scientific councils, International Council of Scientific Unions (ICSU) for the natural sciences and International Social Science Council (ISSC) for the social sciences, have been involved from the start in the process; they produced together a perspective analysis of all the proposed targets, evaluating those which were well developed, those which should be made more specific and those which required significant work (ICSU and ISSC, 2015); and they are now working together in major international research projects like Future Earth.

The SDGs are a major improvement of the MDGs approved at the turn of the century, in the sense that they address key systemic barriers to sustainable development which were not mentioned in the MDGs, such as inequality, unsustainable consumption patterns, weak institutional capacity and environmental degradation. The MDGs captured only to a limited degree all three dimensions of sustainability — social, economic and environmental, and dealt only with developing countries. In contrast, the SDGs deal with all countries and all dimensions, although the relevance of each goal varies from country to country. That's one of the key strengths. Another key strength of the SDGs is a policy planning which is based on transformative solutions, the deployment of new technologies (e.g. information and communications technology), monitoring, real time and intensive learning cycle, high innovation and corporate social responsibility, good governance and public participation, an ethos of solidarity, transparency, honesty and responsibility.

However, although clearly improved with regard to the previous MDGs, the SDGs framework has its own weaknesses: the series of 17 goals and 169 targets is listed and juxtaposed without specifying key trade-offs and complementarities among; goals — and even several targets — are presented using a "silo approach", i.e. they are addressed as separate elements, mostly in isolation from each other. But since many goals are interlinked and many targets may contribute to several goals, some goals and targets may conflict, and action to meet one target could have unintended consequences on others, mostly if they are pursued separately. Groups of targets should, therefore, be pursued in an integrated way, taking care of important trade-offs (for instance, rapid industrial growth can lead to environmental degradation; an increase in agriculture land which is used to help end hunger can result in biodiversity loss; rapid urbanization can foster inequalities between city dwellers and the rural population). The SDGs framework considers only some systemic and structural barriers to, as well as drivers of, change, such as inequality, inappropriate consumption, inadequate institutional capacity, but it lacks a theory of change, an analysis of how the pursuit of specific goals and the related transformative strategies will lead to broader outcomes of social transformation. Moreover, SDGs rightly stress the importance of global networks of universities, business, government, and civil society to promote practical innovative and transformative solutions, but fail to identify the key social groups which oppose this or that goal or target and neglect to analyse conflicts of interests and the ways in which pressure groups with conflicting interests influence policy-making. One has sometimes the impression that cooperation for the common goals is "taken for granted"; the SDGs narrative is plentiful of words like global challenges, universal goals, cooperative partnership, stakeholders engagement, public consultation, whereas there is almost no mention of concepts like power and conflict. But, since the attainment of SDGs greatly impacts on the distribution of costs and benefits and on power relations both at the national and international level, great attention should be paid to the formation of social coalitions capable of opposing and resisting strategies and policies aimed at attaining common goals.

The real challenge is how to verify that pledges to achieve the SDGs are fulfilled by the underwriting governments and how to measure and evaluate their performance. In order to do that we must assess how and to what degree the different goals and targets are considered legitimate priorities by the citizens of different societies and effectively pursued by their governments. However, this analytical exercise is not easy since each SDG is articulated into a set of specific targets and subtargets (from the four ones of Goal 7 to the thirteen ones of Goal 3) and some SDGs lump together more than one objective. Let's take Goal 16 for example. It concerns three different objectives: peace, access to justice for all, and effective, accountable and inclusive institutions at all levels. The related twelve targets are rather diverse as well, from the reduction of all forms of violence — and specifically that against children — to combating all forms of organized crime, corruption and bribery, from promoting the rule of law to protecting fundamental freedoms, from ensuring participatory decision-making to public access to information. Most of these targets lack statistical indicators and available data, and could not be measured without serious difficulty. For instance, Target 1 ("Significantly reduce all forms of violence and related death rates everywhere") is not a target but rather a restatement of the goal; it should have specific targets as, for instance, the reduction in armed conflicts among and within countries, and detailed data on murder, assault, suicide and intimidation. Several targets are very ambitious but rather vague and poorly specified. For instance, Target 4 ("By 2030 significantly reduce illicit financial and arms flows, strengthen the recovery and return of stolen assets and combat all forms of organized crime") and Target 5 ("Substantially reduce corruption and bribery in all their forms"), what do they exactly mean? How "significantly"? How "substantially"? And are reliable data available? Contrary to most other SDGs' targets which specify a deadline for their attainment (generally 2030, sometimes anticipated to 2020), this happens here only in the case of Target 4 and Target 9 ("By 2030 provide legal identity for all, including birth registration"). Target 9 and Target 10 ("Ensure public access to information and protect fundamental freedoms, in accordance with national legislation and international agreements") are actually policy recommendations. Ambitious targets like those concerning violence and criminal activities or Target 2 ("End abuse, exploitation trafficking and all forms of violence and torture against children") would need reliable quantitative indicators. Others, equally ambitious, like Target 6 ("Develop effective, accountable and transparent institutions at all levels") and Target 7 ("Ensure responsive, inclusive, participatory and representative decision-making at all levels") would require good qualitative analyses. Moreover, at the roots of these goals and targets, these are of different conceptions of democracy (representative, participatory, pluralist, centralized, etc.), different criteria of political inclusion, and different models of bureaucracy, which have been developed by a huge literature of political science and sociology and would require a stock-taking of research findings which has not been done. This kind of secondary research analysis is crucial since if we want to assess the feasibility of the various goals and targets, we will need to identify key drivers and major obstacles to transformation of sustainability, and orient effective public policies and private actors' strategies.

This critique of the way in which sustainable development goals and targets have been formulated should not, however, discourage us from trying to assess how different societies are more or less fit to pursue them. In the language of modernization studies, we should ask ourselves whether SDGs can be considered key components of the cultural and political program of modernity and try to evaluate whether specific types of modernity are better equipped than others to cope with the attainment of one or the other of the goals, and one or the other of the targets. In this paper, I will make this exercise with regard to European modernity (one of the two main variants, with the other of the American, of the Western type of modernity); in other words I will discuss the core values and institutions of the modern European civilization, with the further qualification that I will not consider the whole of Europe but that part which coincides with the EU.

This exercise presupposes that it is possible to identify Western civilization as a specific socio-cultural entity, European modernity as a major variety of it and the EU as the contemporary embodiment of European modernity. Two groups of scholars would consider it impossible, although for opposite arguments. The first group of scholars, exemplified by D'Andrea (2001), argued that the core elements of Western identity were no longer exclusive because they had been successfully "exported" and assimilated in other parts of the world. The fact that the civilization of modernity was born in Europe and then spread first to America and then throughout the world induces them to believe that in spreading worldwide, Europe has lost its specific character. In other words, the Europeanization of the world is also the end of Europe as an entity in itself, since European culture, being intrinsically de-territorialized, can no longer define the specificity of a single part of the world. Opposite to this is the view exemplified by Huntington (1996), which claimed that the identification of Western civilization with modern civilization was totally false, since the central characteristics of the West, those which distinguish it from other civilizations, antedated the modernization of the West.

Both views have some grain of truth, but miss two key points: 1) It is possible to identify clear specific features of European modernity, because, distinctive cultural roots of Europe existed since antiquity, but they crystallized into a specific set of cultural and institutional forms only with the advent of Western modernity, fostering bold institutional innovations through a process of historical learning (science and technology, market-led industrial capitalism, representative democracy, nation-state citizenship, research university). The European identity is closely related to the culture of modernity, i.e., to a particular conception of the modern age as an epoch oriented toward the future, conceived as being novel, and as better than the present and the past (Martinelli, 2005). 2) They neglect the fact that the European origin of global modernization does not entail that countries approaching and undergoing the process of modernity do not develop their own distinctive cultural codes and institutions. In other words, both fail to consider that the contemporary world is a world of multiple modernities, especially in its non-Western parts, and that any transition to modernity implies a process of creative adaptation, not the inexorable establishment of a certain type of mental outlook (scientific rationalism, pragmatic instrumentalism, secularism). Traditional culture and modern technology to some extent coexist in many modernizing countries, as well as market economies and authoritarian political regimes. Science, technology and capitalism are the dimensions of Western culture most widespread in the world because they are largely indifferent to ends and able to outperform any other rival instrument. Other aspects of Western culture, such as modern individualism, the critical mind, civil rights, democratic representation and the rule of law, have proved much more difficult to be accepted since they conflict with deep-seated alternative views of the individual-society relationship.

3. The EU as the embodiment of the distinctive features of European modernity

At first glance, the core values and institutions of European modernity that are embodied in the EU seem fit for the pursuit of SDGs. European modernity is one of the main types of global modernity and the EU is its main political embodiment. European modernity shows both strong similarities and key differences with the other most important variety of Western civilization, represented by the United States, which I explored in the book *Transatlantic Divide: Comparing American and European Society* (2007). The EU is a novel political construction, both institutionally and culturally, and a multinational entity with a core of shared values (democratic institutions, basic human rights, free competition, preservation of different cultures and languages, cooperation and coexistence in international relations) that are at the foundations of common institutions.

The value core of European/Western modernity can be identified in the constant tension between rationalism and individualism/subjectivity, seen as opposing and complementary principles. Rationalism and individualism/subjectivity characterized European history from Greek philosophy and Roman law to the Christian religion, but they coalesced into a specific set of cultural values and institutional arrangements with the advent of modernity. They express the tension between individual liberty and social organization. The longing for freedom is universal, but has developed to the fullest extent in Europe, where it has been conceived as the development of the individual together with the social world around him.

Rationalism is the capacity of the human mind to know, control and transform nature (according to a conception of the world as an environment that can be moulded to the purpose of fulfilling human needs and wants), and is the confidence of human beings that they can rationally pursue their own ends and, ultimately, be the masters of their own destinies. It is the product of the critical mind which originated in the Greek philosophical ethos and developed with the Enlightenment's constant critique of its historical era. It has manifested itself in a variety of different forms: from Romanesque architecture to Renaissance painting, from the science of Galileo and Newton to the music of Bach and Beethoven, and from the citizen of liberal democracy to homo economics. Rationalism is closely linked to the relentless quest for knowledge, which was common to various ancient civilizations, but received new impetus in European modernity, when knowledge was liberated from its subordination to a given religious truth or political end. With its confidence in the power of reason to control and transform nature, rationalism has been the breeding ground of scientific discoveries, technological inventions and entrepreneurial innovations. European modernity was the age of "Prometheus Unbound" which metaphorically expresses the absence of ethical and religious limits on the technical domination of nature and belief in constant progress. Reason is related to the perception of an absence of limits, to that particular "restlessness" of the European people portrayed in such paradigmatic figures of European literature as Dante's *Ulysses* and Goethe's *Faust*, and as exemplified in many events of European history, from transoceanic voyages to the spirit of the frontier. At the same time, reason has been conceived as a system of shared rules which make social coexistence possible. Kant did not write an apology for reason, but an inquiry into its limits. The rational mind is strong only if it is aware of its own limits, does not claim to know the Truth with the capital t, and opens the way to an endless search. In this sense, reason is by definition anti-totalitarian and strictly connected to individual freedom.

Rationalism is complementary with, and opposed to, the other core cultural trait of European modernity: individualism/subjectivity. Individualism has many different expressions in European history: evangelical personalism, municipal freedom of late medieval republics, economic competition in the market, citizenship rights in liberal democracies, and reflexive subjectivity of contemporary Europeans. Like rationalism, individualism evolved within the cultural heritage of European history, but it only fully emerged with the advent of modernity. Individualism is at the root of the principles of liberty and equality affirmed by Ius naturalismus (which holds that all human beings are equal insofar as they are endowed with reason), and by English political liberalism and French and German philosophy of the Enlightenment; principles which were recognized in the prerogatives of the English Parliament after the Glorious Revolution of 1688-1689 and solemnly proclaimed in the

American Constitution of 1776 and in the Déclaration des Droits de l'Homme et du Citoyen of 1789. These principles affirm the inviolable rights of the individual to life, freedom and the full accomplishment of his/her existential project. Liberty expresses itself both as negative freedom (i.e. as the protection of human rights against the abuses of power) and as positive freedom (i.e. as the citizen's right to participate in the formation of the common will). Equality was initially defined as the equality of the rights and duties of citizenship and the equality of citizens before the law; soon thereafter it became equality of opportunities and life chances as well, and thus opened the way for the conceptions of progressive liberalism, social democracy and welfare policies which became integral parts of Europe's political culture in the twentieth century. The struggle to strike a balance between equality and freedom is a leitmotiv of the history of European political thought.

Individualism and subjectivity are not identical: the formal term is preferred by scholars who stress positive aspects of European modernity, such as individual rights, scientific progress, secular outlook, cultural pluralism, contractual view of society; the latter term is preferred by critics of such attitudes as pragmatic calculation, the soulless pursuit of money, and the lack of moral passion, to which they oppose the care for the self, spontaneous expression and authentic experience. However, political and economic individualism and aesthetic and moral subjectivity are in fact dimensions of the same principle; they are not the roots of two alternative types of modernity (the supportive and the critical, the societal and the cultural) but rather components of the same cultural and institutional syndrome. Imagination and reason are not enemies; rather, they are allies in the work of both the scientist and the artist, both seek to explore and experience everything without being subject to limits.

The dialectical relationship between the principle of rationality and the principle of subjectivity/individualism manifests itself in the double matrix of change and routine in which the modern self lives. As Gaonkar (2001) wrote, each of those unforgettable figures of modernity — Marx's "revolutionary", Baudelaire's "dandy", Nietzsche's "superman", Weber's "intellectual", Simmel's "stranger", Musil's "man without qualities", Benjamin's "flaneur" (and Schumpeter's "entrepreneur" — I add) — is caught and carried in the intoxicating rush of an epochal change and yet finds itself fixed and formulated by a disciplinary system of social roles and functions (a very European list).

In the European civilization of modernity, these values, attitudes and interpretations of the world coalesce into a distinct cultural program and combined with a set of new institutional formations, the most important of which are the research university, the capitalist market and the industrial firm, the nation state, the democratic polity, and the welfare state.

First, universities. The depth of Chinese and Indian religion and philosophy, the richness of Muslim scientific and religious thought, the advanced astronomical knowledge of Mesopotamia and pre-Colombian America, are only some examples of the historical evidence that Western knowledge is not exceptional at all. What is distinctive, though, is its more marked capacity to unite abstract theory and empirical research and, even more importantly, to link scientific discovery, invention and technological innovation under the constant pressure of either war or commercial competition. Also specific to Western culture, it is its greater ability to design institutions particularly suited to the formation and diffusion of knowledge, from Italian and French universities with medieval origins to the seventeenth-century British scientific academies, from nineteenth-century German research universities to contemporary American research laboratories. European modernity was not simply a package of technological and organizational developments; it was intimately bound up with a political revolution, and with an equally important transformation in the nature of scholarly and scientific practices and institutions (Wittrock, 2000). Europe has invented and perfected an understanding of science which has become a global example and role model. The main characteristics of this understanding of science as it has developed since the Renaissance are, as Rudolph argued, the recognition of mathematics as the measure of exactness in science, the unity of freedom of scientific enquiry and scientific criticism, and the dependence of empirical knowledge on conceptual reflection (Rudolph, 2001).

Market-driven industrial capitalism is a second key distinctive institution of European modernity. The governing principle of capitalism is a constant search for the rational maximization of individual utility in order to compete successfully in the market. Its two basic institutions are the efficient combination of the production factors in the industrial firm, and the exchange of goods and services in the "free" market expanding throughout the world. The Industrial Revolution of the eighteenth century (a most powerful process of innovation, capital accumulation and market expansion) was helped by agricultural and long-distance trade surpluses, and the availability of iron and coal; but it was, first and foremost, generated by a specific linkage with the scientific and technological revolutions of modernity. Trades and markets flourished in the early empires and in many non-European parts of the world as well, but the particular combination of the Industrial Revolution with the free market was a European specificity which gave capitalist growth unprecedented strength and dynamism. Market capitalism has been extensively criticized, first of all in the Marxist tradition, in terms of the dominance of instrumental reason, the overriding concern with efficiency, the "depoliticization" of public life, and the quest for material affluence and passive consumerism. But, in spite of all its internal contradictions and social costs, market capitalism has proved to be resilient to crises and self-transforming.

The nation state is a third key institution of European modernity: a pre-modern institution which slowly took shape in opposition to the multi-ethnic empires and the supranational church, grew historically through a civil bureaucracy, an army and a diplomacy, and developed in the modernization process in combination with representative democracy, the fourth key institution of modernity. The nation state resulted from the encounter between state and nation, i.e. between a sovereign, autonomous, centralized political organization, and a community (real and imagined at the same time) founded on ties of blood, language, shared tradition, and collective memory. The democratic nation state is the institutional embodiment of rational/legal authority in modern society, an impersonal and sovereign political entity with supreme jurisdiction over a clearly delimited territory and population, which claims the monopoly of coercive power, and enjoys legitimacy as a result of citizens' support. The centralized nation state implies the breaking of many local and cultural autonomies, but the risks for individual freedom are kept under control by the development of the institutions of representative democracy, i.e. a political system made up of elected officials representing the interests and opinions of citizens in a context characterized by the rule of law, based on the consensus of citizens, and developing in order to protect their basic rights. The Greek polis, the Roman republic and the free cities of medieval Italy, Germany and the Flanders were all antecedents of this European specificity. The various forms of parliaments, majority rule in government and the protection of minority rights, free and periodical elections, independent judiciary, civil liberties, and free press, are institutional innovations born in European modernity and developed in the United States of America (the "first new nation" constructed by European immigrants) in the course of the three major democratic revolutions — the English, the French and the American, and what were then extended to other regions of the world. In today's globalized world, sovereign nation states are still the key actors in international relations, although subject to the two-fold pressure applied by the growing global interconnectedness of social relations, from above, and by the reaffirmation of regional and local identities and claims of autonomy, from below.

The fifth distinctive institution of European modernity is the welfare state. It developed later than the previous ones, in the course of the twentieth century, partially as a counterbalance to the failures of the market and to the excesses of individualism. It is one of the most important institutional innovations of the twentieth century. Combined with market capitalism, it forms the so-called European social model. The model rejects the notion of the self-regulating market and aims at achieving the joint goals of economic competitiveness and social cohesion. It is an effective way toward the non-violent resolution of redistributive conflicts. The core value at the basis of the welfare state is solidarity, which is based on a sense of belonging, the perception of a common fate, the acceptance of reciprocal responsibilities among fellow citizens, the mutualization of risks through social insurances, and the limitation of economic and social inequalities. The welfare state contributed to fill the void left by the decline of traditional institutions like the church and the local community, and to answer the basic question: Which are the foundations of solidarity in an individualistic society? Welfare policies of EU member states are undergoing a deep transformation as a consequence of the economic crisis, trying to move from welfare state to the social investment state.

This "list" of the distinctive cultural and institutional aspects of the European modernity does not pretend to be complete; functionally organized metropolitan cities and churches are other relevant instances. European cities are part of an old urban system, tracing back to the Roman empire and the Middle Age, which was deeply transformed, first, by nation building and market capitalism and second, by contemporary globalization, in which the most important of them have become hubs of global networks of interdependence. Christian institutions like the Roman Catholic Church (one of the oldest and most durable institutions in history), Christian theology and collective movements have deeply influenced modern European institutions and mentality, sometimes as their source of inspiration, sometimes as their adversary: on the one hand, the highest values and associated norms of European modernity (such as human dignity and its inviolability, the rights of the person, and the individual conscience and responsibility) have, among others, also Jewish-Christian roots. On the other, the notion of the absence of limits and the belief in man as the master of his own destiny have encountered strong opposition in the "anti-modernist" stance of the Catholic Church. And the distinction between temporal and sacred power, which is a well-grounded principle of modern democracy, was achieved only through centuries-long struggles. In today's Europe, the impact of religion is not only a matter of memory in a secularized society but still influences attitude and behaviour. Religion is not (and has not been) a simple undifferentiated unity since there is a great religious diversity internally to Christianity itself and religions other than Christianity, primarily Islam, playing a significant role.

These core cultural and institutional elements have contributed to a specific definition of European modernity, but they are not unambiguous and do not form a coherent system: they have in fact conflicted with each other, as in the cases of capitalism and democracy, religion and science, nationalism and peace. Nor have they produced solely desirable effects or positive outcomes. As Jaspers (1947) remarked, for every position Europe has, it also developed the exact opposite. European history has been constantly marked by deep cleavages, violent conflicts, idiosyncratic controversies, and numerous errors and crimes. The values of rationalism and individualism and the institutions of the market and the nation state have given rise to many contradictions, violations, and deformations, as the profound contradictions between capital and wage labour, economic growth and environmental conservation, colonial and neo-colonial exploitation and the quest for freedom show, not to speak of wars, mass murders and genocide. Indeed, polar opposites characterize almost every core element of European culture: the Christian faith of universal love has inspired some of the most intolerant doctrines and bloodiest religious wars ever; in the heart of the twentieth-century Europe, democracy collapsed into devastating totalitarianism; the free market constantly reproduces monopoly and oligopoly; the quest for political independence has degenerated into aggressive nationalism. In other words, for every value that has been promoted, Europe has also promoted its opposite: faith/reason, tolerance/religious war, democracy/totalitarianism, etc. But this is not a reason for dismissing the importance of the European civilization for human progress (of which SDGs are a basic component): We certainly do not cease to regard ancient Athens as the cradle of democracy because it also experienced tyranny.

Moreover, a salient feature of European modernity today is that history has been subject to reflexive reassertion through a process of historical learning from painful past errors and crimes. The European community was born of the desire to put an end to the centuries-long European "civil" wars. As Therborn (1995) argued, the conception of history that underlies the efforts to establish an ever closer union of the peoples of Europe is not couched in terms of some "manifest destiny" of Europe, or in terms of Europeans as the chosen people, and rather, it is the view of history's disciples and not of its masters. European modernity is not a model to export and, even worse, to impose on others (seeking to do it would be a risky undertaking, widely opposed as arrogant "neo-colonialism"). It is not a model, but a key comparator for other modernities, with which the EU should engage in a process of mutual learning and understanding.

4. How Is the EU Equipped to Meet the SDGs?

The core values and distinctive institutions of European modernity that I have outlined help explain why the EU can be considered a successful example of economic development and political and cultural modernization. The EU is one of the largest economies in the world — in terms of gross national product, market size and scientific potential — and has by far the most developed welfare states: with 7% of the world population and close to 25% of the world GDP, the EU concentrates half of the world welfare expenditure. At the beginning of the twenty-first century the EU was presented as a better societal model than the American one, which "emphasizes community relationships over individual autonomy, cultural diversity over assimilation, quality of life over the accumulation of wealth, sustainable development over unlimited material growth... universal human rights and the rights of nature over property rights, and global cooperation over the unilateral exercise of power... a vision of the future, capable of quietly eclipsing the so-called American dream" (Rifkin, 2004). The ambitious Lisbon strategy, decided in 2000 and aiming at "transforming in ten years the European economy into the most competitive and dynamic knowledge-based economy in the world", reflected the optimism of the time and could, in fact, be seen as the necessary precondition to the attainment of the MDGs.

This optimist view seems outdated today, after the long economic recession following the 2008 global financial crisis; but the EU as the embodiment of European modernity still seems better equipped than most of the other modern and modernizing societies to pursue and achieve the new SDGs. The impact of the economic/financial crisis, together with unresolved problems of an unaccomplished political union, prevented the Lisbon strategy to be effective. Then, in 2010, a new ten-year program, Europe 2020, was launched, which articulated more in detail the previous overarching goal and set five main objectives in order to overcome the crisis and achieve a smart, sustainable and inclusive growth: 1) 75% employment of the 20-64 years of age group; 2) 3% of European GDP minimal investment in research and development; 3) 20% minimal reduction of 1990 greenhouse gas levels; 4) 10% reduction of school drop-outs and at least 30% of people aged 30-34 years holding higher education degrees; 5) 20 million people risking poverty less than in 2010. These objectives and the suggested ways to implement them — from job creation for the young to fighting poverty, from fostering digital innovation to re-launching the common market — are very similar to some key SDGs. But six years later, the objectives of Europe 2020 are far from being achieved. It is therefore necessary to ask ourselves why and to discuss, in more general terms, whether and to what extent the European variety of modernity favours or obstructs the attainment of MDGs.

The EU, as well as the other modern developed societies, such as the United States, Japan and most OECD (Organization for Economic Co-operation and Development) countries, seems better equipped than emerging economies and developing societies to attain most SDGs, from ending poverty and hunger to ensuring quality health and education, from access to modern energy to combating climate change, from achieving gender equality to promoting justice and effective institutions, although there is still much to do to fully attain any of these goals. But significant differences in performance exist also among developed modern societies with regard to the various SDGs. If we compare the European and the American economies, we will find that the former performs better in fostering innovation (Goal 9) and job creation (Goal 8), whereas the latter performs better in ensuring healthy lives and promoting well-being for all and at all ages (Goal 3), combating climate change and its impacts (Goal 13), and making cities inclusive, safe, resilient and sustainable (Goal 11). If we compare the EU with Japan, we find that the former performs better on Goal 5 (gender equality) and Goal 11 (inclusive cities), while the latter performs better on Goal 10 (reducing inequality). If we make comparison not only in space among different modernities, but also through time — analysing European society at different points in time, we will find both improvement — as in Goal 13 (combating climate change and its impact), and worsening — as in Goal 10. On the one hand, in fact, the targets of the EU environmental policy program 20/20/20 are likely to be met by most member countries. On the other hand, inequality has been growing in recent decades both among EU members and within most of them, "absolute poverty" has increased, and even food security and improved nutrition cannot be taken for granted. Economic and social inequalities represent a serious problem of European society, in spite of its developed welfare states which, although suffered restrictions as a consequence of the long economic crisis, have counteracted some of the most negative effects. Even for goals where a European advantage is recognized, like Goal 11, the situation has not improved, quite on the contrary: cities remain a distinctive feature of European society, continue to play a key role as they did in European history, and are comparatively more resilient and sustainable than cities in other regions of the world; and yet their safety and inclusiveness are now challenged by the terrorist threat and by the need to host huge waves of asylum seekers.

The first glance assessment that the EU is reasonably fit to meet SDGs must therefore be better argued and qualified. We could assess the performance of the EU with regard to all 17 goals and all 169 targets, but the evaluation would be difficult for all the reasons I discussed above (interconnected goals, poorly specified targets, lack of significant indicators and reliable data, etc.). It is then easier and more appropriate to focus on two key questions upon which depends the effective capacity of the EU to attain the SDGs for itself, and to contribute to their achievement by other countries in the world: the first question is whether the EU is capable to implement an inclusive and sustainable development as a successful exit strategy from the crisis; the second is whether it will become an ever greater union with enhanced citizens' participation and a more balanced division of power among its main institutions.

4.1 *The First Question: Inclusive and Sustainable Development as a Successful Exit Strategy from the Crisis*

The first question is whether and to what extent the EU will improve its economic performance in terms of innovation, competition and growth, in a socially inclusive and environmentally sustainable way. The 2008 global financial crisis which made the related economic stagnation makes this goal more difficult to achieve. But crises are often also opportunities for changes. A successful exit strategy from the crisis should not only reverse the trend of economic stagnation, but also develop a type of sustainable growth which updates the European social model, i.e. the combination of coordinated market economy and welfare state, adding environmental sustainability. The EU should not go back to business as usual, but develop a new development model, which permits to achieve the ambitious SDGs both in Europe and in the world at large. However, although the underlying values of SDGs are shared by the majority of the European citizens and European institutions committed themselves to pursue them, member states' governments do not agree on common policy priorities and development strategies. The main reason of this disagreement is the different way in which the EU members are affected by and perceive the impact of three different and intertwined crises: the economic/financial crisis, the migrants' emergency, and the threat of terrorism. These crises put at risk the whole EU fabric since they foster the upsurge of nationalist/populist parties which ask for national closures and the re-nationalization of communitarian policies. The first crisis threatens the European social model, the second and the third combined threaten the European integration model of building unity through diversity. In other words, the three crises put at risk the most specific features of the EU and dramatically reduce its capacity to follow a path of sustainable and inclusive development.

The 2008 global financial crisis has been longer affected and has a deeper impact on the EU than on the other main economic regions of the world: the output of several Eurozone countries has yet to return to pre-crisis levels, public debts and unemployment rates have been growing for most EU members. The crisis has reversed the long-lasting tendency toward greater homogeneity within the EU, which had been favored by the free circulation of people, goods, services and capital. In the first decade of the twenty-first century the differences in productivity among the Eurozone countries have increased by 30%; the unemployment rate in Greece and Spain is three to four times the Eurozone average; almost all Eurozone countries are above the Maastricht Treaty requirement of the 60% public debt/GDP ratio, but Greece, Italy and France have higher debts than average. At the root of these differences is not only the crisis that has affected in different ways and to different degrees the economies of the various EU members, but also the introduction of the euro and the response to the crisis given by the institutions of the EU's governance; in other words, it is not the lack of an exit strategy, as many argue, but the specific type of exit strategy that was adopted.

The creation of the euro and the European Central Bank was not a political mistake, since benefits have outdone the costs for the countries involved. The demands for ending the monetary union are based on wrong analyses, and in any case, even most critics of the original decision must admit that dismantling the euro now would amount to great economic losses and political risks. The political hazard of the euro architects was deciding a common monetary policy without common fiscal and growth policies to complement it, on the assumption that the latter would "spontaneously" follow according to the usual "spillover effect". But the fact of having a single currency and central bank with nineteen different economic and fiscal policies of countries with quite diverse economies creates contradictions that are difficult to manage. Moreover, European leaders did not consider that the euro would not only increase the interdependence of members' economies, but also produce relevant differences that had to be managed. These differences could be tolerated in the phase of economic growth of the early 2000s, not in the following phase of recession and stagnation, since they prolonged and worsened the effects of the global crisis. Infra-union differences should have been more effectively managed, and weaker countries should have been helped to recover and allowed to run less stringent public budgets.

On the contrary, the exit strategy chosen by the EU and the Eurozone authorities was a policy of austerity for all, at the expenses of growth and employment, with the richer countries in Europe dictating the poorer ones the austerity cure in order for them to regain the trust of the financial industry. They did it, and continue to do it, in spite of all evidence that austerity is a highly poisonous medicine, an overdose of which will kill the patient rather than stimulate growth and expand the tax base, in which case the weakest Eurozone countries become even more dependent on lenders (Offe, 2014). The EU members policies have become more and more market-conforming and more and more influenced by the strongest members, first of all Germany. At the same time, increasing powers have been transferred to the supranational level, without a parallel transfer of democratic control. The consequence of this state of affairs is technocratic governance and elitist policy-making, together with a growing asymmetry of power among the members. The predominant austerity strategy has a negative impact also on sustainable and inclusive growth policies, since it curtails private and public investments, creates more unemployment and makes combating climate change a second-rate priority which lies well behind fiscal austerity.

If fiscal austerity has such negative effects, why is a different strategy so difficult to agree upon? The main reason is that the different impact of the global crisis on the economies and societies of the EU members has fostered political cleavages along nationalist lines to the point that national interests and the related conflicts have become more important than class interests and related conflicts. It is difficult to take the decisions that are needed since they are unpopular: on the one hand, large-scale and long-term debt mutualization, which would result in massive redistributive measures both among member states and social classes, is rejected by the majority of citizens of Northern "core" members that have been so far less affected by the crisis than those of the South. On the other hand, policies aiming at enhancing competitiveness and adjusting the unit cost of labour (the ratio between real wages and labor productivity) are hard to implement by the governments of Southern "peripheral" countries since are rejected by most of their voters. A divorce occurs between politics and policy: populist mass politics that has no perceptible implication for policy-making on core issues propagates a distorted, simplified picture of complex problems like those of the Eurozone, while elitist policy-making takes place without receiving legitimation through politics. It is difficult for Europe's political leaders to generate the public support needed to create an authentic political and economic union, which would allow a more effective, equitable and strategic management of the crisis; they tend, instead, to muddle through, just doing the minimum necessary for the system to survive.

The situation is complicated by the fact that the North/South cleavage between pro-fiscal austerity Northern states and pro-growth Southern states goes together — and often conflates — with two other main cleavages: the cleavage between continental Europe and the United Kingdom and the cleavage between old Western members and new Eastern members of the EU. The cleavage between continental Europe and the UK has long-standing roots in the "special relationship" between the UK and the United States, in the British imperial past and in the British culture if insular. The UK governments have constantly favoured the European free market and constantly opposed the transfer of sovereignty to supranational institutions. The June referendum in which the UK citizens decided to withdraw from the EU stems from the dilemma between the perceived benefits of the European common market and the perceived costs of limited sovereignty; conversely, for citizens of the other EU members "Brexit" is perceived as a dilemma between weakening the EU financial and military power and the removal of an obstacle to deeper political integration. The best way out from this dilemma is to design of union "at variable geometry" in which a group of core countries — most likely the Eurozone's — move toward greater integration, while the others — first of all the UK — use the opting-out clause, but remain full members of the European common market.

The other cleavage stems from the enlargement of the EU from 15 to 25 (and then 27 and 28, but back to 27) members (most of which from the Eastern Europe). The enlargement has been praised by some as a strategic success, arguing that the EU was capable to take advantage of the "window of opportunity" opened by the collapse of the USSR. But the enlargement has been criticized by others as a strategic mistake, arguing that it took place before "deepening" the political integration, with the consequence of making European governance more difficult and conflict-ridden. In fact, the new Eastern members (Poland, Baltic states, Hungary, Czech Republic, Slovakia, Slovenia, later Romania and Bulgaria and then Croatia) have had a quite different post-Second World War history, after the end of the Cold War have gone through a complex regime change, and have faced partially different problems and sets of policy priorities (first of all in foreign and in migration policies) than the old Western members. Old ethnic and national conflicts, which had been silent during the Cold War years and had been absorbed by the great ideological divide between the United States and the USSR, surfaced again and fostered aggressive nationalism and euro-skeptic government parties, which pursue stubborn re-nationalization, and obstruct the road toward a more developed supranational union. Nationalist/populist right-wing parties, which are in government in Poland and Hungary, do not support the European social model, reject the European open policy toward immigrants and want to restore internal borders, abolishing the Schengen Agreement on the free circulation of people within the EU.

The opposition to the key distinctive aspects of European integration, as social market economy and open internal borders, is not only due to the increasing disparities created by the economic crisis and its exit strategy, but also by the conflation with the two other crises — the consequences of Middle-Eastern and Northern African wars, which push millions of people to look for refuge in Europe and put European cities under the threat of terrorist attacks by the religious radicalism. These crises feed feelings of insecurity, fear and xenophopia, bolster demands for closing the frontiers and building walls, and make more difficult the social integration of immigrants. Nationalist parties with strong populist rhetoric build their consensus on these sentiments and on the illusion that retrenching within national borders and renationalizing European policies can restore political security and economic well-being.

4.2 The Second Question, the Unaccomplished Construction of the EU: Democratic Deficit and Unbalanced Division of Power Among Its Main Institutions

The upsurge of nationalism in the EU is not only fostered by the three crises, but also due to the second key question: the unaccomplished construction of the EU and the unbalanced division of power among its main institutions. The EU is a supranational union in the making, where decisions are taken by a tripartite structure (the Council of heads of governments that represents the governments of member states, the Parliament that represents the peoples of members, and the Commission as a linkage between the other two). The builders of the united Europe did not want to — and could not — reproduce the model of nation state building, first, because they were determined to put an end to centuries-long "civil wars" among the

European nations and avoid the disastrous impact of aggressive nationalism; second, because European supranational institutions lacked fundamental characteristics of a sovereign state like a strong centralized power and a standardized culture articulated through a common language. For the first time in European history the states constituting an organization were not relying on military structures for the integration of such a huge and economically potent body, but rather on a legal and economic community, and did not aim to deprive the members of their cultural diversities and different identities but on the contrary to preserve them as a common resource.

The EU did, however, only partially substitute for the nation states of members, which have been simultaneously strengthened and weakened by European integration. To a certain extent, the EU can be seen as an instance of "consensual democracy" (Lijphart, 1999), insofar as the different socio-cultural components of the European society are recomposed at the political level by democratic elites open to cooperation and agreement. The role of member states in European decision-making has been tempered by multi-level governance, i.e. a system of governance that relies on action taken at different levels (local, regional, national and supranational) by a variety of state and non-state actors who coexist in an integrated hierarchy of decision-making. But insofar as nations remain the building blocks of the supranational union (and have perpetuated themselves through the union), nationalism at the state level continues to be a major obstacle on the way of a deeper integration, especially when it is used instrumentally by political elites to increase their electoral support.

The key contradiction of European union building is the contradiction between the transfer of increasingly growing portions of national sovereignty from the nation-state level to the supranational level (the steel industry, agricultural policy, open European space for the free movement of people, goods, services and capital, and a shared currency) and the still insufficient transfer of commitment and loyalty from the citizens of the member nations to the evolving supranational community and institutions. The two aspects are clearly linked together: policy decisions at the EU level unevenly distribute costs and benefits not only among different social groups but also among different countries, and foster a re-nationalization of conflicts that needs to be held in check by a strong communitarian sentiment and commitment to a shared project. In order to achieve an authentic union, the European peoples and their governments (hopefully of all, but at least those of the Eurozone countries) must solve these two aspects of the contradiction through the development of a European citizenship and the institutional rebalancing of the EU governance. The development of a European citizenship requires the strengthening of institutions that can foster supranational commitment and loyalty, such as the integration of European education, the creation of European-wide media, the use of referenda on key public issues and the adoption of a unique and simultaneous voting system for the European parliament.

Institutional rebalancing is not less crucial. In the tripartite governance the European Council has increasingly enjoyed greater power than the Commission and the Parliament. In the European lengthy and complicated decision-making the member states' heads of governments and their ministers in the European Council tend to pursue first their national interests and negotiate complex and laborious compromises, whereas European Parliament's members and EU commissioners can more easily view problems in terms of a broader

European interest and even share a solidaristic supranational perspective, but they have less influence, since the intergovernmental method increasingly prevails over the communitarian method in policy-making. Moreover, like other intergovernmental organizations, the European Council suffers from a legitimacy deficit, while the secrecy of its debates runs against democratic accountability. It is therefore no surprise that many European citizens feel that their fate is largely decided by foreign governments which defend foreign interests, and/or by global finance and technocratic bodies that are aligned with their views. Finally, the complexity and length of intergovernmental negotiations lead to very slow decision-making in areas like economic governance that would require quick decisions, and hence the increasing reliance on technocratic bodies which are not subject to democratic control.

And yet the EU still has great resources at its disposal. With 18,000 billion dollars European GDP is the world largest. Despite declining productivity, the EU economy still has a high competitive potential, thanks to innovative entrepreneurship, well trained workforce, reliable enforcement of contracts, and efficient regulation and supervision. Despite relevant internal differences among the EU members (in activity rates and labour productivity, international investment and export shares, sovereign debt and budget balance, and business R&D and educational achievements), the EU economy draws significant benefits from its increasing interdependence, free trade and capital movement, and policy coordination and supranational policy steering. In spite of high unemployment, high sovereign debt and constant budget deficits in most member states, the European social model (coordinated market economy with welfare state) is alive and experiencing significant reforms. In spite of its unbalanced structure, long negotiations and complicated compromises, the EU governance provided a management of the global crisis which avoided the collapse of the euro and the breaking apart of the union (with measures like Euro Plus Pact, the European Semester, Sixpack, and Fiscal Compact). But the great resources which the EU still has at its disposal must be pooled together and more effectively used to face the crises.

Great advancements have been made by the European nations and peoples in the sixty-five years since the formation of the European Coal and Steel Community in 1951, but this process is now at a crucial point; the EU is facing the unprecedented challenge of three conflated crises. The conflation of the three crises is sometimes imaginary, as in the use of March 2016 Brussels terrorist bombings made both by British activists to fuel their campaign for Brexit and by the Polish government to question a commitment to accept 7,000 refugees under a previously agreed quota system. But in other cases conflation is quite real as in Greece, where the economy continues to contract and combines with the problem of dealing with the growing mass of refugees trapped in the country since Macedonia closed its border; it is also quite real insofar as it complicated the agenda of European leaders and reduced their ability to agree on effective, consensual solutions. Each unresolved crisis implies in fact an increased loss of trust and political capital and a rise in euro-sceptic attitudes in the population. If the EU is seen as failing to resolve problems, people naturally become reluctant to bestow the union with new powers. National/populist parties and leaders, on the left and the right of the politica spectrum, are on the rise, and exploit union's failures and inabilities to cope with the three conflated crises; but re-nationalization, the solution that they uphold, is a false solution (Martinelli, 2013). In order to cope with the European crises and, more generally, with the problems of the global agenda, as synthesised in the SDGs, the EU must become an accomplished federal union.

Effective crisis resolution requires, in fact, executive power and a common strategy which, in its turn, requires an "ever greater union" with legitimate and policy-effective government institutions. The introduction of the single currency and a central bank were important steps toward political union. But the nineteen members of the Eurozone which already form a monetary union live the contradiction between a common currency and nineteen sovereign debts, open to international financial speculation, and nineteen fiscal policies in harsh competition with each other. In order to solve this contradiction the Eurozone countries should agree on common macro-economic, macro-social policy and security policies. Greater macro-economic policy integration can be achieved gradually through a series of measures, such as appointing a Finance and Treasury minister who could rely on a certain degree of fiscal sovereignty and budget capacity; levying a common carbon, corporate, and financial transactions' tax, while at the same time homogenizing the taxation levels of member states; issuing eurobonds for targeted Europe-wide investments in infrastructures, scientific research, and the digital economy; pooling together part of the sovereign debt of members; completing the banking union and creating a European guarantee on bank deposits; empowering the European Central Bank with the full powers that other major central banks enjoy; and implementing common energy and environmental policy.

The common macro-economic policy should be complemented by a common macro-social strategy, which defines shared rules and minimal standards for welfare policies and implements common measures — like a European unemployment subsidy and a fair redistribution of asylum seekers among members. European governments should agree on a common foreign and security policy focused on defending the external boundaries and enhancing internal security with such measures as the formation of a single European army, a single federal police, and a pan-European border patrolling.

The three key sets of policies in economy, society and security must be developed together in order to avoid that they run against each other as a consequence of their different logics; single market policies and welfare and security policies imply, in fact, two different logics: economic integration implies the breaking of barriers, the opening of national systems, freedom of circulation and rules of non discrimination on the basis of specific identities, whereas welfare and security policies, on the contrary, have developed within the nation state framework and imply a logic of social closure, insofar as people are mostly entitled to protection from want and from criminal acts on the basis of their national citizenship. What the EU citizens should realize is that even their social protection and personal security are better assured by a strong supranational union than by their nation states.

This ambitious set of measures requires, in their turn, the rebalancing of the division of power in the tripartite governance structure (adoption of the generalization of co-decision method of the Council and the Parliament for union legislation and abolition of the veto power within the Council). Given the strict rules and lengthy procedures of the Treaties' revision and given the staunch opposition of some member states to such reform, a smart way out is the creation of a "Europe at variable geometry" with some member states moving toward a deeper integration and others opting-out while fully remaining in the single market. The obvious candidates for the role of the advanced group are the nineteen Eurozone countries which already have a common currency and monetary policy and can more easily implement the policies I suggest above. But in order to provide democratic legitimation to key policy decisions and avoid the criticism that they are taken by a technocracy without control, the Eurozone should have its own parliament, which should be a portion of the existing Parliament of the whole EU (Cavalli and Martinelli, 2015). In other words, the Eurozone countries — with other member countries hopefully joining in due time — should move toward an accomplished union, overcoming nationalist egoism and prejudices that obstruct it. The peoples and governments of these countries have to make a clear choice on whether to move on toward greater political integration or scale back to a simple free trade zone with some legal and administrative agreements in which member states re-nationalize most of their policies. The urgency and scale of the problems of the global agenda (outlined in the SDGs), the increasing world competition, the need for effective and equitable exit strategies from the conflated crises, all push toward the first alternative, i.e. an accelerated process of political integration. A federal solution may be premature but important steps can be taken in that direction. To put it simply, the capability of European modernity to achieve sustainable and inclusive development actually depends on the successful accomplishment of the EU.

References

Acemoglu D, Robinson G. 2012. Why Nations Fail: The Origins of Power, Prosperity and Poverty. Danvers: Crown Publishing Group.
Cavalli A, Martinelli A. 2015. La società europea. Bologna: Il Mulino.
D'Andrea D. 2001. Europe and the West: The identity beyond the origin. In F Cerutti, E Rudolph (Eds.), A Soul for Europe: An Essay Collection. Vol. 2. Leuven: Peters.
Eisenstadt S N. 2000. Multiple Modernities. Daedalus, 129(1): 1-29.
Fabbrini S. 2015. Which European Union? Europe After the Euro Crisis. Cambridge: Cambridge University Press.
Fukuyama F. 1993. The End of History and the Last Man. New York: Harper Perennial.
Gaonkar D P. 2001. Alternative Modernities. Durham: Duke University Press.
Giddens A. 2014. Turbulent and Mighty Continent. Cambridge: Polity Press.
Huntington S. 1996. The Clash of Civilizations and the Remaking of World Order. New York: Simon & Schuster.
ICSU, ISSC. 2015. Review of the Sustainable Development Goals: The Science Perspective. Paris: International Council for Science (ICSU).
Jaspers K. 1947. Vom europaischen Geist. In J Benda et al. (Eds.), L'esprit europeen, Neuchatel, Editions de la Boconnière.
Lijphart A. 1999. Patterns of Democracy: Government Forms and Performance in Thirty-six Countries. New Haven: Yale University Press.
Martinelli A. 2003. Markets, Governments, Communities and Global Governance. International Sociology, 18(2): 291-324 (revised edition of the Presidential Speech ISA World Congress of Sociology, Brisbane, 2002).
Martinelli A. 2005. Global Modernization: Rethinking the Project of Modernity. London: Sage.
Martinelli A. 2007. Transatlantic Divide: Comparing American and European Society. Oxford: Oxford

University Press.

Martinelli A. 2013. Mal di nazione. Contro la deriva populista. Milano: Università Bocconi Editore.

Martinelli A. 2015. Global modernization and multiple modernities. In A Martinelli, C Q He (Eds.), Global Modernization Review (pp. 5-24). Singapore: World Scientific Publishing.

Offe C. 2014. L'Europa in trappola. Bologna: Il Mulino.

Rifkin J. 2004. The European Dream. London: Penguin.

Rudolph E. 2001. Introduction. In F Cerutti, E Rudolph (Eds.), A Soul for Europe: An Essay Collection. Vol. 2. Leuven: Peters.

Sen A. 2009. The Idea of Justice. Cambridge: Harvard University Press.

Therborn G. 1995. European Modernity and Beyond. The Trajectory of European Societies 1945-2000. London: Sage.

Wittrock B. 2000. Modernity: One, none, or many? European origins and modernity as a global condition. Daedalus, 129(1): 31-60.

Moral Capital: An Important Prerequisite for Social Change and Successful Modernization

Piotr Sztompka

Professor of Theoretical Sociology, Jagiellonian University

One of the most seminal theoretical claims to be found in the history of the social sciences is put forward by Karl Marx in *The Eighteenth Brumaire of Louis Bonaparte*: "Men make their own history, but they do not make it as they please, they do not make it under self-selected circumstances, but under circumstances existing already, given and transmitted from the past." (Marx, 1964) Marx asserted, departing from Hegelianism that there was nothing super-human, metaphysical, automatic or inevitable in the course of history. It was clearly a refutation of determinism, fatalism and finalism, mistakenly attributed to Marx as supposed "historicism" (Popper, 1960), or "developmentalism" (Nisbet, 1980).

I have attempted to elaborate Marx's idea into a model of social change which I have labelled as "social becoming" (Sztompka, 1991, 1993, the latter available in Chinese translation 2010). In terms of this model the driving force of social change is a social agency, by which I mean a potential capacity of society for self-transforming praxis. This is a synthetic resource due both to the endowment of actors and the structural arrangements of the social field, or more concretely the intellectual and moral capacities of the people and the organization of their relationships in the interpersonal space. Applied to the specific form of social change known as modernization, one may speak of social modernizing agency as a potentiality for successful modernizing praxis.

Naïve, one may say neo-Hegelian, view of modernization treats it as a necessary, inevitable and irreversible direction of social change. Its proponents commit a categorical error treating time as a determinant; everything that is later in time is treated as more modern. Whereas time is simply a measure or scale of the process which may take the character of modernization, but it may also produce stagnation, backlash or even reversal. Modernization is not something which happily occurs to society, but it is the achievement of society, and the outcome of its own creative efforts (Sztompka, 2015). People make their own history, but what history they make depends on their actions, decisions and choices.

The obvious question arises: how people make their own history; what the necessary traits of social agency needed to turn that synthetic potentiality for change into modernizing direction are. Let us employ a sort of reverse reasoning. A query number one: what kind of actions must be taken to push society toward modernization? A query number two: what type of social fabric must be there as a conducive context mobilizing the people for that kind of action? It is perhaps easy to notice that I am employing similar intellectual strategy to that used by Max Weber in his famous book *The Protestant Ethos and the Spirit of Capitalism* (Weber, 1958). He was asking: what actions must have been taken to give the first push to the arising capitalist system. His answer was: entrepreneurial activities making up "the Spirit of Capitalism". And then he asked what cultural context internalized as personal motivations had been needed to mobilize the people for entrepreneurship. His answer was: a particular religious creed with its moral core, namely "the Protestant Ethos". In my talk I will claim, first, that modernizing praxis requires specific type of actions, to paraphrase Weber, "the spirit of modernization". And second, that modernizing actions are mobilized across society if there are widespread specific social relations internalized as values, namely the moral bonds which in their sum make up the moral capital. Therefore the alternative, shorter title of my talk could be the paraphrase of Weber — "the moral capital and the spirit of modernization".

The modernizing praxis may be described as actions which have at least four traits. First, actions must be innovative and creative, rather than merely reproductive, repetitive and routinized. Second, they must be ready to encounter uncertainty and risk, rather than seek for certainty and safety. Third, they must be based on rational considerations, rather than emotional impulses or mythical beliefs. And fourth, perhaps most importantly, they must be taken together with others, collectively rather than in separation from others. To put it simple they must involve cooperation.

Of course the levels of innovativeness and creativeness are not the same for all people. There is no equality of talent, wisdom, imagination and vision. But even the most brilliant inventor is bound by relations of cooperation either directly with a team, or indirectly, virtually with the authors of earlier innovations in the same area, to use the famous phrase, the origins of which are meticulously traced by Robert K. Merton "the giants on the shoulder of which one stands" (Merton, 1965). And similarly even the most brilliant innovation once attained will remain dormant as long as it is not picked up by others, spread in society, and imitated and applied in practice. In the realm of science it was noticed long ago and expressed in the imperative of publication, as opposed to secrecy of achieved results. To summarize it, the spirit of modernization is expressed in innovative and creative actions, in the conditions of uncertainty and risk, based on rational premises, and carried out in cooperation with others both in the phases of its production and dissemination.

Which social arrangements, and what qualities of a social fabric facilitate, encourage and stimulate this kind of actions? How society is able to mobilize and stimulate widespread modernizing praxis? Here I have to reveal a crucial premise of the argument, namely, what I mean by society, my understanding of that central term. For me society is not a holistic, supra-human entity, some presumed social organism or social system with sui generis properties and regularities. But it is not a bunch of separate and autonomous individuals living their life on their own, neither. Society is a network of relations among the people, and what happens between individuals in the interhuman space. And individuals, distinct from purely biological humans, are merely the unique knots in the network of social relations. All that are humans in ourselves, and our personalities, beliefs, motivations and aspirations are the product of social relations with "significant others" (Mead, 1982). We are whom we have met in life. This relational ontological perspective which I call "the Third Sociology" finds its predecessor and guru in Georg Simmel and his social geometry (Simmel, 1971), and later in symbolic interactionism of George H. Mead (Mead, 1982), dramaturgical theory of Erving Goffman (Goffman, 1971), theory of figuration by Norbert Elias (Elias, 2008) and current theories of social capital by James Coleman (Coleman, 1988), Pierre Bourdieu (Bourdieu, 1980), and Robert Putnam (Putnam, 1995). I explicate and elaborate that perspective in other places (Sztompka, 2012, 2016).

For the purposes of this talk the perspective of "the Third Sociology" implies the search for the prerequisites for social modernization, or in other words the preconditions for widespread modernizing praxis, in the quality of social relations internalized as specific values of interpersonal bonds. It is here that the ultimate driving force for modernization is to be found. There were already Scottish philosophers of the Enlightenment and particularly Adam Smith who claimed that economic development was rooted in some "moral sentiments" (Smith, 1971). I will suggest likewise that modernization depends on the specific syndrome of relations which I label as moral bonds, and their totality as moral capital, to the extent that they are embraced by the personalities of acting individuals as relevant attitudes. It is the crucial social resource which facilitates, encourages and stimulates modernization through the mobilization of innovativeness, risk taking, rational considerations and interpersonal cooperation. Moral capital is a prerequisite for the spirit of modernization.

Six moral bonds which make up the moral capital are the crucial components of the wider social capital. Moral capital as I define it is made of trust, loyalty, reciprocity, solidarity, respect and justice. Let us discuss briefly each of them.

First, trust. As I define it elsewhere "trust is a bet on the contingent, future actions of others" (Sztompka, 1999). The bond of trust means the expectation by A of the beneficial actions of B, and the trustworthiness of B means that it has a right to be trusted by A. Metaphorically speaking trust provides a bridge over the sea of uncertainty. And more concretely, it engenders existential security, predictability of the reactions of others, readiness to initiate interactions, to take risks and to embrace changes in all transactions. Its opposite, distrust produces suspiciousness and anxiety which are paralyzing for actions and interactions.

Second, loyalty. The bond of loyalty means the forfeiting of any harmful action by B toward A, when A trusts B. This makes A even more secure, not afraid of initiating interactions, opening oneself toward others, ready for risk and change, as the others are not perceived as threatening. Its opposite, disloyalty paralyzes actions and interactions as the partners prove not to be worthy of trust, i.e. untrustworthy.

Third, reciprocity. Some authors believe that this is an innate, universal human impulse. Bronislaw Malinowski was discovering it among the primitive tribes of Trobdriand islanders (Malinowski, 1932). Marcel Mauss considered it as a spontaneous reaction to any received gift (Mauss, 1964[1923]). And in contemporary sociology Alvin Gouldner was arguing for its central role among other moral precepts (Gouldner, 1960). The bond of reciprocity strengthens both earlier bonds by making them mutual. If A trusts B, it creates the obligation to reciprocate on the part of B, i.e. to trust A. And if B is loyal to A, it creates the obligation to reciprocate on the part of A, i.e. to be loyal to B. This produces dense network of relations opening the chances of cooperation. The opposite of reciprocity is one-sided exploitation which alienates people from social relations, pushing them toward solitude and building walls against others.

Fourth, solidarity. The bond of solidarity means the recognition and the allegiance to the idea of a common good, accompanied by the readiness to sacrifice some of personal interests for the sake of "we", the whole group, community, or society. It is the expression of typical human craving for social identity. And this is the next fundamental prerequisite of cooperation. If that craving is suppressed by egocentrism, exploitation at the expense of others, or at least by free riding, the atomized society is not ready for any risky innovative ventures.

Fifth, respect. The bond of respect means the mutual recognition of the achievements of the partners, in the currency of praise, fame, prestige, upward mobility, and all sorts of material gratifications. This strongly encourages the innovative and creative actions gaining respect, which by means of the well-known mechanism of the "looking glass self" (Cooley, 1964[1902]) raises self-estimate, an important, highly valued benefit for anybody. If recognition and respect are missing, the investment of effort, energy and time necessary for innovative actions simply does not pay. People drift into resigned passivism.

Sixth, justice. The bond of justice means that the received gratifications are proportional on the one hand to the effort, and on the other hand to the value of the result. This encourages the efforts toward novelty, because it guarantees at least some reward even when innovative results are not achieved, and maximum reward if they are. The propensity toward risky modernizing ventures is therefore enhanced. If distribution of gratifications is arbitrary and based on particularistic criteria (e.g. nepotism), the motivation toward innovative efforts is destroyed.

The strongest result is achieved if such moral bonds are not random and dispersed but become embedded in the culture of cooperation. This is recognized by the common sense which values "team spirit", "high morale", "esprit de corps", and "cooperative climate". When moral capital moves from purely interactional to cultural level, it turns into a widely shared normative expectation. In terms of Emile Durkheim it becomes a "social fact" exerting facilitating and constraining pressure on individual members of society (Durkheim, 1968). Such pressure is expressed in various positive inducements for those who abide, and various negative penalties for deviation. The cultural quality of moral bonds provides one additional asset and its long duration. Culture obtains inertia, and it is resistant to change. Once the moral capital turns into the culture of cooperation, it becomes a lasting tradition conducive to modernization.

Moral capital is contributing to modernization also in a more indirect way. It seems to generate some attitudes, which do not directly produce modernizing praxis, but raise the level of general social activism, helpful also for modernizing actions. There are four attitudes of this sort: first, the forward looking and optimistic perspective; second, the existential security due to the relations with others on whom one can count if needed; third, the feeling of empowerment brought about by rootedness in the dense network of bonds in wider community; fourth, the experience of meaning in life due to the company of the rich "social convoy" of others (Pahl, 2000) moving in their biographies in the same direction as oneself, and realizing some common goals. On the contrary, if moral capital is eroded, various symptoms of alienation are apt to appear: hopelessness, helplessness, solitude, passivism, and loss of meaning (Seeman, 1959).

The comparative research, for example the World Value Survey (Inglehart, 2003) and other similar projects confirm the correlation between the successful modernization and the development of moral capital, particularly in its cultural form as the cooperative tradition. Let us limit the empirical illustrations to China. A number of authors have noticed and discussed the peculiar Chinese form of social capital, known as *guanxi* in pinyin. It is found in China but also in the Chinese diaspora across the world. This very fact indicates that *guanxi* has the character of cultural phenomenon, a particular cultural tradition independent of any concrete political or economic structure. And it seems to be at least partly responsible for the Chinese success in the scale and speed of modernization.

Guanxi literally means "interdependent relationship (…) carefully constructed and maintained relations between persons which carry mutual obligations and benefits" (Qi, 2013: 309). The form and content of such relations are normatively prescribed, included in the long lasting tradition. They are considered as proper and taken for granted, evoking repulsion and sanctions if violated. The foundation of *guanxi* is the idea of reciprocity (*huibao* in pinyin). The main more specific components include three norms. The norm of *renqing* demands that social bonds were preserved for a long period of time, and not broken opportunistically. "The exchanges are used to cultivate and strengthen relationships that are expected to continue. In the process, not only advantages and obligations are achieved but also some degree of trust." (Smart, 1993: 400) Thus the correlative norm of *xinyong* (i.e. credit) demands trustworthiness in relationships i.e. reciprocating the trust received. The norm of *mianzi* (i.e. dignity) demands the acceptance of personal responsibility for harmful actions toward others and the obligation to repair harms done ("preserving face"). The persons linked by *guanxi* are expected to help each other, to support each other, to provide assistance, and in a more general sense to cooperate.

Some scholars (e.g. Hwang, 1987) made distinctions between autotelic and instrumental varieties of *guanxi*, or in other words between "embedded" and "accessing" forms. The earlier form of *guanxi* has a value as spontaneous, emotionally infused way of getting along well with other people, friendly relations producing smooth and satisfying interactions, which are rewarding and advantageous in themselves. The letter form of *guanxi* is strategic, as a purposeful construction of cooperative, solid and lasting relations for mutual business benefits. The means employed consist of gift-giving evoking obligations, and arranged social occasions such as parties, lunches and dinners. Once the bonds of *guanxi* are developed, the sanctioning of misbehavior becomes informal and internal, rather than formal and external. "In a *guanxi* network the cost of opportunism is the potential loss of exchange opportunities with all members of the network." (Standifird and Marshall, 2000: 24) This considerably lowers external costs of any transaction and produces considerable competitive advantage.

It is striking how the Chinese tradition of *guanxi* articulated by their ancient philosophy, historically developed and preserved over centuries, is parallel to the theoretical arguments for the importance of moral capital which I have presented in the first part of this paper. Somehow the brilliance of ancient minds and the evolution of society result in social mechanisms, which are only much later explicated, analyzed and codified by sociologists. Theoretically recognizing the significance of moral capital we should learn from the Chinese not only how to conduct better business but how to live more safely and peacefully, rooted in the rich interhuman space. Both lessons indicate the road toward successful modernization.

References

Bourdieu P. 1980. Le capital social; notes provisoire. Actes de la Recherche en Sciences Sociales, 3: 2-3.

Coleman J C. 1988. Social capital in the creation of human capital. American Journal of Sociology, 94 (supplement): 95-120.

Cooley C H. 1964[1902]. Human Nature and the Social Order. New York: Shocken.

Durkheim E. 1968. The Rules of Sociological Method. New York: Free Press.

Elias N. 2008. Społeczeństwo Jednostek (Society of Individuals, Polish edition). Warszawa: Wydawnictwo Naukowe PWN.

Goffman E. 1971. The Presentation of Self in Everyday Life. Harmondsworth: Penguin.

Gouldner A. 1960. The norm of reciprocity: A preliminary statement. American Sociological Review, 25(2): 161-178.

Hwang K. 1987. Face and favor: The Chinese power game. American Journal of Sociology, 92(4): 944-974.

Inglehart R. 2003. Human Values and Social Change. Leiden: Brill.

Malinowski B. 1932. Crime and Custom in Savage Society. London: Kegan Paul, Trench & Trubner.

Marx K. 1964. Selected Writings. New York: McGraw Hill.

Mauss M. 1964[1923]. Sacrifice: Its Nature and Function. Chicago: The University of Chicago Press.

Mead G H. 1982. Individual and the Social Self. Chicago: The University of Chicago Press.

Merton R K. 1965. On the Shoulders of Giants. New York: Free Press.

Nisbet R. 1980. History of the Idea of Progress. New York: Basic Books.

Pahl R. 2000. On Friendship. Cambridge: Polity Press.

Popper K R. 1960. Poverty of Historicism. New York: Basic Books.

Putnam R. 1995. Bowling alone: America's declining social capital. Journal of Democracy, 6(1): 65-78.

Qi X Y. 2013. Guanxi, social capital theory and beyond: Toward a globalized social science. British Journal of Sociology, 64(2): 308-324.

Seeman M. 1959. On the meaning of alienation. American Sociological Review, 24(6): 783-791.

Simmel G.1971. On Individuality and Social Forms. Chicago: The University of Chicago Press.

Smart A. 1993. Gifts, bribes and guanxi. Cultural Anthropology, 8(3): 388-408.

Smith A. 1971. The Theory of Moral Sentiments. New York: Garland Publishers.

Standifird S, Marshall R. 2000. The transaction cost: Advantage of guanxi-based business practices. Journal of World Business, 35(1): 21-42.

Sztompka P. 1991. Society in Action: The Theory of Social Becoming. Cambridge: Polity Press.

Sztompka P. 1993. The Sociology of Social Change. Oxford: Blackwell.

Sztompka P. 1999. Trust: A Sociological Theory. Cambridge: Cambridge University Press.

Sztompka P. 2012. On interhuman space: Toward the "third sociology". In D Kalekin-Fishman, A Denis (Eds.), The Shape of Sociology for the 21st Century (pp. 26-41). New York: Sage.

Sztompka P. 2015. Modernization as social becoming: Ten theses on modernization. In A Martinelli, C Q

He (Eds.), Global Modernization Review: New Discoveries and Theories Revisited (pp. 25-32). Singapore: World Scientific Publishing.

Sztompka P. 2016. Kapitał społeczny; teoria przestrzeni międzyludzkiej (Social Capital: The Theory of Interhuman Space). Krakow: Znak Publishers.

Weber M. 1958[1904]. The Protestant Ethics and the Spirit of Capitalism. New York: Scribner's.

Global Challenges of Modernization

Edward A. Tiryakian

Professor Emeritus of Sociology, Duke University

More recently, the United Nations (UN), emerging at the end of World War II as a care-keeper and booster of human development, has formulated a set of eight critical targets, or Millennial Development Goals (MDGs) in a framework to be evaluated in 2015 and extended again in 2030. After discussing these, we turn to present conditions which are severe constraints on development and may be viewed as interactive of a global crisis of modernity: These range from a slowdown of world economic growth to environmental degradation.

1. Introduction

"Modernity" as an embracing concept to capture essential aspects of the contemporary world we live in, and experience in our everyday life, was coined by the French literary figure Baudelaire in 1864[①]. From poetic insight to sociological currency, modernity became a shorthand description of the transformations impacting society. The emphasis was placed on change — on patterns of living, on patterns of existence from scattered settlements to greater concentrations of population in urban areas undergoing sharp population growth (urbanization), with the movement taking on rational forms of differentiation and integration, such as the planning of Paris. The entire 19th century, in major Western cities, was characterized by a civilization of modernity, in which the new urban environment was transformed as political, economic and social forces gained dominance over social forces that had been dominant for centuries, if not millennia, before hand. One notable change was a sharp increase in population size, for natural births having greater chances of survival as public health measures became widely disseminated; but urban population also increased from a gradual but steady emptying of the rural countryside, to cities which provided new

---

① Baudelaire indicated that modernity means the ephemeral, the fugitive, the contingent, the half of art whose other half is the eternal and immutable. This transitory, fugitive element, whose metamorphoses are so rapid, must in no account be despised or dispensed with.

forms of (industrial) employment, and new transportation networks[①]. This was accompanied by a new power structure favoring a new middle class that steadily replaced a traditional two-class feudal structure. Overall, modernity provided rising levels of economic well-being for those benefiting from the economic surplus of a machine age. But not everybody benefited, for the modern age also left a residue of those living in the margins, without resources or without the means of obtaining resources. This new class, the underclass, also had a voice, in new class movements and new leaders seeking which are not just reforms but revolutions, drastic social change.

One vehicle for changes in the political structures of society was nationalism, which took on many forms across the world, as a voice of liberation from foreign occupation, even where "foreign" meant a dominant ethnic group (as in the case of Austrian dominance over the Magyar ethnic minority in pre-War Austria-Hungary, or English state dominance over the Scot in the United Kingdom, or Algerian uprising against French imperialism in the 1950s). Sometimes nationalism has taken on an economic form (in establishing and protecting national markets internally), sometimes a political form, sometimes a cultural form (such as a historical narrative relating the current state and its institutions as the matrix for self-development); sometimes a direct violence, sometimes a ballot box and varied symbolic protests. In brief, one may think of nationalism as a "wild card" of modernity, which adds potency to social movements and is often a challenge, rather than a tool of rationalistic development[②].

A related form of nationalism in the 19th century was its extension outside the frontiers of the nation state, with the emergence of imperialism. It rested on new forms of military weaponry, new means of rapid transportation, and a set of ideological beliefs providing legitimation for dominance[③]. Within 100 years — roughly from the Congress of Vienna in 1815 to the start of the World War I — nationalism as imperialism flourished as land grabbing, even in areas where the dominant agent was not the Western state, as shown by Japanese imperialism vis-à-vis Korea during 1905-1945. Nationalism also served as a two-edged sword, used for the state in the formation of the European nation states in the 19th century but also against imperialism in non-Western settings, as is shown in a photograph of Beijing in 1900, the setting of the "Boxer" rebellion. Although the peasant-based, anti-Western movement, lacking modern military might, did not succeed in its siege of Beijing and was brutally

---

① Urbanization as a central process of modernization has been a continuing global process for the past 200 years, marking 2007 as the first time in human history of the global urban population exceeding the global rural population, notwithstanding important regional variations. The latest UN projection anticipates that by 2050, two thirds of the world will be urban, one third will be rural (*World Urbanization Prospects: The 2014 Revision*, Department of Economic and Social Affairs, UN, 2014). I will refer to this trend in the section of this paper devoted to challenges of modernity.

② Tiryakian E. 1997. The wild cards of modernity. Daedalus, 126 (2): 147-181. In an earlier period, I drew attention to a multidimensional aspect of Western modernity in my essay "Three metacultures of modernity: Christian, Gnostic, Chthonic" in *Theory, Culture & Society*, 1996, 13 (1): 99-118. These are deep-seated and often interactive cultural forms, buried deep in the historic past, that provide visions of the future and telic ends for human action. In looking at modernity in East Asia, I would propose that "Chthonic" megaculture in Chinese civilization drew upon pre-historic Taoist tradition, which after its eclipse in the Qing Dynasty is making a popular comeback after the "Cultural Revolution".

③ The beliefs were as much intended for a domestic audience as for targeted colonial populations; among these beliefs, the "mission civilisatrice" in the new French empire, and "white man's burden" for the English, were variants of the new imperialism, superseding earlier, and coarser forms of dominion.

repressed by the multi-national expeditionary force (including Japan and the United States), it was a harbinger of a unified China for the Chinese in the 20th century, with the proclamation of the Republic of China in 1912 providing a new (short-lived) cycle of political modernization.

I have used wide brushstrokes in laying out a canvas for modernization as a general process with which to pinpoint the coming into being of modernity as a forward-going tendency of the modern world. As a summary notation, it was recognized as "progress". Now that we are well into the second decade of the 21st century, how should we evaluate what has been driving individuals and nation states into the arena of modernity, and the basic Enlightenment value of the pursuit of happiness? What I plan to do is to lay out, first, some concrete steps toward "progress", and then discuss serious obstacles to progress, which may even be viewed as "crises of modernity".

2. The Recent Past

2.1 Collective Modernization: The Millennial Development Goals

At the start of the new millennium, after the tumultuous events of the 1990s which saw the collapse of the Soviet Union and an outbreak of civil wars and genocidal perpetration in its former domain boundaries, the task for global reconstruction was felt urgently by many. The UN took up the challenge of providing for global security by an assessment of the least secure segment of mankind. Although one can argue with the selection or non-selection of particular conditions, the UN accepted a set of eight goals as providing a global development framework to be carried out near-term and evaluated in 2015. In terms of its scope and commitment, this was to be the largest collective effort at human altruism. The eight MDGs were:

(1) Eradicate extreme poverty and hunger;
(2) Achieve universal primary education;
(3) Promote gender equality and empower women;
(4) Reduce child mortality;
(5) Improve maternal health;
(6) Combat HIV/AIDS, malaria and other diseases;
(7) Ensure environmental sustainability;
(8) Develop a global partnership for development.

The UN has implicitly taken its mission to be the lead organization for the overall modernization of the world, particularly in replacing the imperialism of a previous era that benefited the few, with a collective responsibility for upgrading the lives of the large segment of humanity in "developing countries". This mission was framed and concretized at the end of the 20th century at the Millennium Summit of the UN as the MDGs, embracing a set of targets to be met in fifteen years. It was an assemblage of earlier proposals intended to uplift voluntarily a large proportion of humanity from basic wants of mankind. One may think of these goals as enabling the "wretched of the earth" to accede at least to the first rung of the civilization of modernity.

In this section, I look at the set of MDGs as they were formulated and adopted with their target of 2015. How has this massive development effort worked? Using 2015 figures from the

Millennium Development Goals Report are the following capsules for each of the eight primary goals.

- Goal 1 — A decline of persons living in extreme poverty dropped from half of the world's population to 14%, or from 1.9 billion in 1990 to 836 million in 2015. Proportion of undernourished people in developing regions fell almost half from 23% in 1990 to 13% between 2014 and 2016.
- Goal 2 — Primary school enrolment rate 91% in 2015, up from 83% in 2000. Sub-Sahara Africa had a 20% increase in net enrolment rate from 2000 to 2015, and 8% increase between 1990 and 2000.
- Goal 3 — Gender equality and empowerment of women. Developing regions as a whole have achieved the target of eliminating gender disparity. In South Asia, 103 girls now enrolled for every 100 boys (vs. 74 : 100 ratio in 1990). Women now represented in parliaments in 90% of 174 countries, though only 1 : 5 are women.
- Goal 4 — Child mortality. Under age 5 mortality declined by more than half from 1990 to 2015. Number of deaths of children under 5 has declined from 12.7 million in 1990 to 6 million in 2015. Measles vaccination has led to a global decline of measles cases of 67% in period 2000 to 2013, as 84% of children worldwide received measles vaccine in 2013.
- Goal 5 — Improve maternal health. Since 1990, maternal mortality rate (MMR) declined by 45% worldwide. In South Asia, MMR declined by 64% between 1990 and 2013; in sub-Sahara Africa by 49%.
- Goal 6 — Combat HIV/AIDS, malaria, and other diseases. HIV infections fell by 40% between 2000 and 2013, with sharp increase in antiretroviral therapy in that period to 7.6 million averted. Between 2000 and 2015, over 6.2 million malaria deaths averted, mainly of children under 5 years. Tuberculosis (TB) prevention saved an estimated 37 million lives between 2000 and 2013, as TB mortality rate fell by 45% between 1990 and 2013.
- Goal 7 — Environmental sustainability. In 2015, 2.6 billion people have gained access to improved drinking water since 1990, including 1.9 billion with access to piped drinking water. 147 countries have met the drinking target, 95 countries the sanitation target and 77 countries have met both.
- Goal 8 — Global partnership for development. Official development assistance (ODA) from developed countries increased by 66% between 2000 and 2014, to 135.2 billion. In 2014, 79% of imports from developing to developed countries were admitted duty-free, up from 65% in 2000.

Undoubtedly, the MDGs program of the UN in its starting period of improving the least-favored segments of humanity has to be registered as having achieved a degree of success in modernization, not across the board but in the aggregate. This was done despite two major crises: the unsettling of the Middle East from the consequences of the American military intervention in Iraq in 2003, and the global economic crisis of 2008.

Drawing upon lessons learned from 2001 to 2015, the UN and its agencies formulated and adopted a comparable list of Sustainable Development Goals for the period 2015 to 2030, with clearly intended targets drawn up[①]. For purpose of illustration, here are some of the indicated targets for SDG 8 ("Promote inclusive and sustainable economic growth, employment and decent work for all"):

8.1 Sustain per capita economic growth... at least 7% GDP grouth per annum in the least developed countries;

8.5 By 2030 achieve full and productive employment and decent work for all women and men, including for young people and persons with disabilities, and equally pay for work of equal value;

8.8 Protect labour rights and promote safe and secure working environments for all workers, including migrant workers, in particular women migrants, and those in precarious employment;

8.10 Strengthen the capacity of domestic financial institutions to encourage and expand access to banking, insurance and financial services for all.

2.2 The Coming Future

While meeting the targets and the goals by 2030 might seems unduly optimistic, if not utopian, yet the past 15 years has given the UN in the new century a sense of a collective effort of solidarity between the better-off and the least well-off segments of humanity. But to make sure that you do not take me for an undue optimist, let me raise in this section what I see as serious contemporary obstacles to continuing modernization and social development. Given that these are interactive, they may be said to be part of our crisis of modernity. They are:

(1) The slowdown of world economic growth;

(2) Increased number of forced immigration;

(3) Border security;

(4) High technology;

(5) Environmental degradation.

2.3 Discussion

Because of length constraint, I will offer only some brief remarks about each of these, although each could well be worth a full day's discussion.

As a preface to this discussion, I would like to invoke materials that have taken much of my attention in previous years, and which I may use today. First, as a normative guideline, I view a given society as ultimately responsible top down and bottom up for the path of modernization it takes. It may be that a chosen path has unanticipated pitfalls, which rather than upgrading conditions, in fact lead to gross losses in population size and resources. That, however, stands subject to correction (either in the short-term if there is an operative political process, or long-term, such as a changing political dynasties), or a new environmental setting. Second, I view the current world crisis of modernity as, at least in part, reflecting the crisis in the transition of the apex of modernity continuing its centuries-old westward path from what

---

① https://sustainabledevelopment.un.org/?menu=1300[2015-10-18].

Parsons and Eisenstadt saw as the "seedbed societies" of the East (Greece and Israel), to the Westward part of the Mediterranean, then to the banking centers of the North, then around 100 years ago crossing the Atlantic to the United States, first to the eastern part, then to western states (California and Silicon Valley notably, but also Oregon and Washington), and at the end of the 20th century, a slow but sure shift across the Pacific to East Asia, notably Japan, Republic of Korea, Chinese Taiwan, and China's mainland. Of course, the geo-political shifts are not smooth processes, free of political conflict; and they do entail changes in collective identity and in structures. How does this large-scale view relate to the items listed in the present section?

2.3.1 World economic growth

If we look at the economic performance of the world since the end of the Cold War, the most striking aspect is the economic performance of China. Starting its economic reform program in 1978 when it was still a low-income country, with primarily an agrarian economy, and about 10 years later sill having nearly 3/4 of its population living in rural areas, it underwent an outstanding economic performance such that in a 20-year period (1990-2010) its annual growth rate increased by 10.4% — by far greater than all other "transitional economies" of the former Soviet system. In 1980, per capita income in China was only 30% of the average sub-Saharan African country, while today it is over 3 times the level of sub-Sahara Africa with a per capita income of $4,400 in current dollars, which qualifies as a middle-income country[①].

China, within a generation, has become a motor force of the global economy as the world's second largest economy, with further recognition from the International Monetary Fund deciding last year that the yuan met the standard of inclusion in the IMF's Special Drawing Rights basket, along with the US dollar, the euro, the pound, and the yen; when added to the IMF basket it will have a 10.92% weighing, reflecting that in 2015, the yuan was the fifth most traded currency. Capitalism has flourished in East Asia, with state assistance and control, though different in form from the Western or American model.

If I list the economic sector at the top of my list (world economic growth), it is because of trouble spots, that are barely covered in an anemic annual growth rate of 2% for Europe and the United States — about 1/3 of a contracting Chinese economy. A rather bleak economy in the developed societies has increased the feeling in a large youthful sector of the labor market that chances for upward mobility are less today than they were for the older generation. In a presidential election year, the two contending American parties are seeking advantage by addressing economic issues: one by appealing to working class voters by supporting increases in the federal minimum wages (and sharply reducing gender economic inequality), while the other party proposes reducing corporate tax rates and cutting back on government expenditures. Cross-cutting the economic situation has been greater attention devoted to income inequality and the distribution of wealth in a given population. This was articulated by French economist Thomas Piketty in his best-seller, *Capital in the Twenty-first Century* (2013) which assessed wealth inequality in coming years as growing faster than the rate of economic

---

① 林毅夫(Lin Y F). 2011. 中国与全球经济. 中国经济杂志, 4(1): 1-14.

growth, barring state redistribution through a progressive global tax on wealth.

Piketty's work on income inequality got much applause and attention in academic circles on both sides of the Atlantic, even becoming a central theme at regional and national meetings of professional societies. It added an intellectual dimension to a short-term but highly significant American social movement that preceded it, the Occupy Wall Street movement, in the fall of 2011. Formally, the latter was a non-violent protest movement of well-educated job seekers in the Wall Street area of high finance, protesting wealth and income disparity between the "top 1% and the bottom 99%". It was a populist, communitarian group that occupied a public area (Zucotti Park), had a General Assembly, focusing on daily activities from food procurement to sanitation disposal, and addressing socio-economic issues of unemployment and economic largesse for the Wall Street elites. It did not last long, and partly because of strict control by alarmed municipal authorities, and partly because it let in its open borders groups of radicals, anarchists and agents provocateur. But it was effective, as a link to similar protest activities against income inequality and austerity programs, in the United States, Spain, and Israel.

The slowdown in the growth rate of the global economy has led to economic nationalism in various forms and various countries. In the United States, one target had been the Trans-Pacific Partnership (TPP, signed on February 4, 2016) among 12 Pacific Rim countries, which awaits coming into force to lower tariffs as trade barriers. Although TPP has been vigorously supported by the Obama administration, it has been chiefly criticized as an opaque and pro-corporate agreement, at the expense of workers in the manufacturing and service industries[①], similarly as had been criticized in the 1990s the North American Free Trade Agreement (NAFTA) endorsed by President Bill Clinton.

Overall, the various strands in the present slowdown of global economic growth may be viewed as a stimulus for reversing the earlier support for economic globalization. Disenchantment with the process of greater coordination and global integration is reflected in the United States in a greater emphasis on a "return home" in manufacturing and in digital capitalism in lieu of an earlier emphasis on "outsourcing" in manufactures and services.

2.3.2 Increased number of forced immigration

As an integral part of modernity, immigrants seeking better employment in one part of a country, or going to a different country for economic advantages, are a normal feature of social change. In the present era of "the Fourth Industrial Revolution", highly skilled immigrants from low-income countries can find remunerative employment in welcoming high-tech areas in developed societies[②], particularly in countries with demographic shortage in the skilled labor force. However, what was a population shortage has almost overnight become an unwelcome population surplus.

In two areas of the world in particular, economic and/or political conditions have led to

---

① https://en.wikipedia.org/wiki/Trans-Pacific_Partnership[2016-9-2]. Among notable American critics have been Nobel economists Paul Krugman and Joseph Stiglitz, Senators Elizabeth Warren and Bernard Sanders, former Labor Secretary Robert Reich, and development specialist Jeffrey Sachs.

② See for example Biradavolu M R. 2005. Globalization from "above" or globalization from "below"? The emergence of transnational Indian entrepreneurship in the software industry. Ph.D. dissertation. Duke University.

massive population movements seeking refuge or resettlements in neighbouring countries. One is the flight of countless civilians from acute civil strife in the broad Middle East, particularly after the American invasion of Iraq in 2003, the ensuing ethno-religious civil war in Iraq and Syria, and the related social protest movements of "the Arab Spring" in 2010/2011 in countries such as Tunisia, Algeria, Egypt, Libya and elsewhere. Conjointly, there appeared the new radical religious movement, the Islamic State in Iraq and Syria (ISIS), using terrorist methods and extreme violence to establish a state, with military leadership from officers in the deposed Iraq regime. From all this vast turmoil in the past five years, millions have sought to leave and find entry into Europe, either in crossing the Mediterranean Sea and seeking asylum in the nearest coastal shelter (in Spain, Italy or Greece), or crossing overland by way of Turkey into Central Europe, with Germany and northern Europe (notably Sweden) as perceived haven. The human stampede has led to publicized tragedies of migrants drowning in waters or overcrowded vessels. Unfortunately, the very rapid and extensive opening has taken place in the general climate of economic slowdown in Europe, weakly recuperating from the 2008 economic crisis. This has produced a political backlash, in Germany and other EU countries, with demands of closing the Schengen area that allows every EU citizen to travel, work, and live in any EU country without special formalities. A border-free Europe had been, until very recently, an accomplishment for the 400 million Europeans in the Schengen states (or candidate states) but at present economic and political issues regarding the new immigrants have impaired the idea of European unity, as different states are seeking new ways of insuring border control, particularly since some of the immigrants are viewed as possibly having ties with terrorist organizations in the Middle East.

At the same time as the potential flood of immigrants, coming from a vastly different cultural setting than that of the European milieu, is a challenge to European unity, and it may also be a long-term opportunity for sustained growth. That is because, for the most part, declining birth rates in European society are causing labor shortage. As International Monetary Fund Christine Lagarde pointed out at the 2016 World Economic Forum in Davos, there is an "upside potential" to the influx of asylum speakers: When they were integrated into the labor force, as producers and consumers, this could raise the GDP for Europe as a whole by about 0.25% by 2020[①]. In brief, the unexpected flood of asylum seekers to secular/Christian Europe from predominantly Islamic Middle East is a two-edged sword.

The other area with a sharp increase in public concern over immigration and attendant economic and political issues is the United States with a large set of immigrants from Latin America, particularly Mexico[②]. Migration between the United States and Mexico has been a long historical process, which in earlier years had an important seasonal aspect of Mexican migrant labor coming to assist in planting and harvesting crops. In 1994, the modernization of North American labor markets (the United States, Mexico and Canada) ensued with the active support of President Bill Clinton, despite reservation at home by American labor unions. NAFTA sought to lower barriers to the movement of goods, capital services and information

---

① http://www.ibtimes.com/europe-refugee-crisis-imf-chief-lagarde-says-refugees-could-boos[2016-7-1].

② For background material, see Massey D S, Durand J and Malone N J. 2004. Beyond Smoke and Mirrors: Mexican Immigration in an Era of Economic Integration. New York: Russell Sage Foundation.

inside the three-country trading bloc. Viewed by government advocates as a win-win situation for all parties in the 1990s, NAFTA has achieved most of its economic targets in ways that need not concern us here, but it has also had some unforeseen consequences, particularly in terms of labor and working conditions for both American and Mexican labor. The severe economic crisis of 2008 and the slowdown of the American economy, together with the threat of terrorism reaching the American border, has generated a xenophobic current against undocumented workers viewed as a security threat (as much an economic as a political one) and requiring a sealing of the border to protect the country from illegal immigration. This apprehension falls on the seeming growing presence of Mexicans in the United States, who make up about half of all unauthorized immigrants (5.6 million in 2014), with a decline of more than a million since their peak in 2007[1].

If one takes the larger integration process of lowering cross-country barriers to the movement of goods, service, information, and people, as a major aspect of modernization, we may term the current backlash in the European Community against massive immigration, and its echo in the United States as a reversal of modernization.

2.3.3 Border security

The preceding discussion of backlash against immigration relates to questions of border security. At the start of the 21st century the simultaneous 9/11 attack on the World Trade Center and the Pentagon made the United States painfully aware of the problem of border security, leading to the creation of the Transportation Security Administration in 2001, and a new Department of Homeland Security (DHS) in 2002. As a first line of federal defense against all forms of attack on American borders — physical and digital — the budget of DHS is that of a privileged organization, with a FY 2017 budget of $40.6 billion in net discretionary funding[2].

While this may well be used in the United States to prevent border crossing by terrorist organizations, it does not eliminate the threat of terrorist cells in the United States, as happened in December 2015 in San Bernardino, California. European countries, with much more open borders in the Schengen area[3] have had has in recent years a flow of alienated second generation Islamic youth leave their country for intensive training by ISIS in occupied Syria and Iraq, before returning "home" to their European habitat to engage in deadly terrorist activity.

Illicit border crossings take other forms besides terrorist organizations. One is that of the vast flow of drugs — marijuana, cocaine, heroin, and the like — from different regions (South America, the Middle East, Afghanistan, etc.) to affluent Western countries, particularly the United States. Drug trafficking has modernized ways of reaching its intended markets as a multitrillion dollar industry in its own era of globalization. A second form of illegal border

---

[1] Pew Research Center. http://www.pewresearch.org/fact-tank/2015/11/19/5-facts-about-illegal-immigration-in-the-United-states[2016-7-1].

[2] https://www.dhs.gov/news/2016/02/09/fact-sheet-dhs-fy-2017-budget[2016-2-9].

[3] Named after Schengen, Luxemburg, where the initial abolition of border controls originated in 1985, the Schengen area takes in 26 Europeans countries which have deregulated passport and other type of border control at their common borders. The sharp influx of migrants and terrorist attacks in France and Belgium have led several European states to reintroduce border controls on borders with other Schengen countries.

crossings, one potentially as lucrative but with much fewer participants as perpetrators, is the penetration of the digital borders — the broad area of cyber attacks on information systems. It is a silent mode of compromising classified data, which has generated a whole industry of perpetrators, including governments, their agencies, and counter-agencies, besides individual "hackers" and cyberware specialists. At the front of public controversy regarding cyber security is the case of Edward Snowden, former contractor for the Central Intelligence Agency and computer analyst, who provided a newspaper (*The Guardian*) with information regarding the National Security Agency obtaining data about millions of Americans and hundreds of world leaders under surveillance in telephone records.

2.3.4 High technology

A prime mover for global development and rapid social change in the age of modernity has been high technology, which is not confined to any one area of human knowledge and application. The Internet has opened up vistas of instantaneous communication and stored knowledge, which in a previous setting of modernity was reserved for an elite and/or elderly population: today, cell phones are available for young children in Africa, alongside adults in Central Asia. The process of modernization has no boundary as high technology unfurls from west to east, as it did at the micro level in the United States from Route 128 in Massachusetts to Silicon Valley in Northern California and Research Triangle Park, North Carolina, locating in areas with access to high-talent universities, trained personnel, venture capital, and an entrepreneurial spirit willing to take risk in research ventures.

Developing countries in East Asia have taken to follow Western development in high technology centers, often in proximity to leading universities, such as Japan, with its enclave in Tsukuba Science City and its Advanced Technology Center at the forefront of research and applications in robotics, nanotechnology, and remote sensing, and India with its high-tech center in Bangalore and its major emphases on software and health applications. As to China, it is anticipated that students returning from advanced training in North America and Europe will in the near future find a government (central or provincial) willing to develop its own industrial, high-technology centers. As an instance of the coming future, it was recently reported that XMC, a contract chip maker owned by the Chinese government, is breaking ground in Wuhan (provincial capital of Hubei Province) to develop the first Chinese-owned plant to produce the most widely used memory chips (dynamic random access memory, i.e. DRAM) used to store data in electronic gadgets[①]. XMC's substantial acquisition of $24 billion will be largely financed by China's national semi conductor fund as well as the provincial government, as a catch-up commitment of China to flash memory chip producers in East Asia, led by Korea, Japan and Singapore. The choice of Wuhan in Central China also follows the model Tsukuba, Route 128, and Silicon Valley by having nearby leading high education centers (Huazhong University of Science and Technology, and Wuhan University of Technology). It seems like a very timely investment for China to make as a major entry into the Fourth Industrial Revolution.

---

① *Wall Street Journal*, March 25, 2016, B1.

2.3.5 Environmental degradation

A civilization of modernity that continues to interlace mankind in the 21st century also renders us more conscious of the millennium goal mentioned earlier in this paper: How to ensure environmental sustainability? It is a question that applies to countries at all levels of development, because human life depends on the air we breathe and the water we drink as bare essentials of life. It has been held for a long time that carbon emission in the atmosphere from industrial development in, particularly in developed societies has had a degrading influence on the habitat, and on human life. A collective effort at finding alternative sources of energy besides fossil fuel has led in Europe to the formation of "green" parties, with opposing factions from the corporate sector, especially producers of energy in oil and coal. Climate change, notably the view of a steadily increasing temperature which can have as consequences massive flooding and meltdown of ice caps, was featured by Vice-President and Nobelist Al Gore in his documentary film *An Inconvenient Truth* (2006), and is one of the chronic factors in making what the late Ulrich Beck treated in viewing how crises of modernity follow from the triumphs of modernity, in his *World at Risk* (Polity Press, 2009). What other forms of energy to favor, if not from fossil fuels, has been a source of debate, since the cost of air and the sun is greater, though less risky, than nuclear. A recent voice in the debate over climactic change is that of developing societies (especially in Africa and Asia) who see the push to curtail carbon emission as a ploy by developed societies to curtail industrial growth in the Third World.

China's astounding high growth rate until recently is also viewed as having contributed to pollution of cities like Beijing, and highest concentrations of dangerous particular matter PM 2.5 responsible for asthma and lung cancer in Shandong and Henan provinces. Joining public demand for governmental action in the face of environmental degradation, ecological restoration was noted in the compendium *Global Modernization Review*: "China will face huge environmental risks in the 21st century if its economic development mode remains unchanged. Actions are to be taken and our basic goals include... gradual clearing of residual environmental pollution and restoration of degraded ecological system."[①] In effect, the government has heeded this call for action in providing for pollution control in its five-year plans, but the ambitious targets for pollution reduction have to be collective efforts of the central and provincial governments and the private sector.

It is in this last sector that perhaps the greatest stride for global cooperation has taken place in Paris, the very site of the destructive potential of religious radical terrorism the month before, 195 countries met in December 2015 for a UN Framework Convention on Climate Change (UNFCCC), whose framework had been advanced in 1992. The agreement, signed by developed and developing countries is the first-ever universal, legally binding global climate deal, entering into force in five years. It provides for global emissions to peak as soon as possible, with a long-term goal of keeping the increase in global average temperature to well below 2°C above pre-industrial levels and requesting countries to submit comprehensive national climate action plans[②]. Funding for this project will be provided by developed countries to improve resilience to

---

① He C Q, Jin J. 2015. Ecological modernization and China's choice. In A Martinelli, C Q He(Eds.), Global Modernization Review: New Discoveries and Theories Revisited. (pp. 262-263). Singapore: World Scientific Publishing.

② http://ec.europa.eu/clima/policies/international/negotiations/paris/index_en.htm[2016-9-23].

climate change impacts in developing countries for another ten years, with new and higher goal set after 2025.

Needless to say, there are many details to be ironed out and many more conferences, but a momentum has already been set, as shown at the January 2016 meeting of the World Economic Forum, where global economic leaders in the public and private sectors meet yearly at Davos, Switzerland. In addition to concerns regarding formidable problems of refugees seeking entry to Europe, this year's discussions of the Fourth Industrial Revolution gave centrality to climate change and the role of business, including heads of energy corporations, in shifting the trillions of dollars needed into clean energy investment to "avoid dangerous levels of global warming"[1].

3. Conclusions

I began this paper with a cursory look at modernity. It has taken place in different settings, east and west, but took a new look of sustaining material with an ideological development in the latter part of the 18th century, continuing so in the 19th century when "modernity" became a term of common currency. Midway in the 19th century, many Western countries underwent an advanced period of industrialization, noted by the wide use of electricity, mass production, innovative scientific knowledge in fundamentals of knowledge, advent of social sciences, and military might that could be used in acquiring and influencing tributary areas. This form of modernity was somewhat like a gigantic house of cards, which unexpectedly crumbled in the 20th century with two global wars and the rise of totalitarian regimes in between.

In the aftermath of World War II, a slow rebuilding process took place, which favored progress in development at various levels — economic, to be sure, but also of other institutions and even of the cultural underpinning of societies. Progress, or going forward to improve conditions, from what has been to what will soon be, is not a continuous linear process, as the historical record demonstrates, but is a broad promise of the state and of higher education. Periodically, progress comes to a halt, for various reasons, and our current situation reflects levels of tension and conflicts, both in the West and the Middle East particularly, which seem abnormally high.

To get a perspective on the state of crisis, we take the UN as a collective representation of countries that comprise a civilization of modernity, and consider what the UN framed at the start of our century as needing core attention regarding the weakest, poorest members of mankind. This took the form of SDGs, which is illustrated in this paper with detail-specific SDG 8, full and productive employment. Going beyond SDGs, with its focus on the least favored segment of mankind, are general obstacles of continuing modernization which are distinct but interactive. We close this part with the problem of environmental degradation, largely global warming, which has been an on-going feature of the success of modernization, but just recognized at the UN Climate Change Conference in Paris in 2015.

So, how to end this presentation? While I tend to a general optimistic view of the basic

---

[1] http://www.eliminatechangenews.com/2016/01/18/davos-climate-change-primer[2016-9-23].

trend of modernization, there are also cultural and normative features of the modernization process in Europe and the United States which I think detract from feeling that the Euro-American zone will be where to watch for the next line of progress. Coming from the United States, I see it as still a center of technological innovations, where it began in the 20th century. But today, unfortunately, I view it as undergoing a cultural degradation more concerned with social issues than structural reorganization.

My last prognosis is that where the civilization of modernity is likely to expand, culturally, economically, and politically, is as a continuing development of East Asia.

Three Paths Towards National Modernization

Chuanqi He

Professor, China Center for Modernization Research, Chinese Academy of Sciences
Academician, International Eurasian Academy of Sciences

According to the second modernization theory (He, 1999, 2013), the world modernization process between the 18th century and the end of the 21st century can be divided into two stages. The first one features the transformation from agricultural to industrial economy and society, and the second one features the transformation from industrial to knowledge economy and society; the countries that have not completed the first modernization at present may promote the coordinated development of the first and second modernization and featuring the transform from semi-industrial to knowledge economy and society — this is referred to as the integrated modernization. From about 1760 to 1970, the basic road of national modernization was the first modernization. From about 1970 to 2100, there are three basic paths, namely, the first, the second and the integrated modernization (Figure 1). This paper discusses the three paths and their major models based on historical data.

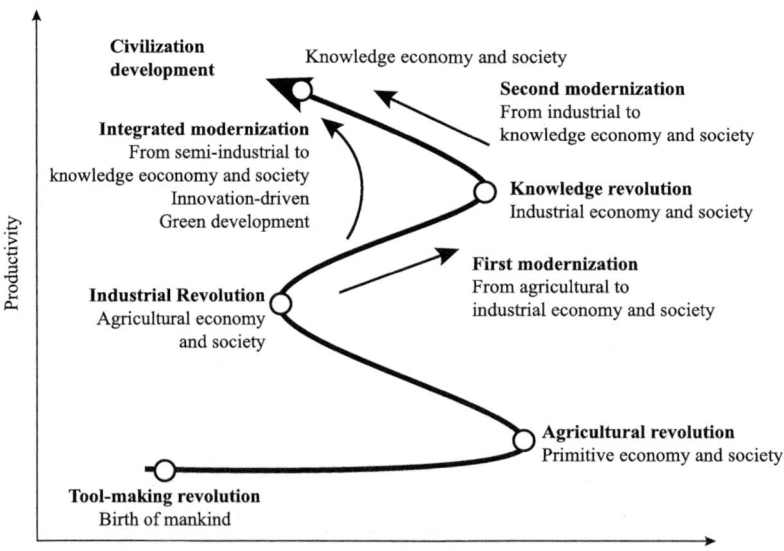

Figure 1 Three Paths Towards National Modernization
Source: He, 2003, 2010

1. Methodology and Data Source

Modernization has been a profound change of human civilizations since the 18th century. It includes not only the great change and transformation from traditional to modern politics, economy, society and culture, but also all human development and the rational protection of the natural environment at present (Martinelli and He, 2015). In the process of national modernization, do the changes of different fields take place at same pace? If not, which take place first and which later? Do these factors affect the results of national modernization?

1.1 Hypothesis

1) National modernization is the collection of the changes of different fields. 2) There are some core elements in each field which can be viewed as modernizing elements. 3) The changes of modernizing elements can be valued by indicators partly. 4) We can analyze the models of national modernization according to the changes and their combinations of modernizing elements.

1.2 Indicators

For the analysis of the models and routes of national modernization since the 18th century, we have identified 12 core elements and 18 development indicators from the fields of politics, economy, society, culture and environment (Table 1).

Table 1 The Core Elements and Development Indicators of National Modernization

Fields	Elements	Indicators	Definitions and units
Politics	Democratization	Universal suffrage	Date of universal suffrage, year
		Coverage of universal suffrage	Proportion of universal suffrage, %
Economy	Industrialization	Proportion of industry	Proportion of industrial value added in GDP, %
		Proportion of agriculture	Proportion of agriculture value added in GDP, %
	Service intensive	Proportion of service	Proportion of service value added in GDP, %
		Proportion of knowledge service	Proportion of knowledge service value added in GDP, %
	Globalization	Trade proportion	Proportion of international trade to GDP, %
		FDI proportion	Proportion of foreign direct investment to GDP, %
Society	Urbanization	Proportion of urban population	Proportion of urban population in total, %
	Suburbanization	Proportion of suburban population	proportion of suburban population in total, %
	Modern education	Proportion of primary education	Enrollment of primary education in total, %
		Proportion of secondary education	Enrollment of secondary education in total, %
	Social welfare	Pension coverage	Proportion of fitted-people involved pension, %

Fields	Elements	Indicators	Definitions and units
Culture	Rationalization	Literacy rate	Literacy rate of adults, %
		Newspaper reading proportion	Proportion of newspaper reading in adults, %
	Knowledge-intensive	Proportion of high education	Enrollment of tertiary education in total, %
	Information-intensive	Proportion of Internet popularity	Proportion of Internet users, %
Environment	Greening	Sewage treatment rate	Proportion of domestic sewage treatment, %

Sources: World Development Indicators on-Line (World Bank, 2015); International Historical Statistics 1750-2005 (Mitchell, 2007); The World Economy: A Millennial Perspective (Maddison, 2006); Economic Growth of Nations (Kuznets, 1971)

2. Paths and Models of the First Modernization

The first modernization, or the classic modernization, is the process and great transformation from agricultural to industrial economy and society, mainly featuring industrialization, urbanization, democratization, social welfare, and emphasis on economic growth. From the 1760s to the 1960s, the first modernization was the basic path of national modernization, but different countries adopted different models for it.

2.1 The main routes of the first modernization

The first modernization took place in the fields of politics, economy, society, culture and environment, etc. The progress and transformation from traditional to modern ones presents the basic trends among politics, economy, society and culture, while environmental degradation occurred sometime (Table 2). The modernity and diversity can be found among the countries in the process of the first modernization.

Table 2 Digital Images of the First Modernization

Fields	Core elements	Indicators	Great changes
Politics	Democratization	Coverage of universal suffrage	Increasing: from 0% to 100%
Economy	Industrialization	Proportion of industry	Increasing: from 5% to 50% *
		Proportion of agriculture	Decreasing: from 90% to 10%
Society	Urbanization	Proportion of urban population	Increasing: from 20% to over 60%
	Modern education	Proportion of primary education	Increasing: from 10% to 100%
	Social welfare	Pension coverage	Increasing: from 0% to 100% *
Culture	Rationalization	Literacy rate	Increasing: from 10% to 100%
		Newspaper reading	Increasing: from 0% to over 60% *
Environment	—	Quality of environment	Decreasing: from friendship to degradation *

* With some varieties among countries

Based on the political challenges and the time and initiation of the modernization process, the American Scholar Black (1966) divided modernization into seven categories: Britain and France, West-derived countries, other European countries, Latin American countries, independent countries, former colonial countries, and African countries.

Gerschenkron (2009) analyzed the experience of European late-comers in industrialization and proposes the so-called "catching-up model". He categorized industrialization into eight pairs of types: local — introduced, forced — autonomous, production centered — consumption centered, inflation — stable currency, quantity change — quality change, continuous — interrupted, agricultural development — agricultural stagnation, and economic motivation — political purpose.

2.2 The main models of the first modernization

The first modernization involves many core elements, e.g. industrialization, urbanization, democratization, international interaction, etc. Different countries may adopt different strategies at different stages, prioritizing some elements over others within a certain stage. Thus, different models are formed (Table 3).

Table 3 Models of Combined Elements in the Process of the First Modernization

No.	Element combinations	Models	Countries for example
1	Industrialization vs. democratization	Industrialization first	Germany, Japan, Republic of Korea, etc.
2		Democratization first	France, Finland, New Zealand, etc.
3		Coordinated development	UK, USA, Sweden, etc.
4	Industrialization vs. urbanization	Industrialization first	France, Finland, etc.
5		Urbanization first	Italy, Australia, etc.
6		Coordinated development	Sweden, UK, etc.
7	Economy vs. education	Economy first	UK, Portugal, etc.
8		Education first	Germany, Sweden, USA, etc.
9		Coordinated development	Italy, France, etc.
10	Market economy vs. planning economy	Free market economy	Western countries in the 19th century
11		Planned command economy	Soviet Union in the 20th century
12		Mixed economy	Western countries since the 1940s
13	Catching-up industrialization	Import substitution	Latin American countries since the 1950s
14		Export orientation	Southeast Asian countries since the 1950s
15		Coordinated development	Developing countries since the 1990s
16	International interaction	National industry protection	Germany in the 19th century
17		Free trade	UK in the 19th century
18		Colonial empire	the 18th century to the early 20th century
19		Dependent development	Some Latin American countries, etc.

Source: Research Group on China's Modernization Strategy et al., 2010

2.2.1 Industrialization vs. democratization

Some European scholars believed there were different models for the different countries to promote the national modernization. For example, from the 18th to the 19th century, the British model was led by industrialization, which then promoted democratization, and facilitated bureaucratization; the French model was led by bureaucratization and democratization, with industrialization coming later; the German model was led by a combination of bureaucratization and industrialization, but always in lack of democratization.

We think that the German model is that the industrialization first and then democratization, the French model is that the democratization first and then industrialization, and the British model is that the coordinated development of the industrialization and democratization (Table 2). As we know that Germany initiated the Industry Revolution in about 1825 and enjoyed universal suffrage in 1918, France enjoyed male universal suffrage in 1790 (the French Revolution) and its Industrial Revolution took place from 1820 to 1870; and the democratization of the UK can be traced back to the Glorious Revolution (1688) and the Reform Act of 1832, and its Industrial Revolution happened from about the 1760s (in the term of 1760 to the 1840s).

2.2.2 Industrialization vs. urbanization

The French model is that the industrialization first and then the urbanization. The Italian model is that the urbanization first and then the industrialization. The Swedish model is the coordinated development of the industrialization and urbanization (Figure 2).

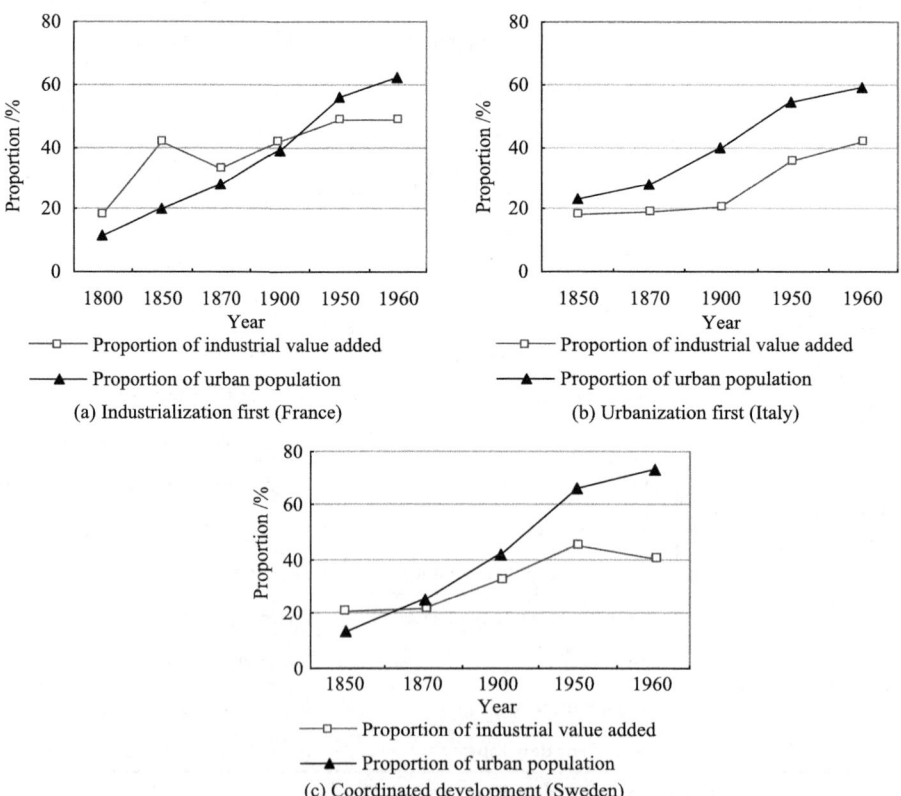

Figure 2   Three Models of the Combination of Industrialization and Urbanization from 1800 to 1960

2.2.3 Economy vs. education

The British model is that the economy first and then the education. The German model is that the education first and then the economy. The Italian Model is the coordinated development of the economy and education (Figure 3).

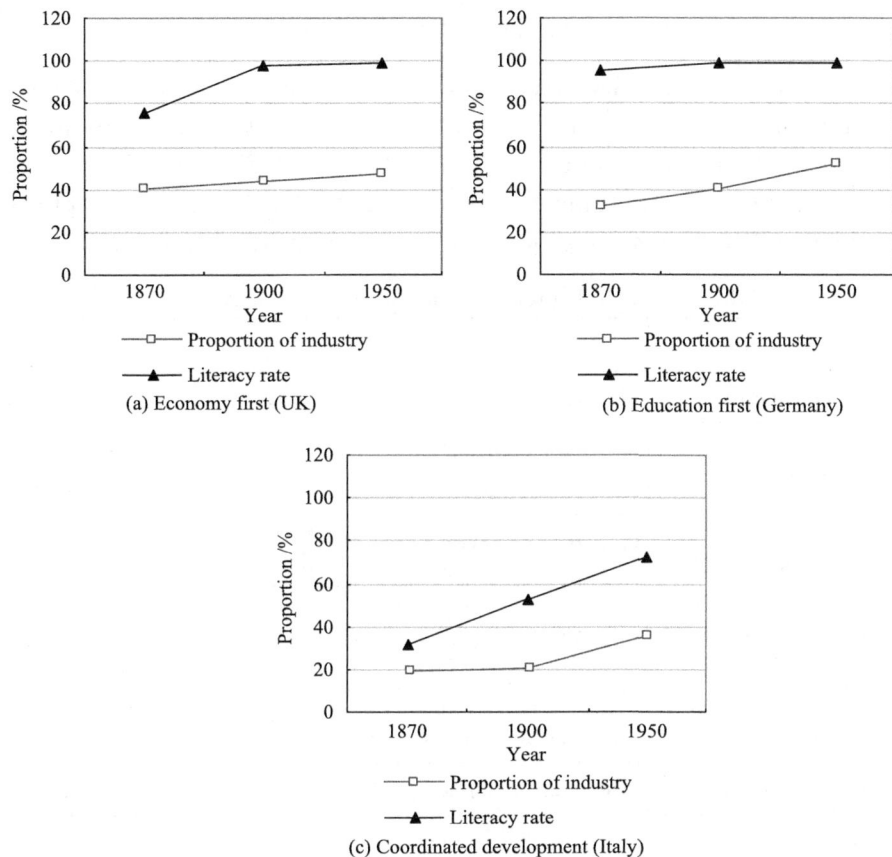

Figure 3   Three Models of the Combination of Economy and Education from 1870 to 1950

Since 1960, developed countries had successively completed the first modernization and have started the so-called post modernization. From 1970, the information revolution, high-tech and environmental movement spread all over the world and more and more countries started the second modernization. Developing countries that had not yet completed the first modernization were bound to be influenced by the tide of the second modernization and bring in factors of the information revolution and environment protection, if they were to continue with their first modernization process. Different countries absorbed the factors of the second modernization to different extents. Here, the first modernization actually became an improved or upgraded version of the first modernization, not the classic modernization any more.

3. Paths and Models of the Second Modernization

The second modernization is a new type of modernization. It is the process and great transformation from industrial economy and society to knowledge economy and society, mainly featuring knowledge-intensive, information-intensive, greening and environmental friendship, innovation driven, the improvement the quality of life, etc. From 1970, developed countries started the second modernization successively. All countries that have completed the first modernization have started the second modernization. Entering the 21st century, more and more countries have started the second modernization.

3.1 The main routes of the second modernization

The second modernization also happened in the fields of politics, economy, society, culture, environment, etc. But the changes occurred in the fields of economy, society and culture can be viewed as a civilization transformation related to the changes of what took place in the first modernization (Table 4). The second modernity and more pluralism can be found among the countries in the the process of the second modernization.

Table 4 Digital Images of the Second Modernization

Fields	Core elements	Indicators	Great changes
Politics	Democratization	Coverage of universal suffrage	Sustained: 100%, internationalization
Economy	Service-intensive	Proportion of agriculture	Decreasing: from 10% to 1% or lower
		Proportion of industry	Decreasing: from 50% to 20% or lower
	Knowledge-intensive	Proportion of service	Increasing: from 40% to 80% or higher *
		Proportion of knowledge service	Increasing: from 20% to 50% or higher
Society	Suburbanization	Proportion of suburban population	Increasing: from 20% to 50% *
	Education	Proportion of secondary education	Increasing: from 60% to 100%
Culture	Knowledge-intensive	Proportion of high education	Increasing: from 10% to 100% *
	Information-intensive	Proportion of Internet popularity	Increasing: from 0% to 100% *
Environment	Greening	Sewage treatment rate	Increasing: from 0% to 100% *

* With some varieties among countries

3.2 The main models of the second modernization

Currently, we have only some 40 years of experience in the second modernization and practices in different countries show both common grounds and special characteristics. The second modernization incorporates a number of elements: knowledge-intensive, information-intensive, greening and environmental friendship, innovation-driven, globalization, improvement of the quality of life, etc., and when different elements are combined, various models appear.

Different countries may adopt different strategies at different stages, prioritizing some elements over others within a certain stage. Thus, different models were formed (Table 5), including knowledge first, information first, greening first, coordinated development, etc.

Table 5 Models of Combined Elements in the Process of the Second Modernization

No.	Element combinations	Models	Countries for example
1	Knowledge vs. information	Knowledge first	USA, Sweden, Finland, etc.
2		Information first	Japan, Netherlands, etc.
3		Coordinated development	Australia, UK, etc.
4	Knowledge vs. greening	Knowledge first	Finland, Belgium, etc.
5		Greening first	UK, Netherlands, etc.
6		Coordinated development	Japan, Norway, etc
7	Information vs. greening	Information first	Norway, Japan, etc.
8		Greening first	Germany, UK, etc.
9		Coordinated development	Canada, Belgium, etc.
10	Globalization	Large-volume trade and investment	Ireland, Belgium, etc.
11		Middle-volume trade and investment	Germany, France, etc.
12		Small-volume trade and investment	USA, Japan, etc.
13	Economy vs. society	Economy first	Japan, Ireland, etc.
14		Society first	Germany, Sweden, Finland, etc.
15		Coordinated development	Belgium, Netherlands, Austria, etc.
16	Economy vs. ecology	Economy first	USA, Australia, Canada, etc.
17		Ecology first	Switzerland, Austria, Spain, etc.
18		Coordinated development	Germany, France, etc.
19	Society vs. ecology	Society first	USA, Australia, Canada, etc.
20		Ecology first	Switzerland, Austria, Spain, etc.
21		Coordinated development	Germany, France, etc.
22	Economy, society, ecology	Coordinated development	France, Denmark, UK, etc.

Source: Research Group on China's Modernization Strategy et al., 2010

Notes: Large-volume trade and investment: share of international trade and FDI in GDP⩾100%. Middle-volume trade and investment: share of international trade and FDI in GDP⩾50% and >100%. Small-volume trade and investment: share of international trade and FDI in GDP<50%

3.2.1 Knowledge vs. information

The American model is that the knowledge first and then the information. The Japanese model is that the Information first and then the knowledge. The Australian model is the coordinated development of the knowledge and information (Figure 4).

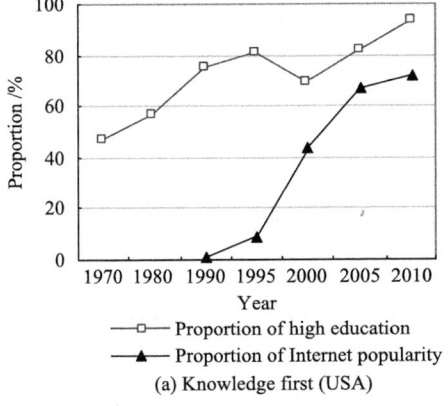

(a) Knowledge first (USA)

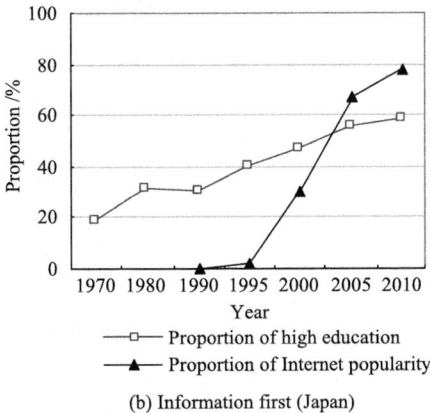

(b) Information first (Japan)

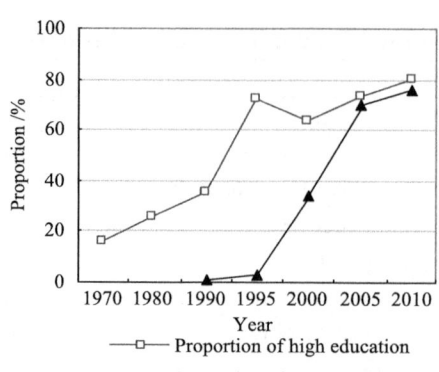

(c) Coordinated development (Australia)

Figure 4 Three Models of the Combination of Knowledge and Information Since 1970

3.2.2 Knowledge vs. greening

The Finnish model is that the knowledge first and then the greening. The British model is that the greening first and then the knowledge. The Japanese model is the coordinated development of the knowledge and greening (Figure 5).

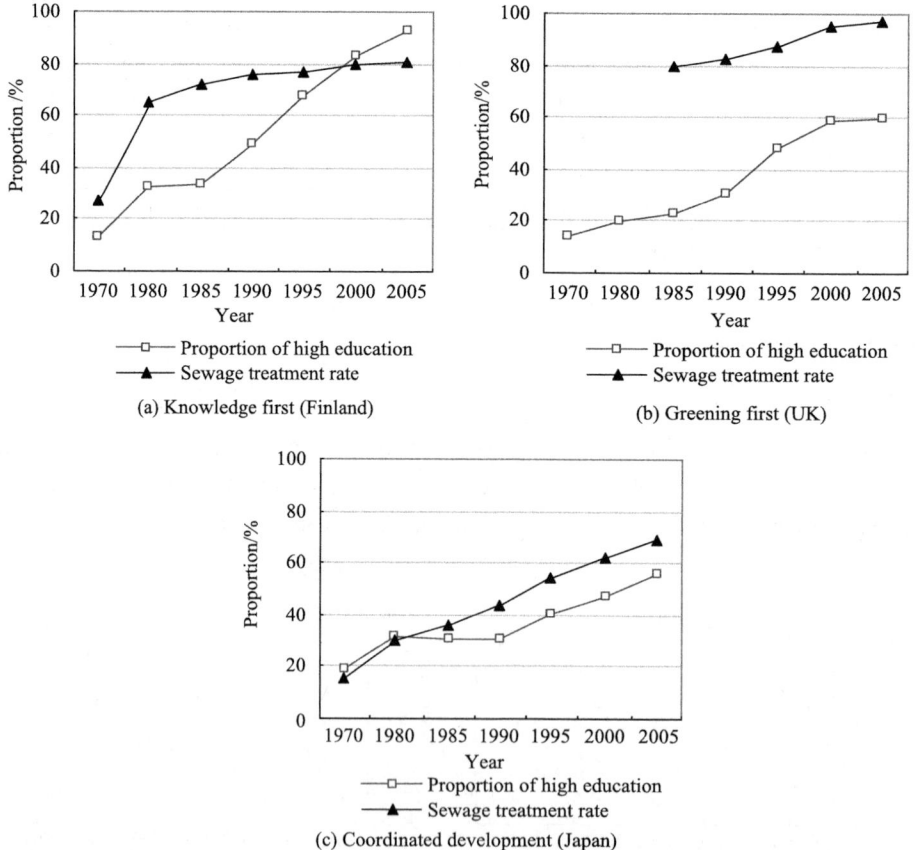

Figure 5 Three Models of the Combination of Knowledge and Greening Since 1970

3.2.3 Information vs. greening

The Norwegian model is that the information first and then greening. The German model is that the greening first and then information. The Canadian Model is the coordinated development of the information and greening (Figure 6).

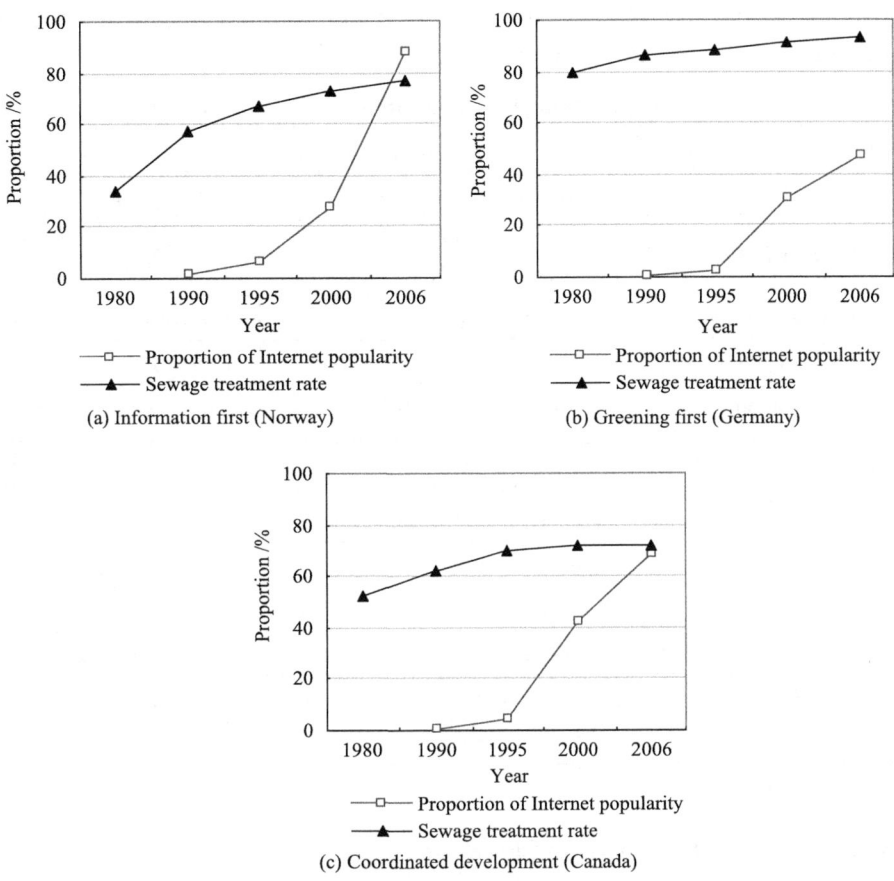

Figure 6 Three Models of the Combination of Information and Greening Since 1980

4. Paths and Models of the Integrated Modernization

Since the 1990s, knowledge economy and knowledge society have become international consensus and the second modernization has been widely recognized as the representation of world frontier and development trend and spread across the world. Countries that had not completed the first modernization were surely attracted by the second modernization and bound to speed up their transformation towards the second modernization. They might advance the first and the second modernization in a coordinate way and gather the essence of the two to reduce errors in the modernization process and reach to the future world frontier of the second modernization. This is the integrated modernization, which starts the transformation towards knowledge economy and society when it is halfway towards industrial economy and society (from semi-industrial economy and society to knowledge economy and society), featuring coordinated industrialization, urbanization, democratization, knowledge-intensive, information-intensive, greening, environment protection, etc.

4.1 The main routes of the integrated modernization

The integrated modernization only fit to the countries which have not finished the first modernization, and also happened in the fields of politics, economy, society, culture, environment, etc, as well as included the main contents of the first and the second modernization (Table 6). The first modernity, the second modernity and diversity can be found among the countries in the process of integrated modernization.

Table 6 Digital Images of the Integrated Modernization

Fields	Core elements	Indicators	Great changes
Politics	Democratization	Coverage of universal suffrage	Increasing: up to 100% *
Economy	Industrialization	Proportion of agriculture Proportion of industry	Decreasing: from 50% to 10% or lower Fluctuated: from 20% to 40% *
	Service-intensive	Proportion of service	Increasing: from 30% to over 60% *
	Knowledge-intensive	Proportion of knowledge service	Increasing: from 20% to 40% *
Society	Urbanization Suburbanization	Proportion of urban population Proportion of suburban population	Increasing: from 20% to 80% * Increasing: from 10% to 30% *
	Modern education	Proportion of primary education Proportion of secondary education	Increasing: from 60% to 100% Increasing: from 50% to 100%
	Social welfare	Pension coverage	Increasing: from 20% to 100% *
Culture	Rationalization	Literacy rate	Increasing: from 60% to 100%
	Knowledge-intensive	Proportion of high education	Increasing: from 10% to 60% *
	Information-intensive	Proportion of Internet popularity	Increasing: from 0% to 80% *
Environment	Greening	Sewage treatment rate	Increasing: from 10% to 100% *

* With some varieties among countries

4.2 The main models of the integrated modernization

First, integrated modernization has three stages. It is the coordinated development of the first and the second modernization and is in fact the combination of different key elements of the two. It is a process of dynamic adjustment. The first stage is dominated by industrialization and supplemented by knowledge-intensive, with elements of the first modernization in a dominant position. The second stage attaches equal importance to industrialization and knowledge-intensive, or to the first and the second modernization. The third stage is dominated by knowledge-intensive and supplemented by industrialization, with elements of the second modernization in a dominant position and the first modernization gradually completed.

Second, integrated modernization has different starting points. Countries may take the integrated modernization at different starting points, which means at that time-point countries may have different completion levels of the first modernization and take different approaches. For a country with a higher level of completion of the first modernization, more elements of the second modernization may be incorporated, and vice versa.

Third, integrated modernization shows differences across countries. Both the first and the second modernization have various models, and integrated modernization has even more different models, with more elements to combine (Table 7). For example, there can be industrialization first, urbanization first, democratization first, knowledge first, information first, coordinated development of knowledge and industrialization, coordinated development of information and industrialization, coordinated development of industrialization and greening, coordinated development of urbanization and information, coordinated development of urbanization and greening, etc. Integrated modernization is the coordinated development of the first and the second modernization, so many models of the first and the second modernization also apply to the integrated modernization, including the economy first, society first, economy-society-ecology coordinated models, etc.

Table 7 Models of Combined Elements in the Process of the Integrated Modernization

No.	Element combinations	Models	Countries for example
1	Knowledge vs. industrialization	Knowledge first	Greece, Panama, etc.
2		Industrialization first	Mexico, South Africa, etc.
3		Coordinated development	Chile, Turkey, Thailand, etc.
4	Information vs. industrialization	Information first	Malaysia, Costa Rica, etc.
5		Industrialization first	Egypt, Algeria, Indonesia, etc.
6		Coordinated development	Turkey, Thailand, Vietnam, etc.
7	Industrialization vs. greening	Industrialization first	Malaysia, Thailand, etc.
8		Greening first	Colombia, Peru, etc.
9		Coordinated development	Chile, Costa Rica, etc.
10	International interaction*	Large-volume trade and investment	Malaysia, etc.
11		Middle-volume trade and investment	P. R. China, etc.
12		Small-volume trade and investment	Brazil, etc.
13	Urbanization vs. greening	Urbanization first, greening first, coordinated development	—
14	Urbanization vs. information	Urbanization first, information first, coordinated development	
15	Economy vs. education	Economy first, education first, coordinated development	
16	Economy vs. society	Economy first, society first, coordinated development	
17	Economy vs. ecology	Economy first, ecology first, coordinated development	
18	Society vs. ecology	Society first, ecology first, coordinated development	
19	Economy, society and ecology	Coordinated development	

Source: Research Group on China's Modernization Strategy et al., 2010

Notes: Large-volume trade and investment: share of international trade and FDI in GDP⩾100%. Middle-volume trade and investment: share of international trade and FDI in GDP⩾50% and <100%. Small-volume trade and investment: share of international trade and FDI in GDP<50%

4.3 Knowledge vs. industrialization

The Panamanian model is that the knowledge first and then the industrialization. The Mexican model is that the industrialization first and then the knowledge. The Thai model is the coordinated development of the knowledge and industrialization (Figure 7).

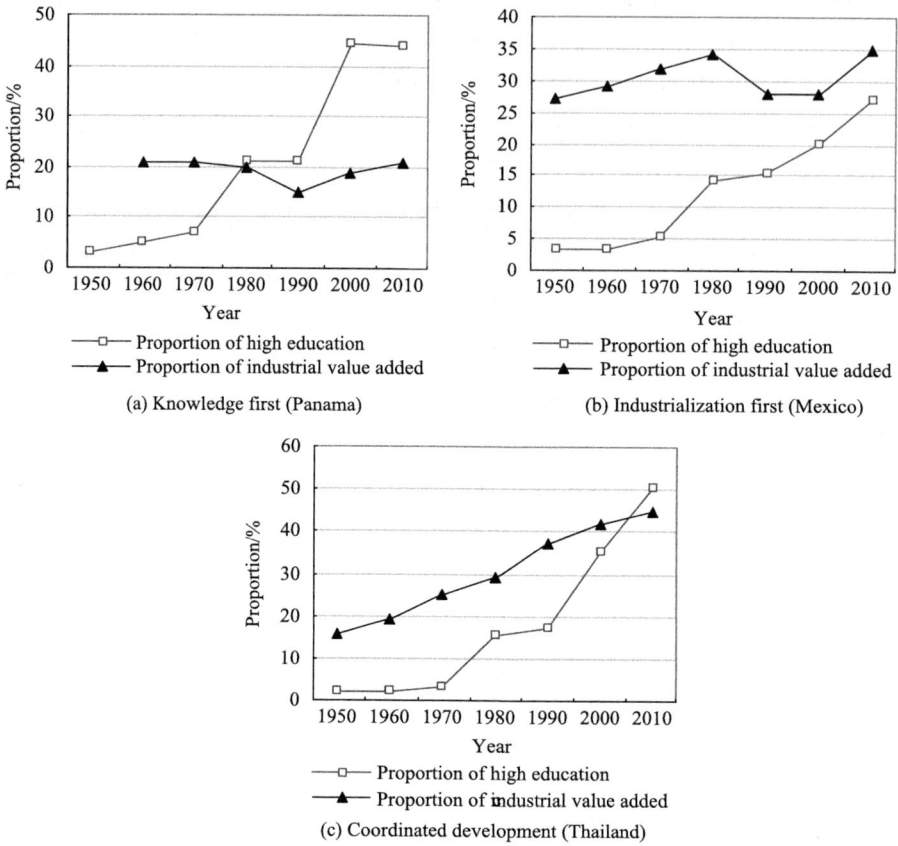

Figure 7　Three Models of the Combination of Knowledge and Industrialization Since 1950

4.4 Information vs. industrialization

The Malaysian model is that the information first and then the industrialization. The Egyptian model is that the industrialization first and then the information. The Turkish model is the coordinated development of the information and industrialization (Figure 8).

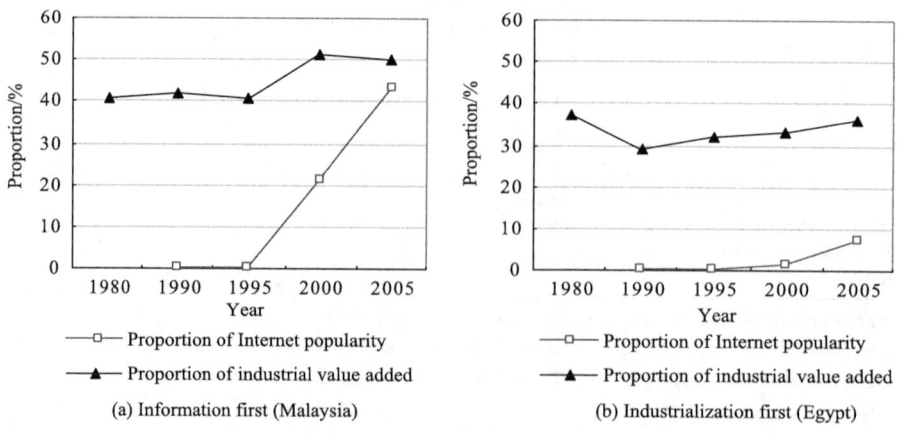

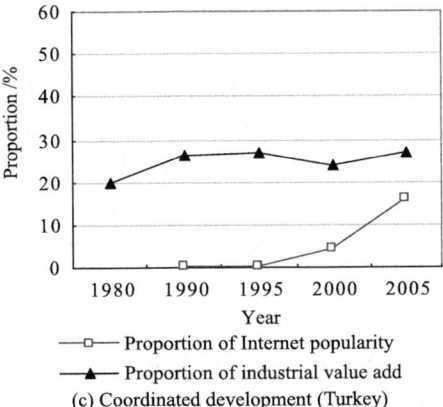

Proportion of Internet popularity
Proportion of industrial value add
(c) Coordinated development (Turkey)

Figure 8 Three Models of the Combination of Information and Industrialization Since 1980

4.5 Industrialization vs. greening

The Malaysian model is that the industrialization first and then the greening. The Colombian model is that the greening first and then the industrialization. The Costa Rican model is the coordinated development of the industrialization and greening (Figure 9).

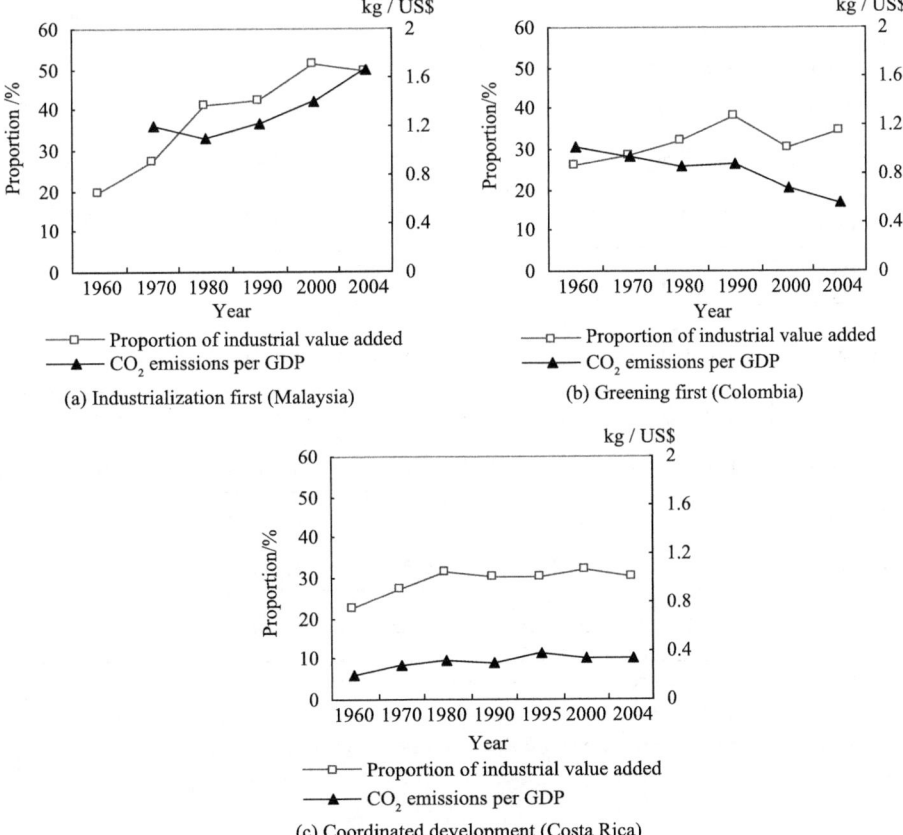

Figure 9 Three Models of the Combination of Industrialization and Greening Since 1960

5. Conclusions

There is no optimal model, only rational choices for national modernization. Over the past 300 years, some countries maintained their status as developed countries, some moved up, some stepped down, and some experienced ups and downs. Comparing their modernization models, we found not clear inclination towards any one model (Table 8). For example, among countries that moved up, some adopted the industrialization first, democratization first, or urbanization first model, but some others prioritized economy, education, or coordinated among multiple elements in the process of their first modernization; in the second modernization, some adopted the knowledge first, information first, greening first model, or coordinated among different elements. Therefore, every country needs to find the model suitable for itself rather than simply copy what any other country did.

Table 8 Combinations of Modernization Elements in Different Types of Countries

Types	Countries	Element combinations'models of the first modernization (1760-1970)			Element combinations'models of the second modernization (1970-2010)		
		Ind. vs. De.	Ind. vs. Ur.	Ec. vs. Ed.	Kn. vs. Inf.	Kn. vs. Gr.	Inf. vs. Gr.
Move Up	USA	CD	Ind. first	Ed. first	Kn. first	Kn. first	CD
	Australia	De. first	Ur. first	—	CD	—	—
	Finland	De. first	Ind. first	Ec. first	Kn. first	Kn. first	Gr. first
	Japan	Ind. first	Ind. first	Ed. first	Inf. first	CD	Inf. first
	Republic of Korea	Ind. first	CD	Ed. first	Kn. first	Kn. first	CD
Up and then down	New Zealand	De. first	Ur. first	Ed. first	CD	CD	CD
	Ireland	De. first	Ur. first	Ed. first	Kn. first	CD	Greening first
Down and then up	Norway	De. first	Ind. first	Ed. first	Inf. first	CD	Inf. first
	Spain	Ind. first	—	Ec. first	Kn. first	Gr. first	Gr. first
Rise first and fall later	Argentina	Ind. first	Ur. first	C&D	Kn. first	—	—
	Venezuela	—	CD	Ec. first	Kn. first	—	—
Move down	Portugal	Ind. first	Ind. first	Ec. first	Kn. first	CD	Gr. first

Source: Research Group on China's Modernization Strategy et al., 2010
Note: Ind., De., Ur., Ec., Ed., Kn., Inf., Gr., CD refer to industrialization, democratization, urbanization, economy, education, knowledge, information, greening and coordinated development separately

References

何传启(He C Q). 1999. 第二次现代化: 人类文明进程的启示. 北京: 高等教育出版社.

何传启(He C Q). 2003. 东方复兴: 现代化的三条道路. 北京: 商务印书馆.

何传启(He C Q). 2010. 现代化科学: 国家发达的科学原理. 北京: 科学出版社.

何传启(He C Q). 2013. 第二次现代化理论: 人类发展的世界前沿和科学逻辑. 北京: 科学出版社.

Black C E. 1966. The Dynamics of Modernization. New York: Harper & Row Publishers.

Gerschenkron A. 2009. Economic Backwardness in Historical Perspective. Beijing: The Commercial Press.

Kuznets S. 1971. Economic Growth of Nations: Total Output and Production Structure. Cambridge, MA: Harvard University Press.

Maddison A. 2006. The World Economy. Paris: OECD.

Martinelli A., He C Q. 2015. Global Modernization Review: New Discoveries and Theories Revisited. Hackensack: World Scientific Publishing.

Mitchell B R. 2007. International Historical Statistics, Europe 1750-2005. New York: Palgrave Macmillan.

Research Group for China Modernization Strategies, China Center for Modernization Research, CAS. 2010. China Modernization Report 2010: World Modernization Outline 1700-2100. Beijing: Peking University Press.

What's Modernization in the 21st Century: A Chinese Version

Chuanqi He

Professor, China Center for Modernization Research, Chinese Academy of Sciences
Academician, International Eurasian Academy of Sciences

Modernization, as a global historical trend, initiated in the about 18th century, diffused in the 19th century, and has become popular in the 20th and the 21st centuries. The contents and characteristics of modernization have changed in many aspects from the 18th to the 21st century. Almost all countries in the world are undergoing some kind of modernization consciously or unconsciously at present, and the modernization drive can also be set as a national goal directly or indirectly (Martinelli and He, 2015). China will enter the stage that modernization becomes the direct national goal in 2020.

The modernization study emerged in the 1950s. And then three waves of modernization researches took place, i.e. modernization study, post modern study and new modernization study. This paper will discuss the three explanations of the modernization from the perspective of new modernization study and a Chinese version.

1. Modernization Is a Worldwide Phenomenon

There is the phenomenon of modernization happening first and the word "modernization" coming later in the world from historic perspective. As a historical phenomenon, modernization can be viewed as the world frontier of human development since the Industrial Revolution in the 18th century, and the practice and process to chase, reach, and maintain a position in the world frontier. Developed countries strive to maintain their positions in the forefront, while developing countries try to catch up with an advanced level. Modernization is like an international marathon campaign of national development; countries in the lead are developed ones, while those lagging behind are the developing ones; developed countries may fall behind, and developing countries may catch up and overtake (Figure 1). The switch between these two groups of countries shows a somewhat set pattern.

Some scholars believe that the modernization phenomenon dates back at least to the Industrial Revolution in Britain and the French Revolution in the 18th century (Bendix, 1967) or before. As early as the 16th century when the Renaissance was near the end, the European society underwent profound changes and the great maritime discoveries made the Europeans believe that a new era — the modern time — was approaching. Then more revolutions that followed, including the Science Revolution, the Enlightenment, the Industrial Revolution, etc., reinforced this belief. By the mid-18th century, the overwhelming changes in Europe made people believe that "to become modern and to meet the modern needs" represented the trend of the time. Thus a new word "modernization" was invented (1748-1770), which was used to describe this new phenomenon (Table 1).

Today, modernization is a polysemant with the basic meanings derived from "modern".

(1) As a noun, modernization has two meanings. 1) It refers to the practice of modernizing. 2) It refers to the status after being modernized. The later is the status of having modern characteristics or having met modern needs, usually the world advanced level, e.g. modernization of nations, etc.

(2) As a verb, modernize stands for the process and act to realize modernization, i.e. the process and act to become modern or meet modern needs, usually the process and practice to chase, reach or maintain the world advanced level, e.g. to modernize agriculture, etc.

(3) Being used as an adjective, modernized refers to the state after the realized modernization, i.e. the state of having modern characteristics or having met modern needs; or simply put, the modernized is the latest, best, and most advanced, e.g. a modernized school, etc.

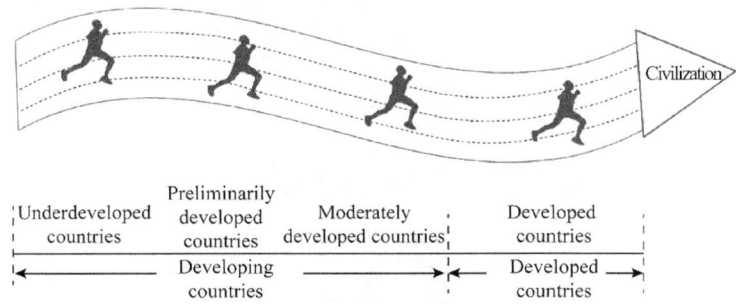

Figure 1   Modernization Is a Worldwide Phenomenon: A Marathon Game of National Development
Source: He, 2011

Table 1   From "Modern" to "Modernization"

Item	Modern	Modernize	Modernization
Meanings	*adj*. Year: 1585 1) relating to, or characteristic of the present or the immediate past. 2) of, or relating to the period from about 1500 to the present.	*verb*. Year: 1748 1) to make or become modern. 2) make suitable for present-day needs.	*noun*. Year: 1770 1) the act of modernizing: the state of being modernized. 2) something modernized: a modernized version.

Source: Webster's online dictionary

2. Modernization Is a Progress of Civilization

Besides being a worldwide phenomenon, modernization is also a progressive change of civilization from academic perspective (Figure 2). The former is the surface, while the latter is the essence. As a civilization change, modernization is a great transformation from traditional to modern civilization as well as the all-round development of human-being and the appropriate protection of the natural environment. It occurs in all fields of human civilization including politics, economy, society, culture, etc. Yet in the meantime, cultural diversity will remain in existence and play its role for a long time. Modernization first occurs in a few early starting countries and then spread all over the world (Bendix, 1967), with some exceptions though in regions or communities.

Modernization occurs to all fields of the human civilization, with different characteristics in different fields. Scholars from various disciplines have studied the phenomenon of modernization and formed a variety of modernization theories. Ten of them attract relatively more attention: the classic modernization theory, the dependency theory, the world system theory, the post modernization theory, the ecological modernization theory, the reflexive modernization theory, the globalization theory, the multiple modernities theory, the second modernization theory, and the integrated modernization theory. They explain the characteristics and principles of modernization from different perspectives. Here I would like to briefly introduce three of them.

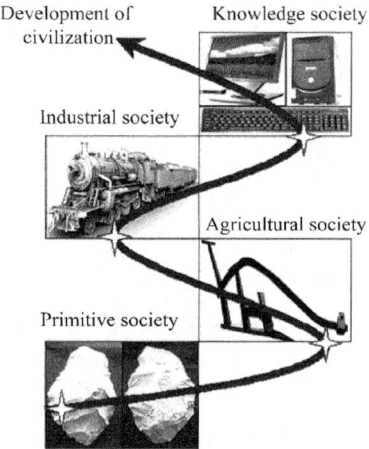

Figure 2   Modernization Is a Change of Civilization: Two Transformations of the Human Civilization Since the 18th Century

Source: He, 2011, 2012

Notes: The transformation from agricultural to industrial society is the first modernization while that from industrial to knowledge society is the second modernization. Stoneware represents the primitive society, and a wood plough represents the agricultural society. Steam engine represents the industrial society, and a computer represents the knowledge society

The classic modernization theory was formed in the 1950s and 1960s. It is not a single theory but a collection of theories on the phenomenon of modernization. It roughly covers six branches and six schools. Scholars of politics, economics, sociology, and history took different approaches in their studies of modernization and the resulted theoretical explanations are also different. For example, sociologists generally believe that modernization is a kind of social change and is the transformation form traditional to modern society (Bendix, 1967; Martinelli, 2005). Luo (1993), as a historian, believed that in the broad sense, modernization is a worldwide historical process, a global change from a traditional agricultural society to a modern industrial society; while in the narrow sense, modernization refers to the process where less developed countries catch up rapidly with advanced industrial countries. Western scholars believe that modernity is an abstract term that describes the results of modernization, such as political democratization, economic industrialization, social urbanization, cultural rationalization, modern science and technology, and universal compulsory education.

During the 1970s and the 1980s, the post modernization theory stepped up onto the academic arena. Instead of a complete theoretical system, the post modernization theory is an assembly of thoughts on post-industrial society, post modernism and post modernization study. For example, the American scholar Bell (1973) divided the development of human society into three stages: pre-industrial society, industrial society, and post-industrial society. French scholar Lyotard (1984[1979]) published *The Postmodern Condition: A Report on Knowledge,* and held that knowledge has become a business good and the most important productivity. The American scholar Inglehart (1997) believed that the transformation from traditional to modern society is modernization, while that from modern to post modern society is post modernization. The German scholar Zapf (1999) believed that modern society needed continuing modernization, while the American scholar Tiryakian(1991) referred to it as "new modernization" and so on.

In the 1990s, the second modernization theory came into being in close relation to the information revolution, knowledge economy, knowledge society, cyber culture, and innovation systems. It was proposed by the Chinese scholar He (1998, 1999, 2013). According to this theory, modernization is not only the situation of the world frontier of human development since the 18th century, and the process to reach or stay at this situation, but also the transformation from traditional to modern paradigm of human civilization, with the mutualism among Human being and Nature and cultural diversity. From the 18th century to the end of the 21st century, the process of world modernization can be divided into two stages, the first modernization or classic modernization, which is the transformation from agricultural economy and society to industrial economy and society, featuring industrialization, urbanization, democratization, rationalization, social welfare, emphasis on economic growth, etc.; and the second modernization or a new type of modernization, which is the transformation from industrial economy and society to knowledge economy and society, featuring knowledgization, informatization, greenization, being innovation-driven, globalization, the improving of the quality of life, etc. Countries and regions that have not completed the first modernization may advance the first and the second modernization in a coordinate way and gather the essence of the two to reduce errors in the modernization process and reach to the future world frontier of the second modernization. This is the integrated modernization, which is the transformation from semi-industrial economy and society to knowledge economy and society, featuring coordinated industrialization, urbanization, democratization, knowledgization, informatization, greenization, etc. It starts the transformation towards knowledge economy and society when it is halfway from the agricultural towards the industrial economy and society.

There are three roads of national modernization in the 21st century, they are the first modernization, the second modernization, and the integrated modernization. There are about 100 countries staying in the first modernization while 30 countries entering the second modernization in 2012. The percentage of countries staying in the first modernization will get down, the percentage of countries entering the second modernization will rise up, and the countries who have not completed the first modernization will push the integrated modernization in the 90 years of the future.

3. Modernization Is a Development Goal

Modernization has been set up as a development goal in many countries and regions from the policy perspective. Among them, the goal of modernized countries and regions is to keep the modernized level, and that of modernizing (or un-modernized) countries and regions is to catch-up and become modernized countries and regions. The national and regional modernization includes the modernization of all fields such as politics, economy, society, culture, environment, and human behavior.

There are three goals for the national modernization (Table 2), and the second and the third are dynamic in the field of new modernization study. For the realization of the third goal, different countries can do it by steps (Table 3).

Table 2 Three Goals for National Modernization

Items	First goal	Second goal	Third goal
Goals	To finish the first modernization, and complete the transformation from the agricultural to industrial society	To accomplish the second modernization, and fulfill the transformation from the industrial to knowledge society	To catch-up, reach and maintain the world advanced level of human development
Notes	All countries may realize this goal with different time. All the developed countries and parts of developing countries have realized this goal at present	All countries can achieve this goal with great different time. No one has realized this goal at present, and developed countries will achieve it at the second half of the 21st century	The countries reaching and keeping the world advanced level are the minority at any time, while others are the majority. Only parts of countries will realize this goal

Table 3 The Three Steps for National Modernization

Items	Low goal	Middle goal	High goal
Goals	To realize modernization basically	To realize modernization averagely	To realize modernization with high quality
Notes	Countries in this level of national modernization surpass 50% of the average level of the high-income countries and world average, and they become moderately developed countries	Countries in this level of national modernization surpass 80% of the average level of high-income countries, and they become developed countries or modernized countries	Countries in this level of national modernization surpass the average level of the high-income countries, and enter the forefront or top-class of world modernization

Based on their modernization level, countries may be divided into two groups: developed and developing countries. And the developing countries can be further divided into three categories: moderately developed countries, preliminarily developed countries, and under-developed countries (He, 2010, 2011). Among the four further-divided groups, the developed countries have the highest modernization level and enjoy the world advance level, the moderately developed countries have a modernization level higher than the world average but lower than that of the developed countries, the preliminarily developed countries have a modernization level below the world average but higher than that of the under-developed countries, and the under-developed countries are of the lowest modernization level, which is usually less than 30% of the average of the developed countries (Table 4).

Table 4 Criteria of Classification of National Modernization Levels

Groups	Modernization levels (based on modernization index and 80% of all modernization indicators)	Ranking (recommended)
Developed countries	80% of the average of the high-income countries or higher	1-20
Moderately developed countries	Below 80% of the average of the high-income countries but higher than 50% of the average of the high-income countries and the world average	21-45
Preliminarily developed countries	Below the world average but higher than 30% of the average of the high-income countries	46-80
Under-developed countries	Below 30% of the average of the high-income countries	81-131

Sources: He, 2010, 2012

Note: The recommended rankings are based on the levels of 2005 and are subject to change annually

According to *China Modernization Report* (He, 2011), in the past 300 years, developed countries accounted for less than 20% of all countries in the world, while developing countries accounted for more than 80%. For example, in 2012, among all 131 countries with a population of over 1 million, 16% were developed countries, while 84% were developing ones. The US and 20 other countries were developed countries, Russia Federation and 19 others were moderately developed countries, China and 42 others were preliminarily developed countries, and Kenya and 46 others were under-developed countries.

In the field of new modernization study, for the convenience of discussion, the developed countries can be viewed as the "modernized countries", while the developing countries can be viewed as the "modernizing countries" or "un-modernized countries". Although the modernization is a dynamic and uneven process, and both developed and developing countries are undergoing some kind of modernization consciously or unconsciously (Martinelli and He, 2015), while some aspects of some developed countries may not reach the world advanced level, and some aspects of some developing countries may reach or maintain the world advanced level conversely. The modernization's goals of the developed and developing courtiers are different (Table 5).

Table 5 The Goals of Developed and Developing Modernization

Items	Developed or modernized countries	Developing or un-modernized countries
Goals	To remain the world advanced level or modernized level, or to realize the modernization in the aspects that they do not reach the world advanced level	To reach the world advanced level, realize the modernization, and become developed or modernized countries in a short time
Notes	—	Among all developing countries, moderately developed ones aim at directly becoming developed countries; preliminarily developed countries aim at becoming moderately developed first and then, developed; under-developed countries need to take three steps: first becoming a preliminarily developed country, then a moderately developed one, and finally, a developed one

4. Conclusions

Modernization has been a polysemous word in the field of new modernization study.

Firstly, modernization refers to a worldwide phenomenon concerning the world frontiers of human development since about the 18th century and the practice and process to pursue, reach and maintain world frontier's levels.

Secondly, modernization has been a progressive change of human civilization with the transformation from traditional to modern paradigm which took place in all fields of civilization such as politics, economy, society, and culture.

Thirdly, modernization can be used as a development goal directly or indirectly, and the modernized developed countries are willing to keep the modernized level, while the non-modernized developing countries are working hard to catch up and reach the modernized level in shorter time. For example, the national objective of China is to become a moderately developed country in the middle of the 21st century and a modernized country in the second half of the 21st century.

References

何传启(He C Q). 1998. 知识经济与第二次现代化. 科技导报, 6: 3-4.
何传启(He C Q). 1999. 第二次现代化：人类文明进程的启示. 北京：高等教育出版社.
何传启(He C Q). 2003. 东方复兴：现代化的三条道路. 北京：商务印书馆.
何传启(He C Q). 2010. 现代化科学：国家发达的科学原理. 北京：科学出版社.
何传启(He C Q). 2011. 中国现代化报告概要：现代化科学概论. 北京：北京大学出版社.
何传启(He C Q). 2013. 第二次现代化理论：人类发展的世界前沿和科学逻辑. 北京：科学出版社.
罗荣渠(Luo R Q). 1993. 现代化新论. 北京：北京大学出版社.
马蒂内里(Martinelli A). 2005. 全球现代化：重思现代性事业. 北京：商务印书馆.
中国现代化战略研究课题组, 中国科学院中国现代化研究中心(Research Group for China Modernization Strategies, China Center for Modernization Research, CAS). 2010. 中国现代化报告2010：世界现代化概览. 北京：北京大学出版社.
Bell D. 1973. The Coming of Post-Industrial Society: A Venture in Social Forecasting. New York: Basic Books.

Bendix R. 1967. Tradition and modernity reconsidered. Comparative Studies in Society and History, IX (3): 292-346.

Black C E. 1966. The Dynamics of Modernization. New York: Harper & Row Publishers.

He C Q. 2012. Modernization Science: Principles and Methods of National Advancement. New York: Springer.

Inglehart R. 1997. Modernization and Postmodernization. Princeton: Princeton University Press.

Lyotard J-F. 1984[1979]. The Postmodern Condition: A Report on Knowledge. Minneapolis: University of Minnesota Press.

Martinelli A, He C Q. 2015. Global Modernization Review: New Discoveries and Theories Revisited. Hackensack: World Scientific Publishing.

Tiryakian E. 1991. Modernization: Exhumetur in pace (rethinking macrosociology in the 1990s). International Sociology, 6(2): 165-180.

Zapf W. 1999. Modernisierung, Wohlfahrtsentwicklung und Transformation. Berlin: Sigma.

Part Two

Multiple Modernities and Cultural Diversity

Part Two

Harmonious Coexistence of Tradition and Modernity — Inspirations from the Lasting Survival of the Amish Community in Modern American Society

Jin Feng

Lawrence Technological University

The ancestors of the American Amish people are the German Anabaptists originally resided in the mountain areas of Switzerland and the Rhine river valley.

Because Anabaptism was considered heresy and the Anabaptists were persecuted in the 16th and 17th centuries. To escape the cruel religious persecution, the Anabaptists emigrated from Switzerland to Pennsylvania of America. They later moved on to settle down in other states in the US and Canada's Ontario. Currently, the population of the Amish communities is about 230,000. The areas that have the highest concentration of the Amish population include the Lancaster area in Pennsylvania, Eastern Ohio, and Northern Indiana.

Historically, the ancestors of the Anabaptist immigrants belonged to the Mennonites named after the Anabaptist leader Menno Simons. In the late 17th century, a group led by Jakob Ammann, the leader of a more conservative movement in the Mennonites became Amish or Amish Mennonite. The term Amish used in the present day usually means all the Anabaptist immigrants including both the Mennonites and the Amish. Generally speaking, the Amish people are more conservative in religion and culture, while the Mennonites are more open. The major characteristics of the Amish are strong religious devotion and their emphasis on community. These two important aspects have made it possible for the Amish culture to resist the influence of the mainstream American culture.

The Amish communities are based on religious congregation. One congregation usually has 30 to 40 families. When the population grows within a community, the congregation will regroup in order to maintain a reasonable and appropriate scale for effective communication. In many communities, there are no church buildings. The congregation events take place in the houses in turn. The clergymen are elected among the congregation members instead of being appointed by the higher level organizations. The consciousness about the size of the congregation effectively preserves the close relationship and affinity among the members of the community.

Based on the interpretation of the Bible, the Amish people believe in a simple and modest life, a humble attitude, and a peaceful way to solve conflicts. To make their life simple and modest, Amish people choose not to use electricity from the grid, automobile, and other modern technologies that may make the Amish community loose its independence and self-sufficiency. Supported by the power of religious devotion, Amish people remain committed to a life style they chose, calmly resisting the popular culture of the modern American society that worships technological progress and material comfort. However, the values of the Amish people are not purposeful anti-technology. In a congregation, people have two times in a year to discuss and determine if they should adopt any modern technology that may help them to improve productivity or to comply with modern product standards, without violating their ethical or religious principles. Since this procedure is carried out in individual congregations, the technologies adopted in different communities are all different. In addition, the Amish people may also refuse to use certain technology purely based on their belief in God's power. For instance, they do not use lightning rod, because they believe that God is in charge of lightning and humans should not interfere. Even when people and animals were hit by lightning in their barns, they would still not install lightning rod.

Based on the collective memories of being prosecuted by state churches in Europe in the 16th and 17th centuries, the Amish people have kept a respectful distance from the mainstream society, the state authority, and other ethnic groups. They have refused the social security benefit from the federal government of the United State, and therefore, do not pay social security tax. The main reason why the most of the Amish communities do not use electricity from the power grid is that they do not want to become dependent on the establishment outside the community. The Amish communities religiously preserve their traditional language — Pennsylvania German or Pennsylvania Dutch. The children in the Amish communities only learn and speak their traditional language before they reach the school age. English is actually their second language for communication with the world outside the Amish community.

Before the Amish youths reach their adulthood at the age of eighteen, they have two years of "free period" to experience the modern American culture outside the Amish communities. And then they will determine whether they will receive the baptism. Receiving baptism means an irreversible life-long commitment to the Amish religious practice and life style. Therefore, this commitment to the religious belief and the traditional life style is not forced. Rather, the determination is made voluntarily under the influence of the close social and familial relationships of traditional society. This process has proven to be beneficial to the sustainability of the Amish life style tradition. Under the pressure of the outside world, there are apostates in the community. In the Amish tradition, the apostates will be treated with shunning to make them return. The so-called shunning is to limit social contact of the apostates until they regret. To the people growing up in the Amish communities with strong communal and familial social bounds, this non-violent punishment by means of social isolation could be felt as harsh and severe, and therefore, effective. About 90% of the Amish teenagers decide to be baptized and accept the traditional life style.

The conviction about religious freedom in the mainstream American society has no doubt provided the constitutional protection to the survival of the Amish culture in the contemporary American society. At the same time, the Christian nature of the Amish religious practice can easily won sympathy from the rest of the society in such a Christian country. However, this does not mean that the traditional Amish life style and social practice have no conflict with laws and regulations. According to the Amish tradition, the younger generation are educated in the community for eight years. The community school usually has only one uncertified teacher and the students are taught in ways like home school. This can be seen as a direct violation of the state legislations that require 12 years of compulsory education for all the school age children. Among the many legal cases, the most well-known is the Wisconsin vs. Yoder case ruled by the US Supreme Court. After three Amish students stopped schooling after the eighth grade in 1962, the families were convicted in a county court with a dollar fine for each family for their violation of the compulsory education law. According to the principles of tradition, they should be in contest with other people even in court. This intrinsic disadvantage of the Amish people in the American legal system caught the attention of a Lutheran minister who formed a non-Amish organization, the National Committee for Amish Religious Freedom, to help the Amish families to appeal the case to the Wisconsin Supreme Court. The court ruled in favor of the Amish families. The state of Wisconsin appealed the case to the US Supreme Court and the US Supreme Court also ruled in favor of the Amish families based on the ground of religious freedom. This ruling provided legal precedent to protect other Amish people to preserve their tradition in education. It is under the constitutional projection that the Amish communities obtained the space for surviving for their cultural traditions.

The existence and continuity of the Amish communities have enriched the local cultural landscape in the US. It is a demonstration of cultural diversity and provides examples of a non-mainstream lifestyle. The Amish farms look very similar to other ordinary farms in the same area in terms of architectural style and building materials. A closer examination will reveal that the Amish farm houses are more complex, reflecting the multi-generational extended family structure. The small windmills used to pump water from wells are indicators of their off-grid living preference, and at the same time add liveliness to the landscape. Although the Amish farm houses are not designated as historically significant for preservation, they represent a special historicity and an on-going historical development. Although the ancient-looking and modest garments the Amish people ware usually provoke a romantic nostalgia, they are not living in the past, but realistically living in the present time. They are not intentionally trying to replay history, but naturally living with their unique attitude toward life. Their buggies are nothing but necessary and simple means of transportation, reflecting the simple life prescribed by God. From the certain point of view, while we are still trying to achieve the modernity that is seen as the extension of history, the Amish people have transcended it.

The unique cultural landscape in Amish communities aroused interests of the public, naturally forming resources of tourism. Visitors can learn about the customs of the Amish countryside in idyllic surroundings, taste delicious food produced using traditional recipes and cooking methods, and appreciate the production of exquisite handicrafts. After all the enjoyment, the visitors can critically reflect on modern social life and mainstream values.

The survival of Amish communities and their cultural traditions perhaps can give us some inspiration. In the Amish communities, we see a cultural tradition that transcends the modern civilization. In this cultural tradition, the will of people determines the extent and manners of their own development. This self-determined way of development is perhaps the best approach to cultural preservation. The self-paced sustainability of the Amish communities is asynchronous to the accelerated development of American mainstream culture and they are not moving in the same direction. In their differences, the social cultural diversity is achieved and the American culture is enriched. From this phenomenon, we should reflect on the issues of cultural diversity in the process of modernization in contemporary China. China has many ethnic groups with rich cultural heritage that provides great conditions to preserve cultural diversity.

The experience of successful cultural preservation of the Amish communities demonstrates that both internal and external factors are necessary. The internal factors include the systematic preservation of the religion, language, education tradition, family, and community; and the external factors include the constitutional protection of the religious freedom and the flexibility of the legislations at different levels of governments.

References

Nolt S M. 2003. A History of the Amish. Intercourse: Good Books.
Scott S. 1992. Amish Houses & Barns. Intercourse: Good Books.
Williamson H R. 2005. The Amish: Current Issues and Historical Background. New York: Novinka Books.

Cultural Diversity and Social Contradictions of the Modernization

Nikolay Lapin

Center for the Study of Socio-Cultural Changes Institute of Philosophy, Russian Academy of Sciences

The theme "Modernization and Diversity" is very important. The Program of 2nd International Modernization Forum(IMF) rightly focuses on the themes that take into account the multiplicity of modernities and paths of modernization, and the main types of diversity — cultural, social, environmental, regional, etc. The author of the report highlights the ratio and methods of measurement of cultural diversity and social contradictions of the modernization in the world and in Russia. Cultural diversity of mankind is obvious, but methods of its measurement, however, are not. Instruments implemented by China Center for Modernization Research (headed by Professor Chuanqi He), Chinese Academy of Sciences, are based on international statistics and allow to obtain reliable indicators and indexes for different countries of the world, including measurement of social and cultural characteristics of each country's modernization. Reports of China Center for Modernization Research contain data allowing to analyze not only the cultural diversity of modernization, but also its social contradictions. This allows not to mix cultural diversity factors and the causes of social contradictions and human woes — poverty, inequality, wars and others.

I recall the characteristic of world modernization trend with 1950 to 2010, which appears in the Feng Zhang and Chuanqi He's report on the 1st IMF: "In the process of world modernization, the divergence and convergence take place across the time and space, the qualitative and quantitative indicators exist from field to field. The structure of economy and urbanization convergence, and cultural diversity are universal. Per capita income increased also, so the per capita income decreased in the regard of relative level in some nations"[1].

Significant cultural differences between countries do not preclude the general trends in the structure of their economy and the evolution of per capita income. French economist

---

[1] Zhang F, He C Q. World modernization indexes 1950 to 2010. In the 1st International Modernization Forum: "Modernization and Global Change" Proceedings. Beijing, 8 and 9 August 2013: 70.

Thomas Piketty clearly demonstrated: On long-time interval in most countries of the world, recapitalization of assets accumulated in the past (*r*), is faster than production and wages grow (*g*) that is valid simple and transparent mechanism: $r>g$[1]. This mechanism determines to a large extent the long-term evolution of the distribution of wealth, not only within countries, but also among countries. This is evidenced by the steady enough composition that 20 to 22 rich countries that have become the most developed on the first, the industrial stage of modernization (since 1960), and then (since 1980), as a rule, retained the leadership on the second, the information stage. They have a comparative advantage in determining their ranks on the integrated modernization indexes. However, their ranks within this set of countries (the Club with most developed countries) markedly changed. There are exceptions to the general rule: In the Club appear 1 to 2 new countries, and some countries are leaving it. This often depends on their culture evolution features.

Center for the Study of Socio-Cultural Changes in the Institute of Philosophy, Russian Academy of Sciences, has adapted the indicators developed by the Chinese colleagues to the peculiarities of Russian statistics and in collaboration with colleagues in 27 regions of Russia calculated the modernization indexes for all 83 regions of Russia. It is allowed to compare regions among themselves and with 130 countries in automatized mode. Analyzing the data, we can study not only the level of modernization in Russia in general (as process of changes of the Russian civilization), but also in the context of socio-cultural evolution of regions and federal districts of Russia.

According to the China Center for Modernization Research, by 2010 Russia as a whole has completed the first, the industrial stage of modernization and during 2010-2012 steady was in the preparatory phase of the second, the informational stage. This progress was achieved thanks to the sustained growth of the modernization indexes of 14 Russian regions. First of all, it's 4 regions that have reached the information stage growth: the most developed Moscow agglomeration (city Moscow and Moscow region), St. Petersburg, and the region, the center of which is the Nizhniy Novgorod. The population of these regions makes up 27.6 million of people. In addition, 10 regions entered the beginning informational stage. Their population is 18.1 million. In the most developed 14 regions of Russia live 45.7 million people, or nearly one-third of the total population of Russia.

However, two-thirds of the population remain in the primary i.e. industrial modernization stage. The proportion is 69 of 83 regions of Russia. The economy of them was destroyed by chaotic deindustrialization during the bureaucratic privatization in the 1990s, so it needed now new industrialization. Several regions are in the early phase of industrialization. The reasons for this status are complex; among them important are their culture features.

The author of this report shows that the main task of modernization now in Russia is to implement the new industrialization in many regions, in conjunction with the development and use of high-tech informational technologies, taking into account the cultural diversity of Russian regions.

---

[1] Piketty T. Le Capital au XXI siec`le. E`dition du Seuil, 2013.

References

He C Q, Lapin N. 2015. Civilization and Modernization: Proceedings of the Russian-Chinese Conference 2012. Singapore: World Scientific Publishing.

Lapin N. 2015. Distances between macro-regions and integrating modernization stages of the Russia. Sociological Studies, 3: 44-55.

Piketty T. 2013. Le Capital au XXI sice'le. Edition du Seuil: appendix.

Zhang F, He C Q. 2015. World modernization indexes 1950 to 2010. In A Martinelli, C Q He (Eds.), Global Modernization Review: New Discoveries and Theories Revisited (p. 70). Singapore: World Scientific Publishing.

Culture Trend of Modernization as Reflected in Office Space Design

Jiang Lv

Eastern Michigan University

The growth of Silicon Valley culture, led by Google, Facebook and other new IT giants, had been touted as the pioneer era that created a variety of new fashionable design trends, including the design of workplace. Walking into today's workplace, one may feel like walking into a coffee shop with coffee bars and seating for relaxed socialization. It is a different corporate culture in a different time — the conceptual age, and it is for a new generation of workers — the creative class.

1. The Current Trend of Modernization in Office Space Design

With the spread of the Google's successful workplace culture in recent years, the traditional hierarchical corporate culture is dissolving in the office landscape. Through the perspective of architectural space planning and design, this paper analyzes the emerging trends in workplace design. The changing layout of offices from the 19th century to the present time reflects the profound changes of the society from the industrial era to the current conceptual time. The traditional workplace for physical labors has given way to new workplace for the creative class. The new workplace forms the new ecology of creativity from which ideas and creative concepts are obtained. The changes in corporate culture are important aspects of modernity.

The newly renovated office space in Smith Group JJR of Detroit and Haworth of Holland, Michigan, where the author visited, representatively reflects the influence of the Google inspired workplace culture. A large portion of the floor area is used for informal exchange of ideas and collaboration in the form of lounge style seating areas, coffee bar, and library with unassigned space. Other employees can use the private offices of senior employees when they are not using the space. The traditional hierarchical corporate culture is dissolving in the emerging creative culture.

2. History of the Workspace Design

Organizational and working culture differs from time to time. The traditional workplace is a bureaucracy consisting of hierarchical tiers of employees. The traditional open floor plan office was born in the 19th century industrial boom. In large-span space with iron beams, executives transplanted their beloved style of factory production line to the office. With clerks seating behind a small desk uniformly aligned and oriented, the office is like a classroom without teacher.

In the 1960s, the office furniture manufacturer Herman Miller created the cubicle workstation system, AO-I and AO-II, which offered possibilities of multi-purpose and adjustable functions for both open floor plan offices and private offices. An office filled with such cubicles is called a cube farm. Within the traditional hierarchical workplace, it is common to see the lower-ranking employees working in a large area with small cubicles.

Within the traditional hierarchical workplace, it is common to see the lower-ranking employees working in a large area with small cubical-type office space. As rank increases, offices become larger and more private, a predominant feature of the workplace identified by the chain of command such as size and site location. Similar to those in the food chain of an ecosystem, the higher-position administrators have their own independent offices, and bosses usually occupy the corner offices with both sides of large windows. The boss's right-hand man same as regular visits observed the lower-ranking employees.

Cube farms are found in high-tech companies, as well as other industries. Many cube farms were built during the dotcom boom. Between 2000 and 2002, IBM partnered with the office furniture manufacturer Steelcase, and researched the software, hardware, and ergonomic aspects of the cubicle of the future (or the office of the future) under the name "Bluespace".

The closed workplace can cause many non-wellness problems, such as phobia or fear and anxiety reaction in a person. Consequently, avoidance behavior towards the workplace or associated stimuli has developed. In some cases, workplace phobia may be a kind of social phobia, social anxiety or extreme shyness. (Florida, 2002)

3. New Trend in the Time of Moving from the Information Age to the Conceptual Age

Concerning the new culture in the conceptual time, new research and products of workplaces were invented to solve the problems. The new workplace forms the new ecology of creativity from which ideas and creative concepts are obtained.

Google, for example, did not adopt the conventional corporate culture and office design. In fact, just by looking at pictures inside the Googleplex, people can see that it looks more like an adult playground, not a place for work. In the shared open space, employees communicate in relaxing environment and work in private spaces on their inspirations. This culture is recognized as happy working environment in order to achieve maximum productivity and real breakthroughs in innovations, which are usually nurtured in environment of "no fear". The private space at Google is heavily personalized to signify individuality and identity. This has been seen as an effective way leading to a positive workplace culture, higher employee morale, and less turnover. Google's success can be attributed to this culture. With the success of this world-changing organization, stories about the Google workplace culture spread quickly.

For office layout, the significant impact is a challenge to the traditional open space. Then Facebook brags that its new building will be the largest open floor plan in the world, consisting of a single, ten-acre[①] open room. These two called "open floor plan" are very different in layout, as well as their profound cultural reasons behind.

In order to comfort and increases employees' satisfaction and decreases illness symptoms, research fellows of Herman Miller paid attention to workplace's personalization which leads to the following important aspects:

(1) A positive workplace culture;
(2) Higher employee morale;
(3) Less employee turnover;
(4) Signifying individuality and identity. (Miller, 2016)

Google's success can be attributed to this culture. Google has people who's sole job is to keep employees happy and maintain productivity. It may sound too controlling to some, but it's how this world-changing organization operates.

With the spread of the Google's successful workplace culture in recent years, the traditional hierarchical corporate culture is dissolving in the office landscape. This paper takes perspectives of architectural space planning and design to analyze the emerging trends in workplace design. The changing layout of the open floor plan office from the 19th century to the present time reflects the profound changes of the society from the industrial era to the current conceptual time. The new workplace forms the new ecology of creativity from which ideas and creative concepts are obtained. The following examples will provide some solutions and practices in the new workplace design.

As the author of *Reconsidering the Startup Open Floor Plan Office* said: "The open floor plan office has become a shibboleth of startup culture. It reflects our rejection of hierarchy, and our embrace of agility, collaboration and creativity, and as a result, many startups take the open floor plan for granted." (Stevenson, 2016)

Startups are young, exciting, extremely small (usually two to six people), and require tons of communication. They're also more casual than older and established companies: coworkers finish the day with a beer and a game of ping-pong. Who doesn't want a pool table, reclining chairs, plenty of greenery, and even a slide at work? That's what employees at Google's EMEA Engineering in Zurich asked for when they were encouraged to voice their emotional and practical needs in a design-led survey on how to best transform a local brewery into 12,000 square meters of office space. Collectively, the 800 staff members were willing to sacrifice their personal office space for larger, more colorful collaborative space — and the result is a zany mishmash of funky pods and thematic rooms that receive loads of daylight. Lest you think the Zooglers doodle all day surrounded by so many these kind of fun, it actually promotes serious creativity and innovation.

[①] 1 acre ≈ 4047m^2.

Aribnb in San Francisco is another a challenge to create a home for new high-technology workplace that would express the company's unique culture, values and brand. Important considerations included connections to the site and its rich history, connections to the local San Francisco communities, sustainability in the design and construction of the space, and the creation of choices for workers in how they could work throughout the day.

To ensure that the Gensler design team fully understood the culture and values that made Airbnb unique, they embedded themselves in Airbnb's offices for four months. During that time the team was able to experience the company culture and participate in events along with Airbnb employees.

The space has been designed to enable workers to choose where and how they want to work on any given day, though workers do have assigned desks. The entire space has an open floor plan, with no private offices, even for the founders. Each collaboration space has a unique look and feel. All in all, the new home for Airbnb is more than an office — it's a home for the spirit and culture of Airbnb.

The author visited the newly renovated office space in Smith Group JJR of Detroit and Haworth of Holland, Michigan, and conducted interviews with the workers. The new renovated space fully reflects the new cultural trend of space planning of the modern office culture in the conceptual age. The floor plans are very open. A large contemporary kitchen occupied the entrance area. The areas facing windows or receiving bright light are sat by lower-ranking employees. The president and chief designer's office of the Haworth are located in the front central area of the office. Everyone can observe their working performance through the transparent curtain walls. Other directors' offices can be shared by everyone of the company when they are out of town or in vacations. The presidents of the Smith Group JJR have no personal office at all. They share conferences, or sit in the sitting area meeting their employees. They told the author that the most important contributors are the people who work in the office every day instead of the managers.

In Haworth, there is private space where several high back sofas are placed. Their backs are very tall and over 200 degrees around a person's head for people making a private phone call. Rest areas for the employees are lager than their working areas. Many employees work there with their laptop computers, drink coffee, lay down, chat, or have a small group meeting. The most popular and busy area is the computer recharge area. Many people sit or stand near by charging high table, like a bar, exchange their ideas, sharing information, and enjoying their happy time.

4. Conclusions

Based on the analyses of the trend of the office plan style from the 19th century to the current century, modern office culture in the conceptual age is recognized as happy working environment in order to achieve maximum productivity and real breakthroughs in innovations, which are usually nurtured in environment of "no fear". The private space at the new space is heavily personalized to signify individuality and identity. It reflects the rejection of traditional hierarchy, and embrace of agility, collaboration and creativity.

References

Florida R. 2012. The Rise of the Creative Class. New York: Basic Books.

Kessler R C, Stein M B, Berglund P. 1998. Social Phobia Subtypes in the National Comorbidity Survey. Am J Psychiatry, 155: 613-619.

Miller H. 2016. Home sweet office comfort in the workplace. http://www.hermanmiller.com/research/research-summaries/home-sweet-office-comfort-in-the-workplace.html[2016-3-26].

Pink D H. 2005. A Whole New Mind: Moving from the Information Age to Conceptual Age. New York: Riverhead Books.

Stevenson S. 2016. Open plan offices: The new trend in workplace design. http://www.slate.com/articles/business/psychology_of_management/2014/05/open_plan_offices_the_new_trend_in_workplace_design.html[2016-3-26].

Vise D A, Malseed M. 2005. The Google Story. New York: Delacorte Press.

Consolidation, Integration, Modernization: From the Shaping of the Framework "Mitteleuropa" to the European Union

Loránd L. Mádly

"George Barițiu" Institute of History, Romanian Academy Cluj-Napoca

1. General Considerations: State, Society and Modernization

Since the years of the Roman Empire, the state tried to introduce measures intended to sustain development, like a uniform language, similar laws for the whole territory or a uniform territorial structure. From the historical perspective, the developments on economic, social, scientific levels were not only market-imposed tendencies or discoveries; many achievements on the path to modernization were the result of complex reforms, introduced by respective states, in order to consolidate, expand or synchronize markets, territories and regions in a complex process which led to the givens of our times, and a process which not only did not cease, but rather increased its speed.

But did the state stand as the proposer of reforms or as a brake for them? Communication became essential during the centuries. From building better roads, then the implementation of telegraph, telephone, later the Internet with its multiple and flexible benefits, this path of modernizing — at times with huge technological inventions as leaps — led to the situation of nowadays, when communication became an important component of the social and economic fabric. From such times, because of the state of the roads and the dangers that travelling implied, oriental goods were measured in gold, we live today in a world in which money can be transferred or practically all existent goods are shipped across the globe. From aspects of the processes which led to this evolution, we can learn essential lessons for the future.

There were different tendencies: the multinational empires, with their tendency to expand, creating a uniform economic or legal space (cite the reforms) or the "closed/isolated" nation states, with a parallel from small medieval/feudal states, which had border tolls and restrictive commercial policies, to the modern nation states, which later, after the fall of the main European empires, developed strong isolationist politics, with closed borders, protectionist measures, product bans, and military build-ups along with belligerent propaganda, characteristic for the interwar period; but there is also to mention that these policies led to the World War II, to a continuity of war in Europe which had a strong impact on the economic and social development, although war periods forced certain innovations on the technical level.

These tendencies led to diverse continuities, whose effects can be observed until our days. In Europe, the evolution of the greater states, like the British, German or Austrian empires, meant a history of integration and modernization with the focus on territorial growth, efforts for establishing an integrative framework, common laws, reforms in all fields of economy and society, industrialization, and political integration. After the World War I, the dissolution of the European empires led to the ascension of the nation states, which did not have the same large hinterland as their predecessors and faced economical and political crises, which partly contributed to the outbreak of a new world war[①]. These two wars determined a rethinking of the political and economical shape of Europe, with a new focus on the supranational organizations, the opening of markets and borders, and economic growth.

In this long path of development, Europe — as many parts of the world itself — comprised regions with different shapes and levels of development; it was a coexistence of areas and regions with huge differences in general development and various specificities. Behind the positive effects of diversity for the economic growth, the "specialized" regions can be easily turned into "problem regions" if not managed with appropriate measures (e.g. ceased industry regions and mining "cities").

The "multi-speed modernization" which was a reality since the first days of industrialization imposed different necessities and policies for them (as today in the EU too). In the old days of the European empires, it was rather a normal situation for all the regions, or even cities or villages, to have a certain economical or social "specialization" — this was a normal state from the beginnings, as the lack of practicable roads and communication in general permitted the local concentration of certain competences, in many cases supported by settlements of certain ethnic groups and strengthened through privileges accorded by the political rulers (kings, emperors). In the later times, not only the development of communication, one of the essential components of modernization itself, but also the change of strategies regarding the local and general development moved the focus on achieving an equal status for all citizens (mainly by renouncing on all sorts of privileges) and relying on communication, supported too by the continuous development of technology. Better roads, followed by the development of railways, steam ships and telegraph, along with reforms which aimed to extend equality in front of the law, facilitating investments in industry and commerce and an equal taxation of all citizens, applied with some particularities in almost all European countries, shaped the beginnings of a common shared space of development, integration and competition. The industrially manufactured goods from Britain, which had the

---

① There are many explanations for the complex reasons and conditions which led to the outbreak of the World War I, which occured in a rather stable and prosper climate and surprised the contemporaries; for more recent views see: Clark C. 2013. The Sleepwalkers: How Europe Went to War in 1914. London: Penguin Books; for a broader view over the wars of the 20th century see: Ferguson N. 2007. The War of the World: The Twentieth-century Conflict and the Descent of the West. New York: Penguin Books.

leading role in industry, reached the peripheral European markets due to the new and cheap means of transportation — a new, in the former centuries impossible situation — and challenged the local manufacturers, determining the lawmakers to establish new conditions and law frameworks. With rather shy steps in the beginning, industrialization made its way on the East European markets too, which was visible on the example of the Austrian Empire too, with smaller achievements as in the Western countries, but concentrated mainly on mining and heavy industry. A certain gap resulted from the difficulty in reforming the set of regulations due to the particularities of the Austro-Hungarian establishment, but from a certain lack of capital too. In this case, these factors, along with the historical tradition of the state, determined a market characterized more by state regulations in almost all fields of economic activity as by the role of the capital or the supply and demand balance. In those days Europe comprised states and markets with different characteristics, and we can observe the effects of these establishments and formulate certain questions: Was for example the British with more free capital and supply-demand-based economy more efficient than the more regulated Austrian model? The answers are not simple due to the different characteristics of each of the societies or economy sectors. The Austrian Empire comprised regions with very different levels of development, different local languages and historical traditions which made the regulatory intervention of the state more necessary in achieving higher levels of development. These answers could help us understand the current differences in the European system, in which a multi-speed model is more and more considered and viewed as a future model. Indeed, there are huge differences among the EU member states and one can notice a lack of experience and models in solving these issues on a broader level, as these aspects, in the historical continuity of the last century, were always regulated on the level of each nation state. This aspect, in a more extended manner, is evidenced by the management of the challenge of migration towards the EU, which set both the European and the national decisional factors in front of a complex situation, which can only be solved together, by means of the same sort of common and elaborate policies which led to the construction of the EU.

One of the most outstanding concepts of the 19th and the 20th centuries was "Mitteleuropa", conceptualized by the liberal philosopher and politician Friedrich Naumann (1860-1919), in the beginning as a free trade and travel zone in the central, mostly German-speaking part of Europe; this concept, which had both its realistic and utopian characteristics, was one of the first modern and scientifically motivated plans for a geographical area with a common market and without inner borders[1]. It served later as well as one of the models for the EU but also for the German expansionist policy. With the later EU model it shared the idea of a common market or customs space and of the gradual expansion, especially towards the eastern European and Balkan states. The intentions to implement this idea had the character of a German expansion and did not consider the interests of other Great Powers, mainly those of Russia; this transformed a rather peaceful idea, pointed initially out by Naumann, into a casus belli, as we can see it in the First Conflagration, and subsequently, in the World War II. Although the "Mitteleuropa" plans were subsequently abandoned and as a consequence of the World War I, some of its ideas remained as a lesson from history;

---

[1] Navmann F. 1916. Mitteleuropa. Berlin: G. Reimer Verlag.

moreover, they grew in importance as the fragmentation of the large markets of the fallen empires in the form of small and rather closed nation states proved to hinder the general economic growth in Europe. Later, the lessons of the two world wars, the desire for more travel freedom, economic ties and cooperation across the continent proved to be strong enough to start a larger, more profound and peaceful European integration process.

2. A Case Study: The Land Register of the Austrian Empire

In this part we will try to point out these aspects, highlighting them with a case analysis — the introduction of the Land Register in the Austrian Empire (the 17th and the 18th centuries) as a means of modernization and territorial consolidation.

In the shaping of a strong framework in all its aspects (political, economical, military and fiscal), the Austrian Empire, one of the biggest European powers, evolved during its evolution phases from the 16th to the 17th century to its end in the World War I, from the struggles between feudal micro-states to a huge political conglomerate, which understood to use all the achievements of the time in establishing a modern state. In this process, the gradual introduction of the cadaster or land register played a very important role, along with the gradual and general introduction of a uniform juridical system and laws. We have to mention that during its whole existence, the Austrian Empire (Austria-Hungary after 1867) comprised territories with different levels of economical development, social structures and law systems, which had to be standardized in order to achieve an even and high development level across the whole state (which, as a historical continuity, is a task for the EU of our days too). The western provinces, then Bohemia and the larger cities and urban areas had a high development level and a more or less strong industrialization; the more rural hinterlands and generally the eastern provinces were, due to the historical conditions, the less they developed and needed concentrated modernization policies with long implementation periods, and some aspects needed several generations to reach the desired level. In this context, the role of the state, which represented at that time the ideas of physiocracy①, Cameral sciences② and Enlightened Absolutism, with a strong role of the bureaucracy and military, with both a controlling and an elite-forming function, proved to be essential, mainly in maintaining a continuity in the implementation of the above mentioned reforms.

The cadaster was important mainly for two reasons: as an instrument in the consolidation of the political power, in the knowledge of the state territory and the drawing of accurate maps, and in the establishing of a certain, mathematically provable basis for the land taxes, with an essential impact on the revenues and state budget. Only in this way, the government would know exactly the extension of the state territory with its subdivisions, the amount of the agriculturally usable land, the exact borders, etc. and could implement the principle of equal taxation of all citizens, which was an important political goal. Moreover, the cadaster system allowed the introduction of "cadastral settlements" which will become the basis of

---

① This was a political and economical concept of the 18th century, which underlined the importance of the agriculture for a society.

② Cameral science/cameralism/Kameralwissenschaften: a scientific view in the 18th century over the state administration, a precursor of the later public administrative sciences.

land organization. The implementation of this complex intent was not easy and could not be realized quickly. The differences between the provinces, the political conditions in each of them, and then the financial and technical details determined an implementation during several generations, but one which shaped a certain structure of the Empire whose effects can be seen even nowadays, e.g. in almost the same structure of the cadaster in the states which formerly belonged to the Habsburg Empire. The implementation of this intent, as every measure which aimed to modernization and improvement, was not easy and quick, passed through decades and historical epochs[①]. The initial revenues were small and disproportionate compared to the huge effort, but the long-term effect was essential: it lasts until our days, when countries which belonged to the former Habsburg Empire have similar laws and land registry systems, simplifying the inner-European cooperation. The continuity of this measure aiming modernization, unification and consolidation, which started in the 18th century and passed through historical conditioned interruptions, find their continuity in the building of the complex framework of the EU.

[①] For example of land register, see Rumpler H, Scharr K (eds.). 2015. Der Franziszeische Kataster im Kronland Bukowina, Czernowitzer Kreis (1817-1865). Statistik und Katastralmappen, Böhlau Verlag Wien-Köln-Weimar; for an Internet-based presentation: http://www.franziszeischerkataster[2016-5-1].

Global Modernization Trend in the Perspective of Human History

Lixing Zou

China Development Bank

Global modernization rests on the basis of history. Looking through the human history, we can see roughly seven stages: 1) anthropoid stage (2 million years ago) when humans walked on two feet; 2) ape-man stage (1.8-0.3 million years ago) when humans could make simple tools; 3) Homo sapiens stage (300,000-40,000 years ago) when humans had some intelligence to improve their living standard; 4) ancient stage of hunting and gathering (40,000-12,000 years ago); 5) middle ancient stage (12,000-5,000 years ago) when humans produced food; 6) ancestor stage (5,000 years ago to the invention of steam engine) of written civilizations; 7) modern human age (the First Industrial Revolution till now) with modern industrial techniques. Corresponding to human evolution, the human society followed a pattern of "unity-separation-unity", moving from one source to pluralism and then to integration. Since the creation of mankind by the Mother Nature, in the primitive age, our ancestors shared the same mind, formed groups to fight against the harsh conditions, and reproduced as required by the need of survival. By the Stone Age, humans made stone tools and were more capable of coping with harsh conditions and more reproductive. People moved to different places in the world, established different groups and cultures of diversity, and developed along separate lines. In the Bronze Age[①], humans created writing systems, developed agriculture and started to mingle. The discovery of a new continent in 1492, in particular, accelerated the pace of integration. Today, we are going through in-depth globalization and some new features are worth close attention.

1. Primitive Integration: Integration for Survival

Humans, as well as all other species, are the results of nature and its laws. According to

---

[①] Humans in different places of the world entered the Bronze Age at different times. In Mesopotamia and Europe, bronze ware was in use in 4000 BC to 3000 BC; in India and Egypt, it was 3000 BC to 2000 BC; and in China it was 3000 BC.

history and palaeoanthropology, 3.75 million years ago, in Africa, the Great Rift Valley in East Africa and today's Ethiopia in particular, the climate was agreeable and anthropoids started to walk on two feet. Walking on two feet set free the two hands of anthropoids and enabled them to grab food and hold it in hand while walking fast. This gave them an advantage in the competition for survival and offered them a chance to evolve towards modern humans[1]. However, during the evolution of anthropoids towards modern humans, they gathered in a small area, collected food and fought against beasts together in joint efforts. Working together and the early form of integration played a crucial role in the birth of human society for only by so doing were they able to survive and thrive[2]. Therefore, the direct predecessor of humans, which was included in the category of humans rather than apes, is called Homo habilis, literally meaning "able man". Primitive integration and working together are the true origin of human society.

About 2 million years ago, primitive Homo habilis knew to some extent how to hunt collectively, how to use animal bones and trees, how to sharpen a piece of stone, and how to use these simple tools to hunt, dig tubers, smash food, and cut off rotten meat. Thus they had ampler food supply. Superior to plants and animals, primitive man could use tools to collect food and thus obtain more and varied foods. This was a precondition of human history and a milestone on the way towards civilization.

Between 1.6 million and 300,000 years ago, Homo habilis developed into its later period and was known among historians as workman[3]. Later-stage Homo habilis was larger and more intelligent than its predecessor, with a cranial capacity 40% larger[4]. They could use and control fire for heating and keeping dangerous animals off; and more importantly, they could use language for communication, which is especially superior to animals, marking their progress towards Homo sapiens.

Primitive Homo sapiens lived around 300,000 to 125,000 years ago. They launched the first globalization process of mankind. When hunting, they chased collectible food from the North to the Middle East, and then some continued west to reach today's Europe and became Neanderthals as we call them today, while some others turned east to reach today's Siberia and Asia and became what is known to us today as Denisovans. In 1856, traces of ancient humans were discovered in the Neander Valley of Germany and the discovered type of humans was named the Neanderthals. They are Homo sapiens of the later stage, around 150,000 to 40,000 years ago, which was the time of the latest Ice Age. The Earth cooled off greatly about 150,000 years ago and the ice sheet covered vast areas, making them suitable for walking and migrating. On the tundra-covered Eurasia continent, many mammals stored large amounts of fat to defense against the harsh coldness during the long Ice Age and humans at that time thus had sufficient prey and could spare more time to study the nature

---

① 菲利普·李·拉尔夫, 罗伯特·E. 勒那, 斯坦迪什·米查姆, 等. 1998. 世界文明史(上卷). 赵丰等译. 北京: 商务印书馆: 12-13.
② 基思·托马斯. 2008. 人类与自然世界. 宋丽丽译. 南京: 译林出版社: 18.
③ 菲利普·费尔南德兹-阿迈斯托. 2010. 世界: 一部历史. 叶建军等译. 北京: 北京大学出版社: 7.
④ 菲利普·李·拉尔夫, 罗伯特·E. 勒那, 斯坦迪什·米查姆, 等. 1998. 世界文明史(上卷). 赵丰等译. 北京: 商务印书馆: 15.

and make tools[①]. Humans in this period were highly skilled at tool-making, invented about 60 large tools including knife, chisel, drill and spearhead. They could build shelters, were good at hunting, enjoyed higher living standards and became more reproductive. As a result, the population surged and they expanded with faster steps either intentionally or unintentionally in the face of climate change and the pressure for survival. They moved while hunting and continued with global expansion.

Entering the Neolithic Age (40,000-12,000 years ago), humans invented bow and arrow, and became more efficient in hunting and more reproductive. They were quite "modern" actually. They enjoyed arts, and they had ambitions, religions, public forums and political practices. Also, they were similar to us in terms of intelligence and physical power. Since it was still Ice Age then (from 10,600 to 8,000 years ago, the temperature was volatile, and ice gradually melted, and the Ice Age gradually ended), they continued to explore new areas, and scattered around the world, building new homes here and there, basically forming the world pattern today.

Figure 1 shows the process of human evolution and spread. Generally, the earliest humans were in Africa and moved to other places later as evolution continued. In the Neolithic Age, migration accelerated, basically forming our world pattern today. This process can be regarded as a kind of globalization.

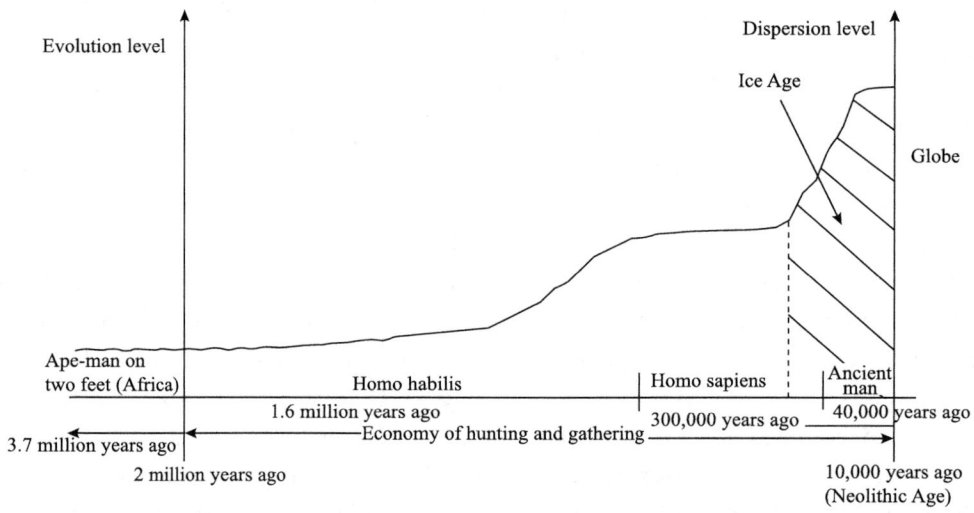

Figure 1 Human Society: From One Source to Pluralism

The Neolithic Age, was a great time for human development. In this age, at all places inhabited by man, the culture shared the same basic elements. All the humans lived on hunting and gathering, used similar techniques, ate similar foods, and had similar levels of material culture. And, based on information available to us, they had similar religious rituals[②]. Therefore, in a sense, we can say this was a time of primitive globalization. Primitive globalization is a globalization formed in the interactions between man and nature.

---

① 菲利普·李·拉尔夫, 罗伯特·E. 勒那, 斯坦迪什·米查姆, 等. 1998. 世界文明史(上卷). 赵丰等译. 北京: 商务印书馆: 19-22.
② 菲利普·费尔南德兹-阿迈斯托. 2010. 世界: 一部历史. 叶建军等译. 北京: 北京大学出版社: 24.

2. Historic Separation: Development Along Multiple Lines

As humans spread out around the world, different species, races and societies were formed and the human society developed along separate lines over a prolonged process. On the ancient Earth, each tribe constituted a separate traditional society, each tradition equaled one unique way of life, and each way of life represented one civilization.

2.1 Species Formed in Migration

Before the Neolithic Age, man lived mainly on gathering or hunting and gathering. Such a way of life means that humans at that time must continuously try to find vegetarian food, or, must migrate along with prey as hunters. For survival and development, humans migrated towards places around the world, tapped into every inch of livable land, adapted to local climate, settled down at different places, and became different species.

History shows that there were generally three branches of humans: ancient African man on two feet, ancient Asian man, and ancient European man (Heidelberg man). According to the archaeological findings, the first and the third started to differ significantly as early as in the middle of the Paleolithic Age (Pleistocene). Evolution may have been more complicated in the region where China is located. Humans here were neither the African branch (Homo sapiens) nor Heidelberg; rather they combined the features of East Asian, European, and African man of the middle of the Paleolithic Age.

About 500,000 years ago, ancient Indians emerged on the subcontinent of India[①]. Between 1926 and 1930, archaeologists found over 40 pieces of bones of Peking man in a cave of Zhoukoudian, 40 kilometers or 25 miles southwest of Beijing, which dated back to no less than 500,000 years ago. This means that Humans lived in the vast Southeast Asia at that time. Archaeologists believe that activities of Homo sapiens dated back to about 65,000 years ago in mainland China[②].

40,000-30,000 years ago, people in the eastern hemisphere migrated to the western hemisphere via the land bridge then existed between Siberia and Alaska. And traces of anthropogenic cultivation were found to date back 30,000 years in Australia[③]. Historians believe that some Asian tribes migrated to North America via the Bering Strait around 30,000 years ago, then to Mexico 21,300 years ago, and to Chile 13,000 years ago[④]. Migration never ceased. About 10,000 years ago, Aryans living in western Russia migrated in three groups. One group moved west to today's Europe and was the ancestors of some of today's European people; one moved eastward to Persia and were the ancestors of some of today's Persians; and the remaining one group moved southeast over the Hindu Kush Mountains to northwestern India and were the ancestors of some of the Indians today.

Evolution differed by environment. Geographic differences resulted in the differentiation of humans. Anthropoarchaeologists found that some distinctive characteristics, e.g. the

---

① 王树英. 2011. 印度文化简史. 北京: 人民出版社: 1.
② 菲利普·李·拉尔夫, 罗伯特·E. 勒那, 斯坦迪什·米查姆, 等. 1998. 世界文明史(上卷). 赵丰等译. 北京: 商务印书馆: 16.
③ 菲利普·李·拉尔夫, 罗伯特·E. 勒那, 斯坦迪什·米查姆, 等. 1998. 世界文明史(上卷). 赵丰等译. 北京: 商务印书馆: 18.
④ 刘文龙. 2008. 大国通史. 墨西哥通史. 上海: 上海社会科学出版社: 7.

relative area of the first palatial molar, differed greatly across races, and geographic locations①. Different environments also resulted in different modern human behaviors. The evolution of ancient human behavior shows temporal and spatial diversity. Based on available materials, about 100,000 years ago, the characteristics of modern humans started to appear in southern China. The modern behavior of Chinese modern humans, though more or less influenced by external humans and technical import, is mainly the result of continuous local evolution②. According to the findings of anthropoarchaeologists, stones sheets and stone ware developed in systematic continuation in northern China; while modern humans in Africa and western Eurasia, and in east Eurasia followed different paths of evolution. This means the evolution of modern humans occurred in different regions③.

2.2 Diversity of Human Civilization

About 10,000 years ago, agriculture appeared and mankind's way of life changed radically. Instead of wandering about, they settled down and formed villages. Life in settlements deepened the development of human society along multiple lines and accelerated the progress of human civilization. From the Agricultural Age to the discovery of the new continent by Columbus, though communication continued, the multiple lines of development remained relatively independent from one another. And this served as the basis for cultural diversity. To a large extent, civilizations and cultures of different regions were influenced by the geographic environment, different natural conditions led to varied ways of life, and various ways of life gave birth to different cultural spirits④. Human civilization and culture developed on the basis of certain natural and geographic conditions and were clearly marked by various geographic conditions.

(1) Different writing systems and legislature. Between 4000 BC and 1000 BC, different writing systems were invented in different areas of the ancient world, laying foundation for the diversity of human civilization.

One of them is the sphenogram of Mesopotamia. Between 3500 BC and 2500 BC, in the area between the Tigris River and the Euphrates River, or Mesopotamia, especially Sumer at the southernmost of Mesopotamia, human society, for the time ever, was civilized and the first city was formed. The Sumerians started to carve images on rocks and invented cuneiform script. They made stylus with triangular tips with reeds and carved cuneiform scripts on clay tablets so as to keep record of dialogues, proverbs, myths and hymns. The script was born in the company of credit lending. Characters carved on clay sheets recorded lending that occurred in 2500 BC and mentioned obligation contribution. This means exchange was already

---

① Institute of Vertebrate Paleontology and Paleoanthropolgy, CAS. 2014. Acta Anthropologica Sinica, 33(3): 400. Science Press; in October 2015, Nature published an article by Wu Liu, Xiujie Wu et al. of the Institute of Vertebrate Paleontology and Paleoanthropolgy, CAS, describing 47 pieces of fossil of human teeth with full characteristics of modern human discovered in Daoxian County, Hunan Province and concluding the existence of modern human in that area 80,000-120,000 years ago.

② Modern behavior is taken by anthropologists as a major distinction between modern and ancient man.

③ 菲利普·李·拉尔夫, 罗伯特·E. 勒那, 斯坦迪什·米查姆, 等. 1998. 世界文明史(上卷). 赵丰等译. 北京: 商务印书馆: 517.

④ 王树英. 2011. 印度文化简史. 北京: 人民出版社: 7.

an important social activity at that time①. The Sumerians also invented the solar calendar, marking the 12 lunar cycles or 12 months as a year and used this system to calculate agricultural cycles. These major inventions made important contributions to the ancient Mesopotamian civilization.

Another writing system is hieroglyph of Egypt. In the Nile River basin, in the predynastic period (around 3100 BC) of ancient Egypt, people had settled down and started farming. Besides stone tools, they had also bronze tools and invented hieroglyphs. Hieroglyphs are made up of pictographs, syllables and letters and were written on flattened and sun-dried papyrus②. Papyrus could be rolled up and easily carried around to be passed on to others, greatly enhancing the administrative efficiency of Pharaohs. Therefore, this was the most important progress in the political history of ancient Egypt. Between 2700 BC and 2600 BC, the pharaohs was able to organize up to over 70,000 people to collect and transport 2,500 tons of rocks for the building of the pyramids. This was undoubtedly a huge management project and documentation played a significant role in this process. Influenced by the Egypt Empire, the ancient Roman Empire that rose later witnessed the emergence of signed contract of tax partnership in written form. This is sort of a prototype of today's companies and was great progress③. Also, the hieroglyph of Egypt is the basis of modern Western writings. It is fair to say that every single letter used today in the West was derived from the writing system of ancient Egypt.

The third is the hieroglyph of India. In around 4000 BC, in the Indus River basin, people started to use wheels to make ceramics, raised various kinds of animals, and created highly developed Dravida cities. By about 3000 BC, the Indus River Valley entered the civilized age and that civilization well rivaled ancient Egypt and Sumer. During that period, stone seals appeared as a kind of tool used to keep record of daily lives. These are known among historians today as the Indus script. It "includes 270 hieroglyphs and letters and has nothing to do with any other writing system"④. The script of ancient India keeps record of hymns and prayers that were orally passed down. *Rigveda* (hymn of wisdom), for example, included over a thousand poems from 1500 BC to 900 BC and was a major source of information for a long period of the Indian history. In the 5th century BC, *Mahabharata* and *Ramayana*, epics of ancient India, both mentioned China and recorded it as "Cina" with Latin letters. The ancient Indian culture was early in having contacts with the outside world and introduced China to the West. Although the Indus River Valley Civilization declined and was cut off later, it was more or less absorbed and carried on by later civilizations and continued its influence on the Indian subcontinent.

The fourth is the Chinese writing system. In the evolution of human civilization, despite regime changes and invasions, the Chinese nation has generally carried through history

---

① 威廉·N. 戈兹曼, K. 哥特·罗文霍斯特. 2010. 价值起源(修订版). 王宇, 王文玉译. 沈阳: 北方联合出版传媒集团股份有限公司: 18-19.

② 菲利普·李·拉尔夫, 罗伯特·E. 勒那, 斯坦迪什·米查姆, 等. 1998. 世界文明史(上卷). 赵丰等译. 北京: 商务印书馆: 95.

③ 威廉·N. 戈兹曼, K. 哥特·罗文霍斯特. 2010. 价值起源(修订版). 王宇, 王文玉译. 沈阳: 北方联合出版传媒集团股份有限公司: 32.

④ 菲利普·李·拉尔夫, 罗伯特·E. 勒那, 斯坦迪什·米查姆, 等. 1998. 世界文明史(上卷). 赵丰等译. 北京: 商务印书馆: 152.

since the Neolithic Age. Different from the civilizations in the Far East, the Mediterranean Basin, and the Indus River Valley, the Chinese civilization has a unique source and a long history. Folklores about Fuxi, Shennong and Huangdi are still widespread in China even today. About 6,000 or 7,000 years ago, Chinese ancestors started to use bronze ware. In 1975, a bronze knife was unearthed in the ruins of Majiayao culture in Linjia, Dongxiang, Gansu Province, which dated back to around 3000 BC, showing that China had entered the Bronze Age by then. The three dynasties of Xia, Shang and Zhou lasted 1,800 years and bronze wares were used as ritual wares and weapons throughout the period. Script was carved into bronze *ding* (vessel) and other artifacts to keep record of major events, forming a special bronze culture of the Chinese nation. Rivaling the bronze culture was scripts carved on ceramics of Liangzhu culture. They also shoed the life of ancient Chinese people. The oracles bones of the Shang Dynasty, in particular, laid down basically all rules of the written Chinese. The Chinese writing, besides pictographic elements, contains also ideographic and phonographic elements. And two different signs and concepts may be combined to form new meanings. For example, when the sun and the moon are combined, the character means light and brightness. In *Shuowen Jiezi*, Xu Shen of the Eastern Han Dynasty summarized the construction of Chinese characters into six categories: pictograms, simple indicatives, compound indicatives, phono-semantic compounds, derived characters and borrowed characters. Each character is like a small picture, showing both the pronunciation and the meaning, as well as the relationship between the two and an overall form. Therefore the Chinese scripts are compound characters providing complicated information in combination with an emphasis on relationship between things. Such a unique writing system gave rise to a unique socio-economic system, e.g. an ancient currency system totally different from the ones of the Mediterranean and West Asia. The oldest currencies of China were bronze coins. These coins did not bear different face values but were used by counting numbers. Upper level units were indicated by stringing coins together. The value of each single coin was determined by the government. This is a major characteristic of the Chinese civilization[①]. As a carrier of social development, Chinese characters have carried on for thousands of years and are now the writing system with the most users in the world.

The fifth is the Mayan calendar and the Minoan Civilization. In Central America, the local Mayans created the Mayan calendar in the 6th century BC. The calendar started in 3114 BC and ended on December 21, 2012, telling the past and the future ending of the human world. Through calculation, the Mayans learned the accurate length of a solar year as 365.2420 days with an error of merely 0.0002 day compared with today's calculation of 365.2422 days. This is to say that over 5,000 years, the error will be only one day. Such high capability left later generations in great awe.

In addition, there were also some other writing systems and traces of ancient civilizations. For example, on the Greek islands on the Aegean Sea, a great civilization was at its prime time around 2000 BC. It was created by Minoans living on the Crete Island and is thus known as the Minoan Civilization. They invented unique linearographs, created the first flushing toilet, and

---

① 威廉·N. 戈兹曼, K. 哥特·罗文霍斯特. 2010. 价值起源(修订版). 王宇, 王文玉译. 沈阳: 北方联合出版传媒集团股份有限公司: 65.

built huge palaces with swimming pools. Facing the Minoan Civilization, we have to acknowledge that many things originally deemed modern actually have their origins deep in history.

(2) Different religions and philosophy. From 1500 BC to 1000 BC, Judaism, Christianity, Islam and Buddhism basically became the classical religion in their respective regions. The first three are somewhat connected: they all originated from today's Middle East, all worship Abraham as prophet, all believe firmly in internal nourishment of the spirit, all are believed to be Western religions, and all are monotheist. However, each of the three believes in one creating prophet, believes itself to be the only one in possession of the complete and concrete explanation to the one and only divinity, and claims itself to be clearly different from the others. Buddhism, as an Oriental religion, differs even more vastly from Western religions, though not without connection to them. To some extent, the emergence and development of Oriental religions went parallel to the dissemination of Western religions.

From the above we can see that mankind developed along multiple lines. Such diversity is manifested on various levels and many aspects. The same things may came into being separately under vastly different geographic conditions and at places far from each other. For example, stories of sudden enlightenment appeared in the religious reforms in both the East and the West. In the 15th century, Martin Luther of Germany obtained enlightenment in the bell tower of an abbey, and acquired the truth of justification by faith. This enlightenment played a fundamental role in the reform of the traditional Christianity. Hui Neng the Patriarch of Chinese Zen obtained the sudden enlightenment that Buddha is in everyone's mind in the process of reforming Buddhism. The two cases are similar in that they both put mind in the most important positions. This means that man may have roughly the same thoughts despite differences in environment and time and achieve similar greatness along different lines. Table 1 summarizes the differences between the three major religions of human society and gives a clearer picture of the development along separate lines.

Table 1 Characteristics of the Three Major Religions

Characteristics	Christianity	Islam	Buddhism
Founder	Jesus	Mohammed	Sakyamuni (Sinicized later)
Divinity	God	Allah	Buddha
Scripture	Bible	Quran	Buddhist texts
Admittance	Baptism	No baptism	Refuge to Buddhism Faith at heart
Doctrines	God is the heavenly father and people are brothers and sisters	Allah is the sole dominator; Mohammed is the missionary of Allah; taking care of both sides	Virtue No greedy cravings Pursuing Nirvana

In the development process of different religions, we can roughly see two lines: one is the path of Western religions and the other is that of Oriental religions. Both Western and Oriental religions nourish people's spiritual world and offers spiritual support. This is something common in various religions. However, the differences between two religions are obvious too. For example, Western religions believe that men are born sinful and need to be salvaged by God or Allah. Thus they are likely to cultivate conflicting personalities. On the contrary, Oriental religions believe that men are born to be virtuous and need to get rid of greedy cravings, have heartfelt faith in Buddha, and achieve nirvana, putting the emphasis on the nurturing of collective personality. Generally, humans are the same as other life forms in that we all have the instinct of pursuing survival. You can't say such an instinct is good or bad. It is a sign of life and shall not be judged with a binary view of good or bad. This instinct gives rise to both good and evil. When you do too much for survival, your private cravings expand and the evil reveals itself; when you remain humble while pursuing survival, you contribute to society and do good deeds. It is right to advocate the good and encourage contribution and devotion, but we should not thus negate reasonable personal interest. Affirming and protecting personal interest is a manifestation of human instinct and is necessary for human development. To contain the evil, we need both external constraints and internal refraining. Both Western and Oriental religions help people build their internal power to refrain. In modern development of the West, industrialization shifted the emphasis of religions towards its role of a social lubricant and the society is relatively healthy. In contrast, China paid little attention to this aspect and in the process of social changes, people's spiritual world was somewhat fragile and empty, and life was impulsive and near-sighted. This is something of great concern and we need to take an appropriate attitude towards it.

3. Global Integration: Globalization of Interpersonal Interaction

Entering the Agricultural Age, though the world continued to develop along separate lines, communication and interaction did occur, driven by the nature of people. Pushed by monsoon and ocean currents, our ancestors might have established connections between the eastern and western hemispheres long ago. In the Bronze Age, they successively learned metallurgy techniques and the use of metals, and thus were better equipped for communication. In the 2nd century BC, the Silk Road connected Eurasia and North Africa, and the maritime Silk Road linked East Asian coasts, South Asia and its islands, and East Africa. However, due to environment and technical reasons, e.g. devastating epidemics caused by the infection of some diseases in new groups of people, population fell sharply along the Silk Road[1]. Therefore, communications conducted by our early ancestors did not have much influence and development along separate lines remained. As a result, societies were diverse, with various independent social groups and political entities, including nomads, tribes, kingdoms and empires. Each of them had a self-sufficient economy, unique local culture, and an independent identity. They did not change themselves easily, and nor did they compare with others[2]. After 1492 when Columbus discovered the new world, both the technological level and people's willingness to interact surged, and 90% of the world population became

---

[1] 杰里·本特利, 赫伯特·齐格勒. 2007. 新全球史: 文明的传承与交流. 魏凤莲, 张颖, 白玉广译. 北京: 北京大学出版社: 307-312.

[2] 彼得·什托姆普卡. 2011. 社会变迁的社会学. 林聚任等译. 北京: 北京大学出版社: 82.

closely connected, giving rise to a high tide of global integration. If previous communications are the prelude of a grand drama, the discovery of the new world is the opening. More and more products and knowledge became globally accepted, global trade expanded, the global markets were more and more connected, political, economic, legal social and cultural interactions grew.

The process of moving from pluralism to integration is shown in Figure 2. Generally, there had always been communications and interactions, but they were not quite influential in the early days. Entering the Industrial Age, communication and interaction intensified and modern globalization started. Modern globalization was formed through interpersonal interactions.

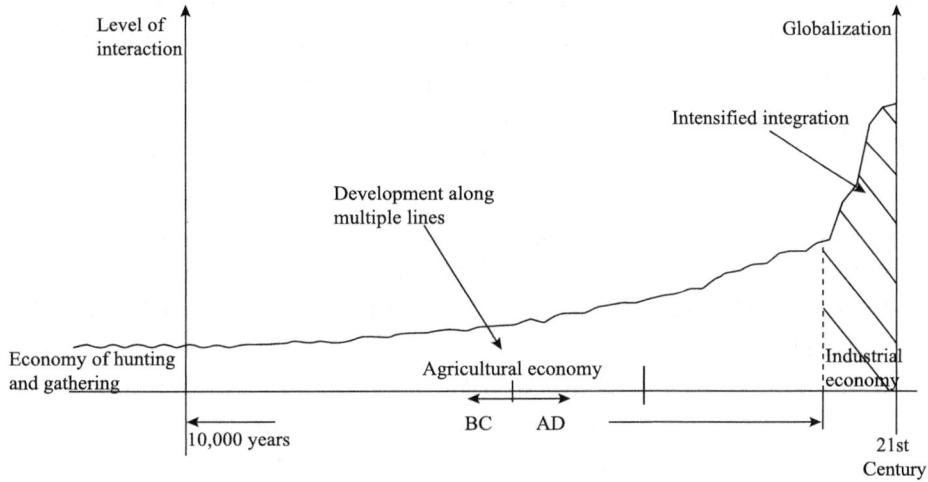

Figure 2　Human Society: From Pluralism to Integration

The modern global integration can be divided roughly into six stages, each with its own driving forces.

The first stage (1492-1831), driven by colonial trade, started from the discovery of the new world by Columbus and ended when steam engine was invented. It mainly involved colonization, agriculture and handcraft trade. Milestones: Marine powers rose after the Renaissance, supported by Protestantism, launched grand colonization efforts in North America, Africa, Australia and Asia, ushering in an era of global travel via inter-continental transportation routes; modern commercial companies such as the East India and West India companies owned by the Netherlands and Britain[①] created new modern models of trade and pushed the sea transportation capacity up from 730,000 tons to 14,600,000 tons between 1570 and 1850, up by 20 times[②]; corporate modernization and regular commercial vessel schedules gave rise to a modern trade system. However, trade was mainly for handcrafts and

---

① Stock company is a delicate organizational form. It is based on an abstract legal person, more stable, and less influenced if one member leaves. Investors do not involve in management directly and may authorize someone else to do it. Such companies offer brand new possibilities for a prosperous market and a flourishing economy.

② 安格斯·麦迪森. 2003. 世界经济千年史. 伍晓鹰, 许宪春, 叶燕斐等译. 北京: 北京大学出版社: 88.

agricultural products during this stage and the total volume was limited.

The second stage (1831-1882), driven by industrial technologies, saw globalization propelled by steam-engine powered industries and transportation. Milestones: The invention of steam engine brought about new production models and radically improved the efficiency of production; railway and relevant equipment made transformation mechanical and improved radically the efficiency of transportation; joint ventures outsourced production tasks to different divisions and improved radically the management and funding capacity. Global trade then involved not only traditional handcrafts and agricultural products, but also machines and railway equipment. Machine-made products were traded in large volumes in particular, promoting radical development of global trade.

The third stage (1882-1931), featured by electronic technologies, witnessed globalization driven by the electrification of industries, transportation and home appliances. Milestones: Thomas Edison successfully launched the power plant in New York and the electrification of production, transportation and home appliances thus started; electronic products, electric equipment, heavy chemical industry products and steel products became an important part of global trade; telegraph, steel rails and steel ships build the transportation capacity and shortened the time of a single trip; a specialized vocational management system (e.g. Taylorism) gave rise to huge factories and greatly expanded the scale of production and trade.

The fourth stage (1931-1980), featured by automation, was the globalization driven by the automation of transportation, and civil and military products. Milestones: Ford automobile production line promoted massive automobile production and consumption worldwide, and the Ford management system accelerated management modernization around the world; radio, high ways, airports and flight routes connected the global market closely; automobiles, tractors, tanks, internal-combustion engines, aircrafts, oil refineries, petro, natural gas and synthetic chemical products became the mainstay of global trade.

The fifth stage (1980-2000) saw globalization driven by finance, especially M&A. Milestones: Financial groups promoted cross-sector and cross-industry global M&A of unprecedented scale, showing a clear trend of powers joining hands; in 2000, multinational M&A had a total value of USD11 trillion, with 109 cases above USD1 billion in value, setting a historical record. M&A intensified within the financial sector, with 12 cases involving more than USD 290 billion of assets between 1995 and 2000; this expanded the overall scale of banks, lowered their costs, improved the comprehensive earnings, and extended their international business.

The sixth stage (2000 till now), featured by information technology, witness globalization driven by IT-based economic development. Milestones: Led by information technology, a lot of technological breakthroughs occurred in clusters; the information highway built the ties of global markets; computers, software, electronic equipment, biotechnology and chips became the mainstay in world trade; regional organizations thrived and EU, ASEAN and NAFTA played major roles in promoting regional and global trade; financial institutions launched multi-business operation and one-stop services, serving their customers from the cradle to the tomb and promoting world integration; global production and distribution networks deepened international division of labor; international network developed, involving all countries and regions in it.

Table 2 gives a summary of the process and driving forces of modern globalization. A major feature of this round of global integration is interpersonal interactions. Interactions occurred between people from the eastern and the western hemispheres, and those from developed and under-developed countries, involving man-made, processed and cultured products. Compared with primitive globalization of mankind, this is great progress of human society and a new stage in the development process of human society.

Table 2 Global Integration: Process and Characteristics

Stages	Driving forces	Characteristics
1	Colonial trade	Discovery of new world, agriculture and handcraft trade
2	Steam engine powered industries	Large-scale mechanization of production and transportation
3	Electrification	Taylorism of production and sales, electric equipment
4	Automation	Highways, heavy equipment and petrol trade
5	Global M&A	Transnational M&A, super banking
6	Computerization	Information network, global production and distribution
Future	Combination of biotech and manufacturing	Intelligent robot, biomedical products, bioindustrial products, bioagricultural products

4. Outlook of Globalization: Globalization Formed in the Interactions Between Man and Nature

Throughout human history, man has gone through the Paleolithic Age, the Neolithic Age, the Bronze Age, the Iron Age, the Agricultural Age, the Industrial Age, the Electric Age and the Automation Age, and we are now in the Information Age. The Information Age is still booming. Informatization is combined with industrialization, and with various industries, and it may give rise to some new industries and offer more space for the development of informatization. For example, wireless technologies will be a major direction for the future development in the industrial sector. Germany launched its Industry 4.0 Strategy, aiming a future where factory equipment and personnel will be connected via wireless network and managed in a visualized way through automation software. As productive technologies change, changes also occur in the ways of production, organization and life of the human society. Every change in the system of human society is the result of changes in material production technologies achieved in interpersonal interactions and interactions between mankind and nature.

By the latter half of the 21st century, people may have achieved major breakthroughs in biosciences and new materials and important development may also occur in bioengineering, bionic engineering and inorganic life forms. A number of new vaccines and diagnostic reagents will be in use for the prevention and diagnosis of major contagious diseases which are major threats to people's health and life. Vaccines and reagents for cancers, in particular, may give rise to an entire biopharmaceutical industry aimed at treating cancers with vaccines to replace the current medication-based approach of fighting cancer with toxins. Also, man-made organs and regenerated organs may also help solve some complicated cases, thus promoting people's health and ushering in an era of new biology. In this new era, biological logic will be stored in computer chips, robot modules, pharmaceutical production processes, software designs and corporate management approaches. Inanimate things may be enlivened, and technologies and industries of medical biology, information biology, and industrial biology may become decisive forces in economic and social development. Table 3 describes possible major events in the coming 300 years.

Table 3 Possible Major Events in the Coming 300 Years

Time	Major events
15 years later	3D holographic virtuality will enter people's life and people will be able to communicate face to face over long distances; the first aerodynamic wingless electromagnetic aircraft (first-generation flying saucer) will come out in the USA; solar glass that absorbs solar energy by applying a layer of coating on ordinary glass will enter our homes; man-made retina will be put into wide use
30 years later	Quantum computer will gradually be put into application and quantum power generator will be created; hydro-fueled car will be put into massive production; human will set foot on the Mars; undersea tunnel will be built in the Bering Strait, and global highway will connect over 100 countries around the world
60 years later	The first experimental positron reactor will be created, marking the start of the era of antimatter energy; people will "migrate" to the future by freezing themselves for enjoyment
80 years later	Vacuum tube maglev train will be in commercial operation around the world, putting Beijing and New York in a one-hour transportation circle; nanometer robots will be the fourth type of blood cells in human bodies to cleanse the grease and clogs and keep blood vessels in good condition
100 years later	There will be a "brain cap" that simulates all sensual information and doctors will feel what a patient feels when he/she puts on this cap; computer will be able to build a man-made brain
120 years later	We will have the first space carrier and small spacecrafts will take off from the space carrier, totally changing the military structure of the world
140 years later	Man-made intelligence will be as good as a human brain, making human-computer intelligent dialogue possible; the Turing test will become reality in some areas, and intelligent robots will replace workers on large scales
180 years later	Man will develop the moon on large scale, use the rich reserve of He-3 there for power generation through nuclear fusion and use the power on the moon by sending it up via huge IR transmitters
220 years later	Major difficulties like radiation feedback will be solved technically, and people will enter the era of time and space travel, with real "pre-history parks" coming into being
250 years later	Physiological research on human brain will break through the critical point, memory will be transplanted, brain chips will be made and our education system will be changed fundamentally
280 years later	There will be fewer and fewer people going without genetic change, and human society on the Earth will be dominated by post humans

Source: Entrepreneurs' Club, May 10, 2015

The new biology era may be the start of a new cycle of human development. While trying to solve the problem of infertility by creating sperm with embryonic stem cell, we may give rise to a conflict between man-made life and human life. Intelligent robots that carry biological chips will be more and more similar to human beings in terms of balance, vision, voice and other aspects, and may even be able to do more than human and replace people or largely reduce the physical or intelligent workload of people. People create the history and labor opens up the future. Industrialization and informatization, while improving labor productivity, cause severe damage to the natural environment we live in as well as the resources. Also, industrialization and informatization have negative effect on human history and culture. For example, pollution by nuclear waste will cause long sufferings, massive industrialization and urbanization cause damage to historic sites and cultural heritage, and underground railway building may result in irreversible loss of historic sites. In addition, industrialization and informatization will also greatly reduce people's workload. This can be good or bad. This is because less labor will definitely hamper human development. That is to say, though biotechnology and other advanced technologies since the Industrial Revolution have, to an extremely large extent, freed people from physical work, reduced diseases, and improved labor productivity, when physical labor reduces, and electronic devices and information have caused more damage to mankind. Examples include more cases of cell phone disease, TV disease, Internet disease and device disease, more negative effect of high and new technologies, possible decline of physical functions and shortened human life. This will be a huge challenge to human development. Human survival and development is an eternal theme. We must value the role of the nature and the effect of the law of balance. We must think it over, reduce the use of various devices, return to nature, increase physical and intelligent labor, including manual work, farming and doing daily work with manpower, and start a new era of manual work. Manual work of this new era may be totally different from traditional manual work. In the new era, handcrafts will adopt natural designs, integrate technology with the nature, combine interpersonal interaction with the interaction between mankind and nature, and take place over the Internet. This will be a hallmark of the civilization of the new biology era. Today, new home-based manufacturing has appeared over the Internet and it may be the herald of the new manual work era. The new manual work era will start a brand new cycle of human development and may witness totally unexpected divisions.

5. Characteristics of the Current Globalization: Integration and Diversification

Entering the 21st century, globalization deepens and people around the world are involved in comprehensive interactions and accelerated development. However, conflicts come along too. For example, shared problems such as global warming, resource shortage and population growth are more and more serious. Moreover, new conflicts that rose in the wake beginning in the financial crisis beginning in 2007 also intensify and call for close attention.

First, there is the conflict between market integration and political diversification. Market integration is speeding up around the world and the economy of various countries and regions are more and more connected, giving rise to more economic and political communities[①] and increasing inner consistency of the global economy. Meanwhile, national conservatism and regional conservatism have revived and differences in the historical traditions, political systems and religions of various groups of people have become clearer.

Second, there is the conflict between economic integration and cultural diversification. As economic globalization deepens, the integration of historical culture is also picking up its pace and responses from the traditional culture and customs of various ethnic groups are intensified, giving rise to conflicts in culture, mindset and behavior. Thus the dispute between globalization and anti-globalization increases.

Third, there is the conflict between information integration and diverse thoughts. In-depth R&D of information technology and industrialized IT development, especially the development and application of big data, is a revolution in the IT industry and has infiltrated to various other industries, creating new models of production and management. Digitalization, intelligentization, networking and global coverage has become a new massive trend and strong social force in the world, pushing mankind towards a more open and better-integrated world. In the Information Age, information spreads faster and faster and nothing stays unknown to the world. Information becomes shared resource. Meanwhile, fragmented information is everywhere. News comes from everywhere about anything, issues are more and more astounding, with more and more weird thoughts. Yet different systems of thoughts have long been formed in history. Thus, the conflict between information integration and diverse thoughts becomes obvious.

Fourth, there is the conflict between global network and personal information security. The Internet connects everyone to form a whole. Companies and individuals alike, depend more and more heavily on the Internet. But in the meantime, personal information goes out more and more easily. This is a conflict. No one is against the Internet, yet no one wants to share his/her personal information with everyone. So the problem is how to keep personal information safe while ensuring smooth Internet use.

Fifth, there is the conflict between global resource allocation and individualized consumption demands. Under the influence of the Internet and the Internet of things, global resources have actually been incorporated into one integrated system and can be allocated in a unified manner to promote the expansion of production scale. Meanwhile, market is divided into more and more refined niches, together with consumption demands. This is also a conflict.

Sixth, there is the conflict between international service standards and traditional local features. In the process of global integration, international standards are a common requirement of the world. Meanwhile, people lay more and more emphasis on traditional local features and such feature are indeed an indispensable part of our life. How to carry forward local traditions while advocating international standards is also a problem of concern.

Seventh, there is the conflict between social equity and gaps in wealth and income. Under the influence and high and new technologies, the world is smaller and flatter, and people

---

① 彼得·什托姆普卡. 2011. 社会变迁的社会学. 林聚任等译. 北京: 北京大学出版社: 83.

pursue equal social status. But the reality is that the wealth gap is widening and the divides between the developed and the developing worlds, between urban and rural areas, and between the rich and the poor are all gaping. A problem of concern is how to uphold equity and justice and reduce the rich-poor gap as global integration progresses[①].

Eighth, there is the conflict between global integration and governance diversification. As global integration deepens, the global society, economy and politics are more and more integrated. However, due to history and social conditions, conflicts between the East and the West, gaps between the North and the South, and disputes between developed and developing countries are growing. The world undergoes huge changes and adjustments, politics go back and forth between multiple powers, and the international strategic situation is in great disorder. This makes global governance complicated and highly uncertain. In today's world, everyone is closely related to and influenced by others, yet we are still in lack of sound global governance. This is a conflict.

Figure 3 shows the conflicts in globalization today. As natural phenomena in economic development of human society, they are the results of globalization and will be solved properly as globalization continues. Conflicts promote social changes in the constitution, structure, function, boundary and environment of human society, and changes will be dispersed at first and then intensify and spread, reshaping the human society as a whole. It is possible that human society will become an integrated community that goes beyond countries and regions. It won't be dominated by either the Western or the Eastern civilization. Instead, it will incorporate and integrate both to form a new holistic global entity.

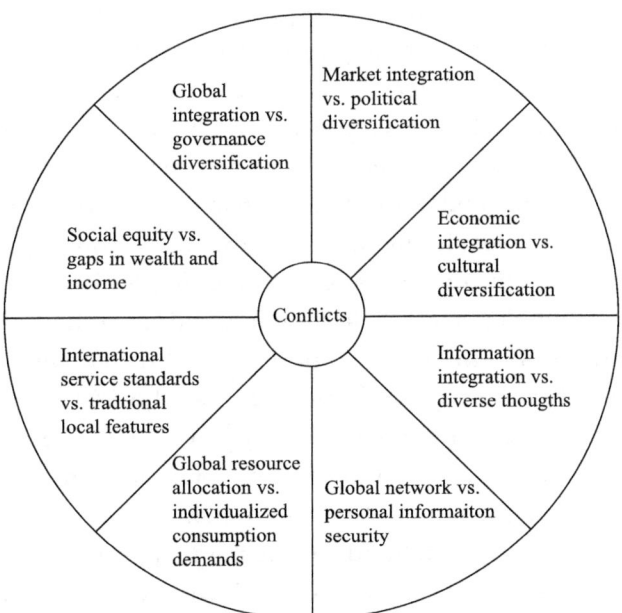

Figure 3 Eight Conflicts in the New Stage of Globalization

---

① 林毅夫. 2012. 新结构经济学. 北京: 北京大学出版社: 87-89.

6. Summary: What We Learn from History

Our world today is featured by integration, profound changes and great challenges, and such a situation is deeply rooted in history. Human history is the history of interaction between mankind and nature, and the history of interpersonal interaction; human civilization is the integration of the past and the present, traditions and innovations, and individual and common features; and the development of human society followed a path that goes from one source to pluralism and then to integration. Mankind has common values, pursues the true, the good and the beautiful, and endeavors for a happy life. Compared with the non-human society that sees little change over long periods of time, the human society is unpredictable and unstable, always undergoing changes, bifurcated development, reestablishment of connections and mutual influences. Influenced by the living environment and innovative tools. The human civilization separates into different parts over time, following different doctrines, gathering followers around different faiths, and forming various groups and sects. However, all these share the same core. All ethnic, regional and national cultures formed over time constitute integral parts of the human culture. Globalization causes different cultures to collide and communicate and brings together different cultures to compete and coexist with one another. Integration, sublation and coexistence are the general trend in the development of human society.

China has an ancient civilization, and the development of the Chinese civilization, like all other human civilizations, finds its foundation in the core values shared with the entire human race. The Chinese civilization has been through ups and downs over time, withstood hardships and garnered rich connotations. Compared with many other countries, China, as a developing country, is still in the preliminary or intermediate stage of modernization. And the top priority for a developing country is reform, opening-up and anti-corruption, all for the one ultimate goal of development. The development of China is comprehensive, balanced and sustainable, with both urban and rural areas given due consideration, with emphasis laid on a reasonable industrial structure, and with efforts made to maintain ecological balance and recycling of resources. China's development is a continuation from its past and long history. It has a vast market and will make contribute to both the modernization of China itself and the human civilization as a whole. The ancient Silk Road is a hallmark of the traditional civilization. The Belt and Road Initiative proposed by China today carries on the excellent traditions coming down from the past and opens up new horizon for the future. It shows to the whole world China's attitude in the new era to open up to the outside world, its political pursuit of peace, communication, cooperation and development, and its intention to create an international environment that facilitates the development of China.

Looking back on the history of mankind from the perspective of the law of balance, we will gain a better understanding of ourselves today, have more inner peace to face the future, and be more aware of the nature, instinct and basics of mankind. Mankind, in nature, is kind and gregarious, and pursues coexistence. This is the ultimate reason why we pursue peace and the ultimate way towards the survival of mankind. Mankind genetically tries for progress, reproduction and excellence, and tends to go all out for survival and for victory. This is the fundamental motivation for human development. Therefore, it is natural that there are competitions and wars in human society. Mankind, in nature, is the combination of existence and consciousness. The former is based on labor, creation and demands for life; while the latter is dominated by thoughts, emotions, intelligence and will power. The nature, instinct and basics of mankind are the internalization of the nature, the enlivening of materials, and the sublimation of life[①]. Mankind cannot live without the nature. Mankind has the spirit of animals but is different from ordinary animals. Mankind is the intelligent on the Earth, has its thoughts, and the ability of cognition, rational thinking and intelligence.

Looking at human civilization from the perspective of the law of balance, we will do better in cultivating our minds, bodies and behavior. To cultivate our minds, we absorb spiritual nourishment, reflect on ourselves, nurture and purify our minds, hone our health and attain perfection of both body and mind to uphold the good nature of mankind. To cultivate our bodies, we learn the skills for survival, train our bodies, improve our behavior, nurture ambitions, defend ourselves against bad habits, build our will power, and enhance our abilities. To cultivate our behavior, we combine the cultivation of body and mind, put together material civilization and spiritual civilization, align our behavior to moral standards, make good use of human qualities and wisdom, and contribute to human development.

Looking at human society from the perspective of the law of balance, we will have better understanding of people's will, livelihood and law. People's will reflects their wishes and such wishes show and determine where the society goes. Therefore, we should establish and improve a specialized investigation and polling system so as to collective people's opinions timely and effectively. People's livelihood is how people live, is the top priority of the world, and is the motivation for social development. Therefore, the government shall take the lead, with social participation, to establish and improve a basic social security system and build a strong safety net for the people. People's law is the civil law, the manifestation of the constitution in civil affairs, and the implementation of the civil law can be taken as a priority in achieving the rule of law in China. Listening carefully to people' voices, caring for people's livelihood, and abiding by civil law are the basic conditions for the healthy development of society.

Human society has entered a stage of in-depth globalization and people around the world are more closely related to one another than ever before. Adapting to social changes and trends, respecting the history and values of mankind, keeping up with the time, incorporating different cultures while maintaining one's own characteristics, building the constructive capacity for communicating with other people and nations, avoiding going to the extremes, preventing self-inflicted setbacks, caring for life, loving your life, serving society, being brave to explore new grounds, making continuous contributions, and pursuing shared development are the basic conditions and driving forces for the sustainable development amid globalization for both the whole world and China.

---

① 李泽厚. 2008. 人类学历史本体论. 天津: 天津社会科学院出版社: 38-41.

Urban Diversification and Social Diversity

Zhongguang Yang

Institute for Urban and Environmental Studies, Chinese Academy of Social Sciences

Urban diversification means that cities, in their course of development, not only vary in process, speed and scale, but also have diverse patterns, forms, ways and models of development, taking on varied and complex processes of development — rather than the simple or singular course of development in which cities grow both in number and population and expand from small cities to large ones. Urban diversification is manifested not merely in form, appearance, planning and design, but also in elements, contents, size and structure. It includes various aspects such as urban economy, society, politics, communities, culture, layout, architecture, construction and administration, is embodied in various fields, systems and dimensions of cities, and reflects not only the reality and status quo of cities, but also their history and course of development. Especially for China which has a long history, a big population, complex ethnicity and a huge number of cities, diversification is an essential character of cities as a whole, and a social expression of Chinese characteristics.

1. The Formation of Urban Pluralism

Fundamentally, the formation of urban diversification is attended by a process of urbanization from the emergence to the development of cities. Specifically, it involves the following reasons and processes.

1.1 Urban Diversification Is Inevitable from the Historical Perspective

Though cities are relatively independent entities, from the social point of view and analyzed in light of the objective of modernization, the term "city" is an umbrella concept, including numerous individual cities. In the course of development of cities as a whole, the emergence and development of individual cities in a country or a region, the change to the number and size of cities, the progress and improvement of urban functions, the development of urban construction and the advancement of modernization happen concurrently, and together they form the course of urbanization and modernization in the country or region concerned. For a region, a country, a continent, or the world as a whole, the emergence and development of cities — a symbol of human progress, and a historical phenomenon — undergoes a very long historical process and extremely complex changes, and those cities continue to develop and make history. In terms of phenomena, some cities are thousands of years old while some were only founded yesterday; there are ancient Chinese and European cities and newly-born ones. There are countless cities in the world, but they are worlds apart in terms of birth origin, development background and development course; almost all of them are deeply marked by times, especially marks of culture, ethos and personality.

1.2 Urban Diversification Is Environment-driven

Cities vary considerably in size, both demographically and geographically. Population can range from tens of millions to several thousand or less, area can be as large as tens of thousands of square kilometers or as small as several square kilometers. The types of city are quite complex and diverse with distinct urban characters. There are numerous and complicated factors that decide or form the size, character and type of cities, but in the final analysis, it is geographic and environmental factors in the forming and developing of cities that play a decisive role. Inland and coastal cities, border and port cities, for example, depend totally on geographic and natural conditions which, in normal cases, won't be changed at will. Physical conditions or elements that form the primary function of a city are closely linked with its geographic environment and natural resources: Coal cities and oil cities rely on the abundance of mineral resources; cities in the cold regions differ from those in the tropical regions in design and construction, structure and materials used, and decoration and appearance. The properties, characters, functions, facilities and buildings of a city have direct effects on its residents' ways of production and life. The change in life cycle of a city is also closely connected with geographic factors and the natural environment.

1.3 Economic and Social Push and Demand

The differences in size, type and nature of cities, which are not only determined by times and the environment but driven by economic and social development, must be adapted to suit the needs of development for a country or a region as a whole and conform to the positions and functions that society endows cities with. The capital city of a country, whether large or small, is different from average cities in various aspects such as function, structure, planning, design and construction. Some cities grew gradually from small cities to middle-sized ones and later to big cities or even megacities, while some have remained small for centuries. For industrial bases, mining cities, transportation and distribution hub cities, financial hub cities, tourist cities as well as cities of other types and characters, their process, pace and scale of development cannot be determined or changed as wished by city administrators, government departments or urban residents, but a result of meeting the needs of economic and social development for cities. Therefore, it makes no sense to require small and middle-sized cities to become large ones. A city cannot see becoming a big city or a global city as its goal, but instead, modernization. A city's modernization accords with its diversification.

Needs of economic and social development are in essence needs of human development. Because economies, societies and human beings are all of diversity, cities as carriers of economies and societies and as places of human existence and activity must be diversified.

1.4 Urban Diversification Is a Result of Cultural Accumulation

It is better to say that a city is a deposit and carrier of culture than to say it is an economic body. A comparison between cities in terms of their status as a cultural body and an economic body will make their differences and characteristics more obvious. Cities in different countries have different cultural deposits and traditions, which deepen and change in the course of time; especially in countries with a long history, a big population and complex ethnicity, cities are more steeped in culture of great diversity. Many small cities or towns in China are very old, and from design to architecture, from structure to layout, from customs to habits, from culture to education and from foods to festivals, a great diversity of culture is displayed in the country; every nationality has its unique culture, and cities dominated by minority groups show national characteristics more fully. Therefore, cities are carriers of culture, and they continue their respective culture that has formed in history; losing cultural differences, they lose their characteristics. It is cultural diversity that accounts for diversification of cities.

Uniformity of cities is not the mark or the goal of modernization. While participating in the 2006 China International Architectural Culture Exchange (IACE) Activity and the 6th International Architectural Design & Urban Planning Exhibition, Anna Kajumulo Tibaijuka, the former Under-Secretary-General of the United Nations and Executive Director of the United Nations Human Settlements Programme (UN-Habitat), said after visiting Yangzhou and Shanghai, that Yangzhou is an ancient city with a long history, while Shanghai is the largest modern city of China. Yangzhou's Slender West Lake and downtown old city represent the traditional style of architecture and way of life centuries ago in China, while Shanghai's majestic buildings on the Bund and financial district Lujiazui represent the modern European style of architecture and construction technology, as well as the latest development of materials.

Modernization is a dream of humanity, and it varies from country to country and from region to region in making this dream come true. But regardless of their cultures, ideology, faith, communities and nationalities, people share one same dream — to own a well-off home and live a life of dignity, security and prosperity.

Diversification makes cities better. In the process of globalization, diversification should not vanish, on the contrary, it should increase new elements, for example social equality, cohesion, new life styles, and higher environmental requirements to improve the quality of life. We should be proud of our cities.

2. Relationship Between Urban Diversification and Social Diversity

Urban development has fueled economic and social development on the whole, and urban construction has become a major driver of modernization. 80% of China's GDP is derived from cities. Cities play a dominant role in modern society, urban modernization leads the modernization of society as a whole, and the pace of urbanization and urban modernization determines the process and space of modernization of the whole society.

2.1 Urban Diversification Is an Intensive Reflection of Social Diversity

In modern society where urban civilization has dominance in social civilization, urban diversification is an intensive reflection of social diversity. In a modernized or modern society, cities represent the mainstream of society, in which the absolute majority of population dwell and which serve as economic, cultural, political and educational centers. Social diversity is primarily manifest in urban diversity or diversification. If cities, from scale and structure to type and pattern, from economic development to construction planning and from the way of life to the content of culture, are all the same without any difference, there would be no social diversity, life would be dull and boring, and modernization would be out of the question. In this sense, therefore, urban diversification is the foundation and precondition of modern diversity.

2.2 Urban Diversification Satisfies the Needs of Social Diversity

Urban diversification embodies diversity of culture and life better. There are marked differences in ways of life between American and Chinese cities and between large and small cities. I have long worked and lived in Beijing, I lived for a time in recent years in a small city called Plano in Dallas, the United States, and every year since my retirement I would go and stay for some time in my native town, a small town (Caota) in Zhejiang. Thus I have first-hand experience of differences in ways of life among Beijing, an American city and a small Chinese town. There are very distinct differences between the three places in many ways ranging from everyday life, family relationship, behavior, means of transportation, community environment to health care, but all residents there can enjoy modern urban civilization as well as regional characteristic culture. It is just those differences that adapt to different people and their varied needs, and make human lives varied and city life better.

2.3 Urban Diversification and Social Diversity Are Functionally Consistent

Urban functions evolve constantly and form part of social change. Urban functions, given by society and geared to the needs of social diversity, represent the implementation in space of the social development function, and both are highly consistent with each other. While urban functions are characterized by a very complex and frequently changing structure, for example residential, economic, political, educational and cultural functions, the distribution in space of social functions works as the fundamental element and lasting priority for the survival and development of cities, and only with urban diversification can social diversity be distributed widest and best in space in the way that urban diversification and social diversity are highly compatible with one another. In other words, different cities carry different social functions and are geared to the needs of change in social functions.

Formerly a little-known small town — both in size and population — Wuzhen has been given the function of hosting international conferences with the advancement of technology, especially the rapid development of transportation and communications. This illustrates that a city's function is not completely decided by its size and administrative level, and different cities may have similar functions. The best example is the fact that in some modernized countries such as the United States, many famous universities are located in small cities or towns.

3. How to Achieve Urban Diversification Compatible with Social Diversity

3.1 Seeking New-type Urbanization Appropriate for Actual Conditions

No matter what urbanization path we take, we must respect nature, cater to the needs of the times, respect laws, and seek truth from facts. The traditional and classical path of urbanization is attracting rural people into cities, especially large ones, where they become part of the urban labor force, then settle down and finally become urban residents (citizens), completing the process of urbanization of an individual (a farmer or a farming family) or a group of farmers and farming families. Therefore, urbanization is inevitably attended by labor transfer and the migration of people, alongside serious problems with migrant workers and urban residency. This seems to be a necessary process, and even the sole path, of urbanization.

Nevertheless, with science and technology advancing fast, social productivity developing rapidly, and transportation, communications and other infrastructure significantly improving, we must take a road of new-type urbanization, i.e. achieving urbanization through multiple paths by putting people first, taking modernization as the goal and adopting urban diversification as the basic model. Particular importance should be given to combining local and migration-based urbanization, and advancing urbanization and modernization side by side. So-called local urbanization means the local implementation of such measures as transferring industries, increasing jobs and sources of income, lifting up resident income, improving living standards, optimizing living environments, improving residential conditions and disseminating modern services, and enabling farmers and family members to change their ways of life and live a modern life while enjoying urban civilization. There have emerged in the country many widely admired and acclaimed exemplary new-type urbanization "villages", e.g. Huaxi Village in Jiangsu, or larger entities of urbanization and modernization, e.g. a township or region. Such urbanization involves no mass migration of labor and population, and can avoid thorny, complex problems relating to migrant workers.

3.2 Respecting Nature and Inheriting Urban History

Many cities are gifts of history, especially in ancient countries like China, where many cities are of so great antiquity that. Though modern building were built in the course of time, they still remain imprints and marks of history. The fundamental pattern and design, traditional street layout, antique buildings and fabulous traditional gardens of these cities are all reminiscent of their glorious history; customs and habits that urban residents have followed for centuries are so indelible and irreproducible that they form unique urban resources, advantages and sights, and become the cities' lasting potential and force of advancement. It is for these reasons that some cities remain forever young and have become the most attractive tourist cities with a worldwide reputation. Urban diversification just means respecting the history of cities, recording and preserving their history, continuing their culture that evolved in the course of history, protecting cultural heritage, and shaping their own urban ethos in the light of historical heritage, culture and requirements of times. Respecting history is to respect laws, which is also a task and goal of urban and national modernization. A city cannot forget, harm or destroy history in the pursuit of modernization. Efforts need to be made so that cities and their residents can conscientiously strengthen awareness about historical heritage protection, enhance the sense of pride and honor about cities and develop their respective urban ethos — the biggest competitive edge that a city can have.

Meanwhile, jobs need be done as much as possible so that cities can associate historical heritage protection closely with everyday urban lives and economic development while promoting modernization, serving local residents and bringing energy to cities.

The currents in recent years in China of discarding old cities and building new ones seem to suggest that all old cities are backward while new cities are modern. What really matters to modernization is the content, the substance, the people, the mode of social production, and how the people live. Old cities can also be modernized and not all new ones are modern.

3.3 Sustaining and Promoting Personality and Characteristics of Cities

We should first admit that differences exist in environments and conditions for the creation and development of cities, or in other words, cities are "innately" different from one another. Some cities were born to be towns or small cities and are unable to reach the scale of a large city no matter how much construction is done for it. Therefore, it is necessary to research and make urban planning in a scientific and objective manner and continue and promote diversified and individualized urban characteristics, rather than replicating one city's planning for other cities and applying one single drawing to all buildings.

Cities in many countries, modernized ones in particular, show features that distinguish them from other cities. In Germany, for example, particular importance is given to highlighting the personality of cities and preserving historical heritage thereof; in some modernized countries, instead of completely "abandoning" such historical cities as coal cities, steel cities and manufacturing cities because of the development of emerging industries and the transformation of energy structure, former industrial facilities or valuable buildings were reused and transformed in an integrated protective manner into cultural facilities like cinemas, museums and rock climbing destinations, taking up an "industrial culture road" that highlights modern industrial heritage, and using the remains of once rapidly rising modern industry as a cultural means to lift up national pride.

A city ought to develop and achieve diversification revolving around its own personality. Neither GDP nor resident income is a measure of how good or bad a city is, or the yardstick of modernization. The key is letting people live a high-quality happy life by putting people above everything.

3.4 Allocating Resources Rationally and in a Balanced Manner

There is a close relationship between urban diversification and the country's resource allocation. Sustaining and fostering urban diversification requires allocating resources most rationally and effectively through multiple means. Favoring some cities over others in resource allocation is detrimental to urban diversification. For example, tilting or intensively allocating some important urban resources, such as scientific research, educational, medical, infrastructure resources, to some cities, large cities or megacities in particular, would make other cities — especially, small and middle-sized cities, towns or remote cities — unable to develop as they should, and even tend to decline. Up to now, we still have no single respectable university located in a small city, let alone a town.

3.5 Establishing and Improving a Legal System Relating to Urban Development and Management

Our country's present theory of law contains no concept of urban legislation, despite a similar notion that cities have certain local legislative powers as Level-I administrative regions or units. But urban legislation differs from local legislation in that they are not completely the same in the object and scope of legal regulation. With the comprehensive development of our economy and society, the rapid advancement of urbanization, the acceleration of modernization, and the comprehensive readjustment in the urban system and structure, conflicts of various sorts in cities are becoming increasingly complex and acute, making it a pressing job to seek urban legislation appropriate for the needs of urban diversification. We already have legal experts who have researched and raised related questions and suggestions, which provide regulatory support for urban diversification, the normal operation of the urban economy and society, and especially for building a normal order of market economy and adjusting and handling as appropriate all kinds of relations among cities and among internal sectors of cities.

At the same time, related urban laws, rules, regulations and policies should pay greater attention to the differences among cities to be more relevant, adaptive and effective for the purpose of urban diversification.

Attitudes Toward Modernization and Rural-Urban Relationship: A Comparison Between Modern China and Japan

Chao Ye

School of Geographic Sciences, East China Normal University

1. Background and Significance

Modernization is a key issue that has long been discussed in social sciences research. And the modernization processes of China and Japan has been a hot topic in the disciplines of modern history, modernization and China-Japan relations. Both countries were forced to open up and launch their modernization processes in the mid- and late 19th century by Western aggressions. However, the two followed different modernization paths and gained widely differed results.

Both countries are located in East Asia, with only a belt of water in between, and have close cultural ties. Then, why are they so different? This is a key issue in modernization theory research and a long-term concern of the author.

Realistically, China has embarked on the path of socialist modernization since the launch of the reform and opening-up policy. This means that China is in the process of modernization as far as its mainstream ideology maintains. In the recent 30 years, as globalization deepens, the processes of industrialization, urbanization and ICTs (information and communications technologies) have made rapid progress in China. The tide of post modernization has been overwhelming too, causing tension between traditions and modernism that has never been seen before. As Zhiwei Zhang put it, "In a sense, it is because of the overlapping of ancient and modern times, and domestic and foreign elements that we are now seeing conflicts between things that were previously existed in different time periods and spaces… China intends to achieve what Western countries have achieved over a time span of several hundred years and thus, it is exposed within several decades to issues that had occurred elsewhere over a longer time of hundreds of years. As a result, the solution to one problem may exacerbate another problem."[1]

---

[1] 张志伟. 2006. 世界性视野下的"中国模式"——现代中国之政治研究的方法论问题. 中国人民大学学报, (3): 108-113.

Therefore, though there may be different understandings of modernization, modernization remains a preferred term among scholars because it represents such temporally and spatially condensed conflicts.

As modernization has rich connotation and extensive denotation, the author chooses to focus on rural-urban relationship which is a representative element of modernization. It is a key issue in the modernization process and reflects different ideological goals. Cyril Black, Gilbert Rozman and many other scholars have all emphasized rural-urban relationship as an important part of modernization. Endeavors toward modernity and modernization have continued throughout the modern history of China. Today, we are facing the problems of rapid urbanization and expanding rural-urban gaps, and it is therefore quite meaningful that we compare China with Japan which has a relatively high urbanization level and sound rural-urban coordination.

A country's attitude toward modernization has crucial influence on the rural-urban relationship in this country as well as the path of modernization it takes. A comparison between China and Japan constitutes a good example. Both countries uphold Confucianism as their cultural orthodox, yet Confucianism was an obstacle in the early days of China's modernization and worked as a propelling force for the modernization of Japan. Why was it like this? To answer this question, we need to analyze the different cultural attitudes and values of the two countries. The renowned historian Edwin Reischauer, for example, once stressed the influence of the different views toward foreign countries, as adopted by China and Japan. China deemed itself as a superior country when it was first challenged by the Western cultures and suffered heavy and radical blows, making it rather difficult for the country to take any step to change; while Japan, since it imported Confucianism from the outside, did not feel as much superiority and was better positioned to accept the Western cultures[1]. For sure, we cannot understand these issues too superficially, and more detailed analysis is required.

2. Attitudes of China and Japan Toward Modernization and Rural-Urban Relationship in the Two Countries

2.1 Attitudes of China and Japan Toward Modernization

Following the Opium War, Western cultures exerted unprecedented impact on the traditional economy, society, politics and culture of China. Like John King Fairbank once said, "What China experienced in the 19th century turned out to be a total tragedy and a huge and unprecedented collapse and fall. It occurred all so slow, yet relentlessly and radically, causing ever more pain. The old order fought to defend itself. It slowly retreated, always at disadvantage. Disaster came one after another, one more tragic than another, until everything of China, from the superiority its people felt toward foreigners and the centralized power of the emperors in Beijing to the ruling Confucian orthodox and the bureaucratic system, was destroyed or ruined one by one."[2]

Due to the Opium War, China was forced to open its gate more than ten years earlier before

---

[1] 赖肖尔. 1992. 近代日本新观. 卞崇道译. 北京: 生活·读书·新知三联书店: 33-35.

[2] 费正清. 1993. 剑桥中国晚清史: 1800—1911(上卷). 中国社会科学院历史研究所编译室译. 北京: 中国社会科学出版社: 4.

Japan, but this did not promise any early starter's advantage for China. China's steps toward modernization were cumbrous and slow, accompanied by extreme conflicts. Rongzu Wang said, "The two East Asian countries, China and Japan, were both changed under external pressures and aggression, but Japan was obviously much more adaptable than China." China witnessed a resurgence during the reign of emperors Xianfeng and Tongzhi, which was before the Meiji Restoration. However, the Meiji Restoration established Japan as one of the world powers in 30 or 40 years, yet around the same time, China was first defeated in the First Sino-Japanese War of 1884-1895, and then suffered the disaster of 1900. Both China and Japan were forced to open their gates to the outside world and seek strength and prosperity. China's setback appeared extremely bitter when compared with Japan's achievements."[1] The vastly different attitudes of the two countries toward the Western culture, foreign trade and education reflected how they viewed modernization and how urbanization and rural-urban relationship progressed in these two countries.

2.1.1 Distinction between China and foreign countries and understanding of civilization

China and Japan held extremely different views toward the West. As an American diplomat in the late Qing Dynasty said, "In regard to learning from the West, it would be unwise and meaningless to compare China and Japan because the two nations were fundamentally different. One discarded the clothing style it borrowed from others in no time, while the other refused to give up on the style it designed, earned through arduous labor, and had been wearing for so long that the clothes were almost part of human body. In discarding the oriental style and learning from the Western civilization, the only thing that Japan gave up on was perhaps the clothing style. But the Chinese, on the contrary, continued in their own way. Through all the years, they had been persistent in making their own cotton coats slowly and with strenuous efforts. Another major difference between the two countries is that from the very beginning of their contact with the West, till the establishment of a set model for them to deal with the relations with the West, things had always been beneficial to Japan, not China. Such a difference from the start resulted in unimaginable and extremely profound influence and outcomes later."[2]

Such different attitudes were actually formed long before the 19th century.

The renowned missionary Matteo Ricci (1552-1610) described the self-centered attitude of China as this: "This country has a vast territory, and borders are far away. But the people know nothing about the outside world and believe that the whole world is within their own country."[3] When Matteo Ricci and other missionaries delivered Western sciences to China, knowledge such as the five continents and that the Earth is round was mostly despised and rejected as absurd by a majority of Chinese officials of the Ming Dynasty due to incompliance to the traditional Chinese belief that China was the center of the world, as well as the Chinese views on geography and civilization. Matteo Ricci suggested using "wanguo" (ten thousand countries) to refer to the world, but it was also rejected. The Chinese continued to call other countries "waiyi" (foreign uncivilized countries) or "siyi" (other uncivilized nations) in official translated works. In

---

① 王荣祖. 2000. 走向世界的挫折——郭嵩焘与道咸同光时代. 长沙: 岳麓书社: 320.
② 切斯特·何尔康比. 2007. 中国人的德性. 王剑译. 西安: 陕西师范大学出版社: 12.
③ 利玛窦, 金尼阁. 2001. 利玛窦中国札记. 何高济, 王遵仲, 李申译. 桂林: 广西师范大学出版社: 33.

comparison, Japan accepted the term "wanguo" as early as the 17th century and had published a lot of geographic books on this topic by the time of the Opium War. Matteo Ricci's world map, though it had China in the center in order to please the Chinese, was not widely distributed in China; while in Japan, his thoughts and map were widely accepted and disseminated by Dutch learning scholars in spite of criticisms from Buddhists, promoting the development of geography and the change of the world view in Japan. Therefore, it is fair to say that the differences had long been in existence in terms of the two countries' attitudes toward the West, but weren't fully exposed until Western aggression occurred.

2.1.2 Different understanding on the roles of Chinese culture and western culture in modernization: Fukuzawa Yukichi vs. Yuan Wei

With a basic concept of distinguishing between what is Chinese and what is foreign, the Qing Dynasty carried on with the mindset of the previous dynasty, holding on to the firm belief that China was the Celestial Empire. Even the defeat in the Opium War did not budge that belief, however hard a blow it was to the country. As a result, China wasn't able to understand the Western civilization in a profound and systematic way. Although there were *Haiguo Tuzhi (Records and Maps of the World)* by Yuan Wei, *Sizhou Zhi (Encyclopedia of Geography)* by Zexu Lin, and *Yinghuan Zhilue (Short Records of the World)* by Jiyu Xu to open people's eyes toward the outside world by introducing foreign countries in terms of their history, geography, politics and culture, China was still confined in the belief that Chinese scholarship should be the fundamentals while Western knowledge was merely skills and that learning Western skills were to contain Western powers. China's understanding of the West remained partial and self-centered. If we compare Yuan Wei's thoughts, which was representative of the mid- and late 19th century China in the late Qing Dynasty, with the thoughts of Fukuzawa Yukichi, the Japanese Enlightenment thinker, we will see clearly how the most advanced thoughts in China and Japan differed at that time.

Yuan Wei (and his followers) and Fukuzawa Yukichi are representatives of the modernization efforts in China and Japan respectively. They were the first in their respective country to introduce the geography of other countries, exerting profound influence on later generations. Yet they differed greatly, mainly in the following aspects.

In terms of values, Yuan Wei emphasized the cultural distinction between China and foreign countries and regarded Chinese culture as superiority, while Fukuzawa Yukichi did not have the judgement and feeling.

In terms of purposes, Yuan Wei aimed at defeating foreign powers, yet Fukuzawa Yukichi intended for Japan to leave Asia and join Europe.

In terms of the content of their thoughts, Yuan Wei emphasized defeating Western powers by learning Western skills, focusing only on the tools, devices and skills of the West, not the culture of spirit; while Fukuzawa Yukichi promoted both Western spirit and materials and advocated spiritual learning as a way to advance people's mindset, which was a sharp contrast to the negligence of the general public in various reforms in China in late Qing Dynasty.

In terms of methodology, Yuan Wei promoted only military and mechanical techniques of the West, yet Fukuzawa Yukichi set priorities for the learning process, putting spiritual learning before material improvement.

Although both countries were aware of the modernization issue, their general attitudes were different. Modern Chinese did not regard the West to be the advanced, instead they believed that the West were advanced only in technologies, especially military and mechanical techniques used in case of emergency. Such an understanding was quite superficial. Also, no theorist in China at that time was as far-sighted and good at combining Western culture with specific national conditions as Fukuzawa Yukichi was. For sure, this also has something to do with the fact that the general public in China did not have any chance to develop as the Japanese people did (Fukuzawa Yukichi promoted spiritual development of the general public as a core part of civilization development, which has much to do with education). Therefore, China was not likely to understand the West deeply and comprehensively. As Albert Feuerwerker pointed out, no reform theorist was able to incorporate all these view points into one relevant plan and no systematic theory was formed. However, the actual proposals were quite clear: The Chinese people were intellectually capable of the same things as others were, and it was just that we were not yet there to finally make it happen. This is how Japan moved forward from an agricultural society to an industrial one[①]. The Japanese scholar Takeshi Hamashita also pointed out that the Westernizationists and the reformists shared one thing in common: They did not make clear who should perform the reforms they proposed and seldom discussed how their proposals were related to internal factors of China. In sum, it should be noted that their understanding of the West was quite limited[②].

2.2 Rural-Urban Relationship in Modern China and Japan

2.2.1 Cultural and geographic patterns of urbanization in China, Europe and Japan

Geographic conditions have their impacts on rural-urban relationship mainly in that they affect the ideology and trade policy. Coastal areas have the natural advantage and inclination to develop trade and the economy and culture are both highly oriented toward the outside. This is the foundation of modern urbanization. Ancient Europe, especially ancient Greece and Rome attached the Mediterranean regions and with a lot of islands, has a long tradition of valuing commerce and foreign trade, and moved from a bifurcated rural-urban structure to urbanization. China, on the contrary, has vast inland territory with only one side facing the sea and, therefore, adopts a more inward looking ideology, preferring stability and holding back China's steps toward modernization. Japan's rural-urban relationship is a middle type between the West and China, as its culture, trade policies and system with the characteristics of both China and the West (See Table 1).

Table 1 Cultural-geographic and Rural-Urban Patterns of Pre-modern China, Europe and Japan

Items	China	Europe	Japan
Geographic characteristics	Facing sea with only one side and many river basins	Mediterranean and many islands	Island country close to China
Cultural characteristics	Double-line monism	Plural and competing	Island culture

---

① 费维恺. 1990. 中国早期工业化: 盛宣怀(1844—1916)和官督商办企业. 虞和平译. 北京: 中国社会科学出版社: 40.
② 滨下武志. 1999. 近代中国的国际契机: 朝贡贸易体系与近代亚洲经济圈. 朱荫贵, 欧阳菲译. 北京: 中国社会科学出版社: 259.

			Continued
Items	China	Europe	Japan
Cultural personality	Stability-oriented inward looking (strong self-center)	Outgoing	Flexible inward looking (weak self-center)
Mainstream ideology	Confucianism	Christianity and other religions	Buddhism, Shintoism and Dutch learning
Attitude toward trade	Promoting agriculture and prohibiting commerce	Emphasis on commerce and foreign trade	Some free trade policies
Attitude toward rural-urban areas	Prioritizing rural over urban areas	Prioritizing urban over rural areas	Shift between the two attitudes
Rural-urban systems	Household registration system	Parliament, laws and economic systems	Tokugawa regime
Rural-urban relationship	Rural-urban integration	Rural-urban separation	The middle type

2.2.2 Comparison of the rural-urban relationship in modern China and Japan

In sharp contrast to the plunge in urbanization rate in China during the late Qing Dynasty, Japan achieved a relatively high urbanization rate in the late 18th and early 19th centuries, around the same as in European countries. Table 2 shows that Japan's urbanization rate was 16% to 17% in 1800, even higher than the level of Europe at the same period, and its commercial development also had a relatively sound foundation, which paved the way for modernization and urbanization.

Table 2 Proportion of Urban Population in the World in 1800

Countries and regions	Total population/million	Urban population/million	Urbanization rate/%
China	300	18	6-7
Japan	30	5	16-17
Russia	39	3	8-9
Europe	160	(20)	12-14
North-South Americas	31	(2)	5-8

Source: 西里尔·布莱克等. 1983. 日本和俄国的现代化. 周师铭等译. 北京：商务印书馆：116

Near the end of the Tokugawa era, urbanization halted for a while in Japan, but especially since the Meiji Restoration, urbanization continued with great momentum thanks to the development of foreign trade and the adoption of the government-supported industrial development policies. The different attitudes toward industrialization of China and Japan determined to a very large extent how industry and commerce developed in the two countries, and industrial development, including its level and structure, in turn, determined the urbanization process and the economic development in urban and rural areas.

Slow industrialization led to delayed urbanization in China. During the 100 years between 1850 and 1950, China's urbanization rate grew by only 5 percentage points. However, in Japan, fast industrialization pushed up the urbanization level rapidly. In 1894, 71% of all households in Japan were agricultural households, yet by 1925, the rate declined by about 21 percentage points to 49.31%. Population in cities with more than 10,000 people increased from 11% of the total in 1887 to 37% in 1925①, up by 26 percentage points within less than 40 years. The trend was more clearly seen in the comparison between agricultural and non-agricultural population. The share of agricultural population decreased from 77.1% in 1887 to 44.8% in 1938, while that of non-agricultural population surged from 22.9% to 55.2% in the same period②. The speed of urbanization was astounding. This corresponded to the industrialization level and speed of the same period.

In terms of the size of cities, almost all Chinese big cities are trading ports or near the sea, while Japan witnessed balanced distribution of small, medium and large cities in modern times. As industrialization and urbanization progressed and after merging some towns and villages, Japan had much fewer villages. The most typical example is that between 1888 and 1893, the total number of villages reduced by over 4,400 and after that, the number of villages continued to decline while the number of cities grew, resulting in a generally balanced distribution of cities, towns and villages. By 1895, there were already more cities than villages, marking a new high in urbanization level and the formation of a highly urbanized society. Also, according to Black et al., respectively 11% and 6% of the total population lived in cities with more than 10,000 and 100,000 people during 1867 and 1878, and these figures rose to 44% to 48% and 30% respectively during 1939 and 1940③. These show the urbanization level of Japan at those times, and reflect a relatively good balance between big and small cities.

Urbanization in modern China increased the conflict between urban and rural areas, but in Japan, such conflicts were avoided wherever possible. Black believed that one of the reasons for this was that there was no strong rural interest groups in Japan, the merger of towns and villages did not hamper the interest of traditional rural powers, and the government thus obtained control over its rural areas without much difficulty; and another reason was that urban and rural areas were conveniently connected and rural residents got information fast and were up to date as for the progress of the reform. The latter reason was in fact the result of universal education in Japan. Universal compulsory education and rural education programs made it easier for rural residents to come to cities, much easier than it was in China. Therefore, urbanization had less resistance and the rural-urban relationship was better coordinated in Japan than in China.

In terms of the influence of the attitudes to modernization on national systems, a major difference between China and Japan lies in that it was an extension and continuation of a set of overall reform (i.e. the Meiji Restoration) in Japan, with consistent guiding principles, major systems and government decrees; but in China, the process was a long winding path from "defeating Western powers with Western skills" to Western skills in a Chinese structure, to "down with Confucianism", then to the "Four Modernizations", people-oriented development and post-modern thoughts, with ups and downs and policy adjustments back and forth along the way. Taking the household registration system which had huge influence on China's rural-urban relationship as an example, rural-urban bifurcation was a serious problem arose from this system and even today, and citizens are still not entitled to the freedom of migration in the Constitution,

---

① 刘天纯. 1995. 日本现代化研究. 北京: 东方出版社: 184-185.
② 张东刚. 2005. 中日经济发展的总需求比较研究: 1886—1936. 北京: 生活·读书·新知三联书店: 111-112.
③ 西里尔·布莱克等. 1983. 日本和俄国的现代化. 周师铭等译. 北京: 商务印书馆: 267.

and China remains in lack of a "household registration law". In contrast, the right to free migration was established in Japan during the Meiji Restoration and its Household Registration Law was issued as early as 1947 and has been in effect ever since. Another example is the attitude toward rural education. Japan promoted rural education with great efforts even when its national strength was limited, and this provided rich human resources for the rapid urbanization. China, on the contrary, did not pay lasting attention to rural areas and rural education on the whole, although there were several famous people who made some efforts in some short time periods when more emphasis was laid there upon.

3. Conclusions

Modernization has been a key issue faced by both China and Japan since the 19th century. Culture and rural-urban relationship are two major topics in modernization research. However, little study delved into the details of the connections between the two. By comparing the attitudes of modern China and Japan toward modernization and their rural-urban relationships, I hereby reach the following conclusion: The different attitudes (values and ideology) of China and Japan toward modernization have had profound influence on the urbanization paths and the characteristics of rural-urban relationship of the two countries.

Generally, before the 20th century, most Chinese people did not deem the West as a separate civilization different from their own, like what most Japanese believed; instead, they thought the West had only some advanced technologies, focusing only on military and mechanical technologies to be used in emergency, and failed to acknowledge the truth that Western civilization is industrial civilization. All in all, China did not understand the West as thoroughly and comprehensively as Japan did. With such a general attitude or ideology, Chinese people did not shift their focus away from agriculture toward industry and commerce in a timely manner like the Japanese did, and thus failed to embark on a path of industrialization and urbanization and missed out on the chance of developing universal education which would have laid solid foundation for urbanization. The different attitudes of China and Japan toward the West or Western civilization, foreign trade and education had great influence on the strategies of the two countries for trade and industrial development, and thus led to differences between the two countries in terms of urbanization and rural-urban relationship.

In the modernization process, the most striking difference in rural-urban development in China and Japan lies in that foreign trade and industrialization propelled urbanization and contributed to a relatively harmonious rural-urban relationship in Japan; while in China, a weak foundation of foreign trade and industrialization slowed down the urbanization process and hampered the coordination between urban and rural areas, widening the rural-urban gap.

Three Trends of Chinese Learning and Construction of Multi-modernity in China

Aiguo He [1], Ying Yan [2]

1 Department of History, Center for Comparative Studies of Modernization, Fudan University
2 Department of History, Shanghai University

In a century during the modern times, China saw Western learning and Chinese traditional learning alternate again and again, which is a historical phenomenon worth deep thinking. It is a serious misunderstanding to simply call the trend of studying Chinese ancient civilization as cultural conservatism or cultural revivalism. Why was a trend of Western learning followed by a trend of Chinese learning? Was the trend of Chinese traditional learning a kind of conservatism? After careful investigation, we find this trend of thought, rather than a conservative one, represents an effort for modernization by absorbing Western learning on the basis of national conditions and culture. Despite different themes and varied thoughts of individuals, all such trends recognized the importance of modernization and called for learning from Western modernity, but rejected to abandon domestic culture, divorce from national conditions and blindly copy foreign models or meaningless repetition. Recognizing several trends of Chinese learning in modern times, a scholar named Yulie Lou holds that "all discussions about Chinese learning, in the final analysis, are communication between Oriental and Western cultures and reflection during the process of modernization on how to properly treat established cultural traditions at home, inherit and carry forward their excellent part, and build a modern state with unique national and ethnical features?"[①] Advocating Chinese learning is neither identical with cultural revivalism nor a gesture rejecting westernization; instead, it is a reflection of modernization. "What is the a-century-long dispute over Chinese learning really for, especially that in recent two decades? It is for finding out where the Chinese society is heading for and how China can realize modernization."[②]

---

① 楼宇烈. 2007-1-11. 国学百年启示录. 光明日报, 3.
② 李宗桂. 2008. 国学与时代精神. 学术研究, (3): 21-32.

1. The First Trend of Chinese Learning: Seeking China's Modernity Through Western Modernity Localization

There were three trends of Chinese learning in the modern times of China. The first one was in late Qing Dynasty at the beginning of the 20th century. Why did it happen at that time? Was there any principle or special meaning for the timing? After the Opium War, the Chinese people has embarked on seeking a way of national salvation by learning from Western countries, and the later Westernization Movement was the first trend of learning from the West. During this period, China followed the principle of "Chinese learning for fundamental principles and Western learning for practical application". Instead of completely Westernized, it insisted on its own political system, ideology and moral customs. However, things became different after the outbreak of the First Sino-Japanese War in 1894. Severely hit by the war, China lost confidence in its own political system and ideology and it became an overwhelming trend to learn from constitutionalism, parliament system, separation of powers and theories about politics and sociology of Western countries. Some suggested taking all Western systems. Scholars in the ram school of thought interpreted Confucianism by using Western modernity thought. The reinterpretation of ideology by intellectuals, providing theoretical support for Constitutional Reform and Modernization in 1898, was also an effort to modernize the ideology by transforming traditional ideology. The trend of complete Westernization became too sweeping to be curbed after another hit on China by the invasion of the Eight-Nation Alliance in 1901. China's home-grown political system and ideology were confronted with an unprecedented crisis, and almost all schools of thought required completely learning from the West. In particular, revolutionists not only advocated adopting political system of the US, France or Japan, but also launched the "revolution on the three cardinal guides" and "revolution on Confucius" to overthrow Confucianism rather than only reform it. Confucianism got the last shot in 1905 when the imperial competitive examination system was abolished by the Qing Court. However, since advocacy for Western learning made such a great clamour, why did people start to pay attention to Chinese learning?

First, rectification and rethink of the westernization trend were needed, so that modernization could suit China's national condition; besides, scholars proposed that China should blaze its own trail of modernization. Advocates for Chinese learning argued that the three decades' Europeanization failed to make desired achievements. "All intellectuals today reach consensus on the way to save the Chinese nation, that is Europeanization. Is it against the natural law and going to bring us into trouble if we advocate our own traditional learning? Will national progress be impeded if we resort to wisdom of ancient sages? No, of course not. Indeed, we encourage Europeanization. However, Western learning was introduced to our country three decades ago, but we see no progress as expected but witness an even worse situation①." Instead of believing in the perfection and flawlessness of Chinese learning, such scholars kept a sober mind about its deficiencies and recognized how necessary to learn from foreign countries. However, they also thought "knowledge from other countries" suited countries where it came from but

---

① 许守微. 1905. 论国学无阻于欧化. 国粹学报, (7).

might not be necessarily applicable for China. The home-grown learning was suitable in the long run and even more suitable in the case of major changes in environment. As long as people kept open-minded, learned from other countries and kept pace with times, local civilization was undoubtedly more applicable and suitable and was easier to be accepted, since it had deep root in local history, customs and people's mind and could hardly be replaced by Westernization. "The most part of Chinese learning should be observed and maintained, but some part of it does not cater to the general trend of the world. That is why we have to learn from foreign countries. However, although foreign civilization might be superior over our local one, it might defeat our purpose due to the sharp differences in environment, customs and habits between China and other countries. Will that let all those who seek to save the country by learning from the West down? Therefore, we cannot improperly belittle our own civilization; instead, we should carry it forward and develop it. In addition, we should not deny or reject all knowledge from the West, but should be open-minded and welcome it." Obviously, advocates of Chinese learning rejected receiving Western learning without understanding it and argued for absorbing it on the basis of Chinese learning. "We should avoid 'eating without digestion' when learning from the West, while reviving the declined Chinese learning."① With its unique Chinese features, Chinese ancient civilization is different from the Western civilization and more advanced than the latter in some cases. As long as we keep open-minded to absorb the good part of the Western civilization and get close to real conditions, the revival of Chinese learning will not lead to fall of this country; instead, it will fuel the development of the country. "All ancient Chinese books about philosophy, medicine or other sciences have special advantages over Western learning in discovering underlying principles. If we carefully study them, develop the good part and avoid flaws, and then integrate such knowledge with Western learning so that the two can complement and promote each other, we therefore can build a new glorious civilization to rejuvenate the country rather than see the country fall." ②

Second, this trend of Chinese learning was not a conservative one but on the basis of Westernization, since, instead of rejecting learning from the West, it strongly advocated absorbing Western learning and was intensively Westernization-oriented to some degree. It only went against Westernization that divorced from actual national conditions, with the hope that Westernization could be implemented in China; in other words, only when western learning and Western modernity were localized and accommodated to China's national conditions, could they belong to China. Jie Huang, Editor-in-Chief of *Guocui Xuebao*, argued that the study of Chinese learning integrated knowledge from both Eastern and Western countries. Not narrow-sensed exclusivism, it was to rejuvenate the Chinese nation and culture and to erect a cultural pillar for the Chinese nation. "The study of Chinese learning is to delimit boundaries of the country as well as the Chinese civilization. Pained by the invasion by other countries and the decline of Chinese civilization, we shall be based on our own civilization to study knowledge from other countries whether in the East or the West, in the hope that one day the Chinese nation and its traditional learning will revive. Nevertheless, we admire scientific achievements made by other countries,

---

① 高旭. 1905. 学术沿革之概论. 醒狮, (1).
② 王天优. 1914. 国学研究会宣言书. 国学丛刊, (1).

and intend to research them, so as to implement them in future."① Advocates of Chinese learning insisted that modernization should proceed from fundamentals. Since European modernization started from Renaissance, China should launch its own renaissance, which meant the revival of the pre-Qin philosophy. "Science boomed in Europe when ancient civilization was revived; however, it is too late to restore ancient civilization in China now"; therefore, "we should start to catch up and try to revive". Studying Chinese ancient civilization did not reject Europeanization and the two did not deny each other; instead, they complemented and promoted each other. "Chinese learning facilitates and promotes Europeanization, rather than defends itself by rejecting the latter. All patriots should study Chinese learning all the time."② In October 1905, Shi Deng, another Editor-in-Chief of *Guocui Xuebao*, published the famous article named *On Revival of Chinese Learning*. In this manifesto of China's renaissance, the author pointed out that reviving and innovating upon Chinese learning was an obliged duty for all Chinese people. "Nowadays, our responsibility to the motherland is to study our traditional learning, search into abstruse subject and indicate the importance and to make new findings. "Books written by ancient philosophers expounded on principles similar with those in Western learning on psychology, ethics, logic, sociology, history, politics and law as well as physics and chemistry. Drawing on each other for reference, they can well complement each other. " Since modernization started from Renaissance in the West, it should also be so in China. The 20th century was the era of renaissance in China and also a century of modernization. "The 15th century is when European traditional learning revived, and the 20th century is when Asian traditional learning came back."③

Third, to save the Chinese nation from crises and build a modern nation state, China needed to revive its traditional learning to establish its own spirit as a nation state, core values and ideology, raise people's awareness of a nation state, arouse patriotism and raise identity awareness. A scholar named Shu Liang pointed out that the first trend of Chinese learning was dominated by the political concept proposed to counter the national crisis, design a path of development and build a modern nation state. "The study of Chinese learning in this period is a political concept rather than an academic one. In the middle of a severe national crisis at that time, advocates of Chinese learning in the late Qing Dynasty paid attention to the relationship between the destiny of the country and the development of academics and proposed that traditional culture should be carried forward at the critical time for the country."④ In July 1906, Taiyan Zhang, a revolutionist, thinker and great scholar in the modern times of China, published the famous *A Welcome Speech to Students from Tokyo* on the No. 6 of *The Chinese Times*, and pointed out that people advocated Europeanization because they had no full understanding of China's history and culture; only by recognizing and deeply understanding the history and culture of their country, could they really love their country and stop boasting of Europeanization. "Recently, some Europeanization advocates gave up on themselves and always said that China will be conquered and the yellow race will perish, since Chinese people are much inferior to Western people. That is because they don't know the advantage of China and see nothing they can love,

---

① 黄节. 1905. 《国粹学报》叙. 国粹学报, (1).
② 许守微. 1905. 论国学无阻于欧化. 国粹学报, (7).
③ 邓实. 1905. 古学复兴论. 国粹学报, (9).
④ 梁枢. 2009-10-26. 新国学之路——访清华大学国学研究院院长陈来. 光明日报, 3.

then their patriotism fizzles out day by day. If they do, I think even the stone-hearted people can by no means stop loving their motherland and race."① Xu Gao emphasized in his article named *Nansheqi* (literally, *Manifesto of Southern Associations*) that Chinese learning carried the spirit of the whole nation, and must provide spiritual support to a nation state. "Countries with a soul would survive while those without it would perish. There is no grief greater than the death of a country. How lamentable it would be if the soul of a country is allowed to perish. Where would the soul of a country lie? It lies in the treasure trove of our traditional teachings. We must preserve the traditional teachings to preserve the soul of our country." Shi Deng said in his article *Defending Against Uselessness of Chinese Learning* that pre-Qin philosophy was the cream of Chinese ancient civilization and the real way to save the country; therefore, the revival of Chinese ancient civilization should start from studying the pre-Qin philosophy. "Any of great thoughts in pre-Qin period, for example, Taoism initiated by Laozi, the thought of equality of things proposed by Zhou Zhuang, universal love advocated by Di Mo, rule by law proposed by Fei Han, art of war by Wu Sun, logics developed by Kuang Xun, idea to develop economy proposed by Zhong Guan, is helpful for the present situation. These great thinkers worked very hard to use their thoughts to save and develop their countries."②

The first trend of Chinese learning was the extension and also a rethink of the first trend of Westernization and represented the start of Chinese people to explore a way of modernization with Chinese characteristics by comprehensively absorbing Western civilization. Given that Chinese learning and Western learning can complement and develop each other, the first trend of Chinese learning and the first trend of Western learning are two sides of the same trend of modernization. The first trend of Chinese learning was open, innovative and modernized, rather than isolated, conservative and old-fashioned. It had a strong orientation of cultural nationalism and represents that the Chinese people embarked on their way to establish a modern China through cultural modernization.

2. The Second Trend of Chinese Learning: Seeking China's Modernity by Rethinking Western Modernity

The second trend of Chinese learning followed the New Culture Movement, during which a strong trend of Westernization swept China. A strong tide of westernization occurred in China after 1895, in which reformists and revolutionists were two schools. In particular, revolutionists even discarded their own ideology and moral customs; however, for the purpose of building a modern nation state, they launched a nationalistic movement to revive Chinese learning and regarded that thoughts of ancient philosophers enjoyed the same status in China like Western learning in Western countries and were the source of the Western learning, and the two were connected to each other. Therefore, since Western modernization started from Renaissance, China's modernization should begin with the revival of such philosophical schools. After the Revolution of 1911, revolutionists learned completely from the West in terms of institutional establishment, but failed to build an effectively functioning freedom and democratic system. The

---

① 章太炎. 1906. 东京留学生欢迎会演讲. 民报, (6).
② 邓实. 1907. 国学无用辨. 国粹学报, (30).

failure of radical Westernization of political systems led to the split of the revolutionists. Some retreated to constitutional monarchy, some insisted on a path of gradual political modernization from stratocracy to political tutelage and then to constitutionalism; and some others became even more radical to attribute the failure of political system's Westernization to the absence of moral Westernization; therefore, Westernization must be complete and cover morals, customs and people's mindset, which was the so-called "last conciousness". Given that, the New Culture Movement was a radical Westernization campaign from the beginning. Activists in the campaign called for overthrowing old culture, literature and morals and replacing them with new ones. Westernization advocates blamed "useless Chinese learning" for poverty in China and justified accordingly complete Westernization. "As Western learning spreads in China, its followers in China attribute the weakness of China to uselessness of Chinese learning and even abandon all Chinese learning."① Westernization was a dominant worldwide tide and also the mainstream in China's society and academia at that time. "Westerners took the upper hand in every part of the world. No one dared challenge their authority. Therefore, Chinese people always thought Chinese civilization much inferior to the Western one, and thus advocated complete Europeanization. That then became a general trend that had overwhelming effects on both domestic politics and academia."②

Why was such a strong Westernization movement followed by a new trend of Chinese learning?

First of all, this trend was to critically reflect on the Westernization movement and absorb reasonable factors in this movement. By reviewing effects of Westernization in the late Qing Dynasty, Chinese learning advocates realized that Westernization did not save China, and their country was troubled with chaos, poverty and backwardness and even hit by several national crises. "Since late Qing Dynasty, China has suffered from political instability, deformity in social development and invasion by other countries. Chinese people were suddenly awaken and so worried about what they were confronted that they thought changes must to be done. They began with using advanced weapons from the West, then adopted Western political systems, accepted Western ethics and morals and finally tried almost all things from the Europe. Militarism, socialism, democracy and anarchism were all transplanted to China, and idealism, materialism, experimentalism and positivism as well as many other thoughts were heard and discussed. Baili Jiang once said, 'In decades, China welcomed and bade farewell to numerous new things from the West. Once new things came, they spread quite quickly…' However, the country saw no changes in political instability or social crisis and its people suffered even more. They were frustrated and thought Western culture was not strong enough to save the country. The only way to save the country and the people is to learn from ancient sages."③ Chinese learning advocates thought that, instead of producing obvious effects on society, Westernization sabotaged morals, customs and ethics to a large degree. "In recent years, Chinese learning scholars were frustrated with the failure of European and American cultures to save their country from crises, and thus returned back to try to revive Chinese learning. The national authority was also worried about the

---

① 姚光. 1923. 国学保存论. 国学丛刊, (1-2).
② 何键. 1935. 研究国学之方法与应具之眼光. 国光, (5).
③ 曹聚仁. 1925. 国故学之意义与价值. 东方杂志, 22.

loss of integrity and found no effective way to make a change. Then it determined to resort to reviving ancient Chinese philosophy. Then the study of Chinese learning had become a general trend both at home and abroad."① During the process of Westernization, we mainly learned science and technology, material civilization and political system from the West. We did not carefully study their moral customs and religious beliefs but sabotaged our own. As a result, materialism, consumerism, hedonism and sole pursuit of benefits appeared. "In decades, domestic intellectuals and officials seemed to follow Europeanization, but China still lagged far behind European countries in terms of improvement of people's life and progress in science and education. In contrast, indulgence in material comfort was as severe as in Europe. People lived in misery and the country suffered from instability due to unlimited desire for material. Therefore, it was said that 'Materialism is the apple of discord for today's China'."② The New Cultural Movement started the second trend of Chinese learning which was a reflection and digestion of the latter based on the Westernization trend. This trend tried to combine Chinese learning and Westernization to blaze a new trail of China's own. "The May Fourth Movement ushered China into an era of renaissance. At the same time, the real soul of Chinese learning began to recover. Since foreign cultures conflicted with the home-grown culture, many far-sighted intellectuals began to study Chinese learning even more carefully in order to explain and solve such conflicts."③ Although the New Cultural Movement was guided by Westernization advocates at the very beginning, these scholars proposed to "revive ancient Chinese philosophy and rejuvenate Chinese civilization". Those who advocating Eastern culture were devoted to reviving Chinese learning, explaining it with Western learning and applying it to find a new path of modernization for China. That is the so-called "aged nation with new movement" and "bringing peace to all generations". Therefore, new Confucianism, Mohism, Taoism and Legalism thrived.

Second, this trend was a critical reflection on Western civilization. The outbreak of the World War I broke the blind worship for Western civilization of Chinese people who then began to rethink deficiencies of the Western civilization and think about advantages of their own traditional learning at the same time. They reconsidered the material civilization, economic and political systems, science and technology, religious beliefs, morals and ethics, and stopped accepting them without doubts. Moreover, they did not doubt, criticize and even deny their own systems and culture any more. Disputes over establishing the country based on agriculture or industry, Eastern and Western culture, and science and metaphysics were all critical reflection on Western civilization. According to Jibo Qian, the second trend of Chinese learning was innovative on the basis of reflection on "materialism" in Europeanization and Chinese traditional "classism", and its theme was "humanism". "Only by 'humanism-based' traditional learning, can people's initiatives be motivated and people's life come back to the right track; this is the reasonable way and will leading us to success. The term 'humanism' is opposite to 'materialism' in Europe and 'classism' for Confucian scholars. 'Classism' was once belittled, while 'materialism' is the ill for now."④ The World War I promoted Chinese scholars to rethink disadvantages in Western

---

① 张树瑸. 1935. 国学今后之趋势. 国光, (12).
② 钱基博. 1929. 今日之国学论. 国光, 1(1).
③ 王皎我. 1928. 中国国学在国际上的新地位及其最近之趋势. 青年进步, 114.
④ 钱基博. 1929. 今日之国学论. 国光, 1(1).

civilization and also forced Western scholars to do so. Thoughts and theories of Bertrand Russell, Henri Bergson, Hans Driesch, Oswald Spengler, Tolstoy, Tagore and many other scholars are products of such reflection. Such scholars were willing to re-understand the Eastern culture and advocate its revival. Thoughts of Chinese and Western scholars spread in China and affected the Chinese academia a lot. Influenced by these thoughts, Chinese scholars did not belittle and cast aside their own culture any more.

Third, this trend of Chinese learning was an effort to seek national identity and China's own development pattern. Chinese learning advocates always believed that Chinese learning was the prerequisite of national identity. Preserving Chinese learning means neither being confined by Chinese learning nor being conservative; instead, it means to carry forward and develop Chinese learning on the basis of understanding and digesting Western learning. "To save our nation at this time, we must preserve our traditional learning. To preserve it, we don't have to be obstinate but should carry forward and develop it. However, a great deal of knowledge from the West is not known to us yet. For this, we should absorb what is good and discard what is bad, and then integrate it with traditional learning. In this way, Chinese learning will be revived."① Three conditions are needed to revive Chinese learning. 1) Chinese learning and Western learning should be compared with and inspire each other, and we should be inclusive and open-minded when developing traditional learning. 2) Chinese learning should be based on actual conditions and target at resolving practical problems, meeting actual needs and seeking the way to save the country. 3) Scholars of Chinese learning should set a good example and have noble spirit. "We know their arguments were biased, but these scholars were in the way of Europeanization and seemed drunk with some wild spring. To waken them and change the current trend, efforts should be made in three aspects. 1) Chinese learning and Western learning should be compared to highlight the advantage of the former. 2) Chinese learning should be understood and applied, to show people that talents fostered by Chinese learning outperform those by Western learning. 3) Those researching Chinese learning should be great in eight virtues to show the reliability and integrity that we have developed by learning Chinese traditional knowledge. Empty words without these efforts will be of no use to advocate Chinese learning." ②

Initiated by the New Cultural Movement, the second trend of Chinese learning was a reflection on the Westernization after the New Cultural Movement and on the crisis of Western civilization brought by the World War I and also digestion and integration of West learning and Western civilization. Like the first trend of Chinese learning, the second one cannot be separated from Westernization advocates. Both Eastern culture and Westernization advocates promoted Chinese learning movement. They did so not for reviving the Chinese learning, but only to anatomize it like dissecting a body; however, they also looked forward to recovering ancient learning of China and reshaping Chinese civilization, by following the pattern of Western civilization though. Westernization advocates stopped blindly worshiping Western civilization after 1930s when the Chinese nation underwent increasingly deepening crises. They began to recognize the significance of Chinese learning and made innovative transformation.

---

① 姚光. 1923. 国学保存论. 国学丛刊, 1-2.
② 何键. 1935. 研究国学之方法与应具之眼光. 国光, 5.

3. The Third Trend of Chinese Learning: Seeking China's Modernity by Reflecting on Paths of Modernization in China and Other Countries

China has been embracing the third trend of Chinese learning since the 1990s. In the 1980s, learning bitter lessons from blindly following Soviet Union and carrying out modernization in an isolated way in the past three decades, China began to learn with an open mind from the Western countries and opened up to the outside world. With great eagerness of absorbing advanced experience of the developed Western countries, China has made whooping progress in modernization. In this period, most socialist countries in the world launched reform and opening-up campaign and learned from the West. A result of learning from the West was sweeping tides of Westernization and it was also true in China. But why was the strong Westernization movement followed by a trend of Chinese learning?

It is a visionary strategic decision, made by the second generation of central leadership in China based on previous lessons, that China should unswervingly uphold the socialist development path with Chinese features. To do so, understanding of and support from China's traditional culture are indispensable. "We are going to build a modernized China with its own characteristics. Then what are such characteristics exactly? Without culture and traditions, I don't think such characteristics can be expressed or reflected. Only when our own cultural tradition is recognized, inherited and carried forward, can we have our special characteristics."① According to the academia, beneath the huge success made in socialist modernization with Chinese characteristics is the support from China's own cultural tradition. "Thanks to the reform and opening up policy for so many years, China has embraced unprecedented prosperity and the development is so stunning despite many problems and hardly expected hidden risks. What are behind such fast and huge progress since China's reform and opening-up policy? Reasons are many of course, but is there any inevitable association between the development and culture, especially between development and Chinese traditional learning or traditional culture? If there is, what is key in the relationship?"② That is the essential reason that the trend of Chinese learning occurred when China determined to carry out socialist modernization with Chinese characteristics.

The third trend of Chinese learning is a new strategic choice to stop blindly believing in and consciously reflecting on Western civilization and to blaze a new trail of modernization. Modern Western civilization is unprecedentedly great since it values technology, material, reasonability, human rights, faith and individual ethics, which are factors for the huge progress in the world history; however, it undoubtedly has severe deficiencies and chronic illness like colonialism, imperialism, materialism, unlimited exploration of national resources, scientism and anthropocentrism. It was confronted with ever more severe crisis after the 1970s. Western civilization is a kind of industrial civilization, which, like a double-edged sword, has created considerably huge wealth but also severe damage, and even threatens the security of physical and

---

① 楼宇烈. 2007-1-11. 国学百年启示录. 光明日报.
② 李中华. 2007. 国学、国学热与文化认同. 北京行政学院学报, 3.

spiritual homeland of human being. "Scientism, individualism and authoritarianism deriving from industrial civilization can solve crises of energy, ecology and environment confronting all human beings; however, responsibility and harmony have new value functions to replace freedom and efficiency as well as other universal values in capitalist society. The revival of Chinese learning today is to seek the inevitability of it, since Chinese learning is a shared spiritual homeland, continuous and special function and unique lifestyle of the Chinese nation."① Mankind has become the master of the planet due to the material civilization, which is the essential feature of the industrialization, but got lost in front of the colossal material wealth. The worship for material and its byproduct power is unprecedented. "There is a new religious belief today, that is fetishism: everything is measured by 'material' and allowed and encouraged only at the level of material; everything is convincing and accepted only when it takes the form of 'material', while all those related to people's value, spiritual life and feelings are abandoned. Another thing that totally matches 'material' is 'power', which reflects the force of 'material'. Power worship is another kind of material worship. It is common to see the unlimited worship of power, which severely damages the integrity and erodes ethics and dignity of our nation."② The third trend of Chinese learning is a profound rethink of Western modernity that prevails and dominates in the globe. The worldwide learning of Western industrialization leads to modernity with distinctive features of industrialization, while the academia sees the deep crisis confronting such modernity, such as environmental damage and pollution, resource consumption and depletion. All these problems should be solved by resorting to Chinese learning. "Since the 1990s, some far-sighted people in the West have reflected on Western modernity. Severe challenges confronting human being, instead of being mitigated, are becoming more severe in the new century. The most severe one is the relationship between mankind and nature, including irreparable damages brought to the nature by energy, environment, ecology and population problems. Industrial civilization based on the separation of mankind and nature or instrumental rationality seems to come to a dead end. Given that, some Western scholars proposed that 'The engine for reforming the way of thinking should be in the Oriental civilization', a cultural idea that was widely echoed."③ Modernity, which successfully defeated traditions, becomes unbridled and brings increasingly more negative effects. An "iron cage" of modernity proposed by Max Weber is formed to prevent human beings from self-improvement and enhancement. Human beings are becoming non-human beings and the slave of science and technology and material, victim of environment, digital machine and byproduct of instrumental rationality. "Modernity, as it goes into its late stage, presents more deficiencies. To date, it has deteriorated severely. Pride and greed of human beings inflates unprecedentedly, development of technology and rationality is distorted, materialism and hedonism overwhelm, and the spiritual world falls. Mature modernity presents the side of deformity after triumphing over traditions."④ Considering such deep crises, we cannot count on Western civilization to save ourselves; instead, we can only depend on ourselves, but not on revivalism. Therefore, we can only resort to innovative

---

① 纪宝成. 2009-12-21. "国学学科问题"高端访谈(上): 该不该为国学上户口？. 光明日报, 5.
② 崔卫平. 2007-1-11. 我们的尊严在于拥有价值思想. 南方周末, 2.
③ 李中华. 2007. 国学、国学热与文化认同. 北京行政学院学报, (3): 96-101.
④ 许纪霖. 2009-7-15. 启蒙如何虽死犹生. 中华读书报, 3.

development of our own civilization. "The contemporary Western civilization is undergoing a profound crisis of nihilism, and Western scholars are pained by completely reflecting on Western learning. Such reflection is as painful as shown by Nietzsche, Martin Heidegger and today's so-called postmodernism. Human beings learn the truth only through pains, and now it is time for both the Westerners and Chinese to learn truth again. It is also at this time that we Chinese people truly realize that our future is not like what is now in the West. It is an inevitable choice to resort to ourselves."[1] Therefore, we have to seriously reflect on the traditional West-centralism and the development pattern of the West, and stick to blazing a trail of modernization of our own, rather than blindly follow the Western countries. "Institutional and ideological deficiencies given away by political hegemony and frequent economic crises of the West are not in line with the historical trend and impede healthy development of human society. We should not blindly follow suit to observe indiscriminately Western political, economic and cultural ideology and use "Western culture centralism" as a standard for value judgment."[2]

The third trend of Chinese learning not only reflects on common crises in Western civilization and development of human beings, but also on special contradictions, prominent problems and all practical issues emerging in the process of China's modernization. "In front of severe conflicts and crises confronting all human beings in the 21st century, contradictions and problems concerning politics, economics, culture, systems, concepts, morals and beliefs that the Chinese nation encounters during the process of development, and also conflicts and integration with dominant Western economy, culture and technology, we should seek solutions from a holistic view and open mind to establish new Chinese learning combining the good part of both the ancient and modern civilization as well as both Chinese and Western civilization."[3]

---

[1] 王德峰. 2006. 依中国精神建设当代国学. 复旦学报(社会科学版), (5): 89-94.
[2] 李慎民. 2010-2-8. 建立马克思主义新国学观和新国学体系. 光明日报, 3.
[3] 张立文. 2007. 国学的度越与建构. 理论视野, (1): 25-28.

The Contours of Russian Modernization

Grigoriy Yu. Kanarsh

Institute of Philosophy, Russian Academy of Sciences

As is known, one of the most important consequences of globalization has been the emphasis of the national originality and socio-cultural specificity. In Russia, public opinion as well as in academic studies, the deviation from the principles of universalism and the emphasis of the priority of the values of the national culture over the universal human values are becoming more and more remarkable (Gorshkov, Krumm and Tikhhonova, 2010: 298-318). At the same time, a contradictory situation remains in Russian political science: There is still a sufficiently strong trend for the conceptualization of Russian socio-cultural experience, including the features of economy and politics in terms of the conception of catching-up development when the West (and particularly the USA) is a kind of cultural sample and Russia, on the contrary, is a "sample" of social maldevelopment. In a predictable manner, some scholars draw a conclusion that there is a lack of options for the movement on the way of Western civilization as well as that there is an exhaustiveness of the historical potential of socio-cultural traditionalism (including traditions of Soviet collectivism) (Suponitskaia, 2010; Rozov, 2011). As for economy, this refers to Western individualistic market (capitalistic) model as the only acceptable way.

Taking into account the newest trends both in the world socio-economic development (economic recovery in a number of non-Western countries from the last three decades of the 20th century to the early 21st century) and changes in the very theory of modernization [a transition from the conception of catching-up development to the theory of the national model of modernization (a term proposed by Valentina G. Fedotova)], this approach is considered to be on the whole inadequate for modern development objectives. In our opinion, there is much more potential in the conceptions emphasizing the role of socio-cultural specificity, not in a negative, but in a positive way (for instance, conceptions of the Russian world or even a disputable conception of a specific distinctive Russian civilization). Nonetheless, we should highlight that the question is not only about the good things and ignoring the bad ones in Russian social history. More likely, what is more adequate is an elaboration of a balanced view on the features of Russian socio-cultural development that takes into account both our "weaknesses" and our achievements to the full extent.

This paper will discuss the ways of socio-economic and political development of Russia by reference to the demands of the imperative of the national model of modernization. Following the ideas of leading Russian and foreign scholars (Harrison and Huntington, 2000; He and Lapin, 2011; Fedotova, 2016), we consider searching for the resources for the development within our own culture to be of high priority. Nevertheless, this search takes in account the similar experience of the Western and non-Western countries.

1. Ways for Socio-economic Modernization

The formation of modern economy is still the main challenge of the development of Russia. Local economists turn to this problem connecting it, in particular, to a very insufficient labour productivity in Russia (in comparison with corresponding indexes in the West, East and Southeast Asia). In such a case, they come to a conclusion that such labour productivity in the Soviet Union and then in Russia (a tenfold economic lag in comparison with Western countries) stems from not only old-fashioned means of production or the lack of modern methods of an effective labour management, but rather from the qualitative characteristics of the workers (Filippov, 2014: 547).

We see a way out of this situation in the change of the population's attitude to labour by means of various measures in accordance with the culturally centrist paradigm." The aim of the development of a rational way of thinking and aura of labour ethics among population is the most important task for Russia.... It is impossible to endorse a national program for the development of a positive attitude to labour in people." (Filippov, 2014: 548).

Accepting the opinion of this work's author in terms of the characteristics of labour in Russia, we raise doubts about the thesis that the development of labour ethics in the population and propaganda of the corresponding values may significantly improve the attitude to labour. Our point of view consists in that we should in some way come to terms with the fact of the lag in the socio-economic field, understand its causes and at the same time try to find some resources within our own culture. We argue that Russia has such resources (spiritual and axiological); the problem is that they are not sufficiently actualized.

From our point of view, among existing approaches to the understanding of Russian socio-cultural specificity, the conception of the Russian world has a significant positive potential. Within its framework, there are other estimations and accents regarding, in particular, the specific character of the economic mode and labour activity in Russia. For example, one of the works underscores that the idea that "the spirit of entrepreneurship" is largely alien to Russian nature is not more than a myth. Indeed, it is said that "any peasant household was basically an entrepreneurial activity" (Pavlovskaia, 2009: 270). Understandably, the character of this entrepreneurship was significantly different from business activity in the West as well as the very attitude to money and wealth in Russia (Pavlov, 2009: 270). However, such an approach, in our opinion, set an absolutely different perspective for the estimation of the historical past (and hence of the future) of Russia.

If we talk about the prospects of contemporary Russian economy then the dynamics of value priorities of the Russians is of a significant interest. It is revealed, inter alia, within the framework of quantitative ethno-social studies. According to the results of the studies conducted in the 1990s, it is possible to say that although Russia had a certain market potential, it belonged to the cultures of collectivist type and was closer to the Confucian type of economy [cf., the Anglo-Saxon Protestant type, the Protestant-Catholic European (Nureev, 2003: 179)]. But according to the analogous 2010 data, our country cannot be referred to such countries unequivocally; if we look at the "mental map of the world", Russia is in the periphery of Western civilization and it is more similar to Israel in comparison with all other countries (Gorshkov, Krumm and Tikhhonova, 2010: 290). From our point of view, the last fact provides evidence that Russia still continues to be a transitional society gravitating towards the West (and having had a chance to assimilate many Western values), but (as well as Israel) retaining a powerful traditionalist layer in its cultural basis.

However, in the light of the drastic changes in social reality and methodology for modernization studies, the last point is not considered as something negative. On the contrary, the existence of a strong traditionalist component in the national character and mentality allows us to say that there is an opportunity to add values and economic mechanisms typical for traditional (and Soviet Union) Russia to new "modernist" trends in economy. Nowadays reputed authors write about the necessity of a new industrialization of Russia (reindustrialization). However, it is conceived not just as a revival of industrial complex resembling the Soviet one, but as a development of new production industries, i.e. industrial facilities of a new type based on the high-end technologies within the scope of modern "knowledge economy" (Fedotova and Kolpakov, 2013). Today this idea is a "mainstream" of economic policy, but we can say that there are other alternatives (in particular, glaring civilization). Traditionally, one of such alternatives is the left-wing idea. Its contemporary essence consists in the revivification of the Soviet experience of industrial as well as of social and political policy, but is adjusted in relation to democratic values, human rights and freedoms (Grinberg, 2012). The idea suggested by conservative scholars of the Center for Dynamic Conservatism gets the essence. It implies a revival of such a tradition for Russia's economic and productive form as the Russian artel' (guild), and in general — of local cooperation based on traditional Russian principles of solidarity which obtain their potential not from the individualistic culture of the Western type, but from the organic world outlook typical for traditional society. It has emerged that the last one (social organicism as a world view and scientific methodology) is unexpectedly popular today (in Western countries as well) in the conditions of the new modernity (or post modernity) (Platonov, 2014).

By and large, the supplement of the newest capitalist modes of modernization ("productive industries") with forms genetically related to various collectivist principles of labour management (within the ambit of the left-wing and conservative models) will, in our opinion, allow overcoming the current downsides of the capitalist system, making economy more "social" and at the same time preserving the historical continuity. Such an approach fully conforms to the challenges of the national-oriented development path that the society faces today.

2. Searching for a National Model of Democracy

One of the key and currently accepted factors of successful modernization of Russian society is the attainment of social justice in diverse areas of public life. Social injustice in its different manifestations (an unfair socio-economic inequality, disparity in opportunities and inequality before the law) is still one of the main issues. That particular fact (as it was both in the 19th and the early 20th centuries) is the main cause that justice in Russia has been acquiring the status of the "national idea" as confirmed by almost all socio-logical studies today (Mareeva, 2013: 17).

In our opinion, the current situation in Russian society raises a pressing problem of the ways and methods of social transformations. As is well-known, since the beginning of the 2000s (when President Vladimir Putin came to power) they have been placing their bets on a variant of authoritative modernization when a "powerful state" implements reforms relying on the public support. This is a traditional Russian model and in the second half of the 1990s to the first half of the 2000s it seemed that it would "work". Especially since this model proposed by the authorities has turned out to be concordant with the etatist moods shared by the majority of the Russians and these moods continue to persist today. However, the logic of the development of Russia in the last one and half decade has led to the development of a model of state-oligarchic capitalism instead of a just society, i.e. there is a close bond between the ruling bureaucracy and big business capital, especially the deterioration of the situation in recent years challenge the adequacy of the model of authoritative modernization for the actual development objectives of Russia. Speaking more clearly, the current situation makes us think of how and in what way the existing model of state power in Russia can and must be corrected in order that its functioning will serve the purpose of the attainment of justice and commonwealth, but not only the interests of the governing class. Such problem statement leads us directly to the objectives of the building of democratic and civil society, the indispensable existence of which in Russian conditions must elaborate and correct the government's actions.

As researchers suppose yet another failure of the democratization of Russian society initiated at the turn of the 1980s-1990s was related not only to the rise of authoritarianism in Russian politics since the early 2000s, but had a deeper social roots. For example, in I. K. Pantin's opinion (Pantin, 2007), the problem mainly consisted in that in the 1990s democracy was being realized in Russia predominantly in the "culminant", Schumpeterian version (by the name of the prominent economist Joseph Schumpeter). This did not allow it to become the result of a conscious choice on the part of the population. In these conditions, Pantin argued, the only case scenario when democracy could have had a real chance for implementation is a overextension of democracy, which radically changes the notion of it not only as a form of the presence of representational regulatory bodies and a regular holding of alternative elections (the Schumpeterian model), but also as the democracy of daily pursuits and everyday participation that demand corresponding competencies and training (Pantin, 2007: 124).

Thus, we may talk about a special topicality of the model of participatory democracy represented in the West (first of all, in the USA) by a number of outstanding political scientists (Batalov, 2014: 458). Alternatively, they call this a model of "developing democracy", because it places the main emphasis not just on the development of democratic institutes, but on the formation of the citizen's competence and certain psychological qualities that are necessary for a full-fledged participation in public (political) life. It is essential that the very participatory model (of all theories of democracy existing at this stage in Western political science) keeps its normative (axiological) meaning. It is per se especially close to the left-wing and socio-democratic conceptions of justice.

Analyzing a number of expert evaluations, we may state that there is a considerably contradictory situation established in contemporary Russia. It predetermines the pathways for the development of democracy and civil society as a necessary precondition for the implementation of the idea of social justice. On the one hand, the state's actions are declared to be ineffective and inconsistent with the main principles of social justice; on the other hand, the state is still considered as the main actor of political and public life, i.e. almost all significant social initiatives unavoidably become marginal without its support. This brings us to the idea that today we should talk not so much as about reorganization, a radical transformation of the socio-political system towards its liberalization and democratization, but as about the traditional "extension" of Russia, the powerful state, and the personified model of power with real (not imitative) structures of democracy and civil society. This being said, we assume that in this respect the participatory model of democracy gives us an important landmark consisting in that real democratization of the political system must be primarily realized on the local level and only gradually "permeate" into the level of "big-league policy".

3. Conclusions

Thus, in Russia, the issue of socio-economic modernization rests not only upon the deficiency of mass labour motivations in comparison to those in the West and the East Asia, but not to a lesser extent upon the inadequacy of existing conceptions of catching-up development that remain almost dominating in Russian socio-political discourse. The solution may consist: firstly, of substitution of these simplified conceptions for more well-balanced (this allows changing both the vector of the socio-political development and, on the whole, the attitude to our own history and culture); secondly, of multi-lateral consideration of Russia's economic and socio-cultural realities, and orientation to those world patterns that demonstrate an effective resolution of socio-economic challenges given a similar difficulty and multistructurality of the society. Therewith, we should pay attention to the fact that in terms of its mental specificity Russia gravitates towards those countries where "national characters" have more realistic naturalness, kind-heartedness, and emotional warmth (France, Belgium, Hungary, Italy, Israel) rather than conceptual prudence and pragmatism (Anglo-Saxon countries, Germany). This, in turn, means that the national development models of these particular countries (and in particular Israel) may be of great interest for us from the practical point of view. An additional point is that while developing a modern economy and society it is necessary to take into consideration such a national and psychological feature of the Russians as their comparatively low capacity for regular and systematic labour, and consequently, the national need for labour stimulus of a special kind — ideologically inspiring, socially creative, and mobilizing (Andreev, 2002: 169-192). This, in its turn, makes the objective of building a socially just society insistent. A number of researchers consider the image of such a society as a new Big Goal, a sort of project of national development for contemporary generations of Russian people.

But if we talk about democracy and the extension of the sphere of public and political freedom as necessary preconditions of a new social creativity of the masses then, incredible as it may seem, the organizing and directing role of the state should remain here quite significant. Foremost, the fact is that the majority of the population of Russia are still as it was centuries ago not ready to live according to clear regulations of the law and what is the key prerequisite and the essential trait of democracy. It seems that this issue is only to a certain degree an outcome of the current paternalist system of domination; we think that its roots are in the natural characterological features of the Russians (Burno and Kanarsh, 2015).

Finally, one more important circumstance we should take into account in national development projects is the significant degree of regional differences and distinctiveness typical for Russia as well as for China. And we should keep our ears open to the opinion of those scholars who emphasize the practical impossibility and theoretical incorrectness of the approach that sensitizes us to the building of a unified national model of economic and socio-political development (Fedotova and Kolpakov, 2013). That is why the most important landmark of modernization should be the comprehension that both the features of economic systems and the peculiarities of civil society may and must differ in a substantial way depending on the specific character of this or that region.

In general, it appears that only this way — of consideration of the national and regional peculiarities — may be profitable for current processes of Russian modernization.

References

Andreev A L. 2002. Politicheskaia psikhologiia (Political Psychology). Moscow: Ves Mir.

Batalov E Y. 2014. Amerikanskaia politicheskaia mysl' XX veka (American Political Thought of the 20th Century). Moscow: Progress-Traditsiia.

Burno M E, Kanarsh G Yu. 2015. Psikhoterapiia zdorovykh, Psikhoterapiia Rossii: Prakticheskoe rukovodstvo po kharakterologicheskoi kreatologii (Psychotherapy of Healthy People, Psychotherapy of Russia: A Guide in Characterological Creatology). Moscow: Institut konsul'tirovaniia i sistemnykh reshenii (Institute for Consulting and System Solutions).

Fedotova V G. 2016. Modernizatsiia i kul'tura (Modernization and Culture). Moscow: Progress-Traditsiia.

Fedotova V G, Kolpakov V A. 2013. Ekonomika i demokratiia v proekte modernizatsii Rossii (Economy and Democracy in the Project of Russia's Modernization). Znanie. Ponimanie. Umenie, (1): 5.

Filippov V S. 2014. Sreda tekhnologii i puti razvitiia proizvodstvennogo kompleksa v Rossii (The Environment of Technology and Ways for the Development of Industrial Complex in Russia) In R S Grinberg, K A Babkin, A V Buzgalin (Eds.), Ekonomika dlia cheloveka»: sotsial'no-orientirovannoe razvitie na osnove progressa real'nogo sektora (Economy for the Man: A Socially Oriented Development Based on Progress of the Real Sector). Moscow: Kul'turnaia revoliutsiia.

Gorshkov M K, Krumm R, Tikhonova N E. 2010. Gotovo li rossiiskoe obshchestvo k modernizatsii? (Is Russian Society Ready for Modernization?). Moscow: Ves Mir.

Grinberg R S. 2012. Svoboda i spravedlivost': Rossiiskie soblazny lozhnogo vybora (Freedom and Justice: Russian Temptations of a False Choice). Moscow: INFRA-M.

Harrison L, Huntington S. 2000. Culture Matters: How Values Shape Human Progress. New York: Basic Books.

He C, Lapin N I. 2011. Obzornyi doklad o modernizatsii v mire i Kitae (2001-2010) (A Survey Report on Modernization in the World and in China (2001-2010)). Moscow: Ves Mir.

Mareeva S V. 2013. Spravedlivoe obshchestvo v predstavleniiakh rossiian (A Just Society as Viewed by the Russians). Obshchestvennye nauki i sovremennost', (5): 12.

Nureev R I. 2003. Ekonomicheskie sub'ekty postsovetskoi Rossii: institutsional'nyi analiz (Economic Subjects of Post-Soviet Russia: An Institutional Analysis). 2nd edn. Moscow: Moskovskii obshchestvennyi nauchnyi fond (Moscow Public Scientific Foundation).

Pantin I K. 2007. Vybor Rossii: kharakter peremen i dilemmy budushchego (A Choice of Russia: The Character of Changes and Dilemmas of the Future), Politicheskie issledovaniia, (4): 13.

Pavlovskaia A V. 2009. Russkii mir: kharakter, byt i nravy (The Russian World: Character, Everyday Life and Morals). Vol. 2. Moscow: Slovo.

Platonov O A. 2014. Artel' i artel'nyi chelovek (The Artel and the Artel Man). Moscow: Institut russkoi tsivilizatsii (Institute of Russian Civilization).

Rozov N S. 2011. Koleia i pereval: makrosotsiologicheskie osnovaniia strategii Rossii v XXI veke (The Furrow and Passover: Micro-sociological Foundations of Russia's Strategy in the 21st Century). Moscow: Rossiiskaia politicheskaia entsiklopediia.

Suponitskaia I M. 2010. Ravenstvo i svoboda, Rossiia i SShA: sravnenie system (Equality and Freedom, Russia and the USA: A Comparison of the Systems). Moscow: Rossiiskaia politicheskaia entsiklopediia.

Part Three

Dynamics and Paths of Modernization

Modernization of Russia: Contemporary Trends

Irina Eliseeva

Institute of Sociology, Russian Academy of Sciences

1. Introduction

Russian scholars actively discuss the problem of modernization of Russia (Krasin, 2011: 213). The entire variety of ideas and explanations of top-priority directions of developments can be generalized due to the acceptance of the need for the modernization process, the main trends of which are globalization, innovation and socialization.

Modernization is the multi-dimensional phenomenon that has the multi-level structure: the country, region, sphere of life, organization, social and professional group, household, individual person. Each of these levels more or less consciously develops its own trends. Altogether, they create a common vector of the state's development. The leading role in arguing for modernization, choice of priorities, etc. belongs to the strategical developments on the state scale. The recession of 2008-2009 vividly demonstrated the direct co-dependence of the countries and regions. The crisis challenged both liberal and Keynesian models of development. Probably, for the first time after the Great Depression of 1929-1933, practically all countries accomplished the global anti-crisis programs, having acknowledged the significance of government control. But even such programs do not decrease a high probability of the violation of the proper sequence of modernization stages, appearance of backwards movements, and proper sequence of reforms and counter-reforms. "Demystification of the state" is also reflected in the public choice theory. "Public choice destroyed a naive view, according to which, to justify the state intervention, this is merely enough to demonstrate that there are market faults that the ideal state can fix." (Lamieux, 2004: 29). "Market faults" are replaced with "state faults".

2. Globalization and Beyond

Global trends and potential scenarios of events concerning the global market development are precisely reviewed in the monography by the scholars from the Institute of World Economy and International Relations of RAS (Dynkin, 2011: 480).

Most countries share some significant features: having resources and using them effectively, and working towards the stable development, international cooperation, etc.

The globalization process preserves the urgency of the interrelation between global and local trends demonstrated by means of the influence of lack of stability of global oil rates and other commodities. The attempts were consolidated to coordinate activities of G7 countries with the most influential developing states — China, Russia, India and Brazil.

Neo-modernistic theory has become the foundation for the comprehension and explanation of the interrelation and inter-influence of globalization and localization.

This development can be effective, if the country pays attention not only to local problems and national specifics. As Karl Marx wrote, "Every nation can and must learn from others." (Marx, 2012) Here, let us mention the saying also used by the academician A. G. Aganbegyan: "A windjammer that does not know where to go cannot have a fair wind." (Aganbegyan, 2012: 106)

There is also the consolidation of the processes of capital transfers among countries, including direct foreign investments. The increasing role in this belongs to the global financial system. Transnational corporations continue to increase their influence too. Still, one can expect the consolidation of the exchange rate volatility, including yuan (starting from October 2016, according to the decision by IMF). For modernization of Russia, direct foreign investments are important primarily as the condition of "catching-up development", while for innovative development the import phase-out policy is more significant, based on the investments from local large-scale business.

The global role of Russia is defined by its huge territory (more than 17 million m^2), which combines Europe and Asia. The global significance in this sense is also determined by the special and ecological potential of Russia, using the natural mechanisms of water self-cleaning from pollutions, synthesis and destruction of organic substances, and support of global hydrologic circle. These mechanisms provide for air purity and water biodiversity, the importance of which grows within the social values system. Forests have the worldwide ecological significance (42% of the country's territory), as well as waterlogged lands and bogs (22%), which regenerates the atmosphere oxygen and provides the geochemical barriers against pollutants; Russia also has the biggest amount of undeveloped lands that are not involved into the economical processes; the same can be said about huge resources of fresh water, 60% of annual stream runoff consists of snowmelt runoff which is the most valuable part of water resources of the world, because the cryosphere of the Earth serves as its effective "cleaning". As Professor N. N. Kluiev (Institute of Geography of Russian Academy of Sciences) has written: "The territory of Russia is the compensation area of the global pollution and natural irregularities and the ecological 'donor' for many national ecosystems." (Kluiev, 2015: 580-581)

Local specifics stability becomes more and more obvious in the context of global changes. There is the growth of the interest towards studies of the influence of ethnic and cultural, religious, civil and other features of countries and regions on current social and economic processes. S. Eisenstadt was the first one who paid attention to the poly-cultural dimension of modernization and emphasized the unacceptance of a simple and strict universality of goal-oriented models of social organization for the entire mankind (Eisenstadt 2000). E. A. Pain emphasized the role of empirical studies and research for investigation of the complicated links between the global and local ways (Pain, 2009: 37-54). The extreme emphasis on universalization leads to weakening national identity, radicalization of controversies between formal and informal institutions. To the contrary, the emphasis only on cultural traditions paying no attention to the role of universal mechanisms of coordination will decrease the effectiveness of transformations, and their quality and speed of development.

3. Innovation

One of the specific features of the knowledge-based economy is the growth of cognitive factor. The constant inner work is being conducted to transform the structure of thinking and the perception of all new things which go through selection and cancelation of what does not seem to be productive; the discussion of discovered priorities takes place. More and more attention is paid to the dimension of cultural diversity, cognitive mapping and formation of the dominant logic for a certain kind of activity in some organizations, professional groups and regions.

The special role in providing for such unity belongs to the large-scale business that is able to invest into R&D, dissemination of new ideas and start-ups. The risk concerned with such investments is quite high: Of 10 start-ups, this is possible that only 1-2 will pay for expenses and even be advantageous, but still such risk is justified. In this sense, this is important here to consider knowledge and intuition to guess the spheres in which there is a reason to be involved, before they are taken by the opponents.

Modernization is essentially connected to the development of science and new technologies. There's a famous saying: "Sooner or later, any fundamental science becomes practical."

Science provides human consciousness with new horizons: new wide perspectives. For Russia now, the top-priority ones are the high-tech developments and projects: genetic engineering, biotechnologies, nanoproducts and nanotechnologies, application of renewable electric energy. The last one is especially urgent for Russia due to the wide area of Arctic, where it's necessary to develop decentralized energetic system. In the world, renewable energy sources provide for the production of 15% of electric energy; in Russia though, it is not more than 8%. Also, the urgent need for development of information technologies grows.

Research and developments require a new language and methods, which is obvious in, for instance, nanodevelopments.

In the context of the growing speed of differentiation of sciences, the thesis by V. I. Vernadsky stays important: "Science is one and single, for, even though the number of sciences grows constantly, and new sciences appear, they are all united into one scientific structure and cannot contradict to one another." (Vernadsky, 1988). This is remarkable that this thought was also expressed by M. Planck: "In fact, there is the single chain from physics and chemistry through biology and anthropology to social sciences." (Planck, 1909) This viewpoint is close to the idea of interdisciplinary approach in studies: the use of the social sciences methods in exact sciences and, to the contrary, the perception within exact sciences of the phenomena that do not directly associate with one particular class or group but having multiple dimensions and aspects and belonging to this or that class of things.

Priority growth of the knowledge economy is the catalyst for innovative development and modernization of all spheres. Today the vast majority of developing countries and countries with economies in transition, including Russia, have the share of this sector in their GDP around 15%

to 20% which is two times lower than in developed countries. In the coming 20-year period, this share will double in the lagging states. And in terms of science, information and biotechnology, maybe even triple. And, of course, developed countries are not standing still. So in 20 years the backlog will continue, albeit in a much smaller size.

Re-industrialization will receive general distribution in the forecast period, which means the translation of most branches of the industry to an entirely new, higher technological base. A striking example is that the look of the entire process of energy transfer is changed with the massive use of combined-cycle plants, heat pumps and other innovations with increasing efficiency in the production of electricity and heat from the current 30%-35% to 50% and higher. Modernization and innovation are related to a significant increase in the proportion of high-tech and knowledge-intensive industries in the composition of the gross output. In particular, the share of Asian developing countries in world production of high-tech products will increase from 25% to 40%. Especially the sphere of intellectual services will grow rapidly, the share of which in the formation of gross domestic product in 2030 will amount to 45% to 50% compared with 35% at present. As a part of the information-communication complex, the share of the service sector in it will rise to 75%.

In the forecast period, increasing distribution will receive a new sixth-generation technology, which is based on the pool of achievements (NBIC system — Nanotechnology, Biotechnology, Information technology and Cognitive science).

Productivity remains as a fundamental factor of modernization. It is especially important in human-nature relationships: extractive industries (Figure 1).

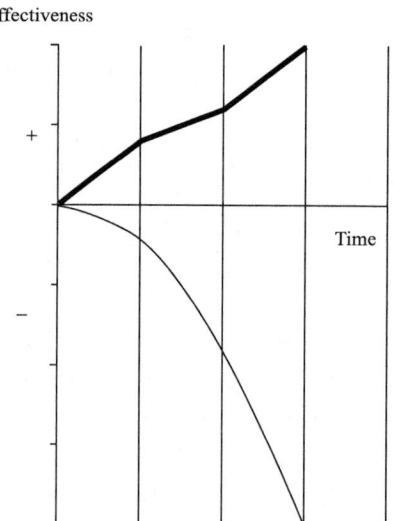

Figure 1 Effectiveness of Human Economic Activities (upper curve) and Nature Reaction (down curve)

Actual task for Russia is increasing the oil extraction ratio: this is equal to 30% (more than 40% in the USA, more than 50% in Norway).

Next important problems of Russian modernization are re-cultivation of land, forest conservation and supplementary works (cartography, meteorology, hydrology, observation points for contamination of surface water and land).

As A. G. Aganbegyan noted, the main branches of international specialization Russian should focus include the petrochemical industry, production of synthetic materials and deep wood processing, the development of which have the best condition in the world in Russia. Russia will develop energy- and electrical engineering, space industry, manufacture of helicopters and different types of airplanes (including cargo); expand the production of software products. There are sectors where we have accumulated considerable scientific, design and production capacity (Aganbegyan, 2012: 112).

4. Socialization

Modernization "from above" is replaced by the modernization "from the bottom". Finally, development depends from the human and his circle well-being, first of all, the families well-being. As to the local trends, the harmonic unity of the interests of the state-business-families-individuals is important. The main condition of this aim is the development of small and middle business in order to provide services for everyday life. Healthy business environment includes tax free periods for small business and decreasing of regulation.

Mega-trend of socialization characterizes a revolution in science, technology and economic development in the human side, in building human capital. This is understandable, because the human role in the socio-economic development increases, as a civilization is growing progressively. Health education, as is already the case in most developed countries, will gradually be put forward on the first place among the priorities in the standard of living. Today in the USA, for example, education expenditures represent 11% of GDP, with an average duration of education of the working population corresponding to the age of 15, and the health share of GDP reaching a record high of 16%. In the vast majority of developing countries and countries with economies in transition, including Russia, the proportion is three times less, the share of expenditure on science is 2 to 2.5 times lower in the lagging countries, the share of information technologies is 3 to 4 times lower and, unfortunately, much smaller share of biotechnology in GDP.

The largest global problem is the problem of poverty. In 2010, only 30% of the world's population lived in countries with a GDP exceeding 10 thousand dollars per capita (that means per capita income of 5 to 6 thousand dollars per year.) Per capita GDP in developed countries exceeds 30 thousand dollars on average and in most developed countries is close to 40 thousand dollars. Moreover, in these countries the proportion of fund for consumption in GDP is about 1 percentage point. So, the difference in income per capita is substantially higher than the difference in the level of economic development. By 2030, there will be fundamental changes: 70% of the world's population will live in countries with a per capita income of over 10 thousand dollars. Accordingly, the middle class will be from 40% to 50% of the population in the world. As a result, the difference in living standards between rich and poor on a global and regional level in the developed world will significantly reduce. The difference in income per capita of 10% of the well-off people in the developed countries today is 5 to 10 times (except the USA, where it reaches 14 times). But in most developing and transitioning countries, this difference is 15 to 20 times higher.

The improvement of people's livelihood inextricably goes hand in hand with democratization and expansion of the rights of citizens in the world. The process of the formation of civil society not only covers a larger number of countries, but gradually moves to the level of a global civil society. Globalization of the labor market across migration will take place.

Both internal and external migration processes function as a more significant factor of modernization. In Russia, much attention is paid to studies of external migration (immigration and emigration). However, the migration inside the country is more important — the amount of cases of moving from one place to another is 10 times bigger than the volume of the external migration flows. The internal migration influences the family structure and intergenerational connections of the population. The entire family can migrate, just as sometimes that happens for separate family members which can cause the split in the family or even divorce, or losing contacts with parents. From modernizational viewpoint, the migration effect is defined by the quality contents of migrants and the ability to adapt to changes: a new environment and a new lifestyle.

The common component of modernization is the growing speed of changes. The problem of managing changes arises on all levels: the state, region, branch, company, family and individual. This is important to predict the development of events and define the character of turning points and when they happen. The charity will be commonly occurring case. Its share in the redistribution of the social product will increase sharply. In the demographic sphere will continue, perhaps even amplify, a trend towards a reduction in fertility. The world's population will increase with a slow rate: instead of growth by 1% per year today, it will be about 0.5% after 2030. Even in developing countries, working-age population will stabilize. In connection to it unemployment can be reduced. Most countries of the world will enter into the second phase of the demography in its development, when mortality and fertility will be both reduced. Among developed countries, many of them will go into the third phase, when cutting the birth rate combined with a stabilization or increase in mortality due to aging population.

Transnationalization in people's lives will become more significant. This will contribute to universal coverage of Internet, thanks to which communities will unite globally basing on similarity of their interests. A characteristic feature of business development will be the growth of its social responsibility and the transition to corporate citizenship. Business partnerships with the state and civil society institutions will be considerably strengthened. The social entrepreneurship will be all the more important area of activity. The role of civil society will increase, especially in the areas of consumer, environmental and other social rights.

5. Conclusions

The concepts of "local" and "universal" lose their former antagonism. Today, local event could instantly become a global one. Modernization is a multiple and non-linear process. Big territory is Russia's main feature, for which Russia is supposed to promote the development of network communications (high-speed railways, highways, air traffic system and water traffic system). Important place in development of communications is kept by the international cooperation, first of all between the Russian Federation and the People's Republic of China.

The modernization is based on human capital development and cognitive factor (i.e. cognitive diversity). Russia, so as in China's modernization, is going across the development of inner market with intensive combination of different regions, urban and rural areas, different kinds of activities and industries. Russian modernization includes "catching-up development" and innovative development with the import replacement.

References

Aganbegyan A G. 2012. Fundamental work about world development. World Economy and International Relationships, (2): 106.

Dynkin A A. 2011. Strategical Global Forecast 2030. Moscow: Magister.

Eisenstadt S N. 2000. Multiple modernities. Daedalus, 129(1): 1-29.

Kluiev N N. 2015. Nature resources sphere of Russia and tendencies of changes. Herald of Russian Academy of Sciences, 85(7): 580-581.

Krasin Y A. 2011. Innovation Modernization of Russia. Moscow: Institute of Sociology, RAS.

Lamieux P. 2004. The public choice revolution. Regulation, 27(3): 29.

Marx K. 2012. Capital (1). Moscow: EKSMO.

Pain E A. 2009. Multicultural modernization: Evolution of theoretical views. Social Sciences and Modernity, (6): 37-54.

Planck M. 1909. Die Einheit des physikalischen Weltbildes (Vortrag, gehalten im Jahre 1908 in Leiden). Physikalische Zeitschrift, 10: 25.

Vernadsky V I. 1988. The Works on the History of Science in Russia. Moscow: Science.

How Did Romania Become Modern? A Southeastern European Experience During the 20th Century

Catalin Turliuc

Romanian Academy, Iasi Branch

1. Brief Preliminary Considerations

These processes of change were of great interest for social historians, sociologists and political scientists since the 1960s. It is clear now that the modernization school of development active in that period underlined that a linear, systematic and desired transition in the less developed countries from traditional values to modern Western like political and economic models is the key to progress and evolution. Modernization was characterized as a phased, gradual and irreversible progression toward relatively homogeneous forms of liberal democracy and free markets[1]. The critics of this vision emphasized that the basic assumptions were ethnocentric, highly abstract, over generalized and finally unethical. These criticisms were listened to and by the late 1970s and the early 1980s some of the basic tenets of the theory were modified in order to include an expanded methodology and historical analysis, a better correlation between internal and external factors, a more appropriate consideration towards local tradition, a diminished role of functionalist assumptions, a less biased approach, etc. In spite of these revisions, modernization was still strongly associated with notions like "the West and the rest" and the belief that development and evolution as exemplified in Western societies could and should be extended all over the world. Furthermore, modernization theory was identified by some of its ardent critics as an ideological weapon developed during the Cold War. One can easily find out that the modernization theories developed in the last decade of the 20th century

---

[1] So A. 1990. Social Change and Development: Modernization, Dependency, and World-System Theories. Newbury Park, CA: Sage; Shapiro I. 1997. Beyond modernization: Conflict, resolution in Central and Eastern Europe. Annals of the American Academy of Political and Social Science, 552(7): 15; Turliuc C. 2015. Modernization and regional development in the 20th century: The case of Romania. In A Martinelli, C Q He. (Eds.), Global Modernization Review: New Discoveries and Theories Revisited (pp. 101-113). Singapore: World Scientific Publishing.

are still keen to reinforce an existing nation state world system in which liberal democracy is held up as the ideal form of political organization and modern free market realities are the predictable future for the whole world. A new development in the framework of modernization theories was added in the early 1990s when the traditional top-down approach to modernization was supplemented by a bottom-up focus on institution building and the development of strong civil societies. Shmuel N. Eisenstadt's research program established in 1986 aimed at the re-systematization and the correction of the classical theory of modernity in the framework of multiple modernities paradigm. Thus, a new theory of modernity emerged. As Gerhard Preyer put it: "Multiple modernities is an alternative paradigm … . Multiple modernities does not assume that global modernity is derived from the West as a single pattern and does not describe a plurality of societal structures … . Modernization does not lead to a unification and convergence of social structures. Therefore, modernization is neither a way towards evolutionary universals, nor is it based on them. Multiple modernities is a structural change that continuously modifies belief systems and their implementation in a process of translation. There are many modernities, not only one single pattern of modernization."[1]

One should not forget the valuable contributions made by Daniel Bell[2], Jean-Francois Lyotard[3] and others to what was called post modernization theory. Anthony Giddens[4] epitomized the reflexive modernization theory[5] and Arthur P. J. Mol[6] as well as Joseph Huber[7] became known promoters of ecological modernization theory. It is worth mentioning the fact that the last decade of the 20th century proved to be a happy ground for many new and innovative approaches towards modernization and modernity. The whole conceptual apparatus put at work in order to refine the sociological and historical research was enriched and improved. Zygmunt Bauman wrote about liquid modernity as a chaotic continuation of the modernization process[8]. The theory of the second modernization[9] and the integrated modernization theory occurred at the dawn of the 21st century as a logical attempt to revive the important theme of modernization. Chuanqi He and his research group even transformed modernization into a kind of science[10]. One Romanian sociologist introduced recently what he called the concept of tendential modernity as a type of evolution of Romanian society towards principles and norms of modernity[11].

---

[1] Preyer G. 2007. Shmuel N. Eisenstadt: Multiple modernities — A paradigm of cultural and social evolution. ProtoSocialogy: An International Journal of Interdisciplinary Research, (24): 10.

[2] Bell D. 1973. The Coming of Post-industrial Society. New York: Basic Books.

[3] Lyotard J-F. 1984. The Postmodern Condition: A Report on Knowledge. Manchester: Manchester University Press.

[4] Giddens A. 1991. The Consequences of Modernity. Cambridge: Polity Press.

[5] An interesting overview is offered by Beck U, Bonns W, Lau C. 2003. The theory of reflexive modernization. Problematic, Hypotheses and Research Programme. Theory, Culture & Society, 20(1): 1-33.

[6] Mol A P J. 2001. Globalization and Environmental Reform: The Ecological Modernization of the Global Economy. Cambridge: MIT Press.

[7] Huber J. 1985. Die Regenbogengesellschaft: Okologie und Sozialpolitik. Fischer Verlag: Frakfurt am Main.

[8] Bauman Z. 2000. Liquid Modernity. Cambridge: Polity Press.

[9] Ulrich Beck coined the term of the second modernity. Beck U. 1996. The Reinvention of Politics: Rethinking Modernity in the Global Social Order. Cambridge: Polity Press.

[10] He C Q. 2012. Modernization Science. The Principles and Methods of National Advancement. New York: Springer.

[11] Schifirnet C. 2009. Modernitatea tendențială. Sociologie Românească, 7(4): 80-97. He already coined the term in 2007 in one of his books titled Formele fără fond un brand românesc.

When in the late 1990s the social change model became out-fashioned and a boom was registered by cultural history and its sub domains, an interesting fact occurred: the historians lost a significant number of conceptual tools in order to explain the social change. Concepts like modernity, tradition, diffusion, adaptation, development, dependency, centre-periphery, unequal exchange, etc. were put in question in new forms and historians who usually ask questions, select and organize evidence and compose accounts were affected being deprived of such strong conceptual references. The normative connotations of ideas like civilized, modern, progress, etc. were put aside favouring new interpretation generated by cultural history. Nowadays, it looks to me that a new historiographical approach towards the concepts enumerated above through the lenses of modernization science will reopen a fertile field of research.

One crucial aspect of the modernization process in Romania, Central and Southeastern Europe and, of course, not only in these areas, was the relationship among national ideology (nationalism), the state and modernization[1]. A quick perusal of the literature concerned with these topics proves that historians and social scientists have taken the historical inevitability of the nation state and nationalism as fundamental prerequisites for the modernization process. The nation state was seen as the single valid option to the agrarian based realities of the "ancien regime". A mature national identity was considered indispensable to modern man's social and moral well-being. To many the coronation of the modernization process was embedded in the establishment of a powerful, well articulated nation state. Moreover, in connection with this way of thinking the modernization process was considered to be deterministic rather than probabilistic.

2. Periodization

During the 20th century Romania, as the case with other countries located in the Central and Southeastern parts of Europe (Hungary, Bulgaria, Czechoslovakia, Yugoslavia, Greece, Poland, etc.), suffered great historical and territorial transformations accompanied by a plethora of significant mutations. A historical periodization of the 20th century concerning the topic of the modernization process in Romania (largely valid as well for the rest of the countries in the region) could be the following: 1) the period from the beginning of the century and up to the end of the World War I (1900-1918); 2) the interwar period (1918-1939); 3) the period of one-party regimes (1940-1989) and 4) the period of one-party to democracy and free market economy (1989-2000). The above mentioned periodization was made according to the main historical events and evolutions which occurred in this area and with the obvious lines of fracture which could be easily noticed.

2.1 Before the World War I

Before the World War I Romania ("Old Kingdom") was an independent state (137.903 km² and 7.5 million inhabitants) surrounded by three great continental empires (Ottoman, Russian-Czarist and Austria-Hungary) with a constitutional monarchic regime, liberal and on the

---

[1] Janos A. 2000. East Central Europe in the Modern World: The Politics of the Borderlands from Pre- to Post-communism. Stanford: Stanford University Press.

path of democratic changes according to Spirit of the Age (Zeitgeist) and the models offered by the Western Powers (mainly France)[1]. Being an "island of stability" during the late 19th century, Romania became a sub-regional power after the Balkan Wars (1912-1913). Its economy was largely based on agriculture, forestry and oil industry (almost 2 million tonnes). The Romanian GDP represented 0.8% from world economy not far behind from Dutch or Austrian economies. The GDP per capita was almost half of the British one (the highest in Europe at the dawn of the World War I) and well above the Serbian, Bulgarian or Greek ones. In 1913, the GDP per capita was 67% of the European average[2]. The Romanian currency (Leu) was strong (1 Leu was the equivalent of 1 French Franc) and the country never experienced inflation. The commercial balance was a positive one with a surplus representing 5% of the GDP. Romania was often called "Belgium of the Orient" or "European Japan" and its capital city Bucharest was nicknamed "Little Paris". 12% of the population was occupied in industry and the rhythm of industrial development was significantly higher compared with the neighbouring countries and even with the rest of Europe between 1900 and 1914[3]. By 1915, the total number of industrial units was 1.149 and the value of their production increased 2.3 times more than in 1900[4]. The Romanian economy was steadily drawn into the international commercial and financial system as Europeans gradually discovered the value of Romanian agricultural goods and raw materials, and, by the outbreak of the World War I, many branches of the Romanian economy were dependent on European banking and commercial interests[5]. These economic data should be accompanied by social indicators such as life span, infant mortality and literacy, and the development of human capital. In this respect, Romania was still at the periphery of Europe.

The main power behind the modernization process was the state and its establishment[6]. While in the Western Europe modernizing change has run its course as an organic "natural" process, issuing from the transformations in the realm of economy and society, in Romania and the countries of its area the driving force was, at least in the beginning, the desire to emulate and sometimes imitate the Western culture and civilization. Once the political superstructure of Western type was put in place in evident absence of corresponding economic and social foundations, this generated a reality in which the above mentioned political structure assigned the role of the main instrument of change. The obvious result was the ascendancy of the state over all aspects of social life and numerous and powerful bureaucracies which became an interest group in its own right[7]. This reality would last for the decades to come. Another relevant aspect

---

[1] See more details in Hitchins K. 2014. A Concise History of Romania. Cambridge: Cambridge University Press. For a comparative view regarding the economic evolution in Southeast Europe, see John R L, Marvin R J. 1982. Balkan Economic History, 1550-1950: From Imperial Borderlands to Developing Nations. Bloomington: Indiana University Press.

[2] See for more data Bairoch P. 1997. Victoires et déboires: Histoire économique et sociale du monde du XVIe siècle á nos jours. Vol. 3. Paris: Gallimard.

[3] All the relevant economic data could be found in Axenciuc V. 1996. Evoluția economică a României: Cercetări statistico-istorice 1859-1947, Vol. 1 Industria, Vol. 2, Agricultura, București: Editura Academiei Române.

[4] Agrigoroaiei I, Cristian V , Iacob Gh. 1989. România de la independență la Marea Unire. Cuza Iași: Universitatea Al I.

[5] Hitchins K. 2014. A Concise History of Romania. Cambridge: Cambridge University Press: 4.

[6] See Lazăr M. 2002. Paradoxuri ale modernizării. Elemente pentru o sociologie a elitelor culturale românești, Editura Limes: Cluj-Napoca.

[7] An interesting discussion of this topic could be found in Rizescu V. 2013. Ideology, Nation and Modernization. Romanian Developments in Theoretical Frameworks. Bucuresti: Editura Universitatii.

was the fact the internal social and economic integration was not so successful as in other European countries. By the beginning of the 20th century, adaptation (Westernization) gradually gave way to innovation, as Romanian scholars and social thinkers helped to shape European values[①]. The political system in Romania during this period was dominated by two main political parties with significant contradictory visions regarding the general development process of the country, namely Liberals and Conservatives. The Liberals, who generally prevailed, were fierce promoters of modernization through protectionist policies aiming at a strong movement towards industrialization, development and encouragement of the national financial capital, building a solid national commercial network and infrastructure, reforming agriculture through agrarian reforms, granting further political rights in order to develop democracy, etc. The absence of a strong entrepreneurial bourgeoisie doubled by a notable commitment to the national cause, namely a solid nation state, also shared by other political groups gave birth to a special variety of liberalism in which state bureaucracy played a central role. The Conservatives, more traditionalists, promoted, generally speaking, the interests and various privileges of large estates holders interested in the development of agriculture without or severely limited agrarian reforms. They did not agree with rapid changes in economy and social realities in spite of the fact that they wanted to be part of Europe and they did not disapprove of the general progress of the society. Also, they were more open to cooperation with the foreign capital and less inclined towards any reforms which could lead to the democratization of the society as seen in certain Western European societies. Among the "modernizers" before the World War I, one can cite important names of Romanian political thinkers of liberal orientation like Mihail Kogălniceanu, A. D. Xenopol, P. S. Aurelian, Ion I. C. Brătianu, and so on. Other important political figures and also founders of a different doctrine more reluctant towards rapid Western like modernization were Petre P. Carp, Titu Maiorescu and Theodor Rosetti. One cannot forget the theoretical contributions developed by such "exotic" trends like *semănătorism*[②] (anti-modern in its essence) or *poporanism*[③]. The socialists[④] were also present, to a smaller degree, in the general debate concerning the modernization of the country and society. The theory of "form without substance" elaborated in the second part of the 19th century by Titu Maiorescu still epitomized the debate around modernization process in Romania in the first decades of the 20th century. One noticeable feature of this period and not only (somehow it became a quite constant reality) was the fact that between the main body of modernizing ideas and the degree to which those ideas and principles were put in practice was a great difference. It seems like the modernization process was a never ending story very often interrupted by various historical events or by the loss of the will to fully implement them.

---

① Turliuc C. 2008. Modernization and/or Westernization in Romania during the late 19th century and the early 20th century. Transylvanian Review, 17(1): 3-11.
② Nicolae Iorga was the prominent figure representing this trend.
③ Constantin Stere was one of the leading personalities.
④ I have to mention here the name of Constantin Dobrogeanu Gherea.

2.2 The Interwar Period (1918-1939)

The World War I was a major event which changed the face of the world and induced through its consequences a plethora of important changes deeply affected the countries and societies of Central and Eastern Europe. The great empires disappeared and new nation states emerged on their ruins (Hungary, Poland and Czechoslovakia); others like Romania or Yugoslavia achieved territorial unity through union with provinces former occupied by neighbouring empires. By the end of 1918, Romania doubled its size and population (295.641 km² and 15.5 million inhabitants). Romania represented 2.52% of the surface of the continent (the tenth place among 28 countries) and 3.60% of the continent population (the eighth place)[1]. A radical agrarian (land) reform took place in the aftermath of the World War I (1918-1921), the most comprehensive in all Europe (6 million hectares were redistributed and 1.4 million peasant families were allotted), the universal vote was introduced and a new democratic Constitution was adopted (1923). By 1938, the Romanian economy could be characterized as an agrarian-industrial one with certain advanced domains like the oil industry (8.7 million tonnes). By 1940, Romania was far and away Europe's leading oil producer excluding the USSR. Much Romanian industry was in the field of production of raw materials (timber, coal, various metals and minerals) which were mainly exported. Foreign investment in industry was very heavy and the participation of foreigners in the domestic economy was higher in Romania than anywhere else in the area[2]. The Romanian industry provided in 1938 78.6% of the internal consumption of industrial goods[3]. By the end of the period, the industrial production of Romania was just 5% of the industrial production of Great Britain. In spite of these realities, during interwar period, Romania faced a lower rate of general development of the economy and society compared with the European average. The growth of GDP per capita was in Romania 1.1% yearly compared with 2%, the European average[4]. The dramatic consequences of the World War I (far more serious than in other cases), the huge effort in order to unify the whole country and the Great Depression from 1929 up to 1933 seriously affected the growth potential. The financial stability was lost (the gold reserve of the National Bank — 105 tonnes of fine gold — was deposited in Moscow during the World War I and was never retrieved), the level of inflation grew almost constantly and the "price scissors" (the ever growing gap between the prices of industrial goods compared with agricultural ones) seriously affected the economic development. The growth of the agrarian sector of the economy was deeply affected by internal as well as by external factors. In the first category, one can easily identify the low technological level used in this domain due to the lack of investments coupled with the economic effects of the land reform (the massive fragmentation of agricultural plots). Concerning the external factor, it was the general context of the unfavourable conditions of the global agricultural market (the price of cereals fell down after 1928 up to 1934). As it is widely known, Romania was a major exporting country for agricultural products. During the interwar period, Romania lagged behind Hungary or Czechoslovakia while still maintaining a

---

[1] Agrigoroaiei I. 2015. România interbelică. Iași: Demiurg: 50.
[2] Walters E G. 1988. The Other Europe: Eastern Europe to 1945. New York: Syracuse University Press: 222.
[3] Walters E G. 1988. The Other Europe: Eastern Europe to 1945. New York: Syracuse University Press: 14.
[4] Bogdan M. 2010. România și Europa. Acumularea decalajelor economice (1500-2010). Iași: Editura Polirom: 216.

superior position compared with Yugoslavia, Bulgaria or other Southeastern European countries. In terms of national income per capita, in 1938, Romania was behind Czechoslovakia, Hungary and Poland, at a similar level with Greece, and in front of Bulgaria and Yugoslavia[①]. In 1939, the national income was produced at a rate of 34.5% in industry and 39.4% in agriculture and the rest in other economic sectors. This general image of the economic development of the country reveals the fact that the gaps in terms of development and implicitly modernization widened compared with other European states. The social indicators during this period demonstrate a serious backwardness which placed Romania at the bottom of European ranking. The economic and social polarization was more evident in Romania as it was in its neighbouring countries.

The modernization process in the interwar Romania was one of the major concerns of the political figures and also of an important group of scholars. More and more significant actors of the social and political scene were concerned with the problem of economic and social advancement of the Romanian society. Of course, the new realities occurred after the World War I generated new and more solid approaches toward modernization process. Besides, the powerful National Liberal Party (centre-right, the main exponent of the bourgeoisie and industrial and financial elites) continued its domination in the Romanian political life; new parties and doctrines emerged as a consequence of the electoral reform and the ongoing democratic transformation of the political scene as it was set by the 1923 Constitution. The second important party in Romania between the two world wars was the National Peasant Party (centre-left, established in 1926) which promoted especially the interests of peasantry, small bourgeoisie and intellectuals. The left wing parties socialist, social-democratic and communist resulted from the split of the labour movement were less influential and significant in terms of power on the political scene and doctrinal debates. The right-wing parties gradually became significant by the end of the interwar period according to the expanded influence of the fascist movements on the European scene and were keen promoters of an exacerbated economic nationalism embedded in an organic corporatist vision. According to the relevance for my topic, I shall further discuss the neoliberal and peasantist approaches to modernization.

The main representatives of liberal or neoliberal current were V. Brătianu, St. Zeletin, I. N. Angelescu, Gh. Taşcă, I. G. Duca, M. Manoilescu, D. (Mitiţă) Constantinescu. All of them, in spite of certain differences, were strong supporters of the private property as the basis of the freedom of economic actions, of the idea of the self-development based on the national forces and focused on the industry, of the promotion of the local capital. They were advocates of state intervention in the development of economy and society. Industrialization was, in their opinion, the safest and only way for the development of the national economy as a whole and to recover the gap which separated Romania from the developed countries in the West. They pointed out that, for Romania, industrialization was a form required by the qualitative evolution of society at a certain stage of development; industry was the only branch of the national economy which could put best value to natural and human resources; industry had higher productivity compared with other branches of national economy; investments in industry were most profitable and ultimately leading to increased wealth of the nation; export of agricultural products could not cover the

---

① Dobre Gh. 1996. Economia României în context European—1938: Editura Fundaţiei Ştiinţifice. Bucureşti: Memoria Oeconomica: 138.

value of imports of industrial products; a strong national industry contributed to an increase in the trade balance of the country[①]. They advocated that the industry growth had to rely on domestic capital and industrialization should be achieved through big capitalist industry which was more stable and profitable than the small industry. They also favoured the heavy industry which could provide machinery and spare parts for all other industries. In agriculture, they favoured the large and medium sized properties and modern intensive farming. They believed that the relation with foreign capital should be limited in what concerns its penetration in the Romanian economy. In other words, local capital must be protected and favoured. One should not forget that economic nationalism was a well-represented attitude in the whole Europe during the interwar years. The great majority of neoliberals who claimed their origins from the old liberals were the promoters of the idea that modernization was not possible without industrialization and the latter was not possible without a protectionist policy. Regarding culture, they believed that educational system should be developed and rationalization of the culture as a must. The all encompassing slogan of the National Liberal Party was "By ourselves".

The National Peasant Party expressed a doctrine which rejected both liberal and socialist ideas. Peasant doctrine was built around democratic ideals and the idea that peasantry is a homogenous social class, fundamental for Romanian society, with specific interests different from the big industrial and financial bourgeoisie and also different from industrial proletariat. The main representatives of this current were Virgil Madgearu and Gheorghe Zane. While the neoliberals favoured state interventionism, National Peasant thinkers favoured state dirigisme. Peasantism prioritized agriculture in the national economy, leaving industry in the background and subordinating it to agriculture. If the neoliberals sustained the development of the industry according to necessity, peasants would favour the development of industry according to existing realities. As a consequence, they disapproved the policy of protecting domestic industry and were adepts of an open-gate policy. Open-gate policy refers also to the foreign capital. In what concerned land ownership, Peasantism advocated small and medium farms organized in co-operatives.

Many of the ideas developed in the interwar period by liberals (neoliberals) and representatives of Peasantism were implemented through legislative measures. It is worth mentioning that the National Liberal Party was favoured by both internal and external contexts and the legacy of liberal modernization policy was more consistent and enduring. Even in the next historical period their example was somehow followed without mentioning the roots of this attitude. By the end of the interwar period, the character of the national economy shifted to an agrarian-industrial one.

2.3 The Age of One-Party Regimes (1940-1989)

From 1940 to 1989 with a small break between 1944 to 1947, Romania was governed by one-party regimes of different strain (extreme right-wing and extreme left-wing) but with an almost similar attitude towards modernization. During the World War II, the one-party regime was keen to mobilize the whole potential of the country in order to sustain the war effort directed primarily to regain the lost territories (in the summer of 1940, Romania lost to its neighbours more

---

[①] Arcadian N P. 1936. Industrializarea României: Studiu evolutiv-istoric, economic și juridic. Bucuresti: Imprimeria națională, Ediția a II a.

than one third of territory and population), and afterwards to continue the crusade against bolshevism. When Romania signed the peace treaty which put an end to the World War II for this country, its territory was reduced to 238.391 km² (80.5% of what was the country's surface in 1938) with a population of approximately 15.9 million, compared with 20 million in 1938. The estimated cost of Romania's participation in the World War II was 3.7 billion US dollars (1938 value)[①]. The national income per capita dropped from 76 US dollars in 1938 to 51 US dollars in 1947. The war efforts and subsequent Soviet occupation took a heavy toll for the Romanian economy.

In the aftermath of the World War II and after the communist takeover, the new regime was ideologically driven to develop the country according to the imposed Soviet model. In the mid-1960s, Romania was transformed in what we can call a "development dictatorship". Due to its heritage and sometime disastrous economic policies, Romania remained by the end of the communist regime at the bottom of the list of the socialist countries in terms of development and modernization. Of course a plethora of explanations were formulated in order to explain this peculiar situation of the country starting with the characteristics of the Romanian socialist regime and its social and economic policies and ending with external factors generated by the international economic scene. Decisions like the complete socialist transformation of the agricultural sector (from the 1950s to the early 1960s), a pro-natalist policy (1967), forced urbanization (from the 1960s to the 1980s) or the payment of all foreign debts of the country (1980s), etc. can be listed as peculiarities of the policies enforced in Romania during the communist regime. Due to obvious limitation of the present paper, I shall pinpoint few of the aspects concerning modernization during this troubled period.

The modernization process during the communist rule in Romania was obviously ideologically driven and the economy was hyper-centralized with strict planning at every five years. Romania registered a forced industrialization and heavy investment in certain fields of its economy. The end result of this kind of policy was a constant growth of industrial production. By 1989, the value of industrial production had been 65 times higher than that in 1938 and 44 times higher than that in 1950[②]. In agriculture, the process of "socialist transformation" through politically enforced measures was disastrous with economic and social consequences hard to assess. In 1989, 27.9% of the population worked in this economic field compared with 74.3% in 1950. The modernization process in agriculture was not favoured by the regime, compared with industry, as one can find out checking the investment policy in this domain. It is certain that Romanian agriculture was not perceived as a valuable tool in order to overcome the differences which separated Romanian economy from the economies of the developed countries. During this period, a lopsided balance between consumption and investment became obvious. All successful developing economies devote part of their current income to investment rather than consumption, so to expand their future ability to consume. That was the Romanian case beginning with the 1960s and up to late 1980s of the 20th century when almost 33% of the GDP was invested each year in the national economy. This feature ensured high rates of GDP growth, sometimes expressed with double digit figures. This kind of economic politics is very difficult to

---

① Mureşan M, Mureşan D. 1998. Istoria economiei. Bucureşti: Editura Economică: 323.

② Bogdan M. 2010. România şi Europa. Aulmularea decalajelor economice (1500-2010). Iaşi: Editura Polirom: 341.

be sustained for long periods (more than several decades) and generates social reactions. The policy of urbanization with all its consequences was noticeable and with spectacular results. In 1989, 53.2% of the population was urbanized compared with 23.4% in 1948. The number of towns grew from 152 in 1948 to 262 in 1989[1]. Some of the social indicators showed certain signs of improvement during socialist period, but in spite of these data, Romania still lagged behind many of its neighbours and the great majority of the European countries. According to the index of human development, Romania was at the bottom of the list of the European states. A general overview of Romania's modernization process as it was planned by the Romanian Communist Party and by its leader Nicolae Ceausescu in the 1970s and 1980s under the title "Programme of the building of a multilateral developed socialist society" show to any interested observer the dark picture of a failed attempt to overcome the gap between Romania and the developed economies and societies of the world. The available statistical data shows that in 1938. the gap in national income per capita between European average and Romania was 2.9 to 1, in 1947, 3.2 to 1 and in 1989, 3.5 to 1[2]. It is clear that the gap deepened in time and various modernization policies failed in their objective to overcome the gap between Romania and the developed countries in the world.

2.4 Post 1989

After the 1989 Romanian Revolution, a new path toward modernization was followed. The main objectives of the transition period were those of achieving a democratic political order, a functional free market economy, a modern society through a sustainable development which will allow Romania to become a fully fledged member of the EU and NATO. The huge transformations in all fields of political, economic, social and cultural life as well as the complicated evolutions in the geopolitics of the region, the dramatic changes in the international arena, the German reunification, the dissolution of the USSR, the violent break-up of Yugoslavia, the "velvet" divorce in Czechoslovakia and so on generated a new environment and new approaches toward modernization policies in the whole region including Romania. The return to private property and the implementation of human rights in the framework of a liberal democratic constitution triggered massive changes in society. One of the main features of the economic evolution in the last decade of the 20th century was the accumulation of huge disequilibrium due to deindustrialization, privatization scheme, exposure to the world economic competition and the rules of the free market economy. Land (agrarian) reform brought initially chaos in the agricultural sector. New economic elites were rising and the polarization of the society was accentuated. One can resume the economic situation by calling this decade one of transitional crises. The general situation of the country and of course of the economy started to improve beginning with 1999 when Romania entered the pre-accession phase in the EU. Up to 2008 when the whole world entered a new crisis, Romania registered a sound rate of growth compared with the previous period and even with some other states. Since the accession of Romania in the EU (2007), the modernization path was defined by the process of economic and social integration required by the newly acquired membership.

---

[1] Bogdan M. 2010. România și Europa. Acumularea decalajelor economice (1500-2010). Iași: Editura Polirom: 350.
[2] Bogdan M. 2010. România și Europa. Acumularea decalajelor economice (1500-2010). Iași: Editura Polirom: 331.

In 2015, the population of Romania numbered 19.8 million and the GDP per capita was 7,800 Euros (155 billion euros in total) and was the 59th in the world according to GDP per capita. The GDP value of Romania represented 0.32% of the world economy as reported by World Bank in 2014. Also Romania is the 50th largest export economy in the world and the 32nd most complex economy according to Economic Complexity Index published by MIT.

3. Final Remarks and Conclusions

Starting from the premise that what I have presented so far can suggest a possible outline of the problems connected with modernization in Romania in the 20th century and being aware that this subject deserves to be investigated more thoroughly and at length, I stress on several conclusions.

The major changes relevant for any observer in the Romanian society during 20th century, as well as in the case of other nation states in the same geopolitical area, were the results of the modernization process.

Various modernization theories developed a conceptual apparatus which hardly can cover the complexity of the processes specific to modernization and modernity. The rise of modernization science could be a possible solution to this problem.

The main sources of the modernization process in Romania were rather institutional than economic. The modern framework of Romanian society and of the Romanian state placed the state on a position of centrality which was seen as a sine qua non prerequisite of the general development.

It is a reality that in spite of a large spectrum of modernizing policies implemented over well one century, Romania diminished its status in the world economy according to statistical data and could not overcome the gap between itself and the developed countries of the world. A plausible explanation beside the general international context which was in general adverse regarding Romanian interests of development could be the fact that political instability and the rapid succession of various political regimes impeded on the resilience of modernizing measures adopted by the successive ruling powers. Of course, no one can neglect the lack of coherence of modernizing policies formulated during this period.

It is obvious that none of the modernization programs formulated during the 20th century by politicians or scholars was not fully implemented due to the lack of adequate means or because of various unfavorable historical contexts.

Since the beginning of the 21st century, Romania entered a new phase of modernization in the general framework offered by the EU, hence a big part of its experience and historical tradition in this field become obsolete. Thus, the normative transfer became an important tool for the modernization process in Romania.

Specifics and Differentiation of the Balance of Modernization Processes in Russian Regions[1]

Lastochkina Mariia

Institute of Social-Economic Development of Territories,
Russian Academy of Sciences

Modernization is defined as a socio-cultural process determining the transfer of traditional society into industrialized. However, it includes not only a technological vector of this direction, but also an innovative one. Since the times of E. Durkheim[2], M. Weber[3], modernization has been regarded as changes leading to innovation, cognitive development of society, not just to division of labor, technical progress and increased economic returns.

Since the moment the modernization theory has been firmly rooted in the paradigm of scientific knowledge, the scientists interested in socio-economic, political and socio-cultural issues use the integral approach to the interpretation of phenomena and patterns of social development. This integrated, interdisciplinary approach unites representatives of various disciplines and scientific fields, especially sociology, economics, ethnology, political science, social psychology, ecology and some others, in shared research efforts that ultimately lead to high authority of the modernization theory in modern social and humanitarian spheres.

Modernization is associated with a complex set of changes — social, economic, political, etc., which inevitably occur in the society undergoing the transition from the traditional to the modern type. The jump from one stage of development to another is significantly different and more highly organized.

In every sphere of society, there are different indicators and criteria of modernization[4]. In the social sphere, modernization involves the following series of objective processes. Sociology uses not a group of people united by a number of criteria, but a separate individual as the main subject

---

[1] The research is performed with the financial support of RFH. Project "Socio-Cultural Determinants of Modernization Development of Russia: Methods of Measurement and Analysis of Causal Dependencies" No. 15-02-00482.

[2] Durkheim E. 1991. The Division of Labor in Society. Moscow: The Sociological Method.

[3] Zarubina N N. 1998. Socio-Cultural Factors of Economic Development: Max Weber and Contemporary Modernization Theories. St. Petersburg: RGGI: 288.

[4] Ermakhanova S A. 2009. Development of ideas about socio-cultural aspects of modernization in Sociology. Humanities in Siberia, (1): 55-59.

of social life and the object of analysis. There is another example: change in the role of the family, which individual functions are transferred to social institutions and kinship ties and highly valued in traditional societies, fade into the background and become irrelevant in the modern world. Modernization is connected with qualitative changes in the demographic sphere, resulting in the decrease in fertility and mortality, rise in life expectancy, growth of the urban population and decline in rural.

In economics, modernization processes are associated with revolutionary changes in economic activity and the change in economic structures of countries. Large-scale and rapid development of technologies, especially information, causes changes in the structure of economic activity, in which secondary and tertiary sectors become increasingly important and the system of labor division deepens and becomes complicated.

Finally, modernization also affects political aspects of the existence of countries, which are increasingly centralizing, uniting into supranational economic and political blocs. Within states there is a sustained trend towards separation of powers, expansion of the role and functions of democratic institutions.

What are the problems of modernization in the Russian Federation (RF)? First, it is the outflow of intelligent layer of the society from the country. Those who have stayed here are deprived of sufficient financing. There is a reduction in the number of persons with higher qualification, high-tech developments, and a decline in R&D volumes. Second, it is the gap among process flows, science and industry. A large share of high-tech products is imported from abroad due to the lag in the organization of the scientific and technical bases for social reorientation of the economy. Third, it is the conservation of primary export and the offshore schemes of business of many Russian companies. Fourth, it is the authorities' corruption. Fifth, it is the lack of socio-cultural potential of the population and its use as capital[1].

Let us consider the analysis of modernization processes in Russian regions. As for the research methods we choose the index approach developed by the China Center for Modernization Research, CAS, which was used to measure modernization indices of 130 world countries[2] and adapted by the Department of Social Philosophy, Institute of Philosophy, RAS[3].

Since the calculation of the secondary modernization index (SMI) is based on 4 sub-indices: knowledge innovation (KII), knowledge translation (KTI), life quality (LQI) and economy quality (EQI). The analysis of these components will help understand the factors hampering and stimulating the dynamics of secondary modernization. The imbalance of secondary modernization processes was characteristic of all RF regions for 12 years (2000-2012). Along with the growth of the SMI there was an increase in the gap from its constituents, especially the sub-indices of knowledge translation (positive growth effect) and economy quality (insufficient growth that contributes to the imbalance). The number of areas with the insufficient growth in the economic component of industrial modernization increased by one and a half times (if in 2000

---

[1] Lapin N I. 2015. Distance between modernization of macro-regions and stages of integrating modernization of Russia. Sotsis (Social Studies), (1): 45-55.

[2] He C Q. 2011. China Modernization Report Outlook (2001-2010): Translated from English. Under general editorship of N. I Lapin. Moscow: Ves Mir: 256.

[3] Lapin N I. Belyaeva L A. 2013. Problems of Socio-Cultural Modernization of Russian Regions. Compiled. Moscow: Academia: 416.

there were 38 regions with $\Delta KII \leqslant -30$, in 2012 there would be 61 such areas). The number of subjects with the sub-index KTI below the SMI decreased from 15 to 1 — it is the city of Moscow. However, the difference is small (0.9 percentage point); besides, Moscow has the highest ratio of balance — 5.333 in 2012 (0.252 in 2000). It is shown as in Figure 1.

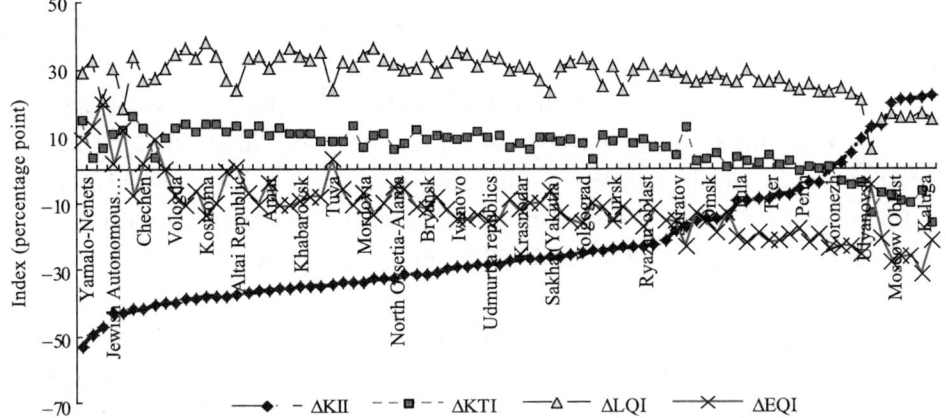

Figure 1　Difference Between the SM Sub-indices and the SMI of Russian Regions in 2000

In 2012, compared with 2000, the situation changed — the difference between the SMI and the sub-index of KTI increased on average by 20 percentage points. As a result, two sub-indices (KTI and LQI) came close by values. This happened due to the growth of life expectancy and infant mortality (whole country). There was a slight increase in the gap between the sub-index of economy quality and the SMI (Figure 2). In some regions, there was a significant increase in the gap between the SMI and the sub-index of EQI. Thus, the imbalance of the secondary modernization process grows in the regions of RF.

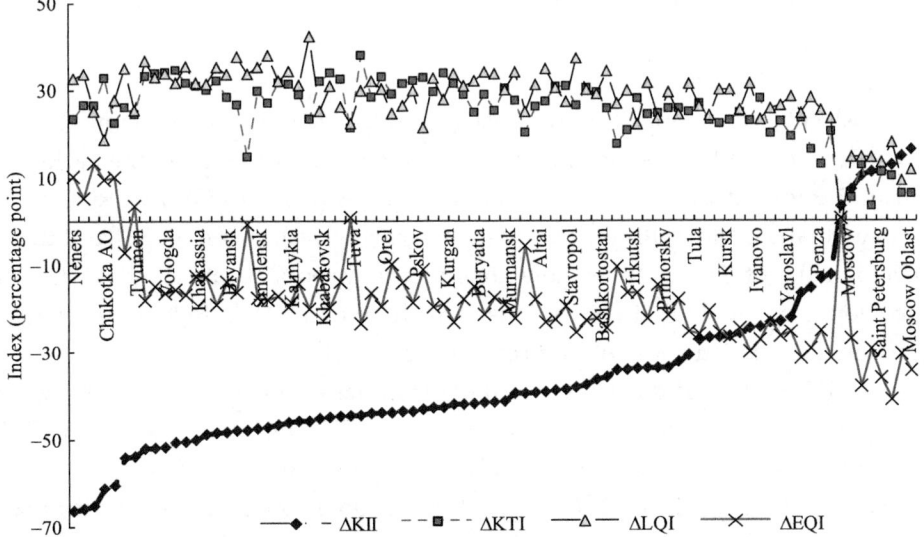

Figure 2　Difference Between the SM Sub-indices and the SMI of Russian Regions in 2012

Let us assess the balance level of the SMI components by means of the secondary modernization balance index (IDSM)[1]:

---

[1] Lapin N I, Belyaeva L A. 2013. Problems of Socio-Cultural Modernization of Russian Regions. Compiled. Moscow: Academia: 29.

$$\text{IDSM} = \frac{100}{\Delta \text{KII}^2 + \Delta \text{KTI}^2 + \Delta \text{LQI}^2 + \Delta \text{EQI}^2},$$

where $\Delta \text{KII} = \text{KII} - \text{SMI}$ is the difference between the sub-index of KII and SMI, $\Delta \text{KTI} = \text{KTI} - \text{SMI}$ is the difference between the sub-index of KTI and SMI, $\Delta \text{LQI} = \text{LQI} - \text{SMI}$ is the difference between the sub-index of LQI and SMI, $\Delta \text{EQI} = \text{EQI} - \text{SMI}$ is the difference between the sub-index of EQI and SMI.

The protracted consequence of the 2008 financial economic crisis — increase in the number of regions with a low balance index, was witnessed in the subsequent period (2009-2012). The negative contribution to the imbalance of the SMI is made by low cognitive and economic components (insufficient number of scientists and engineers and patent application filing, a small share of R&D expenditures in GDP, low GDP per capita, insufficient share of GRP and employment in the service sector).

The calculation of balance indices for Russian regions indicates significant imbalance of the secondary modernization in the RF (the balance index is extremely low: it was equal to 0.087 in 2012, while 0.532 in 2000). Whereas the sub-indices of KTI and LQI reach about 90% of the specified standards of developed countries, the indices of EQI and KII are slightly more than 50%, and in some regions they even do not exceed a quarter. With the growth in imbalance of modernization, we observe widening of contrasts in the socio-economic development and socio-cultural life of the society.

The Russian regions can be divided into several groups depending on the balance degree of the sub-indices (Table 1). Having analyzed the difference (Δ) between the sub-indices and SMI we get the following intervals:

— backward retarded development, if $\Delta \leqslant -15$;
— moderately retarded development, if $-15 < \Delta < 0$;
— moderate development, if $0 < \Delta < 15$;
— accelerated development, if $\Delta \geqslant 15$.

In 2000, all RF subjects belonged to the cluster with the moderate development of KTI and the accelerated development of LQI. Some of them (11 regions) corresponded to the backward retarded development of 2 sub-indices — KII and EQI. A large proportion (59%) of Russian regions (49 regions) belonged to the group with the backward retarded development of KII and the moderately retarded development of EQI. Let us note that in this group 10 areas were characterized by moderate development by EQI. In 9 regions, which fell into the following group, moderate development was characteristic of 2 sub-indices of KII and EQI.

The year of 2012 witnessed the growth in the imbalance of the SM sub-indices: the majority of RF subjects began to conform to the cluster with the accelerated development of KTI and LQI. However, this advantage was reflected in the fact that the other two sub-indices — KII and EQI had the values more lagging from SMI; thus, a large proportion of the territories (52 regions — almost 63%) belonged to the group with the backward retarded development of these sub-indices. In the year under review, only the city of Moscow was characterized by the balanced development of all sub-indices ($|\Delta| < 5$).

Table 1 Clustering of Russian Regions by SM Imbalance Indices (2000 and 2012)

Intervals	Backward retarded development of 2 sub-indices KII and EQI ($\Delta \leqslant -15$)		Backward retarded development of the sub-index KII ($\Delta \leqslant -15$) and moderately retarded development of the sub-index EQI ($-15 < \Delta < 0$)		Accelerated development of the sub-index EQI ($\Delta > 15$) and retarded development of the sub-index KII ($|\Delta| < 15$)		Moderate development of 2 sub-indices KII and EQI ($|\Delta| < 15$)	
	2000	2012	2000	2012	2000	2012	2000	2012
Accelerated development of 2 sub-indices LQI and KTI ($\Delta > 15$)		Kostroma, Vologda, Lipetsk, Belgorod, Kemerovo, Smolensk, Kaliningrad, Orenburg, Tambov, Astrakhan, Orel, Pskov, Kurgan, Kirov, Ryazan, Murmansk, Volgograd, Novgorod, Saratov, Irkutsk, Omsk, Leningrad, Tula, Tver, Kursk, Vladimir, Rostov, Ivanovo, Sverdlovsk, Yaroslavl, Penza, Chelyabinsk oblasts; republics: Adygea, Kalmykia, Udmurtia, Karachay-Cherkessia, North Ossetia- Alania, Buryatia, Mari El, Kabardino-Balkaria, Mordovia, Chuvashia, Bashkortostan, Dagestan, Tatarstan; krais: Krasnodar, Altai, Stavropol, Kamchatka, Krasnoyarsk, Perm (51) Samara Oblast (1) – moderately retarded development of KII	Republic of Khakassia (1)	Arkhangelsk, Bryansk, Amur, Magadan oblasts; republics: Khakassia, Komi, Karelia, Altai, Sakha (Yakutia), Chechen; krais: Zabaykalsky, Khabarovsk, Primorsky; Jewish Autonomous Oblast (14)		Sakhalin, Tyumen oblasts; Tyva Republic; AO: Nenets, Khanty-Mansi - Yugra, Yamalo-Nenets, Chukotka (7) – accelerated development of the sub-index EQI		

Continued

Intervals	Backward retarded development of 2 sub-indices KII and EQI ($\Delta \leq -15$)		Backward retarded development of the sub-index KII ($\Delta \leq -15$) and moderately retarded development of the sub-index EQI ($-15 < \Delta < 0$)		Accelerated development of the sub-index EQI ($\Delta > 15$) and retarded development of the sub-index KII ($|\Delta| < 15$)		Moderate development of 2 sub-indices KII and EQI ($|\Delta| < 15$)	
	2000	2012	2000	2012	2000	2012	2000	2012
Accelerated development of the sub-index LQI ($\Delta \geq 15$) and moderate development of the sub-index KTI ($0 < \Delta < 15$)	Ivanovo, Orel, Volgograd, Kursk, Saratov, Vladimir, Omsk, Ryazan oblasts; republics: Udmurtia, Kabardino-Balkaria, Bashkortostan (11)		Vologda, Lipetsk, Pskov, Kostroma, Arkhangelsk, Smolensk, Orenburg, Kemerovo, Kirov, Belgorod, Novgorod, Astrakhan, Bryansk, Sakhalin, Murmansk, Irkutsk, Magadan, Kurgan, Tambov, Kaliningrad, Amur oblasts; republics: Adygea, Karelia, Kalmykia, Mordovia, Komi, North Ossetia-Alania, Dagestan, Buryatia, Chuvashia, Sakha (Yakutia), Karachay-Cherkessia; krais: Khabarovsk, Stavropol, Altai, Krasnodar, Krasnoyarsk, Primorsky; Chukotka AO (39)	Republic of Ingushetia (1)	Chelyabinsk, Voronezh, Sverdlovsk, Samara, Ulyanovsk, Tomsk, Moscow, Nizhny Novgorod, Novosibirsk, Kaluga oblasts; Kamchatka Krai; Saint Petersburg (13)	Ulyanovsk Oblast (1)	Yaroslavl, Tula, Leningrad, Tver, Penza, Rostov oblasts; republics: Mari El, Tatarstan; Perm Krai (9)	Voronezh Oblast (1) — backward retarded development of the sub-index EQI
			Tyumen Oblast; republics: Ingushetia, Chechen, Altai, Tuva; Zabaykalsky Krai; AO: Yamalo-Nenets, Khanty-Mansi-Yugra, Nenets; Jewish Autonomous Oblast (10) — moderate development of the sub-index EQI					
Moderate development of 2 sub-indices LQI and KTI ($0 < \Delta < 15$)						Novosibirsk, Kaluga, Nizhny Novgorod, Moscow, Tomsk oblasts; Saint Petersburg (6)		Moscow (1)*

*Balanced development of all sub-indices ($|\Delta| < 5$)

Consequently, we can speak about the rise in imbalance in the modernization processes in almost every region of RF and also about increasing imbalance differentiation in the country. This is confirmed by the calculation of SM balance indices in the regions. So if in 2000 8 regions had a high level of balance, in 2012 these were only 2 (the city of Moscow and the Novosibirsk Oblast). There appeared a large share of regions with the level of balance that is low (51 regions) and below average (24 regions).

Thus, in 2000-2012 the modernization processes in RF were characterized by the sharp increase in the number of regions with the SM low balance index (low and below average levels), therefore, by the decrease in the number of regions with the high index and the stable number of regions with the average level. Since much economic, social and cultural process and phenomena have their regional features, such as geographical location, natural resources, labor and socio-cultural potential of the population and other factors, it is impossible to use a single universal approach to the implementation of modernization in the regions. Each region should carry out an individual socio-economic modernization strategy, based on the potential of the modernized society and the advantages of the territory. The central government should both coordinate their development and form a model of healthy competition among the regions on the markets of finished products, factors of production[1]. Only in the way will innovation, application of modern technologies, and efficient use of resources be encouraged in the region. The solution to the problems of transition to innovative (secondary) modernization involves the integration of socio-cultural aspects of society development in the regional economy, the development of theoretical and methodological ways to the analysis of interaction between various regions of the country and the re-orientation on socio-cultural management of regional development. According to N. I. Lapin, it is necessary to work out a strategy of phased modernization and coordinate the evolution of modernization states, so as to ensure the convergence of gaps among RF subjects (federal districts) and increase their internal consolidation and productive interaction[2].

We can single out the key feature of modernization process in the regions, such as multidirectional, asymmetric and non-synchronized development of territories, caused by the existence of the non-diversified economy structure in several regions (fuel, raw materials, metallurgical and agricultural), the economic and social imbalances and the inefficiency of state and municipal management. Besides, the economic and financial crisis led to the change in the development trend and the decrease in the main economic indicators; not all regions were able to fully recover after this crisis[3].

The implementation of social and cultural modernization is hampered by the inconsistency of characteristics of the economic, political and social space. The key parameters affecting the possibilities of modernization are as follows.

A. Economy

a) Lack of the integrated and comprehensive assessment of socio-economic impacts of the

---

[1] Pshunetlev A A. 2014. Regional aspects of Russian economy modernization: Analysis of problems, ways of solutions. Management of Economic Systems, (3). Available at: http://uecs.ru/uecs63-632014/item/2833-2014-03-31-08-08-59[2015-3-17].

[2] Lapin N I. 2015. Distance between modernization of macro-regions and stages of integrating modernization of Russia. Sotsis (Social Studies), (1): 45-55.

[3] Shabunova A A, Lastochkina M A. 2014. Overcoming social inequality as an incentive of socio-cultural modernization. Economic and Social Changes: Facts, Trends, Forecast, 33(3): 69-83.

implementation of modernization programs (projects);

b) Lack of the clear modernization strategy during the crisis and post-crisis periods;

c) Corruption at all levels of governments (federal, regional, local and household), partly supported by the current legislation;

d) Lack of effective mechanisms to guarantee protection of property and security of the citizen[①].

B. Policy

a) Remoteness of the political and governing structures from society, lack of the acceptable optimal model of government and the system of laws, and taking no account the opinions and rights of various strata of the population;

b) Artificial civil society model supported by the authorities;

c) Imbalance of the interests and ideologies of political structure members, low civil activity.

C. Society

a) Division of the population by numerous socio-cultural indicators;

b) Regional differentiation of the level and quality of life of the population;

c) Problems related to the labor mobility of cultures non-traditional for Russia (violation of the legislation, expansion of the shadow economy, formation of separate social structures).

Let us define the main directions that contribute to modernization development:

a) Protection of interests of people (person's merits), prioritizing personal freedom over state interests;

b) Restoration of public trust in the authorities, among people, and mutual understanding among social and cultural strata;

c) Increasing social responsibility of big business (oligarchs), and conducting the anti-corruption reform;

d) Encouragement of businesses to foster innovation and formation of the society based on knowledge;

e) Improvement of the level and quality of people's life.

References

Durkheim E. 1991. The Division of Labor in Society. Moscow: The Sociological Method.

Ermakhanova S A. 2009. Development of ideas about socio-cultural aspects of modernization in sociology. Humanities in Siberia, (1): 55-59.

He C Q. 2011. China Modernization Report Outlook (2001-2010): Translated from English. Under general editorship of N. I. Lapin. Moscow: Ves Mir.

Lapin N I. 2015. Distance between modernization of macro-regions and stages of integrating modernization of Russia. St. (Social Studies), (1): 45-55.

Lapin N I, Belyaeva L A. 2013. Problems of Socio-Cultural Modernization of Russian Regions. Moscow: Academia.

Pshunetlev A A. Regional aspects of Russian economy modernization: analysis of problems, ways of

---

① Sergei N S. Social Aspects of Modernization of Russia. http://www.lawinrussia.ru/sotsialnye-aspekty-modernizatsii-rossii [2015-3-17].

solutions. http://uecs.ru/uecs63-632014/ item/2833-2014-03-31-08-08-59[2015-3-17].

Sergei N S. Social Aspects of Modernization of Russia. http://www.lawinrussia.ru/sotsialnye-aspekty-modernizatsii-rossii[2015-3-17].

Shabunova A A, Lastochkina M A. 2014. Overcoming social inequality as an incentive of socio-cultural modernization. Economic and Social Changes: Facts, Trends, Forecast, 33(3): 69-83.

Zarubina N N. 1998. Socio-Cultural Factors of Economic Development: Max Weber and Contemporary Modernization Theories. St. Petersburg: RGGI.

Progressive Reform: Path of Political Modernization in Britain and Its Inspirations

Jinyuan Liu [1], Yuan Liang [2]

1 Nanjing University, 2 Shandong University[①]

Political modernization is a transformation of the power structure, i.e. a transfer of national power from a certain person (despot) or a group (oligarchy) to the masses of the people, and the ultimate goal is mass democracy. As Gabriel A. Almond pointed out, one of the central issues in political development is political participation, i.e. various social groups pressing for participation in the policy-making concerning the political system[②]. Similarly, as Samuel Huntington put it, political modernization means increasing political participation of all social groups so as to broaden the coverage of political participation and achieve equal political participation[③].

In history, countries of different categories adopted different models of political modernization due to their differences in historical and cultural traditions and specific national conditions. Generally, political modernization follows three models: First, the revolution model completes the transfer of power through a violent revolution where the masses take over political power from a despot or oligarch with armed forces. France is a typical case. Second, the reform model forces the ruler to launch top-down reforms by exerting growing pressure with an aim to achieve peaceful and progressive transfer of political power and ultimately to complete the transformation towards democracy. Britain is a typical case of this model. It is worth noting here that both the revolution model and the reform model are driven by internal factors or forces, which means that the driving force for modernization comes mainly from the nation or country, with little influence from external factors. The third is the model of externally forced reform. When the transfer of political power cannot be achieved with internal forces, the despotic or oligarchic regime can only be overthrown and democracy be established by external forces

---

① Jinyuan Liu, professor in School of History, Nanjing University, Nanjing 210023. E-mail: jyliu@nju.edu.cn. Yuan Liang, lecturer in School of Translation Studies, Shandong University, Weihai, 264209. E-mail: lyraliang@sdu.edu.cn.
② 阿尔蒙德, 鲍威尔. 1987. 比较政治学: 体系、过程和政策. 曹沛霖等译. 上海: 上海译文出版社: 26.
③ 塞缪尔·亨廷顿. 1996. 变化社会中的政治秩序. 王冠华等译. 北京: 生活·读书·新知三联书店: 4.

through military occupation or color revolution. Examples include post-World War II Germany and Japan, and Iraq, Libya and Egypt in the 21st century. Britain is the first industrialized country in the world and the creator of the reform-based path towards political modernization. This paper examines the process, characteristics and inspirations of the political modernization of Britain so as to provide reference for the political modernization of China.

1. Framework of Britain's Political System and Its Problems

A precondition for adopting the reform-based model is that the existing political framework is open. In Britain, despotic monarchy was overthrown after the Glorious Revolution of 1688 and constitutional monarchy was established. However, the surface of its political structure did not change much. The monarch, the upper house, and the lower house remained the main power authorities. The monarch was still at the top with all administrative power and some legislative power. The Parliament, consisted of the upper and the lower houses, i.e. the House of Lords and the House of Commons, was the main legislative institution of the country. The upper house also held judicial power. Nevertheless, essential changes did happen under the surface. First, according to the Bill of Rights, the Parliament became a permanent institution of the country, with meetings convened by the monarch regularly. This put an end to the time when the monarch held no parliament meetings or scarce parliament meetings so as to keep political power in its own hands. Second, the principle of "king under law" was established, which meant that despite the monarch's status of the head of state and the administrative head, everything he did to perform his duty must be permitted by law, i.e. by the Parliament. Third, the Parliament was to determine the order of succession to the throne, which meant that the Parliament had the final say as to who would become the king. For example, William III came back from the Netherlands to England to inherit the throne because the two parties in the Parliament started a coup and ousted his father-in-law James II and his young son. This was an abnormal way to enthrone a new king, which was only possible because the Parliament exercised its power. A similar situation was seen again in the 18th century. In 1701, when Queen Anne's son and successor of the throne the Duke of Gloucester died, in order to shut Prince Charles of the Stuart regime in exile out of the throne, the Parliament adopted the Act of Settlement which forbade any Catholic from taking the throne, thus preventing any possible Stuart restoration. In addition, it was also stipulated in the act that when the House of Stuart ended in England, the throne will be succeeded by Princess Sophia of Hanover, Germany and her offspring[1]. All these changes pointed to one conclusion: The monarch remained powerful after the Glorious Revolution, but not without restrictions. Power was caged and the cage was the laws issued by the Parliament. Thus, the parliamentary sovereignty was established.

Does parliamentary sovereignty ensure democracy? Actually, no! Let's look deeper into the structure of the British Parliament. From the Glorious Revolution of 1688 to the first parliamentary reform in 1832, the power of the monarch declined and the Parliament came gradually to the center of state power. Whoever took control of the Parliament now possessed

---

[1] Stephenson C, Marcham F G. 1937. Sources of English Constitutional History: A Selection of Documents from A.D. 600 to the Present. New York: Harper & Row Publishers: 610.

political power. The British Parliament consists of the upper house and the lower house. Members of the upper house were not elected but status-based, and all seats were taken by secular or religious aristocrats. At the time of the Glorious Revolution in 1688, the upper house had 160 members. At the time of the Dynasty of Hanover, the monarch ennobled a batch of people and expanded the upper house. By 1800, there were 267 seats and the number grew further to about 300 shortly before the parliamentary reform in the 1820s[①]. Exclusive to the aristocracy, the upper house had some of the legislative power.

The lower house, also known as the House of Commons, was elected. Technically it offered a chance for the commons to participate in politic affairs, but as a matter of fact, it did not. Before the parliamentary reform of 1832, the lower house had 400 or 500 members elected from all over the country. But seats of the lower house were in fact also mostly controlled by aristocrats as a result of the electoral system carried forward from the Middle Ages.

Firstly, the distribution of the seats was unreasonable for no change was ever made for hundreds of years in spite of radical demographic changes. Among the 202 boroughs of England in the early 19th century, for example, 56, or more than a quarter, had less than 50 voters[②]. Four of them had 10-19 voters, one had five, and two had no voter at all. In comparison, emerging industrial cities had very few or no seats. In 1820, the three major emerging industrial cities of Manchester, Birmingham and Leeds had a total population of 500,000 but no seats in the House.

Secondly, the criteria for one to qualify as a voter were bizarre. In some boroughs, one had to be a yeoman while in some others, one must have real estate. Generally, real estate is the primary condition for suffrage, which meant that election was controlled by aristocrats who possessed large amounts of land.

Thirdly, the elections were corrupt. The open election system continued till 1872 and as a result some independent voters were faced with pressure from aristocrats. During elections, it was common to gain votes through bribery and the Parliament was actually a club of rich and powerful aristocrats[③]. The consequence of such an unreasonable electoral system was that the lower house, similar to the upper house, gradually slipped into the control of aristocratic oligarchs and parliamentary sovereignty was in fact turned into aristocrats' monopoly of the power. Aristocrats, with the Parliament and Cabinet positions in their control for long, became politically privileged. Therefore, in nature, the constitutional monarchy before 1832 was aristocratic oligarchy.

2. Parliamentary Reform and Political Modernization

Objectively, before the Industrial Revolution of 1760, Britain was an agrarian society centered on land. Real estate was not only a symbol of wealth and economic status, but also a stepping stone towards political power. Therefore, it was to some extent inevitable and justifiable that landed aristocrats, as social elites, monopolized political power. However, starting from the mid-18th century, as industry rose, the middle class and the working class gradually took shape, yet these classes found it difficult to obtain their due political rights. Thus, eliminating aristocratic

---

① 阎照祥. 2006. 英国近代贵族体制研究. 北京: 人民出版社: 70.

② Brock M. 1973. The Great Reform Act. London: Hutchinson University Library: 20.

③ Li J. 2001. Towards Democracy: The First Constitutional Reform of Britain. Nanjing: Nanjing University Press: 19.

oligarchy and achieving mass democracy became the fundamental goal of political modernization in Britain. The model of peaceful reform was adopted for the following reasons. For one thing, the British people learned to settle political conflicts and change the national political system through peaceful compromises in the Glorious Revolution of 1688. Given that compromises worked for restricting the power of despotic monarchs, why wouldn't they work for parliamentary elections? For another, constitutional monarchy had a democratic framework in place with check balance between and powers shared by the monarch, House of Lords and House of Commons, and with the lower house gradually coming into the center of the entire regime. As industrialization progressed, the old political system was challenged not because of the system itself, but because the corrupt electoral system of House of Commons failed to accommodate members of emerging classes. This constituted a framework for peaceful settlement of conflicts and made it possible to achieve political democracy through reforms[1].

From 1760 to 1832, the parliamentary reform prevailed with an aim to change the electoral system of the lower house and give the emerging classes access to the regime. The reform was nearly universal and relevant organizations were established in various classes. They fell mainly into three categories. The first was parliamentary reform organizations of the middle class, mainly consisting of the new industrial and commercial groups emerged during the Industrial Revolution and represented by Society for the Supporters of the Bill of Rights, Society for Constitutional Information, etc. They organized publicity campaigns, assemblies and lectures, submitted petitions, and distributed pamphlets to build people's enthusiasm for political life and were the mainstay in the parliamentary reform. The second category was parliamentary reform organizations of the working class, represented by the London Corresponding Society. Members of the society were mainly skilled laborers and they called for equal voting rights without assets requirements. The third category was organizations established by radical Whigs, represented by Society of the Friends of the People created by Charles Grey in 1792. The Whigs hated the Tories for their lasting control of power and had compassion and offered support for the emerging classes for the parliamentary reform. At the end of the 18th century, they submitted two reform bills in House of Commons and became a force that the emerging groups relied on for the hope of change.

Starting from 1832, the British Parliament went through five rounds of reforms, which lasted till 1928. The first round of 1832, propelled jointly by the middle class, the working class and the Whigs, was the hardest of all. Britain at that time was once on the verge of a civil war but fortunately a compromise was finally reached between those with vested interest and the reformists. Through the reform, the distribution of parliamentary seats was adjusted, with declined boroughs removed. As for the suffrage, assets replaced status as the main criteria, and the middle class thus became eligible. However, such criteria gave nothing to the working class who had fought together with the middle class. The reform bore profound significance nevertheless. It shattered aristocratic oligarchy and laid the foundation of capitalist democracy[2]. Also, it set the direction of a progressive and non-violent approach for a modern industrial

---

① 刘成, 刘金源, 吴庆宏. 2005. 英国: 从称霸世界到回归欧洲. 西安: 三秦出版社: 143.
② 李季山. 2001. 走向民主——英国第一次宪政改革. 南京: 南京大学出版社: 175.

country[①]. Since then, peaceful and progressive reforms have been an established tradition for the political democratization in Britain. A reform, once launched, would not stop halfway. After a successful first round, the second round was much easier. The parliamentary reform of 1867 was completed smoothly within the term of office of the Conservative Prime Minister Benjamin Disraeli. The assets threshold was set at 10 pounds for urban citizens and 5 pounds for rural farmers[②], making most of working class eligible for suffrage (except agricultural workers and miners). In 1883 and 1884 during the time of Liberal Prime Minister William Gladstone, Britain went through its third parliamentary reform. It met almost no resistance, for people had already taken it for granted that the working class should be granted the suffrage in parliamentary elections. The division of urban and rural boroughs was eliminated and boroughs were redefined based on population and one parliament member was to be elected from each borough. It was also stipulated that frauds and bribery in elections must be strictly controlled, no assets requirement remained, and suffrage were virtually granted to all male adults[③].

Entering the 20th century, the universal suffrage for women became a hot topic in society. At the end of the 19th century, when all men had the suffrage, feminists were highly motivated to pursue the same object for women. During the World War I, men joined the army and went to the front, while women came out of their homes to play a crucial role in domestic production activities. More and more people started to recognize the social status of women and support them in pursuing political rights. As a result, the issue of women's suffrage was soon proposed after the war. On January 11, 1918, the Representation of the People Act was adopted by the Parliament, marking a vital victory of women in their fight for the suffrage. It was stipulated in the act that all women of 30 years old or above were entitled to suffrage. This made about 850,000 women legitimate voters for the first time. A decade later, in 1928, the age limit for women was eliminated and women finally became equal to men in terms of universal suffrage[④]. This meant that by 1928, all British adults had the universal suffrage and equal political participation was achieved, fulfilling the fundamental goal of political modernization.

3. Characteristics and Inspirations of the British Path

From a theoretical perspective, Britain took its path because of its conservative traditions. Conservatism in Britain is a manner of prudence that tends to maintain what is achieved by predecessors. It is not obstinacy that refuses development and progress, but a prudent approach towards social changes and their processes. When the existing system can be maintained, the British will hold firmly onto it, pursuing no reform; but when it is no longer viable in new realities, they will allow changes to a certain extent and the changed system will then become what they try to maintain despite pressures for further changes. Edmund Burke, the representative conservative, for example, believes that the British political system after the Glorious Revolution is perfect and there is no need to make any changes. Only when there is no other way out can the existing system be changed, but only to the extent that only necessary

---

① Evans E J. 1983. The Great Reform Act of 1832. London: Methuen: 43.
② 王觉非. 1997. 近代英国史. 南京: 南京大学出版社: 564.
③ Webb R K. 1968. Modern Britain: From the Eighteenth Century to the Present. New York: Dodd, Mead & Company: 401.
④ 陆伟芳. 2004. 英国妇女选举权运动. 北京: 中国社会科学出版社: 283.

changes are made to problematic parts, with an aim to create new national order with existing social factors①. The conservative tradition is the ideological precondition for the progressive approach of Britain.

From a practical point of view, a path of reform relies on preconditions in three aspects. First, the masses must fight unremittingly. The middle class and the working class established political organizations one after another since the start of industrialization in 1760 and exerted pressure on the government through continuous petitions, mass assemblies and other activities. And compromise and reform were finally possible after more than 70 years of efforts. Second, the ruling class must make appropriate and timely compromise. A reform is the redistribution of vested interests. For the aristocratic regime, simple rejection to any change may have resulted in revolutions in the French style, leaving them with nothing to hold on to. In contrast, if compromises have been made when conditions are ripe and the situation is precarious, they would be able to better protect their interests by accepting the reforms. Third, the ruling class must split from inside and offer support to the reform. The success of the British parliamentary reform was the result of joint effects of internal and external factors. On the one hand, the emerging middle class and working class exerted heavy pressure from the outside; on the other, the compassion and concrete support from the Whigs, as part of the aristocracy, was also essential to the success.

Looking through the process of political modernization in Britain, we can't help but pondering the relationship between political democracy and economic development. On the economic side, industrialization started in Britain around 1760 and was completed until around 1840; while democratization led by the parliamentary reform was launched in 1832 and completed in 1928, with almost no overlap. This seems to indicate no positive interaction between the two as emphasized in the classic modernization theory; instead, it appears to hint at a paradox: On the surface, industrialization spanned over 80 years in a regime of typical aristocratic oligarchy where political power was held by aristocrats, with the two emerging classes of an industrial society having no access to ruling positions. Thus, it is to some extent fair to believe that the British economy took off under aristocratic oligarchy, completing the transformation from an agricultural society to an industrial one. This paradox was seen in many a developing countries after the World War II. The Republic of Korea, for example, completed economic take-off and became one of the Four Asian Dragons under the dictator regime of Park Chung-hee and Chun Doo-hwan. Probably, this means that there may not necessarily be any link between political democratization and economic development. Under certain circumstances, a relatively centralized political system may actually be better for economic take-off. However, the parliamentary reform was indeed launched in 1832 when industrialization was almost completed, breaking the ice of aristocratic oligarchy and pushing the country towards democracy. Things were similar in the Republic of Korea in the end of the 20th century. In 1993, the military government was forced to hand over the political power to an elected government led by Kim Young-sam, completing a historical transformation. This shows that when the economy develops to a certain level and the economic take-off is about to complete, the rise of emerging classes will surely exert pressure and challenge on the old political system. And at this point, the group with

---

① 钱乘旦, 陈晓律. 1992. 在传统与变革之间——英国文化模式溯源. 杭州: 浙江人民出版社: 185.

vested interests will have to follow the irreversible trend of the time and adopt appropriate measures for political reform. The British path may be valuable reference for the political reform in contemporary China.

The Guarantee of Progress and Harmony: Modernization and Livelihood Improvement in Modern America

Pengfei Yang

College of History and Culture of Northwest Normal University

Not only a universal historical process, modernization also represents forefront changes and international competition in modern civilization, a process of the formation, development and transformation of modern civilization and international interaction[①]. It's closely linked with a country's productivity and overall strength, and concerns poverty elimination and livelihood improvement. The U.S. industrial society was formed under a liberal system. It created wealth[②] as well as a divide between the rich and the poor and gave rise to various social problems. To mitigate conflicts and establish social harmony, since the late 19th century, successive administrations have taken a variety of measures and achieved great progress. By the 1960s, however, people's livelihood had been extensively challenged. At that time, education and medicine lagged far behind, the rich-poor gap was widening, employment opportunities were unequal and the environment was polluted, severely hindering the American modernization process. The U.S. government made very pragmatic response to all these problems and its efforts proved very fruitful.

1. Implementing the Social Welfare Plan, Expanding the Social Welfare Scope and Addressing Issues That Concerned People the Most

The American social welfare system was younger than its counterpart in Western Europe and

---

① 何传启. 2010. 现代化科学: 国家发达的科学原理. 北京: 科学出版社: 1.

② America's GDP was USD 1.565 billion in 1819, USD 24.055 billion in 1870, USD 88.517 billion in 1890 and USD 52.33 billion in 1961. Though by 1961 the wealth of the American society was more than 30 times that in 1819 when the country was just founded, the increase in wealth didn't make the society more harmonious or orderly. See Bogart E L. 2003. Readings in Economic History of the United States. Stockton: University Press of the Pacific: 313; 黄安年. 1992. 美国的崛起. 北京: 中国社会科学出版社: 242; 黄安年. 1989. 二十世纪美国史. 石家庄: 河北人民出版社: 223.

provided less welfare benefits than some Western European countries did. By the mid-20th century, the abundant social wealth and the low-level social welfare constituted an unharmonious contrast. The situation had severely affected the pace of American modernization. In response, the federal government took a series of measures to fully expand social welfare. The expansion was reflected in the promulgation and implementation of new laws and regulations on medicine, education, housing and urban development.

Measures taken in medicine, healthcare and other social securities are listed as below.

In 1965, the Medicare Bill and the Medicaid Bill were issued. The Medicare Bill covered both hospital insurance and supplementary medical insurance. The hospital insurance provided that anyone at the age of 65 and above eligible for the social insurance system and meeting the retirement conditions for railway staff was entitled to free medical care, with 90 days in hospital and 100 days at home after he/she left the hospital[1]. The supplementary medical insurance had a greater application scope than the hospital insurance. It provided that any senior citizen eligible for the hospital insurance, disabled person and any other person aged 65 or above would be entitled to the reimbursement of general medical expenses and drug bill if they paid extra USD 3 of insurance premium on their own will per month. The Medicare Bill meant a lot. By July 1966, it had benefited over 19 million American people. By 1969, American national insurance expenditure had reached USD 64.142 billion[2]. We may say that this bill to some extent eased the medical burden on the American elderly and was one of the most important welfare bills in American history.

The Medicaid Bill was about welfare subsidies. It provided that the state government should provide medical subsidies to low-income households who were living on social relief, raising children and unable to afford medical expenses. The federal government shall cover 50% to 83% of the expenses, and the exact proportion varied as the per capita income varied from state to state. The bill was soon implemented thanks to the promotion of the federal government. By the mid-1970s, except for Arizona, all American states had formulated their own medical aid plan and the number of recipients jumped from 10 million in 1967 to 23 million in 1973.

Later over 40 more medical bills were issued such as those on nurse training and building neighborhood medical stations[3]. The number of newly-issued bills even surpassed the total of existing medical bills in the U.S. by then[4].

Stimulated by the federal government, state governments also subsidized the disabled including the visually impaired and the elderly. A lot of money was earmarked by each state for this purpose. The amount earmarked was USD 1.8 billion in 1969 alone, according to statistics data[5].

The federal government also took some groundbreaking measures to provide educational aid. Among all the educational aid bills passed by the Congress, the most important were the Elementary and Secondary Education Act and the Higher Education Act, both issued in 1965.

---

① Bedts R F. 1973. Recent American History, Volume II. Homewood: Dorsey Press: 366.
② Congressional Quarterly. 1969. Congress and the Nation, 1965-1969. Congressional Quarterly Inc.: 679.
③ USCB. 1975. Privately Owned Housing Units in Major Federal Programs, 1935-1970, Historical Statistics of the United States, Colonial Times to 1970. Washington, D.C.: United States Government Printing Office: 73.
④ Blake N M. 1972. A History of American Life and Thought. New York: McGraw-Hill: 197.
⑤ 黄安年. 1989. 二十世纪美国史. 石家庄: 河北人民出版社: 299.

The Elementary and Secondary Education Act was the first to provide universal federal aid to elementary and secondary schools. It authorized the federal government to allocate USD 1.3 billion to improve elementary and secondary education. Its issuance and implementation strongly boosted the development of elementary and secondary education in the U.S. Statistics show that in the first year after the act took effect, the Congress allocated USD 775 million for it, benefiting about 19% of students in public schools and about 4% in private schools[1]. By 1968, it had benefited about 6.7 million adolescents[2], including poor students and disabled children.

The Higher Education Act was the first American law granting federal scholarships and low-interest loans to poor college students. It allocated USD 650 million to subsidize universities and colleges, providing scholarships for students and strengthening teaching and research. It meant a lot for higher education development in the U.S. Statistics show that it allowed at least one million poor college students to further their education. In 1967 alone, 225,000 college students obtained the federal scholarship.

The Congress also passed over 60 more educational bills, including the Higher Education Facilities Act of 1963 and the Education Professions Development Act of 1967. The federal government earmarked a huge amount of money for their implementation. Statistics show that from 1963 to 1964, the secondary education fund in the U.S. was USD 24.9 billion and increased to USD 35.8 billion between 1967 and 1968[3]. Throughout the 1960s, the federal higher education fund jumped from USD 6.7 billion to USD 22.7 billion, and the subsidy fund from USD 1 billion to USD 3.8 billion. The above acts helped promote educational development in the U.S. in the 1960s, improved the education for the poor and especially the black and thus the overall qualities of its population, cultivated a large workforce of qualified workers and specialists, and met the human resources demand for modernization.

Fundamental reform was also launched in housing and urban development sectors. The Housing and Urban Development Act was promulgated in 1968, earmarking an amount of USD 7.5 billion for urban reconstruction and providing that a total of 240,000 low-rent public housing units should be built for low-income people; housing subsidy should be provided to anyone who was eligible for public housing, who had to move to make room for government projects such as urban reconstruction and highway construction, who didn't have standard living space, or who was old, disadvantaged, sick or disabled. The law provided that the above families may seek for private housing up to the standard and if the rent took up more than 25% of their income, the government should cover the excess[4]. In 1966, the Congress passed the Demonstration City and Metropolitan Development Act and earmarked USD 900 million to reconstruct shanty towns in 75 cities and improved local schools, hospitals, employment opportunities and residential housing to give them a complete facelift. In 1968, another housing act adopted by the Congress demanded to build or repair 1.7 million housing units for low- and medium-income households. To help these households obtain home ownership, the government subsidized the interests of the mortgage loan of home buyers. The subsidized interest rate might be as low as 4%. These efforts proved

---

[1] Matusow A. 1984. The Unraveling of America: A History of Liberalism in the 1960s. New York: Harper & Row Publishers: 22.
[2] Barnet V D. 1983. The Presidency of Lyndon B. Johnson. Lawrence: University of Kansas Press: 222.
[3] Congressional Quarterly. 1969. Congress and the Nation, 1965-1968. Congressional Quarterly Inc.: 709-711.
[4] Congressional Quarterly. 1969. Congress and the Nation, 1965-1968. Congressional Quarterly Inc.: 187-196.

highly effective. By the end of the 1960s, the number of American households living in substandard housing units had dropped from 8.5 million in the early 1960s to 5.7 million[1].

With the expansion of welfare programs, the federal government's expenditure on social welfare soared. The figure reached USD 53.492 billion in 1965 and USD 86.558 billion in 1969, according to statistical data[2]. The social welfare expenditure of local governments at all levels also increased remarkably. It stood at USD 66.766 billion in 1963, taking up 11.6% of the GDP, and USD 127.149 billion in 1969, 14.1% of the GDP, according to statistical data[3].

2. Implementing the Anti-poverty Program, Improving the Livelihood of Ordinary People and Narrowing Down the Rich-Poor Gap

The U.S. is a highly modernized country and an abundant society. Tens of millions of American citizens live at the highest level of livelihood in the world. But for all the modernization, it still has a poor population, including urban poor groups, farmers, black people and senior citizens. Statistics show that at that time, the poor population in the U.S. was between 40 million and 50 million[4]. The government had to deal with the large poor population and the wide rich-poor gap at the same time.

Poverty elimination is a worldwide challenge. It's not exaggerating to compare anti-poverty to a war, as the American government puts it. To eradicate poverty, we must be creative in how. If we count merely on social relief, it will sabotage the free enterprise system upheld by the American and make the poor persistently depend on social welfare. What the American government did was to help people gain more chance, maximize their potentials, turn tax eaters into tax payers[5], and integrate the disadvantaged into the mainstream society so that they could live a decent life. By so doing, it achieved many things at one stroke.

The federal anti-poverty program covered the following four aspects.

First, children and adolescent education. It provided that preschool education should be provided to children aged 3 to 6 from low-income households; free tutoring should be provided to high school students from low-income households to increase their enrollment rate; a federal fund should be spent creating temporary jobs for about 140,000 adolescents so that they could pay their college tuition with the money they earned. The program was a huge success. Statistics show that preschool education alone benefited about 700,000 children.

Second, job training and retraining, which was rich in content. In particular the Job Corps provided two-year job training and basic skill training for urban youths aged 16 to 21 who had dropped out of school and were jobless and then sent them to protect natural resources; the Volunteers in Service to America sent young volunteers to impoverished areas, mental hospitals,

---

[1] Gordon K. 1968. Agenda for the Nation. Washington, D.C.: The Brookings Institution: 6.
[2] Levitan S A, Tagart R. 1976. The Promise of Greatness. Cambridge: Harvard University Press: 22-23.
[3] USCB. 1979. Statistical Abstract of the United States. Washington, D.C.: United States Government Printing Office: 330-331.
[4] Harrington M. 1999. The Other America: Poverty in the United States. New York: Penguin Books: 1.
[5] Johnson L B. 1964. A Time for Action: A Selection from the Speeches and Writings of Lyndon B. Johnson 1953-1964. New York: Atheneum Publishers: 7.

schools and Indian reservations to serve the poor and ethnic minorities; the Street Youth authorized state and local governments to organize jobless youths and dropouts to serve local communities. There were other projects such as Operation Mainstream, New Economy Initiative and Job Opportunities in the Business Industry.

Third, the implementation of community action plan. The Economic Opportunity Act of 1964 provided that local community action plan with the participation of the poor should be implemented when the community organization must had at least one third of poor representatives. Accordingly, the government handed over anti-poverty projects such as the Day Care Station project, the Neighborhood Health Station project and the Legal Service project to local community organizations participated in by local poor residents. The community action plan was the most revolutionary part of the federal anti-poverty program[1]. It helped solve many problems. For instance, the government hired 1,200 lawyers in 600 law firms in impoverished areas across the country, which provided legal services for one million poor clients from 1965 to 1971[2].

Last but not least, the improvement of economic conditions in backward areas. In 1965, the Congress adopted the Appalachian Regional Development Act which provided that the government should earmark an amount of USD 1.092 billion to develop the Appalachian Region that housed 12 backward states, including building highways, regulating rivers and watercourses, building forests and ranches, and reviving the coal industry. For example, it planned to build 2,350 miles of expressways and 1,000 miles of regional highways, and establish the Appalachian Regional Development Commission to take charge of local development. In the same year, the Public Works and Economic Development Act was adopted, which provided USD 3 billion to develop basic industry in economically sluggish areas and improved local transport conditions to attract businesses from outside. In 1967, the Congress passed the Amendment to the Appalachian Regional Development Act and added another amount of USD 885 million to the project[3]. The implementation of the project not only strengthened the federal government's role in local economic development, but also greatly boosted the development of backward areas in the country.

The above anti-poverty program, though failing to address all the poverty issues in the U.S., did remarkably reduce the American population living under the official "poverty line". Statistics show that in 1964, the population living below the poverty line was 36.1 million, accounting for 19% of the American population, and decreased to 24.1 million by 1969[4], 12%[5]. At the same time, the unemployed also shrank considerably in number. Statistics show that from 1966 to 1969, the American unemployment rate was kept under 4%.

---

[1] Marvin E G. 1967. The Great Society Reader: The Failure of American Liberalism. New York: Vintage Books: 142.
[2] 刘绪贻, 杨生茂. 2002. 美国通史·第 6 卷. 北京: 人民出版社: 244.
[3] Congressional Quarterly. 1969. Congress and the Nation, 1965-1968. Congressional Quarterly Inc. : 286-290.
[4] In 1969, the poverty line stipulated by the American government was an annual income not more than USD 3,986 for a four-member household. See 王怀宁. 1974. 世界经济统计简编. 北京: 生活·读书·新知三联书店: 480.
[5] Levitan S A, Tagart R. 1976. The Promise of Greatness. Cambridge: Harvard University Press: 199.

3. Formulating and Gradually Implementing the Environmental Protection Policy, Addressing New Problems Facing Industrial Modernization and Improving People's Livelihood

As the course of modernization advances and the industrialization level improves, environmental problems attract more and more attention from common people and governments alike around the globe. In American history, Theodore Roosevelt was the first president who made natural resource protection a key national policy, his successors Franklin Roosevelt and John Kennedy also did a lot of work in environmental protection and later the Johnson Administration inherited and carried forward the environmental protection legacies of its predecessors.

The U.S. environmental protection history shows the track of changes from the protection of non-renewable resources, wise and rational utilization of limited resources in the 1920s, to pollution control after the two world wars, then to the protection of public land, wasteland and primitive forests, the construction of national parks and city environment improvement in the 1960s.

While vigorously implementing the social welfare program and the anti-poverty program, the Congress issued a string of laws and regulations on environmental protection, including the protection of water sources, air quality improvement, waste treatment and landscaping.

The Water Pollution Control Act of 1948 granted state governments the power to water pollution control and the federal government provided only technical aid and low-interest loans for local water treatment plants. The Water Quality Act of 1965 set up a special agency under the Department of Health, Education and Welfare — the Water Pollution Control Agency and demanded states to develop an interstate law by 1967 to decide the water quality standards and water pollution control measures in each state[①]. In addition to legislation, the U.S. also significantly increased its investment in water pollution control. Statistics show that the Eisenhower Administration allocated USD 212 million for water pollution control and the figure jumped to USD 847 million during the Johnson Administration[②].

Besides water pollution control legislation, the U.S. government also issued the Solid Waste Treatment Act, the Air Quality Act, the Small Vehicle Exhaust Standards Act, the National Natural Reserve Protection Act, etc.

Highway landscaping was one of America's top priorities in environmental protection in the 1960s. As modernization progressed and the mileage of expressways and highways extended rapidly, the highway landscape in the country was severely damaged with tobacco and alcohol advertisements and auto junkyards littering along highways, presenting a most undesirable look for the modernization project. To improve the image, the Congress issued the Highway Landscape Act in 1965 which provided that from January 1968, any state that failed to dismantle

---

① The Johnson Administration considerably increased the investment in water pollution control. The earmarked fund was USD 212 million during the Eisenhower Administration, more than USD 400 million during the Kennedy Administration and grew to USD 847 million during the Johnson Administration. See Laura E H. 1998. The Beautiful Society: Environment Policy During the Lyndon Johnson Years. The University of Texas: 4.

② Laura E H. 1998. The Beautiful Society: Environment Policy During the Lyndon Johnson Years. The University of Texas: 4.

billboards in non-commercial areas or fail to set up billboards according to national standards on both sides of highways would receive no more financial assistance from the state highway fund; the perimeter of federal control line should be extended to 1,000 m from the edge of highways, and billboards could only be erected in commercial areas on both sides of highways; auto junkyards, motels, restaurants and service stations on both sides of highways and commercial billboards on highways must be moved away by law; each state must spend 3% of federal financial assistance for highway construction on the landscaping of tier 1 and tier 2 highways[①].

These acts promulgated and implemented by the U.S. government to some extent controlled the pollution, beautified the environment and improved people's livelihoods.

To sum up, the livelihood improvement project launched by the U.S. government is an integral part of national modernization. Including actions such as the social welfare scheme, the anti-poverty program and environmental protection, it's an active response to the basic requirements of the times and has produced fruitful results: It addressed some of the poverty issues faced by the abundant American society, eased the American social conflict, maintained political stability, and to some extent re-built the American industrial society. The history of American modernization shows that modernization is a very enormous, complex systematic project, closely linked to not only a country's productivity and overall strength, but also poverty elimination and people's living standards. Livelihood improvement is an integral part of modernization and the progress of modernization is an important guarantee for better living standards.

---

① 王庆安. 2008. "伟大社会"改革——20 世纪 60 年代美国社会改革及启示. 北京: 新华出版社: 171-172.

International Inequality and the Global Crisis: Managing Markets for Sustainable Growth

E. A. Brett

Department of International Development, London School of Economics

1. Managing the Economic Crisis: The Theoretical and Policy Challenge

The global crisis is forcing states to reduce public spending and firms to cut wages and jobs, thus accelerating a global deflationary spiral by reducing demand, investment and tax capacity. Radicals demand more deficit spending to stimulate growth, but weaker economies tried this after the banking crisis in 2007-2008 and increased their debts without producing the growth needed to finance them. Rising interest rates have forced them to implement austerity programmes in exchange for short-term financial support from the EU and/or IMF. The USA has run deficits since 1970, but can still borrow at favourable rates by exploiting the "exorbitant privilege" it enjoys as the largest economy and issuer of the dominant currency, and as an outlet for the surpluses of the strong economies. However, its ability to do this is increasingly constrained because further quantitative easing could increase inflation and devalue the dollar, while spending cuts would intensify the deflationary spiral. The Bank for International Settlements (BIS) identified the threats that these solutions now pose to the stability of the global system:

> *A look at the economy as a whole shows that three groups need to adjust: The financial sector needs to recognise losses and recapitalise; governments must put fiscal trajectories on a sustainable path; and households and firms need to deleverage. As things stand, each sector's burdens and efforts to adjust are worsening the position of the other two. The financial sector is putting pressure on the government as well as slowing deleveraging by households and firms. Governments, with their deteriorating creditworthiness and need for fiscal consolidation, are hurting the ability of the other sectors to right themselves. And as households and firms work to reduce their debt levels, they hamper the recovery of*

governments and banks. All of these linkages are creating a variety of vicious cycles. (BIS, 2013: 8)

These imbalances are being caused by policy interventions that break the liberal rules that govern the market-based global economic system that has prevailed since the 1980s, but, like the regulatory reforms of the 1870s and the 1930s, they were introduced by conservatives, not socialists, who were forced to do so to avert a more serious breakdown caused by "the weaknesses and perils inherent in a self-regulating market system" (Polanyi, 1944: 152). However, they are also having perverse effects because they have been introduced in a peace-meal way to address immediate problems and have ignored the role of free markets in generating the growing imbalances that continue to destabilise the world economy.

This article will substantiate this claim by questioning the theoretical coherence of the liberal assertion that free markets must produce equitable and stable growth by eliminating the "distortions" generated by the state-led or "structuralist" policies that had dominated the previous era. Instead, liberalisation has actually produced uneven development by generating rapid growth in some regions, but reducing investment opportunities and increasing inequality in others. The destabilising effects of this process were initially concealed by the credit bubble fuelled by an unregulated and irresponsible financial sector, but this burst in 2007-2008 was followed by a generalised attempt to sustain growth through an expansion in public sector borrowing. However, this soon became unsustainable as growth failed to recover, reducing tax receipts and increasing safety net costs. Thus the BIS (Polanyi, 1944: 4) therefore directed the authorities' attention with new force to the underlying menace that no longer seemed so far away: the gross underfunding of governments' health care and pension obligations and an unmanageably large public sector that has produced the spending cuts and falling wages and consumption that have produced the "vicious cycles that are impoverishing the weakest economies and people, simultaneously compressing their imports from the strongest ones", thus globalising the crisis and perpetuating the deflationary spiral.

There is now a growing awareness in the policy community of the inadequacy of these responses, but a deeply entrenched inability to recognise the role of laissez faire in creating and perpetuating the crisis, or of the need for interventionist policies comparable to those introduced to address earlier crises. Conservatives blame the crisis on irresponsible governments in weak states, and regulatory failures and perverse incentives in financial markets. Social democrats have jettisoned their old commitment to statist solutions, and call for more spending in opposition but have to adopt austerity programmes in office because they cannot protect their own producers from foreign competition and can only borrow from the financial market at unsustainable interest rates, but no alternative projects that offer equitable and economically viable alternatives to the current system.

We will argue that we can only reverse these vicious cycles and develop sustainable policies by recognising the limitations of the current system by returning to the theories of market failure and uneven development generated by the radical structuralist tradition stretching from Marx and List, to Schumpeter, Keynes, Gerschenkron and Stiglitz. They recognised that competitive markets generate rapid technological and social progress in some parts of the global system but also intensify inequality and marginalisation in others, unless their destabilising effects are offset by redistributive political and social interventions. This article reprises the contribution I made to this tradition during the crisis of the early 1980s, when I claimed that the on-going neoliberal response must intensify inequalities and instability at both national and global levels (Brett, 1983, 1985). These pessimistic predictions were initially falsified by rapid growth in East Asia, and the credit bubble generated by deregulated financial markets, but they have now been vindicated by the intractable nature of the current crisis.

Substantiating these heavily contested claims raises theoretical, policy and political issues that we will take up in the rest of this article. We will first outline the classical liberal theories that tell us why open markets should automatically generate equitable or even development by shifting resources from strong to weak economic systems, then demonstrate that this does not hold in open systems when scale economies derived from technological change offset these processes, and produce uneven development by creating structural inequalities between the most and least successful firms, countries and regions. We will then review the policy implications of this claim by showing that weaker societies have always had to adopt structuralist policies to deal with market failures, that this is also true now, but that current responses fail to recognise the need to impose the primary responsibility for adjustment on surplus rather than deficit countries. We will conclude by reviewing the difficulties involved in generating the political will to introduce viable redistributive policies in a global context dominated by the interests of the strongest states, firms and communities.

2. The Logic of Even and Uneven Development

The stability of the global system depends on the ability of each national economy to balance its imports and exports over the long term; deficit economies can only continue to import by increasing their exports to or borrowing money from surplus countries, or by cutting their imports from them. The stability of the world economy therefore depends on the ability of firms in deficit economies to outcompete firms in surplus countries, pushing the latter into deficit; failure will lead to import compression and impose deflationary pressures on the system as a whole. Thus the survival of a liberal system depends on the extent to which free trade actually generates what I call even development, or a "natural" tendency for weaker economies to move from deficit into surplus without resorting to protectionist interventions that "distort" the play of uncontrolled competition. If free trade creates uneven development because strong economies constantly outcompete weak ones, import compression will first reduce consumption and increase conflict in deficit countries, and then undermine the integrity of the whole system. According to Hager (1980: 15):

> *There is an incompatibility between the extraordinary performance of one or more members in a system and the maintenance of a voluntary rule-based order. The strong tend to believe that a system which allows others the freedom to emulate them is the best of all possible worlds. In the real world, however, the weak have to be bribed to continue playing a game they lose.*

This proposition has crucial political and technical implications, since it implies that growing inequality is a technical as well as normative issue, since the system must break down unless the weak as well as the strong can survive and prosper. Thus the hegemonic status of laissez faire depends on two key claims. First, markets will maximise freedom and efficiency and political constraints will suppress them; and second, free trade will also automatically generate full employment and fair wages, and equilibrate demand and supply at the national and global levels. Serious liberals recognise that viable markets depend on strong states to guarantee property rights, overcome externalities, and provide public and merit goods, but believe that they should create regulatory regimes that do not distort them but enable them to operate better. The collapse of command planning in the East and authoritarian structuralism in the South validated the first claim; unprecedented growth in the East and in South Asia facilitated by tariff reductions in the 1970s and the 1980s has partially validated the second.

These are serious claims since markets do play an indispensable role in modern society, and because many current problems are a function of weak governance and opportunistic behaviour that could have been avoided through better governance and stronger regulatory regimes. Thus we can only continue to benefit from open markets if we make full use of the political and economic insights of liberal theory, but only if they are supplemented by a more realistic analysis of the tendency for even well regulated markets to produce inequality and instability without the redistributive transfers referred to in the last section. We will outline the key claims of liberal theory in the next section, and the logic of the structuralist critique in the one that follows.

3. Accounting for Even Development and Economic Stability: The Liberal Case

The ability of modern neo-classical theory to assume that free trade would automatically produce full employment and even development rests on the work of classical theorists who challenged previously dominant mercantilist arguments that had justified the need for protectionist policies. Instead, Say's theory of supply and demand, Hume's theory of the balance of payments, Ricardo's theory of comparative advantage, and Lewis' theory of surplus labour demonstrated open competition would not only maximise growth, but also generate an equitable and sustainable distribution of the resulting gains. I call these SHRL theory.

Say's theory showed that "supply creates its own demand", since money spent on wages and inputs by firms must reappear as enough demand to buy the goods that they produce; and that competition will actually produce full employment and growth by forcing firms to reinvest their profits in more efficient technology, guaranteeing rising wages in the long term (Keynes, 1943: 18-21).

Hume's theory showed that countries with a chronic trade surplus would have to reinvest this income and incur rising costs while deficit countries would experience falling wages and costs that would soon enable them to move back into surplus (Hume, 1955: 63).

Ricardo's theory showed that even poor countries where the costs of production are higher in all sectors than in rich ones, would still benefit from free trade by importing the goods where their costs are the highest and exporting those where they are the lowest (Haberler, 1961: 7-8).

And Lewis' theory showed that capital would flow from developed regions where capital was plentiful and labour fully employed and expensive to less developed ones where it was scarce and labour was plentiful until full employment and comparable wages existed in both

(Lewis, 1954).

These models have been subjected to rigorous analytical scrutiny, and can also be used to demonstrate that most structuralist policies — protectionism, subsidies and state-enforced monopolies everywhere and punitive taxation, nationalisation, wage and price controls and unaffordable welfare spending in socialist countries — would block these beneficial processes and intensify political conflict and economic breakdowns. The IFIs (International Financial Institutions) used these arguments to explain the generalised balance of payments and fiscal crises in the South and the East that destabilised the global economy in the 1980s and the 1990s, and used their structural adjustment policies to oblige these countries to liberalise in exchange for financial support. The subsequent boom and shift of industry from rich to poor countries that followed seemed to validate their claims and enabled a Nobel prizewinning economist to claim that they had solved the "central problem of depression prevention … for all practical purposes … for many decades"[1].

4. Scale Economies, Market Failures and Economic Crises

The emergence of the latest crisis after most of these "distortions" had been eliminated, clearly undermines the optimistic claims of what I will call SHRL theory, and forces us to return to the analyses of market failure that do explain why free trade has not produced equitable and sustainable development as it predicts. Instead, it has produced growing inequality and unemployment within most countries, and long-term surpluses in the strongest economies like Germany, China and the Asian NICs (newly industrial countries), and long-term deficits in the USA, the European periphery and in the weaker LDCs (least developed countries) that have not benefited from recent increases in raw material prices. Rapid industrialisation has increased wealth as well as inequality in the BRICS (Brazil, Russia, India, China, South Africa), but has destroyed jobs and cut real wages in all but the most successful developed and middle income countries. This has reduced investment despite the fact that the world's leading corporations are hoarding trillions of dollars of cash reserves, and can borrow at negative interest rates. Further, successful industrialisation in East Asia benefited from lower tariffs in DCs (developed countries), but also depended on state-led export-oriented development and not laissez faire. Instead, as Chang (2002: 19) has shown, virtually all early industrialisers have used "a wide variety of industrial, trade and technology policies" that contradict most of the prescriptions of current orthodoxy, and are proscribed by the Articles of Agreements of the IFIs that almost all LDCs have now signed.

These contradictory processes clearly challenge the empirical claims of SHRL theory. The radical theorists who explain this failure do not question the analytical coherence of their models, but do question the validity of their empirical assumptions, and especially their failure to recognise the disruptive effects of economies of scale generated by technological and organisational innovation. This seemingly abstract and technical proposition actually has radical economic, social and political consequences, because, as Schumpeter (1943: 84) showed, scale

---

[1] Lukas R. 2003. Presidential address to the American Economics Association: Macroeconomic priorities. American Economic Review, 93 (1): 1-14.

economies suppress the redistributive processes that would prevail where competition operates "within a rigid pattern of invariant conditions, methods of production and forms of industrial organization". Instead as he also showed, "the essential fact about capitalism" is its tendency to revolutionise technology and therefore produce oligopolistic competition and "creative destruction", but not equitable and stable growth (Schumpeter, 1943: 84):

> ... in capitalist reality as distinguished from its textbook picture, it is not ... competition [within invariant conditions, methods of production and forms of industrial organisation] which counts, but the competition from the new commodity, the new technology, the new source of supply, the new type of organisation (the largest-scale unit of control for instance) — competition which commands a decisive cost or quality advantage and which strikes not at the margins of the profits and the output of the existing firms but at their foundations and their very lives. This kind of competition is as much more effective than the other as a bombardment is in comparison with forcing a door.

These processes enable strong firms and regions to reduce their costs and prices, employ fewer workers and still increase their output and prices, by investing in technical and/or organisational innovations that enable them to destroy weaker firms, raise barriers to the entry of new ones, reduce employment and tax capacity in weaker regions and impose deflationary pressures on the whole system. They operate at every level — the plant, the firm and the region — and produce effects that do explain the depth, persistence and pervasiveness of the current crisis. There are some of their most disruptive consequences as follows.

(1) Automation has eliminated "Fordist" manufacturing and the mass working class in the North, and marginalises everyone without the skills that these complex systems require; the Internet is destroying millions of jobs and small shops.

(2) Multi-plant industrial, banking and retail firms dominate international markets, undermine small independent firms in the North and the South, and raise high barriers to new entrants.

(3) Liberalisation and lower wages have transferred new industries and jobs to some developing countries, but its benefits are concentrated in a few centres with good infrastructure and strong states, and exclude the rural and urban poor. It has destroyed jobs in the North, in weaker economies in the South, and in weaker regions in successful countries too.

(4) Strong economies like Germany and China provide firms with excellent state services that generate external economies, or "economies of aggregation", that offset rising wage costs that their weaker competitors cannot match.

These processes explain growing inequalities between and within nations, the dominant role of global corporations in the world economy, the expansion of an increasingly marginalised informal sector in LDCs, a growing underclass and falling wages in deindustrialised DCs, and the coexistence of long-term export surpluses and deficits that are destroying investment opportunities in weak economics and perpetuating the deflationary spiral that continues at the global level.

Liberal theorists recognise the disruptive effects of scale economies but ignore their consequences or deny their existence. Thus Knight saw that they must "eventuate in monopoly" unless the "normal relation of increasing costs with increasing size" could be re-established (Knight, 1924: 51); while Hicks claimed that monopoly will replace competition, "stability conditions become indeterminate, and the basis of which economic laws can be constructed is therefore shorn away", unless the "supposition" that "marginal costs do generally increase with output at the point of equilibrium" holds (Hicks, 1946: 84-85). The "supposition" that diminishing returns are dominant in late capitalism clearly ignores the powerful processes identified above, and forces neoclassical theory to depend on a "scholastic" approach to policy theory that deduces "real world behaviour from highly abstract arguments that have little or no empirical content" (Lipsey et al., 2005: 385).

This wishful thinking imposes heavy burdens on the weakest members of the global community, because it blames them for their own poverty, forces them to bear the heavy burden of reconstruction, and it denies the need for interventions that do not just regulate markets to allow them to operate better, but that redistribute resources to correct these disequilibrating effects. This clearly demands a fundamental shift in the policy agenda, but one that also takes account of the positive consequences of technological change that we turn to now.

5. Competitive Markets, Scale Economies and Social Progress

The hegemonic influence of market theory is sustained by the ability of the leading countries and corporations to silence the voices of competing paradigms and social movements, but its continuing authority actually depends on our inability to manage the complex global exchanges on which our survival depends without them. The neoliberal revolution in the 1980s was validated by a generalised popular revolt against Stalinism, fascism and statist structuralism, and by unprecedented growth in once poor economies that discredited the claims of dependency theorist who argued that the capitalism was incompatible with third-world industrialisation. Further, scale economies do have disruptive effects, but are crucial to human progress. Thus the problem that confronts us now is to find better ways to control its disruptive effects with sacrificing its manifest advantages. To do this we need to start by identifying the creative consequences of market systems, and the variables that confirm the claims of SHRL theory.

First, while continuous innovation transforms many production processes, many inherently labour intensive activities continue to generate employment, while some innovations, like improved seeds or mobile phones, advantage small rather than large producers and enable them to survive and even create new sectors.

Second, industrialisation in the BRICS has created new investment opportunities there and increased demand for high technology exports from the North, and for raw material exports and labour intensive services in the South. Capitalists in the BRICS are responding to rising wages by investing in poorer LDCs, and particularly in raw material production in Africa. China's ability to finance the American deficit continues to stabilise the global monetary system.

Third, scale economies are responsible for the productivity gains that have contributed most to human progress but they are not generated by small firms working in fully competitive markets, but by "large concerns" operating under "Monopoly Competition" as Schumpeter noted. This has two key implications. First, oligopolistic competition does impose real disciplines on even the most powerful corporations; and second, attempts to restrict the destructive effects of scale economies in the interests of stability or redistribution need to be offset against the positive effects of science-based technological change.

And, fourth, it is these productivity gains that have generated the surpluses that have allowed modern states to provide public goods and safety nets, produce the automated technologies and information systems that have rescued humanity from lives of unremitting toil, facilitated a massive increase in leisure and creative activities, and institutionalised the large-scale resource transfers that have stabilised and legitimised modern capitalism.

6. Political Intervention, Managed Markets and Equitable Development

This analysis provides a technical and normative justification for collective interventions that restructure rather than simply regulate markets by obliging winners to compensate losers and thus offset the inequalities and instability that stem from their tendency to destroy the economic capacity of their consumers. The long slump has validated this claim, but also confronted those who accept it with a technical and political challenge since they must do this without disrupting the complex problems involved in producing the food, clothing, shelter and communication systems for seven billion people, and also generate the political support needed to capture state power and then to manage the transaction and contestation costs involved in transferring scarce resources from dominant to excluded groups.

Now it is far easier to prove the existence of uneven development and the need for systemic interventions to control it than to overcome the technical difficulties and contestation costs involved in dealing with them. Liberals rightly claim that planners can never acquire all the information needed to solve these technical problems, and that only markets can reduce these contestation costs by depoliticising the allocations of scarce resources that must otherwise generate zero-sum conflicts between individuals, classes and nations. Much history attests to the strength of this claim. Mercantilist policies led to the territorial wars and imperialist expansionism that dominated the early modern period; authoritarian socialism in the East and fascism in the West led to beggar-thy-neighbour policies and war in the 1920s and the 1930s; authoritarian statism destroyed state capacity and impoverished whole nations in many post-colonial states. Thus the world would indeed be a safer and less challenging place if competition did indeed produce economic systems "which self-adjust so well that no superior authority (the state) is needed to provide more than a framework of rules and infrastructure not providable by private profit-seeking", as liberal theorists claim (Wade, 2013).

However, the fact that states can also fail does not alter the fact that markets cannot survive without them, so we do need to address the intractable problems, generated by the need for redistributive interventions, however difficult they may be. Thus we will first look at the impact to the anomalous policy interventions that have been introduced to contain the crisis, then at the technical and political issues raised by the need to manage a more equitable and sustainable global order.

7. Perverse Policies and the Intensifying Crisis

Crises occur when the rules and organisational systems that govern an existing social order no longer meet the challenges created by the changing demands it is generating, and must therefore be "systematically modified if [the paradigm that sustains it] is to be reconstituted and put back to use" (Brett, 2009: 16). The current combination of open markets and austerity is clearly producing counter-productive results, but has not yet produced a conscious paradigm shift like the one that occurred between the wars[①]. However, it has forced a reluctant policy community to adopt a number of non-market solutions to avert an even greater catastrophe whose causes and consequences must be clearly understood since they not only demonstrate the weaknesses of the dominant paradigm, but are also modifying the institutional arrangements and implicit assumptions that govern the system and the policy debate that sustains it.

The non-market interventions introduced by right and left-leaning governments in the USA and Europe to protect the system from the effects of the current crisis are well-known. They rescued and partially nationalised major banks in 2007-2008, and are now looking for ways to subsidise credit and develop "industrial policies" that were de rigueur ten years ago. Central banks are maintaining negative interest rates and printing money to stimulate growth. Full-scale Keynesian deficit financing, supported by the IFIs, was introduced in weaker centres immediately after the crisis that provided a temporary stimulus, and was only halted by unsustainable increases in debt and interest payments. However, the resulting double-dip recession that destabilised the weaker states in the EU forced the Eurozone and the IMF to finance bankrupt regimes to safeguard the banks and rescue the currency union, even though falling output and tax revenues means that these debts may never be repaid. It has also forced the Eurozone countries, including Germany at its centre, to recognise the need to strengthen its capacity to finance its weakest members to enable them to stay in the EU, and to take on more of the characteristics of a fully-fledged state in order to do so.

However, the banking and Eurozone crises are only a symptom of the much deeper systemic anomalies stemming from the long-term structural changes that are threatening the USA economy's role as the primary source of global liquidity and provider of the world's main reserve currency. The USA's economic dominance and reserves enabled it to facilitate post-war reconstruction from the 1940s onwards. It played the key role in creating the IFIs that sustain the liberal rules that govern the global economy, and it also financed the post-war reconstruction processes that enabled the world to enjoy a long period of relatively even development. It ensured that the IFIs institutionalised a liberal global order, but also used Marshall Aid and its own international defence spending to facilitate post-war reconstruction, and allowed the war-damaged states to use protectionism, state controls and high redistributive taxation to build new industries and create welfare states (Brett, 1983, 1985).

Thus it was interventionist, not liberal policies that allowed the successful industrialisers —

---

① A major British Academy Conference that asked why economists had failed to predict the crisis, ignored the effects of unequal competition produced by "free" markets, and attributed it to failures of regulation, risk-management and foresight, and their oversight to "a failure of the collective imagination of many bright people, both in this country and internationally, to understand the risks to the system as a whole". See Besley, Henderson, *Letter to the Queen*, June 17th, 2009.

the EU and Japan, the East Asian tigers, then China's mainland and Vietnam — to catch up with the USA and in doing so, to introduce new structural inequalities that the Bretton Woods arrangements have been unable to control. Their achievements have been used to justify SHRL theory, but their actual history tells a very different story. Their state-assisted breakthroughs enabled them to combine cheap labour with best-practice technology and take advantage of lower tariffs to penetrate the USA and other markets and generate unprecedented levels of export-led growth. However, their surpluses did not then turn into deficits as Hume claimed, but have continued over the long term, so their exports have destroyed millions of jobs in the North and less successful middle-income countries in the South, and imposed chronic deficits on many of them, most notably the USA. Its deficits in the 1950s began with defence spending and foreign aid, but were then compounded by the competitiveness of high technology producers in the North, and low wages and now increasingly high technology competitors in the South[①]. Thus global liquidity and the stability of the dollar has depended for many years on the ability of the USA to borrow on an unprecedented scale, because the surplus countries have had "to finance indefinitely US deficits through unpredictable accumulations of dollar claims", or produce a "long-run shortage of liquidity", with serious deflationary consequences for themselves and the rest of the world[②].

This experience is uncannily similar to the history of the long upward wave before the World War I that enabled the now advanced countries to industrialise behind protective barriers financed by British loans and with free access to British markets until Britain's growing deficit stopped it from playing its traditional role thereafter. Thus the current crisis will only end when the deficit countries are able to penetrate surplus country's markets, or protect their own markets from their exports. Their inability to do this, as the BIS pointed out, is also creating a "slowdown" in successful "market economies … whose success has depended on exports" and suggests that they "would do well to speed their efforts to build capacity for internal growth". However, liberalisation means that the political mechanism needed to balance investment in deficit and surplus countries are no longer comparable to those that existed after the war, and this is intensifying the deflationary pressures on deficit countries, and also on the USA where the crisis has now reached a point where it has to choose between balancing its books, or continuing to borrow and print money in an unsustainable way.

The unstable nature of a global system that was generating chronic deficits in weak centres and chronic surpluses in strong ones first became clear when Nixon was forced to repudiate the gold standard and devalue the dollar in the 1970s, followed by a series of banking and fiscal crises in the 1980s and the 1990s in the South and the East that were only contained by the widespread structural adjustment programmes financed by the IFIs. The ability of the USA to continue to sustain global demand and the value of the dollar has depended on the ability USA Treasury to borrow on favourable terms and an increase in fiscal discipline after the 1980s. It also responded

---

① Deindustrialisation has turned the once-great automobile producing city of Detroit, birthplace of "Fordism" into a ghost town that has been forced to sue for bankruptcy with $18-20 billion debts. *New York Times*, 18/7/2013.

② The quotation is from Robert Triffin whose analysis of the contradictory nature of an international monetary system based on the strength of a single national currency is more relevant today than it was in the 1960s when it was formulated. (Triffin, 1966: 288, 290; see also Triffin, 1960)

to the crisis in 2007 with a massive increase in borrowing that has averted a full-scale depression, but only produced very limited growth, together with falling wages and escalating welfare payments. Thus the stability of the international monetary and financial system now depends on its ability to indulge in levels of fiscal indiscipline denied to less privileged debtor countries because "the markets" have few other outlets for their savings, and because withdrawing support would initiate a global depression and devalue trillions of dollars they hold in the USA debt, and as their own international reserves[1]. Indeed a Wall Street commentator recently described the operation of "the U.S. Treasury market" as "a Ponzi market", and also noted that it "has reached levels that wouldn't be sustainable if free market forces were allowed to prevail"[2].

The late 1970s initiated a long period of recession that produced balance of payments, fiscal and debt crises across the South and the East; Serious financial and debt crises occurred in Latin America in the 1980s and in East Asia, the post-communist countries and Africa in the 1990s that were only averted by emergency interventions by the IFIs. These crises were closely linked to badly managed structuralist controls that enabled rulers to adopt unsustainable policies that destroyed state capacity, marginalised whole communities, but also by falling raw materials prices and their inability to compete on domestic and foreign markets with established surplus economies. These crises also created generalised donor-dependence that enabled the IFIs to introduce the structural adjustment and good governance programmes that then produced an almost universal transition to market based systems in the region.

Now these controversial reforms have had very mixed outcomes — they have certainly improved governance and have also removed many irrational monopolies and state controls that blocked investment and entrepreneurship and encouraged unproductive rent-seeking from rulers, crony corporations, and foreign corporations during the structuralist period. Higher levels of fiscal and financial discipline have enabled them to avoid the worst effects of the credit crisis, and the most successful of them have enjoyed significant levels of growth, heavily dependent on increased demand for food and raw materials from the new NICs. These successes do attest to the importance of free markets, and the destructive consequences of bad governance in encouraging growth and freedom, but they cannot be used to justify neoliberal claims, because they, too, have depended on extensive external transfers, and are producing jobless growth that is increasing internal inequalities and social tensions.

In fact, the willingness and ability of the countries to "adjust" their economic and political structures has depended on extensive financial and technical support from the donor community in all of the LDCs without access to resource rents. There were widespread defaults during the debt crisis in Latin America in the 1980s, and most of the poorest countries have depended on significant levels of balance of payments and budgetary support since the 1980s, and had their

---

[1] These risks are huge, as the BIS pointed out: "Today, long-term bond yields in major advanced economies are around 2% .... When interest rates and bond yields start to rise, investors holding government bonds stand to lose huge amounts of money. Consider what would happen to holders of US Treasury securities (excluding the Federal Reserve) if yields were to rise by 3 percentage points ... they would lose more than $1 trillion, or almost 8% of US GDP .... Yields are not likely to jump by 300 basis points overnight; but the experience from 1994, when long-term bond yields in a number of advanced economies rose by around 200 basis points ... shows that a big upward move can happen relatively fast." (BIS, 2013: 8).

[2] A Ponzi scheme involves the fraudulent act of repaying one investor's money with the principal of another, thereby over-inflating the value of assets until the bubble finally pops.

debts forgiven in the 1990s through the Heavily Indebted Poor Counties Initiative. Further, increased demand for their raw materials from the NICs is offset by the destruction of local investment opportunities from their cheap exports producing a classic "infant industry problem" and re-establishing the old-style colonial exchange of raw materials for consumer goods whose limiting effects have produced protectionist policies in the North in the 19th century and the South and the East in the 20th century. These gains, even in the African countries enjoying rapid growth are heavily concentrated in capital intensive extractive industries, mainly benefit politically connected domestic and foreign elites and a small labour aristocracy, confining the overwhelming majority of the population to survivalist activities in informal economies because they cannot compete with low wages and high technology imports from Asia.

8. From Laissez Faire to Managed Markets

The inability of poor people in deficit economies to find the decent jobs or create the businesses that allow them to pay their taxes and repay their loans is not caused by their individual deficiencies but by the uneven development generated by uncontrolled competition. This cannot be corrected by old-style command planning or statist socialism, but it does mean that global and national markets need to be supplemented by far stronger redistributive as well as regulatory processes that offset the asymmetrical nature of the rewards that they now offer to the strongest states and firms, and the austerity they impose on weak ones. Current orthodoxy attributes economic failures to bad governance or excessive wages and fiscal deficits in weak states, and thus imposes the primary responsibility for adjustment on the losers; attributing it to unequal competition, it will transfer the failures to the winners and justify the right of losers to use their political power to protect themselves from its consequences in the absence of some form of compensation for their losses. Command planning and/or beggar-thy-neighbour protectionism would make matters worse for both, but free trade has also created a lose-lose situation that can only be overcome by developing new syntheses that build on the positive structuralist policies that produced far better results after the war.

The current system deploys one-size-fits-all solutions that would succeed if markets did produce a natural tendency to even development as SHRL theory claims, but their failure to so means that we need different policies for societies at different stages of development with different needs and capacities stemming from the success or failure of their earlier developmental experiences. These processes have to be managed at the global level, and must oblige strong states to open their markets to weaker ones, and to facilitate private and public credit mechanisms that transfer resources to them on favourable terms and allow them to adopt structuralist policies until they can compete on world markets on relatively equal terms.

This demand was clearly articulated by deficit countries at the Bretton Woods Conference in 1944 that established the IFIs, and is as relevant and justified now as it was then. Keynes spoke for these countries at Bretton Woods, and attributed the interwar depression to the chronic surpluses generated by the USA, and the corresponding inability of deficit countries to invest and grow. He argued that allowing the creditor country "to remain entirely passive ... [must put] an intolerably heavy task ... on the debtor country" (Keynes, 1943: 28), whose problems could only be resolved without destructive protectionism if the IMF and World Bank could be turned into agencies that would automatically recycle surpluses to deficit countries, by creating:

> ... *a general and collective responsibility, applying to all countries alike, that a country finding itself in a creditor position against the rest of the world as a whole should enter into an arrangement not to allow this credit balance to exercise a contractionist pressure against world economy and, by repercussion, against the economy of the creditor country itself.* (Keynes, 1943: 27)

Unsurprisingly, the USA then, and other surplus countries now, have been unwilling to transfer control more than a tiny fraction of their savings to an international agency, and therefore turned the IFIs into agencies that persuaded deficit countries to remain in an open liberal system by giving them just enough credit to enable them to "adjust" without resorting to anti-market measures. Debtors attempted to impose some limits on surplus countries by introducing a "scarce currency clause" into the IMF's Articles of Agreement that would have enabled them to close their borders to countries in chronic surplus, but American resistance ensured that this clause was so weak that it could never be used, and it soon became a dead letter. This has produced an asymmetrical system that obliges deficit countries to give up the interventionist policies that their predecessors used during their industrial transitions, while absolving surplus countries from any obligation to compensate them for their losses.

Membership of this international system also imposes serious constraints on the domestic policy options available to deficit governments and on left-wing regimes in particular since it imposes serious constraints on the ability of their states to adopt the structuralist policies to protect weaker firms, workers and regions from the effects of unequal competition from dominant firms and regions within their own countries and in the world as a whole. They were introduced by the radical social democratic and corporatist political movement that sustained the post-war boom, but are incompatible with the liberal rules enforced by the IFIs and in free trade areas like the Eurozone. Free trade therefore has radical political consequences because governments can no longer protect high-cost enterprises, trade unions can no longer demand better wages or working conditions without bankrupting their firms and losing their jobs, and states cannot use Keynesian deficit financing to stimulate investment, since much of their spending will finance imports not investment and undermine their capacity to repay their loans, as we have seen.

Thus it was structuralist policies that sustained the post-war boom by limiting the consequences of uncontrolled competition, while inequalities and instability generated by free markets would be far worse now, but for the emergency measures described earlier. They also depend on the survival of the redistributive mechanisms established during the social democratic era that include universal access to safety nets and essential social services, and basic economic infrastructure. The quality of these services depends on the strength of the private sector, but the ability of the state to invest the surplus capital and labour generated by scale economies has been essential to sustain effective demand and full employment and thus guarantee economic stability and the political and social inclusion needed to sustain a moral social order.

Our ability to maintain these symbiotic relationships between welfare states and managed markets has been progressively eroded during the neoliberal era. Deindustrialisation and declining investment opportunities in all but the most successful developed and middle income countries is forcing them to cut wages and services; in some like Egypt and South Africa, the resulting tensions are producing mass unemployment, threatening undermining the social order; in weak states in Africa and elsewhere, a minority has benefitted from rising demand from the new NICs, but the majority are trapped in survivalist occupations in informal economies. The strong surplus countries continue to grow but more slowly as demand for their exports and investment opportunities for their surpluses decline. A serious attempt to reduce borrowing in the USA could further destabilise the system.

These problems cannot be resolved without fundamental reforms of the institutional arrangements that govern the world economy. They do not give the IFIs the resources and power they need to solve the problems of deficit countries, and impose serious limits on the policies that they can use to help themselves. We cannot provide detailed policy prescriptions for the different kinds of countries confronting these problems, but only call for a return to more interventionist systems which strengthen rather than weaken the mechanisms that enable states to regulate markets and redistribute resources, and that oblige stronger states to give weaker ones the right to give more support to their own infant or declining industries and easier access to their markets.

9. In Conclusion: Political Agency and Economic Reform

Thus the need for fundamental policy changes to avert an intensification of the crisis is manifestly clear, but the political obstacles to introducing them are daunting because of problems of conflicting interests, political agency, ideology and organisation that we can only outline here.

The continuing dominance of the neoliberal paradigm is sustained by the political leverage exercised by its well organised beneficiaries — capitalist and managerial elites, skilled workers in successful corporations, and strong states that benefit from their investment and taxes. It has given them immense gains and obscured the costs it has imposed on the losers. They make the investment decisions and credit transfers that create or destroy jobs and services, and thus determine the fate of countries, classes and individuals. Open markets enable them to move to the most favourable locations, and the inability of the IFIs to oblige all states to impose comparable controls over them means that no government or group of workers can ask more from than any other, producing a race to the bottom. Strong states control the surpluses needed to fund structural adjustment and austerity programmes, and this has enabled them to oblige recipients to jettison structuralist policies and universalise the liberal policy agenda. These powerful and largely hidden political levers coexist with their ability to influence political and policy programmes and manage public opinion because they own the global media and fund research agendas, university programmes and cultural events and thus exclude competing views from public debate. They also finance political parties and election campaigns, and create and support interest groups and lobbying agencies with direct access to senior politicians and officials (Wade, 2013).

These structural advantages are offset by the growing gap between the liberal social order's need to maximise freedom, equity and stability and its tendency to concentrate power and increase inequality and crises. This is giving more and more people — marginalised and unemployed workers, less competitive capitalists threatened by unequal competition, an underclass dependent on declining welfare benefits in the North, and on insecure survivalist activities in the South — an interest in collective interventions to protect them from these destructive effects. However, they are socially fragmented, under-resourced, and dependent on the jobs and services provided by the state and capitalist economy, so their capacity for effective political action is highly constrained. A small minority may participate in demonstrations that challenge weak regimes, but protest movements motivated by discontent and linked by little more than mobile phones and social media cannot build the complex political and economic organisations needed to articulate their interests, translate them into viable policies, win mass support, and manage the conflicts and compromises involved in redistributing significant amounts of resources between classes, communities and states when they take power. All radical regimes that capture power have to come to terms with the dominant economic, bureaucratic and military elites that run the current system; expropriation or populist policies destroy crucial assets, intensify zero-sum conflicts and impoverish everyone in the short run at least.

Thus credible attempts to resolve the crisis depend on the ability of old or new political parties and the interest groups that support them to devise more equitable programmes, mobilise support, capture political power, and negotiate difficult compromises between winners and losers. This raises very different problems in DCs and different kinds of LDCs.

In DCs, the crisis has forced the conservative parties that represent the dominant economic elites to adopt some redistributive policies as we have seen, but has yet to challenge their hegemonic authority because of the socio-economic changes that have transformed the interests and identities of the groups that support their social democratic opponents. The parties, trade unions and civic organisations that took power after the war were built over generations by leaders, intellectuals and activists, and supported by the mass working class because structuralist policies protected their jobs and wages, and redistributive taxation sustained the welfare state. However, liberalisation and international competition reduced their ability to defend these gains and deindustrialisation and automation has now virtually eliminated this class, and its ability to sustain old style statist programmes. Most of the people who saw themselves as an exploited underclass with collective interests have been replaced by professional or technical classes with personalised skills, individualised identities and high expectations. They no longer perform routinized tasks, but make informed decisions for their enterprises, or work in small or micro enterprises and would oppose a return to the hierarchical structures that dominated the statist project. They coexist with a marginalised, atomised, and often foreign underclass dependent on welfare benefits, but it lacks the resources needed to organise politically to overcome its own weaknesses.

These radical socio-economic changes forced social democratic movements to jettison structuralism in the 1990s, and looked for a "third way" that would allow them to combine open markets with better services and social protection. The crisis intensified the inevitable contradiction between the need to maximise profits and increase taxation that confronts all regimes attempting to find a sustainable balance between these two needs. Conservatives as well as social democrats need to find ways to resolve this tension, but have failed to do so in all but the most successful economies, producing a political impasse that has led to popular disaffection on the left, and an intensification of racism and economic nationalism on the right.

The problems of political agency confronting reformers are even more complex in LDCs than in DCs. They range from strong states with dynamic export economies at one extreme to fragile states with embryonic capitalist economies at the other. Most people cannot operate as "free" individuals because they are locked into dependency relationships with patrimonial elites or marginalised in segregated informal economies. They have only recently made transitions from authoritarian structuralist regimes, and therefore lack the state capacity needed to regulate open markets, and the democratic traditions and organisations needed to limit the corruption and incompetence that still dominates many political systems. Social systems are often riven by sectarian or ethnic antagonisms that can be exacerbated by the competition and economic inequalities generated by liberalisation. They all adopted structuralist policies after the war, producing predatory authoritarianism and economic failure in the weakest, and successful developmental transitions in the strongest states. Donor dependency then forced weak states to liberalise long before they have solved their infant industry and infant state problems; strong states have only begun to liberalise after their interventionist policies had successfully overcome them.

These experiences suggest that well managed structuralism rather than liberalisation represents the first best policy choice for late developing countries, but the challenges involved in mobilising support for it and more especially of creating the political organisations and state capacity needed to implement it are daunting. The demand for structuralist policies came from uncompetitive local capitalists and workers attempting to defend themselves from foreign competition, while their need for subsidies imposed additional costs on exporters and consumers. The regime's ability to tax and allocate subsidies and monopoly privileges has crucial political implications, since favoured capitalists succeed while others fail; rulers extract rents from allocating these favours and use them for personal enrichment or to finance the patronage networks that sustain their political organisations.

Structuralism failed in some contexts and succeeded in others for reasons we have discussed elsewhere (Brett, 2009). What determines these outcomes, as Kohli (2004) showed, is not the existence of structuralism per se, but the ability to manage the zero-sum conflicts involved in developmental transitions of this kind. Donors and opposition movements now assume that democratisation will increase political accountability and encourage inclusive solutions, but the ability to elect or remove governments does not eliminate these conflicts of interest, and these processes are regularly manipulated by patrimonial elites and intensify sectarian, ethnic or class conflict, as we know (Brett, 2012). Liberalisation alters the ability of regimes to access and manipulate rents, but does not eliminate the ability of the state to allocate of favours, so successful solutions continue to depend on the ability of competing classes, factions, activists and leaders, to build the ideological and organisational frameworks and political coalitions needed to produce effective and equitable policy regimes.

We live in an era that expects growth to continue indefinitely, and that the periodic crises that we confront will always produce new and more progressive solutions. This analysis suggests that our ability to do this after the war was not a foregone conclusion, but the result of exceptionally favourable circumstances that persuaded dominant elites and marginalised classes and communities to produce viable compromises that are no capable of guaranteeing a return to prosperity. We will need far greater concessions from beneficiaries, and far more effective action from losers if we are to build the economic, social and political networks that enable them to demand programmes that offset the disruptive effects of uneven development, networks that will have to operate at the global level. I have outlined the basic principles that should govern these reforms in more detail elsewhere (Brett, 1983, 1985, 2009), the problem confronting radical political activists now is to recognise the dangers of political apathy and the limits of protest politics and to join and strengthen the ability of radical organisations to reconstruct an equitable and sustainable social democratic order. The decline of the mass working class and increasing competition for jobs and markets means that it will be very hard to create cohesive movements and unified programmes, but even to discover "the terrain on which these battles have to be fought". However, a failure to do so will also "lead to a period of dissolution which will have devastating effects upon everything which has been created over the past generation", as I argued during an earlier crisis 30 years ago (Brett, 1983: 245).

References

BIS. 2013. Annual Report 2011-2012. Basel: BIS.

Brett E A. 1983. International Money and Capitalist Crisis: The Anatomy of Global Disintegration. London: Heineman Educational Books.

Brett E A. 1985. The World Economy Since the War: The Politics of Uneven Development. London: Macmillan.

Brett E A. 2009. Reconstructing Development Theory. London: Palgrave Macmillan.

Brett E A. 2012. Problematising the democratic imperative: The challenge of transition and consolidation in weak states. London School of Economics, Working Paper.

Chang H-J. 2002. Kicking away the Ladder. London: Anthem Press.

Haberler G. 1961. A Survey of International Trade Theory. Princeton: Princeton University Press.

Hager W. 1980. Germany as an extraordinary trader. In W Kohl, G Basevi (Eds.), West Germany: A European and Global Power. Toronto: Lexington.

Hicks J. 1946. Value and Capital. Oxford: Oxford University Press.

Hume D. 1955. On the Balance of Trade in Writings in Economics. London: Nelson.

Keynes J M. 1943. Proposals for an international clearing union. In J K Horsefield (Ed.), 1969 The International Monetary Fund 1945-1965: Twenty Years of International Monetary Cooperation (Vol. III: Documents). Washington D.C.: IMF.

Knight F. 1924. Some fallacies in the interpretation of social cost. Quarterly Journal of Economics, (38)4: 582-606.

Kohli A. 2004. State-directed Development: Political Power and Industrialization in the Global Periphery. Cambridge: Cambridge University Press.

Lewis A. 1954. Economic development with unlimited supply of labour. The Manchester School, 22(2): 139-191.

Lipsey R G, et al. 2005. Economic Transformations: General Purpose Technologies and Long-term Economic Growth. Oxford: Oxford University Press.

Lukas R. 2003. Macroeconomic priorities. American Economic Review, 93 (1): 1-14.

Polanyi K. 1944/2001. The Great Transformation: The Political and Social Origins of Our Time. Boston: Beacon Press.

Schumpeter J A. 1943. Capitalism, Socialism and Democracy. London: Unwin.

Scott M. 2013-6-21. U.S. Treasurys are a "Ponzi market". Wall Street Journal, Market Watch.

Triffin R. 1960. Gold and the Dollar Crisis. New Haven: Yale University Press.

Triffin R. 1966. The World Money Maze. New Haven: Yale University Press.

Wade R. 2013. Economist's ethics in the build-up to the second great depression. In G DeMartino, D McClosky (Eds.), Handbook of Professional Economic Ethics. Oxford: Oxford University Press.

A New Institutional Economy Growth Theory from the Angle of the Economic Rights

Zhulan Fang [1], Xiong Kuang [2]

1 The School of the Economics, Renmin University of China
2 The School of Economics and Management, Hainan University

1. Introduction

The paper concerns the relationship between the economy growth and the people's economic rights. As we know, Chinese rapid economy growth since 1978 is related to the transition of the economy institution. The growth depends not only on the increase of the productive factors, but also on the reform, whose complexity and peculiarity exceeds the explanations of the economics theories nowadays.

In order to introduce the factor of the economic rights into the growth theory, as well as substantially explain the reason of Chinese economy growth, the paper tries to study the growth from the angle of the public's economic rights. In Section 2, we first clarify the definition of the economic rights, and then specify the contents and the development process of the economic rights in Chinese transition stage. Based on the classification of the economic rights in Section 2, Section 3 builds a model of the relationship between the economic rights and the supply of the productive factors. Finally, the conclusions of the model are contained in Section 4.

2. The Analysis of the Public's Economic Rights

The economic rights are treated as one part of the human rights in academia. Henkin (1996) indicated that the economic rights mainly contain the private property rights. Tomasevski (2005) provided a basic definition of the economic rights, which include the right to live with a rather high standard, the right to work, and the social security right for those who cannot acquire any income. The reason to define the economic rights into the three parts is that the three rights are the necessary conditions for the realization of the human function — realization of the human's ability (Sen, 1999) and autonomy (Copp, 1992).

According to the Chinese experience, it is not enough to formulate the economic rights that affect the economy just from the angle of the human rights. The definition of the economic rights would be vague based on the notion of the human rights, if we try to demonstrate their action mechanism. To clear the analysis, we define the economic rights as: the social qualifications of the agents by which they can freely and legally engage in economy activities and obtain the most economy benefits through their economy behaviors. According to the natures of the economic rights, we divide them mainly into two parts: the behavioral rights and the bearing rights. The behavioral rights mean the public have the rights to engage in some kind of economy activities, for example, the permission of the people to establish a business. After a behavior, there will be a result. The people's rights to bear the result are called the bearing rights, for example, the rights for the people to obtain the benefit of their production. The two types of the rights, as well as their internal structures, compose the system of the public's economic rights.

In terms of Chinese transition stage, the development of the public's economic rights mainly denotes the growing extent of the public's behavioral rights and bearing rights which are endowed by the government. The endowment of the economic rights is expanded orderly based on the people's process of economy activities. Specifically, it means the public, as the economy agents, gradually obtain the right of venture, the right of competition, the right of transaction, the right of organization, the right of innovation, the income right and the social security right. In the paper, Fang and Miao (2010) raised these seven kinds of economic rights, and detailedly discussed the evolutionary situations of the seven economic rights in the Chinese reformation process. Based on their discussion, we categorize the right of venture, the right of competition, the right of transaction, the right of organization and the right of innovation as the behavioral rights, in that these rights are people's liberty to go in for a sort of economy activity. And the income right and the social security right belong to the bearing rights, because the two rights are the direct and indirect rights for the people to bear the results of their activities. The public's incremental acquisitions of these seven rights are the main content in the process of Chinese reform and openness.

3. A Model of the Relationship Between the Public's Economic Rights and the Supply of the Productive Factors

Based on the analysis of the economic rights above, in this section we build a model of how the economic rights influence the supply of the public's productive factors. Our model economy assumes every individual in the society is homogeneous. To go to work, a representative individual provides a certain amount of factors, x. Here, $0 \leqslant x \leqslant \bar{x}$, $\bar{x}$ denotes the maximal factor that the individual can provide in a certain period of time. Let $Y(x)$ represents the output of factor x. Generally speaking, the output will increase with the increase of factor, so we have $Y'(x) > 0$. $C(x)$ represents the cost of the individual's supply of factor x. Similarly, the cost will rise if an individual wants to increase his supply of factor, so we have $C'(x) > 0$. r_b denotes the index of the public's behavioral rights, where $0 \leqslant r_b \leqslant 1$, 0 means the public don't have any freedom to engage in economy activities by themselves, and 1 means the public have total freedom to do their business. r_a denotes the index of the public's bearing rights, where $0 \leqslant r_a \leqslant 1$, 0 means the public have nothing of rights or obligations to enjoy or undertake the results of their behaviors, and 1 means the public have total rights or obligations to bear the results.

On the condition that the government endows a certain extent of economic rights to the public, the aim of each individual is maximizing his utility by choosing the optimal supply of factors. Therefore, we have the individual's target function

$$\max_x r_a Y(x) - C(x) \tag{1}$$

where $r_a Y(x)$ means the individual's income share after he pays the cost $C(x)$. It can be seen that the bigger of the bearing rights endowed to the public, the more profit the public can gain from his payment.

However, the provision of the public's factors is confined by two conditions: The first is the upper limit of factors, $\bar{x}$, and the other is the extent of the behavioral rights, r_b. Under the two conditions, the formula of the real supply of the public's factors during a certain period of time is

$$x = r_b X + (1 - r_b) x_0 = r_b (X - x_0) + x_0 \tag{2}$$

where x_0 represents the public's willing supply of factors under the compulsive condition (the magnitude of the x_0 depends on the extent of the social supervision or individual consciousness). X represents the public's willing supply of factors under the free condition ($0 \leq X \leq \bar{x}$). From the formula, we can deduce the upper and lower limit of the public's real supply of factors $(1 - r_b) x_0 \leq x \leq r_b (\bar{x} - x_0) + x_0$.

On the base of the public's target function and the constraint condition of supply of factors, the optimizing model of the individual's engaging in economy activities can be depicted as follows:

$$\begin{cases} \max_x r_a Y(x) - C(x) \\ \text{s.t.} \quad (1 - r_b) x_0 \leq x \leq r_b (\bar{x} - x_0) + x_0 \end{cases} \tag{3}$$

Let the Lagrangian function be

$$\Psi(x, \lambda_1, \lambda_2) = C(x) - r_a Y(x) - \lambda_1 [r_b (\bar{x} - x_0) + x_0 - x] - \lambda_2 [x - (1 - r_b) x_0] \tag{4}$$

According to the Kuhn-Tucker theorem, the optimal solutions meet the Kuhn-Tucker conditions

$$\begin{cases} \Psi_x = C'(x) - r_a Y'(x) + \lambda_1 - \lambda_2 = 0 \\ -\Psi_{\lambda_1} = r_b (\bar{x} - x_0) + x_0 - x \geq 0, \lambda_1 \geq 0 \\ -\Psi_{\lambda_2} = x - (1 - r_b) x_0 \geq 0, \lambda_2 \geq 0 \\ \lambda_1 [r_b (\bar{x} - x_0) + x_0 - x] = 0 \\ \lambda_2 [x - (1 - r_b) x_0] = 0 \end{cases} \tag{5}$$

The solutions have three conditions.
(a) The interior point solutions
The solutions subject to the conditions

$$\begin{cases} (1-r_b)x_0 < x^* < r_b(\overline{x}-x_0)+x_0 \\ \lambda_1 = 0, \lambda_2 = 0 \\ r_a Y'(x^*) = C'(x^*) \end{cases} \quad (6)$$

Through the condition $(1-r_b)x_0 < x^* < r_b(\overline{x}-x_0)+x_0$, it can be seen that the optimal supply of the public's factor is within the range of the supply of factor constrained by the behavioral rights, which means the behavioral rights have no constraint function on the optimal supply of factor. In this case, the public can make their optimal decision under a certain extent of behavioral freedom.

From the condition $r_a Y'(x^*) = C'(x^*)$, we can get that $r_a = \dfrac{C'(x^*)}{Y'(x^*)}$. According to the derivation rule, a result can be further deduced

$$\frac{dr_a}{dx^*} = \frac{C''(x^*)Y'(x^*) - C'(x^*)Y''(x^*)}{Y'(x^*)^2} \quad (7)$$

From Formula (7), we can see that if the condition $\dfrac{C''(x^*)}{C'(x^*)} > \dfrac{Y''(x^*)}{Y'(x^*)}$ is satisfied, then $\dfrac{dr_a}{dx^*} > 0$, that is $\dfrac{dx^*}{dr_a} > 0$, which indicates that if the government wants to make the public increase their supply of factor to raise the output, it is necessary to expand the degree of the public's bearing rights. On the general conditions as we know, $C''(x^*) > 0$ (elements marginal cost increases) and $Y''(x^*) < 0$ (elements marginal production declines). Besides, from the above hypothesis, we know that $C'(x) > 0$, $Y'(x) > 0$. Therefore, the condition is satisfied. In this case, if the government enhances the degree of the bearing rights, such as the income rights and the security rights, the public will increase their supply of factor, and finally raise the output. China's reform and opening up in 1978 witnessed this situation. In 1978, the farmers in Anhui Province created the household contract responsibility system, whose substance is releasing the public income rights from the people's commune system. The institution actually linked together the household's payment and income, which improved the farmer's production enthusiasm and liberated the rural productivity. This is a case that the increase of the factor supply results from endowing the bearing rights to the public.

(b) The corner solutions (minimum value)

The solutions subject to the conditions

$$\begin{cases} x^* = (1-r_b)x_0 \\ \lambda_1 = 0, \lambda_2 \geqslant 0 \\ \Psi_x = C'(x) - r_a Y'(x) \geqslant 0 \end{cases} \quad (8)$$

Differentiating the first condition, we can get

$$\frac{dx^*}{dr_b} = -x_0 < 0 \quad (9)$$

Formula (9) indicates that if enlarging the degree of the behavioral rights, the supply of factor will decrease. This situation is based on the third condition $C'(x^*) \geqslant r_a Y'(x^*)$. Now we have two cases to discuss it.

① $C'(x^*) \geqslant Y'(x^*) \geqslant r_a Y'(x^*)$

The case ① means that the marginal cost of factor supply is bigger than the marginal output, so decreasing the factor supply is beneficial to the optimum distribution of resources. Nonetheless, due to the mandatory constraints, the public should provide the factor $x^* = (1 - r_b)x_0$, which brings about the inefficient production. This situation also can be witnessed in China's economy before the reform and opening-up in 1978. In 1958, the government improperly lay down the index of 10.7 million tons of steel output. Millions of people had to take part in the "big steel-making movement". Owing to the low-level technology, most of the steels were actually the scum, which means the marginal output was actually less than the marginal cost. However, because the behavioral rights of people's free work were limited at that time, people had to engage in inefficiency production under the instructions. As a result, in face of the destructive facts, the government had to give up the movement finally. If the public had possessed enough behavioral rights, the inefficiency result would not happen.

② $Y'(x^*) \geqslant C'(x^*) \geqslant r_a Y'(x^*)$

In this case, the marginal cost of the supply of factor is smaller than the marginal output, so increasing the supply of factor is beneficial to the output growth. But due to the few bearing rights endowed to the public, the public's income is smaller than their payment. For that reason, the public only want to supply the minimum factor that the system asks them to provide. This situation is similar to the equalitarianism system in China's planned economy period. Because the public had few bearing rights to enjoy their output in this system, even though the increase of the supply of factor can lead to the increase of the social welfare, individuals had not initiatives to increase their labor factor, but provided the allowable minimum amount instead. In this moment, if the government only enlarges the public's behavioral rights but neglects to enlarge the degree of the bearing rights, the result will be the decrease of the supply of factor as well as the social output.

(c) The corner solutions (maximum value)

The solutions subject to the conditions

$$\begin{cases} x^* = r_b(\bar{x} - x_0) + x_0 \\ \lambda_1 \geqslant 0, \lambda_2 = 0 \\ \Psi_x = C'(x) - r_a Y'(x) \leqslant 0 \end{cases} \quad (10)$$

From the third condition $\Psi_x = C'(x) - r_a Y'(x) \leqslant 0$ and the condition $0 \leqslant r_a \leqslant 1$, we can get

$$C'(x^*) \leqslant r_a Y'(x^*) \leqslant Y'(x^*) \quad (11)$$

The meaning of the formula (11) is that the marginal cost of the public's supply of factor is smaller than the marginal output as well as the individual marginal income. In this case, the public are willing to provide their factor as much as possible. However, because of the restraint of the behavioral rights, they could not provide the upper limit of the factor but only provide the factor satisfying the first condition, that is $x^* = r_b(\bar{x} - x_0) + x_0$. Differentiating the first condition, we have

$$\frac{dx^*}{dr_b} = (\bar{x} - x_0) > 0 \tag{12}$$

Therefore, on the condition that the marginal cost of factor supply is low and the bearing rights are endowed to some extent, if the government enlarges the degree of the behavioral rights to the public, the restrained potential supply of factor will be released and the output will grow. China's economy growth in the transition stage is consistent with this situation. At the beginning of the reform and opening-up, the government have endowed a certain degree of bearing rights to the public, such as implementing the contract responsibility system with remuneration linked to output, improving the distribution according to work and introducing the distribution according to factors of production system. On this premise, the government gradually enlarged the public's behavioral rights: allowing the farmers to do contract business, allowing laboring population to move and work among countries and cities, encouraging town enterprises, individual businesses, private enterprises and foreign-owned enterprises to grow together, reforming the state-owned enterprises to operate independently, reforming the financial system, establishing the capital market, and so on. All of these measures actually enlarged the public's rights of venture, innovation, competition, transaction and organization, which leads to the increase of the public's supply of labor, capital, knowledge and technology. Consequently, China's reform from the traditional planned economy system to the modern market economy system, from the angle of the economic rights, is the development of the public's economy rights, especially the behavioral rights in the early stage.

4. Conclusions

From the angle of the economic rights in the institution, the paper tries to formulate Chinese economy growth in the transition stage by introducing the economic rights factor into the economy growth theories. To achieve the goal of the paper, based on the definition and the classification of the public economic rights, we build a model of how the economic rights affect the public's supply of factor. Through the analysis of the model, some conclusions can be gotten as follows.

(1) The behavioral rights and the bearing rights are two complementary rights. The two types of rights can not work separately.

(2) On the conditions that the marginal cost of the supply of factor is small and the bearing rights are endowed to some extent, enlarging the behavioral rights is beneficial to the increase of the supply of factor.

(3) When the behavioral rights endowed to the public are enough, if we would like to increase the social output continuously, it is necessary to endow more bearing rights to the public.

The conclusions of the model can be verified from China's economy experiences. The implementation of the household contract responsibility system in 1978 is the starting point of China's reform and opening-up, which suggests that endowing the bearing rights to the public can improve the production enthusiasm. On the premises that the marginal cost is low and the bearing rights are endowed in a certain degree, the main reason of China's rapid economy growth in the transition stage is that the government has continuously enlarged the public's behavioral rights — the permission of the people to do businesses on their own, the free movement of the rural migrant workers, the loosening of the private enterprises, the reform of the state-owned enterprises and the establishment of the special economy zone, all basically belong to this phenomenon. The result of the expansion of the public's behavioral rights is the increase of the supply of the social factor, and then the growth of the output. However, as the model implied in the first situation of the solutions, after the behavioral rights have no constraint function, if intending to stimulate further growth, the effective measure should be enlarging the public's bearing rights. Therefore, the reform in the 21th century may be, on the basis of further endowing adequate behavioral rights to the public, perfecting the public's income rights and security rights, such as the medical and old-age security, the constraints of the administrative functions and the transparence of the national public finance. These reforms are proceeding in China now. We'll witness how deeply China can step into and remain its rapid growth.

References

Acemoglu D. 1995. Reward structures and the allocation of talent. European Economic Review, 39(1): 17-33.

Barro R J, Becker G S. 1989. Fertility choice in a model of economic growth. Econometrica, 57(2): 481-501.

Copp D. 1992. The right to an adequate standard of living: Justice, autonomy, and the basic needs. Social Philosophy and Policy, 9(1): 231-261.

Fang Z, Miao D. 2010. A tentative approach of rights economics at China's current stage of transformation and realignment. Journal of Capital Normal University, (2): 37-45.

Henkin L. 1996. The Age of Rights. New York: Columbia University Press.

Lucas R E. 1988. On the mechanics of economic development. Journal of Monetary Economics, 22(1): 3-42.

Murphy K M, Shleifer A, Vishny R W. 1993. Why is rent-seeking so costly to growth?. The American Economic Review, 83(2): 409-414.

North D C. 1987. Institutions, transaction costs and economic growth. Economic Inquiry, 25(3): 419-428.

Romer P M. 1990. Endogenous technological change. Journal of Political Economy, 98(10): 71-102.

Sen A. 1999. Development as Freedom. Oxford: Oxford University Press.

Solow R M. 1956. A contribution to the theory of economic growth. Quarterly Journal of Economics, 70(1): 65-94.

Tomasevski K. 2005. Unasked questions about economic, social, and cultural rights from the experience of the special rapporteur on the right to education (1998-2004): A response to Kenneth Roth, Leonard S.Rubenstein, and Mary Robinson. Human Rights Quarterly, 27(2): 709-720.

A Historical Review of World Industrial Modernization

Lei Liu

China Center for Modernization Research, Chinese Academy of Sciences
University of Chinese Academy of Sciences

In modern society, the industrial sector is one of the pillar sectors that support national economy. In fact, the industrial sector is not only a modern sector, but also a time-honored sector with a rich history. The earliest human industry started in the Stone Age, dating back to over 2 million years ago. The modern industry started from the Industrial Revolution in Britain in the 18th century, and has a history of over 200 years up to now. The development of the modern industry since the Industrial Revolution has introduced the human society to a modern society that is completely different from the past historical stages. The Industrial Revolution is both the starting point of world industrialization and industrial modernization, and the inauguration of the modernization of human society. Since the 18th century, industrial modernization has always been a core part of economic modernization, a strategic cornerstone of national modernization and a driving force for economic modernization and national modernization. To sort through the development path of world industrial modernization and find the intrinsic pattern of important significance to predicting the development direction of the modern society, this paper will depict the basic facts of world industrial modernization and outline the history of world industrial modernization from the macroscopic view of world historical development through quantitative analyses.

1. Connotations of Industrial Modernization

According to standard international division (United Nations, 2006), agriculture is the primary sector, industry is the secondary sector, and the service industry is the tertiary sector. Industry includes mining, manufacturing, construction and public utilities which cover the production and supply of water, electricity, heat and gas. Industrial modernization refers to the modernization of the industrial sector or industrial system. The study of industrial modernization has been going on for over 50 years, yet there is still no standard definition of it. Generally speaking, industrial modernization is both a state of the world's advanced level of modern industry and a process of reaching and keeping up with the world's advanced level of industry. Industrial modernization generally has four connotations, which can be understood as a change, a process, a transformation and a competition (Table 1). These four connotations may be combined to form diverse operational definitions.

Table 1 Four Connotations of Industrial Modernization

Definitions	Basic Connotations of Industrial Modernization
A change	Industrial modernization is an industrial change in the modernization process. It is a change of modern industry since the 18th century, covering the reasonable changes of industrial behavior, industrial structure, industrial economy, industrial technology, industrial institution, industrial mindset, business organization and business management
A process	Industrial modernization is a systematic process. The industrial modernization from the 18th century to the 21st century can be divided into two major periods, i.e., the first industrial modernization (industrialization) and the second industrial modernization (deindustrialization). In the 22nd century, new changes are bound to occur
A transformation	Industrial modernization is an industrial transformation covering the transformations from the traditional industry to the modern industry, and from the modern industry to the smart industry
A competition	Industrial modernization is an international competition, including the international competition and international differentiation, in which countries endeavor to catch up with, reach and keep up with the world's advanced level of industry since the 18th century. Industrial modernization may occur in both early-starting countries of modernization and latecomer countries. International industrial interaction occurs among different countries

It is believed in modernization science (He, 2012) that from the policy perspective, industrial modernization is a type of frontier change and international competition in the world industry since the 18th century. It is the frontier process of the formation, development, transformation and international interaction of modern industry; the composite process of the innovation, selection, propagation and withdrawal of industrial elements; as well as the international competition and international differentiation, in which countries endeavor to catch up with, reach and keep up with the world's advanced level in industry. Countries that manage to reach and keep up with the world's advanced level in industry are industrially developed countries, while others are industrially developing countries. Swap between the two groups happens with a certain probability.

2. Analytical Framework for Industrial Modernization

The time series analysis of industrial modernization is the analysis of the time sequence data and materials of the whole process of industrial modernization as an attempt to discover and summarize the facts and basic patterns of industrial modernization. In the process of industrial modernization, to some extent, the modernization of industrial production is its "micro-foundation", and the modernization of industrial economy is its "macro-manifestation"; some common elements of industry simultaneously act on industrial production and industrial economy, while industrial activities themselves and their surrounding natural environment as well as social environment mutually influence one another (Figure 1).

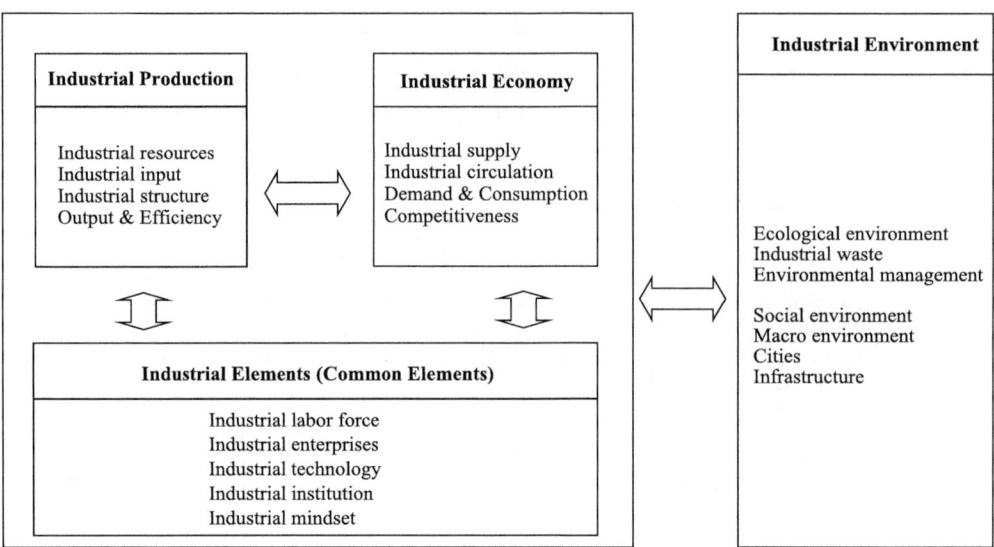

Figure 1　An Analytical Framework for Industrial Modernization

Note: The division between industrial production, industrial economy, industrial elements and industrial environment is relative; they mutually overlap and influence one another

This paper intends to do a time series analysis of world industrial modernization over a time span of over 300 years (1700-2010). We choose 15 countries as samples, including 8 developed countries and 7 developing countries, whose gross national income (GNI) accounts for about 73% of the world's total income, and whose population accounts for about 60% of the world's total population (Table 2). The analysis covers the 4 aspects of industrial production, industrial economy, industrial environment and industrial elements, with over 200 development indictors in 15 categories, as well as a quantitative evaluation on industrial modernization.

Table 2　Sample Countries for the Time Series Analysis of Industrial Modernization (2010)

Countries	Per Capita Income/ US dollars	Percentages of GNI in the World/%	Percentages of Population in the World/%	Countries	Per Capita Income/ US dollars	Percentages of GNI in the World/%	Percentages of Population in the World/%
United States	48,358	23.34	4.49	Mexico	8,885	1.63	1.71
Japan	43,118	8.58	1.85	Brazil	10,978	3.34	2.84
Germany	40,145	5.12	1.19	Russia	10,710	2.38	2.07
United Kingdom	36,703	3.57	0.90	China	4,433	9.25	19.43
France	39,186	3.98	0.94	Indonesia	2,947	1.11	3.50
Canada	46,211	2.46	0.50	India	1,419	2.67	17.51
Australia	51,746	1.78	0.32	Nigeria	1,437	0.36	2.32
Italy	33,761	3.19	0.88	Total	—	72.76	60.45

Source: World Bank, 2014

3. Basic Facts of World Industrial Modernization

Since the 18th century, industrial development in the world has been complicated, but general patterns can still be identified. Since the 20th century, about 68% of industrial indicators have become significantly correlated with the overall economic level of a country, more than 30 industrial indicators have undergone the reverse from an upward trend to a downward one, and industrial modernization progresses in a non-linear way. The following text will outline the history of world industrial modernization in terms of four aspects, i.e., industrial production, industrial economy, industrial elements and industrial environment.

3.1 Basic Facts of World Industrial Production

Since the 18th century, industrial production and industrial distribution in the world have seen overwhelming changes. These changes involved industrial resources, industrial input, industrial structure, industrial efficiency, etc.

First, industrial resources. The reserves of industrial resources are closely related to technological progresses. Progresses in technologies for exploration, drilling and refining have expanded the reserves. The total amount of industrial resources changes slowly, but the per capita amount changes relatively fast. The per capita amount of resources is in direct proportion to the total amount and in inverse proportion to population. In the 20th century, the per capita industrial resources of the world have declined on the whole, but in some countries the per capita amount has increased. The gaps between different countries are large.

Second, industrial input. Since the 18th century, both the share of employment in industry and the share of employment in manufacturing rose first and dropped later. In 2010, the share of employment in industry was around 22% in high-income countries (Figure 2). Since the 20th century, a pattern of rising first and falling later has been seen in the share of fixed asset formation in GDP, the share of industrial energy consumption in total energy consumption, the share of industrial electricity consumption in total electricity consumption, per worker electricity consumption and per worker energy consumption. Constant rises are seen in per worker capital and per worker fixed assets.

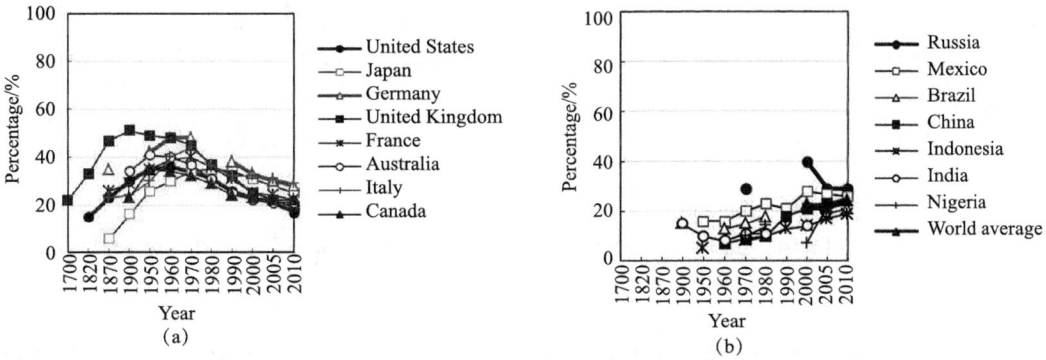

Figure 2   Changes of Employment in Industry from 1700 to 2010
Source: World Bank, 2014; Bannock and Baxte, 2009

Third, industrial output and efficiency. Since the 18th century, a pattern of rising first and falling later has been seen in the share of industrial value added in GDP (Figure 3), the share of manufacturing value added in GDP, and the energy consumption, electricity consumption and freshwater consumption per unit industrial value added. Constant rise is seen in the efficiency of industrial production, including the industrial labor productivity, manufacturing labor productivity, per capita industrial value added and per capita manufacturing value added. Currently, the absolute international gap in industrial labor productivity is near 300,000 US dollars, and the relative gap is over 300 times.

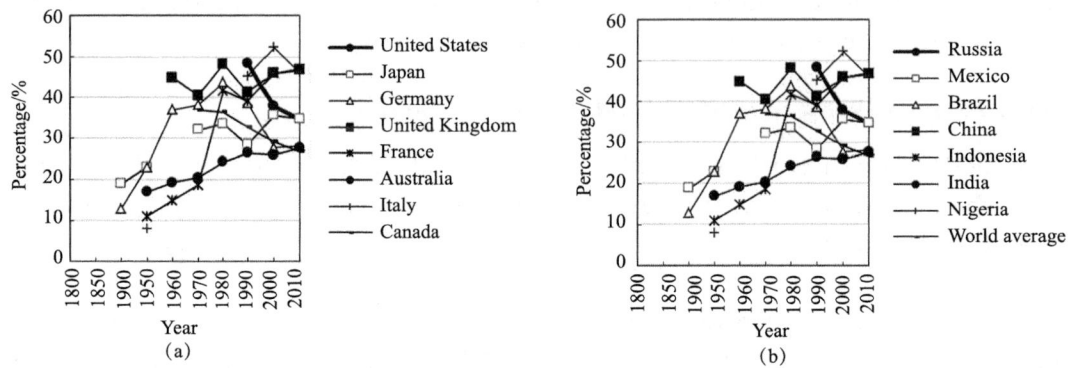

Figure 3   Ratio of Industrial Value Added from 1800 to 2010
Source: World Bank, 2014; Bannock and Baxte, 2009

Throughout the 20th century, the employment in industry (% of total employment) was uncorrelated with the industrial labor productivity and manufacturing labor productivity (Figure 4); the per worker capital, per worker energy consumption and per worker electricity consumption were positively correlated with industrial labor productivity and manufacturing labor productivity; the share of natural resources consumption in GNI was uncorrelated with the industrial labor productivity and manufacturing labor productivity.

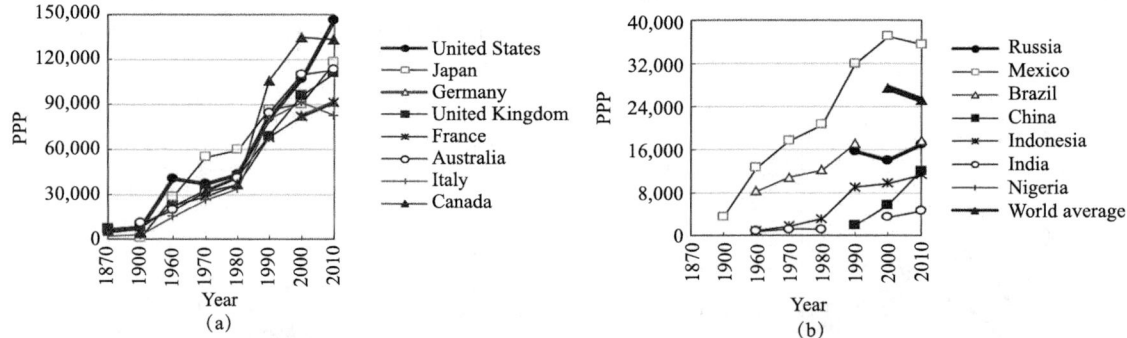

Figure 4   Industrial Labor Productivity from 1870 to 2010 (based on PPP[①] in 1990)
Source: World Bank, 2014; Bannock and Baxte, 2009

Fourth, industrial structure. Since the 18th century, changes in the structure of the national economy are shown in the following aspects: The shares of agricultural value added and

---

① PPP means purchasing power parity.

employment in agriculture both dropped; the shares of industrial value added and employment in industry rose first and then declined; the shares of service value added and employment in service both rose. Within the industrial sector, in terms of gross domestic product (GDP) and total employment, the shares of value added and employment in the mining industry first rose and then fell (with great differences between countries); the shares of value added and employment in the manufacturing industry rose first and then fell; the shares of value added and employment in the construction industry rose first and then fell; the share of value added in public utilities also rose first and fell later, and the share of employment in public utilities changed differently in different countries.

The internal structure of the manufacturing industry includes the technological structure and the industrial structure (Figure 5). Regarding the technological structure of the manufacturing industry, the share of high-tech value added rose, the share of medium-tech value added rose first and fell later, and the share of low-tech value added fell. The share of employment in high-tech industries rose but not without country gaps, the share of employment in medium-tech industries rose first and fell later, and the share of employment in low-tech industries dropped. Regarding the industrial structure of manufacturing, in the late 20th century, the shares of the food, beverage and tobacco industries varied vastly across countries, the shares of the textiles and garment industry fell, the share of the chemical industry rose, the shares of machinery and transportation equipment rose; the change of the shares of other manufacturing industries saw vast country gaps, and the change of the shares of the chemical and machinery industries also saw country gaps.

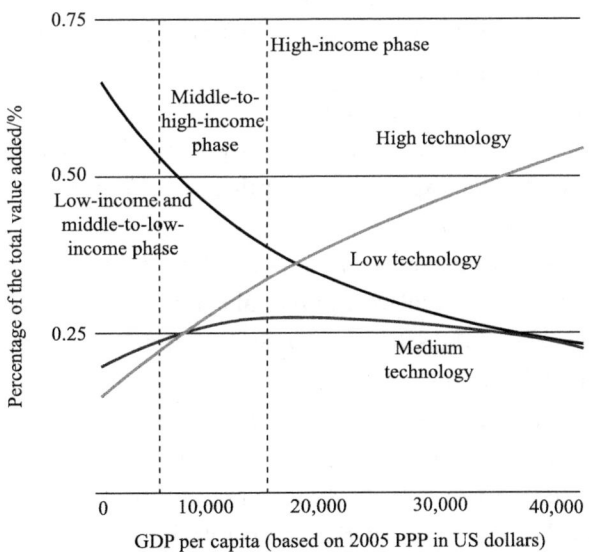

Figure 5 Technological Structure of the Manufacturing Industry in the 20th Century
(Sorted by Income Phase and Technology Group)
Source: UNIDO, 2013

3.2 Basic Facts of World Industrial Economy

From the 18th century to the 20th century, the industrial economy first took over the agricultural economy, and then was soon taken over by the service economy. The result was two transformations of world economy. In this process, profound changes occurred in the industrial supply, industrial circulation, industrial demand and consumption, and industrial competitiveness. Since the 20th century, about 80% of industrial economic indicators have been significantly correlated with the economic level of a country, and over 10 industrial economy indicators have seen the turning point; there is a limit for per capita industrial demand.

First, industrial supply. Since the 18th century, the per capita raw sugar supply has been constantly rising, yet with remarkable country gaps. The per capita output of iron and steel, coal and beer has gone through the pattern of rising first and falling later. Since the 19th century, the per capita output of cement, copper and fertilizers has gone through the pattern of rising first and falling later. Since the 20th century, the per capita output of electricity and natural gas has been on the rise. In 2010, the average per capita electricity supply was 9,524 kW·h in developed countries, and the world average supply was 3,118 kW·h.

Second, industrial circulation. Since the 20th century, the per capita road freight and per capita air transport have been on the rise; the international industrial trade has grown faster but with a large country gap; the simple mean applied tariff rate for manufactured products has declined, with the current world average lower than 10%; the per capita exports of both manufactures and high technologies have been growing, with the highest per capita high-tech exports in the world exceeding 20,000 US dollars and the lowest below 1 US dollar in 2010.

In the 20th century, the share of high-tech exports in manufactures exports increased; the share of medium- and high-tech exports in manufactures exports rose first and declined later; the share of medium- and low-tech exports in manufactures exports rose first and declined later; the share of low-tech exports in manufactures exports declined; the change of the shares of high-tech and medium-tech exports saw vast country gaps.

Third, industrial demand and consumption. Since the 20th century, the per capita consumption has been growing but there is a limit for per capita consumption needs. Currently, a downward trend is seen in the per capita consumption of iron and steel, cement, crude oil, raw sugar and fertilizers in developed countries.

In 2010, the highest per capita crude oil consumption was about 5,130 kilograms, and the lowest was about 64 kilograms, with a relative gap of about 80 times; the highest per capita chemical fertilizers consumption was about 150 kilograms/year, and the lowest was about 0.1 kilogram/year, with a relative gap of about 1,500 times.

Fourth, industrial competitiveness. In 2009, in the Competitive Industrial Performance rankings of 98 countries of the world, the top three were Singapore, United States and Japan (Table 3). In 2010, the manufactures exports of high-income countries accounted for 72.1% of the world total, that of middle-income countries accounted for 27.5%, and that of low-income countries accounted for 0.4%; the high-tech exports of high-income countries accounted for 65% of the world total, and that of middle-income and low-income countries accounted for 35%; in terms of these two indicators, the per capita levels of high-income countries were respectively 3.8 times and 3.5 times of the world average, while the per capita levels of middle-income countries were respectively 39% and 50% of the world average.

Table 3 Ranking of Competitive Industrial Performance Index, 2009

Ranking	Countries	Indexes	Ranking	Countries	Indexes	Ranking	Countries	Indexes
1	Singapore	0.642	60	Mauritania	0.144	89	Bolivia	0.073
2	United States	0.634	61	Jamaica	0.141	90	Mongolia	0.070
3	Japan	0.628	62	Costa Rica	0.135	91	Ghana	0.069
4	Germany	0.597	63	Senegal	0.134	92	Tanzania	0.068
5	Colombia	0.557	64	Albania	0.133	93	Ethiopia	0.068
6	Switzerland	0.513	65	Venezuela	0.131	94	Madagascar	0.059
7	Rep. Korea	0.480	66	Botswana	0.131	95	Panama	0.053
8	Ireland	0.479	67	Uruguay	0.129	96	Rep. Yemen	0.044
9	Finland	0.442	68	China	0.128	97	Algeria	0.042
10	Belgium	0.442	69	Syria	0.128	98	Azerbaijan	0.036

Source: UNIDO, 2009

3.3 Basic Facts of World Industrial Elements

For industrial elements, both quantitative and qualitative elements matter. World industrial development is subject to the influences of a wide variety of factors. Some basic factors, such as industrial labor force, industrial enterprises, industrial technologies, industrial institutions and industrial mindsets, exert influence on both industrial production and industrial economy. Since the 20th century, about 77% of the quantitative indicators of industrial elements have been changing in a relatively continuous and expectable manner.

First, industrial labor force. The industrial labor force is the performer of industrial production and the actor of industrial modernization. Since the 20th century, the quality of industrial labor force has been improving. This is mainly manifested in the growth of schooling years of industrial labor force. The constant increase in the income of industrial labor force is an inevitable result of the constant increase in the industrial labor productivity. The constant enhancement of the welfare of industrial labor force is mainly manifested in less working hours, the decreased rate of work-related injuries and enhanced social security.

Second, industrial enterprises. The industrial enterprises are the main places where industrial activities happen; they are the major sites of industrial modernization. Since the 20th century, corporate management has been improving, and more enterprises have been certified to the ISO system. The organizational structure of enterprises has undergone evolutions, with the corporate management level continuously improving; some industries have seen a higher concentration level, and industrial parks are developing. Quality management in enterprises has roughly gone through four stages: quality test, quality control, comprehensive quality management and international quality certification.

Third, industrial technologies. The development of industrial technologies can be divided roughly into three stages: traditional industrial technology (before the 18th century), modern industrial technology (from the 18th century to the 1970s), and smart industrial technology (since the 1970s): They respectively correspond to the agricultural economy era, the industrial economy era and the knowledge economy era. Since the 18th century, there have been three technological revolutions: the revolution of steam engine and machinery, the revolution of electricity and transportation, and the revolution of electronics and information. Among them, the third can be divided into two halves. The first half is the revolution of electronics and automation, while the second half is the revolution of information and smart technologies. We are currently at the second half of the third technological revolution, which is regarded as "Industry 4.0" by German scholars. The fourth technological revolution is around the corner (Table 4).

Table 4 Industrial Revolutions Since the 18th Century

Industrial Revolutions	General Time Frames	Main Characteristics	Key Technologies	Major Industries
First	1763-1870	Mechanization, steam engine	Steam engine, mechanical loom, machine tool, etc.	Steam engine, textile industry, machinery, coal, metallurgy, railway, etc.
Second	1870-1913	Electrification, internal combustion engine	Electricity, internal combustion engine chemical industry, telecommunication, etc.	Electricity, iron and steel, oil, chemical industry, automobile, aviation, telecommunication, etc.
Third (first half)	1945-1970	Automation, computer	Electronics, automatic control, aviation, other high technologies	Electronic industry, computer, television, nuclear power, aeronautics, automation products, etc.
Third (second half)	1970-2020	Informatization, smart technologies, greenization	Information technology, cloud computing, quantum communication, artificial intelligence, green technologies, etc.	Information industry, e-commerce, smart manufacturing, the internet of things, wireless network, big data, advanced materials, robots, the green industry, etc.
Fourth (predicted)	2020-2050	New biology, bionics, regeneration	Information converter, personality information package, bionics, life creation, regeneration, bio technologies, etc.	Biological industry, regenerative medicine, information converter, personality information package, bionic industry, life creation industry, regeneration industry, artificial intelligence, bionic person, etc.

Note: There is no unified understanding of Industrial Revolutions. Some believe that the first half of the third Industrial Revolution (the revolution of electronics and automation) is the third Industrial Revolution, while the second half of it (the revolution of informatization and smart technologies) is the fourth Industrial Revolution, e,g. the "Industry 4.0" in Germany
Source: He, 2015

Fourth, industrial institutions. According to institutional economists, an institution is a collection of the regulations, routines, ethics and customs that regulate human behavior. There are two interpretations of industrial institutions. One is in the narrow sense, which refers to the institutions established by industrial sectors, including institutions of industrial production, industrial economy and industrial technology. The other is in the general sense, which refers to industry-related institutions, including the industrial institutions in the narrow sense and institutions of industrial trade, industrial enterprises and industrial labor education. The evolution of industrial institutions roughly covers three stages: the industrial institutions for the agricultural economy era, that for the industrial economy era and that for the knowledge economy era (Table 5).

Table 5 Industrial Institutions in Human History (Examples)

Items	Primitive Economy Era	Agricultural Economy Era	Industrial Economy Era	Knowledge Economy Era
General time frame	Before 4000 BC	4000 BC to AD 1763	AD 1763 to 1970	1970 to 2100
Land	Public ownership	Private ownership, royal and church ownership	Private ownership, state ownership, collective ownership	Private ownership, state ownership, collective ownership
Production	Collective labor	Family workshop, etc.	Industrial enterprises, large-scale production	Flexible working, knowledge-based production
Circulation	Real object exchange	Regional trade, high tariffs	National market, GATT, high tariffs	Market globalization, WTO, low tariffs
Distribution	Even distribution	Distribution according to power and land ownership	Distribution according to capital or labor	Distribution according to contribution, adjustment according to needs
Consumption	Real-time consumption	Voluntary consumption	Taxed consumption, high consumption	Green consumption, reasonable consumption
Taxation	None	Land tax, poll tax	Value-added tax, income tax	Income tax, tariff
Science & Education	None	None	Vocational education	Industrial S&T services, pluralistic education
Environment	None	Water conservancy system, forest protection, etc.	Conservation area, national park, etc.	Environmental protection law, ecological security law, etc.

Fifth, industrial mindsets. There are two interpretations of industrial mindsets. One is in the narrow sense, which refers to the mindsets within the industrial sector, including the mindsets about industrial production and industrial economy. The other is in the general sense, which refers to the mindsets of the whole society about industry, including the mindsets in the narrow sense and the mindsets related to industry. The changes of industrial mindsets are manifested in three aspects: The first is concerning academic thoughts — changes of industrial thoughts; the second is concerning industrial norms — changes of industrial ethics; and the third is concerning industrial policy — changes of industrial institutions. The above part has discussed industrial institutions, and industrial ethics requires special study. Generally speaking, the changes of industrial mindsets are complicated and asynchronous, and show great differences across nations and times. The evolution of industrial mindsets roughly covers three stages: the industrial mindsets for the agricultural economy era, that for the industrial economy era, and that for the knowledge economy era. Specifically, it covers the mindsets on resources, production, circulation, distribution, consumption, taxation, enterprises, management, science and education, environment, etc.

3.4 Basic Facts of World Industrial Environment

Since the 18th century, the industrial environment has also gone through profound changes, including both the ecological environment and the social environment. Since the 20th century, the ecological environment has drawn wide attention, and the models of industrial development have been transformed in a green manner one after another. Since the 20th century, about 77% of the quantitative indicators of industrial environment have been changing in a relatively continuous and expectable manner.

First, ecological environment. Since the 20th century, greenhouse gas emission has been increasing, but in some countries it has already started to fall. This phenomenon accords with the Environmental Kuznets Curve (Figure 6, Figure 7).

Since the 20th century, the BOD (bio chemical oxygen demand) emission per worker and BOD emission per unit industrial value added in major countries have followed the pattern of rising first and falling later, and the wastewater treatment rate has been on the rise. The per capita industrial solid waste has been increasing, and the solid recycling rate has been on the rise, too.

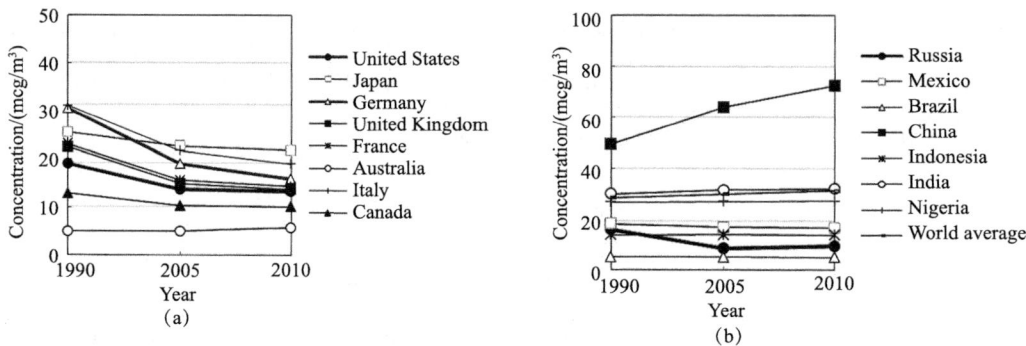

Figure 6 Average PM 2.5 Concentration (Average Concentration of Air Particulate Matter Nationwide)

Source: World Bank, 2014

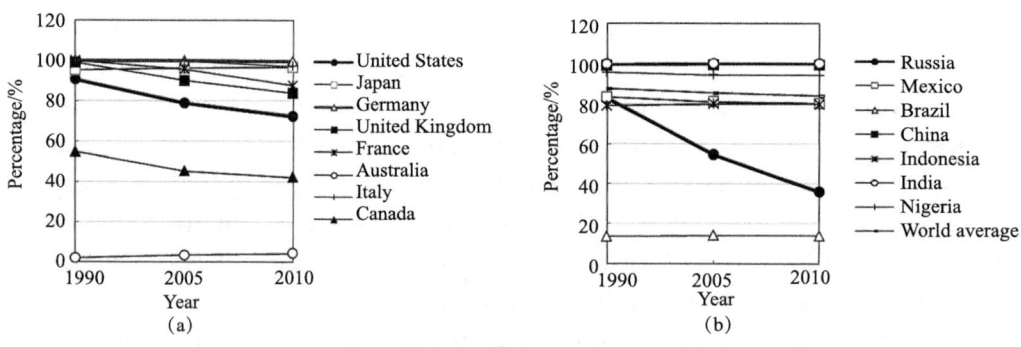

Figure 7 Percentage of Populations Affected by PM 2.5 Pollution (Exceeding the Health Standard of World Health Organization)

Source: World Bank, 2014

Second, social environment. Since the 19th century, the average life expectancy has been rising, the natural population growth rose first and then fell, the share of urban population has been growing (Figure 8); public health conditions have been improving, and the ratio of access to primary education has been increasing. Since the 20th century, progress has been made in universal secondary and higher education, and the computer penetration, and the internet penetration rate has been on the rise.

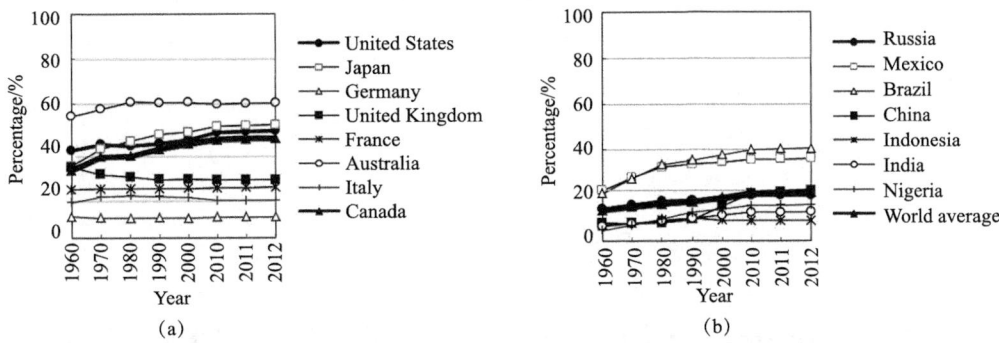

Figure 8   Changing Trend of Populations of Cities with One Million
or More Inhabitants from 1960 to 2012

Source: World Bank, 2014

4. Summary

Industrial modernization is a historical category that is universal and dynamic. This research has built an analytical framework for industrial modernization on four dimensions: industrial production, industrial economy, industrial elements and industrial environment. Then on this basis, it has analyzed the quantitative data in these four aspects, and presented the basic facts of world industrial modernization. It has depicted the development process of world industrial modernization in the past 200 years, and thus provided references for the reasonable choices of China's industrial modernization in the 21st century.

References

何传启(He C Q). 2015. 中国现代化报告 2014～2015: 工业现代化研究. 北京: 北京大学出版社.

Bannock G, Baxte R. 2009. The Palgrave Encyclopedia of World Economic History. London: Palgrave Macmillan.

He C Q. 2012. Modernizaiton Science: The Principles and Methods of National Advancement. New York: Springer.

UNIDO. 2013. Industrial Development Report 2013: Sustaining Employment Growth: The Role of Manufacturing and Structure Change. Vienna: United Nations Industry Development Organization.

UNIDO. 2009. Industrial Development Report 2009: Breaking in and Moving up: New Industrial Challenges for the Bottom Billion and the Middle-Income Countries. Vienna: United Nations Industry Development Organization.

United Nations. 2006. Standard International Trade Classification Revision 4, ISBN 92-1-161493-7.

World Bank. 2014. World Development Indicators Database. http://databank.Worldbank.org/data/reports.aspx? Source=world-development-indicators[2015-11-25].

Challenges and Policy Suggestions on China's Agricultural Modernization

Chuanqi He, Jing Jin

China Center for Modernization Research, Chinese Academy of Sciences

Agriculture is the cornerstone of human civilization. Without agriculture, there is no continuation of humankind or prosperity of human civilization. Agricultural modernization is the world frontier of agricultural development, and the actions and processes of reaching and keeping up with the world frontier. The frontier processes of agricultural modernization during the 18th and the 21st centuries can be divided into two stages. The first agricultural modernization (1763-1970) is the transition process from traditional agriculture to primarily modern agriculture, and from self-sufficient agriculture to market-based agriculture. The second agricultural modernization (1970-2100) is the transition process from primarily modern agriculture to highly modern agriculture, and from industrialized agriculture to knowledge-based and ecological agriculture (He, 2012). In policy terms, there are two major objectives for national agricultural modernization: to improve agricultural productivity and farmers' quality of life, and to maintain the stability of agricultural ecosystem and national food safety. The goal of developed countries is to maintain the world's advanced level in agriculture, while that of developing countries is to catch up with and reach the world's advanced level in agriculture.

China is still a country with preliminarily developed agriculture. Although China's agricultural modernization has made remarkable achievements since 1960, with some agricultural indicators already reaching the world's advanced level and the international gaps of some other agricultural indicators gradually narrowing, it is still faced with great challenges in agricultural efficiency, transformation, etc.

1. Two Large Gaps Concerning China's Agricultural Labor Productivity

The convergence of agricultural and non-agricultural rates of return is an important aspect of agricultural modernization, and the key to reaching such a convergence is the improvement of agricultural labor productivity. Agricultural labor productivity affects agricultural development, farmers' income, rural economic growth, etc. (Gao, 2015). In 2012, China's per unit yield of cereal, rice and wheat reached the level of developed countries, its per unit yield of corn reached the level of moderately developed countries, but China's agricultural labor productivity[①] was only over 50% of the world's average level, about 3% of the average level of high-income countries, and about 1% of that of the United States and Japan. Therefore, China's agricultural modernization is quite unbalanced with "one long leg" (high land productivity) and "one short leg" (low labor productivity). On one hand, China's agricultural labor productivity has increased significantly since 1960; in 2012, China's agricultural labor productivity was 615 dollars per person (Table 1), which was over 5 times of that in 1960 (Table 2). On the other hand, there are still two large gaps concerning China's agricultural labor productivity.

Table 1 Gap Between China's and the World's Agricultural Labor Productivity in 2012

Countries/Regions	Agricultural Labor Productivity/(dollars/person)	Indexes of Agricultural Labor Productivity
China	615	100
High-income countries	19,908	3,237
World average	1,097	178
United States	51,881	8,436
Japan	37,757	6,139
Germany	28,079	4,566
United Kingdom	23,736	3,859
France	59,401	9,659
Australia	41,028	6,671
Italy	39,275	6,386
Russia	4,865	791
Mexico	3,392	552

Note: The agricultural labor productivity is calculated at the constant price in 2000
Source: World Bank, 2015

Table 2 Gap Between China's Agricultural Labor Productivity and Industrial Labor Productivity from 1960 to 2012

Items	1960	1970	1980	1990	2000	2005	2012	2012/1960
Agricultural labor productivity / dollars in 2000	110	164	183	263	364	439	615	5.6
Industrial labor productivity / dollars in 2000	547	609	681	1,263	4,382	5,060	7,958	14.5
Industry − Agriculture	437	445	498	1,000	4,018	4,621	7,343	
Industry ÷ Agriculture	5	4	4	5	12	12	13	

Source: World Bank, 2015

First, there is a large gap between China's agricultural labor productivity and the world's highest level. According to the *World Development Indicators* of the World Bank (Table 1), in 2012,

---

[①] In this paper, the agricultural labor productivity is represented by the agricultural value added of each agricultural laborer, and the agricultural value added is the dollars calculated at the constant price in 2000.

China's agricultural labor productivity was 615 dollars per person, while the world average level was 1,097 dollars per person, which was nearly 2 times of the former; the average level of high-income countries was 19,908 dollars per person, which was over 30 times of that of China. In 2012, France's agricultural labor productivity was 59,401 dollars per person, which was nearly 100 times of that of China. The United States' agricultural labor productivity was 51,881 dollars per person, which was over 80 times of that of China.

Second, the relative gap between China's agricultural labor productivity and its industrial labor productivity has been over 10 times. Since 1960, China's modernization actually follows the strategy of unbalanced industrial development where the agricultural sector is used to support the industrial sector. As a result, industrialization is faster than agricultural modernization, and the gap between the two sectors is widening. For example, from 1960 to 2012, the absolute gap between China's agricultural labor productivity and industrial labor productivity had widened from over 400 dollars to over 7,300 dollars, and the relative gap has widened from about 5 times to about 13 times (Table 2). The difference between industrial labor productivity and agricultural labor productivity has already seriously affected China's labor productivity level.

The relatively low agricultural labor productivity has become a bottleneck constraining China's agricultural modernization. Increasing the agricultural labor productivity will become a fundamental task and priority in China's agricultural modernization.

2. China's Nutrient Structure Has Changed, but Still Has a Gap from High-income Countries

In recent years, the average nutritional status of Chinese people has significantly improved, the consumption of animal nutrition has significantly increased, and Chinese people's food consumption structure is changing remarkably. This is mainly shown in the fact that the per capita demand for and consumption of grain have approached the limit, and that the per capita demands for vegetable oil and fruits, animal nutrition, dairy, meat and feed cereal have all significantly increased.

2.1 China's Consumption Structure for Agricultural Products Has Changed

First, the average nutrition supply of Chinese people is increasing. According to the data of the United Nations Food and Agriculture Organization (FAO), in 2011, the per capita nutrition supply in China was 3,075 kcal/day, which was over 2 times of that in 1961 (Table 3); the per capita animal nutrition supply was over 10 times of that in 1961, and the proportion of animal nutrition was over 5 times of that in 1961 (Table 4).

Table 3 International Comparison of per Capita Nutrition Supply in China from 1961 to 2011
(Unit: kcal/day)

Countries/Regions	1961	1970	1980	1990	2000	2005	2011	2011/1961
China	1,415	1,840	2,146	2,504	2,806	2,877	3,075	2.17
United States	2,880	3,029	3,178	3,493	3,755	3,833	3,639	1.26
United Kingdom	3,231	3,279	3,116	3,242	3,363	3,440	3,414	1.06

								Continued
Countries/Regions	1961	1970	1980	1990	2000	2005	2011	2011/1961
Japan	2,525	2,738	2,799	2,949	2,900	2,828	2,719	1.08
Mexico	2,300	2,539	2,999	2,969	3,037	3,065	3,024	1.31
Brazil	2,209	2,405	2,698	2,720	2,880	3,078	3,287	1.49
India	2,010	2,111	1,994	2,204	2,378	2,267	2,459	1.22
High-income countries	3,016	3,175	3,306	3,374	3,465	3,486	3,523	1.17
World average	2,193	2,388	2,489	2,619	2,726	2,761	2,868	1.31
China ÷ World average	0.65	0.77	0.86	0.96	1.03	1.04	1.07	

Source: FAO, 2015

Table 4 Nutrition Supply and Food Consumption in China from 1961 to 2011

Indicators	Unit	1961	1970	1980	1990	2000	2005	2011	2011/1961
Per capita nutrition supply	kcal/day	1,415	1,840	2,146	2,504	2,806	2,877	3,075	2.17
Per capita animal nutrition supply	kcal/day	58	115	177	313	572	639	689	11.88
Per capita plant nutrition supply	kcal/day	1,411	1,772	2,029	2,299	2,335	2,335	2,386	1.69
Proportion of animal nutrition	%	4	6	8	13	20	22	22	5.50
Per capita protein supply	g/day	40.3	46.9	55.1	67.5	86.2	89.4	95	2.36
Per capita fat supply	g/day	15.6	24.5	35.1	56.4	81.1	87.8	93	5.96
Per capita cereal consumption	kg/year	93	131	157	178	165	156	153	1.65
Per capita meat consumption	kg/year	4	9	15	26	50	54	57	14.25
Meat consumption index (Meat/cereal consumption)		0.04	0.07	0.09	0.15	0.30	0.35	0.37	9.25

Source: FAO, 2015

Second, the per capita cereal consumption in China has a limit. Since 1961, the per capita cereal consumption in China (not including beer consumption) has increased from 93 kg/year to 182 kg/year in 1984, and then gradually decreased to 153 kg/year in 2011 (Table 4).

Third, China's consumption of non-cereal agricultural products has significantly increased. From 1961 to 2011, the per capita consumption of cereal in China increased by about 65%, the per capita consumption of meat increased by over 13 times, and the meat consumption index increased by over 8 times.

2.2 China's Nutrition Supply Lags Behind Some Countries

China's per capita nutrition supply has already exceeded the world's average level, but it still lags far behind the average level of high-income countries. Since 2000, China's per capita nutrition supply has already exceeded the world's average level (Table 3). In 2011, China's per capita nutrition supply, per capita animal nutrition supply, per capita plant nutrition supply, per capita protein supply, per capita fat supply and per capita meat consumption had all exceeded the world's average level, but they still fell behind the average level of high-income countries (Table 5).

Table 5 Comparison of Nutrition Supply and Food Consumption Between China and Other Countries and Regions in 2011

Countries/ Regions	Per Capita Nutrition Supply/ (kcal/day)	Per Capita Animal Nutrition Supply/ (kcal/day)	Per Capita Plant Nutrition Supply/ (kcal/day)	Per Capita Protein Supply/ (g/day)	Per Capita Fat Supply/ (g/day)	Per Capita Cereal Consumption/ (kg/year)	Per Capita Meat Consumption/ (kg/year)	Meat Consumption Index (Meat/Cereal Consumption)
China	3,075	689	2386	95	93	153	57	0.37
United States	3,639	995	2,644	109	162	106	118	1.11
United Kingdom	3,414	989	2,425	103	138	114	83	0.73
Japan	2,719	553	2,166	88	87	104	49	0.47
Mexico	3,024	613	2,411	85	93	158	61	0.39
Brazil	3,287	803	2,484	95	116	114	93	0.82
India	2,459	228	2,232	60	52	152	4.2	0.03
High-income countries	3,523	1,124	2,399	106	152	115	87	0.76
World average	2,868	507	2,362	80	83	147	42	0.29
China ÷ World average	1.07	1.36	1.01	1.19	1.12	1.04	1.36	1.30

Source: FAO, 2015

As the main sector for grain production and nutrition supply, China's agriculture is still faced with many challenges in guaranteeing food supply in the context of consumption structure transformation.

3. Policy Suggestions

China's agricultural modernization can make use of the experience of developed countries, exert its own advantages, make up for the weaknesses in the modernization process, and develop a canal path for agricultural modernization through continuous innovations. The content may include coordinating the two periods of agricultural modernization and continuing to transform towards the second agricultural modernization; coordinating the market-oriented development, mechanization, IT application, green development and internationalization of agriculture; accelerating the industrial restructuring and upgrading in agriculture; enhancing agricultural efficiency and farmers' income; improving farmers' welfare and quality of life; reducing the proportion of agricultural value added and the employment in agriculture; enhancing the international competitiveness in agriculture (He, 2010).

China's agricultural modernization may focus on three key points, make efforts in three aspects, and realize three transformations: 1) The three key points are modernization of agricultural efficiency, modernization of agricultural structure and modernization of farmers. 2) The three aspects are agricultural innovation system, farmers' training and agricultural regionalization. 3) The three transformations are transformation from food-dominated to nutrition-dominated, transformation from yield-dominated to benefit-dominated, transformation from production-and-supply-oriented to market-demand-oriented.

3.1 Establishing the Agricultural S&T Responsibility System, and Improving China's Agricultural Innovation System

Agricultural labor productivity is the weakest point in China's agricultural modernization. Increasing the agricultural labor productivity should become the priority in China's agricultural modernization. The main approaches to increase agricultural labor productivity include increasing farmers' per capita capital and farmers' skills, agricultural technological progress, optimization of resources allocation and economies of scale. Among them, building an agricultural innovation system, increasing the ratio of agricultural scientific and technological input, and increasing agricultural innovation capacity and agricultural technological service capacity are important to increase agricultural production efficiency.

We suggest that a new agricultural science and technology innovation system should be built that adapts to the development of modern agriculture. This innovation system may include two levels: the national agricultural innovation system and the regional agricultural innovation system. The national agricultural innovation system consists of national scientific research institutes, comprehensive universities and central government-owned enterprises pertaining to agricultural science and technology. The regional agricultural innovation system is formed at the provincial scale, agricultural universities are the hinge, and agricultural enterprises are the backbone.

A regional agricultural S&T responsibility system should be built in which agricultural universities are responsible for the agricultural S&T services and personnel training in the local provinces. Efforts should be made to promote the regrouping of agricultural scientific research institutes and agricultural universities, and form a regional agricultural S&T center. Priority should be given to exerting the role of key modern agriculture enterprises and agricultural cooperatives, and enhancing the skills of all farmers.

The specialized agricultural websites should be used as the platform; the research and promotion of agricultural advanced technologies should be used as support; the collection, organization and popularization of information should be taken as the link; the market demand should be taken as the orientation. On such a basis, a virtual and flexible innovation service network should be built to promote cooperative innovation and technological transfer; to improve the responsiveness, adaptability and risk management capacity of agriculture; to enhance the innovation capacity and agricultural efficiency.

3.2 Implementing New Farmers' Training Program and Comprehensively Improving Farmers' Quality

Another important approach to increase agricultural labor productivity is to improve farmers' quality. We suggest that a farmers' training program be carried out to train a new generation of farmers who are adaptable to market and being professional.

We suggest that 12-year compulsory education be gradually popularized in rural areas on the basis of 9-year compulsory education. To young and middle-aged farmers, "free skill training" or "non-profit skill training" should be provided. Full-time farmers who are engaged in farming for over 10 months should receive agricultural skill training; main-job farmers who are engaged in farming for 4 to 10 months or part-time farmers who are engaged in farming for less than 4 months should receive agricultural skill training and work skill training, so that their employability can be enhanced.

The fees for rural free compulsory education and farmers' training may be coordinated and shared by central finance and provincial finance. The trainers may come from teachers of agricultural universities, agricultural research institutes or promotion organizations.

3.3 Revising the Agricultural Regionalization and Realizing the Coordinated Development of the Three Agricultural Types

Accelerating the agricultural restructuring and promoting agricultural transformation is an important aspect of agricultural modernization in China. The main approaches to agricultural transformation include transfer of agricultural labor force, and transformation of agricultural production, agricultural economy, agricultural elements and agricultural ecological environment. Agricultural restructuring not only requires coordination with other material sectors, but also requires reasonable allocation among all agricultural sectors and all crop production, and therefore, the agricultural regionalization is of important guiding significance. The agricultural regionalization can scientifically forecast the development direction of agricultural production, and can effectively guide the current agricultural restructuring and formulation of the medium- and long-term development plans for agriculture.

In 1981, the Integrated Agricultural Regionalization of China divided the country into ten first-level integrated agricultural regions and 38 second-level regions (Agricultural Regional Planning Committee of China, 1981). The tenth region was the marine-fishery region, and the other nine regions were called the nine integrated agricultural regions (Table 6).

Table 6   Integrated Agricultural Regionalization of China

Division Types	Main Regions
Comprehensive division	Northeast China farming-forest region, Inner Mongolia and Great Wall-side pastoral-farming-forest region, Huang-Huai-Hai farming region, Loess Plateau farming-forest-pastoral region, middle-lower Yangtze farming-forest culture region, Southern China farming-forest-tropical-crop region, Southwest farming-forest region, Gansu-Xinjiang farming-pastoral-forest region, Tibetan Plateau pastoral-farming-forest region, marine-fishery region
Geographical division	Southern China paddy farming region, Northern China dry farming region, Northwest pastoral and irrigation farming region, Qinghai-Tibet alpine pastoral and farming region

With the advancement of China's industrialization, urbanization and globalization, and with the formation of a high-speed transportation network, people's nutritional structure and demand have also changed tremendously, and the original agricultural regionalization needs revision.

We suggest that the integrated agricultural regionalization of China should be revised once every ten years according to the three standards which are the principles of "agricultural science, economic geography and ecology". This new integrated agricultural regionalization can be briefly called the "three-dimensional based regionalization" (Table 7).

Table 7 Three Types Based on Human and Economic Geography for Chinese Agriculture

Region Types	Characteristics	Agricultural Types to be Mainly Developed (Examples)
Urban agriculture	High land rent, dense population, close to markets	Capital-intensive agriculture, facility agriculture, factory farming, contract farming, etc.
Suburban agriculture	Relatively high land rend, relatively dense population, close to markets	Organic agriculture, ecological agriculture, leisure agriculture, part-time farming, etc.
Rural agriculture	Low land rent, sparse population, high transportation cost	Large-scale agriculture, specialized agriculture, precision agriculture, tourism agriculture, etc.

Note: The development of the three region types are relative and may overlap

From the perspective of economic geography, Chinese agriculture can be divided into urban agriculture, suburban agriculture and rural agriculture. Different regions have different features and different agricultural focuses.

The above text briefly analyzes the challenges facing China's agricultural modernization process and the policy suggestions for them. Agricultural modernization is a complicated systematic project. According to the past experience of developed countries, the process of agricultural modernization is also a process in which the ratio of agriculture declines (Bai, 2004). To realize this, it is impossible to simply rely on the agricultural sector itself; great efforts must be made to develop the secondary and tertiary sectors, and enhance their capacity to largely absorb the rural labors. In the process of agricultural modernization, the "regurgitation-feeding" of the secondary and tertiary sectors to agriculture would be indispensable.

References

白跃世(Bai Y S). 2004. 中国农业现代化路径选择分析. 北京: 中国社会科学出版社.
高帆(Gao F). 2015. 农业劳动生产率提高的国际经验与中国的选择. 复旦学报(社会科学版), 01: 116-124.
何传启(He C Q). 2010. 现代化科学: 国家发达的科学原理. 北京: 科学出版社.
何传启(He C Q). 2012. 中国现代化报告 2012: 农业现代化研究. 北京: 北京大学出版社.
全国农业区划委员会(Agricultural Regional Planning Committee of China). 1981. 中国综合农业区划. 北京: 中国农业出版社.
World Bank. 2015. World Development Indicators. http: //databank.Worldbank.org/data/home.aspx [2015-4-14].

Analysis on Diversity and Imbalance of Service Modernization: A View Based on the Second Modernization Evaluation

Qing Ye

China Center for Modernization Research, Chinese Academy of Sciences

The term "diversity" originates from biology. In 1995, the United Nations Environment Programme (UNEP) published the *Global Biodiversity Assessment*, which gave a simple definition on "biodiversity": total diversity and variability of living things and of the systems of which they are a part [1]. Many scholars argue that biodiversity is an extensive and complicated concept, and its derivative meaning extends profoundly to all aspects of human life and activities. Nowadays, diversity is increasingly applied to various fields beyond biology, such as cultural diversity, civilization diversity [2], world diversity, democracy diversity, geographical diversity, environmental diversity, landscape diversity, etc. The modernization study also often borrows the concept of diversity as a perspective for analyzing problems, so can service the modernization study.

Service modernization (SM) refers to a profound change of the service sector and service economy since the 18th century; it covers the two shifts from traditional service to mechanized and electrified service, and from mechanized and electrified service to knowledge-based and green service, as well as various changes such as the continuous increase of the ratio of service sector to national economy, changes of service mode and view, improvement of the service technological level, service workers' quality, and the international competitiveness of the service sector, as well as the changes in the structure and international status of the service economy. It is a historical process in that the service modernization from the 18th century to the end of the 21st century covers two periods, i.e., the first service modernization and the second service modernization; it is also an international competition in which countries endeavor to catch up with, reach and keep up with the world's advanced level in service; it also covers the changes of domestic service content, quality, structure, system and mindset.

1. Evaluation Model for Service Modernization

The evaluation of the level of service modernization is conducted via SM indexes, which reflect the actual progress of service modernization and the relative gap between different countries and the world's advanced level. Based on the signal indicators of the progress of service modernization, we can judge the development stages of service modernization. Development levels are not equivalent to development stages. According to the second modernization theory, and taking into consideration the progress of service modernization, this paper has selected some key indicators that can represent the typical characteristics of service modernization, and established an evaluation model for service modernization [3], which includes two parts: level evaluation and period evaluation.

1.1 Level Evaluation

The evaluation of service modernization level covers service content, service quality and service governance (Table 1). The mathematical model is as follows.

$$\begin{cases} SMLI = (I_C \times I_Q \times I_M)/3 \\ I_C = (\sum C_i)/N_C & (i = 1, 2, \cdots, N_C) \\ I_Q = (\sum Q_k)/N_Q & (k = 1, 2, \cdots, N_Q) \\ I_M = (\sum M_j)/N_M & (j = 1, 2, \cdots, N_M) \end{cases}$$

wherein $SMLI$ is the SM index; I_C is the service content index, I_Q is the service quality index, and I_M is the service governance index; C_i is the index of the ith indicator for service content, i is the serial number of the evaluation indicator for service content, and N_C is the total number of the evaluation indicators for service content; Q_k is the index of the kth indicator for service quality, k is the serial number of the evaluation indicator for service quality, and N_Q is the total number of the evaluation indicators for service quality; M_j is the index of the jth indicator for service governance, j is the serial number of the evaluation indicators for service governance, and N_M is the total number of the evaluation indicators for service governance. The values of all indexes are less than or equal to 120, and the standard values are the average values of the indicators across high-income countries in that year (Table 1).

Table 1 Evaluation Structure for SM Indexes

Items	Service Modernization Evaluation	Evaluation Indicators
Evaluation objective	Service modernization progress	
Evaluation dimension	SM index	
Service content (scale, structure)	Service value added in GDP/%	Services, value added of GDP/%
	Service employment in total employment/%	Employment in services of total employment/%
	Per capita knowledge-based service*	Per capita R&D, education and health expenditure
	Per capita producer service*	Per capita air transport, freight /million t/km
Service quality (efficiency, quality)	Service labor productivity	Service labor productivity
	Per capita service value added	Per capita service value added
	Per capita service trade	Per capita service trade imports and exports
	Per capita international travel revenue	Per capita international tourism, receipts

Items	Service Modernization Evaluation	Continued Evaluation Indicators
Service governance (resource, capability, innovation)	Cultural quality of labor force	Labor force with tertiary education of total/% **
	Service infrastructure	Fixed broadband subscription (per 100 people) ***
	Government governance capacity	Average time to clear exports through customs/day
	Service innovation capacity	Percentage of R&D expenditure in GDP/%

* Due to limited access to statistical data, the per capita knowledge-based service is replaced by per capita science and technology, education and health expenditure, and the per capita producer service is represented by per capita air freight. ** The percentage of labor force with tertiary education in 1980 is replaced by the data of 1990. *** The fixed broadband subscription rate in 1980 is replaced by the phone penetration rate

1.2 Period Evaluation

The first service modernization is the process of service mechanization, electrification and automation. The share of service value added, the share of employment in the service industry, the ratio of service value added to agricultural value added, the ratio of service labor force to agricultural labor force, and the SM index can be used as the signal indicators for the first service modernization.

The evaluation model for the development stages of the first service modernization and period-dividing standards for signal indicators can be seen in Table 2.

Table 2   Signal Indicators and Judging Criteria for World Service Modernization Progress

Signal Indicators		Share of Service Value Added in GDP/%	Share of Employment of SM in Total Employment/%	Service Value Added /Agricultural Value Added	Service Labor Force/Agricultural Labor Force	SM Indexes
The second	Maturity	⩾80	⩾80	⩾80	⩾80	
	Development	⩾70, <80	⩾70, <80	⩾35, <80	⩾35, <80	
	Start-up	⩾60, <70	⩾60, <70	⩾15, <35	⩾15, <35	⩾60
The first	Transition	⩾50, <60	⩾50, <60	⩾10, <15	⩾5, <15	⩾50
	Maturity	⩾40, <50	⩾40, <50	⩾5, <10	⩾3, <5	⩾40
	Development	⩾30, <40	⩾30, <40	⩾2, <5	⩾1, <3	⩾20
	Start-up	⩾20, <30	⩾20, <30	⩾1, <2	⩾0.5, <1	
Traditional service		<20	<20	<1	<0.5	

Notes: 1) Four signal indicators are used to judge whether a country is in the first or second service modernization stage. This stage division is consistent with the stage division for world modernization. 2) The criteria for judging whether the second service modernization has been started are the share of service value added ⩾60%, the share of employment in service industry ⩾60%, and the other indicators are used as amendatory indicators. 3) The SM index is used as an amendatory value for stage division: for the start-up period of the second service modernization, the SM index ⩾60; for the transition period of the first service modernization, the SM index ⩾50; for the maturity period of the first service modernization, the SM index ⩾40; for the development period of the first service modernization, the SM index ⩾20. 4) The criteria for completion of the first service modernization are the share of service value added ⩾50%, the share of employment in the service industry ⩾50%, and the SM index ⩾60

$$\left\{\begin{array}{l} P_{fsm} = \sum(P_{\text{Share of service value added}}, P_{\text{Share of employment in service industry}}, P_{\text{Ratio of service to agricultural value added}}, P_{\text{Ratio of service to agricultural labor force}}, SMLI) \\ P_{\text{Share of service value added}} = (4, 3, 2, 1, 0), \text{ the development stage and the assigned value are determined according to the comparison between the actual value and the standard value} \\ P_{\text{Share of employment in service industry}} = (4, 3, 2, 1, 0), \text{ the development stage and the assigned value are determined according to the comparison between the actual value and the standard value} \\ P_{\text{Ratio of service to agricultural value added}} = (4, 3, 2, 1, 0), \text{ the development stage and the assigned value are determined according to the comparison between the actual value and the standard value} \\ P_{\text{Ratio of service to agricultural labor force}} = (4, 3, 2, 1, 0), \text{ the development stage and the assigned value are determined according to the comparison between the actual value and the standard value} \\ SMLI = (4, 3, 2), \text{ the development stage and the assigned value are determined according to the comparison between the actual value and the standard value} \end{array}\right.$$

wherein P_{fsm} stands for the development stages of the first service modernization, $P_{\text{Share of service value added}}$ stands for the development stage determined according to the share of service value added, $P_{\text{Share of employment in service industry}}$ stands for the development stage determined according to the share of employment in the service industry, $P_{\text{Ratio of service to agricultural value added}}$ stands for the development stage determined according to the ratio of service to agricultural value added, $P_{\text{Ratio of service to agricultural labor force}}$ stands for the development stage determined according to the ratio of service to agricultural labor force, and $SMLI$ stands for the development stage determined according to the SM index.

The evaluation model for the development stages of the second service modernization is as follows.

$$\left\{\begin{array}{l} P_{ssm} = \sum(P_{\text{Share of service value added}}, P_{\text{Share of employment in service industry}}, P_{\text{Ratio of service to agricultural value added}}, P_{\text{Ratio of service to agricultural labor force}}, SMLI) \\ P_{\text{Share of service value added}} = (7, 6, 5), \text{ the development stage and the assigned value are determined according to the comparison between the actual value and the standard value} \\ P_{\text{Share of employment in service industry}} = (7, 6, 5), \text{ the development stage and the assigned value are determined according to the comparison between the actual value and the standard value} \\ P_{\text{Ratio of service to agricultural value added}} = (7, 6, 5), \text{ the development stage and the assigned value are determined according to the comparison between the actual value and the standard value} \\ P_{\text{Ratio of service to agricultural labor force}} = (7, 6, 5), \text{ the development stage and the assigned value are determined according to the comparison between the actual value and the standard value} \\ SMLI = (7, 6, 5), \text{ the development stage and the assigned value are determined according to the comparison between the actual value and the standard value} \end{array}\right.$$

wherein P_{ssm} stands for the development stages of the second service modernization, $P_{\text{Share of service value added}}$ stands for the development stage determined according to the share of service value added, $P_{\text{Share of employment in service industry}}$ stands for the development stage determined according to the share of employment in the service industry, $P_{\text{Ratio of service to agricultural value added}}$ stands for the development stage determined according to the ratio of service to agricultural value added, $P_{\text{Ratio of service to agricultural labor force}}$ stands for the development stage determined according to the ratio of service to agricultural labor force, and $SMLI$ stands for the development stage determined according to the SM index.

1.3 Evaluation Standards

The service modernization evaluation takes the average values of the indicators across high-income countries in that year as the standard values (Table 3).

Table 3 Standard Values of the Evaluation Indicators for Service Modernization Level

	Indicators and Units	1980	1990	2000	2010	2013
Service content	Service value added in GDP/%	58.1	69.3	70.5	73.6	73.9
	Service employment in total employment/%	58.2	60.1	66.8	72.4	70.6
	Per capita knowledge-based service/$	612	2,795	3,818	6,892	7,455
	Per capita air freight/(t/km/person)	20.5	40	79.8	108	101
Service quality	Service labor productivity/$	23,943	42,716	48,686	70,705	77,435
	Per capita service value added/$	5,635	13,385	14,388	23,097	24,874
	Per capita service trade/$	586	1,234	1,973	4,532	5,343
	Per capita international travel revenue/$	—	179	268	515	628
Service governance	Labor force with tertiary education of total/%	24.6	24.6	28.1	32.7	34.5
	Fixed broadband subscription/%	25.1	0.23	1.6	23.8	27.3
	Average time to clear exports through customs /day	—	—	14.1	13.4	12.7
	Percentage of R&D expenditure/%	1.6	2.0	2.3	2.4	2.4

Note: The values are the average values of high-income countries or the top 20 developed countries in service in the year. Fixed broadband subscription in 1980 is replaced by the phone penetration rate. The percentage of labor force with tertiary education in 1980 is replaced by the data of 1990

2. Results of Service Modernization Evaluation

The signal indicators are used to judge the world service modernization progress from 1980 to 2013. A total of 131 countries are evaluated, and the overall evaluation results are shown in Table 4.

The coordinates of world service modernization in 2013 are shown in Figure 1.

In terms of SM index, in 2013, 21 countries including Belgium and Switzerland belong to developed countries in the service sector, 23 countries including Estonia and Italy belong to moderately developed countries in the service sector, 29 countries including Argentina and Dominica belong to preliminarily developed countries in the service sector, and 58 countries including Namibia belong to underdeveloped countries in the service sector (Table 4).

It can be seen from Table 4 that in 2013, China ranks the 59th among 131 countries in the world, belonging to the preliminarily developed countries in the service sector and at the intermediate level among developing countries in the service sector; its service modernization level is still far from the world's advanced level. China has not yet completed the first service modernization, nor has it entered the second service modernization. In the past 30 years, China's service modernization level has significantly improved, yet it is still remarkably far from the world's advanced level.

Table 4 Development Stages and Development Levels of World Service Modernization from 1980 to 2013

Countries/Areas	No.	Development Stages					Development Levels				
		1980	1990	2000	2010	2013	1980	1990	2000	2010	2013
Sweden	1	4	5	5	5	6	A	A	A	A	A
United States	2	5	5	5	6	6	A	A	A	A	A
Finland	3	3	4	4	5	5	A	A	A	A	A
Australia	4	4	4	4	5	5	A	A	A	A	A
Switzerland	5	4	5	5	6	6	A	A	A	A	A
Norway	6	4	4	5	5	5	A	A	A	A	A
Japan	7	4	4	5	5	5	A	A	A	A	A
Denmark	8	4	5	5	5	5	—	A	A	A	A
Germany	9	4	4	5	5	6	—	A	A	A	A
The Netherlands	10	4	5	5	5	6	A	A	A	A	A
Canada	11	4	5	5	6	6	A	A	A	A	A
Singapore	12	5	6	6	6	6	A	A	A	A	A
United Kingdom	13	4	5	6	6	6	A	A	A	A	A
France	14	4	4	5	5	5	A	A	A	A	A
Belgium	15	5	5	6	6	6	A	A	A	A	A
Austria	16	4	4	5	5	5	A	A	A	A	A
New Zealand	17	4	4	4	4	4	A	A	A	A	A
Republic of Korea	18	2	3	4	4	4	B	B	B	A	A
Israel	19	4	5	5	6	6	A	A	A	A	A
Italy	20	3	4	5	5	5	B	B	B	A	B
Ireland	21	3	3	4	5	5	B	A	A	A	A
Spain	22	3	4	4	5	5	B	B	B	A	A
Estonia	23	3	2	4	5	4	—	C	B	B	B
Slovenia	24	—	3	4	4	4	—	A	B	B	B
Uruguay	25	4	3	3	3	4	B	C	C	B	B
Russia	26	—	2	2	3	4	—	C	C	C	B
Slovakia	27	—	3	2	4	4	—	C	C	B	B
Greece	28	3	3	4	5	5	B	B	B	B	B
Hungary	29	1	2	4	4	4	C	C	B	B	B
Czech Republic	30	1	3	3	5	4	—	C	B	B	B
Portugal	31	2	3	4	5	5	B	B	B	B	B
Belarus	32	2	1	2	2	3	—	D	D	C	C
Latvia	33	2	2	2	4	4	—	C	C	B	B
Lithuania	34	—	3	3	4	4	—	C	C	B	B
Georgia	35	2	2	1	2	2	—	D	D	C	C

Continued

Countries/Areas	No.	Development Stages					Development Levels				
		1980	1990	2000	2010	2013	1980	1990	2000	2010	2013
Ukraine	36	0	0	1	2	2	—	D	D	D	C
Bulgaria	37	2	2	2	3	3	C	C	C	B	B
Lebanon	38	1	4	4	3	3	—	B	B	C	B
Kazakhstan	39	—	2	1	2	2	—	D	D	D	C
Poland	40	2	2	2	4	4	C	C	C	B	B
Argentina	41	2	2	3	3	3	B	C	B	B	C
Panama	42	3	2	3	4	5	B	C	B	B	B
Croatia	43	—	4	3	4	4	—	B	B	B	B
Saudi Arabia	44	3	3	3	3	4	A	B	B	B	B
Colombia	45	4	2	2	2	2	C	C	C	C	C
Kuwait	46	5	5	5	5	4	A	B	B	B	B
Chile	47	3	2	3	3	3	B	C	C	B	C
Macedonia	48	—	2	2	2	3	—	D	C	C	C
Azerbaijan	49	2	1	1	2	2	—	D	D	D	C
Moldova	50	1	1	1	2	2	—	D	D	C	C
Romania	51	1	1	2	2	3	—	D	D	C	C
Venezuela	52	3	2	2	2	2	B	C	D	C	C
Uzbekistan	53	—	1	1	1	1	—	D	D	D	D
Dominica	54	2	2	3	3	3	D	C	B	B	C
Armenia	55	—	1	1	2	2	—	D	D	C	C
Paraguay	56	2	2	2	2	2	C	D	D	D	D
Costa Rica	57	2	2	3	3	4	B	C	C	B	B
Brazil	58	2	2	2	3	3	C	C	C	C	C
Mexico	59	2	2	3	3	3	C	C	C	C	C
Botswana	60	2	2	2	2	2	D	C	C	D	D
Peru	61	2	2	2	2	2	C	C	C	C	C
Jamaica	62	2	3	3	3	3	—	B	C	C	C
Jordan	63	4	4	3	4	4	A	B	C	B	B
South Africa	64	2	2	2	2	3	B	D	C	C	C
Turkey	65	2	2	2	3	3	D	C	C	B	B
Ecuador	66	2	2	2	2	2	C	D	D	C	C
Iran	67	2	2	2	2	2	C	D	D	D	C
Mongolia	68	2	2	1	2	2	C	D	D	D	D
Morocco	69	1	2	2	2	2	D	D	C	C	C
Malaysia	70	1	2	2	3	3	C	C	B	B	B
El Salvador	71	2	2	2	2	2	D	D	D	D	C

Continued

Countries/Areas	No.	Development Stages					Development Levels				
		1980	1990	2000	2010	2013	1980	1990	2000	2010	2013
Egypt	72	2	2	2	2	2	D	D	D	C	C
China	73	0	0	1	2	2	D	D	D	C	C
Algeria	74	1	1	2	2	2	D	D	D	D	D
Turkmenistan	75	—	1	1	1	1	—	D	D	D	D
Tunisia	76	1	2	2	2	2	D	D	C	C	C
Albania	77	0	0	1	2	2	—	D	D	C	C
Kyrgyzstan	78	1	1	1	1	1	—	D	D	D	D
Tajikistan	79	1	0	1	1	1	—	D	D	D	D
Bolivia	80	2	3	2	2	2	D	C	D	D	D
Myanmar	81	1	0	0	1	0	D	D	D	D	D
Philippines	82	1	2	2	2	2	D	D	D	D	C
Thailand	83	1	1	2	2	2	D	D	D	C	C
Namibia	84	2	2	2	2	2	D	C	C	D	D
Zimbabwe	85	1	1	1	1	1	D	D	D	D	D
Honduras	86	1	1	2	2	2	D	D	C	D	D
Nicaragua	87	1	2	1	2	2	—	D	D	D	D
Vietnam	88	1	1	1	2	2	—	D	D	D	D
Kenya	89	1	1	1	2	2	D	D	D	D	D
Sri Lanka	90	1	1	2	2	2	D	D	D	D	D
Republic of the Congo	91	2	2	1	1	1	C	D	D	D	D
Indonesia	92	1	1	1	2	2	D	D	D	D	D
Zambia	93	1	0	1	1	1	D	D	D	D	D
Guatemala	94	1	2	2	2	2	D	D	D	D	D
Mauritania	95	1	1	1	1	1	D	D	D	D	D
Cote d'Ivoire	96	2	1	2	1	1	C	D	D	D	D
India	97	1	1	1	2	2	D	D	D	D	D
Pakistan	98	1	1	1	2	1	D	D	D	D	D
Lesotho	99	1	1	1	1	1	D	D	D	D	D
Cambodia	100	1	1	0	1	1	—	D	D	D	D
Cameroon	101	1	1	1	1	1	D	D	D	D	D
Eritrea	102	0	2	2	2	2	—	D	D	D	D
Syria	103	2	2	2	2	2	C	D	D	C	D
Ghana	104	1	1	1	2	2	D	D	D	D	D
Chad	105	1	1	1	1	1	D	D	D	D	D
Mozambique	106	0	1	1	1	1	D	D	D	D	D
Guinea	107	1	1	1	0	1	—	D	D	D	D

Continued

Countries/Areas	No.	Development Stages					Development Levels				
		1980	1990	2000	2010	2013	1980	1990	2000	2010	2013
Republic of Yemen	108	0	1	1	2	2	—	D	D	D	D
Papua New Guinea	109	0	0	0	0	0	D	D	D	D	D
Haiti	110	0	0	1	0	—	—	D	D	D	D
Nepal	111	0	0	0	1	1	D	D	D	D	D
Senegal	112	1	1	2	2	2	D	D	D	D	D
Sierra Leone	113	1	0	0	1	0	D	D	D	D	D
Democratic Republic of the Congo	114	1	1	1	1	1	—	D	D	D	D
Laos	115	0	0	0	1	1	—	D	D	D	D
Malawi	116	0	0	1	1	1	D	D	D	D	D
Togo	117	1	1	1	1	1	D	D	D	D	D
Madagascar	118	1	1	1	1	1	D	D	D	D	D
Mali	119	1	1	1	1	1	D	D	D	D	D
Nigeria	120	1	1	1	2	2	—	D	D	D	D
Bangladesh	121	1	1	1	1	1	D	D	D	D	D
Tanzania	122	1	0	1	1	1	—	D	D	D	D
Benin	123	2	1	1	1	2	D	D	D	D	D
Niger	124	0	1	1	1	1	D	D	D	D	D
Angola	125	0	1	1	0	—	—	D	D	D	D
Uganda	126	0	0	1	1	1	D	D	D	D	D
Central Africa	127	0	0	1	1	0	D	D	D	D	D
Burkina Faso	128	1	1	1	1	1	D	D	D	D	D
Ethiopia	129	1	0	1	1	1	D	D	D	D	D
Burundi	130	0	0	0	1	1	—	D	D	D	D
Rwanda	131	0	1	1	1	1	D	D	D	D	D
High-income countries	132	4	4	5	5	5					
Middle-income countries	133	1	1	2	2	3					
Low-income countries	134	—	1	1	1	2					
World average	135	2	3	3	3	4					

Notes: 1) For country's development stages, 0 stands for the traditional service sector, 1 stands for the start-up period of the first service modernization, 2 stands for the development period of the first service modernization, 3 stands for the maturity period of the first service modernization, 4 stands for the transition period from the first service modernization to the second service modernization, 5 stands for the start-up period of the second service modernization, 6 stands for the development period of the second service modernization, and 7 stands for the maturity period of the second service modernization. 2) For development levels, A stands for developed countries in the service sector, B stands for moderately developed countries in the service sector, C stands for preliminarily developed countries in the service sector, and D stands for underdeveloped countries in the service sector

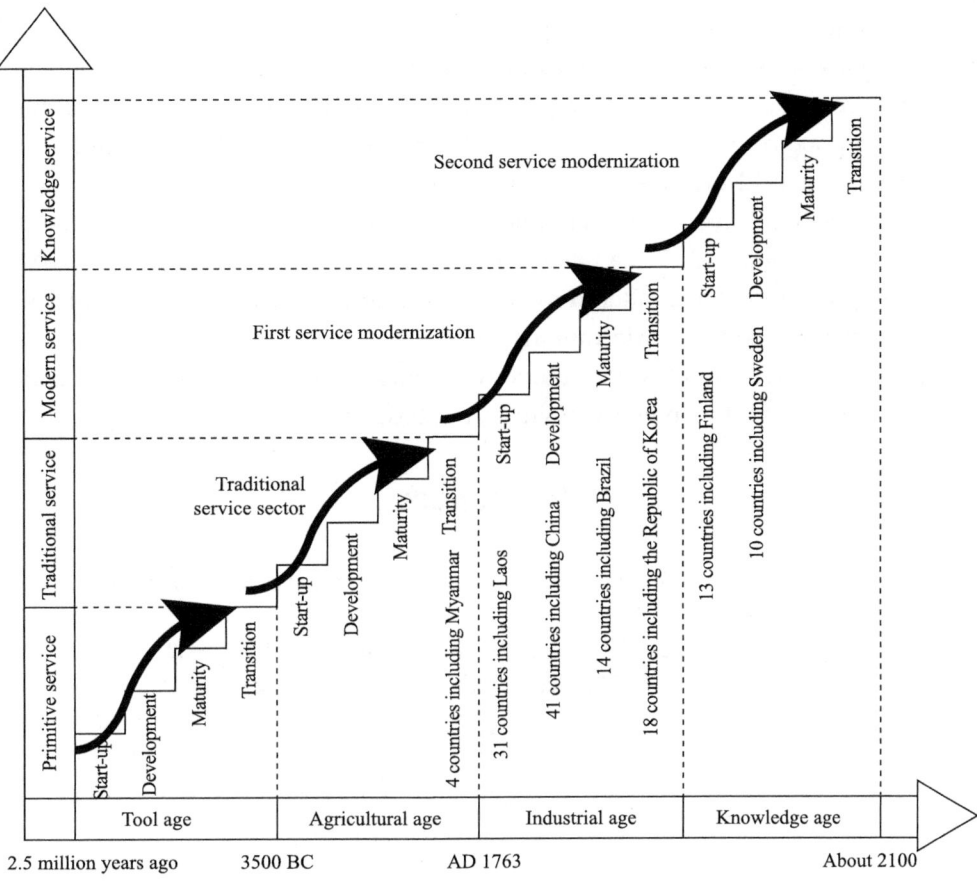

Figure 1 Coordinates of World Service Modernization in 2013

3. Diversity Features of Service Modernization

Take the evaluation results in 2013 for example, the diversity and imbalance of service development across countries are very prominent, which are mainly reflected in five aspects.

First, diversity of service modernization process (Table 4). In 2013, 23 countries at the world service frontiers have entered the second service modernization, 102 countries are still in the first service modernization, while 4 countries are still in the traditional service period. If the average annual growth rate from 2000 to 2013 is maintained, by 2020, 37 countries will have entered the second service modernization; by 2030, 58 countries will have entered the second service modernization; by 2040, 74 countries will have entered the second service modernization; by 2050, 97 countries will have entered the second service modernization. China is expected to enter the second service modernization in around 2030.

Second, diversity of the service modernization level. The relative gap in national service modernization level is 33 times. There are 18 countries with a SM index above 100, which are Belgium, Switzerland, Finland, the Netherlands, United States, France, Denmark, Sweden, Israel, Singapore, Germany, Australia, United Kingdom, Norway, Austria, Ireland, Canada and New Zealand; 37 countries including Haiti have a SM index below 20.

Third, diversity of service indicator development. The difference among the indicators is remarkable. None of the countries have all the 12 indicators up to the reference value (average value of high-income countries). The development of service indicators is unbalanced.

Fourth, diversity of service modernization speed. Some countries undergo rapid growth while some undergo negative growth. Compared to that in 2000, the vast majority of the countries in 2013 have undergone positive growth in the SM index, except for Chad, which has undergone negative growth. The world average of the annual average growth rate of the SM index is 3.4%. Among the countries that have not yet completed service modernization, from 2000 to 2013, 69 countries including Georgia and China have moved up in the world rankings of the SM index, 57 countries including Lebanon have fallen down in the world rankings, while 5 countries including Greece remain unchanged in the world rankings.

Fifth, geographical diversity of service modernization. Africa remains the most underdeveloped area. This is consistent with the diversity of world modernization.

References

[1] Heywood V H. 1995. Global Biodiversity Assessment: Summary for Policy-Makers. Cambridge: Cambridge University Press.
[2] 盖光(Gai G). 2007. 从生物多样性走向文化多样性. 科学技术与辩证法, 24(2): 24-32.
[3] 何传启(He C Q). 2013. 现代化科学: 国家发达的科学原理. 北京: 科学出版社.

Part Four

Ecological Modernization and Green Development

Staging Pathways Towards Ecomodernity[1]

Atle Midttun

BI Norwegian Business School

1. Introduction

We live in an age that harvests the fruits of modernity. Cultural values in Europe released in the Enlightenment era have emancipated us from dogma, promoted individual freedom, and unleashed entrepreneurship in science and technology. On this basis the world productivity has developed on a scale never seen before, fostering a material basis for human welfare that has allow the human species to more than quadruple since 1900.

As several scholars, including Eisenstadt (1992, 2003), Parsons (1971) and Matrinelli (2005), have pointed out, modernity is closely connected with the processes of economic development, permanent innovation and the unprecedented growth of technology and economic expansion under the emergence of the industrial society. Anthony Giddens has argued that this made modernity vastly more dynamic than any previous type of social order (Giddens, 1998: 94). He attributed this to the complex of economic institutions, especially industrial production and a market economy together with political institutions and mass democracy.

Yet modernity in the 21st century has reached a scale and scope that challenges its very foundations, particularly as the modern industrial society is still largely carbon-based. In what has been called the age of the anthropocene, the footprint of modern human societies on the planet has exacerbated ecological crises thus bringing modernity into a confrontation with itself.

Paradoxically, it is precisely the dynamism that Giddenes points to, which has led modern development to transcend its ecological limits. Berger (1977) has shown — combining the insights from Karl Marx and Niclas Luhman — that the dynamic market economy, once set free, developed into an autopoietic system which might subordinate both the society and environment to economic exploitation. Modernity's hyper dynamism is therefore also its weakness.

---

[1] Based on Midttun A, Witoszek N. 2016. Energy and Transport in Green Transition: Perspectives on Ecomodernity. Oxon and New York: Routledge.

One of the contentions of this paper is that modernity is now in need of a serious revision. Indeed there are many indications that modernity is moving to its next phase: ecomodernity. Ecomodernity seeks to rebalance modernity's relation to its natural environment and social context, and to set continued modernization on a more sustainable course. At a stage when the massive expansion creates problematic side effects, industrial creativity needs to be redirected, and the ecological and social limitations need themselves to be brought into the commercial equation. Terms such as the "circular economy", "resource efficiency" and "pro-sociality" indicate a reorientation of the commercial process to ecological and social considerations, and to aim at advanced industrialization to serve human welfare and well-being.

However, ecomodernity does not only imply adjustment at the level of technology, but also entail a deeper change of mindset and overarching world view. Inspiration for this change may interestingly come from early roots of modernity itself. The Renaissance and early Enlightenment humanists developed thinking that inspired sceptical scientific examination replacing blind traditionalism and theocratic dogma. This type of thinking is equally valid for a pivotal revision of modernity. As Toulmin (1990) has famously argued in his *Cosmopolis: The Hidden Agenda of Modernity* that the limited mechanistic atomism that characterized modernity at its technocratic heyday, moved away from the broader holistic outlook inherent in the Renaissance, namely humanist foundations of modernity.

Facilitated by modern systems thinking, ecomodernity reconnects with modernity's early scientific and critical roots in seeking solutions to modernity's technocratic exploitative excesses. This involves addressing the socialist critique of commercial exploitation of workers to establish pro-sociality in a hyper-competitive world. Similarly, ecomodernity highlights the consequences of commercial over-exploitation of our natural habitat, and lays a basis for ecological correctives.

As opposed to the Romanticism, which was a critique of the Enlightenment's reason, ecomodernity resorts to reason and science to scrutinize its own excesses. Big data, system analysis and simulation models allows us to better understand the complex interplay between markets, technology, ecology and social behavior.

This paper explores the transition to ecomodernity with a particular focus on climate change. It does so by highlighting new ways of reconciling modernity with ecological concerns. These ways can be called revolutionary approaches, but are not revolutions themselves, which can trigger the reform processes and evolve into major systemic changes after a period of time. This paper discusses important mechanisms of ecomodern transition.

(1) It highlights the need to introduce a cultural/visionary perspective into our thinking around techno-economic evolution. Transformation of our cognitive outlook thereby becomes an integral part of the innovation process.

(2) The paper recognizes that ecomodern transition may be controversial and may entail a "battle of modernities" that compete for hegemony. It therefore includes the challenges to forging changes, not only at the product level, but also at the industry and societal levels.

(3) The paper argues that the complicated and controversial nature of transition entails a need for staging complex pathways across commercial, political and technological realms. It therefore explores transition to ecomodernity from a strategic game perspective.

(4) The paper shows how green pathways may evolve across the globe. It therefore analyses innovation journeys where technology migrates from market to market, thriving on global

variation.

(5) The paper ends by illustrating how radical changes towards ecomodernity may take place by triggering exponential green growth. It therefore contends that ecologically unsustainable conventional growth can be countered by creative staging of green growth.

2. Triple Cycles of Innovation

While technology and business are obviously critical to emerging ecomodernity, we argue that the parallel evolution of visions and institutions is also essential to understanding the complementary societal changes. In our application to the broad green transition, we therefor argue that the process towards ecomodernity may be fruitfully analyzed as an interplay between three cycles: a generic product cycle, where new green innovations that launch technological revolutions create new industrial actors and commercial dynamics; a visionary cycle, where a new societal vision develops and matures; an institutional cycle, which codifies and formalizes supportive organizational frameworks. The paper thus expands the concept of the product cycle from innovation studies, which highlights the process from emerging new prototypes towards novel mature products, to also including visions and institutions.

Green transition, as this perspective suggests, plays out through the dynamic interface between the three cycles. As visions consolidate, they motivate public interventions and stimulate new components of the green product cycle. If successful, these new components feedback to — and strengthen — the original vision and gradually institutionalize it. Transition to ecomodernity may thus be driven by a mutual interplay between technology, visionary policy and green institutionalization, where the three cycles may reinforce one another and together drive green transition in a manner that would not have been possible with only one alone (Figure 1). Firstly, visionary public engagement based on stories, images and role models may trigger policy support for dynamic technology development and commercial entrepreneurship. In turn, successful commercial entrepreneurship confirms the validity and attractiveness of the original vision and mobilizes further visionary development, which is gradually consolidated by supportive institutional structures.

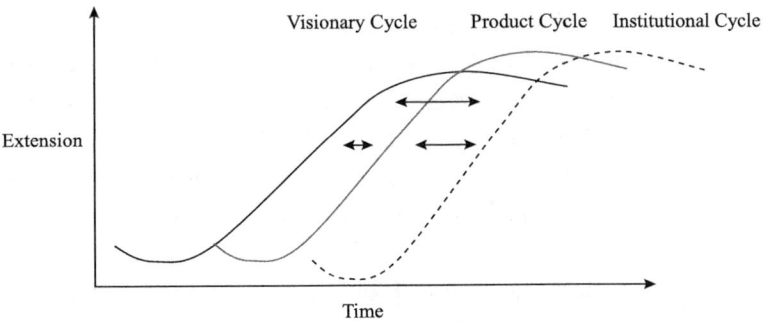

Figure 1   The Visionary, Product and Institutional Cycles

As in the case of early emergent product innovation, visionary and conceptual innovation towards ecomodernity began from inspiring but often unrealistic initiatives. The pioneering "prototypes" have ranged from "small is beautiful", deep and shallow ecology, sustainability, corporate social responsibility, "green-dark religion", and ecological villages and cities, to massive public mobilizations for the Earth manifested in the success of the social mobilization platforms such as 350.org and Avaaz.

These visions were initially dismissed as mere chimeras by the apostles of the carbon industry. And yet there are reasons to believe that they were crucial to the emergence of the agenda of ecomodernity based on incremental green innovation. As scenarios of ecomodernity mature and interface more closely with mainstream politics and business, there are signs that the balance is changing not only towards realism, but also towards deeper penetration.

There have been rich and manifold visions of ecological correctives to industrial modernity. They grew out of movements such as the Sierra Club in the USA that mobilized one of the USA's major grassroots societies. The club focused strongly on protecting wilderness, but eventually moved into clean air, clean water and endangered species. More recently, the club has engaged against fossil fuels that cause climate disruption and toward a clean energy economy. In Britain, the Coal Smoke Abatement Society — formed in 1898 and one of the oldest environmental NGOs was instrumental in promoting clean air legislation, notably after the Great London Smog of 1952, when several thousands died. The society gradually moved on to campaign against emission beyond air quality and took on a broader environmental agenda, rebranded as the Environmental Protection UK. Together with numerous other similar initiatives, visions of alternative and ecological paths for modern development have evolved and matured.

In line with business and economy in general, environmental NGOs have also scaled up to embrace the global arena. Organisations like Greenpeace and Friends of the Earth are cases in point. Through non-violent direct actions and outspoken initiatives, they have captured the public's imagination, and have triggered debate around major parts of industrial modernity.

The visionary contributions to redirecting modernity in an ecological direction have also come from leading intellectuals like Schumacher, Amory Lovins and Dennis Meadows. Lovins has systematically promoted energy efficiency and the use of renewable energy sources, and has advocated a "Negawatt Revolution" arguing that utility customers don't want kilowatt-hours of electricity, and they want energy services. Meadows has raised public attention to the need for modern industrial development to come to terms with its limitless resource use and pollution (Meadows et al., 1972). Numerous thinkers have followed their footsteps and helped generate the intellectual underpinnings of an alternative vision of modernity.

Green visions have gradually diffused into most political parties, but in particular through green parties that have specialized in ecomodern transformation. One of the most successful green parties in Europe has been the German BUND. The party is committed to a broad ecomodern agenda, including issues such as fostering the use of renewable energies, banning the production of genetically modified food and fodder, and reducing the amount of toxic chemicals in everyday life.

The growing strength of the ecological re-framing of modernity is demonstrated through its gradual accommodation by governments and international organizations. For instance, the International Energy Agency's (IEA) global development scenarios have broken down barriers by challenging several dogmas in the carbon-dominated energy supply: 1) Renewable energy (except large hydropower) was not scalable and was able to play a significant role in the energy supply; 2) intermittent renewable energy could not provide a modern stable energy supply; and 3) renewable energy could not deliver energy at cost-effective prices. Another visionary contribution to green innovation has been the EU and the Green Peace's joint report, "Energy Revolution: A Sustainable World Energy Outlook" (2007). The report insisted that all that was missing from the feasible cuts of CO_2 emission was the right policy support — a point which started a policy mobilization across continents. Still another contribution to the visionary cycle came with the "Vision 2050 Report" published by the World Business Council for Sustainable Development in February 2010. Its novelty lays in defying the perception of the green transition as a cost-incurring exercise and identifying unprecedented opportunities for business in the green economy. A multitude of commitments to green transition by governments, unions and regions have followed, including the European Commission's "Energy Roadmap 2050" (2011), indicating that the visionary cycle is reaching a maturing stage, where green transition is penetrating into mainstream thinking. These programs and agendas and their steady impacts both on the perceptions of green transition and on techno-economic practice show that ecomodernity has made some progress within existing commercial and political structures.

The visionary roadmaps for green transition have been strengthened by an explicit tie and a trend toward green growth. This trend has emerged through a series of international programs and agreements that are gradually redefining the global outlook on ecology and economy. Those programs and agreements witness the pioneering United Nations Environment Program (UNEP) launched in 1972, followed by the Green Economy Initiative, or the United Nations Economic and Social Commission for Asia and the Pacific, which released the "Low Carbon Green Growth Roadmap for Asia and the Pacific" (UNESCAP, 2012).

Moving from the visionary toward the institutional cycle highlights how green reorientation of modernity has fostered the buildup of new organisation and numerous regulatory initiatives. To take the EU as an example[1], its environmental reorientation has been institutionalized through a series of so-called environmental action programmes. They have evolved over almost half a century, from controlling a broad range of pollution problems in the early 1970s and 1980s to new complex and holistic framework legislation, such as the "Ambient Air Quality Directive" and the "Water Framework Directive" in the 1990s. The current 7th environmental action programme enhances broad and inclusive ecomodernity by protecting, conserving and enhancing the EU's natural capital; by turning the EU into a "resource-efficient, green, and competitive low-carbon economy"; by safeguarding the EU's citizens from environment-related pressures and risks to health and wellbeing. In addition, the programme signals a special focus on the greening of cities and on international environment and climate challenges.

The environmental action programmes have been followed up by a multitude of specific measures that serve to take the vision down to tangible actions. For example, the EU targets for 20% reduction of greenhouse gasses, 20% increase in energy efficiency and 20% increase in the share of renewables, all by 2020. To realize these specific targets, the EU will negotiate with individual member countries, and the EU emission trading scheme, which was launched as a major tool for CO_2 reduction, will be carried out. In addition, tariffs and certificate markets have been developed by individual countries. In the building sector, the EU has set a goal of nearly zero energy use in new buildings by 2019. In the transport sector, the measures include energy efficiency targets for ships, emission limits for cars, as well as the demands for halving

---

[1] http://www.hiz.hr/icttrain/en/trainings/01/01.html.

conventionally fueled vehicles in cities by 2030 and fully phasing them out by 2050.

The EU has imposed demands on all sectors of the economy to benchmark lifecycle's resource efficiency. Furthermore, the EU has taken measures to eliminate waste landfill by 2020, and has taken measures for vast recirculation and for the improvement of drinking water's quality, as well as bathing water's quality. Measures to improve management so as to avoid over exploitation of natural resources are also taken.

Finally, with regard to product cycle, the reorientation of policy, institution and regulation from narrow industry towards broader ecomodernity has stimulated technological innovation on a broad front. This includes a whole set of renewable energy technologies, as well as efficiency improvement in conventional energy generation. For example it includes transition to new engines and drive trains in the transport sector, alongside efficiency improvement in the conventional combustion engine. Across many other sectors of economy, environmental concerns, regulatory requirements and incentives have triggered rethinking of products, processes and business organisations. One example is the development of building standards in construction industry, where the sector is rapidly moving towards passive house and zero emission buildings.

3. Battle of Modernities

Implication in the understanding of ecomodern transition as a broad, transformative process lies in the recognition that we may see changes not only in products and technologies, but also in business models leading to a radical remaking of industries and indeed also of societies. At the product and process level, business may engage in innovation by refining, reconfiguring or inventing green products and processes, while at the same time maintain stability within business and industry. At the business level, innovation becomes more comprehensive and involves re-engineering of business processes or combining new business concepts. At the industry level, radical innovation forges new industry structures. Such structural changes obviously also have wider social and cultural implications, and as previously argued social and cultural visions may in fact trigger industrial and technological changes.

Transition towards ecomodernity therefore easily entails rivalry with other alternatives. We have called this rivalry the "battle of modernities", where technologies, business models, interests and visions compete for hegemony. Taking energy as an example: What we have defined as "carbon modernity" grew during the late 1800s and through much of the 1900s as a dominant economic mode which allowed modern industrial society to produce goods for mass consumption. In the next phase, nuclear electrical modernity was launched as a civilian application of nuclear technology, which had been developed for military weaponry during World War II. This peaceful application was designed to transcend the limitations of carbon-based energy and give the world oxygen back through the abundance of clean energy. Today's emerging of "ecomodernity" is a new wave that stems from the critique of carbon and nuclear excesses, while encompassing shifts in culture and politics. It is focused on an alternative, post-carbon and post-nuclear economy based on renewables.

In energy, ecomodernity comes in two stages: The first stage is supply-driven, and depends on solar, wind and hydroelectric energy as well as adequate management of these resources. There is also a looming second, demand-driven stage of ecomodernity which is less dependent on outside supply and uses resources located close to the consumer. Concepts such as "energy-plus" houses, "smart grids" and "prosumership", present alternatives to carbon, nuclear and renewable-based technologies which are supplied via the central grid.

In the beginning of the 21st century, these various modernities competed to reinvent themselves to answer today's energy and climate challenges. The carbon and nuclear modernities imply a continuation of the scale and scope of existing centralized systems, though with improved climate performance. Supply-driven ecomodernity adds new resource bases with extensive relocation of electricity generation and raises new demands for balancing intermittent solar and wind supply. Finally, demand-driven ecomodernity moves the focus out of the energy system and implies a radical involvement on the consumers' side, with energy efficiency and self-supply becoming dominant concerns.

Ecomodern transition therefore easily ends up as disruptive (Christensen, 1997) when seen from the incumbent industry's perspective. Both wind power and photovoltaics are now taking over substantive market shares from the mainstream carbon-based energy supply. From simple applications at the bottom of the market, they have moved up in the market, to some extent displacing established competitors, thereby disrupting existing structures and markets. In combination with information technology that has opened up avenues for new sharing economy and customer-centric green energy "prosumership", they now challenge conventional centralized electricity industry.

In line with our triple cycle perspective, the battle of modernities — exemplified in energy above — is not only a battle of technologies, but also a battle of visions and definitions. The proponents of carbon modernity have traditionally held hegemony in the field by coupling energy, growth and employment. The cognitive formula that buttresses their position is as follows: a carbon-based energy supply delivers cheap power, which in turn delivers industrial competitiveness and growth, and hence generates employment (Figure 2).

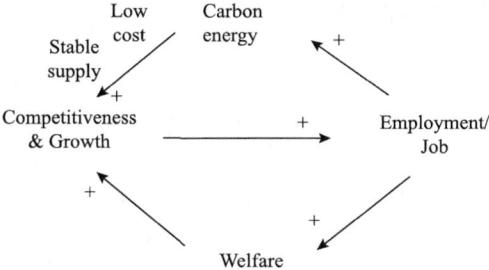

Figure 2 Cognitive Assumptions of Carbon Modernity

When seen from this perspective, ecomodernity in its initial stage represents the unappetizing alternative: high costs of green technologies and increased energy costs associated with alleged weaker competitiveness, less growth and unemployment.

However, carbon modernity's cognitive hegemony is breaking up, and the pivotal link between renewable energy, growth and employment is increasingly becoming recognized. Most importantly, from the wider ecomodernity's perspective, the link between green growth and job goes beyond economic welfare; its benefits include an increase in human well-being and an increase in the quality of life (Figure 3).

The shifting relationship between growth and job from carbon to ecomodernity is eminently illustrated in California: In 2012, broad popular mobilization called the "California New Environmental Movement" defeated the initiative financed by oil company which was aimed at

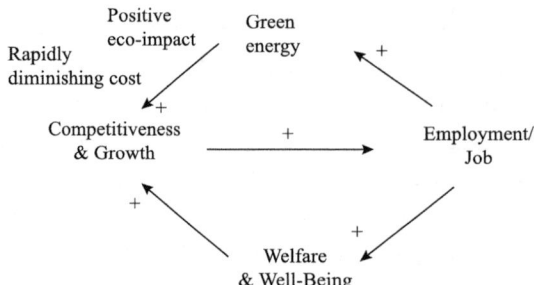

Figure 3　Cognitive Assumptions of Ecomodernity

overturning the state's global warming legislation, which was recognized as the toughest in the nation. The initiative, which was sponsored by Texas-based oil companies Tesoro and Valero Energy Resources, funded a campaign under the catchphrase — "California Job Initiative," which claimed that too many incentives for clean energy and energy efficiency had destroyed California's economy and had cost thousands of jobs. According to the companies' "Proposition 23", California's pro-climate legislation was to be suspended unless the state's official unemployment rate fell to 5.5% or below for four quarters in a row. Clearly, while the stated goal was to protect job and economy, the de facto objective was to repeal existing environmental legislation. As a response, Californians organized a massive "No to Proposition 23" campaign which led to the defeat of the oil companies' "California Job Initiative". The result of this campaign was the creation of a network of "Communities United Against the Dirty Energy Proposition", which had morphed into "Communities United for Clean Energy and Job". The latter has organized to promote green innovation and job in California and around the nation.

4. Staging Complex Pathways

Given the complex interplay among technology, commerce and culture, as well as the "battle of modernities", transition to ecomodernity becomes a complex journey — to paraphrase a widely known US innovation study (van de Ven et al., 2008). As carbon, nuclear and ecological strains collide and struggle for hegemony, there are surprising turns, discontinuities, shifts and quantum leaps: a process reminiscent of "punctuated equilibrium" in evolutionary biology, where development is marked by raptures, retardations and sudden advances.

Our suggestion is that the transition towards ecomodern sustainability resembles, in many ways, a relay race, where various factors can drive innovation at different stages (Figure 4). At one point, changes may be driven by politics or governance, while at another point, the baton is taken by market and technology. Still at a later stage, civic mobilization and cultural influence become the main advancing agents. Causality may therefore change as in a relay run, across governance, product and cultural cycles. In addition, chance events may transform the contest. Strong policies may easily lead to a backlash, while softer and less confrontational policies with triggering effects in other institutional domains may have a better chance of success. The sequential triggering may build momentum behind green policies and stimulate a stronger, de facto green effect. In this way, transitions that at first would appear impossible because of the massive counter-forces, may become possible as sequential triggering gradually builds up momentum.

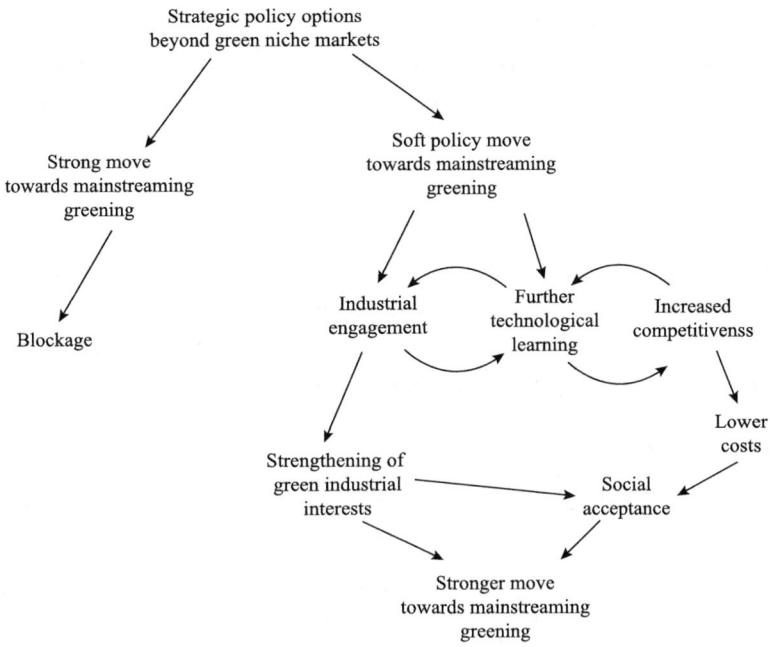

Figure 4   The Relay Model in Open Game Form

5. Innovation Pathways in a Heterogeneous World

In addition to building momentum through relay processes, green transition may also rely on niches where green initiatives can find favorable conditions at a given stage of their development[①]. Global diversity in industrial institutional and cultural conditions may hence be essential to eco-modern development. The story of photovoltaics (PVs) is a case-in-point — indicating how the interplay among diverse regions may create opportunities for technology development that no single region alone could accomplish.

In a recent study (Midttun and Toporowska, 2014), we have followed PVs from its early stages in the US space industry, to later phases in Japan and Germany, and finally its mass production in China, from where PVs is now spreading on a purely commercial basis. We found that regional specialization across the world — with diverse cultural, political, financial, entrepreneurial and technological competencies — has provided unique lead-market conditions that at the right moment were crucial to drive technology down the learning curve. The shift from one lead market to another has typically come as the first market failed. Let us briefly recapitulate the stadia of this journey.

5.1 US Initiates PVs

The early start of PVs in the US space program in the late 1960s marked an important move into operative industrial use. By coupling PVs to the space-industrial complex, the US provided a pioneering niche market for early technology development as well as an advanced arena for technological research. Yet the US did not have institutional preconditions or political will to take PVs towards deployment in mainstream competitive energy markets. The result was that the US

---

① There is, in other words, likely a parallel to the "niche" concept in biology, where some species find locations with natural characteristics that they then adapt to and survive under.

lost out as a leading market for PVs. While the application in the space industry was highly successful, it did not manage to penetrate into larger-volume markets. The technology therefore remained a niche product with a strong research base, but with very limited applications in the US.

5.2 Japan Follows up

Pressure from resource's scarcity combined with high technology competence and strong political commitment turned Japan into the second leading market for PVs. Japan took the leading role in PVs development in the 1980s with the "Sunshine Project" — a national research and development (R&D) project aimed at developing new energy sources. Japanese PVs development stagnated in the mid-1980s due to poor incentives for market deployment.

5.3 Germany Takes Over

The red-green German political coalition in 1998 set ambitious targets for green energy and staged a combination of technology adjusted tariffs with unconditional rights to feed PVs energy into the electricity grid, all of which were proved to be forceful tools for boosting PVs expansion. With the German Energiewende, PVs was given a formidable boost in a critical phase of development. In less than a decade, Germany drove volumes of PVs energy up to unprecedented levels, and in 2004 surpassed Japan. From that point, PVs gained the status as a significant contributor to the energy market.

5.4 Chinese Market Leadership

Chinese market domination emerged as the result of a two-step process. In the first step, China geared up its industry for PVs export to lucrative western markets. In the next step — as western markets collapsed in the wake of the financial crisis — China boosted its home market and soon overtook Germany as the market leader. The technology learning undertaken in mature western markets thus allowed cost-efficient production at rates that were attractive to a catch-up economy.

5.5 The Learning Curve Perspective

This innovation journey of PVs makes good sense in a learning curve perspective, which brings techno-economic improvement centrally into the analysis: The stand point is that deployment brings increased efficiency and decreased costs, and technological learning is particularly strong in the early phases of technological development. The sequence of niche markets, visionary policy initiatives and institutionalised support systems may trigger a technological learning process that eventually results in competitiveness in regular markets. Figure 5 illustrates how visionary policy interventions through public deployment may be crucial in triggering industrial learning before private investors are ready to engage — polygon a. That is to say, when early publicly stimulated deployment has created sufficient industrial learning, private investments may be attracted to niche markets that are willing to pay for the next deployment round — polygon b. At the final stage — if successful — the new technology has the potential to dominate the slower, developing incumbent technologies and establish itself profitably at the heart of the mainstream economy — polygon c.

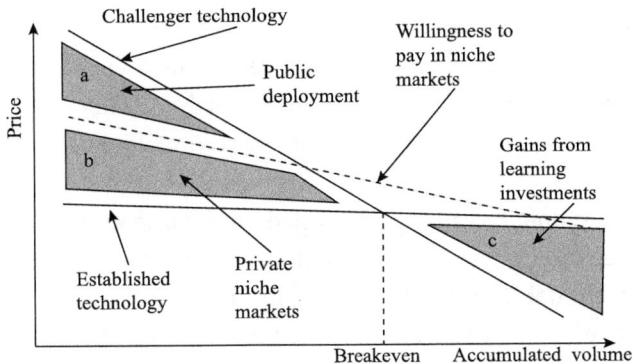

Figure 5 Essentials of Experience Curce and Technology Deployment
Source: Adopted from IEA/Wene, 2000

Back to the PVs example, the global innovation journey has taken PVs down the learning curve from over USD 500/watt in the 1960s to less than EUR 1/watt[①] in 2013, with the prospect of a further price-decrease (Figure 6). Each leading market has taken its share of development costs, but gradually experiences limitations which halt further development. Termination or slowdown has occurred because of the limited scope of niche markets, weathering of political support and institutional weaknesses. However, new lead markets have emerged as a result of the technology learning which has already accomplished. New interests and capabilities have been mobilized to take technology to the next step. A sequence of leading markets therefore has been necessary to continue the journey to a successful end.

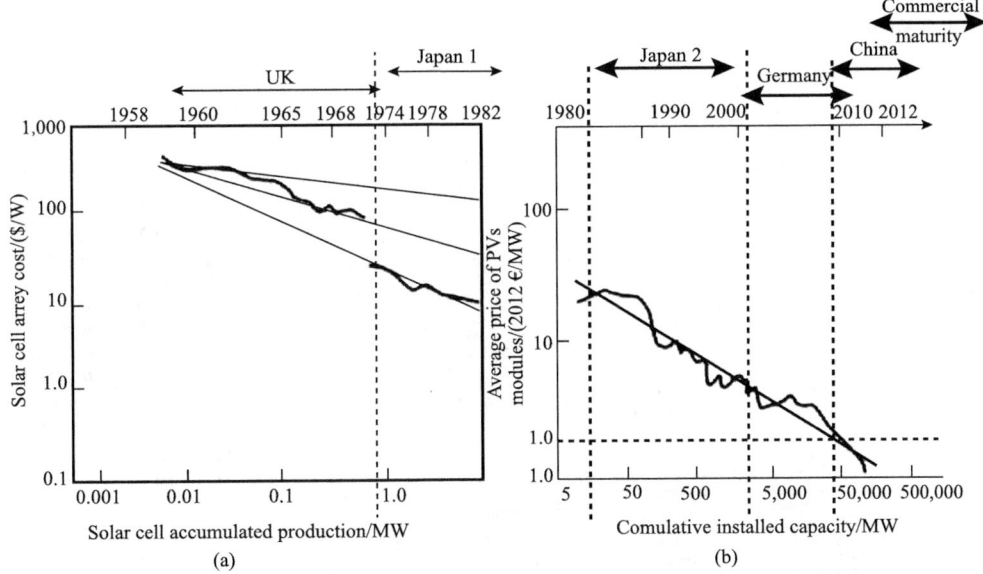

Figure 6 Learning Curve with Sequential Leading Markets for PVs
Sources: Etzkowitz, 1984; Wirth, 2013

5.6 Back in the USA

A good success indicator is that the PVs market is now taking off in several locations on a

---

① 1 EUR=1.1698 USD.

purely commercial basis. California and several other US states now feature firms like Sungevity, which offer installment of solar systems with guaranteed savings vis-à-vis conventional power. The cost efficiency of PVs in sunlight-rich environments, furthermore, has made PVs an attractive energy source for Africa. Large programs of solar deployment are therefore emerging in South Africa, for instance.

While the core photovoltaic technology has made a commercial breakthrough, innovation in important supportive technologies, such as battery technology and smart grids, carries the promise of making PVs available in new fields of application. In the second decade of the 21st century, the PVs' innovation journey can now be considered an obvious success, while the "commercial journey" is only starting.

6. A New Wave of Modernisation

In a broader historical perspective, ecomodernity may be seen as the emergence of a new wave of eco-industrial modernity, with a potential to be a dominant economic growth factor in the coming decades. Innovation scholars like von Weizsäcker et al. (2009) and Perez (2014), put green transformation, or the Age of Sustainability, on a par with such breakthroughs as the Industrial Revolution; the Age of Steam and Railways; the Age of Steel and Heavy Engineering; the Age of Oil, Electricity, Automobile and Mass Production; the Age of Information, Telecommunications and Biotechnology (Figure 7)[1]. These were all based on breakthroughs for new generic technologies, which establish platforms for further innovation, development and refinement, and for proliferation of applications to new fields. These in turn create new leading industrial or commercial sectors.

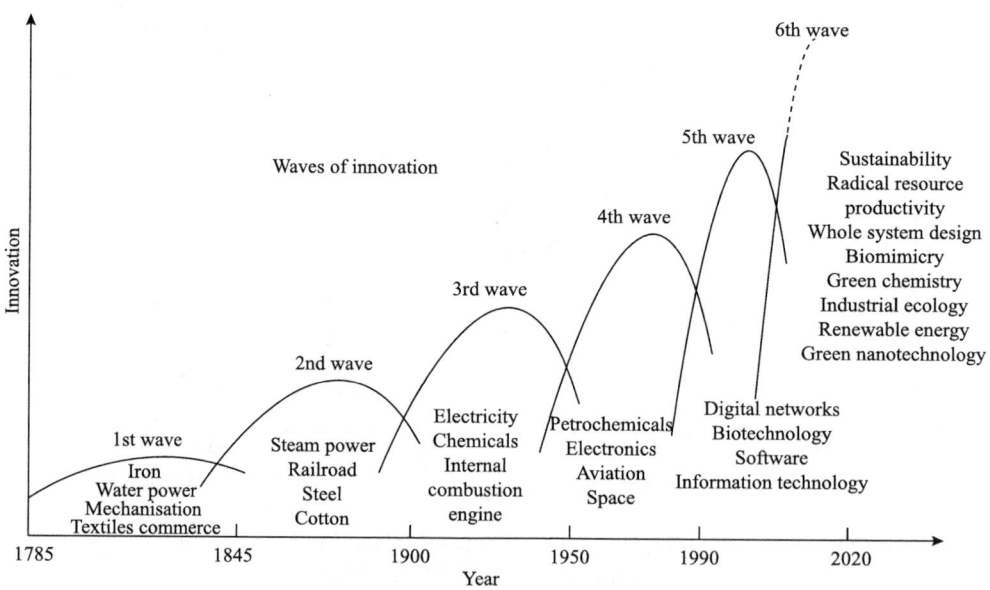

Figure 7 Waves of Industrial Modernisation
Source: von Weizsäcker et al., 2009

---

[1] von Weizsäcker here draws on the Russian economist Nicolai Kondratieff's theory of long waves in economic development and further refinement by several generations of innovation scholars, including Joseph Schumpeter, Christopher Freeman and Carlota Perez.

While ecomodernity shares many of the typical characteristics of previous industrial waves, it introduces a strong focus on resource efficiency, as opposed to previous waves that focus more on labour efficiency. While labour productivity rises considerably with industrialisation, and dramatically after World War II with extensive mechanisation and automatisation, the focus is now shifting. With the impact of industrialisation on our natural surroundings growing rapidly, resources and the carrying capacity of eco-systems have become our central focus more and more. Demands for resource efficiency, recirculation and renewable energy — all central to ecomodernity — have come to stimulate green innovation over a broad frontier of industrial applications.

7. Visions and Collective Actions

In addition to its emphasis on resource efficiency, ecomodernity does, more than other waves, rely on collective actions, and visionary public policies. The new wave of renewables focused and resource efficient ecomodernity could only, however, emerge with the support of visions and policy interventions as a strong driver. Other major industrial transformations thrive on attractive technological opportunities within the reach of business on a commercial basis. In the case of ecomodernity, however, core concerns such as the climate challenge, transcend the confines of conventional business models both with respect to scope and time horizon. The ability to mobilize public interest behind green transition is therefore of more paramount importance than in previous transitions, where commercial entrepreneurship is more readily at hand. Civic support and visionary public policy are, thus, needed to set a direction for handling compelling potential long-term ecological imbalances, and bridging the relatively long-lead time to early commercial applications. In other words, to a large extent green transition is dependent on decisions where members of society act in their own enlightened self-interest overriding the immediate, narrow self interest of business as usual①.

In a complex global economy with multiple vested interests, one can hardly expect full consensus around "Kantian" enlightened self-interested solutions. However, it suffices that dominant actors adopt "Kantian" strategies and thereby trigger new directions of growth, which in turn drives technological evolution that over time will replace undesirable outcomes of narrow short term which focuses on self-interested strategies. Admittedly, some parts of the green transition could reap win-win opportunities where ecology and economic efficiency go hand in hand, but other crucial parts are dependent on long-term technological development and the buildup of infrastructure that transcends normal business horizons.

Given the need to motivate collective action beyond short-term commercial interest, the ability to create visions and mobilise political support is crucial in triggering changes in policies and business strategies that subsequently drive the actual techno-economic transformation on the ground. Hence our previous focus on the triple cycles of innovation visions shapes the policy outlook by defining preferred societal agendas; they also consolidate value bases and ethical

---

① From a game theoretical perspective, we do, in other words, need to see a move from a Nash towards a Kantian equilibrium where strategies that lock-in to maximization of short — run competitiveness only, need to be supplemented with "enlightened in the long run" self-interest following Kant's categorical imperative — an imperative that demands strategies should be sustainable if followed by all.

frameworks that remain central fundaments for shifts in policy and technology. In other words, visions and images are the "software" of innovation in policy and economy. Without the compelling, value-laden ideas, images and modes of action which have laid the contours of ecomodernity, the very idea of the "green transition" would have had much less public resonance, appeal and selling power.

8. Ecomodernity and Climate Change

While the scale and scope of green transition as a new Kondratieff wave are debated, so is our capacity to meet the climate challenge. This challenge currently represents the largest ecological threat to modernity. The literature on responses to climate change features widely different opinions: According to the Oxford energy specialist Helm (2013: ix), very little has been achieved in addressing climate change in the last two decades. Coal power stations continue to be built on an enormous scale in China and India. He pointed out that, indeed, Europe was back to the new coal power stations business and the EU's Emissions Trading Scheme had come perilously close to collapse.

But according to the Roland Berger consultancy company (Berger, 2011: 1), the world has turned green. They argue that we are experiencing a revolution, perhaps as profound as Industrial Revolution, which has altered every facet of life as it is known and understood.

How to square these opposing scenarios?

Judging by the long-term trends, Helm appears to be right: In the 20 years after the Rio summit in 1992 — the period when climate change became recognized — the EU had reduced its CO_2 emission from electricity and heat at an average rate of 0.40%, while the US had increased its own emission by 0.5% annually. This is a trend towards serious climatic disruption on the planet. If we had extrapolated CO_2 rate of decline just since 2011, the picture would have become only slightly more encouraging (–2.5% for the US and –3.2% for the EU). At these rates the two regions would reach 80% emission reduction from the 1992 level in 2080 (the US) and 2063 (the EU) — far behind the schedule for getting climate change down to tolerable levels.

Predictably, the biggest challenge is that rapid growth economies like China aim to catch up with the Western countries. If China were to continue its present CO_2 emission growth curve — around 9% — until it reached the US per capita level of 9.5 tons, there would be a massive emission spike, peaking at 14 billion tons in 2024, which would dwarf any decline in the US and the EU economies combined. If, after China peaked at the US level, we assumed a decline rate equal to the high EU rate (–3%), we would be well into the next century before reaching 80% reduction of today's level. Even halving the Chinese CO_2 growth rate and assuming a maximum CO_2 emission per person at 5 tons before starting reduction would grossly overshoot the 2% goal (Figure 8).

It is, however, possible to chart a second scenario, which is built on trends of radical innovation taking place as part of green transition towards ecomodernity (Figure 9). To take the EU electricity sector as an example: At its basis lies the extrapolation of a slow growth rate for the total electricity consumption of 0.5 % from recent trends. The scenario shows the prolongation of recent exponential growth trends for wind and PVs in the European market and estimates how

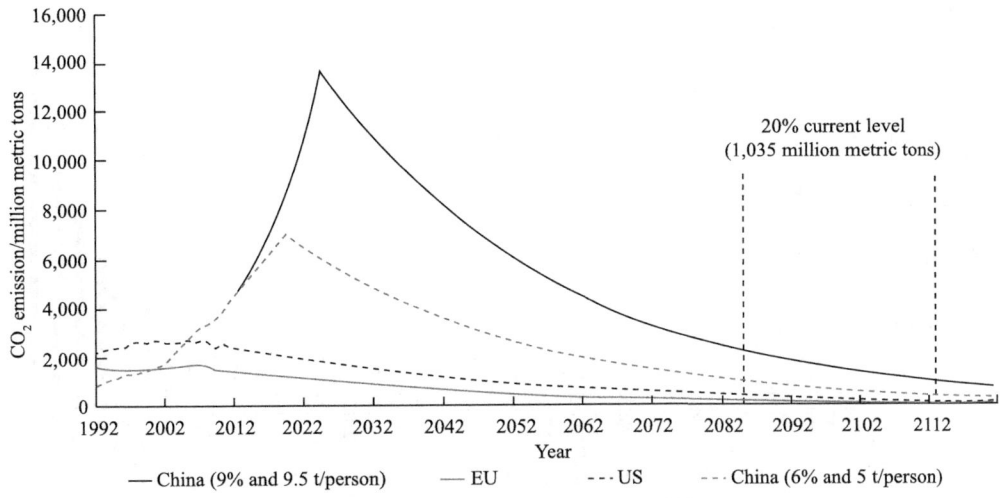

Figure 8   Projecting CO$_2$ Trends for Electricity and Heat Production

Source: Compiled by authors based on World Bank Indicator (http://data.worldbank.org/indicator/EN.CO2.ETOT.MT)

long it will take before the European electricity supply is completely renewable-based. Hydropower is assumed constant throughout the period at its present level of 600 terawatt-hours (TWh), while biomass is expected to grow by 10 % until it reaches the same volume as hydropower. Under these conditions, the European electricity supply will be expected to be completely based on renewables with a good margin by 2025.

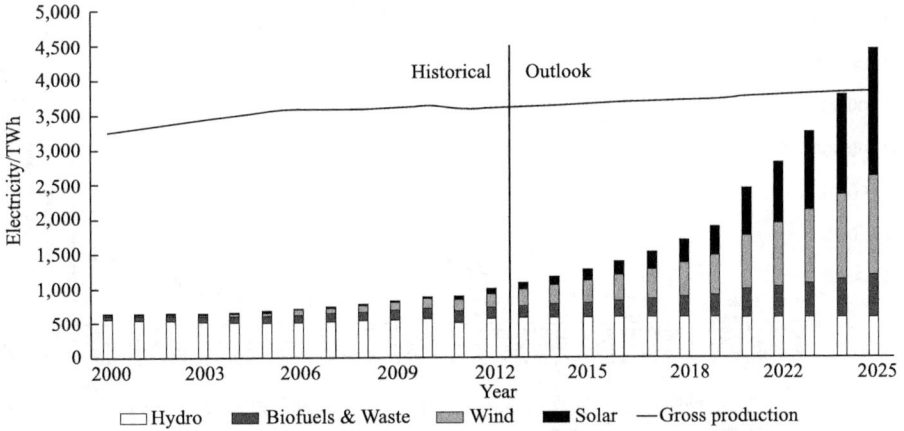

Figure 9   Projecting Trends for the Greening of the EU Electricity

Source: Data are smoothly estimated across time based on given data of the years 1973, 1980, 1990, 2000, 2005, 2010, 2011, 2012

The picture for the US is not very different. Under assumption of a continued growth of electricity consumption of 0.3% — the average annual growth rate for 2005-2015 — the US electricity supply could also become completely renewable-based by 2025 (Figure 10). This development assumes a continuation of the last decade's extraordinarily high growth rates for solar and wind energy.

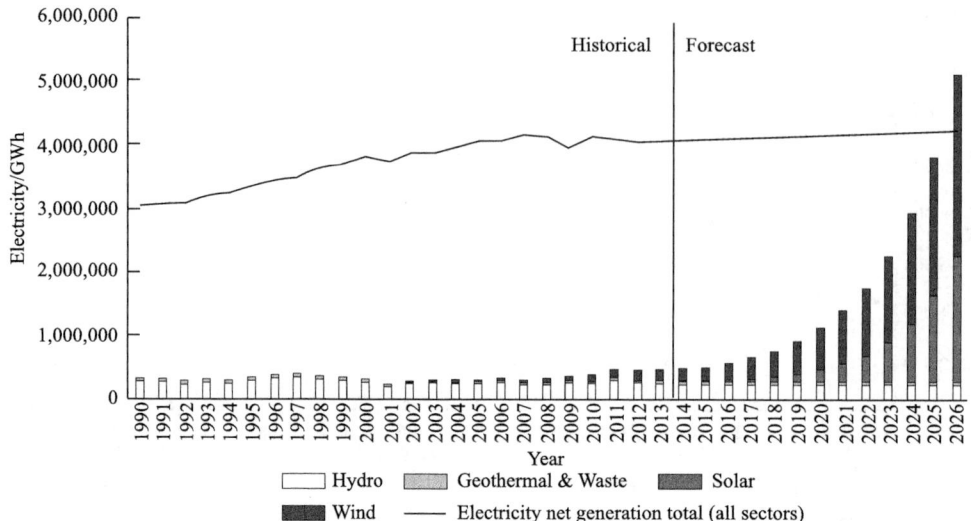

Figure 10 Projecting Trends for the Greening of the US Electricity

Source: http://www.lea.org/statisticssearch/report/?country=CHINA&product=electricityandheat&year=1990

Even the Chinese rapid growth economy could produce a renewables-based electricity supply before 2013 if renewables' growth rate continued at only half of the current level (Figure 11). We are then assuming halved growth rate in total electricity consumption (about 6%) as opposed to almost 12% over the last decade (2003-2013).

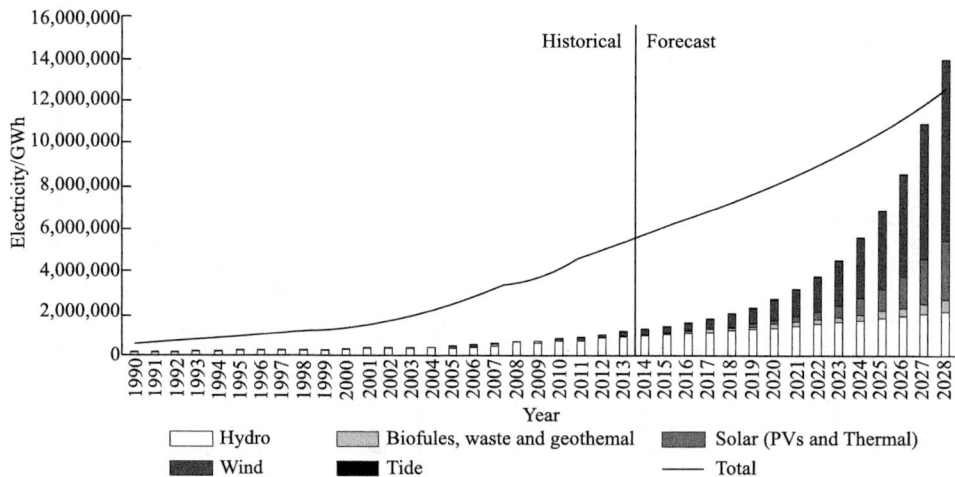

Figure 11 Projecting Trends for the Greening of Chinese Electricity

Source: http://www.lea.org/statisticssearch/report/?country=CHINA&product=electricityandheat&year=1990

The above scenarios are not predictions. They are alternative and conditional projections of possible futures and possible modernities. There are signs, however, that the energy system has come to a turning point where changes in the direction of the renewables dominated scenario are taking place in advanced nations, and may drive disruptive changes at a speed that overruns the smooth trend of the first. The fact that climate mitigation with the 2015 Paris Agreement has moved on from being largely a European endeavor to also becoming embraced and supported by major economic powers like the US and China, is a sign of progress.

9. Multiple Modernities and Innovation Pathways in a Heterogeneous World

The scenarios in Figure 8- Figure 11 indicate the challenge involved in classical industrial modernity is meeting one of the major ecological challenges of our time. Yet they also illustrate the potential for ecomodern transition. The contention in our paper is that by deploying the very strengths of modernity that have triggered the climate threat — today's major ecological challenge to humanity — ecomodernity may be about to come up with the solution. Yet, as the green transformation must take place on a global scale, spanning vast differences in economic and societal conditions, we are dealing with multiple modernities where there is no single, one-size-fits-all trajectory towards ecomodernity. Our comparison of transformation in mature economies such as the US and Western Europe, rapidly growing economies such as China, and developing economies such as those that dominate in Africa (Midttun and Witoszek, 2016), illustrates some of the existing models of green transition.

Mature economies such as the US and the EU are characterized by saturation and slow decline in crucial climate sectors such as energy and automotive industry, which reflects a combination of incremental innovation, growing energy efficiency, and changing behavioral patterns. As illustrated in Figure 10 there is evidence that these economies are doing too little and too late, given their starting points of sharp CO_2 over-emission — particularly in the US. However, ever new breakthrough green technologies which signal the potential for more radical transformation and at a much higher pace. Photovoltaics and wind have thus seen exponential growth rates. The same goes for the electric car.

China, the dominant catch-up economy, has become the world's largest CO_2 emitter, and is rapidly approaching the EU's per capita emission. However, while China is championing growth in the carbon economy, it is also championing growth in green energy and green transport. China's booming expansion gives room for anything and everything, resulting in the unique situation where the conflict between carbon modernity and ecomodernity can be avoided. Puring the 21st century China runs both trains at full speed. Here, the strong motivators of exponential green growth are resource scarcity, local pollution, foreign policy imperatives and trade balance.

Sub Saharan Africa is often locked into structural problems that on one hand limit growth, and on the other hand, sustain energy-inefficient technologies. Not only Africans, but also developing nations, are rightfully "unapologetic about growth", but CO_2 efficiency, for instance in the automotive sector, is constrained by low-quality refineries and petrol, bad roads, older vehicles and mechanics with competencies suitable only for older cars. The energy sector shows weak or missing grid infrastructure and reliance on extensive backup from local diesel generators. However, even here, both sectors show signs of breakthroughs. The limited fixed-line electricity supply in the countryside, as well as frequent urban electricity blackouts leave entry points open for photovoltaic solutions which are gradually emerging in several African countries. Increasingly, a growing urban, middle-class consumers demand advanced energy efficient cars, which slowly raises ecological standards of African car markets. (Yaro, 2016; Mahamma, 2016)

The strength of the global economy is that it allows these cultures and economies to play together. As indicated in our own story of PVs, technologies for green transition may profit extensively from cultural and institutional variation found in diverse "habitats" at different stages of development. If wisely stimulated, this could provide the boost needed for taking modernity one more step to ecomodernity. As Freya Mathews has argued:

> [T]he hallmark of modernity is radical change — in the form of development, control, management, design, intervention, progress, improvement, even salvation. [...] This is reflected in the very etymology of the word "modern", which is derived from "mode", meaning "of the present", as in "a la mode", keeping up with the latest. Modernity is that period which is characterized in terms of its commitment to the ever-emerging new, its dissatisfaction with the given. (Mathews, 2012: 227)

In this sense, ecomodernity — although undermining some of modernity's "holy cows", such as the rule of the carbon economy — is ultimately the child of modernity. It is a product of modernity's eternal impatience with the crisis-ridden here and now. But it is also the result of modernity drawing upon its roots, revisiting the holistic outlook of the late Renaissance and the critical reason of early Enlightenment. It is these roots that give it the power to reform and correct itself.

References

Berger P L. 1977. Facing up to Modernity. New York: Basic Books.
Berger R. 2011. Green Growth, Green Profit: How Green Transformation Boosts Business. London: Palgrave Macmillan.
Christensen C M. 1997. The Innovator's Dilemma: How New Technologies Cause Great Firms to Fail. Boston: Harvard Business School Press.
Eisenstadt S N. 1992. A reappraisal of theories of social change and modernization. In H Haferkamp and N J Smelser (Eds.), Social Change and Modernity. Berkeley: University of California Press.
Eisenstadt S N. 2003. Comparative Civilizations and Multiple Modernities. Leiden and Boston: Brill.
Etzkowitz H. 1984. Solar versus nuclear energy: Autonomous or dependent technology? Social Problems, 31(4): 417-434.
EU. 1996. Ambient Air Quality Dirvective. http://eur-lex.europa.eu/legal-content/EN/TXT/?uri=CELEX: 31996L0062 [2016-4-14].
EU. 2000. Water Framework Directive. http://eur-lex.europa.eu/legal-content/EN/TXT/?uri=CELEX: 32000L0060 [2016-4-14].
EU and Green Peace Joint Report. 2007. Energy Revolution: A Sustainable World Energy Outlook. http://www.energyblueprint.info/fileadmin/media/documents/energy_revolution.pdf. [2016-4-14].
EU. undated. Environmental Action Programme. http://ec.europa.eu/environment/action-programme/process.htm [2016-4-14].
European Commission. 2011. Energy Roadmap 2050. http://ec.europa.eu/energy/energy2020/roadmap/index_en.htm[2016-4-14].

Giddens A. 1998. Conversations with Anthony Giddens: Making Sense of Modernity. Stanford: Stanford University Press.

Helm D. 2013. The Carbon Crunch. New Haven: Yale University Press.

IEA (International Energy Agency). 2006. Energy Technology Perspectives 2006: Scenarios and Strategies to 2050. Paris: Organisation for Economic Cooperation and Development, International Energy Agency.

IEA/Wene. 2000. Experience Curves for Energy Technology Policy. Paris: OECD/IEA.

Mahamma A. 2016. Growth versus green transition: Energy in Sub-Saharan Africa. In A Midttun and N Witoszek (Eds.), Energy and Transport in Green Transition: Perspectives on Ecomodernity. London & New York: Routledge.

Martinelli A. 2005. Global Modernization: Rethinking the Project of Modernity. London: SAGE.

Mathews F. 2012. Ecology and Democracy. London: Routledge.

Meadows D H, Randers J, Meadows D, et al. 1972. Limits to Growth. New York: Universe Books; London: Chelsea Green.

Midttun A, Toporowska E. 2014. Sequencing lead markets for photovoltaics. In A Brunnengräber and M R Di Nucci (Eds.), Im Hürdenlauf zur Energiewende. Von Transformationen, Reformen und Innovationen. Berlin: Springer Verlag.

Midttun A, Witoszek N. 2016. Energy and Transport in Green Transition: Perspectives on Ecomodernity. London & New York: Routledge.

Parsons T. 1971. The System of Modern Societies. Englewood Cliffs: Prentice-Hall.

Perez C. 2014. A Green and Socially Equitable Direction for the ICT Paradigm. Working Paper No. 2014-01. http://www. globelics[2014-9-21].

Toulmin S E. 1990. Cosmopolis: The Hidden Agenda of Modernity. New York: Free Press; Chicago: University of Chicago Press.

UNESCAP. 2012. Low Carbon Green Growth Roadmap for Asia and the Pacific. Bangkok: United Nations.

van de Ven A, Polley D, Garud R, et al. 2008. The Innovation Journey. Oxford: Oxford University Press.

von Weizsäcker E U, Hargroves C, Smith M, et al. 2009. Factor Five. London: Earthscan.

WBCSD. 2010. Vision 2050: The new agenda for business. Report from World Business Council for Sustainable Development. http://www. wbcsd. org/pages/edocument/edocumentdetails. aspx?id=219&nosearchcontextkey=true[2016-4-14].

Wirth H. 2013. Aktuelle Fakten zur Photovoltaik in Deutschland, Frauenhofer report: Recent facts about photovoltaics in Germany Version as of September 12, 2013. Compiled by Dr Harry Wirth Division Director Photovoltaic Modules, Systems and Reliability Fraunhofer ISE. http://www.pv-fakten. de[2014-12-10].

Yaro J. 2016. Squaring Growth with Green Transition in Africa's Automobile Sector. In A Midttun and N Witoszek (Eds.), Energy and Transport in Green Transition. Perspectives on Ecomodernity. London & New York: Routledge.

Ecological Modernization and Resilience of Resource Communities

Juha Kotilainen

University of Eastern Finland

This paper explores two issues related to the processes of modernization. First, it deals with the issues of ecological modernization and green development that bring with them a need for the extraction of raw materials which are utilized, for example, in the production and consumption of cleaner energies. Second, the processes of modernization are essentially about changing social structures as well as the relations of humans to their environment. This paper discusses how resource extraction could deal with the challenges of change. To this end, this paper focuses on the potential trajectories and evolution of resource communities. It is typical for resource communities that they experience evolution which is dependent on the cycles of extraction of a specific natural resource, and the policies related to them have to struggle to find suitable ways to overcome periods of crisis. In other words, resource communities face the challenge of how to be resilient in the face of larger scale social and economic transformations and resource depletion. This paper investigates the resilience approaches with the aim of analyzing the trajectories of resource communities, and outlines the various ways in which resource communities might be resilient in the course of modernization.

1. Resource Extraction, Resource Communities

The extraction of natural resources is essential for society, and minerals have already been vital for the functioning of the society in the pre-industrial era (Bardi, 2014). Despite efforts to recycle and recover minerals, deposits of primary minerals are still important raw material sources for industries. Changing needs for commodities have also transformed the locations for mining, while many old minerals retain their value as commodities, there are also new minerals, such as rare earth elements, that have emerged as sources of new technologies and have redirected exploration and extraction schemes. While a global tendency since industrialization has been shifting minerals extraction to developing countries and peripheral locations, new technologies and applications for extracting resources, such as hydraulic fracturing and deep mining, have been reintroducing mining to industrialized countries. There are political initiatives that aim at increasing the extraction of minerals in industrialized countries, a goal that is related to the success of industries and the employment they should provide. On a European scale, a political initiative concerning raw materials supply incorporates the goal of increasing minerals extraction within the territory of the EU in order to secure a steady supply of raw materials to the European industries (European Commission, 2013).

It is crucial for the exploitation of natural resources that have been spatially organised. A traditionally common way for arranging the exploitation is through human communities that emerge in the vicinity of the resource. Resource communities therefore have played a crucial role in the spatial organization of industrial production and labour. Natural resources, including minerals and metals, have for long been transported for long distances globally, which has led to the evolution of resource peripheries (Hayter et al., 2003; Halseth, 2017). After industrialization, with a shift from the industrial society towards the post-industrial society, and with the easiness and relatively low costs of transportation, the locations of resource extraction have become more far away from the core urban areas of consumption. Typically resource communities are therefore located outside commercial and administrative centres, but supply these centres and other regions with raw materials and products that are necessary for their existence. Today, societies and regions which used to procure raw materials for their industries in a relative vicinity to their core areas, tend either to import or recycle the raw materials; the past mining regions of Germany and the UK are examples. However, as noted above, the new developments in raw materials policies and politics are re-organizing the spaces of resource extraction.

Not only has there been a shift in the locational relations of deposits, manufacturing and consumption, but also the distance from which labour operates the deposits and commutes to the mining sites has been under transformations. During industrialization, resource communities are largely organized in a way that allows the daily work to be carried out within a distance that is easy to cover daily to a mine. In recent decades, in industrialized countries and societies as diverse as Canada, Australia and Russia, there have been new forms of organizing labour to the sites of extraction, and the fly-in-fly-out model has replaced long-term place-based communities located in the immediate vicinity of the extractive activities (Storey, 2009; Spies, 2009). Thus a model, which allows the workers to live in places remote from the locations of extraction and commute to the mineral extraction sites where they spend periods of time labouring on the deposits, has been expansively employed. The communities of today are therefore in many ways different from those of the past, yet there are communities nevertheless which are comprised of the staff working at the mines. A challenge therefore lies in how to understand a local resource community.

A resource community is defined here as a spatially bounded local community that is substantially linked to natural resource extraction, at the same time acknowledging the relational connections from any place to social and economic structures and processed at other scales. Resource communities are therefore understood as local communities dependent on the exploitation and processing of natural resources available in a specific location. Resource communities are often located in resource regions, a significant part of whose income is from the extraction of natural resources. There are many existing and planned resource communities in the regions, and they are characterised by multiple medium to large-scale extraction and processing facilities, typically including extensive roads, rails and port infrastructure (Kinnear and Ogden, 2014).

There are several controversial issues related to resource communities. The extractive and industrial activities have been a source of environmental and health problems to the inhabitants in the communities operating the resource exploitation, and these problems in mining cities have been recognised as amongst the earliest causes for environmental concerns in modern societies (Radkau, 2008: 142-151). Resource extraction also has impacts on communities and inhabitants other than those directly involved in the resource exploitation, and an important aspect in resource extraction is related to the impacts of industrial resource exploitation on other livelihoods in a region (Yakovleva, 2014). Furthermore, mining often utilises workforce from its surroundings and provides employment to pre-existing communities, thereby transforming them into new forms of resource communities (Tiainen et al., 2014). Since much of the exploitation of resources takes place in resource peripheries, often indigenous communities, cultures and livelihoods are closely related to the deposits, which is a concern running through diverse societies from the Arctic to the Global South (Gilberthorpe and Hilson, 2014). With overall global resource depletion, the expansion of the extraction of minerals to lower grade deposits is likely to emphasize the issues related to sustainability in the future (Prior et al., 2012). Regardless of their locations, it is inevitable for resource communities to experience evolution that is dependent on the cycles of extraction of a specific natural resource, and they have to struggle to find suitable ways to overcome periods of crisis (e.g. Martinez-Fernandez et al., 2012). These issues related to changing conditions for resource communities can be brought together by conceptualizing them with the concept of resilience. The notion of resilience focusses attention on the challenges brought about by changes (Brown, 2016), and thus is useful for understanding resource communities which are prone to facing the challenge of how to be resilient in the face of larger scale social and economic transformations and resource depletion.

2. Conceptualizations of Resilience of Resource Communities

The origins of resilience thinking lie in a concern over the functioning of ecosystems (Holling and Gunderson, 2002), and at the core there is a focus on human-environment relations and integrated social-ecological systems (Walker and Salt, 2006). From the foundational perspective that societies (social systems) and nature (ecological systems) are interlinked and mutually dependent, the argument has been put forth that the focus should be on the social-ecological system, which comprises ecological processes as well as social actions and decisions. Within resilience thinking, different meanings for resilience have been differentiated (Folke, 2006), ranging from an idea of a stable equilibrium to which the system could return, through persistence and robustness of a system to ideas of integrated systems feedbacks and cross-scale dynamic interactions, with a focus on reorganization, adaptive capacities, transformability, learning and innovation within social-ecological systems. A significant aspect in resilience thinking is the emphasis on including multiple scales in the analysis (Walker and Salt, 2006), as the key is that occurrences on any single scale can have repercussions on the structures, functions and capacities on some other scales.

One of the traditional ideas exploring resilience focuses on systemic loops (Holling and Gunderson, 2002). While this is easily observable within ecosystems, it is not that easy to accept a view that societies would return to a stable state after a disturbance. Nonetheless, there is resemblance of the idea of loops to research on the cyclical nature of economy (Hassink, 2010). This applies especially well to resource extraction with its booms and busts, which also drive the economic expansion of resource communities and cause their decline. Resource communities may follow the cyclical nature of the resource industries, although it is unlikely that a resource community would return to the exact state that it was in prior to a shock.

Resilience as a notion has also been taken on by scholars associated with evolutionary economic geography, with an interest in the persistence and adaptability of regional and local economies (Christopherson et al., 2010; Martin, 2012; Martin and Sunley, 2015). Regional economic resilience has been defined, for example, as "the capacity of a regional or local economy to withstand or recover from market, competitive and environmental shocks to its developmental growth path, if necessary by undergoing adaptive changes to its economic structures and its social and institutional arrangements, so as to maintain or restore its previous development path, or transit to a new sustainable path characterized by a fuller and more productive use of its physical, human and environmental resources" (Martin and Sunley, 2015: 13). There are various ways in which regional and local economies could deal with changes, including resistance, return to the previous state, adaptation to changes and preparation to future changes (Martin, 2012).

Some issues can be recognised for how to achieve an overall resilience in regional economies. As occurrences on larger or smaller scales can have impacts on the resilience of systems at other scales, attempts at securing resilience at one scale may hamper resilience at other scales. For example, from the perspective of national economy, it might be wise not to support recessive peripheral regions, which would hinder the possibilities for development in (resource) communities in these regions. Or it could be beneficial for the global economy if industries could be relocated as flexibly as possible, yet the regions experiencing the relocations as loss of industrial production, employment and income, may suffer from loss of capacity that creates preconditions for regional economic resilience, if their economic diversity decreases, and also their resilience for future shocks decreases (Boschma, 2015). Moreover, resilience of some livelihoods may be in contradiction with others, such as the inconsistencies between the development of the extractive industries, tourism and northern nomadic cultures (Kumpula et al., 2011).

Another approach on resilience research can be seen to focus on an analysis of the capacities of human communities to deal with pressures to change, either by resisting these pressures or adapting these pressures (Wilson, 2012: 11). The research on community resilience has had an interest in natural resource dependent communities (Adger, 2000). Community resilience has been analysed as an indicator of social sustainability and has been defined as the existence, development and engagement of community resources by community members to thrive in an environment characterised by change, unpredictability and surprise (Magis, 2010). Community resilience has also been defined as a result from a balance between the economic, environmental and social needs of communities (Wilson, 2012: 25). A difference to regional economic resilience, which may also include a focus on communities (Martin and Sunley, 2015), is that community resilience has a more varied interest on the development of a community than just the growth of the local economy.

A crucial issue for the understanding of community resilience is whether communities are seen to remain unchanged when faced with any kind of pressure. Regarding natural-resource-dependent communities, two definitions for resilience have been differentiated: One is about the time that it takes for a system to recover from a disturbance, and the other is the amount of disturbance a system can absorb before transforming to an entirely different system (Adger, 2000). While both of them stress the ability of a community to remain unchanged, a community being resilient does not necessarily need to be about success in remaining unchanged. There are other definitions of resilience which see it as the capabilities of a community to change its non-essential elements enough in order to maintain its essential elements and functions (Manyena, 2006), and community resilience has also been connected with transition theories (Wilson, 2012). Such perspectives pay attention to the extent which communities change over a period of time and the benefits these changes can bring to communities.

3. Understandings of Resilience of Resource Communities

Mining operations are prone to bringing changes to regions and localities. Each of the various phases of mining — mineral exploration, establishment of mining operations and mine closure — leads to transformations that are experienced in resource communities. Environmental impacts that result from mining are causes of changes in the landscape and therefore in the surroundings of local communities. When mining is planned, mine closure should be considered and planned from a local community perspective, since it can be assumed that an important local livelihood disappears with mine closure, and the physical impacts of mining remains in the landscape. Technological transformations have an impact on local economies through the decreasing employment that adoption of new technologies often causes, and fluctuating prices of minerals affect the profitability of mining operations. Overall, mining can be seen as an activity that is inherently constituted around various sorts of factors that cause regions and communities to change, which is the reason why resilience, as a concept focused on dealing with changes, is an apt notion for examining resource communities.

Following the broadest understanding of resilience, attention could be paid to the amount of disturbance that a resource community would be able to absorb and still keep the same field of activities of resource extraction and processing as significant for its existence. Resource depletion, the decrease in the value of resource, or environmental and other political occurrences leading to the decrease in resource extraction, could undermine this existence. It could be estimated how well a resource community is able to adjust and organise itself instead of being reorganised by external forces, actors and policies. Often the evolution of resource regions and communities is related to larger-scale development policies, and together with the local-scale actors, national-scale actors and policies may play a significant role in how a resource community manages changes (Halonen et al., 2015). Distinguishing between internal and external capabilities of an organization in a resource community is not straight-forward.

As to the interpretation of resilience as the capacity of resistance by the local economy and communities against adverse impacts, with a well-planned establishment or closure of mines, the existing situation in communities which are in the vicinity of the new mine will not change.

However, this is unlikely, as a new mine will inevitably have an impact on landscapes and communities, even if the magnitude of impact varies depending on the types of mining and the technologies used. Also with mine closure, the community and the composition of the local economy will change. With a key employer closing down, there is likely to be out-migration. Diversification strategies may help with the performance of the local economy, but the social structures and networks inevitably will be transformed with other livelihoods taking over. Overall, we can hardly speak about regional resilience in the sense of resistance in terms of mining.

Resilience in the sense of bouncing back from the local and regional economy with regard to mining is more likely to occur. Mining business and a mining community may be hit by impacts caused by decreasing prices of minerals, which may cause the industry operating a specific mine to reduce its workforce in order to adapt to the situation. Following an increase in the prices of minerals, the mining operations would be restarted, and the positions of employment could possibly be regained. A mine could also be reopened due to the advancement in mining technologies, but in this case probably the local economy would not regain the previous level of employment, as more advanced technologies by rule require less workforce. This would turn the local economy to rise again but with the same industry, mining, providing the elements for the regrowth, so that there would be no need for major restructuring of the foundations of the local economy. If a mining site ceases to operate for good, the community is not likely to be able to bounce back to the previous state that existed before the mining operations, as mining often transforms the landscape permanently.

In terms of resilience as an adaptive capacity, the establishment of new mining operations could lead to a situation where the local economy is facing a serious disruption, and the local communities have to find ways to adapt. Adaptation could occur by the inhabitants taking positions of employment with the mining industry. The physical landscape may be transformed to the extent that in a later phase of regional economic evolution, returning back to the previous activities in the area is not a feasible and possible option. Therefore, there has to be an adaptation, or in other terms a reorganization or a renewal of the local economy (Martin, 2012). In the sense of the local economy finding a new growth path with the inauguration of mining operations, the local economy can transform to one with a different economic and industrial structure. The aim of any local economy and community is to adapt by discovering new ways of finding livelihoods after mine closure, which has also become a conscious target for some responsibility policies within the extractive industries. A new growth path would mean that timely and early diversification of the local and regional economies takes place, thereby making it possible for local economies to find paths for evolution in ways that prevent a recession of local or regional economies after mine closure.

A challenge relates to the ability of local communities to gain the capacities to adapt when facing pressures to change. In terms of mining, this could mean, for example, that while a local community might be prepared to deal with the impacts of mining by learning to live with mining operations and taking advantage of the positions of employment becoming available in the mining industry. Its possibilities to manage the later situation of mine closure could be undermined by the lack of diversification of the local economy, and thereby its capacity for adaptability could be low. One way to increase the capacities to manage changes locally could be through corporate social responsibility policies of mining companies (Dashwood, 2012). These policies can bring resources to local communities for dealing with the adverse impacts of mining. However, the corporate social responsibility policies also demonstrate that there are serious challenges of finding ideal solutions for increasing the resilience of local communities in the face of mining operations. It has been observed that negotiations over corporate social responsibility of mining companies tend to lead to uneven spatial results (Heisler and Markey, 2013). Resilience in one place may be in contrast to the lack of similar positive development in other places with similar mining operations (MacKinnon and Derickson, 2013). A further problem is the issue of who or which group it is in the local community whose resilience we are focussing on, as there are usually multiple voices in any community, and it may not be clear who is allowed to represent a resource community and whether this representation is accepted by the local inhabitants.

4. Conclusions

Resource communities and questions over their resilience are important aspects of ecological modernization for two reasons. First, a central aspect of ecological modernization is that there is a need for minerals in ecologically modern societies, and an increasing need for new minerals which are used for new technologies created for the needs of ecological modernization, for example, new technologies produce energy in new ways or store this energy in more efficient ways. This aspect of ecological modernization causes there to be a need for new extractive activities, which turn the focus to the impacts on existing and emerging resource communities. The communities which emerge do so in places and regions where they are likely to have impacts on pre-existing communities, sometimes turning them into new resource communities. In the course of time and with depletion of a resource locally, being resilient becomes a challenge for a resource community. Second, in a more general sense, modernization has always been a process about changing conditions. Therefore, focuses on resilience as such, and on resilience of resource communities as a specific case, can provide new insights into the impacts of and reactions to the processes of modernization by societies at various scales.

References

Adger N W. 2000. Social and ecological resilience: Are they related? Progress in Human Geography, 24(3): 347-364.

Bardi U. 2014. Extracted: How the Quest for Mineral Wealth Is Plundering the Planet. White River Junction (Vermont): Chelsea Green.

Boschma R. 2015. Towards an evolutionary perspective on regional resilience. Regional Studies, 49(5): 733-751.

Brown K. 2016. Resilience, Development and Global Change. Abingdon: Routledge.

Christopherson S M J, Tyler P. 2010. Regional resilience: Theoretical and empirical perspectives. Cambridge Journal of Regions, Economy and Society, 3(1): 3-10.

Dashwood H S. 2012. The Rise of Global Corporate Social Responsibility: Mining and the Spread of Global Norms. Cambridge: Cambridge University Press.

European Commission. 2013. On the Implementation of the Raw Materials Initiative. Paper presented on the

Commission to the European Parliament, the Council, the European Economic and Social Committee and the Committee of the Regions. 2013-06-24.

Folke C. 2006. Resilience: The emergence of a perspective for social-ecological systems analyses. Global Environmental Change, 16(3): 253-267.

Gilberthorpe E, Hilson G. 2014. Natural Resource Extraction and Indigenous Livelihoods: Development Challenges in an Era of Globalization. Farnham: Ashgate.

Halonen M, Kotilainen J, Tykkyläinen M, et al. 2015. Industry life cycles of a resource town in Finland — The case of Lieksa. European Countryside, 7(1): 16-41.

Halseth G. 2017. Transformation of Resource Towns and Peripheries: Political Economy Perspectives. Abingdon: Routledge.

Hassink R. 2010. Regional resilience: A promising concept to explain differences in regional economic adaptability? Cambridge Journal of Regions, Economy and Society, 3: 45-58.

Hayter R, Barnes T J, Bradshaw M J. 2003. Relocating resource peripheries in the core of economic geography's theorizing: Rationale and agenda. Area, 35(1): 15-23.

Heisler K, Markey S. 2013. Scales of benefit: Political leverage in the negotiation of corporate social responsibility in mineral exploration and mining in rural British Columbia, Canada. Society and Natural Resources, 26(4): 386-401.

Holling C S, Gunderson L H. 2002. Resilience and adaptive cycles. In L H Gunderson, C S Holling (Eds.), Panarchy: Understanding Transformations in Human and Natural Systems. Washington: Island Press.

Kinnear S, Ogden I. 2014. Planning the innovation agenda for sustainable development in resource regions: A central Queensland case study. Resources Policy, 39: 42-53.

Kumpula T, Pajunen A, Kaarlejärvi E, et al. 2011. Land use and land cover change in Arctic Russia: Ecological and social implications of industrial development. Global Environmental Change, 21: 550-562.

MacKinnon D, Derickson K D. 2013. From resilience to resourcefulness: A critique of resilience policy and activism. Progress in Human Geography, 37 (2): 253-270.

Magis K. 2010. Community resilience: An indicator of social sustainability. Society & Natural Resource, 23(5): 401-416.

Manyena S B. 2006. The concept of resilience revisited. Disasters, 30(4): 434-450.

Martin R. 2012. Regional economic resilience, hysteresis and recessionary shocks. Journal of Economic Geography, 12(1): 1-32.

Martin R, Sunley P. 2010. The place of path-dependence in an evolutionary perspective on the economic landscape. In R Boschma, R Martin (Eds.), The Handbook of Evolutionary Economic Geography. Cheltenham: Edward Elgar.

Martin R, Sunley P. 2015. On the notion of regional economic resilience: Conceptualization and explanation. Journal of Economic Geography, 15: 1-42.

Martinez-Fernandez C, Wu C T, Schatz L K, et al. 2012. The shrinking mining city: Urban dynamics and contested territory. International Journal of Urban and Regional Research, 36(2): 245-260.

Prior T, Giurco D, Mudd G, et al. 2012. Resource depletion, peak minerals and the implications for sustainable resource management. Global Environmental Change, 22: 577-587.

Radkau J. 2008. Nature and Power: A Global History of the Environment. New York: Cambridge University Press.

Spies M. 2009. Oil Extraction in Extreme Remoteness: The Organization of Work and Long-distance Commuting in Russia's Northern Resource Peripheries. Joensuu: University of Joensuu.

Storey K. 2009. Fly-in/fly-out: Implications for community sustainability. Sustainability, 2: 1161-1181.

Tiainen H, Sairinen R, Novikov V. 2014. Mining in the Chatkal Valley in Kyrgyzstan — Challenge of social sustainability. Resources Policy, 39: 80-87.

Walker B, Salt D. 2006. Resilience Thinking: Sustaining Ecosystems and People in a Changing World. Washington: Island Press.

Wilson G A. 2012. Community Resilience and Environmental Transitions. London: Routledge.

Yakovleva N. 2014. Land, oil and indigenous people in the Russian North: A case study of the oil pipeline and Evenki in Aldan. In E Gilberthorpe, G Hilson (Eds.), Natural Resource Extraction and Indigenous Livelihoods: Development Challenges in an Era of Globalization. Farnham: Ashgate.

Ecological Civilization Construction Demonstration Areas in China from a Three-dimensional Theoretical Perspective

Qingzhi Huan

Peking University

Since the 18th National Congress of CPC in 2012, eco-civilization and its construction has become one of the key parts of socialist modernization strategy and its implementation of the Chinese government. The major follow-up political documents and measures, including the Decision to Comprehensively Deepen the Reform of Several Major Issues (November 2013, hereinafter referred to as The Decision), the Suggestions on Promoting the Construction of Eco-civilization (April 2015, hereinafter referred to as The Suggestions) and the Overall Plan for the Reform of Eco-civilization System (September 2015, hereinafter referred to as The Overall Plan), not only highlight the importance of practical dimension of eco-civilization and its construction but also raise more and clearer questions for further theoretical research on eco-civilization and its construction. How we expound and practice eco-civilization construction depends ultimately on the actual conditions of our time. This does not mean that theoretical guidance or the theories themselves are not important for eco-civilization. Rather, it means only when a theory is firmly rooted in practical needs can it possess the realistic power to reshape or forge eco-civilization construction. Therefore, the various pilot or demonstration areas launched around the country for eco-civilization construction should be of great concern to philosophical and social science researchers today.

1. Eco-civilization and Its Construction: A Conceptual Analysis

As far as the terms themselves are concerned, eco-civilization is not the same as eco-civilization construction. So far the former draws more attention from scholars in environmental humanities and social sciences, with an emphasis on the new characteristics of the structure of human-nature relationship or the form of human civilization. Therefore, it involves mainly philosophical ethics or political philosophy. On this basis, eco-civilization and its practice are to a large extent a kind of negation and transcendence of modern industrial and urban civilization, and are associated with a new (post-modern or non-capitalist) economic, social and cultural system and mindset (Huan, 2010).

For example, according to Lu (2013: 13), eco-civilization is a civilization built under the guidance of ecology, with an aim of pursuing harmonious coexistence and coordinated evolution of human and nature. Specifically, it involves seven levels: artifacts (green products produced by an eco-industrial system), technology (environment-friendly and ecological technologies), systems (democracy, rules of law and restricted market), customs (moralized customs), arts (diverse arts, including multiple types of arts independent of commerce), concepts (non-materialism, non-economism, holism, non-anthropocentrism and transcendental naturalism) and language (multiple ethnic languages). In his opinion, such a process of ecologicalization and ecological transformation extending from the artifact level to the institutional level and further to the mindset level will surely usher in a new era or form of civilization that departs from and transcends modern industrial civilization. We can also interpret it in the following way: Without the reconstruction and rebirth of modern industrial civilization on the seven levels mentioned above, eco-civilization will never be created, and human society will never be able to march into that era.

In comparison, eco-civilization construction has more to do with policies and attracts more attention from CPC and the governmental departments, with an emphasis laid on guidelines and strategies for governance (or "policy tools"). Arguably, "eco-civilization construction" and raising "eco-civilization perceptions" in the working report of the 17th National Congress of CPC, "five-in-one" (*wu wei yiti*), "three developments" and "four key strategies and general tasks" in the working report of the 18th National Congress of CPC, "four items of institutional and system reform" in The Decision of 2013, and "greening" and "the eight core tasks" in The Suggestions of 2015①—all should be understood in this context. Therefore, while there are disputes over the connotation of eco-civilization, the meaning of eco-civilization construction is relatively clear. The efforts for eco-civilization construction led by CPC and the Chinese government are to deal with (solve) the serious dilemma of population, resources and environment or the growing tension between human and nature as well as between the society and nature in a comprehensive, systematic and forward-looking manner. In this view, we may even say that the most realistic effort (practice) to construct eco-civilization is to contain the spreading fog and haze in urban and rural areas, and to improve the quality of water polluted in various rivers, lakes and seas.

Here we can see that there is an obvious alienation or "disjunction" between the theoretical domain of eco-civilization and the practical efforts of eco-civilization construction. For example, it is difficult for theoreticians to clarify how China today who is (or claims to be) in the process of modernization can take the lead in opening up a new form (era) of civilization which is totally

---

① "Five-in-one" (*wu wei yiti*) refers to integrate eco-civilization construction into all aspects and the whole process of economic construction, political construction, social construction and cultural construction (Hu, 2012: 39); the "three developments" are green development, low-carbon development and circular development; the "four items of institutional and system reform" are establishing natural resource assets property rights system and use control system, defining ecological protection redline, implementing the system of paid use of resources and the ecological compensation system, reforming the management system of ecological environment protection; the "eight core tasks" are strengthening the main function orientation to optimize the pattern of land and space development, promoting technical innovation and structural adjustment to improve the quality and efficiency, comprehensively promoting resource conservation as well as its circular and efficient use to make a fundamental change of the way of use, increasing the natural ecological system and environmental protection to improve the quality of ecological environment, perfecting the eco-civilization system, strengthening the statistical monitoring and supervision of law enforcement in eco-civilization construction, speeding up the formation of good habits to promote the building of eco-civilization, strengthening the organization and leadership.

different from that before. Similarly, grass-root professionals are confused about how our energy-saving and emission-reduction policies, or new energy promotion policies, are associated directly with the creation of a new civilization or a civilizational transformation, though they may help remove the unfathomable fog and haze. Confusing as it may be, it fundamentally stems from the serious imbalance of economic and social development in China and the highly heterogeneous nature of historical and cultural traditions of China. The specific reasons are very complicated. But one thing is clear: Such a mismatch between theories and practices is harmful to both the theoretical research on eco-civilization and the practical efforts for eco-civilization construction.

Based on this, the author proposed in an article (Huan, 2014a) that eco-civilization and eco-civilization construction in a broad sense can be conceptualized as two levels of theory and practice, or "quadruple implications". Specifically speaking, in philosophical terms, eco-civilization is a kind of natural/ecological relationship and ethics of weak (quasi) ecocentrism; in terms of political ideology, eco-civilization is an alternative economic and social choice which is different from the capitalism-dominated paradigm in the world today; eco-civilization construction or practice refers to the part of appropriate natural/ecological relationship in the entire socialist civilization and the process of its creation, i.e. ecological environment protection in a broad sense as we usually terms it; in the context of modernization or development, eco-civilization construction or practice refers to the green dimension of socialist modernization or economic and social development. Compared with the definition given by Professor Feng Lu, such a comprehensive or eclectic definition highlights the nature of political and philosophical innovation of eco-civilization construction and its requirements for institutional innovation, especially the "red-green" facet or characteristic of a radical green politics it necessitates. Moreover, it combines the theoretical and practical dimensions of eco-civilization and its construction by means of methodology, indicating that no civilizational innovation can be mono-dimensional.

Furthermore, the author proposed in another article (Huan, 2015a) that, a complete theory for eco-civilization and its construction contains three sub-dimensions or levels based on different perspectives of environmental political analysis: a "green-left" ideological discourse on the development of governing political party, an environmental political-social theory insisting on a comprehensive transformation or re-construction of contemporary society, and an organic way of thinking as well as philosophy with a strong link to the Chinese and/or classic tradition. In the author's opinion, eco-civilization no matter as a theoretical and academic concept or as a systematic environmental political-social theory or an ecological cultural theory points at and requires a profound and radical green transformation. Or it is not only a theory of social realistic criticism or of future social building, but also a theory of rather radical green transformation or ecological transcendence (Huan, 2014b, 2015b).

2. Major Programs of Eco-civilization Construction Demonstration Areas in China

It is fair to say that the conceptual analysis above forms the discursive context or methodological precondition based on which the author will proceed to present his theoretical thinking over the practice of eco-civilization construction demonstration areas in China. On the one hand, we cannot assume a priori that every local experiment of eco-civilization construction naturally pursues or involves an idea or strategy of eco-civilization, but when there are a sufficient number of cases of extensive attempts available, some substantial changes on the level of ideas or strategies are bound to emerge. On the other hand, cases and local experiences are always full of practical meanings, but they are case-specific and hard to replicate (this may be especially true when it comes to eco-civilization construction) (Huan, 2013a). However, the inherent consistency of theory and the relatively sufficient comparison should be able to reveal to us some typical and trend-setting changes. In other words, the metaphor of an oasis in the desert or dispersed sparkles may not mean any definite conclusion or outcome, yet they are for sure the most important or convenient access to the future.

Specifically speaking, "eco-civilization construction demonstration area" is a comprehensive concept, referring extensively to various pilot or pioneering schemes of demonstration areas established by national ministries or commissions, or the authorities of provinces, municipalities and autonomous regions. Among them, the most authoritative ones so far are those designated by the Ministry of Environmental Protection (MEP)[①], the National Development and Reform Commission (NDRC) and six other ministries and commissions, the Ministry of Water Resources (MWR), and the Ministry of Land and Resources (MLR)[②].

MEP launched its demonstration program in 1999 when it designated Hainan for the building of an "ecological province". The program was later extended to a total of 14 provinces, municipalities and autonomous regions, namely, Hainan, Jilin, Heilongjiang, Fujian, Zhejiang, Jiangsu, Shandong, Anhui, Hebei, Guangxi, Sichuan, Liaoning, Tianjin and Shanxi. In 2008, MEP issued the Suggestions on Promoting Eco-Civilization Construction, laying down clear guidelines and basic principles for eco-civilization construction and proposing requirements for building industrial systems, cultural ethics, institutions and mechanisms in line with the requirements of eco-civilization, and also decided to launch a national pilot program for eco-civilization construction. By October 2013, MEP had approved in six batches a total of 130 national pilot and demonstration areas for eco-civilization construction, including 19 prefecture-level cities and two trans-regional or trans-river basin areas. There are no province-wide pilot areas and 70% of the pilot areas are in Jiangsu, Zhejiang, Liaoning, Guangdong and Sichuan.

In May 2013, MEP released Indicators for National Pilot and Demonstration Areas for Eco-civilization Construction (trial), which was generally a continuation from the evaluation system stipulated in Indicators for the Building of Ecological Counties, Cities and Provinces (revised edition) (HF [2007] No. 195) which was issued six years before that. The indicator system covered five sub-systems, namely ecological economy, ecological environment, ecological human habitat, ecological systems, and ecological culture with 29 Level-3 indicators for ecological counties and 30 for ecological cities (MEP, 2013).

The major characteristic of this indicator system is that it sets different benchmarks for Level-3 indicators respectively for the key development areas, the optimization development areas, the restricted development areas and the prohibited development areas, with a distinction between binding indicators and reference indicators. As a result, eco-civilization construction has

---

① The Ministry of Environmental Protection now has changed its name as the "Ministry of Ecology and Environment".
② The Ministry of Land and Resources now has changed its name as the "Ministry of Natural Resources".

different but clear goals for cities and counties in regions of different functions, and the evaluation criteria vary for different types of indicators. In addition, though the basic criteria are generally the same for ecological cities (and prefectures) and ecological counties (and cities/districts), the specific benchmarks differ significantly. In particular, for ecological cities, more emphases are laid on the control over the intensity of human activities and economic development covering wider geographic and ecological spaces, and on the harmony between humans and nature. Another characteristic of the indicator system is that it pays more attention to plans and policy measures for eco-civilization construction. For example, there are five Level-3 indicators for ecological culture, yet only the indicator for public energy saving and water saving efforts and that for public transportation truly reflect the ecological advancement of a city. The share of expenditure on environmental protection initiatives in the total public-interest expenditure of enterprises above a certain scale may also serve this purpose partially, yet the remaining indicators seem sort of far-fetched for showing the actual progress towards ecological culture, and they may be difficult to measure accurately. Therefore, we may as well call it a "plan evaluation indicator system" (Huan et al., 2013: 74-81).

After the 18th National Congress of CPC, a number of other ministries stepped up their efforts in pilot projects for eco-civilization construction and launched various programs or plans of their own. In December 2013, NDRC, together with the Ministry of Finance, MLR, MWR, the Ministry of Agriculture [1] and the State Forestry Administration, proposed a plan for eco-civilization pioneering demonstration areas in China based on the National Functional Zoning Plan which was approved in 2010. In June 2014, NDRC and five other ministries jointly issued the Notice for Issuing the Constructing Plans of National Eco-civilization Pioneering Demonstration Areas (trial), formally launching the project for constructing such pioneering demonstration areas. Soon, 57 areas were designated as the first batch of demonstration areas (the applications of Fujian Province and Huzhou City were approved respectively by the State Council and the six ministries in advance), and selection of the second batch started in June 2015 (with the Ministry of Housing and Urban-rural Development as the seventh authority). A total of 100 administrative regions, river basins and ecological areas were designated as planned.

Different from the program of MEP, this program incorporates more regions above the prefecture level and more river basins and ecologically sensitive areas. The first batch includes five provinces and 28 cities/prefectures (including nine special regions), accounting for 73% of the total. The increased attention to trans-regional river basins and ecological sensitive areas is reasonable and scientific from the perspective of eco-civilization construction, and policy pilot programs in this regard may be able to better tackle some governance difficulties faced today within the current system. However, the wide geographic and administrative coverage of eco-civilization demonstration areas hints more or less at a lowered threshold or standard. In comparison, it may be more appropriate to stick to the approach of MEP, which selects ecological counties, then eco-civilization counties, and then move up to the provincial level.

In May 2014, MWR released the first batch of national water eco-civilization construction cities, and 40 out of all 46 designated cities were at the prefecture level (another 59 cities were selected in the second batch). In this program, designated cities will devote themselves to

---

[1] The Ministry of Agriculture now has changed its name as the "Ministry of Agriculture and Rural Affairs".

exploring ways to ensure water safety. The major goal is to coordinate water resource protection and ecological development, to improve the restoration and protection of water ecology, to achieve a sound ecological balance in regard to water resources and water environment, to enhance city safety level in case of flood, to create good urban ecological environment, and to develop regional industrial layout and development frameworks in line with local water resource conditions.

Early in February 2013, the State Oceanic Administration under MLR also released the first batch of national oceanic eco-civilization demonstration areas: Weihai City, Rizhao City and Changdao County of Yantai City of Shandong Province; Xiangshan County of Ningbo City, Yuhuan County of Taizhou City and Dongtou County of Wenzhou City of Zhejiang Province; Xiamen City, Jinjiang City and Dongshan County of Zhangzhou City of Fujian Province; Zhuhai Hengqin New Area, Xuwen County of Zhanjiang City and Nan'ao County of Shantou City of Guangdong Province. This program emphasized that national oceanic eco-civilization demonstration areas would be limited to the four provinces (Shandong, Zhejiang, Fujian and Guangdong) designated by the State Council as pilot provinces for the development of oceanic economy. The goal is to improve the industrial structure, to transform the development pattern, to enhance pollution control, to improve oceanic environment, to strengthen oceanic ecological protection and development, and to ensure oceanic ecological safety in coastal areas.

It is clear that the programs of MWR and MLR are targeted at certain elements of eco-civilization. With clear targets, they can improve the control over certain ecological elements, e.g. water ecosystem or oceanic ecosystem. However, their shortcomings are also clear and may even be fundamental. For any geographically or administratively larger area, it is hard to implement or even imagine such specifically targeted ecological measures.

Therefore, though there are more similar programs targeted at specific elements of eco-civilization, the program of MEP and that of the seven ministries led by NDRC are undoubtedly more typical and authoritative. The author's discussion in the following section will mainly focus on them instead of elaborating on more other programs such as "Beautiful Countryside" of the Ministry of Agriculture (fully rolled out in 2013 as a breakthrough or symbol of agricultural eco-civilization construction), the pilot program for national (forest) park construction led by the State Forestry Administration (Yunnan was designated as a pilot province in 2008), the national smart city pilot program organized by the Ministry of Housing and Urban-Rural Development and the Ministry of Science and Technology (covering 97 cities, districts and towns as well as 41 dedicated projects in 2014), the national city of public transportation program led by the Ministry of Transport (with demonstration projects in 30 cities around the country within the 12th Five-Year Plan period).

3. A Three-dimensional Theoretical Framework in Studying Eco-civilization Construction Demonstration Areas

A precondition for philosophical thinking on eco-civilization construction demonstration areas is that we must be clear about what is philosophy. This is indeed not an easy question. Generally speaking, Marxist dialectical materialism (materialist dialectics) and historical materialism (materialist outlook on history) are the theoretical or methodological bases for the author's observations and analysis in this paper. Specifically, the nature of an eco-civilization construction pilot or demonstration area is an attempt to improve or restructure the relationship between humans and nature as well as between society and nature at different levels or in different dimensions of the human society. And the primary role of materialist dialectics and materialist outlook on history is to help (require) us view our understanding and practice of eco-civilization construction in an objective, dialectic and historical manner. To be objective, we must see the reality as it is and base everything on the reality. The most important reality we must face is the vastly diverse ecological environment in different regions. Individual natural ecological elements can be made with the support of modern science and technology, but an organic and holistic ecosystem is more likely to remain natural. Therefore, the adaptation and protection of natural ecosystems are always the top choices for the human society (subject). To be dialectic, we must be aware and reflect upon the fact that all our understandings and practices, their forms and results, have two sides. Both intuitive experience and rational understanding, and both truth revealed by a great man and wisdom generated among the general public, reflect the coexistence and balance between the right and the wrong, the reasonable and the limited, the active and the passive. The human's capability to understand and act on the nature is not merely manifested in conscious changes made to the natural environment. It also involves active and initiative maintenance or nurturing of the ecological environment. Moreover, to fully tap into the potential human's capability to maintain the nature with its understandings and practices, we will have to initiate profound changes to the existing social practice, especially under the current social conditions. To be historical, we will have to be clearly aware that all human understandings and practices are historical and practical. This means our understandings and practices of the nature, like our understandings and practices of everything else, are not born to be like this or the result of any individual's preference; instead, they can be changed but cannot change whenever anyone wants them to.

Based on this, the author believes that we can examine eco-civilization construction demonstration areas in China from the following three-dimensional theoretical perspective: The first dimension focuses on the mechanism and path for realizing "five-in-one" (*wu wei yiti*) or "integrating the five key elements"— its management philosophy or strategic dimension, which involves the question of what kinds of subject-object relationship, institutional configuration, and economic, political and social dynamic mechanisms are needed for a healthy and smooth development of eco-civilization demonstration areas. The second dimension is to compare the effectiveness and efficiency of administrative authorities at provincial, municipal and county levels in promoting the development of these demonstration areas — its spatial dimension, which involves the question of which administrative level is more suitable for making progress of eco-civilization construction. The third dimension refers to the socialist nature or orientation of eco-civilization construction — its political dimension, which involves the question of whether and to what extent eco-civilization construction will lead to the realization of a socialist vision.

Under the management philosophy or strategic dimension, in terms of both the definition of eco-civilization and the strategies for eco-civilization construction, it points at or hints at a new structure of relationship between humans and nature as well as between society and nature. Or we can say that it refers to a combination of economy, politics, society, culture and ecology which are in line with "five-in-one"(*wu wei yiti*) or "integrating the five elements" emphasized in the report of the 18th National Congress of CPC, namely, eco-civilization construction shall pervade in all aspects and the whole processes of the other four elements. Based on this, we may also say that the "five-in-one"(*wu wei yiti*) approach or "integrating the five elements" shall be interpreted in terms of what our goals are and in terms of which path to follow towards our destinations. In the former sense, it embodies the achievements or standards of eco-civilization construction, while in the latter sense, it is an important propeller or focal point for promoting eco-civilization construction. Therefore, it must be emphasized that eco-civilization construction and its pilot and demonstration projects are important as both a purpose in itself and a path towards our goals; these two sides shall receive equal attention.

Here, two specific issues require particular notice. First, the fundamental nature of eco-civilization construction pilot areas is to create a brand-new relationship between humans and nature as well as between society and nature, which is different from that of the contemporary industrial civilization, or a holistic economic, political, social, cultural and ecological system of eco-civilization. That is to say, concrete and substantial civilizational reforms on the whole or results of eco-civilization construction are the most important and most convincing. Special efforts should be made to avoid the tendency of substituting concrete progress towards an eco-civilization with merely policy measures or initiative endeavors on the level of path, or even single-dimensional endeavors within local areas. For example, take the number of trees planted in a year as the level of ecological improvement achieved or take the achievement in energy saving and emission reduction (closing, merging or transforming relevant enterprises) as the improvement of local air quality. Such substitution may not actually be appropriate. Second, eco-civilization construction may have diverse specific goals and may take multiple paths, so the relationship between the goals and the paths may be extremely complicated in a certain area or a certain region. This means that the experience or guiding role of any eco-civilization construction pilot area may be relatively limited. It is especially worth noting here that even if some areas have similar natural and ecological conditions, it may not mean that they can share the same goal and strategy for eco-civilization construction because they may have vastly different economic and social conditions as well as largely different historical and cultural traditions.

Of course, for newly designated pilot or demonstration areas of different types in China, the most realistic concern may have more to do with the paths rather than the goals. Specifically, it is about how an area or region can initiate a brand-new process that can be called eco-civilization construction. As far as an objective and dialectic analysis on the strengths and weaknesses of ecological conditions of a certain area and its strategy for choosing an impetus of eco-civilization construction are concerned, the author believes that the following three elements are important in terms of paths.

First, an appropriate subject-object relationship. This can be summarized as a clear division of labor for all social actors in a certain area or a certain region so that appropriate tasks are assigned to appropriate people. For sure, social actors in a modern society can be divided into governments and their officials, business owners and their employees, mass media and new media as well as media professionals, college teachers and students as well as research staffs, non-governmental organizations (NGOs) or civil organizations as well as their members and advocates, individuals, etc. In this regard, a core issue is how to forge a "green political consensus" or "green mass culture" in all the above social groups, which is beneficial to eco-civilization construction. It should not only be widely and democratically participated in by the general public (with concrete and institutionalized traditional channels for democratic participation), but also be of deliberative democracy in nature (any organization or individual should be prepared to change its ideas or behaviors on the basis of eco-civilization progress). By so doing, we will nurture the majority of the society into "citizens of eco-civilization" or "green new man" (Huan, 2013b). Also, the traditional division between social elites and the general public, if it still remains, should have only limited significance. This is because both of the groups will have to receive green education or undergo a process of rebirth as a social subject. When comparing the two, traditional social elites may not have higher ecological literacy than the general public. More importantly, any concrete progress in practices for eco-civilization construction (the "object") will ultimately be transformed into (manifested in) the lifestyle and daily conducts of a new-generation general public.

Second, a scientific institutional framework. As mentioned above, the core of eco-civilization construction and its pilot projects is the attempt to create a holistic governance system and an operational mechanism covering economy, politics, society, culture and ecology (Huan, 2015c, 2014c). In comparison, the environmental economic policy tools belonging to the category of economic system and mechanism (e.g. environmental tax or "carbon market") and the environmental administrative supervision policy tools belonging to the category of ecological management system and mechanism (e.g. the "ecological red line" and national parks) are only of secondary importance. On the national level, at the minimum, the backbones of an institutional framework for eco-civilization construction should be a system of "eco-civilization state" or "environmental state", comprising the three parts of legislation, justice and law enforcement based on a clear authorization of (people's) sovereignty. This means that the progress in the eco-civilization construction of China and its achievements will gradually be incorporated into our "rule of law" system (e.g. by inscribing it clearly into the constitution or other relevant laws), rather than remaining at the level of "political system" of CPC and the government for long (e.g. mainly promoted by issuing decisions and recommendations of the Central Committee of CPC and the State Council). Similarly, it can be expected that at the sub-national levels (provincial, municipal and county levels), eco-civilization construction should also be based on or supported by the national "rule of law" system and mechanism at the corresponding levels (e.g. local laws and regulations). This is the core and an important part of our pilot programs for eco-civilization construction today (Huan, 2013c).

Third, an economic, political and social dynamic mechanism which is full of vitality. Friedrich Engels made the famous proposition of "historical resultant force" when talking about realistic propelling force for historical development (Engels, 2012: 605, 649), emphasizing that for the realistic development process of human history, the explanation should not be too simple or metaphysical, rather it should be understood as a result of the synergy of multiple forces (including theoretical ideas and political elites). Also, eco-civilization construction as a civilizational transformation, or any true and lasting change (or improvement) towards it, must be tested once and again in history, and it must be made clear that initiative efforts of a society in any time have its own cognitive and practical boundaries, and that no abrupt breakaway from the past or creation of the future can ever happen within a short period of time (as the old saying goes, "Rome was not built in a day"). Moreover, any true and lasting change or improvement toward eco-civilization can only be brought about by the joint force of economic, scientific, political, legal, social and cultural factors. Neither high-tech decree or administrative decree alone can lead effectively toward a clear and positive direction, though they may cause rapid and widespread changes to the way of social production or people's lives. A good example in this regard is people's way of transportation and daily habits, and how they change. The enhanced public transportation system is the ultimate solution to today's transportation problems in modern cities. This is the green transportation consensus widely accepted today. However, green transportation or green travel is still far from the mainstream of how urban transportation is organized or what way of transportation people choose. This is mainly because various social systems and mechanisms do not match one another as well as common people's "rigid" habit of modern transportation. These are undeniable facts and cannot be expected to change within a short period of time. Therefore, we should be prudent about any single-element measures and their effectiveness. Examples include administrative or economic restrictions for purchasing and driving private cars.

As for the second spatial dimension, i.e. the administrative level is the best for the initiation and smooth progress of eco-civilization, and the author believes that the core lies in discussing and determining an appropriate time and range for launching such efforts and programs. Or in other words, we need to elaborate on when and on which level we should launch eco-civilization construction efforts. Specifically, the appropriate time depends on an overall judgment about the progress of our economic modernization and its negative ecological effect, while an appropriate range involves how big a geographic scope we should consider for building (restoring) the balance between economy, society and ecology so as to ensure reasonability and effectiveness. In regard to the former, political announcement and strategic deployment at the national level are clearly laid out in the report of the 18th National Congress of CPC, The Decision, The Suggestions and The Overall Plan, etc. Vigorously promoting eco-civilization construction is now part of our overall approach toward socialist modernization. However, for some remote and relatively poor provinces and regions, awareness and attitude in this regard may still be problems. For example, the pilot program of MEP is obviously tilted toward southeastern provinces. This may hint at more than just a gap in the capacity for eco-civilization construction.

As for the latter, the author's general view is that the provincial level (provinces, autonomous regions and municipalities) maybe the best choice. In the author's opinion, this is mainly because provincial governments enjoy more independence and autonomy in the following three aspects (Huan, 2015d).

The first aspect is administrative zoning. In a unitary system with relatively centralized power in China, the level of provinces, municipalities and autonomous regions is the main level and possesses more power, resources and higher efficiency than the other levels (prefecture, county, town and village levels). Therefore, at the provincial level, public administration and service are more at the government's own discretion, and this includes promoting eco-civilization construction. In this regard, we may even say that just placing the primary supervision responsibility on the governments of provinces, autonomous regions and municipalities, the primary responsibility of promoting eco-civilization construction should also fall on the governments of provinces, autonomous regions and municipalities (besides the central government, for sure). The existing and launched national strategies such as the coordinated development of Beijing-Tianjin-Hebei Region, the Yangtze River Delta city cluster, and the Pearl River Delta city cluster show that it is necessary and important to launch trans-provincial initiatives for eco-civilization construction, but the provincial level remains a crucial substantial administrative level.

The second aspect is ecosystem. Though it is an objective fact that ecosystems nationwide and worldwide are largely connected as a whole, the diversity of climate, river basin, mountain system, soil, vegetation and living species will always differ in one way or another as geographic conditions change. Moreover, generally, most of our provinces, municipalities and autonomous regions have a coverage that corresponds with a special and complete ecosystem. Perhaps only Inner Mongolia, Gansu and Hebei are exceptions. It is quite understandable that the smaller an administrative region is, the more likely that ecosystems will overlap, causing difficulties in issuing and implementing various administrative measures. The same is true for eco-civilization construction. Therefore, in comparison, we are more likely to respect the specificity and the completeness of ecosystems, and launch initiative actions to change human activities and their structure as well as the coordination with natural and ecological laws at the provincial level, for we will have wider vision and ample room to take various measures. Based on the above aspects, we should be prudent when creating or talking ecological villages and towns.

The third aspect is historical and cultural traditions. Historical and cultural traditions have always been an important reference when administrative zoning is made throughout the history of China. For example, place names such as Qinjin, Qilu, Yanzhao, Jingchu, Xiaoxiang, Wuyue, Lingnan, Saiwai, etc. of the Spring and Autumn Period in Chinese history still correspond largely to how we divide provinces today. More importantly, the complicated interactions between the historical and cultural traditions of a region and the characteristics of ecosystems constitute an important precondition for the eco-civilization construction in China today. Therefore, when we try to innovate various forms of systems and institutions, we must be fully aware of and do everything possible to adapt to the different historical and cultural traditions of different provinces. In other words, the historical and cultural traditions of a province will provide considerable incentives or "positive energy" for the path selection and exploration of eco-civilization construction in China.

Without doubt, counties (cities/districts) in China have their own characteristics and advantages, too. Since the adoption of the prefecture-county system in the Qin Dynasty, counties have always been a key unit in the social, economic and political structures of feudal China, and there comes the old saying that once prefectures and counties are in a good order, the country will be at peace. Coming into the modern age, as medium and small cities began to play more important roles in the economic system, counties' economic status declined. However, after the founding of the People's Republic of China, counties, as well as cities and districts of the same level, remained significant in the existing economic and political structures. Before the adoption of the reform and opening-up policy, most counties in China had relatively complete economic and industrial systems of their own. After the reform and opening-up policy was launched, many counties in China embarked on the path of market-based competition and division. As a result, counties in the southeastern provinces see faster economic development, while the development in the counties of some central and western provinces is slower. For example, in the "Top 100

Counties of China" selected by Zhongjun Institute — a social think tank, 63% of all counties were in Jiangsu, Shandong and Zhejiang provinces, having 24, 21 and 18 counties on the list respectively; while nine provinces had no county selected, namely Gansu, Guangxi, Guizhou, Hainan, Heilongjiang, Ningxia, Qinghai, Tibet and Yunnan (*Life Daily*, 24 August 2015). Jiangyin City and Zhangjiagang City, tied at the top of the list, respectively registered RMB 275.4 billion and 220 billion in regional gross product (RMB 169,000 and 146,700 per capita), roughly the same as the total economic volume of Ningxia Hui Autonomous Region and Qinghai Province (RMB 275 billion and 230.1 billion respectively).

From the perspective of eco-civilization construction, counties are very important geographic and administrative spaces or platforms, though less independent and autonomous than provinces. On the one hand, county governments in China have relatively strong comprehensive administrative power and coordination capacity, play a connecting role between the provincial level and the town and village levels, and thus are able to adopt to a certain extent a holistic way of thinking and strategies for the economic, social, cultural and ecological development within the scope, rather than simply implement the policies and laws of the CPC and the national government. In particular, county governments usually lead directly the refining of the goals of eco-civilization construction as well as the operationalization of the paths and strategies. On the other hand, county economies remain and should be to a large extent local. This means that the relationship between humans and nature as well as between society and nature can be more localized or face-to-face. Localized economic production and marketing processes enable and promote people, as producer and operator, to use local natural resources in a wiser and more ecological way and to do more to protect the local natural ecology. Face-to-face material consumption and living activities help people, as consumers, to better experience the material metabolism among individuals, society and nature, and the heavy dependence that humans have on natural ecosystems for their survival and daily life. This will foster the awareness of green consumption and the community sense of being the subject.

Of course, the prefecture level also has its unique advantages in promoting eco-civilization construction compared with the provincial and county levels. On the one hand, a prefecture covers a geographic space that is smaller than a province yet larger than a county, and is therefore positioned to tackle the excessive natural and ecological diversity at the provincial level and the overlapping of natural ecological systems at the county level. So it is more suitable to adjust and restructure the relationship between humans and nature as well as between society and nature on the basis of the completeness of a natural ecosystem and the uniqueness of historical and cultural traditions, thus striving for the realization of "five-in-one" (*wu wei yiti*) or "integrating the five elements". On the other hand, over the past nearly 40 years since the launch of the reform and opening-up policy, as economic and social modernization progressed continuously in China, economic and social integration advanced rapidly, especially in the economically more developed southeastern provinces (e.g. the Yangtze River Delta, the Pearl River Delta and the Beijing-Tianjin-Hebei Region). Accordingly, we need to take a broader perspective for both economic developments in the narrow sense and more comprehensive initiatives like eco-civilization construction — for example, in regard to the tourism development of a natural ecological landscape and the effective control of ecological environment pollution. For this very reason, there has been a trend in recent years that prefectures are gaining importance as an administrative level. This trend can be seen in the fact that the prefecture level is taken as the main level for pilot projects of eco-civilization construction in the program of the seven ministries led by NDRC and the program of MWR.

As for the third political dimension, i.e. the socialist nature or orientation of eco-civilization construction, the author believes that though the answer may seem sure and clear without any doubt, it may actually require discussion or even argument. It is about the political ideology and the institutional orientation adopted by CPC and the national government when leading the efforts for eco-civilization construction. For most scholars and the general public, the answer to this question may be clear and definite, requiring no proof at all (Lin, 2015). This is because the path of socialism with Chinese characteristics and the leading position of CPC determine the political correctness and ideological leading position of socialism in eco-civilization construction in China. Generally, this is indisputable. However, in an international economic and political order dominated by capitalism and its discourse hegemony, a clear socialist nature of eco-civilization construction points at a clear-cut and radical political preference and choice, or a red-green politics (Huan, 2009a, 2014d), which has been avoided in researches of eco-civilization and its construction today, either intentionally or unintentionally.

Specifically, this question can be understood and answered in the following two aspects (Huan, 2013d): The first is how to determine the universality or limitedness of the western interpretation of ecological and environmental issues and the experience in tackling with them, and the second is the relationship between the basic socialist economic and political systems and eco-civilization construction.

In regard to the former, we must acknowledge that the western capitalist countries were faced with unprecedentedly serious ecological and environmental problems or public hazards, and such problems and crises were largely relieved and alleviated after the late 1980s. But questions are: How did it happen? To what extent and on what level is it universally meaningful? It is adequately proved by facts that the international economic and political order has long been dominated by these countries, the export of excessive capital and the transfer of dirty and backward industries, massive domestic environment campaigns, and the rise of green parties in these countries, as well as the economic reform and opening-up of later emerging economies and various other factors all contributed to the shift of western countries toward a "light green" economic and industrial structure, ecological governance and massive green awareness (culture). That is to say, the relative improvement of the ecological and environmental quality in western countries was conditional rather than unconditional because it was the result of the transfer rather than dissolution of its ecological and environmental problems or burden. Or, in other words, the reason why these countries appeared to have achieved win-win results in regard to economic development and environmental quality is that heavily polluting industries were transferred to various developing countries (emerging economies including China). As a result, the overall ecological and environmental pressure of the Earth as a whole was not reduced but increased. This also explains why, 40 years after the Conference on Human Environment held in Stockholm in 1972, we are facing a worse ecosystem and living environment on the Earth today. On this basis, we can see that the western way of "eco-modernization" and "ecological capitalism" is indeed a realistic way to deal with ecological crises and challenges, but it may not be appropriate to take it as a universal way, especially when it comes to the sustainable development of the human society as a whole and the continuation of civilization.

As for the latter, we must see that we started our reform and opening-up policy by learning and adopting the science and technology as well as economic management methods of developed industrial countries in the West, and that we shifted our attention away from and avoided the once-excessively-emphasized political division between the two different social systems by focusing on the vaguely-defined "integration with international (mainstream) society". However, on the one hand, capitalism is never a political tag or a void slogan, but rather, it is an organic combination of lifestyle and cultural values. That is to say, it is not easy to simply "disentangle" or "dialectically absorb" the so-called "advanced experience" of developed capitalist countries in the West. It is more likely that a capital-inclined political mindset or one that follows the logics of capitalism will gradually erode our economy, society and culture, without us knowing it. This is because in the logics of neo-liberalism, a market dominated by private capital and the logic behind it should not have any boundary (Huan, 2009b). As a result, we may not have established a market system in line with classic liberalism or the Western standard.

4. Conclusions

Basic theoretical discussions on eco-civilization and its construction, especially profound theoretical questions and challenges proposed in regard to the practices of pilot or demonstration areas of eco-civilization construction, which require answers, are topics of deep concern on the author's part, and many efforts have been made to analyze them. In this regard, the author's basic view is that scholars have done little to elaborate on and build theories for eco-civilization construction, and that we can borrow a lot from the broad environmental political social theories or ecological cultural theories, eco-Marxism (socialism) or "green-left" theories when trying to create independent theories for eco-civilization and its construction.

Without doubt, the three dimensions discussed above cannot cover all aspects of the theoretical and practical importance of pilots or demonstration projects of eco-civilization construction in China. They are at most concerns and focuses of attention of the author in regard to the various forms of existing pilots and demonstration areas of eco-civilization construction. Based on this, the ultimate question that the author tries to answer can be summarized as whether and to what extent the eco-civilization construction, which was fully rolled out after the 18th National Congress of CPC, can promise a concrete turning point in the worsening of our ecological conditions since we adopted the reform and opening-up policy, and constitute a milestone in our way toward socialist modernization with Chinese characteristics or a civilizational transformation.

References

恩格斯(Engels F). 2012. 1890 年 9 月 21 日《致约·布洛赫》和 1894 年 1 月 25 日《致瓦·博尔吉乌斯》//马克思恩格斯选集(第 4 卷). 北京: 人民出版社: 605, 649.

胡锦涛(Hu J T). 2012. 坚定不移沿着中国特色社会主义道路前进 为全面建成小康社会而奋斗——在中国共产党第十八次全国代表大会上的报告. 北京: 人民出版社.

环保部(MEP). 2013. 国家生态文明建设试点示范区指标. http://www.zhb.gov.cn/gkml/hbb/bwj/201306/W02013

0603491729568409. pdf. [2013-07-22].

林安云(Lin A Y). 2015. 社会主义生态文明建设的政治推进方略. 哈尔滨工业大学学报(社会科学版), (4): 122-126.

卢风(Lu F). 2013. 生态文明新论. 北京: 中国科学技术出版社.

郇庆治(Huan Q Z). 2009a. 社会主义生态文明: 理论与实践向度. 江汉论坛, (9): 11-17.

郇庆治(Huan Q Z). 2009b. 终结无边界的发展: 环境正义视角. 绿叶, (10): 114-121.

郇庆治(Huan Q Z). 2010. 重建现代文明的根基: 生态社会主义研究. 北京: 北京大学出版社.

郇庆治(Huan Q Z). 2013a. 多样性视角下的中国生态文明之路. 学术前沿, 01(下): 17-27.

郇庆治(Huan Q Z). 2013b. 生态文明建设与环境人文社会科学. 中国生态文明, (1): 40-42.

郇庆治(Huan Q Z). 2013c. 论我国生态文明建设中的制度创新. 学习月刊, (8): 48-54.

郇庆治(Huan Q Z). 2013d. "包容互鉴": 全球视野下的"社会主义生态文明". 当代世界与社会主义, (2): 14-22.

郇庆治(Huan Q Z). 2014a. 生态文明概念的四重意蕴: 一种术语学阐释. 江汉论坛, (11): 5-10.

郇庆治(Huan Q Z). 2014b. 绿色变革视角下的生态文化理论研究. 鄱阳湖学刊, (1): 21-34.

郇庆治(Huan Q Z). 2014c. 环境政治学视角的生态文明体制改革与制度建设. 中共云南省委党校学报, (1): 80-84.

郇庆治(Huan Q Z). 2014d. 再论社会主义生态文明. 琼州学院学报, (1): 3-5.

郇庆治(Huan Q Z). 2015a. 生态文明理论及其绿色变革意蕴. 马克思主义与现实, (5): 167-175.

郇庆治(Huan Q Z). 2015b. 中国生态文明的价值理念与思维方式. 学术前沿, (01)上: 64-73.

郇庆治(Huan Q Z). 2015c. 环境政治视角下的生态文明体制改革. 探索, (3): 41-47.

郇庆治(Huan Q Z). 2015d. 志存高远创建生态文明先行示范省. 福建理论学习, (6): 4-9.

郇庆治, 高兴武, 仲亚东 (Huan Q Z, Gao X W, Zhong Y D). 2013. 绿色发展与生态文明建设. 长沙: 湖南人民出版社.

After Paris: Global Trend of Green Development and China's Ecological Modernization Strategy

Huiming Li

University of Jinan

1. The Paris Agreement Infused New Momentum to the Global Trend of Green Development

Over the past years, as global climate change intensifies, various countries have been making adjustments to their development directions, targeting their technological development, international trade, and domestic and foreign investment efforts at green development in the future, and launching strategies for green transformation. At the Organisation for Economic Cooperation Development (OECD) Ministerial Council Meeting in 2009, 30 member countries, together with Chile, Estonia, Israel and Slovenia, making a total of 34 countries, released the Declaration on Green Growth, calling for green growth. The United Nations Environment Programme's (UNEP) reported Towards a Green Economy: Pathways to Sustainable Development and Poverty Eradication released in 2011 pointed out that if we invested 2% of the global gross product each year in 10 major economic sectors from 2011 to 2050, we would be able to accelerate our transformation towards a green economy that is low-carbon and resource-efficient[①]. *China 2030: Building a Modern, Harmonious, and Creative Society* released jointly by the World Bank and the Development Research Center of the State Council of China emphasized that "the world's development process is at a crossroad. Given the unsustainability of current economic growth in both China and the world, a new approach to development is needed. The concept of green development is such an approach. Green development can become a potentially transformative process for the economy, the society, the environment, and the role of government. It is an opportunity: an open door"[②]. Against such a background of green transformation, the Paris

---

[①] UNEP. 2011. Towards a Green Economy: Pathways to Sustainable Development and Poverty Eradication. http://www.unep.org/pdf/GER_Chinese/Green_Economy_Full_report_ch.pdf[2016-1-19].

[②] 世界银行, 国务院发展研究中心. 2013. 2030 年的中国: 建设现代、和谐、有创造力的社会. 北京: 中国财政经济出版社: 239.

Agreement reached at the 2015 Conference on Climate Change undoubtedly infused new momentum to the global trend that has already been in action, heralding the end of the fossil fuel era[①] and spreading green development wider across the world[②].

1.1 The Paris Agreement Sets Clear Long-term Goals for Global Warming Control with Upper Limits for Global Greenhouse Gas (GHG) Emission

It was made clear in the Paris Agreement to "hold the increase in the global average temperature to well below 2℃ above pre-industrial levels and to pursue efforts to limit the temperature increase to 1.5 ℃ above pre-industrial levels, recognizing that this would significantly reduce the risks and impacts of climate change"[③]. This sets clear requirements and targets for the global climate governance and shows a clear direction for the transformation of the world economy. According to the Global Risks Report 2016 released by the World Economic Forum (WEF)[④], the first risk among the top five global risks for the past three years is "failure of climate change mitigation and adaptation", meaning that this risk is deemed as the most influential risk in 2016 and the No. 1 single threat faced by the world economy. For over a decade, this is the first time that climate change is listed by experts as the No. 1 risk faced by the world, sending out an unequivocal signal to policy makers, entrepreneurs and investors around the world that as the Paris Agreement is reached, all countries in the world are determined to take more rigid measures to address this global risk. In order to achieve the long-term temperature goal of 2℃ or even 1.5℃, parties of the Paris Agreement aim to "reach global peaking of greenhouse gas emission as soon as possible, recognizing that peaking will take longer for developing country parties, and to undertake rapid reductions thereafter in accordance with best available science, so as to achieve a balance between anthropogenic emissions by sources and removals by sinks of greenhouse gases in the second half of this century, on the basis of equity, and in the context of sustainable development and efforts to eradicate poverty"[③]. This will require all countries to cooperate and control the use of carbon-intensive fossil fuel, and low-carbon clean energy and relevant technologies will surely become the general trend of economic and social development in all countries soon.

1.2 The Paris Agreement, Together with the 2030 Agenda for Sustainable Development Shows a Clear Path of Green Development for Future Economic Development of the World

The year 2015 is critical in the history of global environmental governance. Since various countries are concerned about the sustainability of world development, especially since it was pointed out with more certainty that anthropogenic GHG emission is "extremely likely to have been the dominant cause of the observed warming since the mid-20th century", it is now more

---

① Vidal J. 2015. Paris Climate Agreement May Signal End of Fossil Fuel Era. http://www.theguardian.com/environment/2015/dec/13/paris-climate-agreement-signal-end-of-fossil-fuel-era[2016-1-19].

② 胡鞍钢. 2012. 中国: 创新绿色发展. 北京: 中国人民大学出版社; 张梅. 2013. 绿色发展: 全球态势与中国的出路. 国际问题研究, (5): 93-102.

③ UNFCCC. 2015. Adoption of the Paris Agreement. http://www.360doc.com/content/15/1216/08/1180205_520756935.shtml [2016-2-7].

④ WEF. 2016. Global Risks Report 2016. http://www3.weforum.org/docs/GRR/WEF_GRR16.pdf[2016-10-25].

clear that anthropogenic factors are the causes of climate change. Meanwhile, global greenhouse gas emission continues to rise, and it is more and more urgent that we take measures to address climate change. With these consensuses strengthened in the scientific circle, it is clearly more urgent for us to address climate change, and the international community is therefore more willing to take major actions. On September 25, 2015, the United Nations General Assembly adopted *Transforming Our World: The 2030 Agenda for Sustainable Development*, deciding on new goals for global sustainable development. In the next 15 years, there would be 17 sustainable development goals, seeking to build on the millennium development goals and complete what they do not achieve[①]. The Paris Agreement is an active response to the *Transforming Our World: 2030 Agenda for Sustainable Development* and they together form two milestone international laws in the history of world development. If the latter shows the direction and path for future sustainable development of the world in a more comprehensive way, the former will confirm the path from the perspective of global climate governance. It was made clear in the *Transforming Our World: 2030 Agenda for Sustainable Development* that "we envisage a world…in which consumption and production patterns and use of all natural resources — from air to land, from rivers, lakes and aquifers to oceans and seas — are sustainable". It was also pointed out that "climate change is one of the greatest challenges of our time and its adverse impacts undermine the ability of all countries to achieve sustainable development. Increases in global temperature, sea level rise, ocean acidification and other climate change impacts are seriously affecting coastal areas and low-lying coastal countries, including many least developed countries and small island developing states". To "take urgent action to combat climate change and its impacts" is one of the 17 goals in the *Transforming Our World: 2030 Agenda for Sustainable Development*. And the Paris Agreement confirmed this goal and laid out the details for it. With these two combined, a clear goal and requirements are set, together with well-defined path and direction for the development and transformation of the world economy. Green development will surely pick up its pace (Figure 1).

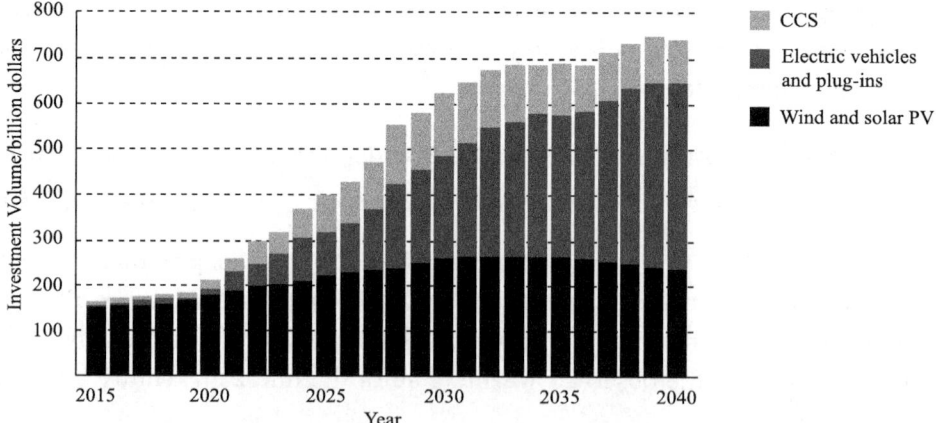

Figure 1 Global Investment in Variable Renewables, Carbon Capture and Storage (CCS) and Electric Vehicles in the 450 Scenario

Source: International Energy Agency. 2015. Energy and Climate Change: World Energy Outlook Special Report. p. 143

---

① United Nations General Assembly. 2015. Transforming Our World: 2030 Agenda for Sustainable Development. http://www.mw.one.un.org/transforming-our-world-the-2030-agenda-for-sustainable-development/[2016-1-23].

1.3 The Paris Agreement Will Further Change the Direction of Global Investment and Promote the Radical Change of the Global Energy Structure Towards Clean Energy

It was mentioned in the Paris Agreement that by the latter half of this century, i.e. after 2050, we are to achieve a balance between the anthropogenic GHG emission and the carbon sink, that is, zero net GHG emission by the latter half of this century. By then, the energy structure will have been dominated by new and renewable energy, and the consumption of coal and other fossil fuels will approach zero. To achieve this, we need an energy revolution in which new and renewable energy gradually replaces fossil fuel, and low-carbon transformation of the economy is achieved. Only by so doing can we ensure development and mission reduction and thus achieve sustainable development while controlling global climate change in the same time[①]. According to the latest statistics of the International Energy Agency (IEA), GHG emission from the energy sector represents roughly two thirds of all anthropogenic GHG emission, and effective actions in the energy sector are, consequentially, essential to tackle the climate change problem[②]. Figure 1 shows the global investment in variable renewables, CCS and electric vehicles if we are to achieve the goal of keeping the temperature increase below 2℃ over the pre-industrial level. We can see that the investment will grow annually, the growth must be especially fast after 2020 and the overall level will gradually reach USD 700-800 billion after 2030. Figure 2 shows the number of countries adopting renewable energy policies and a trend of annual growth is also clear. In this scenario, the Paris Agreement is a clear commitment of state parties to develop low-carbon green economy, and it is a strong signal that the path of low-carbon and green development is a must for the future of mankind, and green development will be a core concept in the global climate governance in the future.

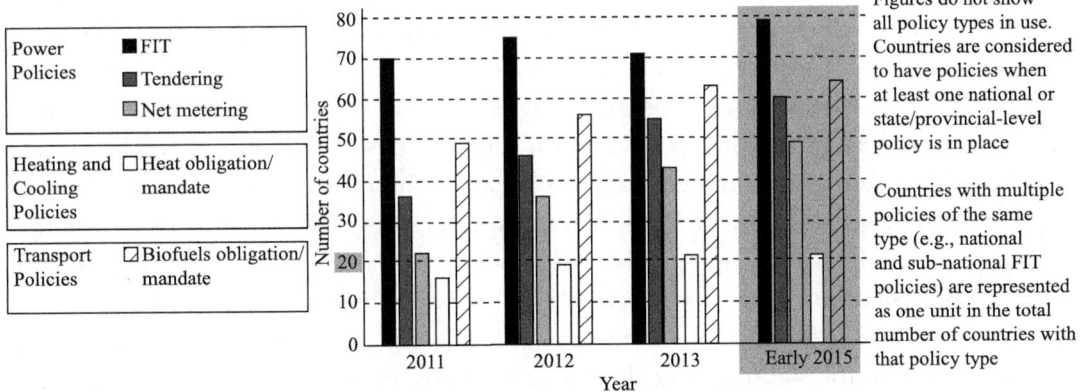

Figure 2　Number of Countries with Renewable Energy Policies in 2011 to Early 2015
Source: Renewable Energy Policy Network for the 21st Century. Renewables 2015 Global Status Report: 15

---

① 杨雪杰, 刘丹. 2015. 巴黎协定: 开启应对气候变化新征程——访清华大学低碳经济研究院院长何建坤教授. 环境保护, (24): 24.

② International Energy Agency. 2015. Energy and Climate Change: World Energy Outlook Special Report. http://www.docin.com/p-1855693743.html[2016-1-8].

2. Ecological Modernization Theory and Its Green Connotation

In the early 1980s, the ecological modernization theory first emerged in Germany. As a theory of ecological politics strongly oriented towards realistic problems, it is clearly characterized by a close combination with reality, and the core viewpoint is to promote forward-looking and preventive environmental policies, to facilitate technological innovation, to prevent and control environment pollution from the very beginning, and, more importantly, to show a clear direction and path for win-win development of the environment and the economy[①]. Ecological modernization offers an economic and technological path for the green reform of the contemporary society. From the economic and technological perspective, which is one of the core dimensions of modernization, it offers realistic policy options for the green reform, providing not only direct economic driving forces, but also a clear direction, possible tools, political support and strong momentum for the green reform.

2.1 Ecological Modernization, with Technological Reform as the Medium, Offers a Relatively Realistic Direction for the Green Development of the Contemporary Society

Technology and its reform have always taken a core position in the economic and social modernization process. By "science and technology are the first productive force" we mean that science and technology are the No. 1 propelling force for economic development. In ecological modernization, it is emphasized that science and technology, not only being the first productive force, but also being the first element we can count on the green development of our economy and society. Traditionally, science and technology are usually believed to be a fundamental cause of ecological and environmental problems. Some believe that science and technology are out of control in the process of their applications, especially the applications of chemical and nuclear technologies, severe ecological crises are caused, and technological progress is to blame for the modern environmental disaster. In contrast, ecological modernization believes that technological reform and the development of clean technologies are the keys to environmental problems. Instead of blaming environmental problems on technologies, it regards technology as a key weapon to fight against such problems and to improve the overall environment. If we define modernization as the process in which machines or technical devices take the place of manpower, and then in a certain sense, the process of modern economic and social development is irreversible. Our use of machines and electricity today undoubtedly represents huge progress of the human society and great improvements of people's living standards. Therefore, technological reform offers tools for the solution of ecological and environmental problems. With technological progress, we can minimize the ecological and environmental impacts of economic activities, and reduce or even eliminate negative impacts. Therefore, by strongly promoting new technologies, we will be able to improve the efficiency of today's economic activities, to use material resources in a more efficient way, and to create a modern society that is cleaner and more economical. This is undoubtedly a realistic path of economic and social development that may be accepted and supported by the majority of people.

---

① 李慧明. 2013. 生态现代性理论的内涵与核心观点. 鄱阳湖学刊, (2): 61-72.

2.2 The Political Modernization Required by Ecological Modernization Sheds Light on the Reform of the Government's Position and Role, and Provides Political Support for the Green Reform of the Contemporary Society

Ecological modernization requires political modernization as its precondition and basis. Essentially, ecological modernization is a political concept. Ecological and environmental protection is undoubtedly one of the major responsibilities of governments at all levels today, and the way this responsibility is performed needs to change, too. This is what ecological modernization reveals to us. Economic and social activities are complicated and full of changes in a modern society, with various factors intertwined. The way governments try to protect the ecological environment must conform to the requirements of such a society. Ecological modernization calls for a more dispersed, more flexible and more consultative way of governance, and it provides the conditions for stakeholders on various levels to participate in the decision-making process, so as to exert restriction on corporate behavior with voluntary actions and promote the "greenization" of society with the power of civil society. Public participation and supervision serve as external forces that push forward the reduction of negative environmental impacts of economic and social activities as well as internal forces that raise people's environmental awareness and improve their behaviors. In the end, guided and led by a law-based government, all kinds of social forces will move towards the shared goal of environmental protection along a green path. Political modernization of a country will promote technological improvements in enterprises and the supervision by the civil society, and ultimately achieving truly sustainable development across the society.

2.3 Ecological Modernization Tries to Coordinate Between Government, Market (Enterprises) and Society (General Public) as well as Unite All Political Forces Around Environmental Protection so as to Promote Green Reform in the Contemporary Society

Ecological modernization believes that some agreements may be reached by the government (the governing power), the market represented by enterprises and consumers, and social forces (public participation in the government's decision-making on environment affairs, supervision over environmental behaviors of enterprises and the governing behaviors of the government, as well as NGOs) on environmental protection as well as this agreement tap fully into the social forces by forming an extensive "united front" for the green reform and by pushing the society towards green development. This practical proposal, to some extent, solves the problem of "what force to rely on" for the green reform of the contemporary society, which is actually the "agent dilemma"[①], a long-term difficulty faced by radical ecologists. According to this proposal, the green reform of the contemporary society may rely on the governing power of the government (including technical bureaucratic system), enterprises (investors, producers and business operators), social consumption forces, which constitute a major part of economic activities (consumers), and the general public (participants and supervisors in the decision-making process). To some extent, media may also be counted on as some one believes media to be the

---

① 郇庆治. 2006. 生态现代性理论与绿色变革. 马克思主义与现实, (2): 90-98.

fourth force of the contemporary society. This is highly realistic in today's society for it offers an effective strategy for the contemporary society, especially the government, to form alliances for environmental protection, making it possible to create a multi-center mechanism for ecological and environmental governance featuring coordination and cooperation[①], which will promote the green reform effectively.

2.4 Ecological Modernization Emphasizes Market Mechanism, Aims at Developing Lead Market, and Offers Director Economic Driving Force for the Green Reform of the Contemporary Society with Ecologization of the Economy and Economization of Ecology

Lead market plays a significant role in the ecological modernization process, and offers another "rational choice" for the contemporary society with growing ecological rationality. On the one hand, it makes economic activities more compliant to ecological principles and incorporates ecological principles into economic ones; on the other hand, it helps ecological principles create economic benefits, make ecological compliance a kind of productive force, and make the ecological industry an important part of the contemporary economy with growing significance. According to the ecological modernization theory, to protect the natural ecosystems bears not only ecological value but also growing economic value in terms of sustainable economic and social development. Ecologization of the economy and economization of ecology are both the means and ends of ecological modernization, and they achieve coordination between the economy and ecology together.

3. Ecological Challenges in China's Modernization Process and China's Ecological Modernization Strategy

Still on its way towards modernization, China has achieved a lot in economic development but is faced with unprecedented pressures in terms of resources and environment. This is the end of our pursuit of economic growth at the expense of resources and environment, and it is urgent that we launch a green transformation.

3.1 China Is Facing Growing Ecological and Environmental Challenges

China is a huge consumer of energy, mainly coal. As its economy develops, it is now challenged by both energy security and global climate change. Moreover, China has also been pressed by the international community to cut its emission, with people spreading ideas that China is a energy-wise or environment-wise threat. Since China is undergoing rapid industrialization and urbanization, its energy consumption and CO_2 emission will continue to rise for now and for some time in the future. It is and will continue to be one of the major sources of CO_2 emission increase in the world. Under such a circumstance, China will surely face huge pressure from the international community to shoulder more responsibility for quantified emission reduction. Meanwhile, internal pressures of resources and environment have also been

---

① 肖建华，赵运林，傅晓华. 2010. 走向多中心合作的生态环境治理研究. 长沙: 湖南人民出版社.

growing, and CO₂ emission control has become a hard constraint for China's economic development and the modernization process. Over the past decade, environmental degradation and resource depletion have cost it nearly 10% of GDP, with air pollution accounting for 6.5%, water pollution 2.1%, and soil degradation 1.1%. Though air pollution is retreating continuously, population aging, growth of urban population and the increase in urban residents' income, lead to the fact that people are spending more money on diseases caused by pollution[1]. The extremely high economic growth of China is achieved at huge environmental expenses, and it is summarized by the World Bank into an economic model of high growth and high pollution where it is hard to pursue growth without pollution. According to a research group of the Chinese Academy of Sciences, "high resource consumption, environmental pollution and ecological damage have become the by products of the rapid economic growth (in China)"[2]. The World Bank pointed out that "China's current pattern of development has also placed considerable stress on the environment land, air and water, and has imposed increased pressure on the availability of natural resources. The challenge going forward will convert these pressures into new sources of growth by adopting a green growth model that taps into new global markets in green technologies while at the same time solving many of China's own pressing environmental concerns"[3]. It is clear that China's modernization path is still facing unprecedented challenges and constraints in some sense. We are now at a critical turning point. Facing pressures from resources and environment, bearing in mind the strategic considerations for the realization of the Chinese dream of a great rejuvenation of the Chinese nation, we need to turn things away from this growingly unsustainable "borderless" development model[4] and towards green development, going beyond the somewhat "unidimensional" western pattern of modernization.

3.2 Dimensions and Direction of China's Ecological Modernization Strategy

In the Recommendations for the 13th Five-Year Plan for National Economic and Social Development released at the Fifth Plenary Session of the 18th Central Committee of CPC, green development was listed as one of the five major development ideas for China during the 13th Five-Year Plan period, saying that "Green, which represents an eco-friendly outlook, is a necessary condition for ensuring lasting development as well as an important way in which people pursue a better life. We must stick to the basic national strategy of energy conservation and environmental protection, carry on with sustainable development, adhere firmly to the development path of production development, well-off life and good ecological conditions, accelerate the building of an energy-efficient and environment-friendly society, form a new pattern of modernization featuring harmony between man and nature, promote the building of a

---

[1] 世界银行, 国务院发展研究中心联合课题组. 2013. 2030 年的中国: 迈向现代、和谐、有创造力的社会. 北京: 中国财政经济出版社: 44.

[2] Asian Development Bank. 2012. Toward an Environmentally Sustainable Future — Country Environmental Analysis of People's Republic of China. Manila: ADB: 5.

[3] 世界银行, 国务院发展研究中心联合课题组. 2013. 2030 年的中国: 迈向现代、和谐、有创造力的社会. 北京: 中国财政经济出版社: 9.

[4] 郇庆治. 2009. 终结"无边界"的发展: 环境正义视角. 绿叶, (10); 2012. "发展主义"的伦理维度及其批判. 中国地质大学学报(社会科学版), 12(4): 52-57.

beautiful China, and make new contribution to global ecological security"①. This lays solid theoretical and practical foundations for green development, and the ecological modernization strategy is the key to green development. If China wishes to do more amid the great tide of profound ecological transformation, it must make efforts in the following four dimensions.

First, develop green economy to reinforce the material basis and economic support for green transformation with technological reform. From a relatively realistic perspective, in China today, technological breakthrough is a must in the face of growing ecological and environmental difficulties. Though the author doesn't really favor technological determinism, in current circumstances, technology may be a "better than nothing" solution. Technological reform and the successful use of new technologies are the keys to the green transformation of the current pattern of economic and social development as well as major benchmarks gauging whether our economic modernization is on an ecological track. This is also one of the key points of the western ecological modernization theory②. On the basis of technological reform, we shall strongly promote ecological economy, including the industry of ecological and environmental protection, ecological tourism and ecological services, so as to lay solid foundation and provide strong economic support for the green transformation of economy and the society. Only by continuously incorporating ecological rationality into economic rationality and ultimately achieving economic ecologization③ can we gradually enable ecological rationality to prevail over economic rationality and turn ecology into a natural orientation as well as a internal criterion of the economy. Only by doing so can we lay solid material foundation and provide realistic support for the green transformation of economy and the society.

Second, create ecological systems to ensure correct path and direction for the green transformation. The Decision of the Central Committee of the Communist Party of China on Some Major Issues Concerning Comprehensively Continuing the Reform of the Central Committee of CPC pointed out that "to promote ecological progress, we must put in place a systematic and complete set of ecological systems, implement the most rigorous systems for protection at sources and accountability, and improve our environmental governance and ecological restoration system, so as to protect the ecological environment with sound systems"④. Systems are the keys to building the rules of law in China and improving the national governance and the capacity for it. In particular, for the direction and path of economic and social development that we need to make strenuous efforts to turn around, system building bears very high significance. To some extent, our modernization process is now on the old track that has repeatedly been proved by the West to be unsustainable, which features "pollution first and treatment later" and is deeply

---

① 中共中央. 2015. 中共中央关于制定国民经济和社会发展第十三个五年规划的建议. http://www.xinhuanet.com/fortune/2015-11/03/c_1117027676.htm[2016-2-19].

② Jänicke M. 2000. Ecological Modernization: Innovation and Diffusion of Policy and Technology. Forschungsstelle für Umweltpolitik (FFU) Report, No. 8. Berlin: Free University of Berlin; 2008. Ecological modernisation: New perspectives. Journal of Cleaner Production, 16(5): 557-565.

③ Mol A P J. 1999. Ecological modernization and the environmental transition of Europe: Between national variations and common denominators. Journal of Environmental Policy & Planning, 1(2): 167-181; 2002. Ecological modernization and the global economy. Global Environmental Politics, 2(2): 92-115.

④ 习近平. 2013. 中共中央关于全面深化改革若干重大问题的决定. http://www.xinhuanet.com/politics/2013-11/15/c_118164294.htm [2016-2-19].

trapped on it. The logic of capital and the profit-seeking nature of the market have pushed up the track to a point where it is extremely difficult to turn around. Path dependence and a certain level of the "lockdown" effect have posed huge constraints on our efforts to shift the track. Difficult as a shift of the track may be, more political determination and will are required from the ruling party, and more rigid system support and driving force are needed to achieve it. Therefore, the government must give full play to its governing role in economic and social development. To create a set of ecological systems, we must incorporate the idea of ecologically sustainable development and a series of accountability rules into all aspects of our economy and society. The system shall have a very extensive coverage from the general direction of national economic and social development to large investments relevant to national strategies and people's livelihoods, from major adjustments of the economic structure to the evaluation of officials' performance, and from the launch of industrial and agricultural construction projects to the restoration and treatment of water rivers, lakes and seas. As the renowned German environmental politician Martin Jänicke once pointed out, "technological reform, market mechanism, environmental policies and the preventive principle are the four core elements of ecological modernization, and the most important among the four is the formulation and implementation of environmental policies"[①]. This means that the ecologization of the national economy and the society is a comprehensive reform of technology, market, policy and mindset. For any of these, national policies and their implementation play a key role because no ecological theory and system can be effective without the political power that ensures their implementation.

Third, improve the green market to build internal motivation safeguards for the green transformation with market mechanisms. To some extent, the development of a modern society is now driven more and more by the market. It was emphasized by the Central Committee of CPC that "we should deepen the reform of the economic system by centering closely on the decisive role of the market in resource allocation, carry on and improve our basic economic regime, enhance the modern market system and macro regulation system, open economic system with quickened steps, accelerate the transformation of our economic development pattern, and speed up the building of a country of innovation, so as to enable the economy to develop in a more efficient, fairer and more sustainable way"[②]. It is fair to say that China today has embarked on the track of marketization, and the market has become an irreversible driving force, pushing forward the entire economy and society. As is pointed out earlier in this paper, the key to achieving the green transformation of the national economy and society is how we channel this force towards ecologization, for the market is the central force in promoting technological reform and applying new technologies in the economy and society. For the overall development of the country, we must stick firmly to the idea of giving full play to the role of market mechanisms, and rely on market mechanisms to guide technological reform and the market launch of the achievements. This is because marketization contains in it the basic motivation and path towards green development, and it ensures that technological forces and economic factors are channeled towards green development under the effect of interest. Only by relying on the innate force and

---

① 郇庆治, 马丁·耶内克. 2010. 生态现代性理论: 回顾与展望. 马克思主义与现实, (1): 175-179.
② 习近平. 2013. 中共中央关于全面深化改革若干重大问题的决定. http://www.xinhuanet.com/politics/2013-11/15/c_118164294.htm [2016-2-19].

the logic of the market can we ensure that the ongoing ecologization process continues on the right track and gains strong momentum for moving forward on its own.

Fourth, promote green culture to change people's mindset and lay solid foundations as well as provide strong spiritual support for a green society. In a sense, when an ecological and environmental dilemma we face in the process of development is actually the result of people's cultural values, people's behaviors, especially consumption, will be closely coupled with and supported by the logic of the capital, and will push things towards unsustainability until it is no longer possible to turn them around. The ecological and environmental dilemma has profoundly rooted in philosophy and culture, and only by changing people's mindset and then making their behaviors in line with ecological rules, can we lay solid cultural foundation for a green society. Fundamentally, a green society must be strongly supported by a green culture, and a basic condition for green development is that a green culture becomes a social mainstream and people's habits change fundamentally. Green development and green transformation, at the very basis, are changes of the paradigm of human civilization. They will not be possible without a change in people's mindset. Development concept and outlook on the national level must also change fundamentally towards sustainability before we can infuse strong spiritual motivations into green transformation, provide favorable public opinion support and cultural atmosphere for ecological progress, and promise "Green China Dream" a hopeful future.

Establishment of Low-carbon City Construction Policy Toolkit and Analysis of the Policy Tools' Effectiveness[①]

Dong Du, Shaoyang Ge

Institute of Information Management, Hohai University

1. Introduction

Climate change is a common challenge for mankind. To cope with global climate change, all countries across the world have been engaging in low-carbon city construction. Currently, China's low-carbon city construction is in the full swing stage, and the theoretical findings emerge one after another. In particular, China has done considerable work in building the evaluation indicator system for low-carbon city development [1], but the existing researches play a very limited role in guiding actual low-carbon city construction. The indicator system only plays a guiding role. Actually, the policy tools are essential to promote low-carbon city construction since the policy tools represent important means and effective paths for the government to promote low-carbon city development. The policy toolkit for low-carbon city construction in response to the needs of developing the low-carbon city construction evaluation system facilitates the overall examination and investigation of the urban low-carbon policy. If we go further to analyze the effectiveness of the urban low-carbon policy toolkit, we are in a position to make policy suggestions on developing and implementing the urban low-carbon policy on a well-informed basis.

2. A Brief Review of Relevant Literature

The literature review reveals that the domestic scholars seldom study the urban low-carbon policy since they mostly discuss China's low-carbon policy from the macroscopic perspective. To be exact, the scholars have approached the issue on how to improve the low-carbon policy system

---

[①] The research is supported by the National Major Social Sciences Funded Project: Research on Evaluation Indicator System of China's Low-carbon City Construction (Approval No.: 15ZDA055).

from different angles. Specifically, Qian and Zhang [2], from the perspective of the policy system, held that in the process of policy planning, the low-carbon policy system consisted of the sub-systems of policy actors, policy tools and policy changes. Jia [3] discussed the low-carbon policy system in urbanized areas, which covered the industrial policy, fiscal policy, investment and financing policy, land policy, environmental protection policy and lifestyle-related policies. Attaching importance to the planning and construction of low-carbon policies, these researches are predominantly qualitative studies.

Some other scholars approach the low-carbon policy structure from the perspective of policy tool theory. For example, Li et al., [4] on the basis of related studies, conducted content analysis and developed an analysis framework in light of the low-carbon policy tool promulgated by the Chinese central government. Still based on content analysis, Luo and Zhu [5] carried out a quantitative analysis upon China's low-carbon policy tools over the years, namely, textual quantitative analysis. Doubtlessly, the content analysis — a quantitative analysis upon literature — is an important way to dig out the implications of the documents. However, this research holds that whether a policy is good or not is determined by its enforcement. How the policy tools — a bridge and a bond between the policy goal and the policy implementation result — work determines the actual implementation of the policies. On this account, this paper proposes that it is essential to put a premium on building a low-carbon policy toolkit and researching the effectiveness of the policy tools.

3. Establishment of Low-carbon City Construction Policy Toolkit

The policy tools are more often than not referred to as "policy measures". The policy tools are what the government depends on to implement related policies. In the broad sense, the policy tools refer to the means that are adopted or likely to be adopted by decision-makers and policy implementation parties to fulfill the policy goals. Many policies are in themselves policy tools. Therefore, in a less strict sense, policies are policy tools. But in the strict sense, policies are made up of a series of policy tools somehow organized and matched.

According to different standards, policy tools fall into diverse categories. According to the Canadian public policy scholars Howlett and Ramesh [6], policy tools are divided into three categories: compulsory, mixed and voluntary. In this case, the policy tools are categorized by the degree of the government's intervention. By the use of policy tools, Gu and Wu [7] categorized the policy tools into three types respectively for control, stimulation and information dissemination. Luo among others, according to the basis underpinning the policy tools' functions, classes the low-carbon policy tools into three types: regulative, economy stimulating and society-oriented [5]. These categorizations, though nominally different, have basically the same connotations.

This paper categorizes low-carbon policies in light of the application fields of the policies (including five major fields, namely, low-carbon energy, low-carbon industry, low-carbon architecture, low-carbon transportation and low-carbon consumption [8]) to facilitate pertinent policy research and analysis of the policy effectiveness, with the priority laid on the selection of low-carbon policy samples and the screening of policy tools as well as the development of the policy toolkit.

3.1 Selection of the Low-carbon Policy Samples

The low-carbon policies refer to the laws, regulations, plans, opinions, measures and notices related to low-carbon development issued by the government departments, which usually come out in policy documents.

As for the low-carbon city construction, relevant polices include not only national low-carbon policies, but also the local ones, and in particular the low-carbon policies of certain cities (like the low-carbon community construction policies). The former two are the upper polices of corresponding cities, which shall be implemented unconditionally.

Each of the five fields mentioned above is taken as the key term for research whose result discloses the relationships among the policies (in succession or quotation). On this basis, the policy document most related to the five fields is studied as the typical case. A preliminary search shows that among the five fields, there are many policies on low-carbon energy, and especially on energy conservation and emission reduction; still there are quite some policies on the low-carbon industry, including the financial and taxation policies as well as the investment and financing policies; the last three aspects (about low-carbon architecture, low-carbon transportation and low-carbon consumption) are related to the lifestyle and corresponding polices in these regards.

3.2 Selection of the Low-carbon Policy Tools

The identification and differentiation of policy tools are apparently simple, but it is actually not the case. All the collected policy documents are not policy tools or policy measures, and thus it is necessary to go through the policy documents to screen out the ones that lack policy tools, like those on monitoring and evaluation, technique solicitation and promotion. Moreover, to make the follow-up researches easier, we need to standardize the chosen policy tools, for instance, to put together the policy tools with similar implications and to unify policy tool expressions with the same connotations.

3.3 Development of the Low-carbon Policy Toolkit

The development of the low-carbon policy toolkit means to develop the knowledge base in the low-carbon city construction evaluation system we have developed.

The knowledge base is also known as the knowledge element management system [9]. Its mainly functions are sorting through the knowledge elements, and making them ready for search, check and update. The knowledge base supports the functions of complicated search and personalized management based on knowledge elements in addition to the document and network management systems. Different from the traditional knowledge document management system, the knowledge bank incorporates background information about knowledge elements rather than registers relevant contents only. Specifically, the low-carbon policy toolkit not only concerns coding the standardized policy tools to make the search of policy tools by key terms easy, but also contains such information as the policy background, issuing agency and categorization of the policy tools.

This paper, based on the establishment of the low-carbon policy toolkit knowledge base, proposes to build a system of three groups of layered indicators in the logic of "structure-process-result". The first-layer indicators evaluate the concreteness of the policy tools. In different areas, these indicators evaluate the relevance of various low-carbon policy tools. The second-layer indicators evaluate the execution abilities of these policy tools; they are mainly intended to evaluate the operation mechanism and implementation process of the low-carbon policy tools to see whether corresponding organizations and necessary management mechanisms are in place to realize the policy goals. The second-layer indicators also measure to what extent the goals have been realized by the policy tools. All these are conducive to quantitative treatment and effectiveness analysis of the policy tools.

4. Effectiveness Analysis of Low-carbon City Construction Policy Tools

One of the focuses of the policy tool research is policy output or policy effect [10]. Different categories of tools construct different policy activities, leading to different effects. Therefore, the evaluation of the policy tools' effect is one of the most important issues and has a very important position in the research of low-carbon city construction policy tools since the policy tools' effect reflects the government's governing capacity and how far the low-carbon city construction has been promoted. But at present the research in this regard has just got started because the low-carbon city construction is nascent and the policy tool research is emerging.

The evaluation of the policy tools' effectiveness can be conducted through internal and extern frameworks of policies [11]. From internal framework of policies, the research focuses on the characteristics of the policy tools, as reflected in their effectiveness measurement from the two dimensions of acceptability and predictability; from external framework of policies, the research mainly measures how far the policy tools and goals are appropriately matched. For a long time, the academic community takes the former as the dominant force to measure the policy tools' effectiveness, failing to break through the limitations caused by the policy tools. With the deepening and expansion of the research, the scholars begin to have keen interest in the latter. This paper adopts the policy tools' effectiveness perspective to analyze the links between the goals and the means (tools) to achieve them. In the initial research, we have built an evaluation indicator system for low-carbon city construction, and have determined the low-carbon city construction goals and evaluation standards for different types of cities [12].

Yin et al. [13] analyzed the foreign industrial policy and discussed its effectiveness; Zhong et al. [14] conducted a quantitative study on the innovation policies and explored the coordination among policies; Zhang and Gao [15] carried out a quantitative research upon the energy conservation and emission reduction policies, and measured and discussed the impacts of policies and measures upon energy conservation and emission reduction. Based on the existing researches, this paper, in view of the preliminary work related to the low-carbon city construction evaluation indicator system and the demand for building the low-carbon city construction evaluation system, presents the framework of effectiveness analysis upon low-carbon city construction policy tools as follows.

4.1 Dimensions of the Low-carbon City Construction Evaluation Indicator System

The foregoing researches have built the low-carbon city construction evaluation indicator systems respectively corresponding to different types of cities, cities in different phases of development and five fields. According to their stages of development, i.e., the short-term, middle-term and long-term development stages, the cities can search in the database for the target indicator and standard value for their low carbon construction. See Table 1 for details.

Table 1 Low-carbon City Construction Evaluation Indicator System

Five Fields	Indicators	Remarks
Low-carbon energy	(1) Ratio of zero-carbon energy in primary energy (2) Emission from unit energy production (3) Forest coverage	Reflecting the status of resources and ecological environment
Low-carbon industry	(1) Carbon emission from unit economic output (2) Energy consumption of unit output	Reflecting the status of low-carbon production
Low-carbon architecture	(1) Carbon emission from unit economic output (2) Energy consumption of unit output	
Low-carbon transportation	(1) Carbon emission from unit economic output (2) Energy consumption of unit output	
Low-carbon consumption	Carbon emission per capita	Reflecting the low-carbon living status

4.2 The Basic Policy Tool Dimension for Low-carbon City Construction

The policy tools are a mechanism that in policy implementation converts the policy goals into concrete policy acts. The tools roughly fall into six types: direct regulation, carbon tax, carbon emission trading, financial subsidy, policy recommendation and government procurement [16]. The direct regulation is the most common. The carbon tax and the carbon emission trading are the two most important low-carbon policy measures proposed in the United Nations Framework Convention on Climate Change; the financial subsidy means to stimulate organizations and individuals to reduce carbon emission by adopting financial incentives; the policy recommendation is meant to persuade the organizations and individuals into certain behavior; in comparison, the government procurement has far less influence than the preceding tools.

4.3 Quantitative Study of the Policy Tools for Low-carbon City Construction

To analyze different influences of policy tools upon the low-carbon city development, we need to conduct the quantitative analysis upon the low-carbon city construction policy tools, so as to better understand how the policy tools are used, and provide recommendations and suggestions for the future policy-making. According to the backgrounds, issuing authorities and types of the policies, and more importantly the detailedness, enforceability and goal-orientedness of the policy tools, each of the policy tools is assigned a 1-5 value (respectively denoting fail, pass, medium, good, excellent) so as to quantify the effects of policy tools, as seen in Table 2. The experts' scores for each item concerning the policy tools shall be averaged to get the total score of the said policy tool.

Table 2 Scores for Policy Tools

Policy Tools	Detailedness	Enforceability	Goal-orientedness	Total Score
Direct regulation				
Carbon tax				
Carbon emission trading				
Financial subsidy				
Policy recommendation				
Government procurement				

It must be made clear that the policy tools get different scores under different indicators.

4.4 Effect Analysis of Low-carbon City Construction Policy Tools

According the development stages (the ages) of specific cities, the evaluation indicators and actual data are drawn from the database of the low-carbon city construction evaluation system to be taken as dependent variables while the policy tools are taken as independent variables to build a basic calculation model and discuss the policy tools' influence upon the cities' low-carbon development. In view of the influence of the previous years' development levels on this year, the following analysis model can be established for each indicator.

$$Y_t = C_t + \alpha \times Y_{t-1} + \sum_{i=1}^{6} \beta_i \times X_{ti} + \varepsilon_t$$

In the model, Y_t means the level of the year t; Y_{t-1} refers to the level of the previous year; X_{ti} denotes the policy tool adopted in the year t; C_t is the constant; α and β_i are co-efficients of variables; ε_t indicates the influence of random factors upon dependent variables. It needs to be made clear that the low-carbon technology is also an important factor affecting the urban low-carbon development; as this paper focuses on the low-carbon policies' impact upon the low-carbon city construction, the low-carbon technology's role is implicated in C_t and ε_t.

Additionally, the indicated level of a certain year is the ratio between the actual value and the standard value. It is a precondition to clarify the standard for each indicator.

With the annual data during the observation period collected, we can conduct the relevance analysis to make clear of the policy tools' impact upon concrete indicators of a certain field, and on this basis evaluate the effectiveness of the policy tools. With all relevant indicators treated as thus, we can have an overall evaluation upon the effects of policy tools.

5. Conclusions

In developing the low-carbon city construction evaluation system, we stress the development of policy toolkit to strengthen the policy analysis, which distinguishes this research as an innovation. The policy toolkit includes not only a series of policy tools, but also the background data, experts' views and analysis results concerning the policy effectiveness. The greatest contribution of this paper lies in the study of the policy tools' effectiveness. A combination of the quantitative study of the policy tools and the low-carbon city construction evaluation indicator system helps improve the way to use policy tools, and sheds light on developing more effective low-carbon policies.

This paper also has drawbacks, since it only makes the systematic analysis and gives solutions concerning the policy tools as well as the policy analysis involved in the low-carbon city construction evaluation system. In the follow-up study, we should conduct empirical researches and case studies, improve the development of policy toolkit and analyze the policy tools' effectiveness on a better-informed basis, so as to contribute to the formulation and implementation of appropriate policies for low-carbon city construction.

References

[1] 朱婧, 刘学敏, 姚娜(Zhu J, Liu X M, Yao N). 2013. 低碳城市评价指标体系研究进展. 经济研究参考, (14): 18-28.
[2] 钱洁, 张勤(Qian J, Zhang Q). 2011. 低碳经济转型与我国低碳政策规划的系统分析. 中国软科学, (4): 22-28.
[3] 贾若详(Jia R X). 2014. 城市化地区低碳政策体系探析. 中国经贸导刊, (12): 51-54.
[4] 李健, 高杨, 李详飞(Li J, Gao Y, Li X F). 2013. 政策工具视域下中国低碳政策分析框架研究. 科技进步与对策, (21): 112-117.
[5] 罗敏, 朱雪忠(Luo M, Zhu X Z). 2014. 基于政策工具的中国低碳政策文本量化研究. 情报杂志, (4): 12-16.
[6] M. 豪利特, M. 拉米什(Howlett M, Ramesh M). 2006. 庞诗等译. 公共政策研究. 北京: 生活·读书·新知三联书店: 144.
[7] 顾建光, 吴明华. 2007(Gu J G, Wu M H). 公共政策工具论视角述论. 科学学研究, (1): 47-51.
[8] 杜栋, 王婷(Du D, Wang T). 2011. 低碳城市的评价指标体系完善与发展综合评价研究. 中国环境管理, (3): 8-13.
[9] 李东, 蔡剑(Li D, Cai J). 2005. 决策支持系统与知识管理系统. 北京: 中国人民大学出版社: 322.
[10] 顾建光(Gu J G). 2006. 公共政策工具研究的意义、基础与层面. 公共管理学报, (4): 58-61.
[11] 姜国兵(Jiang G B). 2008. 对公共政策工具五大主题的理论反思. 理论探讨, (6): 133-136.
[12] 中国社会科学院城市发展与环境研究所(Institute of Urban Development and Environment, Chinese Academy of Social Sciences). 2013. 重构中国低碳城市评价指标体系: 方法学研究与应用指南. 北京: 社会科学文献出版社: 1-2.
[13] 殷华方, 潘镇, 鲁明泓(Yin H F, Pan Z, Lu M H). 2006. 中国外商直接投资产业政策测量和有效性研究: 1979—2003. 管理世界, (7): 34-45.
[14] 仲为国, 彭纪生, 孙文祥(Zhong W G, Peng J S, Sun W X). 2008. 政策测量、政策协同与经济绩效——基于创新政策的实证研究(1978—2006). 南方经济, (7): 45-58.
[15] 张国兴, 高秀林(Zhang G X, Gao X L). 2014. 我国节能减排政策措施的有效性研究. 华东经济管理, (5): 45-50.
[16] 叶托, 李金珊, 吴乐珍(Ye T, Li J S, Wu Y Z). 2013. 面向低碳经济发展的政策工具研究. 中共宁波市委党校学报, (3): 76-82.

Rural Ecological Modernization: Evaluation Indicators and Case Study

Li Li

China Center for Modernization Research, Chinese Academy of Sciences

1. Introduction

In recent years, although China's industrialization and urbanization levels have been rising, the urban-rural bifurcation is still obvious. The gap between the per capita disposable income of urban residents and the per capita net income of rural residents widened from 2.5 times in 1978 to 3 times in 2013. Gaps in industrial development, labor productivity, infrastructure, supply of public goods and environmental governance, between urban and rural areas do not narrow with the enhancement of national, urban and industrial modernization levels. Moreover, non-point source pollution and ecological degradation frequently occur in rural areas. These pose a threat to the sustainable development of agriculture and rural areas as well as to farmers' income growth. Besides, these also weaken the capacity of rural areas to provide resources and energy, to serve as pollution buffer and to help with ecosystem protection to urban areas. Without rural modernization, there will be no regional modernization on the whole. Therefore, in regard to China's rural modernization, we should not sit back and wait for it to happen, neither should we blindly follow what some developed countries did — develop agriculture and rural areas at high price of resources and pollution; in particular, rural areas should not be measured by the criteria of urban modernization. It is of important theoretical and realistic significance that we explore evaluation criteria and practical paths for the modernization of the vast rural areas and avoid the traditional path of urbanization and industrialization that feature pollution first and treatment later or simultaneous pollution and treatment. It will not only help break the urban-rural bifurcation, facilitate urban-rural integration, release the potential for economic growth and offer equal access to public services, but also enable us to save more natural resources, environmental capacity and ecological capital for national and regional modernization, realizing the coordinated development of population, resources, environment and economy.

Ecological modernization was first put forward by German scholars in the 1980s, and then was further studied by Dutch, British and American scholars (Mol, 1992). Ecological modernization is the mutually beneficial coupling of modernization and the natural environment, and it is the ecological transformation of modernization (He, 2008). Its core is to realize the ecologization of economy and the economization of ecology through various technological and institutional innovations, to separate economic growth from environmental degradation, and eventually to realize the mutually beneficial co-existence between humans and nature. Throughout global history, industrialization and urbanization are the keys to promoting modernization, but nowadays more and more environmental crises occur against the background of industrial mass production; therefore, industrial ecological modernization and urban ecological modernization are the key points in ecological modernization study.

As environmental pollution and ecological damage spread gradually to agriculture and rural areas, agricultural and rural ecological modernization is receiving more and more academic attention. In as early as 2003, some EU countries have noticed the negative aspects of the rapid agricultural modernization, including the environmental pollution caused by fertilizer and pesticide overuse; they began to shift toward a new rural development model which involved new agricultural practices and rural development policies (Wiskerke et al., 2003). The Farm Bill of the US also emphasizes integrating environmental friendly technologies into agricultural production so as to protect the agricultural environment (Reimer, 2015). Scholars from different countries had discussed rural ecological modernization from different perspectives, including ecological agriculture practices, the effects of ecological agriculture on ecological environment and economic output, the coupling between agriculture and rural sustainable development modes (Horlings et al., 2011), the development of new sources of rural energy (Carrosio, 2014) and the development of rural ecotourism.

Chinese scholars had conducted many studies on ecological modernization (Yang, 2007; He, 2008; Chen, 2010), but the studies on rural ecological modernization did not thrive until 2008, and are still very limited compared to the studies on ecological modernization in other fields. They mainly focused on agricultural ecological modernization (Tan, 2010; Tan et al., 2011; He, 2013; Teng, 2012; Li, 2012; Zhang, 2013) and small-range empirical researches (Chen, 2008; Xu and Li, 2009; Du, 2009; Li and Miao, 2010), and a small part involved the ecological transformation of rural governance system (Zhang et al., 2010), rural culture (Li, 2007) and farmers themselves (Guan, 2009).

This paper builds evaluation indicators and an evaluation model for rural ecological modernization under the theoretical framework of modernization study, and evaluates the level of rural ecological modernization in different regions. It is a further development of the national, regional and urban modernization study.

2. Rural Modernization and Rural Ecological Modernization

Modernization is the global frontier of human development, as well as the process of reaching and keeping up with the global frontier. It is also a profound change of human civilization covering the tremendous transition from traditionality to modernity as well as the all-round development of humankind and the reasonable protection of natural environment. Rural modernization is a type of frontier change and an international competition of rural areas and rural systems. It includes the formation, development, transformation and international interaction of new modern rural areas; the innovation, selection, propagation and withdrawal of rural elements; as well as the international competition and international differentiation in which rural areas endeavor to catch up with, reach and keep up with the world's advanced level in rural areas[①].

Rural ecological modernization is an ecological transformation of rural modernization. Various technological innovations and institutional innovations are adopted to realize the separation of rural economic growth and social progress from environmental degradation, and to complete the transition from traditional rural form to modern rural form, and from traditional rural civilization to modern rural civilization. Rural ecological modernization mainly covers four dimensions which include rural ecological production, ecological living, ecological culture and ecological environment.

3. Evaluation of Rural Ecological Modernization

3.1 Evaluation Model

Since the 1960s, Chinese and foreign scholars have put forward a series of modernization indicator systems, which including the four following systems: 1) The black index system that measures modernization based on economic development and social mobility. This is the first one featuring quantitative study of modernization. 2) The Inkeles index system put forward by the American scholar Inkeles in 1985, which includes 10 indicators and is still influential. 3) The UN Millennium Development Goals, which includes 8 goals, 18 targets and 48 specific indicators. 4) The national and regional modernization index system of China Center for Modernization Research, Chinese Academy of Sciences (CAS), including the first modernization, the second modernization and the integrated modernization evaluation index systems.

This study is based on current research findings on ecological modernization, agricultural modernization and rural modernization. It builds an index system for rural ecological modernization evaluation, which involves four dimensions, i.e. rural ecological production, ecological living, ecological culture and ecological environment. Twenty-two indicators are screened to reflect the characteristics of rural production, living and ecological environment as well as the changes in rural environment and human activities (Figure 1). In practice, some core indicators are selected from the collection according to the scope and characteristics of the research area as well as the data availability.

Regarding evaluation method, this study adopts the standard formula of UN Human Development Index as follows.

Indicator value = (Actual value − Minimum value)/(Standard value − Minimum value) × 100%

---

① Source: The website of China Center for Modernization Research, CAS, http://www.modernization.ac.cn/document.action?docid=2753.

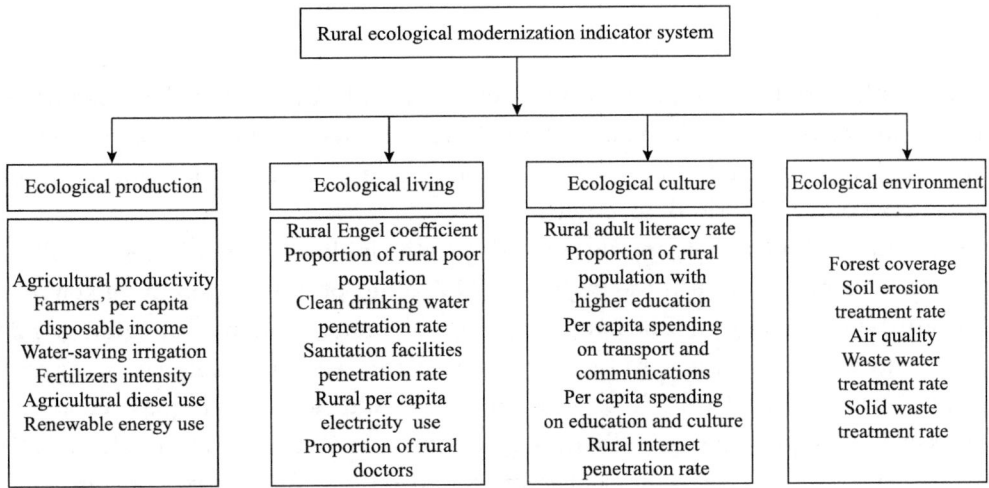

Figure 1 Rural Ecological Modernization Index System

3.2 Provincial Rural Ecological Modernization Evaluation

Based on the statistical data in China Rural Statistical Yearbook, China Statistical Yearbook, China Statistical Yearbook on Environment and local statistical yearbooks, we use the evaluation model for rural ecological modernization to evaluate the rural ecological modernization level of the 31 provincial-level regions in China (except for Hong Kong, Macao and Taiwan). As some indicators involve data that are unavailable or unreliable after further screening, such as data on rural internet users and population with access to clean drinking water, we select 10 core indicators for this evaluation (Table 1).

Table 1 Evaluation Indicators and Standard Values for Provincial-level Rural Ecological Modernization

Level-1 Indicators	Level-2 Indicators	Units	Standard Values	Minimum Values
Ecological production	Agricultural productivity	USD	21,775	301
	Farmers' per capita disposable income	USD	38,811	533
	Fertilizers intensity	Kg/h	90.6	10.4
Ecological living	Rural Engel coefficient	%	10	60*
	Sanitation facilities penetration rate	%	100	42
	Rural per capita electricity use	kW·h	8,253**	206
	Proportion of rural doctors	‰	2.8	0.2
Ecological culture	Rural adult literacy rate	%	100	87
	Proportion of rural population with higher education	%	40	1
Ecological environment	Forest coverage	%	31.1**	3.1

* Determined based on the UN categorization of living standards of all countries in the world. ** The average value of OECD countries in 2010 is used as the standard value. The standard values of other indicators are determined based on the average level of high-income countries

3.3 Results

We have evaluated the rural ecological modernization of 31 provincial-level regions based on the evaluation indicator system. The base year is 2014. Standard values are the average values of high-income countries, and minimum values are the average values of low-income countries in 2010 as obtained from the World Bank database.

The evaluation shows that among the 31 provincial-level regions, the rural ecological modernization level of Shanghai is the highest at 49.7; other provinces and municipalities among the top 10 are Beijing, Jiangsu, Zhejiang, Liaoning, Yunnan, Tianjin, Guangdong, Fujian and Ningxia. The highest ecological production indexes are seen in Shanghai, Jiangsu, Hainan, Liaoning and Hubei, respectively 50.0, 48.4, 46.6, 46.5 and 46.4; the highest ecological living indexes appear in Shanghai, Jiangsu, Shandong, Tianjin and Beijing, respectively 95.5, 76.6, 65.2, 64.6 and 60.9; and the highest ecological culture indexes are for Beijing, Shanghai, Liaoning, Guangxi and Hebei, respectively 62.4, 57.7, 50.6, 45.6 and 44.5 (Table 2 and Figure 2).

Table 2   Evaluation Results of Rural Ecological Modernization in 31 Provincial-level Regions (Except for Hong Kong, Macao and Taiwan)

Regions	Ecological Production Indexes	Ecological Living Indexes	Ecological Culture Indexes	Ecological Environment Indexes	Overall Indexes
Beijing	44.1	60.9	62.4	116.9	43.5
Tianjin	46.3	64.6	44.2	24.2	32.5
Hebei	44.9	47.7	44.5	88.9	26.7
Shanxi	42.5	40.8	42.7	53.2	19.1
Inner Mongolia	12.1	36.5	30.9	64.0	17.5
Liaoning	46.5	48.9	50.6	120.0	35.1
Jilin	45.6	45.7	41.7	120.0	22.0
Heilongjiang	26.7	45.0	43.2	120.0	17.9
Shanghai	50.0	95.5	57.7	27.3	49.7
Jiangsu	48.4	76.6	32.9	45.4	39.1
Zhejiang	46.0	55.6	35.8	120.0	35.8
Anhui	43.3	33.6	10.1	87.3	16.9
Fujian	46.2	51.8	27.7	120.0	31.7
Jiangxi	40.7	47.2	32.1	120.0	21.8
Shandong	45.2	65.2	34.9	48.7	29.0
Henan	43.5	47.4	31.8	72.1	22.0
Hubei	46.4	46.5	30.8	120.0	24.0
Hunan	43.6	35.4	39.5	120.0	19.1
Guangdong	44.7	52.2	40.0	120.0	32.1
Guangxi	43.0	39.5	45.6	120.0	18.9
Hainan	46.6	33.5	31.7	120.0	17.2

Continued

Regions	Ecological Production Indexes	Ecological Living Indexes	Ecological Culture Indexes	Ecological Environment Indexes	Overall Indexes
Chongqing	43.1	33.9	24.6	120.0	18.3
Sichuan	23.6	36.7	24.7	114.7	14.5
Guizhou	25.5	23.9	0.4	120.0	29.3
Yunnan	26.0	32.2	2.7	120.0	33.2
Tibet	2.0	33.7	0.0	31.7	19.2
Shaanxi	43.1	35.7	28.3	120.0	18.3
Gansu	19.5	37.8	0.9	29.2	24.1
Qinghai	2.8	53.0	0.0	10.7	23.1
Ningxia	42.4	36.0	0.0	31.4	30.2
Xinjiang	21.2	41.9	35.1	4.1	14.9

Notes: Some regions see actual indicator values high above the average of high-income countries or OECD countries and thus index values are far above 100; some actual values are far below the average of low-income countries, leading to negative index values. In order to prevent these extreme values from affecting the results, and to eliminate the noise effect, the evaluation indexes are set to be no higher than 120 and no lower than 0

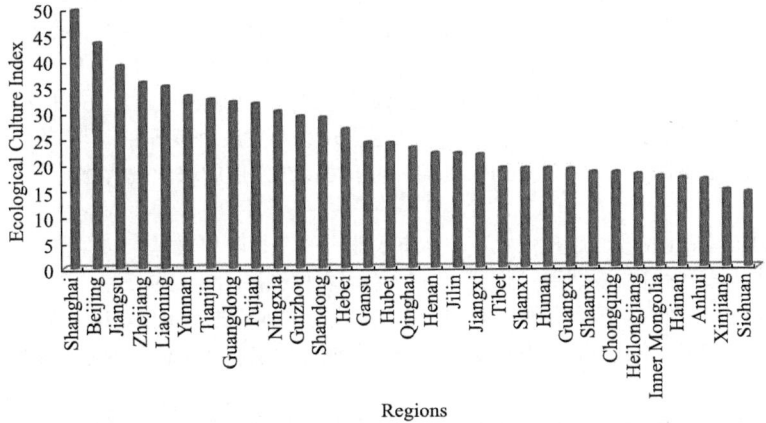

Figure 2 Ranking of Rural Ecological Modernization Levels of 31 Provincial-level Regions (Except for Hong Kong, Macao and Taiwan)

4. Discussions

Urban and rural areas differ greatly in natural resource, ecological structure and social structure; therefore, rural ecological modernization and urban ecological modernization have different connotations and extensions. Meanwhile, different from pure agricultural ecological modernization and industrial ecological modernization, rural ecological modernization is not merely a matter of industrial development, but has to do with more aspects including rural production and living as well as social development. Since researches in this regard are still preliminary, studies on the mechanism of rural ecological modernization are not mature yet, lacking relevant statistics and monitoring data. Therefore, how to further deepen the study on rural ecological modernization and improve the relevant evaluation index system is a priority in the future.

Besides, China's rural ecological modernization should not blindly copy what some developed countries did — develop agriculture and rural areas at high price of resources and pollution. Instead, we can draw on the experience of countries that start ecological modernization early. However, due to the differences in natural resource conditions and economic and social development stages, their experience should not be blindly copied either. How to strengthen field study on rural ecological modernization so as to improve the standard values for the evaluation on various indicators is also an important issue awaiting further efforts.

References

陈涛(Chen T). 2008. 生态现代化视角下对皖南农村发展的实证研究——兼论当代中国生态现代化的基本特征. 现代经济探讨, 07: 37-41.

陈瑜(Chen Y). 2010. "两型社会"背景下区域生态现代化评价与路径研究. 中南大学博士学位论文.

杜萍(Du P). 2009. 新农村建设中农村现代化评价指标体系及评价的研究——以江苏省为例. 安徽农业科学, 37(26): 12722-12724, 12768.

管爱华(Guan A H). 2009. 农村生态文明建设中农民的价值观转换. 马克思主义与现实, 01: 152-154.

何传启(He C Q). 2008. 中国现代化报告 2007——生态现代化研究. 北京: 北京大学出版社.

何传启(He C Q). 2013. 中国现代化报告 2012——农业现代化研究. 北京: 北京大学出版社.

李富军(Li F J). 2012. 高效生态型农业现代化体系的构建与完善. 商业时代, 18: 112-113.

李家寿(Li J S). 2007. 重视和加强新农村传统文化的生态保护与发展. 生态经济, 12: 164-167.

李梅, 苗润莲(Li M, Miao R L). 2010. 北京农村生态文明建设现状及发展对策研究. 广东农业科学, 4: 325-328.

谭爱花, 李万明, 谢芳(Tan A H, Li W M, Xie F). 2011. 基于可持续发展的农业现代化目标的构建. 生态经济, 9: 113-116.

檀学文(Tan X W). 2010. 现代农业、后现代农业与生态农业——"'两型农村'与生态农业发展国际学术研讨会暨第五届中国农业现代化比较国际研讨会"综述. 中国农村经济, 02: 92-95.

滕明兰(Teng M L). 2012. 广西农业现代化测评与路径探析. 南方农业学报, 43(10): 1600-1605.

徐合雷, 李豫新(Xu H L, Li Y X). 2009. 农村城镇化与新疆绿洲生态农业现代化的互动研究. 资源开发与市场, 09: 808-810.

杨思涛(Yang S T). 2007. 走向生态现代化——海南现代化路径选择历史过程研究. 复旦大学博士学位论文.

张磊, 罗远信, 喻元秀, 等(Zhang L, Luo Y X, Yu Y X, et al.). 2010. 农民专业合作社在农村环境治理新格局中的角色. 云南师范大学学报(哲学社会科学版), 04: 65-71.

张新颖(Zhang X Y). 2013. 粮食主产区农业现代化问题研究. 学习与探索, 12: 106-110.

Carrosio G. 2014. Energy production from biogas in the Italian countryside: Modernization vs. repeasantization. Biomass and Bioenergy, 70: 141-148.

de los Ríos I, Rivera M, García C. 2016. Redefining rural prosperity through social learning in the cooperative sector: 25 years of experience from organic agriculture in Spain. Land Use Policy, 54: 85-94.

Horlings L G, Marsden T K. 2011. Towards the real green revolution? Exploring the conceptual dimensions of a new ecological modernisation of agriculture that could "feed the world". Global Environmental Change, 21(2): 441-452.

Li G H, van Ittersum M K, Leffelaar P A, et al. 2016. A multi-level analysis of China's phosphorus flows to identify options for improved management in agriculture. Agricultural Systems, 144: 87-100.

Li P, Ryan C, Cave J. 2016. Chinese rural tourism development: Transition in the case of Qiyunshan, Anhui

2008-2015. Tourism Management, 55: 240-260.

Mol A. 1992. Sociology, environment, and modernity: Ecologicalmodernization as a theory of social change. Society and Natural Resources, 5 (4): 323-344.

Reimer A. 2015. Ecological modernization in U.S. agri-environmental programs: Trends in the 2014 Farm Bill. Land Use Policy, 47: 209-217.

Wiskerke J S C, Bock B B, Stuiver M, et al. 2003. Environmental co-operatives as a new mode of rural governance. NJAS-Wageningen Journal of Life Sciences, 51(1-2): 9-25.

Time to Reinstate Poise of Nature

R. V. Karanth

Department of Civil Engineering (Geoscience), IITRAM

Some of the most important aspects of modernisation are planning of smart cities, development of infrastructure and necessity of large engineering constructions. Such requirement leads to exploitation of natural resources and possible interference with the composure of nature (both geological and biosphere). Rush to development could ignore many aspects such as ecological, geological and biological considerations, and the inevitable needs to be anticipated in the early stage and be thwarted accordingly. Any failure that leads to frustration could lead to the decline of the progress. It is required to formulate a scale/index for developing an establishment, which includes considerations on its geology, structure, geomorphology, erodability, stability of the site, situation, approachability, extent, structure, vulnerability to natural disasters and palaeoseismicity.

Uncontrolled exploitation of natural resources is the foremost issue to be addressed. The green coverage of the earth, particularly the equatorial rainforest is erased such as that of the Amazon basin and Congolese basin for exploration and mining activities or for growing oil palms. Such activities not only curtail rich rainforests, but also influence the precious biodiversity. Deforestation leads to intense erosion of nutrient-rich soil cover, and the resultant "on-site" and "off-site" problems are now well established facts. Lust for animal tusk horn, fur, claws and other parts is pushing them to be tagged in the "endangered species" list. Despite several well publicised examples of vanished species in the recent past such as "dodo" and "elephant bird" are frequently quoted, there are unabated attempts to push more members into this list. Lion, the "king of animals", is unable to defend itself amidst the well-informed modern setup with efficient technological preventative devices. Some of the laws today even defend the killers. Let apart the dense tropical forests, even the forests in the temperate-subarctic climatic zone are not spared. Greed for extracting sand-oil, the boreal forests and wetlands makes Alberta, once home to 600 plant species and 300 animal species, being targeted. After all Canada is not a developed country which is in need of extra resources for its growth. No doubt, for the development and modernization, the foremost substance required is "fuel" which is the source for energy. Intensive research for developing more and more efficient "alternative renewable energy generated from natural resources" has to be ventured rigorously.

Historically, during each era, certain realms are considered as model cultures, whose way of living and thinking are imitated by the rest of the world. Industrial revolution in the western world in the 19th century introduced the "Modern Era" during which the world was gifted with numerous discoveries and inventions such as steam power, electricity and various mechanical tools replacing manual labour with mechanisation that added to the "luxurious living" and the ability to explore places further than our planet, even into the solar system and beyond. At the same time mechanical sustenance was also accompanied by the invention of enormous destructive devices. In the present era, the style of the western regime led by the United State of America is imitated by the rest of the world; in other words, the rest of the world is aping the West. At the same time our population is increasing, and proportionately our demands are increasing; our diversity as well as resources are increasing, and thus our productivity is increasing. With the accessibility to enormous resources, we have developed a tendency to possess materials more than the necessity. We are now living in the "use and throw world", in other words in the "throw away world". The net result is the Earth has turned into a polluted globe whose poise is largely disturbed resulting in erratic climatic regime and alarming global warming. It is the time to restore the "poise" of nature on our planet — the Earth. As the rest of the world is following the "footsteps" of the successful-glamorous "western world", it could also set a model for restrained simple living by shunning away extravagance.

On Promoting the Construction of Ecological Civilization from the Perspective of Ecological Modernization Theory: A Case Study of the Wuhan International Garden Expo

Jingxuan Li, Sixue Li

Central China Normal University

1. Main Points on the Theory of Ecological Modernization

In the 1980s, the scholars of Germany, Holland, Britain and other countries first proposed the theory of ecological modernization. Martin Janicke, a German scholar, first used the concept of "ecological modernization" in 1982. Janicke initially believed that technological innovation, market mechanism, environmental policy and precautionary principle are the four core elements of ecological modernization [1]. German scholar Joseph Huber first used the concept of "ecological modernization". He believed that ecological modernization theory belongs to the theory of industrial society; at present, the main problem lies in that the social atmosphere and biosphere are enslaved by industrial system (technology), which must be overcome through social and ecological reconstruction for the circle of technology. This process is the ecological modernization[2](P335). Arthur P. J. Mol, a Holland professor, who takes ecological modernization as a kind of social change theory from the relationship between system and environmental evolution, pointed out that the ecological modernization is not the essence of material improvement, but the social and institutional transformation, and this transformation is the core of the theory of ecological modernization. At present, most of the core issues of ecological modernization theory are not material improvement itself, but the five types of changes in the society and system: The change of science and technology, science and technology are not only from the perspective of "causing environmental problems", but also consider the practical role and potential role of themselves in the management and prevention of environmental problems; the importance of market dynamics and economic activities (such as producers, customers, consumers, credit institutions and insurance companies) is increasing as economic adjustment and reform carrier; the role of nation-state has changed, and the governance is more decentralized, more flexible, and puts more emphasis on consensus; the position and the role of social movement and ideology have changed, and social movements are increasingly involved in the public and private decision-making systems; the discourse practice has changed, and the new ideology has been produced [3](P6-7). He Chuanqi, an expert on Chinese modernization, believes that the basic requirements of general ecological modernization includes four aspects: non-physical, green, ecological and unhook connections between economy and environmental degradation. Specifically, the production and consumption are non-physical and green; economy and society are ecological and unhook connections between modernization and environmental degradation [4](P111). Zhou Xin, a young scholar in China, summarized six basic ideas of the western ecological modernization theory on the basis of systematic analysis of the theories of western scholars: promoting technological innovation, paying attention to the market, emphasizing the role of government, highlighting the civil society, paying attention to the ecological rationality and promoting the ecological transformation (environmental change) [5](P58-68).

In a word, the theory of ecological modernization has its common views: paying attention to technological innovation, market mechanism and government role. In addition, citizens' ecological consciousness, life style, consumption concept, behavior and so on will have an important impact on the process of ecological modernization with the rise of civil society. Therefore, the citizens' participation should become one of the core ideas of the theory of ecological modernization. So we believe that there are four main points of ecological modernization: promoting technological innovation, paying attention to the market mechanism, emphasizing the role of government and focusing on citizen participation. At present, our country is comprehensively promoting economic construction, political construction, cultural construction, social construction and ecological civilization, and summarizing the main points of ecological modernization theory not only has certain theoretical significance, but also has important practical significance.

2. Wuhan International Garden Expo: A Microcosm of the Construction of Ecological Civilization

The 18th National Congress of the CPC made a strategic decision to "make great efforts to promote the construction of ecological civilization". In May 2015, the CPC Central Committee and the State Council promulgated the Opinions on Accelerating the Construction of Ecological Civilization, which makes an overall plan for the construction of ecological civilization, and points out the basic principles of constructing ecological civilization: Persist in taking the economization priority, conservation priority and natural recovery as the basic policy; persist in taking the green, circular and low-carbon developments as the basic way; persist in taking reform and innovation-driven as the basic power; persist in taking the cultivation of ecological culture as an important support; persist in taking breakthroughs and overall promotion as a way of work [6]. In September 2015, the 10th International Garden Expo opened in Wuhan, whose theme is "Ecological Garden Expo, Green Life". Wuhan Garden Expo architecture consists of four main buildings and two (east-west) service areas. Its main building includes the International Garden Art Center, Yangtze River Civilization Pavilion, Flying Garden and Creative Life Pavilion, respectively showing the classical garden art, culture achievement of Yangtze River, Wuhan garden art and Wuhan urban culture. Wuhan Garden Expo adheres to the concept of "science and technology, innovation, ecology, green", implementing the principle of ecological civilization construction, which is a microcosm of the ecological civilization construction in China.

First, Wuhan Garden Expo contains a large number of science and technology elements adhering to creating science and technology garden. The Garden Expo shows green technology with engineering ration at the technical level. It uses the program "aerobic repair" and "closure governance" to accelerate the garbage degradation, and uses special materials to make the underground garbage to be closed. Aerobic technology is one of the most advanced technologies to treat waste in the world. It's principle is that the fresh air and water pressure are piped into the deep underground garbage; at the same time, the carbon dioxide and other gases are drawn out, monitor the reactant temperature, humidity and gas, and activate the microbial regeneration of waste, thereby changing the anaerobic state into aerobic condition, and accelerating the garbage degradation. Closure treatment is that after being dealt with aerobic technology, the garbage is put on 4 layers of "coats", the 4 "coats" are the exhaust layer, seepage layer, drainage layer and vegetation layer. After the completion of the treatment, the garbage dump is a piece of "pure land" with no odor, no flying of sewage. In addition, the specific techniques used in Wuhan Garden Expo also includes green roof overburden, rainwater collection system and intelligent irrigation system. At the same time it uses energy-saving construction, and the exhibition hall gets available natural lighting and natural ventilation through the adjustable roof, which makes efficient use of natural resources and greatly reduces energy consumption of air conditioning and lighting. Wuhan Garden Expo cleverly combines the elements of science and modern gardening, showing the unique charm of the innovation of science and technology in the construction of ecological civilization.

Second, Wuhan Garden Expo adheres to the concept of innovation, insists on innovative garden. Wuhan Garden Expo breaks through the previous divisions of other gardens, and innovatively exhibits around the three major personal themes: "Garden and human art, Garden and science, Garden and happy life". It realizes the ecological vision, the vision of ecological restoration, the vision of cultural heritage, the vision of green life and the vision of friendly people based on the overall planning and innovative design. Other gardens also embody the concept of innovation. Shanghai park has been attempting and exploring on innovation. The Shanghai Park — "360°green garden", designed by the Shanghai Garden Institute — makes many attempts on the innovation of urban garden. It attempts to extend the green space to the roof greening, vertical greening, indoor greening and other forms of greening in order to show the "beautiful Shanghai". Innovation is one of the highlights of Wuhan Garden Expo, and it is a core concept from design to completion, and realizes the goal of innovative garden.

Third, Wuhan Garden Expo implements ecological idea, and builds "ecological park". "Ecology" is the theme of it. Yangtze River Civilization Pavilion is a true portray of the development of ecological civilization of the Yangtze River. Yangtze River Civilization Pavilion is located in the central park, and it is a public cultural institution to collect, study and demonstrate the Yangtze River's ecology and human civilization with natural hall, humanity hall, experience hall and temporary exhibition hall. The main line of Yangtze River Civilization Pavilion is the Yangtze River's natural ecology and human civilization, and the natural ecological part mainly displays the Yangtze River's landforms, hydrology and water resources, ecological environment, rare animals and plants; the part of human civilization mainly shows archaeological objects and non-material cultural heritage. The pavilion shows the development of natural ecology and human civilization through the simulation of realization and interactive experience, etc. Sheng Park meaning "rebirth", reflects the ecological concept of Wuhan Garden Expo. It is one of the nine creative gardens. Sheng Park uses many kinds of bottles. The boundary of the garden is surrounded by waste bottles, and the garden is full of flowers in bottles; the vertical wall is also stacked by large and small bottles, and then flowers are planted, that's very interesting. Walking in the park, visitors will see a large number of beautiful landscapes made by waste.

Fourth, adhering to the idea of green for constructing "Green Park", Wuhan Garden Expo deals with 5 million cubic meters and 1 million tons of waste, implements 213 hectares of garden greening, basically completes 9 parks and Zhang Gongdi Urban Forest Park of 31 square kilometers. It builds 117 green ecological gardens, and brings all kinds of gardens, such as north gardens, Bashu gardens, Jiangnan gardens, Lingnan gardens. Nantong's" Jin Garden" with the concept of "low-carbon environmental protection, energy saving" is divided into four parts, forming clear, green and ecological landscape, and showing the theme of "Ecological Garden Expo, Green Life".

3. Enlightenment of China's Ecological Civilization Construction with the Ecological Modernization Theory

The emergence and evolution of the ecological modernization theory is a historical response to social development on the ecological environment and economic development. It originates in the western capitalist industrialization to re-examine, trying to realize the organic combination of ecology and modernization in a certain way. Ecological modernization is the realistic choice of socialist modernization with Chinese characteristics, and we are promoting the construction of ecological civilization in a certain sense which can be understood as China's ecological modernization. The ecological modernization theory has certain enlightenment to promote the construction of ecological civilization of our current country.

First, change the role of science and technology. The representatives of western ecological modernization theory — Joseph Huber and Arthur Mol, have emphasized the role of technological innovation in the ecological modernization, but they also believed that the role of science and technology innovation has undergone great changes. "In fact, in the dimension of technology ecological modernization, there are two kinds of very eye-catching technology innovation. One is the role of technology in environmental problems, which has been from the end to the assistant auxiliary preventive, common development of clean technology. The other is from the innovation and development of a single technology to a complex social system — development and application of technology. These two kinds of transformation are developments of technology innovation in the ecological modernization discourse, and represent the new direction of the development of modern science and technology."[5](P60) In fact, recalling the development path of China's economy, especially during the reform and opening-up period, we can find that with the science and technology innovation as well as rapid economic development, ecological environment is deteriorating, appearing to the reverse development of science, technology and ecology. Therefore, in the process of promoting the construction of ecological civilization, our country must change the role of science and technology. On the one hand, to realize the transformation of science and technology from governance to preventive role in the construction of ecological environment. Science and technology not only play the roles of ecological management and ecological restoration, but also play a preventive function role, to integrate science and technology into agricultural, industry and service industries and other areas, to improve the output and input of science and technology, and to establish a resource-saving and environment-friendly society. On the other hand, simply playing the role of science and technology is not desirable. John Bellamy Foster said: "To solve the problem is not technology, but the social and economic system itself. In the developed social economy, there is a kind of social production mode, which establishes a sustainable relationship with the environment, just social relations of production hinder the change. "[7](P95) Therefore, contact technology innovation and mechanisms of the development of society with the social and institutional transformation to promote the construction of ecological civilization.

Second, change the mode of practice of the main body of the market. The main body of the market and the market economic behavior are regarded as carriers of ecological reconstruction and the change of environment, which play an important role in the theory and practice of ecological modernization. Huber believed that "government intervention has little effect, the effect of new social movements (such as environmental movement) is not large either, just as the market and economic behavior are the most parts in the role of ecological modernization process" [5](P61). This conclusion is mainly based on Hubers' free market capitalism, but faces the main body of the market economy which is an important role in promoting the ecological modernization process under the condition of socialist market economy. Under the market economy, the main body of the market is important to the construction of ecological civilization. At present in China's economic development, high input, high consumption, high pollution as well as unbalanced, uncoordinated and unsustainable issues appear gradually, and the shortage of resources, environmental pollution and ecological damage has become the bottleneck of sustainable development; the main body of market practice is not without relevance. Therefore, on the one hand, the behavior of the main body of the market has to change the concept of development and adhere to long-term and sustainable development; on the other hand, the main body of the market is to establish the concept of green development and low carbon development. Enterprises should intensify science and technology research and development, make full use of clean and efficient implementation of green technology and clean production, promote the green transformation of the traditional manufacturing industry and the establishment of industrial development system of green low carbon cycle, and continuously improve enterprises' productivity and core competitiveness. For the market, it is of great significance to guide the ecological transformation and to promote ecological civilization construction.

Third, strengthen the leading role of the government. The early Huber despised the government's role in ecological modernization. In his view, "to some extent, the government is counter productive.... In the 1980s, the industry developed countries often appeared to outweigh the environmental protection agency. The government in any case could not produce ecological modernization" [8](P50-51). But Martin Janicke didn't agree with this view, Who stressed the importance of the government which is a positive role in the environmental change: "As the whole social intervention authority legalization level system of government, it should be regarded as indispensable, especially when we seek to develop an effective balance of global growth of the huge ecological impact the modern industrial system. In environmental protection to social intervention decisions, form marks unpredictable, government intervention can be negotiated in the form of waiting period Play an important role. "[9](P38) Mol tended to a decentralized and bottom-up government, and he advocated a promotion alliance of ecological modernization including government officials, managers and environmental non-governmental organizations. In short, in the western theory of ecological modernization, the government plays an indispensable role. In our country, facing the deteriorating ecological environment, the government must play a leading role in promoting the construction of ecological civilization. First of all, the government should adopt all sorts of ways and means to increase the ecological value of propaganda, through necessary ecological culture education, to make the ecological concept deepen into the society and the hearts of people, and the whole society should look at and solve problems from the angle of ecological civilization, forming ecological civilization and building consensus beliefs. Secondly, the government should improve and perfect the system of ecological civilization construction. Construct clear environmental property rights, environmental economic system, and improve the ecological compensation mechanism, environmental regulation mechanism, environmental protection and economic development comprehensive decision-making mechanism providing a security system for the construction of ecological civilization. Thirdly, strengthen the administrative supervision. To further strengthen the management of the administrative supervision departments of the government, completely reverse the local government's working style which is out of the strategy of implementing local protectionism for local interests, and change the unreasonable government functions' evaluation criteria; further increase the law enforcement administrative, and strengthen the social responsibility of the enterprise on the construction of ecological civilization.

Fourth, Citizens play participation roles. The western theory of ecological modernization thinks that the civil society is an important force in the process of ecological modernization. Albert and Marten Hajar all attached great importance to the public's participation in the process, and they thought "one of the connotations of ecological modernization is a more open attitude for a kind of decision-making. This is in addition to participate in the government, also a partnership includes three party power, which includes the neighborhood, community and environmental non-governmental organizations" [5](P65). Delaizek also believed that "ecological modernization means a kind of partnership including government, enterprises, mild environmentalists and scientists" [5](P65). Therefore, the civil society is indispensable in promoting ecological modernization. Ecological civilization as a kind of public goods or services, because of the lack of social forces, easily falls into the double predicament of "market failure" and "government failure", and the establishment of the citizens' participation mechanism helps to break the dilemma. On the one hand, ecological civilization is a public product, and citizens are the direct victims of environmental pollution and ecological deterioration; citizens' participation in social mobilization and extensive supervision as well as reasonable rights, can effectively balance the illegal behavior of enterprises. On the other hand, citizens ask the government to publish a large amount of information of environmental pollution to the public, to urge the government to listen more the views and suggestions of the citizens in the decision-making process, and to improve the effectiveness of public policies. The citizens' participation in the construction of ecological civilization must change from "formal participation" to "essential participation". Mu said that "at present, the public participation in environmental protection in our country mainly concentrates in the end of participation, namely, after the environmental pollution and ecolgecial destruction, the public begin to participate in environmental protection after suffering contamination threat, while less involve in the whole process of protecting the rights of environmental participation and expression; in fact it is still the government plays the leading role and the public seldom participate"[10]. Therefore, in promoting the construction of ecological civilization, citizens should fully and effectively play the role of participation. The government should unblock the communication channels between itself and citizens, and listen to citizens' advice; enhance citizens' participation attitude, participation level and ability, to establish the incentive mechanism of citizens' participation in the protection of the ecological environment, and to encourage more people to care about environmental protection and participation in ecological construction; at the same time, the government should further establish and perfect the three party dialogue mechanism of the government, enterprises and citizens, to open effective channels about public opinion expression and complaint, and to expand expression space for citizens on ecological protection and governance.

References

[1] 郇庆治, 马丁·耶内克. 2010. 生态现代化理论: 回顾与展望. 马克思主义与现实, (1): 175-179.

[2] Spaargaren G, Mol A P J. 1992. Sociology, environment, and modernity: Ecological modernization as a theory of social change. Society & Natural Resources, 5(4): 323-344.

[3] 阿瑟·莫尔, 戴维·索南菲尔德. 2011. 世界范围的生态现代化——观点和关键争论. 张鲲译. 北京: 商务印书馆.

[4] 中国现代化战略研究课题组. 2007. 中国现代化报告 2007——生态现代化研究. 北京: 北京大学出版社.

[5] 周鑫. 2012. 西方生态现代化理论与当代中国生态文明建设. 北京: 光明日报出版社.

[6] 中共中央 国务院关于加快推进生态文明建设的意见. 2015-5-5. 新华网. http://news.xinhuanet.com/politics/2015-05/05/c_1115187518. htm[2016-1-18].

[7] 约翰·福斯特. 2006. 生态危机与资本主义. 耿建新, 宋兴无译. 上海: 上海译文出版社.

[8] Huber J. 2009. Ecological modernization: Beyond scarcity and bureaucracy. In A P J Mol, D A Sonnenfeld, G Spaargaren (Eds.), The Ecological Modernization Reader: Environment Reform in Theory and Practice. London and New York: Routledge.

[9] Janicke M. 2009. Ecological and political modernization. In A P J Mol, D A Sonnenfeld, G Spaargaren (Eds.), The Ecological Modernization Reader: Environment Reform in Theory and Practice. London and New York: Routledge.

[10] 穆书涛. 2015-8-30. 生态文明建设应发挥公众的主体作用. 光明日报.

Part Five

Social Modernization and Human Development

Social Modernization and Quality of Life Measurement in Russia

Lyudmila Belyaeva

Institute of Philosophy, Russian Academy of Sciences

One of the important signs of social modernization in a society is the improvement of the population's quality of life. The improvement of quality of life contributes to more successful human development, and it is an increase in the level of the population's welfare and satisfaction with their life.

The quality of life is a derivative of living standards, the key components of which are income and wealth. Over the past 25 years, the living standards have been rising unevenly for different population groups in Russia. Income differentiation has notably grown and the Gini coefficient has reached 0.416. Apart from income, another indicator of quality of life is wealth obtained by individual social groups at the first stage of reform due to privatization and business activities, and later through the incomes of top income groups. The difference in the rates of pay between the top and bottom 10% groups amounted to 14.5 times in 2015. The income gap was even wider, reaching 16 times. The top 10% population group that can boast of the highest income accounts for 30.6 % of all incomes, while the 10% population group with the lowest income accounts for 1.9% of all incomes (Figure 1).

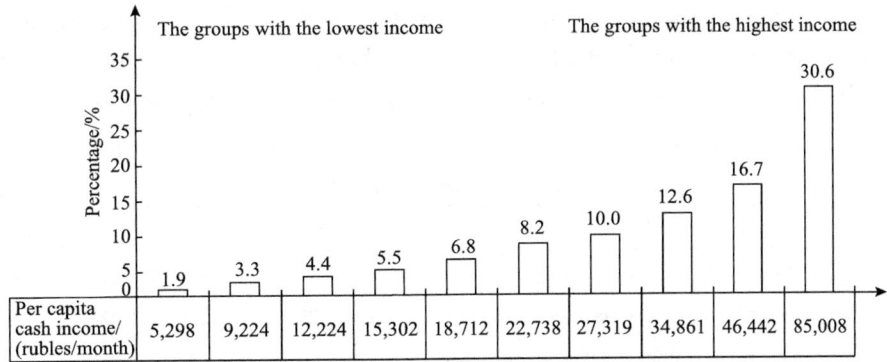

Figure 1　Percentages of Different Income Groups of Russia in 2015

---

① The research was carried out by the grant RHF, № 14-03-00338.

The average income growth acceleration begins from the eighth group, while the starkest difference is observed between the top ninth and tenth groups — 1.83 times. According to the *2012 World Wealth Report*, Russia substantially outpaced many major countries in terms of income inequality level, yet it still falls behind the USA, Latin American states and some African countries. At the same time, Russia is an absolute "champion" in terms of wealth distribution inequality. The income inequality develops primarily at the expense of property incomes and business revenues in the first turn. Naturally, the top income groups can boast of the highest volume of resources for forming wealth and investments. For instance, according to the Russian Federal State Statistics Service, the growth of savings in 2014 amounted to 55.4% of resources available for the fifth top 20% income group, 24.8 for the fourth group, 10.8% for the third group, 6.1% for the second group, and only 2.9% for the first one with the lowest level of resources. The 10% R/P ratio for growth of savings amounts to 33 times, which is substantially higher than the 10% R/P ratio for incomes (16.0 times) and wages paid (14.5 times).

Income differentiation is one of the indicators of the differentiation of quality of life in post-soviet Russia, and is also its prerequisites.

The author defines "quality of life" as a complex characteristic of the population's living environment that has objective indicators and subjective evaluations of meeting material, social and cultural needs, and is connected with people's perceptions of their position depending on cultural peculiarities, value system and social standards existing in the society.

The quality of life category differs from living standards. The differences are primarily connected with the characters of indicators. Objective statistical indicators are predominantly used to assess one's living standard. However, they are often not credible enough (so called "misleading figures"). Besides, they do not allow taking into account the living standards of separate groups of population in detail for making comparison.

The important defect of these methods lies in the fact that they do not take into account the influence of the population itself to the various aspects of life. Meanwhile, the total volumes of material benefits and living conditions that the residents of both the country in general and separate regions have are distributed unevenly among population categories and are perceived differently by them.

The subjective characteristics of living standards are reflected by the evaluations that the respondents offer in comparison with the standards that exist in the society and closest social environment. The dynamics of these evaluations during 1994-2015 in Russia is shown in Table 1.

Table 1 Which Statement Better Describes Your Financial Standing (of the Total Number of Respondents, Russia) (Unit: %)

Self-perceptions of Financial Standing	1994	1998	2002	2006	2010	2015
Not enough money to live to paycheck, so I have to borrow	7	24	13	11	13	11
The salary is enough to cover daily living expenses alone	31	29	23	22	18	18
Enough money for daily living needs, yet the purchase of clothes is challenging	28	21	30	21	21	22
Enough money in general, yet I have to borrow money to buy expensive items	22	14	22	29	31	33

Quality of life indicators are a more credible source of knowledge about the correspondence of population's living conditions to social standards existing in the society. They comprise both objective indicators of living standards and subjective evaluations, and they can characterize the quality of life of different population groups: gender, age, settlement, professional, status, etc.

The all-Russia monitoring performed by the Institute of Philosophy of Russia Academy of Sciences (RAS)(1990-2015) makes it possible to analyze the quality of life in terms of evaluations offered by Russia's population[①]. It has demonstrated that the quality of life in Russia correlates with a place in social hierarchy, professional position, type of settlement and respondents' age.

The subjective perceptions as to the quality of life in the country, differentiated with respect to regions, settlements, social groups and tiers, are as important as the objective characteristics of living standards. It is the subjective opinion that enables us to talk about social bonds, satisfaction with individual life and life in general, social stability or conflict and other vital processes that modern statistics cannot reflect. In this context, the quality of life means the person's satisfaction with both his/her life in general and its individual components expressed on the basis of his/her personal subjective evaluation.

The author suggests using four components to analyze the subjective indicators of the population's quality of life.

(1) Living standards (welfare): specific indexes — material living standards; satisfaction with one's housing conditions; medical care accessibility; education accessibility.

(2) Quality of the closest social environment: specific indexes — self-identification with one's own settlement; protection from crime; protection from poverty; protection from functionaries' arbitrariness; protection from law enforcement agencies' arbitrariness.

(3) Quality of environmental conditions: specific indexes — protection from environmental threat; air purity assessment; water purity assessment.

(4) Social well-being of the population: specific indexes — confidence in the future; satisfaction with one's life; independence.

Thus, we calculate 15 specific indexes, and on the basis we form four general indexes that fit the four components of quality of life. The report presents the algorithms of calculating specific, general and integral quality of life indexes.

The analysis excludes such components of quality of life as political stability and democracy. To measure the impacts of these components, we need them to be perceived by the population as personally relevant, and need the population to see direct dependence of political institutions upon the opinions and interests of all social groups, comprising the society. The absence of such dependence does not allow us to suggest that this component makes impact on the perception of the quality of life by the population today. Table 2 presents the four components of quality of life and names of specific indexes for each component.

Table 2 Subjective Indicators of the Population's Quality of Life

Quality of Life Components	Specific Indexes
Living standards (welfare) (General index of living standards)	(1) Index of material living standards
	(2) Index of satisfaction with one's housing conditions
	(3) Index of medical care accessibility
	(4) Index of education accessibility

---

① Data are obtained in the course of all-Russia monitoring performed by the Center for the Study of Social and Cultural Change, the RAS Institute of Philosophy.

Continued

Quality of Life Components	Specific Indexes
Quality of the closest social environment (General index of social environment quality)	(1) Index of self-identification with one's own settlement (2) Index of protection from crime (3) Index of protection from poverty (4) Index of protection from functionaries' arbitrariness (5) Index of protection from law enforcement agencies' arbitrariness
Quality of environmental conditions (General index of environmental conditions quality)	(1) Index of protection from environmental threat (2) Index of air purity assessment (3) Index of water purity assessment
Social well-being of the population (General index of social optimism)	(1) Index of confidence in the future (2) Index of satisfaction with one's life (3) Index of independence
Integral quality of life index	

The integral quality of life index is built on the basis of the four general indexes. It enables us to compare in principle the quality of life of different social groups and tiers, as well as the quality of life in the regions on the basis of the residents' perceptions as to the various sides of their life.

To calculate the subjective indexes for each component of quality of life, we use the method applied for calculating the index of economic expectations in European countries.

The formula for calculating specific index is as follows.

$$\text{Specific Index} = (X-Y) + 100$$

Where X is the share of positive answers (evaluations), Y is the share of negative answers (evaluations), the values of specific index may change in the range of 0-200. The index is equal to 200 when the population at large evaluates a certain aspect of life positively. When positive and negative evaluations account for equal shares, the index value amounts to 100. If the index's value is lower than 100, it means that negative evaluations prevail.

The general index for each component is calculated as arithmetic average of specific index.

$$\text{General Index of Component} = (\text{Specific Index 1} + \text{Specific Index 2} +\ldots \text{Specific Index } N)/N$$

The integral index is calculated as arithmetic average of general indexes.

The attempt to limit the quality of life's characteristic to integral index alone, leaving out both specific and general indexes, would be precipitant, as in such case we lose a great deal of information that describes individual components of life and eventually allows one to judge how well Russia's residents live. All of them are important, though such indexes as the ones of living standards and social optimism appear to be the weightiest ones. However, it is true only for the present situation, when ill-being, poverty and economic insecurity are the most disturbing problems for many people, and the ones that people mostly want to get rid of. Yet after we manage to overcome the problem of low living standards, other issues (environmental conditions, social environment, political liberties and personal rights) will make increasingly stronger impacts on the perception of quality of life in the country by the population.

According to the monitoring data, the estimates for the general indexes of quality of life are the following: Index of Living Standards — 116, Index of Social Environment Quality — 94, Index of Environmental Quality — 78, Index of Population's Social Well-Being — 130.

The index values vary around 100, demonstrating minor deviations up or down for gender and education groups. The situation as to social and professional groups, as well as urban and rural dwellers, is different, however. The index value of leaders can boast to the level of 127, outpacing other professions by a significant margin. Rural population also evaluates the quality of their life by 14 points higher than urban dwellers. In this context, a natural question arises: Which specific index makes the most substantial contribution to the leveling or differentiation of the integral index of quality of life for those groups that we consider? Figure 2 allows us to trace this influence. It presents the integral index and specific indexes dealing with four components for the two most differentiated groups — the ones related to professions and places of residence.

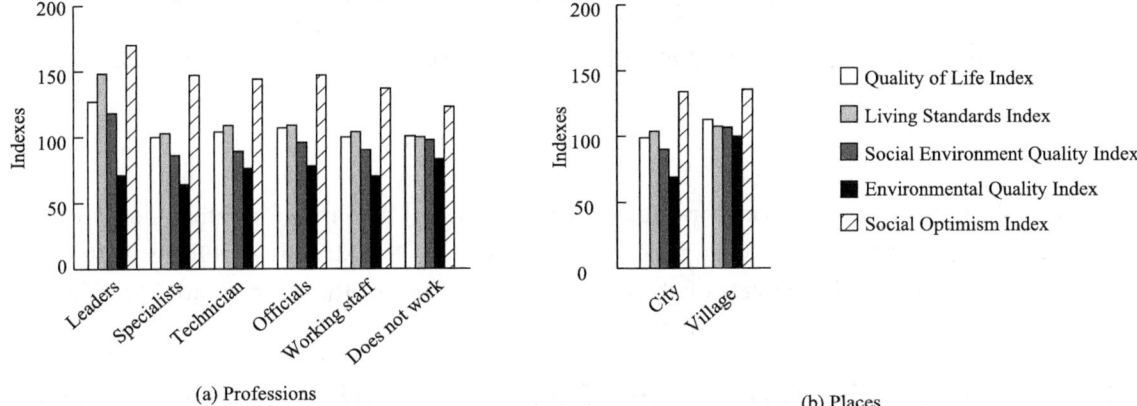

Figure 2 Quality of Life of People from Different Professions and Places

We can clearly see that the leaders enjoy the highest quality of life index due to the values of three general indexes — the ones of living standards, social environment quality and especially social optimism. However, we should pay attention to the fact that in terms of environmental safety, the leaders show little difference from the majority of other professional groups. Their quality of life seems being directly connected with individual resources and social networks that they are involved in. The factors beyond their control do not facilitate the increase in their evaluation of quality of life. Here the leaders' positions are close to the ones of other professional groups.

Thus, the use of suggested methods in addition to the objective indicators of well-being level offers the opportunities for taking into account the subjective opinions on the part of the country's population on the essential sides of their life with consideration of cultural and social capital typical of various social groups living in different social environments as to the standards of quality of life.

A Study on China's Structural Reform in Social Fields

Yiyong Yang, Yan Gu, Haiyuan Wan, Yifang Wei

Institute of Social Development, National Development and Reform Commission, China

Structural reform occurs not only in the economic field, but also in the political field; it is also seen in cultural and social fields. This paper mainly discusses the structural reform in the social field and focuses on the social aspects of structural reform as part of the effort to adapt to, navigate and guide the new normal economic growth.

1. Social Structure Is an Important Factor That Influences Sustainable Economic Growth

Social structure is the historical result of a long-term interaction between various social policies and factors. Since it is a slow variable or a basic variable, for a long time many people consider it unadjustable. However, that is not the case. When a particular emphasis has been put on innovative development, coordinated development, green development, open development and shared development, we cannot merely stress the adjustment of economic structure or only excel at using economic policy instruments, but at the same time we should adjust irrational social structure as much as possible and learn to make good use of social policy and other tools. Taking initiative in adjusting social structure is conducive to the sustainable economic development, and more importantly, to the coordinated economic and social development.

1.1 The Impact of Demographic Structure on Economic Growth: Coordinated Development

Long-term economic growth is determined by the potential economic growth rate, and a high proportion and a large size of labour force are important factors that support a high potential economic growth rate. In 2011 and 2012, the proportion of working-age population in China's total population and the size of the working-age population declined in succession and the trend would last two to three decades. This demographic change has a negative impact on long-term economic growth. It is predicted that the contribution rate of labour force to economic growth will continue to decline with the demographic change.

1.2 The Impact of Income Distribution Structure on Economic Growth: Shared Development

At present, as China is seeing a significant economic slowdown, the idea of "stable growth" is proposed once again. However, to maintain stable growth we cannot go back to the old path of relying on investments and exports which sometimes are able to guarantee a high economic growth rate, but will delay economic restructuring and economic transformation. The costs of economic adjustment will be even greater in the future. Therefore, the most reliable, timely and reasonable way to keep a stable growth is to start applying the third solution of the troika for economic growth, namely to boost consumption.

Adjusting income distribution structure and properly narrowing the income gap will help to achieve shared development, including sharing between the rich and the poor, between labour force and enterprises as well as between urban and rural areas.

1.3 The Impact of Social Governance Structure on Economic Growth: Innovative Development

Since the reform and opening-up policy, especially in the 21st century, China's tertiary industry has been developing rapidly. As of the end of 2014, there were 606,000 social organisations which was four times those of 2000; the average annual growth rate of social organisations from 2000 to 2014 was 10.3%, covering various areas of social life such as science and technology, education, culture, health care, labour, civil affairs, sports, environmental protection, legal services, social intermediary services, business services, as well as rural and agricultural development. Social services provided by social organisations directly form an important part of the economy, and in 2014 the added value of social organisations was 63.86 billion yuan, an increase of 11.8% over the previous year which was 0.9 percentage point higher than the growth rate of the tertiary industry. In addition, the economic activities of social organisations directly create jobs in various fields, and in 2014 the number of people employed in social organisations amounted up to 6.823 million, an increase of 7.2% over the previous year which was 4.4 percentage points higher than the growth rate of urban employment over the same period.

2. The Current Social Structure Is Unfavourable to Sustainable Economic Growth

There are basically three types of possible relationships between social structure and economic growth: The social structure is conducive to economic growth; the social structure is neutral which at least does not drag economic growth; the social structure is unfavourable to economic growth. As for a long time the reform in social fields is lagging, and the third type is currently the case in China.

2.1 The Impact of an Ageing Population on Potential Economic Growth: The Failure of Labour Transmission Mechanism

In 2000, as the percentage of citizens aged 60 or above reached 10.3%, China became an ageing society as internationally recognised. In 2010, this proportion rose to 13.3%, which means that within ten years the proportion of the elderly population increased by nearly 3 percentage points. In the four decades to come, the population will be ageing rapidly. Every ten years the proportion of senior citizens will increase by 4.7, 8.0, 5.2 and 5.3 percentage points respectively. Until 2050, the percentage of the population aged 60 or above will reach about 37%, amounting to around 440 million (Table 1).

Table 1 The Proportions of Citizens Aged 60+ and 80+   (Unit: %)

Year	60+ Proportion in the Total Population	80+ Proportion in the Total Population	80+ Proportion in the Elderly Population
2010	13.3	1.3	9.8
2020	18.0	2.1	11.7
2030	26.0	3.2	12.3
2040	31.3	5.5	17.6
2050	36.6	9.4	25.7

Source: Calculated according to the data of the 6th national population census in 2010

At the same time, the trend of a lowering birth rate and ageing is increasingly significant. From 2000 to 2012, the proportion of children aged between 0 and 14 rapidly dropped from 22.9% to 16.6%. With a significant increase in the number of families of low birth rate, China became a society with a moderately declining birth rate[1]. The declining birth rate is accompanied by an ageing population. In 2010, there were 17 million very old people aged 80 or above in China, accounting for 9.8% of the elderly population; in 2020, the number will grow to 27 million, accounting for 11.7% of the elderly population, and then enter a stage of rapid growth. By 2050, the number will have reached 120 million, accounting for 25.7% of the elderly population. The trend of a lowering birth rate and ageing is increasingly becoming one of the key issues that China needs to tackle in responding to the ageing population.

Before China's population reaches its peak, the working-age population will have reached its peak value first. In 2012, China's population aged from 15 to 59 for the first time saw an absolute decrease, down by over 3.45 million than the previous year. Among the working-age population, there is a more significant decreasing trend in young labour force. Assuming the current policy remains unchanged, the working-age population will continue to decrease; after 2030, the trend of declining and ageing will further accelerate.

At the same time, China's total dependency ratio[2] also hit bottom in 2012, reaching 33%; afterwards it will gradually rise and it is expected to rise to over 50% in 2035 and around 65% in 2050. This shows that China's quantitative demographic dividend tends to decline. A horizontal analysis demonstrates that after 2030, China's dependency ratio will exceed that of India, and China's advantages in the demographic structure will be significantly reversed (Figure 1).

---

[1] Generally speaking, a proportion of the population aged between 0 and 14 below 20% indicates a low birth rate, below 15% a severely low birth rate, between 15% and 18% moderately low birth rate and between 18% and 20% a mildly low birth rate. Currently, Japan, Italy and Spain have a severely low birth rate; Germany, China and Russia have a moderately low birth rate; France and Britain have a mildly low birth rate; the proportions of the United States and the Republic of Korea are still above 20%.

[2] Total dependency ratio is the number of non-working age population in the total population to the number of working-age population. Total dependency ratio can be divided into aged dependency ratio and child dependency ratio.

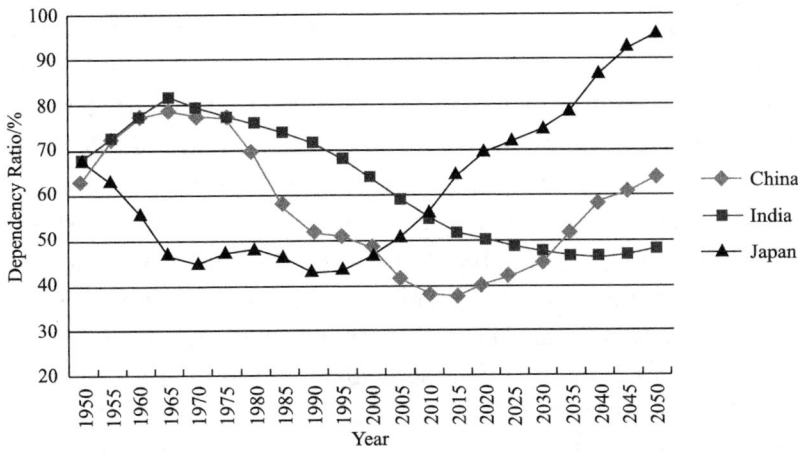

Figure 1 Dependency Ratios of China, Japan and India

2.2 The Great Negative Impact of Income Distribution Structure on the Expansion of Consumer Demand: The Failure of the Transmission Mechanism of Purchasing Power

In the primary distribution, the share of the income of the household sector shows a downward trend while that of the corporate sector and the government sector are on the rise. From 1992 to 2013, the share of the household sector in the total income of the primary distribution fell from 66.1% to 61.6% with a decline of nearly 5 percentage points. Over the same period, the share of the income of the corporate sector rose from 17.4% to 25.3% with an increase of nearly 8 percentage points; that of the government sector rose from 16.6% to 17.5% with an increase of almost 1 percentage point.

In secondary distribution, the government sector obtains income, the corporate sector provides income, and there is little change in the income of the household sector. In recent years, with the regulation by secondary distribution, the total disposable income of the government sector was more than 20% higher than its total income of the primary distribution, the income of the corporate sector decreased by over 13%, and the income of the household sector grew by less than 1%. Compared with the primary distribution, the share of the corporate sector decreased by 3.3 to 3.7 percentage points, that of the government sector increased by 3.5 to 3.8 percentage points, and that of the household sector dropped slightly by 0.1 to 0.3 percentage point.

The increased income of the government sector in secondary distribution comes from income taxes and social security contributions, respectively accounting for 46% and 54% of the government's current transfer income. Two thirds of income taxes come from the corporate sector and one third from the household sector. Social security contributions come from the household sector, but they are still larger than the expenditure on social insurance and welfare; the former is about 25% higher than the latter. In other words, in secondary distribution, the government sector obtains income from the corporate and household sectors (which contribute respectively 30% and 70%), and 40% of the transfer income is returned to the household sector.

The key to adjusting income distribution structure is to achieve the shift from an inverted T-shaped social structure, characterised by a large low-income group, a solidifying underclass and a small and unstable proportion of the middle-income group, to an olive-shaped social structure which has two pointed ends and is wide in the middle. We should promote the low-income group to transfer to groups of higher income, and at the same time, prevent the middle-income group from descending to groups of lower income. In general, the current income distribution in the household sector in China demonstrates a shape of an inverted T and it has the following features.

First, the income of most people is below the social average. In 2013, among the urban households divided into five groups according to their incomes, per capita disposable income of the 20% households in the middle was 24,518 yuan, while that in the urban area was 26,955 yuan, which indicates that the average is 10% higher than the median and the income of most urban residents is below the average; among rural households, the per capita net income of middle-income households was 7,942 yuan, while that in the rural area was 8,896 yuan, which indicates that the average is 12% higher than the median and in the rural area the income of most people is also below the average level.

Second, there is a low proportion of middle-income population. At present, the middle-income population in China is small in size and unstable. According to the standard that the per capita income of a family of three is 20,000 yuan, the proportion of the middle-income group in China is only about 10%, and they are in an unstable position in the household income distribution. During a period of five years, their probability of transferring to a group of lower income is about 40%, that of transferring to a group of higher income is only 25%, and that of remaining at the original level is only 1/3.

Third, there is a great resistance to moving from the low-income group to the middle-income group. Among the urban low-income households, more than 2/3 will remain at the same income level during the 5-year period, and the probability of moving up to a group of higher income is just slightly higher than 30% while this number is 50% in the United States and about 60% in the United Kingdom and Finland. In a country which is in transition, the household sector should move more actively among different levels of income, but in China the situation is that there is a high probability of downward mobility, a small probability of upward mobility and an unstable middle-income group; it is difficult for the low-income group to reach a higher-income level, and a trend of a certain degree of solidification and rigidity is emerging in the underclass of society.

2.3 The Negative Impact of Social Governance Structure on Sustained and Stable Economic Growth: The Failure of the Transmission Mechanism of Social Stability

In recent years, China's social organisations have been developing rapidly, but the quantity and quality of social organisations have yet to be improved; their vitality falls short and they haven't reached the full potential for promoting economic growth. In 2014, the added value of China's social organisations accounted for only 0.21% of that of the tertiary industry, and was about one thousandth of GDP (some research has argued that the official data underestimated the GDP contribution rate of social organisations in China and the actual proportion is about seven thousandths), far lower than that of developed countries and the global average (Table 2). In terms of scale, currently China has less than 5 social organisations per 10,000 people, much lower than that of developed countries (97 for Japan, 63 for the United States, and 18 for Singapore). In terms of the regulation of social organisations, it is apparent that the efforts of the management departments in charge focus more on registration than regulation, and there is a lack of effective oversight both during and after the handling of matters; in terms of the autonomy of social organisations, as some social organisations still need to improve the internal governance structure and their credibility, it is difficult for them to play a full and active role; in the interaction between the government and social organisations, government administration is not separated from the management of social organisations, which are run, regulated and used by the government; efforts still need to made to improve the public service platform provided by social organisations and encourage nongovernmental participation.

Table 2 Contribution of the Tertiary Industry to Economic Growth   (Unit: %)

Scope	GDP Contribution Rates	Employment Contribution Rates
China (2014)	0.1	1.7
World (1990s)	4.6	5.0
US (2014)	5.3	9.2

Source: National Bureau of Statistics of China, National Centre for Charitable Statistics of the United States. *Global Civil Society: Dimensions of the Nonprofit Sector*

3. Promote Sustainable Economic Growth with Structural Reform in Social Fields

Structural reform is significantly different from aggregate reform. Over the past thirty years, China's economic reforms have been aggregate reforms that focus primarily on incremental reforms, avoiding substantial transformation as much as possible. In the future structural reform, since mere incremental reform is unable to solve the problem, substantial transformation must be actively carried out. The social structural reform, which is compatible with the economic structural reform, is designed to continuously improve relevant social structures by reducing what is excessive, making up what is insufficient, reflecting on what has been accustomed to and changing what is not suitable for the current situation.

3.1 *Optimise Demographic Structure: Maintain a Relative Balance Between Generations*

To promote the optimisation of demographic structure, population policies must be improved. For one thing, the momentum of population overgrowth has been effectively curbed, and with the improvement of living standards, people's attitudes towards having children are also changing gradually, which provides a favourable social environment for the further improvement of family planning policies. For another, international experience demonstrates that when per capita GDP reaches a certain level, it usually results in a decline in the fertility rate. In general, the total fertility rate (TFR) and per capita GDP have a significant negative correlation (Figure 2). Currently, China is ranking among the upper-middle income countries in per capita GDP, and the impact of sustained economic growth on the fertility desire of the Chinese starts to appear, which is basically consistent with the relevant national circumstance. In the context of sustained and sound economic development, the fertility rate is unlikely to rebound, and policy adjustments may not cause the volatility of the fertility rate.

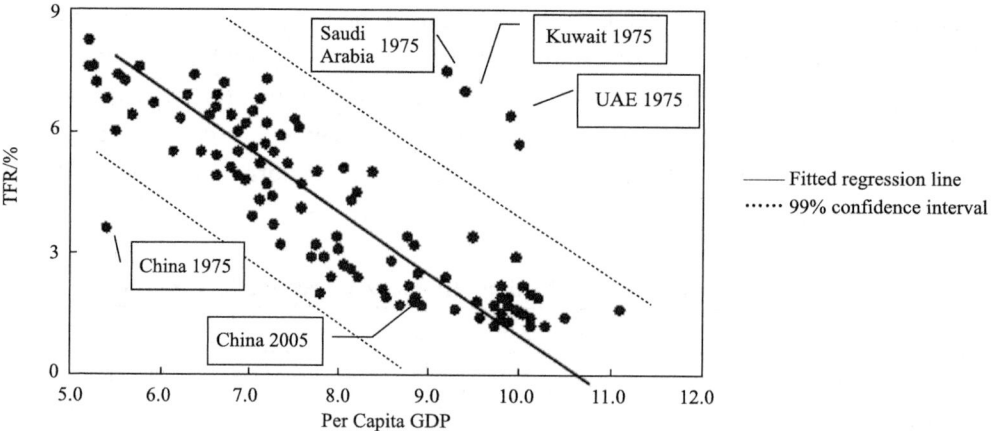

Figure 2 Per Capita GDP and TFR of Various Countries
Source: UNDATA

Improving family planning policy is an important matter that will produce a far-reaching and profound social impact, and it is a complex project of social system which requires us to pool our wisdom together, to have a comprehensive assessment, to design and implement relevant plans in a scientific way, and to carry forward the work soundly and orderly. First, we must unswervingly adhere to the basic state policy of family planning, focus on improving the policy, and maintain the continuity of the family planning policy, which is conducive to the balanced development of population in the long run. Second, we should adhere to risk control and maintain a moderately low fertility rate to avoid falling into the trap of low fertility, which will result in a rapid and irreversible shrink of the population size, and to effectively prevent the rapid rebound of birth rate which will again lead to an unfavourable situation of population overgrowth. Third, we should adopt a holistic approach, and better handle the relationship among population, economy, society as well as the resources and environment to promote coordinated development; further narrow the policy gap between urban and rural areas and different regions as well as different groups of people to promote social fairness and justice.

Based on the population prediction model we have established, the changes in the total population under different policies are compared, and accordingly preliminary suggestions are made to further improve family planning policy (Table 3).

Table 3 A Comparison of the Total Population Under Different Family Planning Policies
(Unit: hundred millions people)

Year	Two-child Policy Applied to Couples with Both Parents Being the Only Child	Two-child Policy Applied to Couples with Either Parent Being the Only Child	Since 2015 Two-child Policy Applied to All Couples	Since 2017 Two-child Policy Applied to All Couples	Since 2020 Two-child Policy Applied to All Couples
2013	13.61	13.61	13.61	13.61	13.61
2015	13.72	13.74	13.74	13.74	13.74
2020	13.94	13.99	14.09	14.03	13.99

					Continued
Year	Two-child Policy Applied to Couples with Both Parents Being the Only Child	Two-child Policy Applied to Couples with Either Parent Being the Only Child	Since 2015 Two-child Policy Applied to All Couples	Since 2017 Two-child Policy Applied to All Couples	Since 2020 Two-child Policy Applied to All Couples
2030	13.86	14.09	14.29	14.24	14.21
2040	13.44	13.79	14.07	13.99	13.90
2050	12.65	13.21	13.82	13.61	13.46

Source: Calculated by the research group

From the perspective of the total population and the sustainable development of the population, the policy allowing two children for couples in which both parents are the only child implemented before 2013 has a prominent policy risk that a substantial decline in population will happen following its peak. In contrast, the policy allowing a couple to have the second child if one of the parents is the only child has certain advantages, being able to delay the population peak and slow the population decline after the peak. Implementing the universal two-child policy will further optimise population development.

3.2 Improve the Income Distribution Structure: Maintain a Relative Social Equity

First, improve the primary income distribution. The policy of the primary income distribution should be mainly aimed at solving the problems of market distortion and market imperfection. In particular, a competitive environment with equal opportunities should be created, and the primary distribution mechanism, in which labour, capital, technology, management and other production elements participate in distribution according to their contributions, should be improved.

Second, improve the policy system of secondary distribution. The policy of secondary income distribution should be primarily aimed at giving more consideration to low-income people from the perspective of "consideration to fairness".

Third, improve supporting policies. The primary step is to improve the income supervision system. An important reason for the confusion in the income distribution procedures lies in the diversification of income forms and sources. Various subsidies and incomes beyond wages can foster corruption for related posts, especially in the public sector, and they also make it hard to carry out income supervision and regulation.

3.3 Establish a Modern Social Governance Structure: Realise a Relative Balance of Rights

First, improve the way of social governance and consolidate the safety net securing sustained and stable economic growth. Second, inspire the vitality of social organisations to create a booster for sustained and stable economic growth. Third, establish and improve cross-regional governance mechanisms to ensure the successful implementation of regional strategies. Fourth, strengthen network governance to promote the sound development of the internet economy. To reach this goal, the first step is to promote the application of the big data and the internet in the field of social governance. Improve the information platform that maintains social stability, enhance the intelligent analysis of public opinions and the ability to respond to online public opinions, and strengthen the ability of scientific decision-making in public affairs through information technology. The second step is to strengthen the internet security monitoring and control so as to maintain a good order in the online world.

4. Conclusions

In general, most of the periodic problems are aggregate problems which can be resolved through policies and measures based on aggregate reform. However, the problems leading to periodic confusion and the prolonged period are mostly structural problems which need to be resolved through policies and measures based on structural reform. As great achievements have been made in the reform of economic system, sufficient studies have been conducted on the issues of economic structure; however, since the issues of social structure have just been proposed, we must give a high priority to them. In fact, the structural reform in social fields is rich in content, additionally including issues such as social capital, the household registration system, inner quality structure and psychosocial structure; structural reform in social fields has a complicated transmission mechanism for sustainable economic growth, including cooperative issues as well as non-cooperative issues which can be divided into confrontational non-cooperative issues and unintentional non-cooperative issues. This paper starts with three social structural issues that are the most simple and are directly related to economy, making a preliminary exploration into the structural reform in social fields. In the future, we will continue to have an in-depth research on the structural reform in social fields.

Historical Experience of Modernization in Russia[1]

V. G. Burov

Institute of Philosophy, Russian Academy of Sciences

There have been several stages of modernization in Russia. The first stage began during the reign of Peter the Great in the first quarter of the 18th century. It was triggered by his trip to Europe during 1697-1698. During the trip Peter got acquainted with European civilization, culture and the way of life of the people in Europe. According to a graphic expression by an outstanding Russian historian, Kliuchevsky (19th century), Europe appeared before him in the form of a noisy and smoky workshop with machinery, ships, shipyards, factories and plants. Influenced by what he saw in the West, Peter the Great began to modernize Russia. The modernization was continued by his successors during the 18th century and the first half of the 19th century. It took the form of transition from manufactory to factory production and the introduction of some elements of market relations. However, the social system of Russia remained unchanged for a long period of time. Russia was ruled by an autocratic system with special privileges for the nobility and the absolute lack of rights for serfs.

The next stage of modernization in Russia is connected with the name of the emperor Alexander II (1855-1881). The main reform undertaken during his reign was the abolition of serfdom, in other words the liberation of the peasants from feudal dependence. However, owing to resistance from the landlords, land ownership was not transferred to individual peasants but to rural communities. The communal lands were not subject to purchase or sale, i.e. they were excluded from the market. A peasant had to buy his land plot from his landlord; moreover, the buy-out was mandatory. If the peasant refused to pay, the authorities would forcibly exact the payment, so the peasant would obtain his freedom but get no land. Indeed, the Russian agrarian reform under Alexander II was a major step towards the modernization of the country, but it did not create a class of small owners and there was no transition for small private enterprises.

Under the reign of Alexander III, who came to the throne after the assassination of Alexander II, the reforms continued, although on a smaller scale. A number of measures were taken to

---

[1] The paper is based on a research done by Russian and Chinese scientists.

promote the development of industry and trade, extensive railway construction was conducted, and a monetary reform was carried out (the introduction of gold into circulation). According to some historians, Russia under the reign of Alexander III was following the "Chinese way": the inviolability of the autocratic regime and absolute monarchy, with the expansion of market relations in the economy. The "Chinese way" refers to the policy of "self-strengthening" initiated by Li Hongzhang and his associates in the last quarter of the 19th century in China.

A characteristic feature of Russia's modernization in the second half of the 19th century was that the state retained control over all aspects of social life, and the industrial sector did not have sufficient freedom for its development, so the claims proposed by Russian historians that Tsarist Russia had a thriving and booming economy are groundless.

Nevertheless, at the end of the 19th century, Russia was undergoing industrialization. New structures inherent to advanced economies come into play: financial capital, a developed banking system, joint-stock companies, the formation of a nationwide Russian market, etc. As a result of the transformation of the productive forces, the transition from manual labor to machines and from manufactory to factory production took place; the industrial bourgeoisie and its antagonist — the proletariat — were developing fast. However, under the strict control of the despotic state there was no mechanism to resolve the growing social and class contradictions in the society.

The further modernization of Russia in the early 20th century is associated with the name of the chairman of the Council of Ministers — P. Stolypin. The main objective of the reforms proposed by him was the destruction of the peasant community and the transition to the farming industry based on small private landowners. Before the World War I, in 1909-1913, the modernization made it possible to achieve significant progress in economic development. In terms of the total volume of industrial production, Russia occupied the 5th or 6th place in the world. However, in terms of per capita industrial development, Russia lagged far behind the advanced countries in the West. In 1913, Russia's per capita output was 40% of the level of France, 20% of Great Britain, 10% of the US. The shares of Russia and other countries in world industrial production were as follows: Russia 5.3%, US 35.8%, Great Britain 14%, Germany 15.7%, France 6.4%.

After 1917 Russia's modernization began to be carried out on entirely different principles due to the power of the Communist Party. The party embarked on a course of industrialization and the implementation of a cultural revolution. Over the years of Soviet authority, Russia became a modern industrial power with a powerful educational and scientific potential. This is because the country's leadership had a clear strategic plan for the modernization of the economy by industry, region and timeframe. The development strategy was defined by the desire to catch up with the advanced capitalist countries. It was a "catch-up modernization".

It should be stressed that the Russian scientific and expert communities are still debating over Soviet modernization — its nature and the methods of its implementation. It has been suggested that a too high price was paid for its implementation. What is meant is that in the absence of sufficient funds, the necessary resources had to be obtained within the country, primarily in the countryside.

The collectivization of agriculture in the early 1930s not only provided substantial finance for industrialization, but also freed up much labor. In the course of collectivization, approximately 1/3 of the peasants left for the city, where they became workers and city builders. However, in the process of collectivization the slogan of "liquidation of the kulaks" was put forward, i.e. the rich peasants' property was confiscated, and they were relocated forcibly to remote areas of the country, along with other repressive measures. In some areas, the directives for the implementation of collectivization were not carried out on the principles of voluntariness and mutual benefit, but by making peasants join collective farms by force. In a number of areas, in order to accomplish the government's task of procuring grain, the grain was confiscated from the peasants forcibly and in full, which led to famine in some regions; consequently many peasants died of starvation. These measures inflicted serious damage on the economy and had long-term negative impacts on the development of agriculture in the Soviet Union.

As a result of modernization, the industrial base of the economy was created. At the end of 1937, the industrial production of the Soviet Union increased by 8.2 times in comparison to that in 1913. In pre-revolutionary Soviet Union, the gross industrial output constituted only 2.6% of the world total, while in the pre-war Soviet Union, it reached 13.7% of the world total; in 1937, the gross industrial output amounted to 77.4% of the entire national economy; the level of industrial production rose from the 5th place in the world and the 4th place in Europe in 1913 to the 2nd in the world and the 1st in Europe for the Soviet Union. As a result of industrialization, the Soviet Union developed new branches of economy such as heavy machinery, automobile and tractor industries, large military and aerospace industries, machine tool construction and precision instrument production industries. At that time the Soviet Union became one of the few countries in the world being able to produce almost the entire range of industrial products. Such existing industries as mining, metallurgy, chemical industry and transportation underwent a complete technical modernization, and their technological levels were significantly improved. As a result of the improvement in the level training of personnel, workers' productivity and their technical levels grew significantly. Modernization demanded literacy and mastering the basics of technical knowledge. A major achievement was the creation of the public system of free general and special education. Much attention was paid to the creation of the scientific and technical intelligentsia. As a result, the overall economic and national power of the country increased significantly.

Chinese scientists gave an objective assessment of the modernization carried out in the Soviet Union: "If you approach the matter from the point of view of the international and domestic situation of that time, the Soviet Union stimulated the rapid development of the socialist economy by unlocking the advantages of an economy based on public ownership, and firmly prioritized the development of heavy industry and the use of planned economy, which was absolutely necessary and correct. But in terms of operational policies, there was a tendency to ignore the real level of development of the productive forces and to make a one-sided focus only on public ownership, even to resort to coercive methods of destructing economic elements based on private ownership. Some of the employed methods far exceeded simple cruelty. The implementation of a highly centralized planned economy gave too much importance to prescriptive policies; there were a rigid and excessive control and a disproportionate centralization. The economy was managed by administrative means, ignoring economic instruments and the regulatory roles of the market. While the heavy industry was prioritized, the necessary balance among the various branches of the national economy was not maintained, which affected the development of agriculture, light industry and the production of consumer goods. As a result, this led to imbalances in the national economy, etc. The appearance of these errors to a certain degree was a result of violation of objective laws; furthermore, the long absence of corrective actions and solutions in no way contributed to the development of the economy"①.

The obvious achievements of modernization allowed the Soviet Union to defeat Nazi Germany and, in the postwar period, to achieve breakthroughs in scientific and technical areas, as evidenced by the creation of nuclear weapons and space exploration. Nevertheless, for all its shortcomings, the focus on a "mobilization economy" in the pre-war period was largely justified.

In 2000, J. Heckman, an American professor from Chicago and a Nobel laureate in Economics, noted that the scientific and technological progress of the second half of the 20th century was completely determined by the competition of the Soviet Union and the US. He also said that it was "a great pity that this competition was over".

For the sake of historical justice, it must be said that during the 1970s-1980s there was a slowdown in the economic development of the Soviet Union. This was due to the fact that the previous economic model (in Chinese research it is referred to as a highly centralized management system) had exhausted itself; it had no use of market mechanisms, the structure of the economy remained the same, there continued to be an emphasis on the development of heavy industry and the military-industrial complex, and there was a growing technological gap with the West.

M. Gorbachev, who came to power in 1985, was aware of the need of a new modernization of the country, and advocated the acceleration of scientific and technical progress at the beginning of his rule. However, later he prioritized the restructuring of the socio-political system, i.e. a political modernization. Glasnost and pluralism became its slogans. Instead of serious practical work in the field of economic development, the Communist Party structures held endless and ultimately futile debates on how to reform the party and the society. The reform of the economic system became secondary in importance. The result was a split in the Communist party and the loss of its leading role.

In the context of a multinational and multi-religious country with different levels of political and cultural traditions, and different levels of development of the regions, Russia was fraught with dangerous consequences. The Communist Party was the supporting structure of the social and political systems of the Soviet Union. It should also be noted that in the 1980s the prevailing trend in the Soviet Union and later the Russian intellectual community were universal admiration for the political and economic achievements of Western countries. The successes of the Chinese modernization ongoing since 1978 were completely disregarded. Nevertheless, a number of experts, including the author of this paper, spoke and wrote about the necessity of applying Chinese experience in the course of Russia's modernization. They referred to the common social and political history of the two countries, which was due to the fact that the Soviet Union and China both were socialist countries and that the Communist Party was the leading force in both of them. However, these arguments were not taken into account. The typical argument of the opponents of this approach, including those in M. Gorbachev's inner circle, was the lack of democracy in China.

The result of Gorbachev's policies is well-known — the collapse of the Soviet Union. Z. I. Alferov, a famous Russian scientist, a Nobel laureate in physics, an internationally recognized authority and an academician, recently wrote the following: "By itself, the collapse of the Soviet Union is a terrible thing as it undermined the entire economic system of the country, regardless of its political and social structures. We destroyed the high-tech industry, so the country is now

---

① 国际共产主义运动史编写组. 2012. 国际共产主义运动史. 北京：人民出版社：222.

developing through the sale of natural resources, especially oil and gas. In some respects, Russia has become a rentier state, where millions of people live off the sale of natural resources without making any real contribution to development, including to the development of these industries".[1]

The first decade of post-Soviet Russia can be characterized as a period of political instability, ethnic conflict and economic chaos. Only in the 21st century with the advent of the new political leadership did the process of Russia's revival begin. The government again embarked on the course of modernization of the Russian society as a whole and the Russian economy in particular. However, this process is slow and difficult. The fact is that there is still no consensus on the path of Russia's modernization and the methods of its implementation.

Just like before, representatives of the political and economic elite and the expert community place greater emphasis on the balance between economic and technological modernization and political reforms, and on the subject of modernization, its scope and stages. All participants agree that modernization is imperative for Russia's development, and its rejection is fraught with the loss of the country's global position in the world community.

There is also a consensus that the shortcomings of the modernization process are largely if not mainly due to the lack of a concrete forward-looking modernization program and, simultaneously, due to the insufficiently effective work of the state apparatus. As some experts pointed out, the Russian economy is divided into two sectors which use different mechanisms of management. The first sector has functioning market laws, where everything depends on one's business decisions. The second sector, as the famous expert Iosif Diskin put it, has "grown out of 'friendly' modernization of the 1990s and maintains a strong dependence on the disposition of the authorities and is in need of their support". The fact is that the privatization of state-owned enterprises in Russia was carried out not according to the norms of a market economy but according to the position of its participants in the system of power relations and their proximity to the center of decision-making. Due to these circumstances, the government comes to the aid of this sector in times of crisis.

Another serious obstacle on the way to the successful implementation of modernization is the serious defects in the system of governance and the lack of trust in state institutions. All these entail interventions by the country's senior government officials — the president and the prime minister — for solving day-to-day — that is day-to-day rather than long-term — issues of development. In Russia, there has in fact emerged a manual system of running the state. An example of this is the frequent (almost weekly) meetings of all members of the government on specific economic issues, often with the participation of the president.

The discussion on modernization, of course, touches on the question of how the project of Russian modernization fits into the mainstream of the previous Russian and the modern global processes of modernization. If this is a "normal" complementary modernization, there is no need to "reinvent the wheel", and we should only take advantage of the experience gained by other countries. Another matter is if Russia's modernization has its own specifics and is unique. The experience of successful experiences of modernization shows that they are based on proprietary national models, because precisely such models are able to solve the problems facing a country.

Russia has its own specific features (historical, cultural, geographical) distinguishing it from

---

[1] Sovetskaya Rossiya, March 12, 2016.

the developed European countries. Thus a simple transfer of modernization experience to its territory is impossible, just like the experience of China should also be refracted through the specifics of the modern conditions of Russia's development. The experts who spoke in the 1980s in favor of learning from Chinese experience did not by any means suggest transferring it mechanically to the Russian soil.

Modernization, as many Russian experts emphasized, is a political project designed to make the transition from one path of development to another. When speaking about modernization as a political project, one should mention the following. In Russian society, there continues the struggle between the supporters of modernization through the so-called liberalization and the supporters of conservative modernization.

The former suggests either starting Perestroika number two, which would involve an attack on the current regime (we all know how Perestroika number one ends), or returning to the 1990s, when the state had no control over business at all.

The connection between political liberalization and economic changes seems self-evident to the modern Russian liberals, just like the connection between glasnost, democratization as well as solving urgent social and economic problems seems self-evident to the "foremen of Perestroika" (M. Gorbachev and his associates). The deplorable results of this approach are obvious. After the collapse of the power vertical, the resulting vacuum is filled with unrestrained journalist demagoguery similar to the slogan of "bombard the headquarters", the struggle for the redistribution of power and, accordingly, property, which locally often takes a nationalist character.

The latter supports the course proclaimed by the government. Conservative sentiments are widespread in the Russian society. Indeed, in the minds of ordinary Russians there are still fresh memories of the 1990s, when the country plunged into economic chaos and the living standards of the population declined sharply. Therefore, the idea of conservative modernization is popular in Russia. It means a rejection of ideological doctrinairism, both right- and left-wing, of adventurism, and appeals to the practical experience and careful consideration of the project. The conservative approach means the development of a realistic minimum program and a consistent and gradual progress.

Speaking of the criteria of the modernization project, we should name two of them: economic and sociological ones. The economic criterion is well-known: It is the reduction of dependency of the economy on commodity prices, especially oil and gas. Russia has now effectively become a raw materials appendage of the developed countries in the West and the developing countries in the East. As for the sociological criterion, it is about creating a macro-social environment for the realization of the potential of skilled and talented people. Russia has a significant intellectual resource concentrated in the field of higher education and fundamental science. It could have a serious impact on the economic and social development of the country. However, due to the country's leadership policy, after 1991 Russia has emerged such a phenomenon as "large-scale brain drain". According to some sources, over the last twenty years Russia has lost more than 300,000 scientists (three recent Nobel Prize winners in physics are scientists who left Russia in the post-Soviet period). Unfortunately, the process of "brain drain" continues. It is clear that modernization is impossible without a radical change of policies in relation to the scientific and technical personnel, without efficient use of their potential for the benefit of the country. The main disadvantage of the current modernization, as some experts pointed out, is that it does not create demand for Russian intellectual resources, for quality education and for the innovation potential in general.

Modernization is impossible without innovation. When there is no innovative development, there is no demand for talent and no end to the "brain drain". Here we can note some changes that have occurred in recent years in mobile telecommunications and information technologies in general, in oil and gas industry, in ferrous and non-ferrous metallurgies, etc. The economic sanctions imposed by the West force the Russian industry and agriculture to seriously engage in importing substitutions, which inevitably demands innovative technological approaches.

Experts rightly make the public aware the serious lack of attention to fundamental research, although it is known that fundamental research is the source of breakthroughs of technologies and projects. Indeed, not all of them lead to applied results. However, at present Russia has in fact no state agency that would be responsible for linking fundamental research with practical needs, and for identifying potential applications of the results. In fact, fundamental studies very often do not contain direct reference to the possibility of their applied use.

According to many Russian experts, the current efforts to create new and innovative structures are naive and hopeless. A few years ago "Skolkovo" innovation project (modeled after Silicon Valley in the US) was established for the development of fundamental research, but hopes should not rest solely on it because powerful innovative structures take decades to create. In the meantime, the scientific structure with strong potential such as the Russian Academy of Sciences has been barely used since 1991, and its funding has been cut, resulting in a much reduced inflow of young staff and a generation gap between scientists.

The reform of the system of science management started two years ago. The reform has been reduced to the creation of the Federal Agency for Scientific Organizations, which is primarily interested in the financial and economic activities of scientific institutions. At the same time the three academies — the Russian Academy of Sciences, the Academy of Medical Sciences and the Academy of Agricultural Sciences — merged into one. As a result, the present-day Russian Academy of Sciences has effectively become a club of scientists.

Speaking about the priorities of the policy of modernization, one cannot ignore the views of experts and the public on why Russia is lagging behind the leading countries of the world. The fist and foremost here is the high level of corruption. Next comes the ineffectiveness of governance, the incompetence of the authorities, and the loss of industrial capacity in the course of reforms.

These problems manifested themselves in the two socio-economic crises — the one of 2008-2009 and the current one which began in 2015, which is related to the economic sanctions imposed by Western countries. The country's leadership is aware of the gravity of the problems and is trying to respond to them. A separate matter is whether its reaction is adequate. It is important to choose the right priorities and avoid populism. The current Russian leadership has done a lot to improve the living standards of the people. However, in crisis there are no conditions for the continuation of such a course, so there is an opinion in the expert community that it is necessary to focus on those sectors of the economy and those social groups that are important to the success of modernization.

And here the author cannot but again refer to the article wrote by academician Z. I. Alferov. He is absolutely convinced that the oil age will end due to the development and successful implementation of new technologies, including the photovoltaic method of converting solar energy, which will solve almost all problems of humanity related to electricity and energy. In fact, according to him, we are very close to solving this problem: We are talking about the 2030s, when this method will become both economically beneficial and dominant. After all, it would effectively solve the problem of power industry for the whole planet for many centuries... According to Z. I. Alferov, what is extremely important for Russia is that only the implementation of this method may lead to the situation where millions of people not only have jobs but also have interesting jobs that can bring them both good income and the feeling of satisfaction from work[①].

[①] Sovetskaya Rossiya, March 12, 2016.

The Deepening of the Division of Labor, Social Structure and the Modernization of National Governance

Xiaowei Xuan

Development Research Center of the State Council

1. Introduction

Although there are many controversies over what is the modern society and there are diversified opinions about the merits and demerits of the modern society, yet it is acknowledged that "substantial and sustained increase in the economic growth rate" (i.e., "modern economic growth phenomenon") is one of the most prominent features of the modern society as compared to the traditional society, and is also one of the most remarkable achievements of the modern society[①]. Due to the remarkable rise of the productivity level, even the material conditions of common people have been greatly enriched. Adam Smith has already commented in his time that the life of an ordinary laborer in Britain is more affluent than that of an Indian Chief[②].

It is exactly because "modern economic growth" is so important to the modern society that massive studies are carried out to explore why modern economic growth happens and how it can be sustained. China is currently at the stage of upper-middle-income countries[③]. There are already plenty of discussions on whether China can avoid the "middle-income trap" and find a way into the club of high-income countries (Liu, 2011). Under the new normal, China's economic growth rate is under heavy downturn pressure. Therefore, it is very beneficial to discuss the factors affecting

---

[①] From the pre-historic age of mankind to the age before the industrial revolution, the global GNP grew extremely slowly, but since the modern society began, as the famous British historian Hobsbawm put it: "Some time in the 1780s, and for the first time in human history, the shackles were taken off the productive power of human societies, which henceforth became capable of the constant, rapid, and up to the present limitless multiplication of men, goods, and services. This is now technically known to the economists as the 'take-off into self-sustained growth'". See Hobsbawm (2014: 34-35).

[②] See Cannan (1982: 177).

[③] The upper-middle-income countries are defined by the World Bank as having a GNI per capita between 3,976 and 12,275 US dollars (2010 standard). China's current GDP per capita is 7,594 US dollars (2014), and it is at the transitional stage from a middle-income country to a high-income country. See http://siteresources.worldbank.org/DATASTATISTICS/Resources/ OGHIST.xls.

economic growth from the perspective of modernization transformation, with a view to providing some references for the future growth of China.

2. Economic Growth and the Deepening of the Division of Labor

There has been much attention as well as plenty of research findings on the modern economic growth phenomenon (Kuznets, 1989). However, as it takes time to establish and improve the national economy accounting system, to collect and sort statistical data, and to adopt and apply mathematical tools, the formal analysis on the modern economic growth phenomenon with economic theories (especially the standardized model study on the economic growth of different nations) does not truly thrive until after the 1950s. Considering the importance of capital in modern economic growth, the initial economic growth theories focus on how to form capital accumulation and expand investment, giving rise to the "classic theory of economic growth" represented by the Solow model. However, since the beginning of the 20th century, the total factor productivity growth resulting from technological progress is playing an increasingly important role in modern economic growth. For example, in the United States, the contribution of total factor productivity to economic growth has grown from 36% in 1855-1890 to 70% in 1890-1927 (Yujiro Hayami, 2003: 143). Economists gradually focus on discussing how innovation and technological progress promote economic growth, giving rise to the "endogenous growth theory" in the 1980s represented by Robert Lucas and Paul Romer. Meanwhile, some economists are not satisfied with the "institutional neutrality"[1] hypothesis in the above theoretical model, and focus on discussing in what institutional environments the technological progress and economic growth can be sustained, giving rise to the "new institutionalism"[2] represented by North.

It can be seen that in order to explore the secret of modern economic growth, economists have tracked all the way from "capital" to "technology" and then to "institution", deepening people's understanding of modern economic growth in different aspects. However, the theories of new classical economics tend to study how to enhance the quantity and quality of different inputs (capital, labor, technology) to promote economic growth on the condition of fixed labor division level and product structure. In other words, the growth theories of new classical economics do not consider the increasing returns to scale brought by increased specialization level due to the deepening of the division of labor (Yang, 1998: 13-16); they can hardly bring in the benefits of new products and new professions resulting from the division of labor on economic growth.

But to classical economists, it is the continuous deepening of the division of labor that fundamentally drives modern economic growth. As Adam Smith pointed out in *The Wealth of Nations*: "The greatest improvement in the productive powers of labour, and the greater part of the skill, dexterity, and judgment with which it is anywhere directed, or applied, seem to have been the effects of the division of labour". The continuous expansion of market scale is conducive to the

---

[1] In new classical economics, the optimal behaviors of producers and consumers are merely a technical requirement; the resulting supply and demand are adjusted by the price signals in the market, which do not contain any ideological and institutional meanings. In other words, the influences of different institutional arrangements on resource allocation efficiency and economic growth are simplified; the institution is neutral. See Furubotn et al. (2006: 1-2).

[2] The above review of economic growth theories is highly simplified. For detailed discussion, see Jones (2002) and Helpman (2007).

continuous deepening of the division of labor, and the deepening of the division of labor results in roundabout mode of production and increased production efficiency, leading to reduced product costs and increased product quantity, which will in turn promote the expansion of market scale; thus, it forms a circular accumulation process of "deepening of the division of labor — market expansion", which forcefully promotes sustained economic growth (Young, 1928). In the above process, the introduction of material capital (machinery)①, accumulation of human capital, technological progress and corresponding institutional changes all are reasons why the division of labor can be continuously deepened, and are also the results of the deepening of the division of labor. It is thus clear that the perspective of the division of labor can take the capital concerned by the classic growth theory and the technology concerned by the endogenous growth theory, and the institutions concerned by new institutionalism all can be made into a unified analytical framework. Therefore, the deepening of the division of labor becomes one of the most central factors in the economic growth process. With the expansion of the market, it is involved in close bilateral interaction with capital, technology and institution, and thus determines the performance of economic growth. The infinite deepening of the division of labor has also become one of the most prominent and important features of modern economic growth.

If we regard "the infinite deepening of the division of labor" as a synonym for "sustained modern economic growth", then the following important questions are "Why does the infinite deepening of division of labor (i.e., acceleration of economic growth) happen in the modern society rather than in the traditional society?" and "Why can some countries realize continuous deepening of the division of labor (maintain sustained economic growth) and gradually transform from low-income countries to high-income countries, but others cannot?".

3. The Division of Labor and Differentiation: From Stratified Differentiation Society to Functional Differentiation Society

The comparison between the systematic features of the traditional society and the modern society will help explore why the infinite deepening of the division of labor is unlikely to happen in the traditional society. German sociologist Niklas Luhmann has differentiated different society types according to the forms of system differentiation. System differentiation refers to the process of repeatedly building systems within a system, i.e., how a system produces different sub-systems②. Luhmann argued that the differentiation of a social system mainly includes three ideal types: segmentary differentiation, stratified differentiation, and functional differentiation. Segmentary differentiation means the whole society is divided into some identical sub-systems, stratified differentiation means the whole society is divided into different upper and lower classes, and functional differentiation means the whole society is divided into some sub-systems with different functions (such as economic, political, legal, religious and educational functions)③.

The primitive society is a social system formed from segmentary differentiation; its segments

---

① Adam Smith has also pointed out that "the invention of all those machines by which labour is so much facilitated and abridged seems to have been originally owing to the division of labour", see Smith (2003: 10).

② See Kneer (1998: 148).

③ See Kneer (1998: 181).

(such as family and tribe) are all self-sufficient small social units with the same functions. Segmentary differentiation results in expansion on the quantitative dimension without qualitative change. It does not have complicated social relations and social structures, cannot carry more delicate social functions, and cannot induce deeper division of labor.

The traditional society mainly features stratified differentiation. Although there are various fields with different functions, it is in essence a pyramid structure with distinct hierarchies dominated by unified values (such as religious ideology). As Weber put it, in the Western European traditional society, "religion interprets the power relationships in this world in a metaphysical way. All occupations and social classes are determined by God's will, and each one of them is assigned with some specific and essential duties expected by God or determined by the norms of the objective world"[①]. Stratified differentiation gives different professions different classes according to a unified ideology; the ruling class (King or bishop) at the top of the pyramid can dominate different fields including politics, economy, law, culture and religion by right of their own class. In other words, although the whole society is divided into several fields with different functions, there are no clear boundaries between these fields. The group with a higher social class can carry out multiple functions simultaneously, showing a functionally diffused mode of governance, which features unification or integration of the politics and the belief.

The modern society mainly features functional differentiation. Its prominent feature is the independence of individuals from the traditional society. Unified ideology gives way to plural values and beliefs, and different fields with different functions increasingly become well-defined and mutually independent autonomous systems. Durkheim described the formation of the modern society as the transitional process in which the communication and coordination among social groups transform from "mechanical solidarity" to "organic solidarity" after the unified ideology breaks apart (Durkheim, 2000). Although there is still a hierarchical order in every field of the modern society (for example, in the political field, there are bigger and smaller power levels; in the academic field, there are higher and lower professional ranks), the hierarchical division in each field only conforms to its own rule, and the rules of different fields shall not mix (for example, the academic field should not bring in the rules of the political field; otherwise, one with the bigger power level will end up with a higher professional rank). Luhmann argued that in a functional differentiation society, all functional fields such as economy, politics and law separately conform to an operation rule called "binary codification". For example, the rule in the economic field is "pay/not pay", in the political field it is "powerful/powerless", and in the legal field it is "legal/illegal". The allocation of resources in the economic field is only based on the size of the bid (regardless of power)[②]. The modern society with functional differentiation is a network-structured society with multiple fields and rules co-existing. The whole society does not have a single rule of hierarchical division; instead, it conforms to a functionally differentiated mode of governance with all fields being relatively independent from one another.

Literally, the division of labor means one devotes more and more work time to fewer and fewer work fields, i.e., a process of specialization. However, the advancement of the division of labor does not only involve individuals' specialization wills and efforts, but is also greatly affected

---

① See Weber (2004: 277).
② See Kneer (1998: 181-182).

by the differentiation form of the whole society. In the traditional society with stratified differentiation, admittedly, there are various occupations as well as social divisions of labor with considerable scale and depth. However, first, the range of occupations one can choose is restricted to different extents by one's class. One's family background and class origin can greatly restrict one's occupational choice (an extreme example is the caste system of the traditional Indian society, where one's caste corresponds one by one to a type of occupations)[①]. Second, people's specialization level is also restricted by the hierarchical structure. As the deepening of the division of labor progresses to a certain extent, it will hit the ceiling of unified ideology and hierarchical rules and be forced to stop. The restriction of a pyramid social structure on the deepening of the division of labor is similar to the confinement of the Braudel Bell Jar on the capitalist sectoral extension as described by Braudel[②]. Third, in the functionally diffused mode of governance, the relative independence of different fields cannot be guaranteed, and people in different fields can hardly gain reasonable returns with their own specialization levels, which hinders the sustained deepening of the division of labor.

In the modern society with functional differentiation, after the unified ideology and single stratified rule are shattered, individuals are entitled to independently choose their own occupations, and people can climb up to a higher class in different fields with their own specialization efforts. Although the society still has a general distinction over elites/common people and upper class/lower class, the elite classes in different fields conform to separate rules, and the upper class of a field cannot arbitrarily step into another field[③], thus guaranteeing the relative independence and specialization of different fields, and enabling sustained deepening of the division of labor in different fields.

Therefore, on the surface, the deepening of the division of labor is only a matter of continuous increase in a specialization level in the economic field, but the differentiation form of a society and the resulting social structure and governance mode will deeply affect the level of division of labor in this society. In the traditional society with stratified differentiation, although there is a fair extent of social division of labor and a certain economic growth, the pyramid social structure and the functionally diffused mode of governance have fundamentally restricted the continuous progress of the deepening of the division of labor, and cannot induce an effective increase in economic growth rate. It is only in the modern society with functional differentiation that the shackles around the deepening of the division of labor are truly shattered, and a reasonable environment is created in which increased specialization level can bring corresponding returns, thus propelling the infinite deepening of the division of labor, leading to modern economic growth.

---

① The Indian caste system divides the whole society into different ranks (the four classes are Brahmins, Kshatriyas, Vaishyas and Shudras, and within the four classes hundreds of ranks are differentiated). People at different ranks take up different occupations. The occupation that one is going to pursue for a lifetime has already been determined at one's birth. Even people at different ranks in the same class should take up different occupations and should not mix up. For example, the Brahmins that host weddings should not replace the Brahmins that host funerals because they belong to different ranks even though they belong to the same Brahmins class.

② See Bruadel (1982) and de Soto (2000), quoted from Wei (2009: 56).

③ For example, an elite can gain great wealth with his or her business capability, or obtain a high academic rank with his or her own academic capability, but he or she cannot gain a real academic rank with his or her wealth.

4. Modernization of China's National Governance System: From a Pyramid Structure to a Network Structure

Compared with other traditional societies, Chinese traditional society features relatively fewer hereditary factors and higher social mobility. After the first emperor of Qin Dynasty abolished the enfeoffment system, and implemented the prefecture and county system, government officials dispatched by the state rather than hereditary peers gradually became the real governors of local places. Qian argued that in Chinese traditional society, only the royal family was hereditary, and there were no other occupations in the government or other families that could be inherited like this[1]. More importantly, the implementation of the imperial examination system had in theory carried out the goal of "opening the political rights to anyone". Most people, regardless of their family backgrounds, as long as they had talent and learning, might be able to access the upper class of the society through examination. "In the morning, he is still a peasant farming on the land; in the evening, he is already an official in the imperial court." Even many prime ministers were born in poor families and started from scratch. Some researches found that the vertical mobility in the upper society of the Ming and Qing dynasties was even beyond reach by modern western countries[2]. Therefore, although the Chinese traditional society is also a pyramid structure featuring stratified differentiation, the people in different classes were not completely fixed; the older generation of a family might be in the lower class of the society but the next generation might move up to the upper class, and vice versa. Fewer identity hereditary factors and higher social mobility allow people to have more freedom of choice and bigger chance of class change, making the stratified social structure more flexible and loose, which could produce and allow higher scale and depth of social division of labor. This is also closely related to the fact that compared to other traditional societies, the Chinese traditional society is able to achieve a relatively high level of economic development.

However, the Chinese traditional society also has distinct characteristics of stratified differentiation, that is, the bureaucrat-oriented system and functionally diffused mode of governance under a single stratified rule. Supported by a unified ideology dominated by Confucianism, the whole society is divided into different ranks according to a single rule, resulting in the bureaucrat-oriented system, which has lasted for thousands of years in the traditional society till now. The bureaucrat-orientation means people are oriented towards seeking administrative power in the political field (i.e., to become a bureaucrat). In the context of the bureaucrat-oriented stratified differentiation, the principle of the division of administrative ranks is applied to various social fields, and the development of other fields is more or less directly affected or even dominated by administrative power. The functionally diffused mode of governance is clearly shown in the "scholar-official politics" of the traditional Chinese society. The scholar-officials, as a class combining various identities including scholar, bureaucrat, landlord and country gentleman, carry out multiple functions including safeguarding Confucian orthodoxy, serving the imperial court and civilizing common people. They are the main actors of the governance of the whole society as well as the adhesive maintaining social operation. However, the negative consequences are the amateur

---

[1] See Qian (2001: 3).
[2] See He B D. The Ladder of Success in Imperial China: Aspects of Social Mobility 1368-1911. Quoted from He (2011: 20).

of the bureaucrat class and the functionally diffused governance. Therefore, although the Chinese traditional society has a looser social structure and a higher level of social division of labor, it still could not break away from the restrictions set by stratified differentiation. The bureaucrat-oriented system and the functionally diffused mode of governance have fundamentally restricted the infinite promotion of the division of labor and the specialization level, and are unlikely to give rise to modern economic growth.

Although the current Chinese economy and society have undergone tremendous changes compared to the past, from the theoretical perspective of the division of labor and differentiation, the features of bureaucrat-oriented system and functionally diffused governance are still prominent. On the whole, China is still in the transitional process from stratified differentiation to functional differentiation. The boundaries among different fields of the society are still not clear enough; such illegal phenomena as power-for-money, power-for-academic-rank and power-for-legal-right are not uncommon; the relative independence and specialization levels of different fields urgently need improvement; the functionally diffused phenomena are still common; the responsibilities of the government, enterprises, government-affiliated institutions and social organizations as well as the relationships among these units all require further clarification. Therefore, under the new normal, in order to facilitate technological progress, increase productivity and maintain sustained economic growth, China needs to promote the further deepening of the division of labor and the continuous increase in the specialization level. This means the society should transform from a stratified differentiation one to a functional differentiation one, which will cause the social structure to gradually transit from a pyramid structure to a network structure, and the governance to transit from a functionally diffused mode to a functionally differentiated mode. At present, to shatter the bureaucrat-oriented system and to separate government administration from the management of enterprises, public institutions, social organizations and state assets[①] should be the top priority of the tasks of modernization of national governance.

References

埃米尔·涂尔干 (Durkheim E). 2000. 社会分工论. 渠东译. 北京: 生活·读书·新知三联书店.
艾瑞克·霍布斯鲍姆 (Hobsbawm E). 2014. 革命的年代: 1789—1848. 王章辉等译. 北京: 中信出版社.
弗鲁博顿, 芮切特 (Furubotn E, Richter R). 2006. 新制度经济学——个交易费用分析范式. 姜建强, 罗长远译. 上海: 上海人民出版社.
何怀宏 (He H H). 2011. 选举社会: 秦汉至晚清社会形态研究. 北京: 北京大学出版社.
赫尔普曼 (Helpman E). 2007. 经济增长的秘密. 王世华, 王筱译. 北京: 中国人民大学出版社.
坎南 (Cannan E). 1982. 亚当·斯密关于法律、警察、岁入及军备的演讲. 陈福生, 陈振骅译. 北京: 商务印书馆.
库兹涅茨 (Kuznets S). 1989. 现代经济增长: 速度、结构与扩展. 戴睿, 易诚译. 北京: 北京经济学院出版社.
刘世锦 (Liu S J). 2011. 陷阱还是高墙: 中国经济面临的真实挑战和战略选择. 北京: 中信出版社.
钱穆 (Qian M). 2001. 中国历代政治得失. 北京: 生活·读书·新知三联书店.
琼斯 (Jones C I). 2002. 经济增长导论. 舒元等译. 北京: 北京大学出版社.

[①] See Decision of the Central Committee of the Communist Party of China on Some Major Issues Concerning Comprehensively Continuing the Reform, adopted at the Third Plenary Session of the 18th Central Committee of the Communist Party of China on November 12, 2013, Xinhua News Agency.

速水佑次郎 (Yujiro Hayami). 2003. 发展经济学——从贫困到富裕. 北京: 社会科学文献出版社.
韦伯 (Weber M). 2004. 宗教社会学. 桂林: 广西师范大学出版社.
韦伯 (Weber M). 2010. 新教伦理和资本主义精神. 桂林: 广西师范大学出版社.
韦森 (Wei S). 2009. 再评诺斯的制度变迁理论. 经济学(季刊), 8(2): 373-398.
亚当·斯密 (Smith A). 2003. 国民财富的性质和原因的研究. 郭大力, 王亚南译. 北京: 商务印书馆.
杨小凯 (Yang X K). 1998. 经济学原理. 北京: 中国社会科学出版社.
Kneer G, Nassehi A. 1998. 卢曼社会系统理论导引. 鲁贵显译. 北京: 巨流图书公司.
Young A A. 1928. Increasing returns and economic progress. Economic Journal, 38: 527-542.

The Youth Entrepreneurship as a Factor of Social Modernization of Society

Pavel Deryugin, Alena Smelova, Reseda Salakhutdinova,

Anna Shilyaeva, Liubov Lebedintseva

St. Petersburg State University

In this paper we will discuss youth entrepreneurship as a proven force for social change. We suppose that the phenomenon should be analyzed not only as a factor, but also as an integrative indicator of the success and prospect of social modernization of the society. We argue that, in fact, values, motivations and interests of young people are the keys to the implementation of natural, cultural and historical potential of any society. They guide young entrepreneurs' behaviors, and so that determine the direction of a country's development: Whether the country will be the next metropolis of developed capitalism or its periphery, and wherever the country will be able to realize its potential and become one of the leaders of the world development or not. The numerous sociological studies show that the underdevelopment of youth entrepreneurship mainly leads to the collapse of the socialist economic system in the Soviet Union, because young people are guided primarily by the totalitarian principles in management and economic activity (e.g., Eriashvili and Djafarov, 2010; Kharseeva, 2015). So, it is obvious that the social modernization is an impracticable task without the integrative activities of young entrepreneurs. As studies show, the collapse of the Soviet system is not the result of defeat in the Cold War with the West, but, to a greater extent, due to its own rebirth. In addition, the successes of China, Singapore, India and many other countries, which manage to stimulate entrepreneurial initiatives among young people demonstrate that in a short historical period, the society is able to overcome the centuries-old backwardness and achieve a resounding success.

1. Some Critical Moments in Studying Youth Entrepreneurship

Since the revival of the private property institution in the new history of Russia, youth entrepreneurship has been a major factor of social change — the social relations and the whole social structure. In the development of modern entrepreneurship and the implementation of market reforms in Russia, young people play a decisive role in many respects. In fact, the efforts of the youth lay practices of modern business. As in the early 1990s, the bulk of small and medium non-state businesses (i.e. 70%-80% of these companies), were created by young people under the age of 35. So new challenges have arisen, the solutions of which have provided versatile studies of youth entrepreneurship, social aspects, dynamics and trends of its transformation.

The general economic perspective on youth entrepreneurship is often limited to the analysis of the predominant economic activities paying little attention to those socio-institutional changes and value contradictions that have developed in studying this phenomenon. Meanwhile, the youth entrepreneurship can not only elevate or lead the society into the leaders of global development, but also can be its brake. Recent history shows that entrepreneurship is not necessarily a means of salvation of the society. Conversely, it may ruin the society. Anyway, this threat is very real for those countries, where entrepreneurship becomes predatory in nature, and focuses exclusively on making profits and assertions of selfish interests. That is a common practice in the contemporary history of post-Soviet space. Therefore, the analysis of youth entrepreneurship is of keen scientific interest. The modern Russian legislation still contains no definition of the concept that characterizes youth entrepreneurship. Moscow adopts a separate resolution on youth entrepreneurship and establishes financial assistance to young entrepreneurs. It discusses a number of practical issues related to the organization of youth entrepreneurship, resource allocation, assessment, the funding of youth projects, etc. So, this topic starts to attract the attention of researchers, as it is poorly covered.

What is the danger of such disregard to the study of the entrepreneurial initiatives of young people? The importance of the analysis can be demonstrated by eloquent figures about the unrealized possibilities of the active parts of young people striving to start their own business. The percentage of young people wishing to start their own business in several times is greater than the proportion of those who have already started their business. According to various studies, 78% respondents believe that opening a small business is a great way of self-realization, and 60% respondents prefer to start their own business, because they aim to obtain a higher level of income compared to employment (Ilinuh, 2015). Today, however, only 5% of young people have their own business. Thus, the entrepreneurial spirit among Russian youth is high; however, only a small part of young people are able to implement this initiative in practice.

Youth entrepreneurship is an integral part of the entrepreneurship institution in Russia, with its own characteristics and specificities. First of all, youth entrepreneurship is a part of small business: 94% of youth entrepreneurs own small business enterprises. That is the reason why the sociodynamics of Russian youth entrepreneurs' values, its history and genesis of the formation are essential to consider in the light of general trends in the development of the market space and small entrepreneurship. In general, these trends characterize the youth entrepreneurship around the world — its concentration on the small business space.

The analysis of the youth entrepreneurship development in the Russian context shows that there is an apparent number of phases, which differ from one another by special characteristics. First of all are the special values of the youth in the field of entrepreneurship. Based on the main provisions of the activity-activist approach, the values are viewed as the results or products of the diverse activities of young entrepreneurs, who sacrifice their material or spiritual needs. This understanding of the values mostly reflects the idea of entrepreneurship not only as an active action to transform the socio-economic development of the society, but also as activities that are always aimed at a certain result. In accordance to this provision, there are four stages in the development of the Russian youth entrepreneurship.

2. The Periods of Youth Entrepreneurship Institutionalization

The first stage (1985-1992) is the beginning of the legalization of youth entrepreneurship, the period of breakthrough of accumulated and unrealized creative potential of youth, the period of takeoff and initial failures, and the stagnation in youth entrepreneurship. There were only 4.2% extreme pessimistic assessments among young Russians about starting a business in Russia in the late 1980s. Most respondents welcomed the advent of market reforms, believing that these changes will give the opportunity to manifest such yesterday enterprises that have long been secretly acting in the youth environment. From this environment later came the people, who have used their entrepreneurial talents not only for the benefit of the society, but also for financial speculations (e.g., Sergey Mavrodi). So, to be an entrepreneur was recognized as a new previously unprecedented opportunity to realize one's potential. Entrepreneurship was considered as a prestigious and promising economic activity for the youth.

The second stage (1993-2001) is a period of turbulence and transformation, a period that showed youth entrepreneurship inside out — its implicit limitations to the real potential of economy. By the mid-1990s, the share of poor Russians had increased, and according to some experts' opinions, the gap between wealthy and poor individuals reached 30-35 times. Amid this hypertrophied poverty social stratification of Russia, youth entrepreneurship, starting business in almost all cases implied making it with private capital, became more volatile and mainly weak, almost always teetering on the verge of bankruptcy. A new competitive environment had been formed, however monopolies arose in every sector of the economy. Besides, large business and foreign companies entered the Russian markets, and others factors pressed youth entrepreneurship, pushing it to peripheral and unprofitable markets, and even in the shadow spheres of the economy.

The third stage (1999-2008) is a phase of steady growth and institutionalization of youth entrepreneurship, when it has reached a qualitatively new level. At the junction of the end of 1990s and early 2000s, there have been important events in the socio-economic spheres of the country that formed a strong background for a new stage of development of youth entrepreneurship. The year 2001 is the first year of the implementation of the strategic program initiated by Putin, called Gref Program, designed for the next decade. From this period, youth entrepreneurship began to show a tendency for continuous growth. With all the vagaries of the market during these years, young successful entrepreneurs (at the expense of profitable business) could reach a 5-7 times gap in the income level in comparison to non-entrepreneurial activities. The prestige of this profession, according to surveys of the public opinion, remained the highest — in the 2nd place and more times higher than other professions. This allowed young entrepreneurs to have expensive cars, to visit exotic countries and to spend huge amounts of money on consumption.

The fourth stage (2009-present) is the decline of latent phase of youth entrepreneurship. A new stage in the development of youth entrepreneurship originated from another crisis — the global financial crisis. A strong decline in GDP (7.9%), the decline in investments in the Russian economy (17%) and the increase of unemployment by 1/3 significantly reduced opportunities of the youth in starting their own business. Later the political-economic sanctions were an important factor of the slowdown of the Russian economy. These factors also affected the status of youth entrepreneurship.

Since the late 1980s, young entrepreneurs were 83%-90% of all entrepreneurs, and to date, their percentage composition decreased almost twice. In the 2010s the demographic portrait of the average Russian entrepreneurs is as follows: It is men of 38-40 years old (Vavakina, 2014). As for women, they usually start doing entrepreneurial business at the age of 35, after having children. At this age they are even slightly ahead of their male counterparts in the quest to do it. This data differ from the results of studies in 1988-1997, when the average Russian entrepreneurs' age was 33.5 (Barsukova, 2000). And only the pioneers, i.e. those who did business in the earliest periods of perestroika, turned 36 years old. In fact, in the 1990s small- and medium-size business entrepreneurs were young people. Thus, over the past two decades of research, the average age of Russian entrepreneurs increased by 2.5 years. This rate is almost twice higher than that in advanced economies. Despite many contradictions in the formation of the Russian youth entrepreneurship, one may recognize the transitional forms of youth business like co-working, anticafes, freelancing, outsourcing and outstaffing, including social entrepreneurship, which became particular research interest after the global financial crisis.

3. Social Entrepreneurship as a New Phase of Youth Entrepreneurship Institutionalization

In fact, social entrepreneurship can be defined as that "a form of economic activity aims at solving problems of specific groups of people who, due to market failures and the state insolvency, do not have access to essential benefits" (Aray, 2015: 4). The term is coined by B. Drayton, CEO and founder of Ashoka — the Center for Social Entrepreneurship at the University of Oslo. Social entrepreneurship is hardly a new phenomenon, however, in recent years it actively develops in the world economy. According to Web of Science (ISI Thomson Scientific), the number of publications on this topic from 1995 to 2014 has increased almost 10 times. Research interest has raised due to the new trend of the development of capitalism, the so-called philanthrocapitalism (Bishop and Green, 2009), which globally mobilizes private capital (i.e. financial and social capital, time and expertise knowledge) for the betterment of the society. Thus, social entrepreneurship is one of the tools of philanthrocapitalism, which serves not only to solve current social problems, but also to cause changes in the entire social system with the aim of complete eradication of these problems.

The reason for the evolution of capitalism is a social criticism, which changes the direction of its development, indicating the main problems: social injustice, unemployment, income inequality, environmental pollution and resource degradation areas. Financial capital is no longer exclusively involved in speculative transactions, in order to obtain astronomical profits. It acquires a social dimension. The subject of its financing and developing innovative solutions to problems (using the institute of entrepreneurship) becomes a social environment between man and man.

Legislatively Russia social entrepreneurship is allocated in a special kind of entrepreneurial activity. So, according to the No. 411 order of Ministry of Economic Development of the Russian Federation by July 1st, 2014, social entrepreneurship is a "socially-oriented activity of small and medium-sized businesses aimed at solving social problems". In particular, it provides employment to people with disabilities, women with children up to 7 years old, orphans, graduates of orphanages, pensioners in difficult life situations, and persons released from prison over the past 2 years. The share of employees with disabilities in the enterprises should be no less than 50% of the average headcount, while the share in the salary fund is no less than 25%. The fields of social entrepreneurship are health, physical training and sports, children and youth vocational training, social tourism, cultural and educational activities, assistance to victims of natural disasters, the production of medical equipments, prosthetic and orthopedic products, vehicles, etc. For prevention of disability and social rehabilitation of the disabled, and social rehabilitation of socially disadvantaged persons released from prison no more than 2 years, and persons suffering from alcoholism and drug addiction, social entrepreneurs can receive grants of no more than 1 million RUB. In condition, the co-funding of the project will be no less than 15%. A specific law on social entrepreneurship has currently not developed.

In addition, the tax on the profit of socially responsible companies is abrogated (Mulyukov, 2015), and at present the criteria for the assignment of legal entities to the category of subjects of small and average businesses, and questions about ownership of companies to investors, including foreign ones, are being discussed. In the future, it can give an impetus to the development of the Russian stock market, where shares of small and medium enterprises will be traded. Today social entrepreneurship in Russia is in the institutionalization process. As in other countries it takes the form of social movement (Arjaliès, 2010), whose primary goal is to compete for changing norms, values, shared meanings and making economic processes in the country.

Gradually, the philosophy of social entrepreneurship is integrated in the cultural life of the society. Its conductors become public organizations (e.g. the fund "Our Future", the Agency of Strategic Initiatives, the Russian Microfinance Center "Opora Rossii", the Russian Union of Industrialists and Entrepreneurs, the all-Russia public organization "Business Russia", Russian Association of Managers, and the Agency for Social Information), banks (Petrocommerc Bank — since 2015 it became the financial group "Otkrytie", URALSIB, etc.), resource extraction companies (LUKOIL, Norilsk Nickel, RUSAL, etc.), non-profit organizations (GLADWAY, Impact HUB, etc.), universities, etc. There established several awards for contribution to the development and promotion of social entrepreneurship (e.g., the "Impulse for Good" by the fund "Our future"), and for contribution to social development and environmental security ("FERD Social Entrepreneur"). Besides that, the leading Russian universities organize business competitions for students: best startup of the year" in National Research University (nomination of "the Best Socially Significant Startup" with the support of the foundation "Union"), which is a business plan competition; "Godwin Wong" in the Graduate School of Management at St. Petersburg State University (special nomination of "the Best Business Plan in the Field of Social Entrepreneurship" with the support of the fund "Our future"); the best social project of the year in the Russian State Social University, with the support of the Ministry of Economic Development of Russia and Expert Council for Development of Social Innovations of the Russian Federation in the Federation Council. Besides that, social media about social entrepreneurship are actively developing: the internet-portal "New Business: Social Entrepreneurship", "Sustainable Business", "Hometowns", etc.

Russia have opened several schools on social entrepreneurship, mostly for people under the age of 30, such as the school organized by the "Social Investment Fund". The company's experts conduct educational seminars in the fields of social investment, entrepreneurship and design, give specific instructions to students launching their own projects, as well as provide assistance in seeking financial resources for the project implementation from Russian and foreign investors. The following projects should be noted: In 2012-2014 the "School of Aspiring Entrepreneurs" in Novotroitsk was supported by the company Metalloinvest; in 2014-2015, the "School for Social Entrepreneurs" in Penza was a project of the Center for Innovation in Social Sphere of the Penza region; the ongoing federal acceleration program "Social Innovation" by the support of the Ministry of Economic Development of the Russian Federation held in Moscow City, as well as in Moscow, Samara, Sverdlovsk, Krasnodar, Krasnoyarsk, Primorsky Krai and several other regions of the Russian Federation.

The integration tool that connects globally circulating finance and local needs of the societies into a single is the institute of online social exchange. The online social exchange is an online platform that connects potential investors and social entrepreneurs. Their mission is to assist social entrepreneurs in gaining access to financial capital and providing financial expertise to guarantee the transparency of transactions and assess the potential impacts of the investment projects. All social companies and social entrepreneurs are required to undergo an audit. Only after this procedure, the profile becomes available to potential investors. However, contracts are traded online over the internet (the online dating service). Besides that, in 2009 Rockefeller Foundation initiated the creation of a global network of social investors (GIIN, has functioned since 2013), one of the objectives of which is the establishment of the global social exchange.

At the moment one can only talk about the formation of online social exchange in Russia. However, there are prototypes of social exchanges which have been used for a long time, such as INPROEX, the exchange of investment projects that has been operating since 2011. The investment projects there are structured by a geographical and sectoral basis. The projects are presented from 3 countries: Russia (85 regions), Belarus and Kazakhstan. The following types of projects are available: ready business, business project or business idea. The projects are divided into investment, real estate, municipal and innovative sections. It contains the projects in 37 sectors of the economy: agriculture, industry, logistics, trade, real estate development and other industries, which include media, finance and credit, medicine, securities, sports, education, tourism, internet projects, leasing, services, entertainment industry, etc. The responsibility for the information about the projects lies with the initiators of investment projects. The administration of the portal only provides the adjustment of the information to the format. However, it proposes additional consulting services: the examination of investment projects, development of business plan and its adaptation to the Russian economy and other services.

Thus, one of the factors of economic development and social transformation is youth entrepreneurship. The process of institutionalization of entrepreneurship in Russia has passed through different historical stages: from "dealers" and "shadow entrepreneurs" up to legal entrepreneurs. Today social entrepreneurship, which mainly focuses on young people under 30 years old, has the potential to be a significant force of social modernization and human development. It embodies the ideas and values of philanthrocapitalism i.e. the concerns about improving human life and society. However, it should be remembered that social modernization is a slow and capital-intensive process. However, it will result in global social change, creating a new "human ecology", which is achieved through a responsible approach to sustainable development in social, environmental and financial spheres.

References

Aray Y N. 2015. Business Models in Social Entrepreneurship: A Typology and Features of Formation (Unpublished PhD thesis). St. Petersburg, Russia.

Arjaliès D L. 2010. A social movement perspective on finance: How socially responsible investment mattered. Journal of Business Ethics, Supplement 1 (92): 57-78.

Barsukova S. 2000. Business appeals from the old guard to new recruits. Sociological Research, 3: 53.

Benedikter R. 2011. Social Banking and Social Finance: Answers to the Economic Crisis. New York: Springer.

Bishop M, Green M. 2009. Philanthrocapitalism: How Giving Can Save the World. New York: Bloomsbury Press.

Eriashvili N D, Djafarov N K. 2010. Entrepreneurship in the USSR and the present stage. Education, Science, Scientific Personnel, 1: 49-53. (In Russian)

Ilinuh S A. 2015. Entrepreneurship in Russia: The analysis of influence factors. The Problems of the Modern Economy, 2 (54): 35-38.

INPROEX. 2016. The exchange of investment projects. http://www.inproex.ru/[2016-1-12].

Kharseeva N V. 2015. Economic culture and business in the USSR. Fundamental Research, 2-8: 1972-1976. (In Russian)

Martinelli A. 2005. Global Modernization: Rethinking the Project of Modernity. London: Sage Publications.

Muljukov A. 2015. The abolition of income tax will hike up public services to a higher level. http://www.kommersant.ru/doc/2758351[2016-1-12]. (In Russian)

Soros G. 1998. The Crisis of Global Capitalism: Open Society Endangered. New York: Public Affairs.

Vavakina T S. 2014. The analysis of representations of Russian entrepreneurs about business partners and relationships: Regional and gender features. Modern Technologies of Management, 2(38): 12.

To Explore a Chinese Discourse of Modernity Research Paradigms[①]

Yuan Gao [1]   Feile Gao [2]   Jianbiao Guo [1]

1 Fujian Jiangxia University   2 Fujian Administration Institute

As a historical phenomenon of specific development stage in the process of human evolution, modernity inherently has its own essential stipulation which constitutes the core of modern industrial civilization — modernity. As the core of modern industrial civilization, modernity stipulates the modernization of the world, which deeply influences the historic vicissitudes of various countries and nations from the pre-industrial civilization to the industrial civilization. Since modernity is the core of industrial civilization and embodies the essence of modernization, in that way regardless of the merits or demerits of industrial civilization, and results or problems of modernization, its origin should be explored in modernity.

1. The Review on the Modernity Research Paradigms in Chinese Academia

After entering the 1990s, Chinese academia began a theoretical reflection on the problems which appeared during the period of rapid changes of the society and the acceleration of modernization. An obvious feature of this reflection is affected by international intellectual debates on the problem of modernity, and the core problem is close to Chinese contemporary social change and modernization — Chinese modernity. Over the past 20 years, Chinese academia has gradually formed three paradigms named "modern", "modernity" and "post modernity" in the process of reflection of Chinese modernity, due to different theoretical resources, value orientations and path selections.

On the problem of Chinese modernity, most Chinese commentators believe that the historical task is not to abandon it, but to construct it. Because of the differences in theory resources and

---

[①] This paper is the stage research result of China National Social Science Fund Project, 2015 — "The Research on Contemporary Chinese Social Development in the Perspective of New Modernity" (Approval No. 15BZX009).

research paths, the theorists of modernity sum up research paradigms for understanding and explaining the formation of "capital modernity", "cultural modernity" and "modern system". The "capital modernity" paradigm focuses on the analysis in historical movement and logical relationships between capital and modernity. The main theorists include Feng Ziyi, Zhang Xiong, Lu pinyue, etc. They believe that modernity is the production of capital movement based on modern production, and because of the inherent requirements of capital, it contributes to the formation and development of modernity in politics, economy and other aspects of social life. The "cultural modernity" paradigm is mainly from the dimension of value and the meaning of human to understand and interpret modernity. The representa-tives of the theory are mainly Yi Junqing, Zhou Xian, etc. They believe that in order to prevent the subversion of the values and the foundation of significance modernization by the one-sided development, it must be corrected through the modernity of culture for today's social modernization. The "modernity of system" paradigm emphasizes that the system construction for the realization of modernity is an indispensable fundamental condition; therefore, as China gradually blends into the modern world tide today, the key is not those problems like how to maintain their national consciousness and national spirit and the like, but is the political system problem of how to construct the Chinese modern constitutional system which must be solved fundamentally. Ren Jiantao, Gao Quanxi et al. mainly hold the viewpoint.

The "anti-modernity" theory is divided into two paradigms in Chinese academia: One is the conservative "anti-modernity" theory, and the other is the radical "anti-modernity" theory; both of them are vehemently criticizing and opposing modernity, but their positions and views are greatly different. After the 1990s, with the rise of "Craze for Traditional Chinese Culture" in China, some "New Confucianism" representa-tives blame the problems which appear in Chinese sharp social changes in modernity from the standpoint of cultural consideration. They are calling for a return to the Chinese culture stand point to solve the development problems of China, and trying to build an ideal mode of future Chinese culture system and political structure. They are asking for modernization that presents the Chinese traditional manifestation of "Nature Law". At the same time the rise of another batch of theorists who have the radical "anti-modernity" tendency are referred as the "New Left" by their left-wing sense. In Chinese academia, Wang Hui is one of these leading figures, and the representatives are Gan Yang, Cui Zhiyuan, etc. They mainly borrow the left-wing social theory of modernity in contemporary western cultural resources to criticize modernity, and then make their own theoretical researches on path selection. They believe that the double historical context history which China is looking for is decided by the extension of imperialism and historical exhibition of social crisis in modern capitalism.

In the middle of the 1980s, by the introduction of the American scholar Jameson, Chinese scholars began to understand, disseminate and research post-modernism. In the 1990s, some scholars began their theoretical thinking which combined the contemporary Chinese realistic practical problems and gradually formed a "post-modernity" paradigm. The main theorists include Zhang Yiwu, Chen Xiaoming, Wang Ning, etc. Although the characteristics of post-modern diversification and anti-homogenization determine that they can't form a complete theoretical system and a unified academic view point, it still can sort out the theorist demands of "post-modernity" paradigm which would terminate modernity and rise to post-modernity from the analysis on each post-modernity theorist's basic viewpoint: First, the contemporary problems can not be simply attributed to single "modernity"; second, the end of "modernity" is an unavoidable topic of China today; third, "from modernity to post-modernity" is the sign of social and cultural process of contemporary China; fourth, to critique and liquidate modernity in the position of post-modernity must jump out of the trap of modernity.

The "modernity" commentators are observing the correlation between modernity and Chinese modernization, seeing the positive role of modernity for Chinese social development and emphasizing the truth that the view of modernity should not be abandoned in the process of transition from the traditional agricultural society to the modern industrial society in China today, but there are three important problems that "modernity" theorists also failed to make a fundamental answer to in theory: First, the overall problem about modernity; second, the time problem about modernity; third, the problem of nationality on modernity. Conservatives of "anti-modernity" disregard the basic fact that the modern concept has been widely recognized by the Chinese people in the historical process of Chinese modernization during the 100 years, and consider that Chinese future direction should construct Chinese characteristics of benevolent politics and ritual laws based on the restoration of traditional Confucian culture which is undoubtedly a historical reversing choice of path. The radicalism "anti-modernity" theorists simply equate modernity with capitalist modernity in revealing and criticizing the malpractice of capitalist modernization, and thus deny the general value and basic concept of modernity for the universal significance of modern society. Although the "post-modernity" theorists note that negative factors exist in the process of modern western social modernization, and maintain vigilance on the negative function in Chinese modernization development, they are likely to hinder the process of Chinese modernization due to their misplacement of time and space in trying to dock the post-modernity theory of western post-industrial society with China.

At present, there are limitations in three forms — "modernity", "anti-modernity" and "post modernity" of theoretical paradigms on the modernity research of Chinese academia. All of them can not offer strong theoretical social transformation and modernization in the research of contemporary Chinese social transformation and the problem of modernization development. It requires that our vision must go beyond the theoretical barriers of "modernity", "anti-modernity" and "post modernity", and establish a reasonable interpretation for the direction of development, development path, development model and development law. It can effectively analyze the realistic problems in the process of social transformation and modernization in China today, and it can effectively respond to doubts and criticism in the problem of Chinese modernization development from the international intellectual. There is no doubt that the construction of such a new paradigm has very important significances, as it could not only promote China to solve the practical problems in the process of modernization, but also promote the contemporary Chinese academic development and enhance the international academic exchanges and dialogues in the ideological discourse.

The precondition of building a reasonable and effective analysis theoretical paradigm of Chinese modernity is to have an objective understanding and a basic judgment on modern development of contemporary China. In the time dimension of human society modernization development, we see that the historical process of modernization has undergone the enlightenment period and the industrialization period, and is entering a post-industrialization and globalization period now. In the space dimension of human society modernization development, we see the modernization as a universal historical movement of human social development in modern times. Although it is only originated from the Western Europe, it has been spread around the world, especially in China today. The modernization movement is moving rapidly. Just based on this space-time intersection, we choose the theoretical study of social transformation and modernization of the development in contemporary China, and try to put forward a new research paradigm — "new modernity", and treat it as the interpretational framework of law of development, roads, forms and problems for the historical process of Chinese modernization. Since the new paradigm of modernity research is an alternative theoretical framework of interpretation, it must have its own core theory circle, and the logical framework should include the theoretical resources, core concept, basic principles and empirical analysis. Firstly, the first level is the theoretical resources of the research paradigm, using Marx's theory of social development as the guiding ideology, critically absorbing the beneficial factors of Chinese traditional culture and western culture in the implementation of the comprehensive innovation, and learn widely from others. The next level is the core concept of this research paradigm — "new modernity", which should be established at the intersection of the two space-time dimensions of "globalization" and "China in the process of modernization". The third level, from the perspective of "new modernity" as the core concept, reflects the essential characteristics of some basic principles of the main principle of diversity — the subject pluralism principle, the essential multiplicity principle, the narrative diversity principle, the multi-dimensional development principle and the dynamic balance principle. The fourth level is the empirical analysis using a new paradigm of new-modernity research to analyze the major problems in the construction of Chinese socialist modernization including the problems of subject, social nature, culture and thoughts, development path, development mode, etc. in the construction of the socialist society with Chinese characteristics (Figure 1).

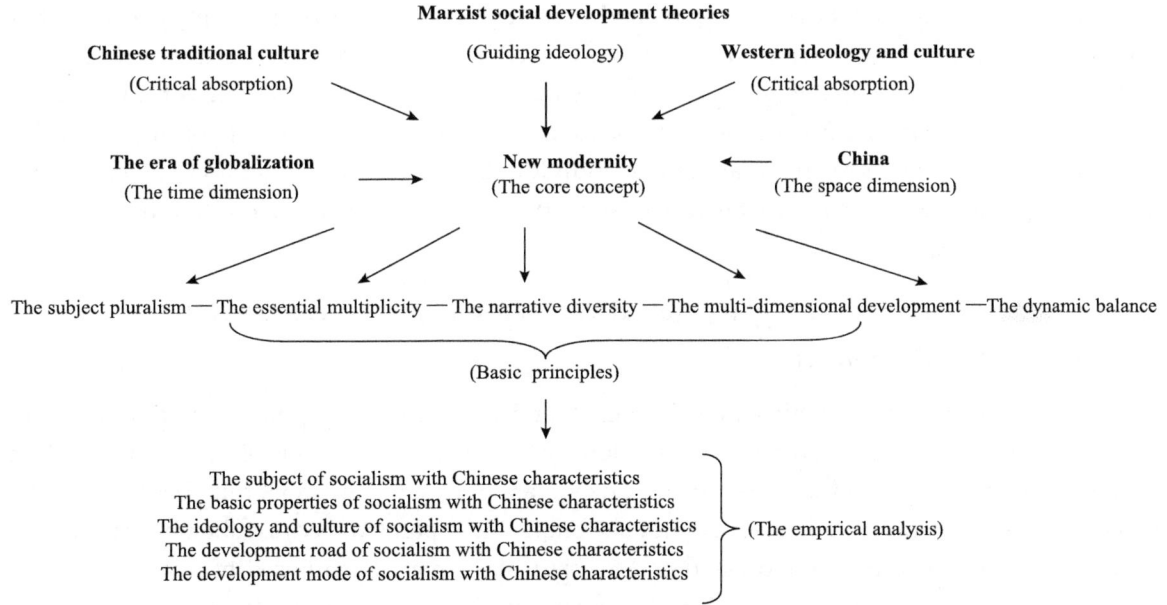

Figure 1 The Logical Structure of the New Modernity Research Paradigm

2. The Basic Connotations of the New Modern Research Paradigm

2.1 The Core Concepts of the New Research Paradigm — "New Modernity"

"New modernity" gives "new" to "modernity", and its meaning can be grasped respectively from two dimensions of time and space. From the perspective of time dimension, the formation of modernity has experienced the enlightenment period, the industrialization period and now has entered the post industrialization and globalization period, so "new modernity" does not refer to the modern enlightenment era, nor the modern industrialization era, but refers to the modernity of globalization and industrialization at present. From the perspective of space dimension, "new modernity" mainly characterizes this new type of modernity in the space scope of China. In addition to the general nature of modernity, it also shows the distinctive characteristics of Chinese modernization development. In short, "new modernity" is the essential multiplicity of new-type Chinese modernization in globalization era.

2.2 The First Basic Principle of the New Research Paradigm — the Principle of Subject Pluralism

New modernity emphasizes that subject has distinct characteristics: First, subject has hierarchy. The so-called subject refers to the behavior of a body with independent action ability, regardless of the size of this behavior. Subject can be divided into different levels from large to small as all mankind, nation, class (stratum), family and individual. Second, subject is relative. Mankind can be the subject because it is relative to the natural world; a state, a nation, a class (stratum), families and individuals can constitute the subject which is relative to other states, nations, classes (stratums), families and individuals.

Based on the characteristics of hierarchy and relativity of subject, new modernity considers that subject should not be an element, but should be diversified. The diversity of subjects is showing multiple levels verti-cally, that is to say, it not only has macro-level subjects such as humanity and state, but also has medium-level subjects such as nationality and class (stratum), and has microcosmic-level subjects such as family and individual. The diversity of subject is showing the mutual recognition horizontally, that is to say, at every level, subject is numerous and diverse, even mutually recognized.

2.3 The Second Basic Principle of the New Research Paradigm — the Essential Principles of Multiplicity

Essence is an important philosophical concept, and new modernity puts forward a viewpoint which is different from post modernity and modernity for relational problems of the essence of object as well as how to understand the essence and phenomenon. Firstly, new modernity believes that the essence and phenomenon of an object can not be completely separated, because the object itself is an inherent unity of phenomenon and essence. An object like onion is composed of many scales (fact elements), and each layer of scales (each fact element) can be seen as the epidermal (phenomenon), and can also be considered as the kernel (essence). In this way, we can get the first conclusion about the essence of new modernity, that is, the essence and phenomenon are homogeneous.

Secondly, new modernity considers that since the internal structure of every object like onion exists different levels, and each level can be regarded as the essence (or phenomenon) of a presentation, it is clear that the essence of object is not unitary and indivisible; on the contrary, the essence of object can be divided into multiple levels. The internal structure of object demonstrates the process from shallow level to deep level of essence, and then primary essence, intermediate essence and senior essence... From this we can get the second conclusion about the essence of new modernity, that is, the essence and phenomenon have multiplicity.

Thirdly, new modernity considers that every level of objects has duality of phenomenon-essence: It is essential in a shallow level, and in a deeper level it is phenomenon. This shows that any level in the structure of objects can not absolutely attribute to the essence or phenomenon, only to grasp the relative logical relation. Thus, we can get that the third conclusion about the essence of new modernity, that is, the essence and phenomenon have reciprocity.

2.4 The Third Basic Principle of the New Research Paradigm — the Principle of Diversity

Advocating the "grand narrative" is an important feature of modern discourse system. In 300 years, with the development of western modernization, the grand narrative is the basic form of expression by the mainstream discourse of Western intellectual circles. Western bourgeois democratic revolution makes the grand narrative of modernity gradually become the mainstream discourse in the Western society, and with the expanding of Western discourse in social knowledge system, the grand narrative of modernity has become the dominion discourse monopoly, and eventually will become a general and exclusive ideology. At this point, it is the main reason for the rejection of post-modernity of grand narrative. Although the critical discourse of post-modernity has some truth in debates with the discourse of modernity in the grand narrative of the exclusivity and homogeneous discourse monopoly, it is not advisable to completely deny the grand narrative but replaced by the so-called "micro narrative".

Through the critical analysis of grand narrative of modernity and micro narrative of post-modernity, new modernity has established its own narrative principle: Narrative level should be more diverse, and not only needs the grand narrative, but also needs ordinary narration. The grand narrative manifests the development power of whole human survival and historical process, the forward direction and goal as an abstract overall; the ordinary narration highlights each person's fresh and colorful features of life and tracks of activities. Only through the levels of diverse narrative for the real world, the way of narrative is full of vitality.

2.5 The Fourth Basic Principle of the New Research Paradigm — the Principle of Multi-dimensional Development

On development, new modernity identifies the views of the development progress of human society is under the action of general laws. However, new modernity has some significant differences on the understanding of human social and historical development with traditional modernity in the premise of recognizing the law of social development. In the view of traditional modernity, the historical process of human society is under the control of a common law according to an established direction to evolve and develop. New modernity believes that there are rules in human social movement, evolution and development, but it should not be understood as a certain law of causality, and should be understood as the common possibility of opening. In this sense, new modernity's emphasis on social development is not single and one-dimensional, but is multi-line and multi-dimensional, and thus, the multi-dimensional development constitutes an important principle of new modernity.

The fundamental difference between traditional modernity and new modernity in the concept of "development" is as follows: Traditional modernity development is defined as a unidirectional vector, and it is in a one-dimensional linear space; the unidirectional vector length shows the degree or stage of development to achieve. The development of new modernity is defined as a multi-dimensional vector; it is in a multi-dimensional (infinite dimensional) vector space, and the development of any dimensional vector is composed by the strength and direction of its development. The multi-dimensional vector development principle tells us that the development of human society has stage and direction, and social development is the organic combination of stage and direction. Society as a whole is a organic combined form by technical form, economic mode, political structure, cultural type, ethnic composition and natural environment. So the development of society is the inevitable result of each part of the whole social comprehensive development.

2.6 The Fifth Basic Principle of the New Research Paradigm — the Dynamic Balance Principle

Modernity advocates the struggle concept of binary opposition. In dealing with the relationship between people and people, the concept causes contradictions, confrontations and conflicts between individual and individual, class and stratum, ethnic and ethnic, and countries and countries. It has made the historical tragedy of countless lives and property destruction of to human society. In dealing with the relationship between man and nature, it has led to a worse relationship between man and nature. The avaricious plunder of human has been revenged by the nature. Based on the profound reflection on the lessons of history, new modernity suggests that we must follow the "dynamic balance" principle, and advocate new thinking, new ideas that man and man, man and society, man and nature could in the coexistence of multiple harmony and common prosperity .

The forward of the "dynamic balance" principle of new modernity has generally acknowledged the existence of differences and contradictions between objects, and at this point new modernity has similarities with modernity and proposes a criticism on post-modernity which denies the existence of contradictions and struggles between objects. Second, new modernity denies the absolute point of both sides against each other based on binary opposition. Third, new modernity thinks that the multivariate tolerance advocated by post-modernity and the Confucianism concept of moderation and harmony have the factors which are desirable for our time, but the common defects of them are that they ignore the internal contradictory movement. Fourth, new modernity acknowledges that paying attention to how to receive the dynamic balance between different objects is conflicting and competing under the premise of different objects that have differences and contradictions, which makes the whole system more harmonious.

Part Six

Regional Modernization & Reduction of Poverty and Inequalities

Socio-economic Development of Region in the Context of Modernization Processes: A Case Study of St. Petersburg

Liubov Lebedintseva

Faculty of Sociology, St. Petersburg State University

The Russian Federation consists of seven federal districts. The most developed districts are the Central Federal District and the North-Western Federal District. The first modernization in these districts is above average, but in large megalopolis (Moscow and St. Petersburg) the first modernization is completely ended. The subject of our study is the process of socio-economic development of St. Petersburg as a Russian region. It should be noted that the concept of a region may have two meanings. In the first sense, a region is the whole country and we can discuss the modernization process taking place in it. According to the second sense, a region means one part of a country. In this case, there are different levels of understandings: A region could be a large area, for example, the North-Western Federal District, and could be a separate area with the center and even the city (statistically significant). The unique status of a city or a region in the Russian Federation have two subjects — Moscow and St. Petersburg.

In all statistical sources, St. Petersburg represents a region in the Russian Federation. In our opinion, this fact provides additional opportunities for researchers. Socio-cultural and socioeconomic characteristics of urban space allow us to consider it as a separate, local, complex and holistic community. To understand the characteristics of such a region as a space of interaction, and its unique and special features, problems and prospects of modernization is the purpose of this paper.

The city as a historical phenomenon initially is varied in all aspects of life. The level of organization of the modern society allows us to consider the fact that urbanization process enhances the role of cities in society development. Special sociological theories of the city consider it as a unit cell of a larger social organism, that is a society. As a part of concrete historical society, the city reproduces complete social structure, elements and relationships of the holistic social system. In this case, in his theory of the division of labor in society, E. Durkheim noted that the professional division of labor is the basis of urbanization and the progressive development of a society, and the main way of historical development. Two positions of this theory are most relevant in our case: the city as a concentration space of life produces interaction of intensification; the city as a new form of socio-cultural integration is a transition to another society type (Durkheim, 1996). According to M. Weber, the emergence and logic of urban development depend on economic, political, cultural and spatial-temporal influences of the society (Weber, 1994: 309-447).

The city brings people together through new forms, based on changes in production, in particular the emergence of rationally organized economic sector. In these circumstances, human relationships begin to create their social environment (social and symbolic connectedness), and design and transform it (for example, community members of the same organization, professional identity, etc.). Even F. Tennis wrote about the difference between a community (rural community) and a society (urban, public association of people), mainly due to the presence of formal rationality in the second case. The development of trade, manufacturing and then large machines, establishes other relations with nature, which are different from that with agriculture. The mechanism of the capitalist mode of production in the city is fundamentally different from agricultural production in the feudal household in the village. The gradual development of economic activities is less directly dependent on the natural environment, and more needs the artificially created environment, which is understood as the market. Economic relations, created on the basis of rational and utilitarian principles of doing business, where a priori assumes the existence of commodities and money (economic exchange), can only exist where there is a market. The relationship between the natural environment and a person in these circumstances is necessary only indirect.

Thus, the city has a greater opportunity of choosing the place of occurrence, because natural factors have a smaller impact. Economic production in urban environments dictates the need for intensive development of spatial areas, and it also creates the preconditions and conditions of its successful economic functioning, which, unfortunately, does not always coincide with the concept of social efficiency. But in any case there is social space, which, according to G. Simmel, is only possible because of the energy activity of people (Simmel, 2001: 138-170). According to A. Giddens, the city also has a unique social space that gives the "form" of social relations and helps to establish social order. The uniqueness of cities is due to the fact that each of them is a result of social construction in specific historical conditions. There are common features for all cities and regions, according to which we can always assume upcoming opportunities for development.

For example, R. Park's theory of social ecology argued that social space was the same for all cities. R. Park wrote that the city was "a special organization with a typical biography, and that individual cities are similar enough to ensure that the knowledge about one city could be considered (in some measure) true to other cities" (Park , 2002: 3-12). Park compared the city with a social laboratory in which social experiments are constantly conducted due to the different social environments and conditions, and allocated according to the principle of local organization (different urban areas).

New forms of social and cultural integration are developed on the basis of cultural patterns of behavior, and the structure and communication tools are also changed. Such socio-cultural changes are unique to the new urban space. The major socio-cultural aspects of city regional modernization are heterogeneity, diversity and orientation towards novelty, etc.

Effective studies of regional life actualize the socio-economic reality of the city. It is largely expressed in ideas about the city's different actors of urban life. The modern city is the result of social construction, and it is intended to implement not only vital human needs, but also needs for creativity and self-realization, and to create a comfortable environment for work, rest and leisure.

Depending on the degree of satisfaction of needs, the levels of social, economic and cultural dynamics and mobility as well as innovation activity form attractiveness of urban space. Thus, socio-economic modernization and socio-cultural modernization as kinds of social transformation are inseparably linked.

1. The Space of Modernization in the Modern Region

There are new forms of urban structure in the modern society — the megacities, "global" cities. Urban spaces begin to explore creative, network, dataflow structures. This "fluidity" of the modern city involves the rejection of rigid structures, whether they are based on territorial, professional, social, etc. principles of dividing and producing new types of social relations and communities. There's a great significance of the economic and professional relationship (as opposed to kinship and neighborhood), and further development occurs in the context of removing the rigid forms of spatial, semantic and organizational structures. The emergence of creative clusters, creative spaces and free forms of professional activities, requires overcoming the rigid dichotomy between home and work (the concept of "work at home" is based on high level of information, computer development and technologies), overcoming the necessity for external management ("own boss" — a freelancer), waiving activities in professional sphere, with the possibility of returning (downshifting), and the transition to new forms of territorial organization of working activities, when, for example, professional identity is built not on the basis of belonging to one type of work (or profession), but through involvement in the professional community on a single limited area (as a rule, these are artificially created areas such as creative clusters). New spatial forms and modernization processes are formed by the dynamics of the social structure. From the perspective of the social modernization theory, space is the material support for social practices of time sharing in the sense that space brings together practices which are performed simultaneously. So, the space of flows appears as a new spatial form, and the material organization of time in a divided social practice that works through flows as purposeful and repetitive sequences of exchange and interaction between physically disconnected positions (which may be social actors in the economic, political and symbolic structures of society). Rigid structures are replaced by smooth transitions and fluidity of forms in postmodernity cities. To stop the development of cities is impossible in the modern society, their development leads to the emergence of megacities. All above-mentioned content applies more to metropolises, but gradually penetrates into the "social fabric", which is less populous settlement.

2. Modernization "Gene" of St. Petersburg

At the moment, the metropolis is the major form of urban settlement with inclusion of the surrounding settlements. For the first time the cities have been allocated in a separate group by the known scholar J. Gotman in the 1960s. The peculiarities of the metropolis, in addition to large sizes, include the leading role of business, political and financial centers of national and world levels, the presence of international organizations, outstanding importance as a center of culture and art, the role of major international transport hub, the development of the service sector, the concentration of highly skilled types of activities (Maximov and Semenenko, 2012).

Modern megalopolises play an important role in the economy of the country. For example, in

European countries, cities account for up to 50% of GDP: Copenhagen provides 49.6%; Dublin, Brussels, Helsinki and Budapest 42%-47%; Vienna, London, Paris, Stockholm and Tokyo 28%-34%. St. Petersburg is the largest city in Russia after Moscow, the fourth city in Europe (after Moscow, Paris and London), the only European city, wholly included in the UNESCO World Heritage List. It's no longer the official capital of the Russian Federation, but known by everyone as the "cultural capital"; many new phenomena of our (Soviet and new Russian) life for the first time implement at St. Petersburg's (Petrograd, Leningrad) territory. The importance of strategy and creativity is the original idea of the city proposed by Peter the First. St. Petersburg is the center of huge cultural and human capital, the returns from which in the future should be much more significant in comparison with the natural resources of those financial and political capitals, and will play a significant role in the modernization of the country.

In fact, modernization implies an endless process of "modernizing" society. Chinese method of analyzing modernization in relation to Russian regions is used in our research (He, 2011). N. Lapin and L. Belyaeva as scholars from the Center for the Study of Social and Cultural Changes (Institute of Philosophy) design instruments adapting this method to Russian conditions.

So, according to the estimates of researchers and the available statistical information, St. Petersburg has already completed the first modernization. Assessing indices of the first modernization and the second modernization shows positive dynamics of index growth for the period of 2000-2012. The conclusion is that St. Petersburg is in a phase of maturity of evolution. Gross regional product (GRD) is among the factors: more than 4.6% of the total GRP of Russia is in St. Petersburg. It should be noted that St. Petersburg is in full measure metropolis of post-industrial economy; in the structure of it, 67.7% GRP belongs to the service sector. There is a high level for Russia's region life expectancy — 73.5 years old almost, 100% literacy rate of the population, and the high proportion of university students — for every 100 young people aged from 18 to 22 years old, the students in St. Petersburg account for 76. The index of the second modernization is 97.8. This index includes the index of innovation in the knowledge (based on the share of research and development expenditures in GDP, the number of scientists and engineers per 10 thousand people and the residents who file patent applications is 109.1), the index of knowledge transition (considering the students of secondary and higher education institutions, the number of televisions and personal computers per 100 households is 101.2), the index of the quality of life (the number of urban population, physicians per 1,000 people, infant mortality rate, life expectancy and energy efficiency is 112.4), and the index of the quality of the economy (68.4). In general, there have shown the good indicators of GRP in St. Petersburg. But GDP per capita and purchasing power parity have very low rates (indices for these indicators are only 34.2 and 61.9, respectively). For this reason, the index of the quality of the economy in St. Petersburg has such a low value compared to other more "optimistic" looking indicators. According to the index of human development among Russian regions, St. Petersburg is the second, after Moscow, with a value of 0.89.

The result of the integrated modernization as a coordinated interaction of both phases of St. Petersburg is also at a high level (81.3%). This index reflects not only the level of economic development (growth of productivity), but also the level of social characteristics (the standard of living), the achievements in the field of knowledge production and reproduction, and the distribution of knowledge.

The growth of economic modernization is limited by the unclaimedness of cultural (creative) potential of the population and the lack of its distribution into an active cultural capital in Russia. So, N. Lapin wrote that the greatest contribution to the imbalance between processes of the second (informational) modernization introduces three indicators: the low proportion of residents applying for patents, the low level of GDP per capita, and a relatively large share of the employed in material production and insufficient share of services in GDP (Lapin, 2012: 4-23). As to the second and third indicators mentioned above in St. Petersburg, things are pretty good. However, as to active participation in patenting, the picture is complicated. On the number of patents issued for inventions, the situation for nine years in the region has changed so slightly that it is difficult to talk about any clear trends. After the surge in 2009, the indicators returned to the level of 2005 and was even lower: In 2005, 1,376 patents for inventions were issued; in 2009, 1,778 patents; in 2013, 1,357 patents. The situation was different with the granting of patents for utility models: The growth rate was 33.4 % (from 696 patents in 2005 to 1,045 patents in 2013). This is largely due to the fact that to obtain a patent for the utility model is easier and cheaper than to obtain a patent on invention. The utility model provides rather convenient option protection solutions for small and medium businesses. Currently in Russia only one of the 500 patented inventions is used in the industry. The percentage of patents granted to foreign applicants almost annually increases, which indicates the interest of foreign investors in the Russian market and the desire to take an active part in it. The number of annually obtained patents for industrial designs of international applicants surpassed that of Russian in 2009, and in 2010 every one in fourth patents was owned by the applicants from other countries. Unfortunately, the results of the Russian research and development are almost not in demand abroad. Russia is on the border of the second and third dozen countries on the activity in the foreign market of research and development.

The basis of the GDP of developed countries is the service sector. So in this sense, Russia is a society which is still only in the process of establishing their post-industrial way of life. The "smart economy" demands the development of science and rapidly implements its achievements in high technology. For example, information technology is the basis of world economic development. In this direction, much has been done in St. Petersburg. In 2010 the federal target program "Electronic Russia" was ended, and in 2011 another program was started, "Information Society 2011-2020", in which the city actively participates. In addition, St. Petersburg operated its own regional program — "Development of Information Society in St. Petersburg in 2013-2016". As a result, there are very attractive socio-economic conditions of innovative activities in the region. For example, the development of information and communication technologies every year enables to grow the amount of information services. Experience in internet has the vast majority (almost 80%) of the adult population of St. Petersburg. The majority of consumers have a choice of different types of services depending on access speed, service, quality and price (the region has more than 100 organizations that provide access to internet resources).

The activities of ICT companies in St. Petersburg demonstrate how intensively the north-western region of Russia is developing all the existing directions of communication, and suggest that St. Petersburg is moving towards integration into a global information space. The importance of ICT industry is reflected in the constant increase of the number of graduates in IT-specialties and the share of this sector in GRP (estimated as 5.2%). For comparison, in developed countries, this share to date reaches 10%-15%.

According to the index of preparedness for information society, St. Petersburg occupies the second place among regions of Russia with an index of 0.612. St. Petersburg has a high value of electronic development factors: human capital, and ICT infrastructure. But the importance of the economic environment factor in St. Petersburg is only 0.526 (12th place).

It should be noted that citizens participate in the innovation processes. So, according to the poll, the respondents taking part in the creation of a new company occupy 6%, new product 12%, new technology 9%, and new services 13%. According to another study "Higher School of Economics" conducted by the National Research University jointly with the Institute for Statistical Studies and Economy of Knowledge, the rating of innovative development is created. It represents a ranking of regions in Russian about innovation index. Only by one sub-index — the quality of innovation policy, St. Petersburg falls to the 11th place in the second group of regions; for other indices, St. Petersburg traditionally occupies the first or the second place, competing only with Moscow. It can be argued that St. Petersburg as a city with a high level of modernization "requires" a greater involvement of social community and institutions in the process of creating a new one.

Social well-being of citizens in a survey is at a high level. So, about the question "Do you think the people of our region live better or worse than the residents of the neighboring regions?", 55% of respondents answer positively. The most attractive features of this region include: a perspective region for life (56%), many opportunities for enterprising people (48%), and beautiful scenery (30%). Positive emotions in relation to their region are experiencing an overwhelming majority of respondents — 84%. However, this does not preclude the vision of gaps and opportunities to improve the social aspects of life in this region. It can be stated that the high integrated ranking of St. Petersburg does not mean the disappearance of most of the problems inherent in the Russian society. So the answers to the question "What needs to be done to improve the life standards?" rank all the main problems of St. Petersburg: to bring order, to combat crime and corruption (48%), to improve health care (41%), to build affordable housing (34%), to develop small and medium business (30%), to revive the nature (30%), to reform education (22%), and to create new work place (20%). As well as other regions throughout the country, the inhabitants of St. Petersburg do not feel protected from these dangers in modern society such as poverty (29% of respondents) and the arbitrariness of officials (55%). Extortion, bribery and corruption were encountered by 42% of citizens in 2014.

The complexity of the social organization of the city's life and the difficult situation in the country influence the respondents' answers about their future: More than 20% of respondents are not confident about their future, 22% can't say for sure, but more than half of respondents say they are confident about their future. The overall inhabitants are satisfied with their life (71% of respondents).

The study shows that there is a positive approach to solve existing problems, and it also reveals that there are problems inherent in all Russian regions (low level of life, a sense of vulnerability from social and economic risks, the compression space of socio-political freedom and rights of citizens). These problems as well as traditional personal values and attitudes, hamper the positive process of transformation and modernization of society as well as the realization of accumulated human potential. The main problems, in particular, are high-level population stratification and poverty, wealth inequality, as well as social, professional and educational differentiation in this region.

3. The Growth Points of the City

About cultural capital of St. Petersburg, as often referred to the "northern capital", it is known by everyone and we cannot deny it still has relevant values. However, we would like to mention a new and important process, sometimes unexpected, in cultural and economic spheres of the city, which has a strong impact on the urban environment. The emergence of the city is directly related to its potential ability to relatively rapid reconstruction and transformation.

Complex and dynamic analyses of the situation demonstrate the type of integrated modernization, which measures the aggregated level of both stages of modernization in the region and shows the strategy for its development.

Modern metropolis is in a state of transition from rigid structures and relations to more soft and blurred structures and relations. The qualitative transformation of the urban structure of the population can be observed in the emergence of the creative class, which requires certain conditions for its development. R. Florida defined it as a group of people with common interests and tending to think, feel and behave similarly, which depends on what kind of work a person does. The reason for the formation of a new social class is economic needs for creativity, new ideas, new technologies and new creative content of work. This class is filled with professionals engaged in the fields of science, technology, education, health and related fields as well as art, design, business, finance, etc. (Florida, 2005). The urban environment provides such professionals necessary conditions. Active energy of the subject appears as a social space through "creative ethos", which is shared by all representatives of the creative class and in which important creativity, individuality, personal merit, and technological, cultural, and economic implications can become unified and interrelated. St. Petersburg has always been a tolerant city, including the expression of their own identities. Changes in economy have given rise to this class, and the city is involved in this situation.

For the definition and development of creativity, Charles Landry offered the concept of "the cycle of urban creativity" as a tool designed to create a special energy in the city, being a renewable resource development, a strategic management tool, and a mechanism for assessing the strengths and weaknesses of urban creative projects. Landry identified five interrelated phases of the cycle of urban creativity, ending with turning ideas into real practice (Landry, 2005). It should be noted that some cities only declaratively appeal to creative industries, copying the experience of other cities, without analyzing the existing urban assets, and often neglect the need to combine the organizational arrangements at the municipal or district level with proactive creative-minded inhabitants. Thus, the request by the society for creative products and ideas sets the dynamics, which structures the creative process and further promotes the generation of new ideas that arise in the new environment — creative clusters. Creativity produces creativity, creating new circles and involving more and more people and resources.

The main characteristic of the creative clusters of technology parks and business incubators is that they are directly integrated into the urban environment. For the first time the concept of creative blocks as a parallel development of cultural and economic life of the territory appears, which is formed not so long ago. In the UK the creative industries are supported by government policies since 1998. St. Petersburg from 2012 to 2013, held an open debate on the "Concept of Producing a Creative Cluster in St. Petersburg" with the possibility of further stating support for the funding of the project. In 2012, with the support of administration, St. Petersburg created five creative quarters for mixed-use developments, with one operator providing all conditions for comfortable working of the cluster. Each quarter should unite various workshops, exhibition and educational space, recreation and creative activity, retail space, offices, creative organizations, business incubator, hotel, clubs, cafes and restaurants. The project should support themselves independently, and doesn't need almost any investment budget. At the same time it is transforming depressed urban areas of the city into attractive places for tourists and citizens. As potential platforms for creative clusters, they propose the building of the detention facility "Kresti", admiralty shipyards, Levashovskiy bread baking, spinning-thread combination named after Kirov, rope factory of Goth, etc. In addition, creative entrepreneurs in St. Petersburg organize such famous creative spaces as "Tkachi", "Etazhi", "Architector", "Fligel", "Tretii cluster", "Multiplase 17/26". Similar examples of new forms of activity in the city suggest that the city is a living system, and is able to fill a "frozen" form of continuing to develop content.

Today, world exports of goods and services of creative industries contribute significantly to total GDP growth. Since 2002 it has annually increased by 14.4% on average and has amounted to 59,208 billion (2.73% of the total world exports). Combining the interests and efforts of the state, business and creative organizations are able to form additional direction in the development of the economy of the region. The creative sector has considerable export potential and is based on copyright law, and in addition, refurbishment of the emergency facilities and industrial buildings contributes to the recovery of depressed areas.

Thus, the analysis shows that one of the main ways to reduce socio-economic problems is to develop new forms of economy activity such as creative clusters, which helps to realize measures of social policies to improve living standards, reindustrialization of production, etc. Overall, both existing spaces and newly created spaces have the potential to solve many social and economic problems of the city.

References

何传启(He C Q). 2010. 世界和中国现代化报告概要(2001—2010). 北京: 北京大学出版社.
Belyaeva L. 2012. The modernization of Russia — modernization of regions. Philosophical Sciences, 7: 5-6.
Durkheim E. 1996. The Division of Labor in Society. Moscow: Nauka (Science). (In Russian)
Florida R. 2005. The Rise of the Creative Class and How It's Transforming Work, Leisure, Community and Everyday Life. Moscow: Classica-XXI. (In Russian)
Gokhberg L M. 2012. Rating of innovative development of subjects of the Russian Federation: The analytical report. Moscow: High School Economics. (In Russian)
Khvatova T, Lebedintseva L. 2013. The process of innovation infrastructure creation in Russia: An exploratory study of St. Petersburg. In Impact: The Journal of Innovation Impact, 5(1): 31-42.
Landry C. 2005. The Creative City: A Toolkit for Urban Innovators. Trans. by V Gnedovsky and M Khrustaleva. Moscow: Classica-XXI. (In Russian)
Lapin N I. 2012. Measurement of modernization of the Russian regions and sociocultural factors of its strategy. Sociological Researches, 9: 4-23. (In Russian)
Maximov S N, Semenenko V V. 2012. Features and problems of development of modern megalopolises. http://www.m-economy.ru/ art.php?nArtId=4113 [2015-12-18]. (In Russian)
Park P. 2002. City as social laboratory. Sociologicheskoe obozrenie (Sociological review), 2(3-12). (In Russian)

Simmel G. 2001. Sociology of space. In D Frisby and M Featherstone (Eds.), Simmel on Culture (pp. 138-170). London: Sage Publications.

Veselov Y V. 2012. Economic sociology of one city (space of St. Petersburg). The Magazine of Sociology and Social Anthropology, XI (2): 153-185. (In Russian)

Weber M. 1994. City. In M Weber (Ed.), Favourites (pp. 309-447). Moscow: Lawyer. (In Russian)

Regional Modernization and Sustainable Development in a Mining Region from the Habsburg Monarchy (Transylvania) in 1750-1914

Iosif Marin Balog

The "George Barițiu" Institute of History, Cluj-Napoca
Babeș-Bolyai University, Cluj-Napoca, Romania

1. The Regional Economic Area of the Apuseni Mountains in the 19th Century (1800-1914) as well as Specific Features, Modernization and Development

Ever since the 18th-19th centuries, geological academia has recorded the fact that the Apuseni Mountains represented the richest gold-field region of Europe. The travelogues and the geological maps compiled in the 18th-19th centuries by various specialists sent here by the Erarium Province pinpointed the existence of myriad locations with extremely rich gold ore deposits[1].

A territory of about 800 km² was thus circumscribed, comprising, at the end of the 19th century, over 77% of Transylvania's total production of gold. There were, thus, 33 larger or smaller settlements, four of which have enjoyed, since the 18th century, the status of mining cities, endowed with privileges during previous periods or after the installation of the Austrian administration in 1691[2]. Moreover, in the 18th century these urban or quasi-urban settlements had a special status, as regards both the fiscal system and mining law. They were organized into the so-called mining domains (or districts).

An attempt at identifying the stages in the evolution of mining in "auriferous quadrilateral of Transylvania" during the modern period reveals the existence of three distinct periods: 1745-1850,

---

[1] Edler Ignaz von Born, Briefe über mineralogische Gegenstände auf seiner Reise durch das Temeswarer Banat, Siebenbürgen Ober-und Nider Ungarn, Frankfurt u. Leipzig: Johann Jakab Ferber Verlag, 228 S. See also Johann Ehrenreich von Fichtel, Mineralogische Bemerkungen von den Karpaten. Wien: Joseph Edlen von Kurybeck k. k. Hofbuchdrucker, 2 Bände, 736 S.

[2] See, in this sense, Gustav Gündisch. Deutsche Bergwerksiedlungen in dem siebenbürgischen Erzgebirge. In Aus Geschichte und Kultur der Siebenbürger Sachsen. Ausgewälte Aufsätze und Berichte, Köln- Weimar-Wien, 1987: 85.

1850-1880, and 1880-1914. This periodization has more of an orientative function, because it is impossible to establish strict chronological boundaries.

The first period of modern gold mining began in Transylvania in 1745-1850, when the region came into the attention of the Vienna authorities, who realized the economic potential of mining in Transylvania, not only in the field of gold and silver, but also in that of iron, copper, lead ores, etc., and started to reorganize these activities on new grounds. Since the spirit of a mercantilist policy has already enshrined throughout the whole Habsburg Empire, the activity of mining was supported in every way possible, both in the mines owned by the state (Erarium) and, especially, in the private sector that was a dominant share in Transylvania, providing most of the gold delivered at the exchange offices. Indeed, the revival of gold mining in the Apuseni Mountains was achieved after many decades of stagnation, thanks to the measures imposed by Empress Maria Theresa. In addition, the state was involved in the development and construction of new collector lakes to ensure the water necessary for the operation of stamp mills, since there were long periods throughout the year in which these stamp mills could not function because of the lack of water, negatively affecting the quantity of gold dispatched to the exchange offices. The majority of the institutions that had to ensure the functioning and supervision of mining (the mining inspectorate, the main exchange office, the mercury shop) were, in fact, concentrated in this region. Particular attention was paid to the functioning of the exchange offices, which were constantly supplied with sums of money necessary for the weekly acquisition of the precious metal. Vienna's principle of conduct as regards the gold mining conducted by private miners could be summed up in the phrase: "Work and pay me!" In the same sense, the Vienna authorities considered that it was extremely important to encourage, in the long term, mining activities in the area of the Apuseni Mountains and to reconfirm the old individual and collective privileges of the miners. Since serf labour had an important share in agriculture and mining in Transylvania, including on the domains from the area of the Apuseni Mountains, the state got involved in taking measures in favour of the mining serfs, who had to be protected from their feudal masters. The latter generally tried to impose new obligations upon the serfs, both on those who worked mainly in agriculture and those who, in theory, earned a living from mining and had no obligations to the agricultural landlords. It should be emphasized that up to 1848, serf labour played a significant role in the gold mining activities of the state. This aspect was regulated on several occasions, including by means of contracts of the Erarium with the local communities, under which they were bound to carry out mining-related activities, such as those involving the transportation of wood required for the foundries, road repair work and all other activities adjacent to mining. Another characteristic of this period was the disputes between the provincial and the higher mining authorities, i.e. between the Gubernium of Transylvania and the Vienna officials. On the one hand, the latter saw the intensification of the obligations imposed on serfs as serious obstacles in the way of increasing the production of gold and silver; on the other hand, the Gubernium had no such interest, being concerned only to protect the interests of the local landlords, who also represented the local administration and often regarded by Vienna as incompetent and corrupt.

The legislation passed in 1747 and the administrative measures adopted during the reign of Maria Theresa and Joseph II endorsed the reorganization of mining in Transylvania on new bases, in keeping with the practices of the time. Their main aim was, on the one hand, to systematize the multitude of old and unsystematic local regulations, bringing them, as far as possible, under the umbrella of uniform principles and practices, and on the other hand, to give a new impetus to gold mining, both through private enterprisers and, above all, through the active involvement of the state, in the spirit of a mercantilist policy[①]. The state was aware of the importance and the potential of private mining. In particular, the so-called peasant mining provided the bulk of the gold extracted and the state endeavoured, through various administrative measures, to support it. Moreover, Vienna aimed to become involved in the opening of new mines, with the meagre resources, and it was willing to invest in them with the meagre resources, so as to exploit deep ore deposits for whose exploitation the private enterprisers lacked the necessary capital and opportunities. The strategy was that the state should open these mining operations and then rent them to private mining companies.

In addition, a specific feature of gold mining in Transylvania up to 1850, whether we talk of large-scale or peasant enterprises, was the persistent use of the old technologies. Certainly, the mining administrations sought to introduce technological innovations that enhanced productivity and reduced human effort, but they were limited to technological and energetic resources that were locally available. These were solutions that were independent from technological developments in other parts of Europe. The state's investment strategies were no exception in this regard; although there sometimes were such initiatives and the specialists sent to the scene of the place carried out serious studies, as in the case of Baia de Arieș or Roșia Montană, these initiatives were quickly abandoned when it was found that necessary capital was lacking or when the higher mining authorities in Vienna refused to approve more consistent and long-term investment plans. Every time the problem of investment came up or technical problems emerged and the costs of exploiting the galleries were high, the Erarium preferred either to abandon them or to lease them out or sell them, when new and easily exploitable deposits were discovered.

The second period 1850-1880 may be associated with a new stage in gold mining. While no major or significant changes occurred from a technological viewpoint, certain transformations were visible at the level of legislation or institution, as regards the administration and supervision of the mining activities. Last but not least, some of the changes were the results of the new entrepreneurial strategies adopted by the state in its own exploitations.

The economic policies of the state in an era of administrative authoritarianism and political conservatism as well as economic liberalism led to the adoption of new economic legislation, in keeping with the realities of the time, including the field of mining. Thus, the Mining Law of 1854 was an act of exceptional importance, because alongside other legislative measures regulating industry and trade, it deeply influenced regional economic life. In fact, during the period 1850-1885 gold mining in the Apuseni Mountains perpetuated the so-called "predatory" mining practices, including the search for rich ore deposits and native gold ores as well as the avoidance of poorer ores due to the high costs of extraction and smelting. Still, there was an intense activity of the private mine owners in Transylvania, primarily due to the state's permissive policy, with protectionist tendencies against foreign capital that had ambivalent effects in the region: While annual production was maintained at 1,000-1,500 kg annually[②], the actual income of both the entrepreneurs and the workers underwent a

---

[①] Wollmann V. Der siebenbürgische Bergbau im 18. Jahrhundert. In Silber und Salz... Bd. 1., S. 41-58.

[②] The data also appear in L Vajda's Locul mineritului..., but the author cited does not make reference to the manner of calculation and the sources used.

rather noticeable decline amidst the general growth of prices.

The year 1885 marked the entry into the third period of the modern history of gold mining in the Apuseni region. The launching of major investments naturally led to a concentration of mining exploitations in the region, as many individual owners decided to sell their galleries or perimeters they had leased. Foreign capitals and local entrepreneurs engaged in land transactions, buying land from private owners, leasing it from the state and opening new exploitation perimeters and galleries. Basically, a process of fierce competition began, dozens of mining properties passing quickly from one owner to another. Multiple mergers took place, as big companies, especially the foreign ones, attempted to concentrate their production capacities in compact areas in order to create conditions for profitability and cost reduction. Along with the French, Belgian and British capital, the German capital proved to be the most active. Thus, thanks to capital investments and technological innovations, the area along the valleys of the Arieș and White Criș rivers turned, within only a few years, into the most modern and the largest gold exploitations in Europe. Here worked around 2,195 employees in 1910.

2. Demographic Developments

The analysis of the demographic evolution in the "auriferous quadrilateral" in the period 1850-1910 reflects, to some extent, the socio-economic processes that took place in the region. What can be seen clearly from the analysis of the demographic data, in conjunction with the evolution of mining in the area, the dynamics of exploitations (reflected in the amount of gold mined) and the number of those involved in specific gold mining activities, is the existence of a visible correlation of the quantitative data that reveal all these indicators. Without aiming to highlight the economic factor as an absolute determinant, we should underline a series of aspects that indicate both convergences with and divergences from similar demographic evolutions at the level of entire Transylvania.

According to Figure 1, which takes into account 33 localities from the region studied[1], from 1850 to 1910 the population increased in absolute figures, from 34,906 to 44,354 inhabitants. This represents an actual numerical increase of 9,448 inhabitants by 27.06%.

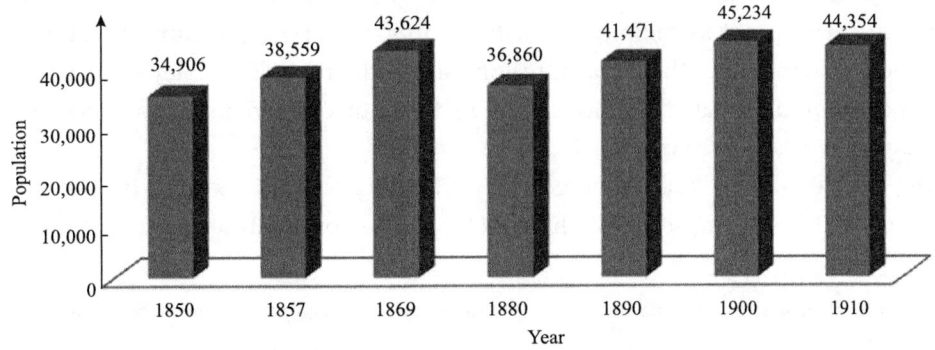

Figure 1   The Demographic Evolution of the "Auriferous Quadrilateral" 1850-1910

---

[1] Schumacher's map recorded 33 localities, as mentioned in our table. Although there were small mountain villages adjacent to these administrative units, we will focus only on the 33 localities where gold was exploited, one way or another.

Correlating these numbers with the population growth at the level of entire Transylvania during this period, we can notice that although this is an upward trend, it is far below the general average of 40.4%[1].

Like at the level of the entire province, demographic growths occurred both in the period 1850-1857 and in the next decade were 10.46% and 24.97%, respectively. From an economic point of view, the region was on an upward trend, marked by the new economic and legislative atmosphere. Private enterprises experienced an unprecedented expansion. Although the old technological processes continued to be used, the amount of gold extracted underwent a steady growth during this period: If the area produced around 820 kg of gold in 1850, 1864 saw a maximum production of 1,420 kg, the annual average exceeding 1,100 kg[2].

The decade 1871-1880 witnessed a demographic decline of 15.51% at the regional level, far above the average in Transylvania, which during the same period showed a population decline by 5.8%[3]. This was the period of the economic crisis triggered in 1873, which strongly affected the mining activities in the region. Thus, while in 1873 there were no less than 516 larger or smaller exploitations that employed 8,369 permanent and temporary workers, in 1876 there were only 383 mining exploitations, employing 6,613 workers[4], most of the small-scale private enterprises have suspended their activities due to their lack of capital and rudimentary technological equipment that led to very low profitability levels and revenues. Of course, we should not omit other demographic causes, above all the virulent cholera epidemic that broke out in the Apuseni Mountains in 1873.

By contrast, the following period revealed a higher demographic growth in this region (by 12% compared to the previous decade) than that at the level of the entire province, the Transylvanian average for this decade being 8.3%[5]. As regards the economic development, a radical change occured in the gold mining sector after 1884, when foreign capital made its appearance in the region. This was the period when towns and villages like Brad, Ruda and Crișcior underwent spectacular demographic growth, the most important investments being concentrated here. This demographic growth was partly due to immigrations outside the region, these settlements becoming attractive centres for those looking for a job.

Ten years later, we find the same upward trend of demographic growth (9.7%) compared with the previous decade, revealing a convergence with the average of Transylvania (9%)[6], amid generally positive economic development in those areas where the volume of investments was higher. Technologization and the concentration of production at the level of several mining companies made them dominate the gold mining sector in this region, in terms of both productivity and the number of workers employed.

However, the evolution was divergent in the decade 1901-1910: Whereas Transylvania witnessed an overall demographic growth of 8.3%, the region analysed revealed a demographic

---

[1] Bolovan I. Transilvania între revoluția de la 1848 și Unirea din 1918. Contribuții demografice. Cluj-Napoca: Fundația Cluturală Română, 2000: 35.

[2] Statistisches Handbuchlein für die Österreichische Monarchie von der k. k. Direktion der administrativen Statistik, Wien, 1864.

[3] Ioan Bolovan, op. cit., p. 36.

[4] Vajda L. Locul mineritului din Săcărâmb în cadrul exploatării metalelor prețioase din Transilvania în a doua jumătate a secolului al XIX-lea. In Studia Universitatis Babeș-Bolyai. Historia fasciculus 1, 1973: 68.

[5] Ioan Bolovan, op. cit., p. 37.

[6] Ibidem, p. 45.

decline by nearly two percentage points (1.94%). The situation may seem paradoxical if we consider that the mining activity continued to intensify, and having been dominated, for a good while, by a few large companies with foreign capital. On the one hand, a significant restriction affected the small private exploitations, whose land tended to be leased to larger companies. Given the new technologies they had implemented and financed, these companies limited the number of workers they employed. This maximum level reached a peak value around the 1900s, after which it stagnated. On the other hand, in the case of state-owned mines in Roșia Montană and Săcărâmb, mining activities stagnated and even declined amid a lack of investments and up-to-date technologization. At Săcărâmb, the gold deposits were nearing exhaustion. As a result, the surplus workers in the region who failed to find employment in the gold mining sector were forced to choose the path of emigration. One of their destinations was the Jiu Valley, an area whose economic profile was similar to that of the Apuseni Mountains, and the Jiu Valley was relatively close to the Apuseni Mountains in geographical terms, so it attracted, during this period, an important demographic contingent.

The relationship between the economic development and the demographic trends in the goldfield region of the Apuseni Mountains can also be highlighted at the level of villages and towns. The author has chosen for this purpose nine situations where the mining activities were carried out in different ways and at specific rhythms. These situations can be grouped into three patterns.

(1) The first pattern is a pattern of significant demographic growth, at Brad, Crișcior and Ruda, where the activities of large foreign-owned companies were concentrated at the end of the 19th century. The most important company of this kind was Harkort'sche Bergwerke und Chemische Fabriken zu Schwelm und Harkorten AG in Goth, whose headquarter was located in Brad and who gradually took over vast auriferous perimeters at Musari, Ruda, Valea Morii, etc., creating the largest mining area administered by this company in the Apuseni Mountains[1]. These localities had the highest demographic growth rates in the entire "auriferous quadrilateral". Thus, from 1850 to 1910, the population had increased by 126.39% at Brad, by 165.60% at Crișcior, and by 76.29% at Ruda (Figure 2).

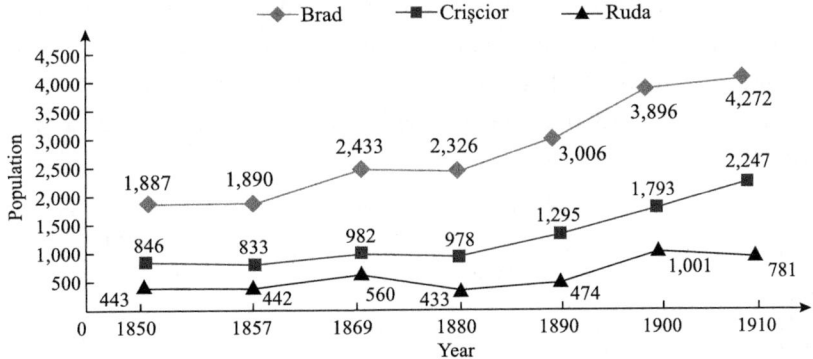

Figure 2　A Comparative Demographic Evolution in 1850-1910

(2) The second pattern — demographic decline — was detectible at Căraci, Roșia Montană and

---

[1] Wendenborn B A. Die Goldindustrie in der Umgebung von Brád (Siebenbürgen). In Slotta R, Wollmann V, Doredea I, (Hrsg.) Silber und Salz in Siebenbürgen, Vol. 10, Part Ⅱ, Bochum 2010, pp. 1319-1356.

Săcărâmb. It should be noted that in these localities, the state owned the largest share in the gold mining sector. Roșia Montana was an exception, because there were numerous small private exploitations. Although the production of all these mines had been very good right up to the end of the 19th century, the lack of high-profile investments, the declining ore concentration and the technical problems associated with poorly designed underground exploitations generated a drop in productivity and a rather large fluctuation of employment possibilities. The demographic decline at Roșia Montană was 7.18%, evincing a continuous process of population decline after 1870. The same process affected Săcărâmb, where the population decreased throughout the period 1850-1910. By 1910, the population had declined by 54.79% there. At Căraci the population dropped by 20% (Figure 3).

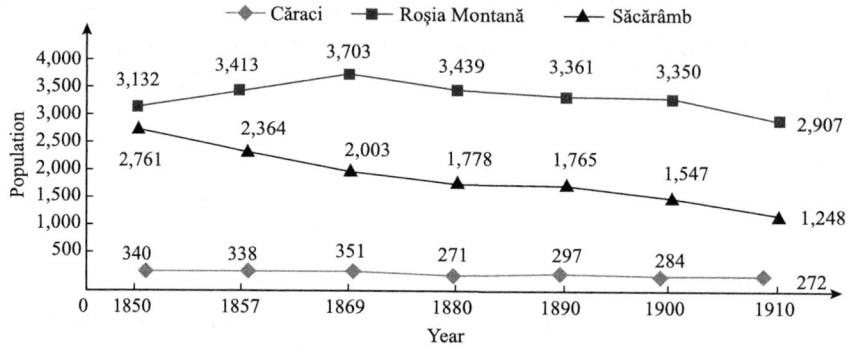

Figure 3   A Comparative Demographic Evolution in 1850-1910

(3) The third pattern — demographic "stagnation" — was encountered in several villages in the region. In the three examples we have chosen, mining was done mostly through small private operations, which, alongside agriculture, provided the inhabitants of the area with modest livelihood sources. There were many such exploitations, both at Bucium and at Țebea, which were carried out with traditional technological means by the local, these areas being insufficiently dynamic and attractive to absorb workforce from the outside. At Certeju de Sus, the closing of the smeltery in 1882 resulted in a significant decline in economic activities, and demographic growth was just over 2.53%. In Bucium there was an increase of 13.25%, well below the region's average (27.06%). The situation in Țebea revealed a special case: If we look at the data reported at the two chronological extremities (1850-1910), there was a demographic decline of 0.16%. It should be noted, however, that the period 1890-1910 witnessed an increase of 14.99%, and in 1910 the decrease was 54.79% (Figure 4).

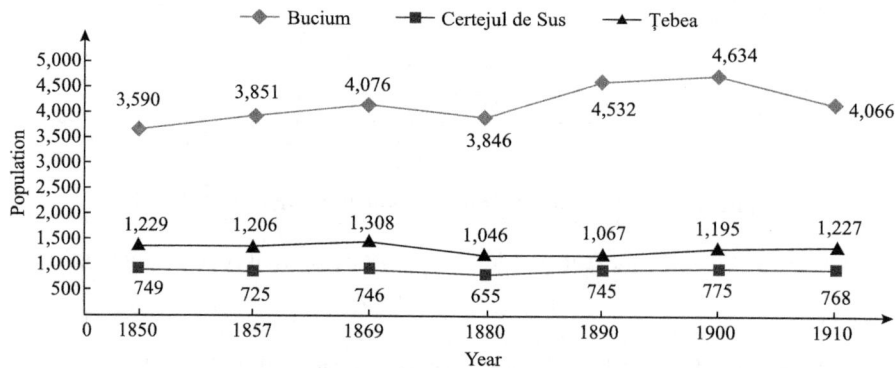

Figure 4   A Comparative Demographic Evolution in 1850-1910

Another demographic aspect that reveals the modernization of a region is the share of urban population. From the very beginning, it should be noted that only two of the 33 localities were towns (Abrud and Zlatna). In 1850 the population of these two towns amounted to 5,083, i.e. 14.56% of population in the region studied. In 1910 they had 7,255 inhabitants, i.e. 16.35% of the region's population, the percentage share being above the average of Transylvania's urban population, which at that time was 12.4% (Figure 5)[1].

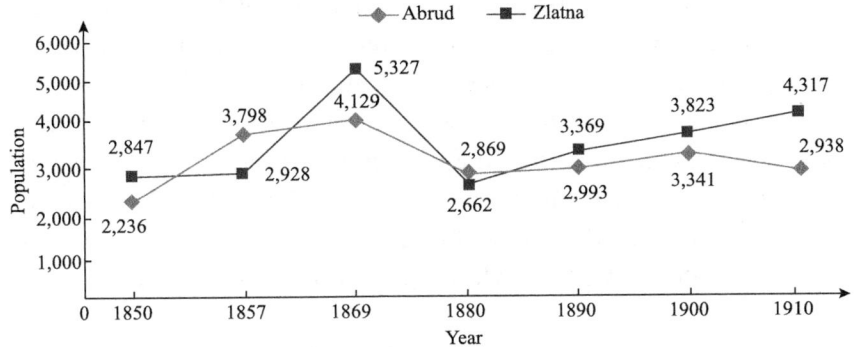

Figure 5　A Comparative Demographic Evolution in 1850-1910

However, it cannot be claimed that the region was urbanized. These small mining towns lacked the force of attraction, the resources and the potential necessary for becoming urban centres. They relied on a restricted set of activities: Abrud was a mining town and, in addition, it concentrated several commercial activities that ensured a market of modest demands for the surrounding villages. A series of administrative functions of local interest were added to it as well (the town housed the headquarter of a circle/district or plasă). Zlatna was an important mining centre and was also the mining captaincy that coordinated, along with the Directorate of Mines and Salt Mines in Cluj, the mining activities across most of Transylvania.

The analysis of the socio-professional evolution of the "auriferous quadrilateral" from 1850 to 1910 is difficult to undertake because of a lack of statistical data that might suggest a necessary continuity and uniformity. Up until 1900, every census was operated with different indicators, so the computation could not provide accurate quantitative data. For instance, the census of 1857 recorded the social structure down to the level of localities, but operated with different rubrics than the one conducted in 1910. In 1857, there were no explicit rubrics, for example, for the people who were employed in the mining and metallurgical sectors. Hence, even though their numbers may be inferred from other categories recorded in the census, it cannot be regarded as accurate. In the case of the 1869 census, it provided no statistical data on the socio-professional structure of the towns and villages of interest for our study. Under these circumstances, taking necessary precautions, we will analyse the socio-economic profile of the region from a comparative perspective, taking 1910 and 1857 as benchmark years respectively. The social composition of the "auriferous quadrilateral", both in 1857 and in 1910, revealed their specific profiles from the vantage point of the economic activities that were carried out here. The analysis of the data enables us to distinguish among three

---

[1] Bolovan I. Transilvania între revoluția de la 1848 și Unirea din 1918. Contribuții demografice. Clui-Napoca: Fundația Cluturală Română, 2000: 35.

types of settlements.

(1) The first type is the mining settlements, including Abrud, Băița, Bucium, Roșia Montană and Săcărâmb. It can be easily noticed that most of the population here was employed in the mining and industrial sectors[1], and that agriculture had a low share in the occupational structure. Thus, in 1857, 13.94% of the population in Roșia Montană carried out activities related to mining[2]. By 1910 this percentage had reached over 27.68%, while employment in agriculture had undergone a sharp decrease from 18.16% to 1.65% (Table 1), well below the average of the region (20.51%) or that of Transylvania in general. The situation was also valid in the case of Bucium, where more than 20% of the population carried out mining-related activities, while agricultural occupations did not exceed 3.34%. In these cases, of course, we should take into account the fact that the landscape and the climate favoured agricultural activities only to a very limited extent. This conclusion is reinforced by the cumulative analysis of the five settlements mentioned above: basically, in all of three cases, in 1910 16%-19% of the population was employed in the mining sector or carried out related activities, while agriculture accounted for a marginal share of 1.83%-5.57% (Table 1).

(2) A second category includes the localities marked by a complementarity between specific mining occupations and those related to the practice of agricultural activities. Such situations were encountered in Baia de Criș, Crișcior, Ruda and Zlatna. In Baia de Criș, the ratio between the number of those employed in mining and those employed in industrial activities was around 11%, while more than 9% of the population was employed in agriculture. In Crișcior, where mining activities gained impetus toward the beginning of the 20th century, there occurred a significant demographic growth. Moreover, the social composition reflected the profound changes that had taken place compared to the mid-19th century. Thus, while in 1857 only 1.08% of the inhabitants were employed in mining, in 1910 over 20% of the population carried out mining activities. Agriculture also maintained an important position, since over 14% of the local population continued to practise it as their main source of livelihood. As an urban settlement, Zlatna had a specific situation: the level of employment of the population in industrial and mining activities was 12.77% in 1910, but agriculture also had a share of over 11.53%, which was a lot, in any case, for a town in 1910.

(3) There was a third situation that could be encountered in numerous localities from the "auriferous quadrilateral" featured agriculture as the dominant sector, mining activities being carried out at small exploitations, the great majority of which were private. Basically, in 22 out of the 33 localities, agriculture accounted for over 20% (Table 1). The villages that illustrated this situation were Almașu Mic, Buceș and Căraci, where the population employed in agriculture had a share of over 40% (in fact, with the exception of the village Căraci, where there were gold exploitations, the others belonged to the "auriferous quadrilateral" geographically, but no large-scale mining activities were conducted there).

---

[1] The author refers to them because in statistical terms it is difficult to make a clear dissociation between the two categories of occupations.

[2] Rotaru T. Recensământul din 1857 –Transilvania. second edition. Cluj-Napoca, 1997: 62-63.

Table 1 Socio-economic Structures in the "Auriferous Quadrilateral" in 1910

Localities	Population in 1910	Employed in Industry	Percentage/%	Employed in the Mining and Metallurgical Sectors	Percentage/%	Employed in the Trade and Banking Sectors	Percentage/%	Employed in Agriculture	Percentage/%	Day Labourers	Percentage/%
Abrud	2,938	364	12.3	118	4.01	125	4.25	54	1.83	155	5.27
Almașu Mare	1,356	17	1.25	22	1.62	0	0	549	40.48	4	0.29
Almașu Mic	518	6	1.15	0	0	2	0.38	231	44.59	0	0
Baia de Arieș	956	51	5.33	19	1.98	8	0.83	235	24.58	22	2.3
Baia de Criș	1,001	110	10.98	7	0.69	27	2.69	96	9.59	0	0
Băița	1,220	73	5.98	193	15.81	6	0.49	68	5.57	0	0
Brad	4,272	278	6.5	120	2.8	89	2.08	803	18.79	15	0.35
Buceș	821	9	1.09	3	0.36	1	0.12	376	45.79	0	0
Bucium	4,066	126	3.09	689	16.94	26	0.63	136	3.34	0	0
Bucureșci	627	7	1.11	56	8.93	0	0	171	27.27	0	0
După Piatră	2,240	26	1.16	1	0.04	2	0.08	777	34.68	0	0
Căienel	597	2	0.33	26	4.35	0	0	224	37.52	0	0
Căraci	272	2	0.73	7	2.57	1	0.36	123	45.22	0	0
Cerbăl	568	7	1.23	29	5.10	1	0.17	180	31.69	7	1.23
Certejul de Sus	768	20	2.6	64	8.33	3	0.39	193	25.13	4	0.52
Criscior	2,247	98	4.36	354	15.75	21	0.93	317	14.1	0	0
Curechi	941	6	0.63	1	0.1	1	0.1	394	41.87	0	0
Fizeș	458	4	0.87	15	3.27	0	0	141	30.78	0	0
Glod	441	14	3.17	0	0	0	0	160	36.28	0	0
Hărțăgani	1,764	21	1.19	14	0.79	0	0	618	35.03	0	0
Hondol	1,126	46	4.08	44	3.9	5	0.44	348	30.9	0	0
Luncoiu de Jos	714	15	2.1	3	0.42	0	0	258	36.13	0	0
Porcurea/Vălișoara	478	7	1.46	14	2.92	0	0	183	38.28	0	0
Rișca	479	14	2.92	0	0	0	0	203	42.37	6	1.25
Roșia Montană	2,907	93	3.19	712	24.49	44	1.51	48	1.65	35	1.2
Ribița	892	18	2.01	0	0	0	0	304	34.08	0	0
Ruda	781	14	1.79	186	23.81	2	0.25	81	10.37	2	0.25
Săcărâmb	1,248	31	2.48	279	22.35	7	0.56	36	2.88	5	0.4
Stănija	1,097	8	0.72	5	0.45	0	0	508	46.3	0	0
Techereu	428	5	1.16	20	4.67	1	0.23	124	28.97	0	0
Trestia	589	11	1.86	11	1.86	0	0	189	32.08	3	0.5
Țebea	1,227	11	0.89	14	1.14	2	0.16	535	43.6	0	0
Zlatna	4,317	315	7.29	237	5.48	89	2.06	498	11.53	326	7.55
Total	44,354	1.829	4.12	3,263	7.35	463	1.04	9,161	20.65	584	1.31
Total Transilvania*/average	5,243,180	286,151	5.45	29,113	0.55	55,885	1.06	1,546,082	29.48	48,390	0.92

* We refer to the total population of Transylvania as it appears in the Census cited below

Source: The data were selected and processed after Recensământul din 1910. Transilvania, vol. 2, Populația după ocupații, Traian Rotaru (Ed.), Cluj Napoca, 2006

Recourse to general quantitative data does not, of course, suffice for providing a satisfactory explanation on the relation between the dynamics of economic activities in the region and demographic phenomena: It is also necessary to study deeper mechanisms, the sources of demographic growth and decline, the dynamics of internal and external migrations, the rate of natural increase, and changes in birth or death rates. However, this would exceed the framework and the aim of this study. What is certain, however, as demonstrated by the examples above, is that there was a visible and direct relationship between the evolution of mining activities and the socio-demographic realities in the region.

The situation was, in fact, specific to all mining and, in general, all mono-industrial regions, which depended on large-scale activities, correlated with the existence of exploitable resources. This can ultimately reveal, alongside other indicators, how fragile and unstable or untenable economic growth can be in such a region. When the natural resource disappears, when interest in it dwindles or when it is no longer profitable to exploit it, what is also basically disappears is the sustainable source of economic growth and, in fact, the source of livelihood for the local population, which can find viable alternatives and diversification resources in other domains only with great difficulty.

We believe that the aspect of the school education promoted by state policies or the initiatives of local communities should also be considered in this context. From a historical point of view, the analysis of the three basic elements of this equation — education, social discipline, and the formation of practical and entrepreneurial skills — leads to the idea of a causal relationship between them and the process of economic modernization and community development. It is clear that when these elements converged and expanded, the process of modernization acquired substance and durability, ensuring the prerequisites for self-sustained development[1].

In terms of the rate and pace of literacy in the "auriferous quadrilateral", the analysis of the centralized data regarding elementary and secondary education, regardless of whether it was confessional or state-run, reveals a rather similar situation to that of other regions in Transylvania. For example, in Săcărâmb, where, as already indicated, there was a relatively well-developed education system, and the rate of literacy was 35.46% in 1880, reaching 40.54% in 1910[2]. Another example was that of Zlatna, a town where the rate of literacy was 19.94% at 1880, improving to 37.80% in 1910[3]. In Roșia Montană, the rate of literacy was 20.03% in 1880, evolving towards 47.60% in 1910, at a convergent pace with that of Transylvania as a whole. In the case of Abrud, the evolution was somewhat better: Against the same chronological horizon, there was an increase from 25.19% to 58%, which can be considered a good pace compared to the province as a whole. It should be noted, however, that the percentages identified above represent average figures, valid for the entire population, regardless of ethnic origin and religious denomination.

We can thus conclude that within the timespan 1890-1910, the situation of literacy in the "auriferous quadrilateral" registered a relative improvement, consistent with the general trends

---

[1] See Westermann A. (Hrsg.) Montanregion als Sozialregion. Husum: Mathiesen Verlag, 2012: 11 sqq.

[2] For numbers close to the average in Transylvania, see Rotaru T Recensământul din 1880-Transilvania. Cluj-Napoca, 1997; Rotaru T Recensământul din 1900-Transilvania. Cluj-Napoca, 1999; Rotaru T Recensământul din 1910-Transilvania. Cluj-Napoca, 1999.

[3] The data are calculated after the above-cited censuses.

identifiable throughout the province during this period. Although denominational schools, communal state-run schools and schools patronized by mining companies exist now in most of the villages in the Apuseni Mountains, the advancement of literacy did not exceed the average recorded at the level of entire Transylvania①.

---

① Thus, in 1890, 27.5% of the total civilian population in Transylvania could read and write, while in 1900, the percentage was around 35%. If we refer to the population aged over 6 years old, the percentage amounted to 32.9% and 41.1%, respectively (significantly lower than that at the level of the entire Kingdom of Hungary, where 59% of the total population aged over 6 years old could read and write in 1900). Source: Ungarisches Statistisches Jahrbuch, Neue Folge, XIII, 1905, Budapest, 1906: 324.

Evaluation of Regional Modernization of China's 52 Regions

Yang Li, Li Li

China Center for Modernization Research, Chinese Academy of Sciences

1. Introduction

According to Deng Xiaoping's three-step development strategy and the strategic deployment made at the 18th CPC National Congress, China will have completed the moderately prosperous society in all respects (MPSIAR) building by 2020, and will have become a modern socialist country by 2049, achieving the "two centenary goals". The "Thirteenth Five-year Plan" period is vital to China's MPSIAR building, and 2020 is the key time node for China's modernization drive. In 2020, the nation will enter into a new stage of striving to basically complete modernization, and most areas in China will start a new march into basic completion of modernization.

The report of the 18th CPC National Congress also pointed out that we should encourage areas with good conditions to keep taking the lead in pursuing modernization and to make greater contributions to nationwide reform and development. According to the documents of the State Council, the Yangtze River Delta will have basically completed modernization by 2020; the South Jiangsu Modernization Construction Demonstration Zone has been launched and is planned to basically complete modernization by 2020.

It can be predicted that in the next five years, the advanced areas that have already completed MPSIAR building will continue to march towards the "second centenary goal" of basically completing modernization, and are likely to take the lead in basically completing modernization; whereas the relatively advanced areas that have just completed MPSIAR building will immediately march towards the same goal.

Regarding MPSIAR, the reports of the 16th, 17th and 18th NPC National Congresses have already specified the goal and requirements, and the National Bureau of Statistics has already put forward ten basic criteria for MPSIAR building. The core indicators include: a per capita GDP of 3,000 US dollars (based on the exchange rate in 2000), an urban per capita disposable income of RMB 18,000 yuan, a rural per capita net income of RMB 8,000 yuan, an Engel coefficient of 40%, an urbanization rate of 50%, and 2.8 doctors per thousand people.

Regarding "basic completion of modernization", there is no universally acknowledged criterion yet. *China Modernization Report* has completed an evaluation of the national modernization level of 131 countries in the world from 1950 to 2012 as well as the regional modernization level of 34 provincial-level areas in China from 1970 to 2012. It can provide a scientific basis for the macroscopic decisions of the central government and provincial governments on "basic completion of modernization". However, on the prefecture level, there are no systematic and internationally comparable research findings yet. *China Modernization Report* has found that the modernization of provincial-level areas shares much commonality with national modernization, but the modernization of prefecture-level areas is greatly diversified and flexible, where the criteria of national modernization cannot simply apply.

This research selects as objects of evaluation 52 prefecture-level cities in three provinces (Guangdong, Henan and Gansu) respectively located in the east, middle and west of China; builds on the experience of the modernization evaluation on 131 countries in the world and 34 provincial-level areas in China; takes as comparison the modernization level of high-income countries, middle-income countries, low-income countries, the world average, China and Chinese provincial level-areas; collects data from the statistics of the World Bank, the United Nations Statistics Division, OECD and Chinese statistical departments; builds an evaluation index system and evaluation model on regional modernization; conducts continuous dynamic evaluation on the modernization level of the areas. It can provide a scientific basis for the macroscopic decisions of prefecture-level areas on basic completion of modernization.

2. Study Object and Data

The objects of this study are 52 prefecture-level cities in Guangdong, Henan and Gansu provinces.

This study selects the year 2013 as a cross section of research, and collects data from the following sources: *China Statistical Yearbook for Regional Economy 2014*; provincial yearbooks in 2014 of the three provinces; *China Statistical Yearbook 2014*; *China Statistical Yearbook on Science and Technology 2014*; *China Statistical Yearbook on Education 2014*; *China Statistical Yearbook on Environment 2014*; *China Statistical Yearbook on Energy 2014*; *China Statistical Yearbook on Cities 2014*; population census data 2010; World Bank database; OECD database; UN International Labour Organization database.

3. Evaluation Model

3.1 Index System

Considering the indicator connotation, policy orientation and data availability, we select 32 quantitative indicators of four categories including economic quality (8), living quality (8), innovation drive (8) and environmental friendliness (8), and one category of qualitative indicators about satisfaction evaluation, and use them to build an initial index system for this regional modernization evaluation, as is shown in Table 1.

Table 1 Index System of Regional Modernization Evaluation

Types of Indicators	Indicator Items	Units of Indicator and Calculation Methods
Economic quality	GDP per capita	RMB/person, GDP per capita
	Agricultural productivity	RMB/person, Added value of the primary sector ÷ Employees in the primary sector
	Industrial productivity	RMB/person, Added value of the secondary sector ÷ Employees in the secondary sector
	Per capita disposable income	RMB/person, (Per capita disposable income of urban residents × Urban population + Per capita net income of rural residents × Rural population) ÷ Resident population at year-end
	Industrial structure level	Ratio, Ratio of industrial to agricultural value-added
	Industrialization level	RMB/person, Per-capita industrial value-added (Added value of the secondary sector ÷ Resident population at year-end)
	Informatization level	%, Number of internet users (households) ÷ Resident population at year-end ×100
	Market competitiveness	RMB/person, Per capita export value (Total export ÷ Resident population at year-end)
Living quality	Urban population (% of total)	%, Urban population ÷ Resident population at year-end
	Average life expectancy	Years, Average life expectancy
	Proportion of doctors	‰, Number of doctors (licensed doctors + licensed assistant doctors) ÷ Resident population at year-end ×1,000
	Coverage of medical insurance	%, Participants of medical insurance ÷ Resident population at year-end ×100
	Private car penetration rate	‰, Private automobile ownership ÷ Resident population at year-end ×1,000
	Cellphone penetration rate	%, Number of mobile phone users ÷ Resident population at year-end ×100
	Average wage of urban workers	RMB/person, Average wage of staff and workers
	Engel coefficient of urban residents	%, Per capita spending on food ÷ Per capita consumption spending ×100, Inverse indicator
Innovation drive	Proportion of patent application	10,000/10,000 people, Number of patent applications ÷ Resident population at year-end × 10,000
	Proportion of revenue from new products	%, Sales revenue from new products ÷ GDP × 100
	Proportion of expenditure on science and technology	%, Internal spending of R&D funds ÷ GDP × 100
	Proportion of S&T personnel	Parts per 10,000, R&D personnel full time equivalent ÷ Resident population at year-end × 10,000
	Average years of schooling	Years, Average years of schooling
	Proportion of adults with higher education	%, Population aged 16 and above with a college degree or above ÷ Resident population at year-end × 100
	Secondary enrollment (%)	%, Students at regular secondary school ÷ Population aged 12–18 × 100
	Proportion of expenditure on education	%, Fiscal expenditure on education ÷ GDP × 100

Continued

Types of Indicators	Indicator Items	Units of Indicator and Calculation Methods
Environment-friendliness	Per capita energy consumption	Kilogram standard oil, Total energy consumption ÷ Resident population at year-end
	Energy consumption per unit GDP	Gram standard oil/RMB, Total energy consumption ÷ GDP, inverse indicator
	Energy consumption per unit industrial value-added	Gram standard oil/RMB, Total industrial energy consumption ÷ industrial value-added, inverse indicator
	Density of industrial organic waste water	Gram/RMB, Industrial chemical oxygen demand discharge ÷ Industrial value-added, inverse indicator
	Density of industrial solid waste	Gram/RMB, General industrial solid waste output ÷ Industrial value-added, inverse indicator
	Solid waste disposal rate	%, Temporally replaced by "domestic garbage safe disposal rate"
	Domestic waste water treatment rate	%, Temporally replaced by "urban waste water treatment rate"
	Urban air quality	$\mu g/m^3$, PM2.5 concentration or PM10 concentration, inverse indicator
Satisfaction	Satisfaction with material life	(Sampling survey)
	Satisfaction with cultural life	(Sampling survey)
	Satisfaction with social safety	(Sampling survey)
	Satisfaction with environment quality	(Sampling survey)
	Satisfaction with public services	(Sampling survey)
	Satisfaction with social equity	(Sampling survey)

Based on the data available, we further sift and simplify the initial index system and eventually obtain a simplified index system with three categories (economic quality, living quality and innovation drive) and 10 sub-categories (Table 2).

Table 2 Index System of Regional Modernization Evaluation (Simplified)

Types of Indicators	Indicator Items	Indicators	Indicator Explanations	Units of Indicators
Economic quality	Per capita income	Per capita disposable income of urban residents	Disposable income of urban residents ÷ Resident population at year-end	US dollar/person
	Industrialization level	Per capita industrial value-added	Added value of the secondary sector ÷ Resident population at year-end	US dollar/person
	Informatization level	Broadband network penetration rate	Internet broadband users (households) ÷ Resident population at year-end × 100%	%
	Greening level	Energy consumption per unit GDP	Total energy consumption ÷ GDP, inverse indicator	Kilogram standard oil/US dollar
Living quality	Urbanization level	Proportion of urban population	Urban population ÷ Resident population at year-end × 100%	%
	Medical service level	Doctors per thousand people	Number of doctors (licensed doctors + licensed assistant doctors) ÷ Resident population at year-end × 1,000	‰
	Average wage of workers	Average wage of workers	Average wage of urban employees (RMB)	US dollar/person
	Engel coefficient	Engel coefficient	Per capita spending of urban residents on food ÷ Per capita consumption spending of urban residents × 100%	%

Types of Indicators	Indicator Items	Indicators	Indicator Explanations	Units of Indicators
Innovation drive	Proportion of expenditure on science and technology	Proportion of expenditure on science and technology	Internal spending of R&D funds ÷ GDP × 100	%
	Proportion of adults with higher education	Proportion of people with higher education	Population with higher education ÷ Population aged 16 and above × 100%	%

3.2 Calculation Formula for Regional Modernization Index

We adopt the evaluation methods of the UNDP Human Development Index: relative index and geometric mean.

The regional modernization index (RMI) consists of economic quality index (EQI), living quality index (LQI) and innovation drive index (IDI).

$$RMI = (EQI \times LQI \times IDI)^{1/3}$$

wherein

$$EQI = (GNI\ per\ capita \times Trio\ index)^{1/2}$$

wherein

$$Trio\ index = (Industrialization\ index \times Informatization\ index \times Greenization\ index)^{1/3}$$

$$LQI = (Urbanization\ index \times Medical\ service\ level\ index \times Average\ wage\ index \times Engel\ coefficient)^{1/4}$$

$$IDI = (Index\ of\ proportion\ of\ expenditure\ on\ science\ and\ technology \times Index\ of\ proportion\ of\ adults\ with\ higher\ education)^{1/2}$$

3.3 Maximum Value and Minimum Value

In this study, the maximum value and the minimum value are based on the data of high-income countries and OECD countries in the World Bank database.

Specifically, the maximum value is the average value of high-income countries or OECD countries in the World Bank database; the minimum value is 1% of the average value of high-income countries or OECD countries in the World Bank database.

The maximum value and the minimum value of each indicator in the simplified index system are shown in Table 3.

Table 3 Maximum Value and Minimum Value

Indicators	Indicator Explanations	Units of Indicators	Maximum	Minimum	Notes
Per capita income	Per capita disposable income of urban residents	US dollar/person	30,682	307	Estimated*
Industrialization level	Per capita industrial value-added	US dollar/person	9,068	91	
Informatization level	Broadband network penetration rate	%	27.3	0.27	

Continued

Indicators	Indicator Explanations	Units of Indicators	Maximum	Minimum	Notes
Greening level	Energy consumption per unit GDP	Kilogram standard oil/US dollar	0.12		Inverse indicator
Urbanization level	Proportion of urban population	%	80.5	0.81	
Medical service level	Doctors per thousand people	‰	3.1	0.03	
Average wage of workers	Average wage of workers	US dollar/person-year	44,837	448	
Engel coefficient	Engel coefficient	%	20.0		Inverse indicator
Proportion of expenditure on science and technology	Proportion of expenditure on science and technology	%	2.42	0.02	
Proportion of adults with higher education	Proportion of adults with higher education	%	35.0	0.35	Estimated**

*Estimated method = Per capita disposable income = GNI per capita * 80%; **Estimated according to OECD countries

3.4 Calculation Method for the Standardized Index of Single Indicators

Index of a positive indicator = (Actual value − Minimum value) ÷ (Maximum value − Minimum value) × 100

Index of an inverse indicator = Maximum value ÷ Actual value × 100

The index of a single indicator falls between 1 and 120, with 1 representing any values less than 1, and 120 representing any values greater than 120.

3.5 Categorization of Regional Modernization Level and Criteria

(1) Developed area: regional modernization index above 80 and above 80% of the average value of high-income countries.

(2) Moderately developed area: regional modernization index above the world average value yet below 80.

(3) Preliminarily developed area: regional modernization index below the world average value yet above 30.

(4) Underdeveloped area: regional modernization index below 30.

(5) Criteria for completing modernization: regional modernization index above 80 and above 80% of the average value of high-income countries.

(6) Criteria for basically completing modernization: regional modernization index above the world average value yet below 80.

4. Evaluation Results

4.1 Modernization Index Scores of the Three Provinces

Table 4 shows the modernization index scores of the 52 prefecture-level cities in the three provinces. It can be seen from the table that the regional modernization index ranking is not completely consistent with the rankings of GDP per capita and GNI per capita; instead, it can more comprehensively and objectively reflect the comprehensive development level of regional modernization.

Table 4   Regional Modernization Index Scores of the 52 Prefecture-level Cities of the Three Provinces

No.	Areas	Regional Modernization Indexes	GDP per Capita	GDP per Capita Ranking	Income per Capita	GNI per Capita Ranking
4401	Guangzhou	60.3	119,695	2	42,049	3
4403	Shenzhen	59.7	136,948	1	44,653	2
4404	Zhuhai	56.5	104,786	3	36,375	5
4406	Foshan	49.4	96,310	5	38,038	4
6202	Jiayuguan	45.9	96,335	4	24,294	12
4419	Dongguan	45.6	66,109	8	46,594	1
4101	Zhengzhou	44.7	68,073	7	26,615	9
4420	Zhongshan	44.2	83,393	6	34,274	6
6201	Lanzhou	40.2	48,852	13	20,767	31
4413	Huizhou	40.0	57,144	10	32,991	7
6203	Jinchang	38.1	53,854	12	23,786	14
4407	Jiangmen	36.5	44,546	16	29,772	8
4103	Luoyang	35.6	47,569	15	24,820	11
4402	Shaoguan	33.9	35,063	22	25,595	10
6209	Jiuquan	33.2	58,041	9	22,389	17
4108	Jiaozuo	32.6	48,545	14	22,058	21
4107	Xinxiang	32.6	31,138	27	22,105	20
4110	Xuchang	31.5	44,297	17	21,717	22
4104	Pingdingshan	30.8	31,496	25	22,482	16
4412	Zhaoqing	30.7	41,479	19	23,930	13
4417	Yangjiang	29.9	42,017	18	21,434	25
4405	Shantou	29.7	28,661	32	22,206	19
4408	Zhanjiang	29.4	28,859	30	22,371	18
4102	Kaifeng	28.8	29,327	28	19,492	38
4112	Sanmenxia	28.0	53,863	11	20,938	30
4409	Maoming	27.9	36,063	21	20,036	36
4418	Qingyuan	27.7	28,928	29	21,368	26
4414	Meizhou	27.3	18,603	46	20,737	32
4105	Anyang	27.2	33,100	24	23,019	15

Continued

No.	Areas	Regional Modernization Indexes	GDP per Capita	GDP per Capita Ranking	Income per Capita	GNI per Capita Ranking
4109	Puyang	26.9	31,483	26	21,571	24
4451	Chaozhou	26.8	28,837	31	19,674	37
4416	Heyuan	26.1	22,499	41	18,436	42
4111	Luohe	26.1	33,568	23	21,174	28
6204	Baiyin	25.8	27,004	35	18,280	43
4113	Nanyang	25.8	24,692	39	21,653	23
4415	Shanwei	25.5	22,560	40	20,485	33
6207	Zhangye	25.3	27,788	33	15,877	48
6210	Qingyang	24.5	27,261	34	18,761	41
4452	Jieyang	24.5	26,866	36	20,980	29
4453	Yunfu	24.3	24,863	37	20,440	34
4106	Hebi	22.9	38,919	20	21,228	27
6206	Wuwei	22.9	20,975	44	17,368	45
6208	Pingliang	22.5	16,364	47	17,351	46
6230	Gannan Tibetan Autonomous Prefecture	22.1	15,658	48	15,065	51
4114	Shangqiu	21.3	21,073	43	20,214	35
6205	Tianshui	20.8	13,820	49	16,892	47
4117	Zhumadian	19.6	22,296	42	19,431	39
4115	Xinyang	19.6	24,754	38	19,150	40
4116	Zhoukou	18.5	20,359	45	18,046	44
6212	Longnan	17.7	9,699	50	15,555	50
6211	Dingxi	17.6	9,106	51	15,723	49
6229	Linxia Hui Autonomous Prefecture	15.8	8,440	52	12,617	52

4.2 Modernization Index Score of Henan Province

Table 5 shows the scores of the regional modernization index and economic quality, living quality and innovation drive indexes of the 17 prefecture-level cities in Henan Province. It can be seen from the table that Zhengzhou City of Henan has a regional modernization level that is only slightly above the world average level, an economic quality level that is below the world average but above the national average level, a living quality level and an innovation drive level that are high above the world average. There are 11 prefecture-level cities (Luoyang, Jiaozuo, Xinxiang, Xuchang, Pingdingshan, Kaifeng, Sanmenxia, Anyang, Puyang, Luohe and Nanyang) whose regional modernization levels are below the world and national average levels, yet above the average level of middle-income countries. The other 5 cities (Hebi, Shangqiu, Zhumadian, Xinyang and Zhoukou) have a regional modernization level that is below the level of middle-income countries but above the average level of low-income countries.

Table 5 Modernization Index Scores of the 17 Cities of Henan

Areas	Economic Quality Indexes	Living Quality Indexes	Innovation Drive Indexes	Regional Modernization Indexes
High-income countries	99.4	100.0	100.0	99.8
Zhengzhou	25.9	51.9	66.4	44.7
World	34.0	47.3	49.5	43.0
The whole country	21.5	45.8	53.6	37.5
Luoyang	22.5	44.9	44.6	35.6
Jiaozuo	20.6	44.5	38.0	32.6
Xinxiang	18.9	41.4	44.3	32.6
Xuchang	21.3	41.6	35.1	31.5
Pingdingshan	18.8	42.1	36.9	30.8
Kaifeng	17.3	40.1	34.2	28.8
Sanmenxia	20.2	46.7	23.3	28.0
Anyang	18.7	40.6	26.5	27.2
Puyang	18.9	38.3	26.9	26.9
Luohe	19.5	38.1	23.8	26.1
Nanyang	19.2	35.5	25.2	25.8
Middle-income countries	16.6	33.6	25.1	24.1
Hebi	18.9	43.3	14.7	22.9
Shangqiu	16.2	36.5	16.4	21.3
Zhumadian	16.2	36.0	12.9	19.6
Xinyang	16.1	32.2	14.5	19.6
Zhoukou	16.4	35.9	10.7	18.5
Low-income countries	1.7	6.7	4.8	3.8

4.3 Modernization Index Score of Guangdong Province

Table 6 shows the scores of the regional modernization index and economic quality, living quality and innovation drive indexes of the 21 prefecture-level cities in Guangdong Province. It can be seen from the table that there are 6 cities in Guangdong (Guangzhou, Shenzhen, Zhuhai, Foshan, Dongguan and Zhongshan) whose regional modernization levels are above the world average level. Among these cities, Guangzhou has an innovation drive index that is already very close to the average level of high-income countries; Huizhou has a modernization level that is between the world average and the national average level; the other 14 cities have a regional modernization level that is below the national average level but above the level of middle-income countries. The overall modernization development level of Guangdong is higher than that of Henan.

Table 6 Modernization Index Scores of the 21 Cities of Guangdong

Areas	Economic Quality Indexes	Living Quality Indexes	Innovation Drive Indexes	Regional Modernization Indexes
High-income countries	99.4	100.0	100.0	99.8
Guangzhou	39.2	61.9	90.4	60.3
Shenzhen	44.5	57.9	82.4	59.7
Zhuhai	37.5	58.3	82.6	56.5
Foshan	38.4	52.1	60.3	49.4
Dongguan	39.0	46.9	51.8	45.6
Zhongshan	34.4	49.0	51.4	44.2
World	34.0	47.3	49.5	43.0
Huizhou	29.7	46.0	46.9	40.0
The whole country	21.5	45.8	53.6	37.5
Jiangmen	27.2	42.8	41.6	36.5
Shaoguan	20.0	43.1	45.3	33.9
Zhaoqing	22.4	36.4	35.4	30.7
Yangjiang	21.3	37.9	33.3	29.9
Shantou	21.1	38.4	32.4	29.7
Zhanjiang	20.1	34.6	36.4	29.4
Maoming	17.8	36.3	33.6	27.9
Qingyuan	17.1	39.6	31.3	27.7
Meizhou	15.7	38.3	34.0	27.3
Chaozhou	17.4	37.8	29.4	26.8
Heyuan	16.7	34.7	30.8	26.1
Shanwei	19.1	37.6	23.3	25.5
Jieyang	19.6	36.4	20.5	24.5
Yunfu	16.6	31.7	27.5	24.3
Middle-income countries	16.6	33.6	25.1	24.1
Low-income countries	1.7	6.7	4.8	3.8

4.4 Modernization Index Score of Gansu Province

Table 7 shows the scores of the regional modernization index and economic quality, living quality and innovation drive indexes of the 14 prefecture-level cities in Gansu Province. It can be seen from the table that only Jiayuguan City of Gansu has a modernization level that is above the world average, an economic quality level that is below the world average but above the national average level, a living quality level and an innovation drive level that are high above the world average level. The regional modernization levels of Lanzhou and Jinchang are between the world and the national average levels. There are 4 prefecture-level cities (Jiuquan, Baiyin, Zhangye and

Qingyang) whose regional modernization levels are below the national average level, yet above the level of middle-income countries. The other 7 cities have a regional modernization level that is below the level of middle-income countries but above the level of low-income countries. The overall regional modernization level of Gansu is slightly below that of Henan.

Table 7 Modernization Index Scores of the 14 Cities of Gansu

Areas	Economic Quality Indexes	Living Quality Indexes	Innovation Drive Indexes	Regional Modernization Indexes
High-income countries	99.4	100.0	100.0	99.8
Jiayuguan	29.2	60.6	54.8	45.9
World	34.0	47.3	49.5	43.0
Lanzhou	19.5	54.4	61.0	40.2
Jinchang	23.4	51.9	45.4	38.1
The whole country	21.5	45.8	53.6	37.5
Jiuquan	20.2	44.0	41.1	33.2
Baiyin	14.4	38.0	31.5	25.8
Zhangye	13.3	38.7	31.5	25.3
Qingyang	14.4	35.3	29.1	24.5
Middle-income countries	16.6	33.6	25.1	24.1
Wuwei	12.6	33.8	28.2	22.9
Pingliang	11.6	36.2	27.2	22.5
Gannan Tibetan Autonomous Prefecture	9.3	37.7	30.6	22.1
Tianshui	10.4	32.4	26.5	20.8
Longnan	8.3	30.1	22.0	17.7
Dingxi	8.0	30.6	22.2	17.6
Linxia Hui Autonomous Prefecture	6.6	30.3	19.6	15.8
Low-income countries	1.7	6.7	4.8	3.8

5. Conclusions

This paper has produced a complete set of methods and procedures for regional modernization evaluation through expert consultation and data testing, including a complete index system for regional modernization evaluation (32 qualitative indicators and 6 quantitative indicators) and a simplified version of the index system. It is of important theoretical and practical significance to future regional modernization evaluation, and also provides technical support for regional modernization evaluation of areas below provincial level.

It can be seen from the evaluation analysis of the three provinces in this paper that the current statistical data in China do not suffice to support the complete index system of regional modernization evaluation. Based on the simplified version of the evaluation index system, the current statistical data and the analysis of the three provinces, it can be seen that the current regional modernization level in China is still below the world average, and there is a remarkable difference among the east, the middle and the west regions, as well as a remarkable imbalance within a province. If we want all areas to basically complete modernization by 2020, certain areas need to catch up in certain fields.

Interactive Mechanism Between Regional Economic Integration and Regional Modernization

Xijun Zhao

China Center for Modernization Research, Chinese Academy of Sciences

Regional economic integration was first presented in the form of international customs union in the 1940s in Western Europe, and then became the main research area of economy. Regional economic integration can facilitate production transfer and investment transfer, bring huge economic benefits to the members of the integrated organization, and actively push forward regional economic development and regional modernization. Therefore it has always been the focus of attention.

1. Connotations and Development of Regional Economic Integration

1.1 Main Connotations of Regional Economic Integration

After World War II, some developed countries started to establish regional development communities that aimed at promoting production exchange and free flow of factors in order to boost their own economic development. This gave birth to the initial form of regional economic integration. In 1954, Tinbergen was the first to present a definition of economic integration, which is "the creation of the most desirable international economic structure by removing artificial barriers to the optimum operation of economy and introducing all desirable forms of cooperation and unification". In 1961, Balassa further developed Tinbergen's definition of economic integration by proposing that economic integration was the movement of products and factors which were free from any discrimination or restriction from the governments. Afterwards, a number of world-renowned scholars (Wonnacott and Lutz, 1989; De Melo et al., 1992; Ethier, 1998) carried out plenty of studies on regional economic integration from various perspectives such as trade optimization, customs union, industrial organization and development dynamics. Now, the customs union theory, the free trade zone theory, the common market theory and the theory of agreed international division of labor have become the core theories of economic integration. Based on the above studies, this paper argues that regional economic integration is mainly the creation of a transnational and regional economic group among geographically close countries, which can guarantee the free flow of goods, capital, human resources and labor force by formulating common economic and trading policies and mutually removing artificial barriers to the free flow of production factors and products to achieve the maximum overall interests for the country or the region.

1.2 Main Organizational Forms of Regional Economic Integration

Large-scale regional economic integration worldwide has generally gone through three waves, i.e., the wave represented by Europe in the 1950s and 1960s, the wave represented by the United States in the 1980s, and the wave dominated by developing countries afterwards. Currently there are about hundreds of regional economic integration organizations of various forms and scales, almost involving countries all over the world.

The most typical successful cases of regional economic integration are the European Union (EU), North American Free Trade Agreement (NAFTA) and Asia-Pacific Economic Cooperation (APEC), all of which are basically dominated by developed countries. Developing countries have also made active attempts to promote regional economic integration. Some influential organizations include the Association of Southeast Asian Nations (ASEAN), Latin American Integration Association, Caribbean Community, Arab Common Market and East African Common Market. In terms of the current organizational forms of regional economic integration, there are roughly four types, i.e., customs union, common market, free trade zone and economic union (Table 1).

Table 1 Typical Organizational Forms and Characteristics of Regional Economic Integration in the World

Main Organizational Forms	Main Characteristics and Operating Forms	Representative Cases
Customs union	Two economies mutually remove trade barriers against each other and establish common customs to others, forming prominent differential treatment to non-members in the inflow of goods	German Customs Union in the 17th century
Common market	Based on the free flow of goods and services, further promoting the free flow of services, capital and human resources, achieving unification of internal markets	The European Union in 1992
Free trade zone	Two or more economies reach an agreement based on negotiations and mutually remove trade barriers. The barriers are only removed among members, and non-members do not enjoy the same treatment	North American Free Trade Agreement
Economic union	On the basis of a common market, an economic union is an organizational form of regional economic integration that extends the supranational coordination and management mechanism to almost all areas of national economy of member countries. For example, currency unification within the region makes trade among member countries as easy as that within one country, thus greatly reducing transaction costs	The EU; Belgium and Luxembourg have formed such an organization since 1921

Note: Summarized according to Qu C. Review of trend in regional economic integration Studies. Commercial Times, 2008, 4: 28-30

2. Interaction Between Regional Economic Integration and National Modernization

2.1 Regional Economic Integration Promotes Regional Economic Growth

Regional economic integration is in essence the removal of barriers to optimally allocating production factors, enhancing trading freedom, and forming trade diversion, production transfer and investment transfer effects, which helps to improve the overall welfare level of the integration region (An and Li, 2007). Wang (2008) studied the case of ASEAN economic integration. Using the "turbine" model, the research has verified that regional economic integration mainly promotes economic power and degree of affluence, international competitiveness as well as business environment or the three "blades" of the "turbine", through static and dynamic economic effects, and thus to enhance regional competitiveness and accelerate the achievement of regional modernization.

Take the EU for example, the EU evolved from the Union Economique Benelux and the European Community, and it officially became the European Union, or the EU, in 1992, so as to expand the scope of integration. Economic integration has a remarkable effect on economic growth. During the transition period from 1958 to 1969 when the customs union was established, the total amount of foreign trade grew at 11.5% on average, while the internal trade among member countries grew at 16.5%. From the 1950s to the 1970s, the proportion of internal trade within the European Community to the total trade of the member countries rose from 30% to 50%. From 1985 to 1989, the industrial production of the European Community has increased by 20%, while the trade volume within the region has also increased from 55% in 1982 to 62% in 1988. Compared with the US, in 1958 when the customs union was established, the total industrial production of the 6 member countries accounted for less than half of that of the US, the gold and foreign exchange reserves only accounted for 55% of that of the US, and the export trade volume was similar to that of the US. But in 1979, the export trade volume of the 9 countries of the European Community was more than twice of that of the US, and the gold reserve was more than 5 times of that of the US.

As Figure 1 shows, after 1990, especially after 1992 when the EU was officially established, the percentage of its goods and service trade volume in GDP has been growing at an even faster rate. From 1990 to 2000, the average annual growth rate reached 10.5%, which was maintained until 2010. The outbreak of the global financial crisis in 2009 seriously affected the economy of the EU. Nevertheless, the percentage of its goods and service trade volume in GDP has been still quite steady. Therefore, it can be seen that economic integration has a powerful facilitating effect on regional economic development, and can enhance the region's ability to withstand external economic risks.

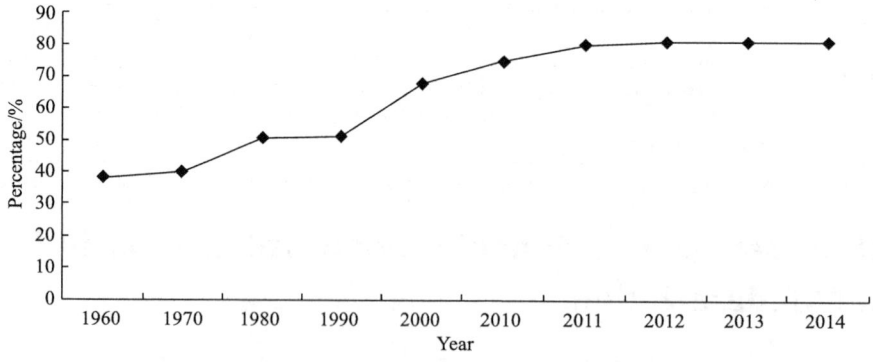

Figure 1   Change of the Percentage of Total Goods and Service Trade Volume in GDP in the EU

2.2 Regional Economic Integration and Regional Modernization

Regional economic integration can accelerate the development of regional modernization. According to the monitoring of the integrated modernization level (He, 2015), among the 28 EU countries, only 4 countries (Germany, Sweden, Denmark and the Netherlands) ranked in the top ten in 1980, but with the advancement of EU economic integration, in 2010, 6 countries (Germany, Denmark, Sweden, etc.) ranked in the top ten. This somehow suggests that the advancement of the EU economic integration plays a significant propelling role in the development of modernization level; the development levels of them are closely related (Table 2).

Table 2 Integrated Modernization Indexes and Rankings of Major EU Countries in 1980-2010

Member Countries	1980		1990		2000		2010	
	Indexes	Rankings	Indexes	Rankings	Indexes	Rankings	Indexes	Rankings
The United Kingdom	88.4	14	88.7	13	88.4	10	90.3	14
France	89.2	12	89.8	12	85.6	15	91.4	9
Germany	93.0	3	93.5	5	94.7	5	96.7	2
Italy	74.6	23	84.6	16	77.9	19	82.5	22
Belgium	90.9	10	94.4	4	85.7	14	90.8	11
The Netherlands	91.0	9	95.8	3	90.2	8	90.4	13
Denmark	92.8	4	97.7	2	95.1	4	95.1	3
Ireland	68.3	29	71.0	20	75.0	20	87.2	15
Greece	68.8	28	67.4	23	60.4	28	73.3	26
Portugal	52.5	46	60.5	31	69.3	23	76.5	24
Spain	72.7	26	83.5	17	74.0	22	84.5	20
Austria	87.2	16	92.0	8	86.9	12	92.4	8
Sweden	98.0	1	98.1	1	98.3	1	94.2	5
Finland	87.0	17	91.8	9	89.4	9	93.1	6
Poland	65.2	32	50.8	50	53.3	39	65.4	38
Hungary	63.0	34	57.9	33	58.2	30	68.1	33
Czech Republic	72.7	25	58.7	32	57.0	31	73.0	27
Slovakia	—	—	69.3	22	53.1	40	65.9	37

Note: The modernization report monitors 131 countries in the world; some EU countries such as Luxembourg, Malta and Cyprus are not included

3. Interactive Mechanism Between Regional Economic Integration and Economic Modernization

3.1 Analysis of Factors Affecting Regional Economic Integration

There are many factors that affect the process of regional economic integration. At the macro level, there are social and cultural gap generated by differences in deep-level ideology, protection of local interests caused by differences in political system, economic potential difference produced by different stages of economic development, and geographical distance induced by non-neighboring geographical locations. These four aspects are also the deep-level factors that restrict the development of regional economic integration. At the micro level, there are market segmentation and trade barriers caused by artificial means such as technological protection, tax rate control and administrative regulation as well as industrial structure barriers resulting from differences in resource and environmental conditions and development stages.

3.1.1 Effects of local interest protection on regional economic integration

Local interest protection includes protection of political interests and protection of economic interests. Protection of political interests has a very significant negative effect on regional economic integration. Each country may adopt various closing measures to realize self-protection, but some countries may form a regional cooperation organization for political interests, such as the Black Sea integration agreement initiated by Turkey. However, with the increase of interdependency in regional economy, economic factors will occupy the dominant position and develop from a means or a tool to maintain and achieve integration to a critical factor that decides its development, stability, efficacy and interests or even "evolve" into the main objective that integration pursues (Zhang, 1997). Due to the aggravation of protection of local interests, some established integration organizations will be dismissed such as the East African Community dismissed in 1977. All in all, protecting local interests can greatly decrease the static resource allocation efficiency of production factors. It prevents factors from flowing among regions according to market signals and makes them cannot be allocated to the production with the highest marginal output. Therefore, it seriously hinders the development of regional economic integration.

3.1.2 Effects of regional factor market segmentation on regional economic integration

Regional factor market segmentation mainly refers to the failure of the free flowing of production factors such as land, capital, labor force and technology among regions according to market rules, so the optimal allocation in the production factor market cannot be realized. The main manifestation is that the government sets up various barriers and obstacles through tariff and technological protection measures to prevent foreign products from entering the local market so as to protect its own products. It attempts to prevent foreign products that may have an impact on local region from entering the local market, and meanwhile prohibits local human resources, capital and raw materials from flowing outside. Within the country, due to various reasons such as incomplete market system, nonstandard transaction order, administrative intervention and control on pricing, and the fact that a market environment that allows all market players to equally use production factors has not yet formed, the factors' allocation efficiency within the region is also seriously restricted, thus affecting the process of regional economic integration.

3.1.3 Effects of different economic development levels on regional economic integration

Neighboring countries or regions are usually greatly different in terms of political status, economic foundation, technological conditions and resource conditions. Such a "potential difference" usually becomes an important obstacle to regional economic integration. According to Friedman's core-periphery theory, regions with higher development levels are usually in the dominant position, and will further strengthen their dominant position through "polarization", while regions with lower development levels are usually marginalized and can hardly achieve breakthroughs. As the two parties cannot simultaneously achieve the same "welfare effects", the integration organization can easily fall apart. Currently, the NAFTA is a successful attempt in which neighboring developed countries and developing countries can achieve regional economic integration, but the member countries are largely different in their comprehensive national strength and market maturity. Compared with the EU, the NAFTA lacks high-level economic cooperation.

3.2 Interactive Mechanism Between Regional Economic Integration and Regional Modernization

3.2.1 Analysis of the effects of regional economic integration

Regional economic integration can bring about many effects. As early as the 1950s, Viner has argued in *The Customs Union Issue* that the customs union can produce trade diversion and trade creation effects. Later, these effects are considered as main causes of regional economic integration. In addition, in the process of regional economic integration, the restrictive factors such as trade barriers, market segmentation and protection of local interests that hinder the free flow of production factors and products can be removed so that resources can be reallocated. It is easy to generate the size effect and agglomeration effect of production factors, and these effects will be amplified under the mutual effect of integration, thus accelerating regional economic development and realizing regional modernization, as is shown in Table 3.

Table 3 Analysis of the Main Effects of Regional Economic Integration

Effects of Regional Economic Integration	Main Effects	Interaction with Regional Modernization
Effects of production and investment transfer	The reduction of trade barriers within the region guides external industries to transfer into the region, resulting in capital being transferred into the region from outside. Production transfer also means investment transfer	Capital is re-allocated, which, together with the amplifying role of the local market, will accelerate local economic growth
Effects of trade creation and trade diversion	A customs union implements a unified tariff on non-members, resulting in less foreign imports and more imports from partner countries, changing the direction of trade and producing "trade diversion"	It reduces the tariff barriers within the integration organization, reduces production costs, increases trade volume and promotes regional economic development
Effects of economies of scale	A proper scale can produce the optimal economic interests. In the microeconomic theory, it refers to the phenomenon where the expansion of production scale leads to reduced long-term average costs	An integration organization can integrate dispersed resources and markets to reach the optimal economies of scale and enhance regional economic efficiency
Effects of specialization and cooperation	Cooperation can strengthen the communication between specialized departments and enterprises, continuously expand the scope of cooperation and facilitate the continuous development of interdependency in production	Through the reinforcement of specialization and cooperation within the region, it enhances the overall economic operation efficiency and promotes economic development
Effects of agglomeration economies	It refers to the economic effect generated by the spatial concentration of all industries and economic activities as well as the centripetal force that attracts economic activities to approach a certain region; it is also one of the important factors that can enhance regional competitiveness	Through the agglomeration of production factors, the effects of scale economy and external economy are realized, which play an important facilitating role in local development
Effects of economies of scope	When the costs of an enterprise simultaneously producing two types of products are lower than the sum of the costs for separately producing each type of product, the situation is called economies of scope	An integration organization can concentrate the human resources as well as supply and sale of raw materials and semi-finished products that local enterprises need; it can easily reduce production costs and form economies of scope

Note: All effects may overlap, such as the economies of scale, economies of scope and agglomeration economies

3.2.2 Interactive mechanism between regional economic integration and regional modernization

From the perspective of the division of labor and cooperation, regional economic integration is in essence the deepening of regional labor division and cooperation. According to Adam Smith's theory, the deepening of labor division and cooperation can greatly enhance the productivity of the region. The formation of regional economic integration can provide spatial advantages for the division of labor and specialization, allow free flow of factors within the regional economy, and thus expand the scope of factor market. Furthermore, the expanded factor market can deepen the division of labor, facilitate enterprises to redivide the work and re-cooperate, and form an even more interactive correlation effect among them, thus realizing industrial agglomeration and expanding the market (Ethier, 1998). Similarly, only by continuously reducing transaction costs within the established region can regional economy achieve better development.

From the perspective of cost reduction, regional economic integration can promote the optimal allocation of production factors among regions, realize free flow of population, sharing of technological development, smooth operation of capital and interconnectivity of information, and thus greatly reduce the transaction, transportation, information and learning costs of production factors, enhance the efficiency of production factors' allocation, and realize benefit sharing among regions. Cost reduction is conducive to the further agglomeration of production factors, can facilitate economies of scale, economies of scope and agglomeration effects in the region, and greatly promote regional economic development. Regional economic development will further promote regional benefit sharing and further realize regional economic integration, as is shown in Figure 2.

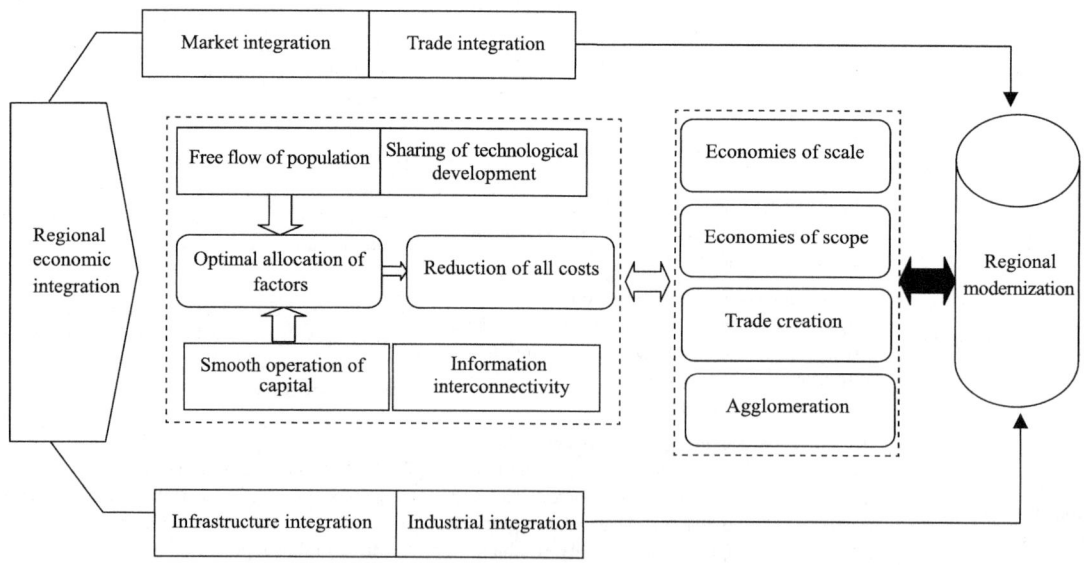

Figure 2   An Interactive Mechanism Between Regional Economic Integration and Regional Modernization

From the perspective of market transaction, based on the free flow of all factors and resources owing to market integration, the economic efficiency of the region will further improve, and the development strength will further grow. As enterprises are the main body of economic development, modulated by the market mechanism and under the action of economies of scale, enterprises will carry out horizontal alliance and vertical merger for the sake of profit maximization and long-term development, which will greatly promote regional economic development. Meanwhile, the free flow of production factors among the regions will realize proper division of labor and the regional economic integration goal of optimal allocation of resources. On the contrary, in regions with serious restrictions on the inflow and outflow of factors, the factor's reward is low, capital accumulation is slow, and production cost is high; in regions with serious restrictions on the inflow of competitive products, local enterprises lack the enthusiasm for improving production and management, causing productivity to grow slowly. Both situations will hinder regional economic development.

4. Policy Suggestions for Promoting Regional Economic Integration in China

As the second largest economy in the world, China must establish a regional economic integration strategy that centers on itself, no matter for the sake of global strategy or regional strategy. Currently, China has started to value and has actively participated in regional economic cooperation. For example, China has joined the WTO, has established Shanghai Cooperation Organization with Russia and Central Asian countries, and has been actively promoting the China-ASEAN free trade area. But considering the essence of economic integration, these cooperation organizations have not yet reached the level of integration, so current China is nearly not involved in regional economic integration.

4.1 Taking the Opportunity of Promoting the Silk Road Economic Belt to Build a New Economic Integration Organization

The Silk Road Economic Belt is an important passageway that connects East Asian, Central Asian, South Asian and Mediterranean countries. In 2013, the construction of the Silk Road Economic Belt was officially recognized as a national initiative, with priority to strengthen the cooperation with countries along the belt in transportation, energy, industries and trade. In 2015, the Asian Infrastructure Investment Bank (AIIB) was established, which marks a firm step towards the integration construction of the Silk Road Economic Belt. Therefore, this paper suggests that China should take the establishment of the AIIB as an excellent opportunity, fully utilize the fact that the countries along the belt value China's capital, technologies and geographical advantages as the hub connecting Asia and the Pacific, and cooperate with these countries in the form of free trade zone to co-establish the "New Silk Road Economic Cooperation Organization" to carry out cooperation in transportation, energy, trade and finance in an orderly manner. Considering that the countries along the Silk Road Economic Belt have different political systems and varying development levels, it is not proper to adopt the competition-oriented integration mode of the EU. Instead, the cooperation-oriented integration mode is more suitable (Li, 2014). In a word, China should carry out innovative and orderly integration to eventually transform the initial function of the Silk Road Economic Belt as a transportation hub into an integration organization in all fields, making it become a real regional economic integration organization with smooth flow of factors, complementary markets, openness and cooperation.

4.2 Continuing to Strengthen Economic Structural Reform and Vigorously Promoting the Construction of Market Economy

The market plays a decisive role in regional economic integration. It will play a fundamental role in the smooth flow and reasonable allocation of production factors in the region, that is, regional economic integration inevitably requires market integration. For a long time, the planned economy adopted in China had seriously hindered the reasonable flow of factors. After the reform and opening-up, although China works hard to promote the construction of market economy, the influence of the planned economic system still lingers. The government plays a significant role in the market, while the enterprises are seriously dependent on the government, and their enthusiasm and initiative haven't been encouraged. So the full market integration is far from complete. In the third plenary session of the 18th CPC Central Committee, the Chinese government has proposed to give full play to the decisive role of the market in resource allocation, which has fundamentally clarified the functions of the government and the market. This means that in the future, China should vigorously strengthen the economic structural reform, promote further the marketization of monopolized resources, encourage the government to delegate more powers to the market, and gradually form a modern market system with free flow and equal exchange of goods and factors. That is to say, China should continuously promote the free flow and reasonable allocation of production factors among regions through the development of marketization, further enhance the efficiency and equity of resource allocation, and truly lay a firm foundation for the advancement of regional economic integration.

4.3 Vigorously Strengthening Infrastructure Construction and Breaking the Fundamental Obstacles to Economic Integration

Spatial distance is usually the natural obstacle to regional economic integration. When the spatial distance is large, the transportation is less convenient, and the transportation cost is higher. Infrastructure integration, especially transportation infrastructure integration, can provide important guarantee for the flow of human resources, materials, capital, technologies and information across regions, or even realize "zero-distance" exchange, which can greatly reduce transaction costs and is conducive to the achievement of regional economic integration. For example, in 1990, the North Xinjiang railway of China was linked to the Turkestan-Siberia railway of the Soviet Union in Alashankou, forming an integrated international transportation trunk line that traverses through Asian and European continents. The transportation integration has undoubtedly reduced the transportation and time costs, and has accelerated the economic and trade exchanges between China and other Asian and European regions. Infrastructure integration is not only the easiest one to achieve in economic integration, but also the most important and most critical breakthrough point. Only with the interconnectivity of infrastructure can the first step to regional economic integration be started.

4.4 Innovating Regional Coordination Mechanism and Building a New Mechanism for Regional Economic Integration

During economic integration, as different countries have varying development foundations and conditions, the benefits they gain also vary hugely. If the benefits for both parties after the cooperation are larger than those before the cooperation, but the benefit increase for one party is smaller than that for the other party, the former will adopt political boycott. Krugman also pointed out that as long as the market scale varies across countries or regions within an integration organization, production and investment will increasingly concentrate in the country or region with the largest market scale with the enhancement of the integration level. Under this circumstance, adopting appropriate compensation mechanism is critical to maintaining the sound advancement of economic integration. Moreover, China should make efforts to improve the information communication mechanism, market development mechanism, mechanism for scientific and technological cooperation with talented personnel and factor flow mechanism, to form a new organizational system that can promote regional coordinated development. Meanwhile, China should launch the union between enterprises and non-governmental institutions, foster and improve non-governmental economic organizations such as chambers of commerce and guilds, and adopt various coordinating measures to solve the important and major problems in regional integration, so as to facilitate the progress of regional integration.

References

安虎森, 李瑞林 (An H S, Li R L). 2007. 区域经济一体化效应和实现途径. 湖南社会科学, 5: 95-102.
何传启 (He C Q). 2015. 中国现代化报告 2014~2015. 北京: 北京大学出版社.
李建民 (Li J M). 2014. "丝绸之路经济带"合作模式研究. 中国党政干部论坛, (5): 87-91.
李瑞林, 骆华松 (Li R L, Luo H S). 2007. 区域经济一体化: 内涵、效应与实现途径. 经济问题探索, 1: 52-57.
王竞 (Wang J). 2008. 国际区域经济一体化与区域竞争力研究——以东亚为例. 浙江大学硕士学位论文.
张纪康 (Zhang J K). 1997. 区域经济一体化的决定因素及形式比较. 当代亚太, (06): 16-21.
Balassa B. 1961. The Theory of Economic Integration. London: Homewood Irwin.
De Melo J, Montenegro C, Panagariya A. 1992. Regional Integration Old and New. World Bank Working Paper, No. 985.
Ethier. 1998. The new regionalism. Economic Journal, 108 (449): 1149-1161.
Tinbergen J. 1954. International Economic Integration. Amsterdam: Elsevier.
Wonnacott P, Lutz M. 1989. Is there a case for free trade areas? In J J Schott (Ed.), Free Trade Areas and U.S. Trade Policy (pp. 59-95). Washington: Institute of International Economics.

Appendix

World Modernization Indexes in 2015

Countries/Regions	First Modernization			Second Modernization			Integrated Modernization	
	Indexes	Ranking	Phases	Indexes	Ranking	Phases	Indexes	Ranking
Denmark	100.0	1	F4	109.3	1	S2	100.0	1
United States	100.0	1	F4	107.3	2	S2	97.7	4
Switzerland	100.0	1	F4	106.7	3	S2	97.3	7
Sweden	100.0	1	F4	106.6	4	S2	98.7	3
Netherlands	100.0	1	F4	106.1	5	S2	97.7	5
Singapore	100.0	1	F4	103.7	6	S2	96.9	8
Belgium	100.0	1	F4	102.5	7	S2	98.8	2
Ireland	100.0	1	F4	101.3	8	S1	94.5	10
United Kingdom	100.0	1	F4	99.0	9	S2	91.6	15
Finland	100.0	1	F4	98.8	10	S2	97.4	6
Norway	100.0	1	F4	98.7	11	S1	92.9	13
Germany	100.0	1	F4	98.0	12	S1	94.5	9
France	100.0	1	F4	97.5	13	S2	91.7	14
Japan	100.0	1	F4	96.8	14	S1	93.2	12
Austria	100.0	1	F4	95.1	15	S1	94.0	11
Australia	100.0	1	F4	93.1	16	S2	90.9	16
Israel	100.0	1	F4	90.5	17	S2	89.3	17
Canada	100.0	1	F4	90.3	18	S1	89.1	18
Republic of Korea	100.0	1	F4	87.7	19	S1	84.2	20
New Zealand	100.0	1	F4	84.2	20	S2	87.3	19
Spain	100.0	1	F4	77.9	21	S2	79.4	21
Italy	100.0	1	F4	73.4	22	S1	78.1	22
Greece	100.0	1	F3	72.2	23		69.1	27
Portugal	100.0	1	F4	71.2	24	S1	69.6	26
Slovenia	99.9	1	F4	70.6	25	S1	71.7	23
Estonia	100.0	1	F4	63.9	26	S1	65.7	30

Continued

Countries/Regions	First Modernization			Second Modernization			Integrated Modernization	
	Indexes	Ranking	Phases	Indexes	Ranking	Phases	Indexes	Ranking
Czech Republic	100.0	1	F4	63.5	27		69.9	25
Hungary	100.0	1	F4	62.2	28	S1	66.5	29
Lithuania	100.0	1	F4	59.7	29		65.4	31
Latvia	100.0	1	F4	57.8	30		64.8	32
Slovak Republic	100.0	1	F4	56.4	31		63.7	35
Croatia	100.0	1	F4	56.3	32		62.2	36
Poland	100.0	1	F4	54.6	33		59.0	40
Uruguay	100.0	1	F3	54.0	34		64.2	33
Russian Federation	100.0	1	F4	53.9	35		59.1	39
Saudi Arabia	100.0	1	F4	52.8	36		71.4	24
Argentina	100.0	1	F4	52.6	37		64.0	34
Chile	100.0	1	F4	51.1	38		62.1	37
Kuwait	100.0	1	F4	50.3	39		66.6	28
Costa Rica	100.0	1	F3	50.2	40		56.9	42
Belarus	97.5	53	F4	48.1	41		53.9	46
Brazil	100.0	1	F3	47.0	42		57.3	41
Bulgaria	98.6	51	F4	46.4	43		55.2	44
Turkey	100.0	1	F3	46.2	44		56.2	43
Malaysia	100.0	1	F3	44.9	45		49.9	54
Panama	100.0	1	F4	44.8	46		52.2	49
Lebanon	99.2	49	F4	44.7	47		54.7	45
Romania	100.0	1	F3	44.7	48		52.6	48
Colombia	98.2	52	F3	42.3	49		52.2	50
China	99.2	50	F3	41.1	50		44.4	63
Venezuela, RB	100.0	1	F3	40.4	51		61.5	38
Kazakhstan	100.0	1	F3	39.7	52		51.3	52
Islamic Republic of Iran	96.2	57	F3	39.6	53		47.9	58
Mexico	100.0	1	F4	38.3	54		51.6	51
Dominican Republic	97.2	54	F3	38.0	55		53.3	47
Ukraine	93.1	65	F3	37.7	56		46.4	60
Ecuador	96.9	56	F3	37.7	57		45.2	62
Jordan	94.5	61	F4	36.3	58		50.8	53
Macedonia	95.4	59	F3	36.1	59		48.0	56
Georgia	91.4	71	F2	35.3	60		42.2	66
Jamaica	83.8	87	F3	35.3	61		43.3	64

Continued

Countries/Regions	First Modernization			Second Modernization			Integrated Modernization	
	Indexes	Ranking	Phases	Indexes	Ranking	Phases	Indexes	Ranking
Albania	88.6	76	F2	35.1	62		40.8	70
Thailand	89.0	74	F3	34.5	63		36.9	76
Peru	97.1	55	F3	34.2	64		48.0	57
Botswana	88.6	75	F3	34.1	65		38.7	75
Tunisia	94.4	63	F3	33.3	66		41.7	67
Paraguay	92.6	66	F3	32.8	67		40.2	72
Armenia	90.9	72	F2	32.6	68		47.4	59
Moldova	91.6	70	F3	32.5	69		41.6	68
Sri Lanka	85.3	83	F3	32.5	70		34.0	79
Azerbaijan	95.5	58	F3	31.6	71		45.5	61
Mongolia	94.3	64	F3	31.4	72		42.4	65
Algeria	95.0	60	F3	30.9	73		39.1	74
South Africa	92.0	68	F4	30.6	74		40.2	71
Morocco	87.3	79	F3	30.6	75		36.3	77
El Salvador	94.4	62	F3	30.0	76		41.1	69
Namibia	81.4	89	F2	29.7	77		33.3	82
Philippines	92.0	69	F3	29.6	78		40.0	73
Vietnam	83.6	88	F2	29.5	79		30.6	84
Syrian Arab Republic	88.1	77	F3	28.9	80		49.1	55
Indonesia	84.9	84	F3	28.1	81		28.9	88
Kyrgyz Republic	86.6	81	F3	27.4	82		32.3	83
Egypt, Arab Republic	90.0	73	F3	27.1	83		33.9	80
Bolivia	87.7	78	F3	25.9	84		33.7	81
Guatemala	92.6	67	F3	25.6	85		34.8	78
Honduras	86.1	82	F3	23.8	86		29.3	86
Angola	74.3	93	F3	23.7	87		28.5	90
Nicaragua	87.1	80	F2	23.4	88		28.4	92
Uzbekistan	83.8	86	F2	23.2	89		28.6	89
Ghana	71.6	96	F2	22.6	90		28.4	91
Turkmenistan	84.7	85	F3	22.0	91		30.2	85
Papua New Guinea	56.3	117	F1	21.7	92		14.9	122
Kenya	57.5	116	F1	21.5	93		18.5	114
Nigeria	69.6	98	F2	21.2	94		24.9	97
Republic of Congo	72.6	95	F3	21.0	95		26.8	94
Senegal	65.5	104	F2	20.4	96		21.9	103

Appendix 413

Continued

Countries/Regions	First Modernization			Second Modernization			Integrated Modernization	
	Indexes	Ranking	Phases	Indexes	Ranking	Phases	Indexes	Ranking
Republic of Yemen	70.6	97	F3	20.2	97		26.2	95
Bangladesh	76.8	91	F2	20.2	98		25.0	96
India	77.5	90	F2	20.0	99		24.7	98
Tajikistan	75.8	92	F2	20.0	100		29.1	87
Lao PDR	65.9	103	F2	19.9	101		23.5	99
Madagascar	58.8	112	F1	19.9	102		18.6	113
Lesotho	69.1	100	F3	19.9	103		19.8	108
Myanmar	73.3	94	F3	19.7	104		19.8	109
Zambia	65.2	105	F2	19.4	105		22.4	102
Zimbabwe	64.1	106	F2	19.4	106		20.1	107
Cambodia	63.2	109	F2	19.2	107		17.8	116
Cote d'Ivoire	57.9	114	F1	18.5	108		21.0	104
Cameroon	69.3	99	F2	18.5	109		27.2	93
Guinea	55.5	119	F2	18.5	110		19.4	110
Pakistan	68.1	101	F2	18.5	111		23.2	100
Benin	61.5	110	F2	18.3	112		22.6	101
Mozambique	50.6	122	F1	18.0	113		15.8	119
Malawi	47.7	126	F1	17.8	114		13.5	126
Nepal	67.4	102	F1	17.8	115		18.7	112
Tanzania	54.9	120	F1	17.7	116		15.3	121
Eritrea	57.8	115	F1	17.7	117		20.8	105
Mauritania	58.6	113	F2	17.4	118		19.3	111
Rwanda	59.3	111	F1	16.8	119		18.0	115
Sierra Leone	42.6	129	F0	16.7	120		12.6	129
Togo	56.0	118	F1	15.9	121		14.0	124
Haiti	64.0	107	F2	15.9	122		20.7	106
Ethiopia	49.0	124	F1	15.6	123		12.9	128
Uganda	53.1	121	F1	15.4	124		14.7	123
Burkina Faso	46.9	128	F1	15.3	125		13.6	125
Mali	48.3	125	F1	15.3	126		17.6	117
Democratic Republic of Congo	63.7	108	F2	14.2	127		15.6	120
Chad	37.1	131	F0	14.2	128		10.5	131
Niger	38.9	130	F1	14.1	129		13.3	127
Burundi	49.4	123	F0	14.1	130		10.8	130

Continued

Countries/Regions	First Modernization			Second Modernization			Integrated Modernization	
	Indexes	Ranking	Phases	Indexes	Ranking	Phases	Indexes	Ranking
Central African Republic	47.0	127	F1	13.8	131		16.2	118
High-income Countries	100.0		F4	99.7		S2	100.0	
Middle-income Countries	95.3		F3	29.3			37.2	
Low-income Countries	99.6		F3	40.0			48.1	
World	55.4		F1	15.7			15.1	

Notes: F0, F1, F2, F3 and F4 refer to the agricultural society and the starting, developing, mature and transitional phases of the first modernization respectively. S2 and S1 refer to starting and developing phases of the second modernization. When the FMI reaches 100, the rank of nation will be 1 at all

Source: He C Q. 2018. China Modernization Report 2018: Modernization of Industrial Structure. Beijing: Peking University Press